Power Pack

Business English

Robert Tilley

Compact Verlag

© 2001 Compact Verlag München
Alle Rechte vorbehalten. Nachdruck,
auch auszugsweise, nur mit ausdrücklicher
Genehmigung des Verlages gestattet.
Chefredaktion: Ilse Hell
Redaktion: Karina Partsch, Alexandra Pawelczak
Fachredaktion: Ted Hall, Anthony Moore, Till Nassif
Übersetzung: Marc Hillefeld
Produktion: Martina Baur, Claudia Schmid
Gestaltung: Hendryk Sommer
Umschlaggestaltung: agenten.und.freunde

ISBN 3-8174-7246-3
7272461

Besuchen Sie uns im Internet: www.compactverlag.de

Vorwort

Englisch ist die länderübergreifende Sprache der Wirtschaft. Angesichts der zunehmenden Globalisierung der Märkte werden gute Englischkenntnisse immer wichtiger für den beruflichen Erfolg.

Power Pack Business English bereitet auf unterhaltsame und zugleich zielgerechte Weise darauf vor, die unterschiedlichsten Situationen des Berufsalltags erfolgreich in der Fremdsprache zu meistern. Er trainiert speziell die Kommunikationssituationen am Telefon, in Verkaufsverhandlungen, in Präsentationen und beim Erledigen der täglich anfallenden Geschäftskorrespondenz.

Dies geschieht anhand einer Story, die die Erlebnisse des Deutschen Peter Brückners, der von seiner Firma nach England versetzt wurde, in humorvoller Weise darstellt.

Alle Dialoge sind praxisnah und sowohl in englischer Sprache als auch in der deutschen Übersetzung angegeben. Die Schlüsselbegriffe sind im Text besonders hervorgehoben. Nach jedem Dialog folgen zur Überprüfung und Vertiefung des gelernten Wortschatzes kurze Übungen.

Daneben findet der Benutzer zahlreiche sprachpraktische und kulturelle Zusatzinformationen. Hierzu gehören Tipps zum korrekten Sprachgebrauch und landeskundliche Hinweise zur Vermeidung typischer Fehler.

Eine Zusammenstellung der wichtigsten Redewendungen ermöglicht eine zielgenaue und rasche Vorbereitung auf bestimmte Situationen des Geschäftsalltags in englischer Sprache. Über aktuelle Entwicklungen im Business und Internet gibt eine ausführliche Trendwörterliste Auskunft. Mit einem abschließenden Test kann der Kenntnisstand überprüft und etwaige Lücken geschlossen werden.

Die englische Kurzgrammatik und weitere wichtige Informationen rund um den Business-Alltag, die wichtigsten Suchmaschinen des Internet sowie Umrechnungstabellen zu Maßen und Gewichten befinden sich im Anhang.

Das **Compact Power Pack** wird durch die anwenderfreundliche CD-Rom mit einem umfassenden Fachwortschatz Business English ergänzt.

Verschiedene Symbole zu Beginn jedes Abschnittes ermöglichen einen zielgenauen Zugriff auf die relevanten Passagen:

 Here we go: kleine Einleitung am Anfang des Kapitels

 Talk Talk Talk: praxisnahe Dialoge mit deutschen Übersetzungen, die wichtigsten Stichwörter sind hervorgehoben

 Train Yourself: abwechslungsreiche Übungen trainieren den gelernten Wortschatz

 Background Information: Wissenswertes zu Business und Landeskunde

 Do's and Don'ts: Tipps zum korrekten Verhalten in Geschäftssituationen

 False Friends: Hinweise auf mögliche sprachliche Fehler

 Vocabulary: Vokabelliste mit dem Wortschatz des Kapitels

 Auf einen Blick: die wichtigsten Redewendungen rund ums Telefonieren, Korrespondieren, Verkaufen und Präsentieren

 Business- und Internet-Trendwörter von A bis Z: alles Wichtige, um in der modernen Berufswelt aktuell zu bleiben

 Anhang: englische Kurzgrammatik, Maße und Gewichte, Feiertage in GB und den USA, Suchmaschinen im Internet

 Abschlusstest: im Abschlusstest zeigt es sich: Was haben Sie gelernt? Wo sind vielleicht noch Ihre Schwächen?

 Glossar: Zusammenfassung aller neuen Vokabeln

 Lösungen: die Lösungen zu Übungen im Text und zum Abschlusstest

Inhalt

Vorwort	**3**
Story	**7**
Telefonieren	**8**
Die ersten Tage im Unternehmen	8
In der Verkaufsabteilung	32
In der Marketing-Abteilung	61
Kundenbetreuung	89
Auf Geschäftsreise	119
Korrespondenz	**144**
Anfragen	144
Empfehlungen und Reklamationen	174
Angebote	199
Bewerbungsschreiben	224
Antwortschreiben	248
Verkaufsgespräche	**276**
Kunden akquirieren	276
Produkte präsentieren	299
Geschäftsabschlüsse erzielen	323
Angebote unterbreiten	352
Vertragsbedingungen aushandeln	380
Präsentationen	**404**
Informelle Besprechungen	404
Interview mit der Presse	429
Pressekonferenzen	456
Präsentation auf der Messe	480
Präsentation vor der Handelskammer	501

Auf einen Blick **526**
    Redewendungen rund ums Telefonieren   526
    Redewendungen rund um die Geschäftskorrespondenz   536
    Redewendungen rund ums Verkaufen   543
    Redewendungen rund ums Präsentieren   557

Business- und Internet-Trendwörter von A bis Z **565**

Anhang **598**
    Englische Kurzgrammatik   598
    Unregelmäßige Verben   608
    Wichtige Abkürzungen   612
    Maße und Gewichte   615
    Feiertage in GB und USA   616
    Suchmaschinen im Internet   617

Abschlusstest **619**

Glossar **628**

Lösungen **651**

 **Story**

Peter Brückner ist 30 Jahre alt. Nach seinem BWL-Studium wurde er als Assistent des Vertriebsleiters bei der internationalen Firma ERGO Ltd. beschäftigt. ERGO Ltd. ist ein innovatives Unternehmen und hat sich auf die Produktion von Zubehörteilen im IT-Bereich spezialisiert.

Um Peter Brückner auf eine spätere Führungsposition vorzubereiten, wird er in die Filiale nach London versetzt, damit er dort die Abläufe des internationalen Vertriebs kennen lernt. Wie viele andere Unternehmen, legt auch ERGO Ltd. großen Wert darauf, dass künftige Führungskräfte Auslandserfahrungen sammeln.

Power Pack Business English zeigt, wie Peter Brückner das tägliche Geschäftsleben in englischer Sprache erfolgreich meistert.
Tatkräftige Unterstützung erhält er dabei von seinen neuen Kollegen, die ihm jederzeit mit nützlichen Tipps zur Seite stehen und ihn auf die kulturellen und sprachlichen Feinheiten hinweisen. Dies sind:
– James Morgan, Managing Director, direkter Vorgesetzter von Peter
– Steve Blackman, Leiter der Verkaufsabteilung
– Melissa Walker, Marketing Managerin
– Lucy Scott, Sekretärin und »gute Seele« des Büros.

Schon bald ist Peter Brückner mit den wichtigsten Strategien vertraut und weiß, wie man in englischer Sprache sicher telefoniert, richtig korrespondiert, erfolgreich verhandelt und überzeugend präsentiert.

The first days in the company
Die ersten Tage im Unternehmen

 Here we go

Das erste Kapitel beginnt an Peters erstem Arbeitstag, an dem er viele neue Menschen kennen lernt und die ersten Hürden am Telefon zu bewältigen hat.

 Talk Talk Talk

L. Good morning, ERGO Limited. **May I help you?**

P. Yes, it's Peter Brückner **speaking**. I am supposed to be starting today, but I had difficulty in **reaching** Mr Morgan yesterday to ask when I should arrive. I'm **phoning** now to **find out**.

L. Oh, Mr Brückner. We did **try to get hold of** you, but they appear to be **mending the lines** in your street. Come along whenever you like. Mr Morgan won't be in for half an hour or so.

P. Fine! I'm leaving the apartment now and I'll catch a bus from the end of the street. It shouldn't take me more than ten minutes.

L. Guten Morgen, ERGO Limited. **Kann ich Ihnen behilflich sein**?

P. Ja, hier Peter Brückner **am Apparat**. Ich sollte heute bei Ihnen anfangen, aber ich hatte Probleme, Herrn Morgan zu **erreichen**, um ihn zu fragen, wann genau ich da sein soll. Ich **rufe an**, um noch einmal **nachzufragen.**

L. Oh, Mr Brückner. Wir **haben versucht, Sie zu erreichen,** aber in ihrer Straße scheinen gerade **die Leitungen repariert zu werden**. Kommen Sie einfach vorbei, wann es Ihnen am besten passt. Mr Morgan wird vor einer halben Stunde sowieso nicht hier sein.

P. Sehr schön! Ich gehe gerade von meinem Apartment los und versuche, einen Bus am Ende der Straße zu erwischen. In 10 Minuten bin ich da!

L. Oh, dear me – you're an optimist, Mr Brückner. This is London, you know - you'd probably be quicker to walk. Or you could take the tube – there's a station just down the road from you. The Tottenham Court Road station is right on our doorstep.

P. Do you know what line I have to take? I'm quite new here.

L. Take the Central Line. Tottenham Court Road is just five stops. And buy a day ticket. I'll arrange for you to get a permanent travel pass.

P. Thank you so much. I'll **see you shortly**.

L. Oh, wei! Sie sind ein Optimist, Mr Brückner. Sie sind jetzt in London – es würde wahrscheinlich schneller gehen, wenn Sie laufen. Oder Sie nehmen die U-Bahn – eine Station ist ganz in Ihrer Nähe. Die Haltestelle Tottenham Court Road liegt genau vor unserer Tür.

P. Wissen Sie, welche Linie ich da nehmen muss? Ich kenne mich hier noch nicht so aus.

L. Nehmen Sie die *Central Line*. Bis zur Tottenham Road sind es nur fünf Haltestellen. Und kaufen Sie sich am besten eine Tageskarte. Ich werde mich darum kümmern, dass sie eine Dauerkarte bekommen.

P. Haben Sie vielen Dank. **Bis gleich**.

 1. Train Yourself

1. Setzen Sie die nachfolgenden Sätze eines Telefongesprächs in die richtige Reihenfolge:

- I tried to call Mr Morgan yesterday.
- Good morning! May I help you?
- I couldn't get through.
- This is Peter Brückner speaking.
- The phone seemed to be out of order.
- I'm calling to find out when I should start.
- Mr Morgan will be calling in shortly.

2. Füllen Sie die Lücken!

Sagen Sie, wer Sie sind.	Good morning, ▒▒▒ Peter Brückner ▒▒▒ ing.
Erklären Sie, warum Sie erst jetzt anrufen.	I tried to ▒▒▒ yesterday, but I couldn't ▒▒▒ through.
Fragen Sie, ob Sie Herrn Morgan zu Hause anrufen sollten.	Should I try to ▒▒▒ Mr Morgan at home?
Fragen Sie, ob das Büro versucht hat, Sie zu erreichen.	Has the office tried to ▒▒▒ me?

 Talk Talk Talk

P. (enters office) Good morning. I'm Peter Brückner.

L. Oh, Mr Brückner. **How nice to meet you**. Please come in and make yourself at home. I've tried to **reach** Mr Morgan at home, but he must have left for the office already. But I expect he'll call from his **mobile** on the way. He always likes to check if there's any urgent business to attend to before he gets to the office. Oh, that'll be him now. Good morning! ERGO Limited. Oh, good morning, Mr Morgan. Mr Brückner has arrived. Yes, I've told him to make himself at home. Yes, I shall. **See you later**, Mr Morgan. (Phone rings again) Oh, we are busy this morning, aren't we? Good morning, ERGO Limited. Oh, **I'm terribly sorry** but we have been so busy

P. (betritt das Büro) Guten Morgen. Ich bin Peter Brückner.

L. Oh, Mr Brückner. **Schön, Sie kennen zu lernen**. Kommen Sie doch herein und fühlen Sie sich wie zu Hause. Ich habe schon versucht, Mr Morgan zu Hause zu **erreichen**, aber er muss schon auf dem Weg ins Büro gewesen sein. Aber ich denke, dass er unterwegs von seinem **Handy** anrufen wird. Er fragt immer gerne nach, ob etwas Dringliches anliegt, bevor er ins Büro kommt. Oh, das wird er schon sein. Guten Morgen, ERGO Limited! Oh, Guten Morgen, Mr Morgan. Mr Brückner ist gerade angekommen. Ja, ich habe ihm gesagt, er soll sich wie zu Hause fühlen. Ja, das werde ich. **Bis später**, Mr Morgan. (Das Telefon klingelt erneut) Meine Güte, ein ganz schön hektischer

that I just didn't have time to check when you called yesterday. I'll **attend to it** right away. Can you **phone again** in an hour or so? Just ask for Lucy. That's right. Bye for now. Now, Mr Brückner, what about a nice cup of tea?

Morgen, was? Guten Morgen, ERGO Limited. Oh, **es tut mir furchtbar Leid**, aber wir hatten so viel zu tun, dass ich nach ihrem Anruf von gestern noch gar keine Zeit hatte. **Ich werde mich** sofort **darum kümmern**. Könnten Sie in etwa einer Stunde noch einmal **durchrufen**? Fragen Sie einfach nach Lucy. Ganz genau. Bis später. Also, Mr Brückner, wie wäre es mit einer schönen Tasse Tee?

J. (enters) Well, hello, Peter. **I'm very glad to see you.** I tried to **reach** you **on the phone** yesterday, but I couldn't **get through** for some reason. But I see you have found your way safely here and that Lucy has made you at home. I'll have a cup too, please, Lucy. Now come into my office, and then I'll **show you around.**

J. (kommt herein) Na so was, hallo Peter. **Ich freue mich, Sie zu sehen.** Ich habe gestern schon versucht, Sie **telefonisch zu erreichen**, aber aus irgendeinem Grund **kam ich nicht durch**. Aber wie ich sehe, haben Sie ja sicher hierher gefunden und Lucy hat sich Ihrer angenommen. Ich hätte auch gern ein Tässchen, Lucy. Aber kommen Sie doch mit in mein Büro, und ich **führe Sie herum.**

J. (calls from his office) Lucy, can you **connect me please** with Melissa's office, and if you see Steve tell him to look in. Melissa is our **Marketing Manager,** and Steve is **Head of Sales.** You'll be working from time to time with both.

J. (telefoniert aus seinem Büro) Lucy, können Sie mich bitte mit Melissas Büro **verbinden** – und wenn Sie Steve sehen, sagen Sie ihm, er möchte bitte mal hereinschauen. Melissa ist unsere **Marketing-Managerin** und Steve der **Leiter der Verkaufsabteilung.** Sie werden sicher von Zeit zu Zeit mit den beiden zusammenarbeiten.

L. Hello, Mr Morgan. I'm **putting you through** now to Miss Walker's

L. Hallo, Mr Morgan. Ich **stelle Sie** jetzt zu Miss Walkers Büro **durch**.

Telefonieren

office. Just **hang on** one moment. Her number is **ringing**.	Bitte **bleiben Sie** eine Sekunde **in der Leitung**. Ich **läute** gerade bei ihr **durch**.
J. Hello, Melissa, could you **come into** my office for a moment, please. I'd like you to meet Mr Brückner, our new man from Germany.	J. Hallo, Melissa, könnten Sie bitte kurz in meinem Büro **vorbeischauen?** Ich würde Ihnen gerne Mr Brückner vorstellen, unseren neuen Mann aus Deutschland.
M. (enters) Good morning, Mr Morgan. (To Peter) **How do you do?** I'm Melissa Walker.	M. (kommt hinein) Guten Morgen, Mr Morgan. (Zu Peter) **Wie geht es Ihnen?** Ich bin Melissa Walker.
S. (also enters) Good morning, Mr Morgan. (To Peter) Hello, I'm Steve Blackman - **just call me Steve. Pleased to meet you.**	S. (kommt ebenfalls hinein) Guten Morgen, Mr Morgan. (Zu Peter) Hallo, ich bin Steve Blackman – **sagen Sie einfach Steve. Freut mich, Sie kennen zu lernen.**
C. (enters after knocking) Oh, sorry, sir. I didn't know you were having a **meeting**. I should have **given you a buzz** first of all.	C. (klopft und tritt dann ein) Oh, Entschuldigung, Sir. Ich wusste nicht, dass Sie in einer **Besprechung** sind. Ich hätte zuerst **kurz durchrufen** sollen.
M. That's all right, Chip. Mr Brückner, this is our driver and courier, Charles Collyer – he likes to be called Chip.	J. Schon in Ordnung, Chip. Mr Brückner, das ist unser Fahrer und Kurier, Charles Collyer – aber er hat es lieber, wenn man ihn Chip nennt.
C. Well, it's easier, isn't it Mr Morgan? Hi, Steve. **How're you doing**, Melissa? I'm pleased to meet you, Mr Brückner. Welcome to London – it'll be a change from Hamburg. But there again, per-	C. Na ja, das ist doch viel leichter, oder Mr Morgan? Hi, Steve. **Wie geht es Ihnen**, Melissa? Freut mich, Sie kennen zu lernen, Mr Brückner. Willkommen in London – das wird eine ganz schöne

haps it won't! Not after you've seen Soho! Although it's not like it used to be!

Umstellung verglichen mit Hamburg sein. Aber andererseits – vielleicht auch nicht! Nicht, nachdem Sie Soho gesehen haben! Obwohl das auch nicht mehr ist, was es war!

2. Train Yourself

Geben Sie die richtige Begrüßung an:

...., Mr Morgan, my name is Peter Brückner. *(Good morning, hello, hi!)*

....? I'm very pleased to meet you at last. *(Good day, how do you do, good afternoon)*

.... Lucy! Lovely day today. Can I have a cup of tea, please. *(How do you do, good day, good morning)*

.... Chip! Can you take this packet to the Post Office, please. *(Good day, hi, pleased to meet you)*

.... Steve, fancy seeing you in the office so early! *(Hello, good day, good afternoon)*

Background Information

The British love to substitute colloquial words for everyday activities. The telephone itself is still referred to in some quarters as a »**blower**«, although the term itself is very old-fashioned. Even business people promise to give each other a »**buzz**«, meaning they'll call each other on the phone.

Handy Information: German »**handy**« is a »**mobile**« in Britain. You'll also hear new arrivals from English-speaking countries such as South Africa or the US refer to it as a »**cellphone**«.

Do's and Don'ts

Office relations in Britain are very **informal** when viewed from a German perspective, although senior staff – particularly the boss – are treated with correctness and respect (particularly department heads or the boss!). Colleagues are almost always on first-name terms, so don't be surprised to find yourself addressed that way from day one. Respond in the same way – if Peter is addressed by his first name and then gives his colleagues a »Mr« or »Mrs« title he'll be dismissed as a »cool Hamburger«! You'll be offered a hand to shake on first introductions, but after that shaking hands is not a British custom.

Talk Talk Talk

J. Well now, Mr Brückner, please **step into** my office and we'll **tackle the formalities.** Please sit down. I have your **CV** here and I must say I'm very impressed. It's rare for us to receive a CV written so accurately and concisely. Let me just **go through the details.** You were born, I see, in Hamburg on June 30, 1969. There is one **gap** here for the years 1985-86.

J. Gut, Mr Brückner, dann **kommen Sie doch bitte hinein** in mein Büro und **wir nehmen die Formalitäten in Angriff**. Setzen Sie sich doch. Ich habe hier ihren **Lebenslauf** vor mir liegen und ich muss sagen: Ich bin sehr beeindruckt. Es ist sehr selten, dass wir einen Lebenslauf bekommen, der so genau und vollständig ist. Lassen Sie mich noch einmal **die Details durchgehen**. Wie ich sehe, wurden Sie am 30. Juni 1969 in Hamburg geboren. Aber hier gibt es eine **Lücke**, 1985 bis 86.

P. I took two years off and toured North America. I thought it wasn't that important to mention in the CV.

P. Oh, ich habe mir eine Auszeit von zwei Jahren genommen und bin durch Nordamerika gereist. Ich dachte, es wäre nicht wichtig, das im Lebenslauf zu erwähnen.

J. It certainly explains your good command of English. May I just pause here to **call in** Mr Jenkins of the **Personnel Department.** He will want to explain to you certain points in your **contract**.

(He **lifts the telephone receiver** and presses one of the buttons on the console in front of him)
Hello, David. It's Morgan here. I have Mr Brückner in the office. Could you **come in** for a moment, please?

(David Jenkins enters)
J. David, **I'd like you to meet** Mr Brückner, who has joined us from Hamburg. Mr Brückner, this is Mr David Jenkins of our Personnel Department.

P. How do you do?

M. And now let me show you your office, Peter. It's right next to mine.

P. It's really very nice. And very well equipped.

M. We obviously have the very latest hardware and software. You have Windows 2000 already installed, and also the Microsoft »Office« programs. You have **instant Internet access**, and **don't**

J. Es erklärt zumindest Ihr gutes Englisch. Lassen Sie mich an dieser Stelle eine kurze Pause einlegen, um Mr Jenkins von der **Personalabteilung dazu zurufen.** Er wird mit Ihnen bestimmte Details Ihres **Vertrages** durchgehen wollen.

(Er **nimmt den Hörer ab** und drückt einen der Knöpfe auf der Konsole vor ihm)
Hallo, David. Hier Morgan. Ich habe Mr Brückner bei mir im Büro. Könnten Sie bitte einen Moment **vorbei kommen?**

(David Jenkins tritt ein)
J. David, **ich würde Ihnen gern** Mr Brückner **vorstellen,** der aus Hamburg zu uns gestoßen ist. Mr Brückner, das ist Mr David Jenkins aus unserer Personalabteilung.

P. Wie geht es Ihnen?

M. So, lassen Sie mich Ihnen Ihr Büro zeigen, Peter. Es liegt gleich neben meinem.

P. Wirklich sehr nett. Und sehr gut ausgestattet.

M. Wie Sie sehen, verfügen wir tatsächlich über die allerneueste Hard- und Software. Windows 2000 ist bereits vorinstalliert, ebenso wie die Microsoft Office-Programme. Sie haben einen

Telefonieren

be shy to use it. Our service package includes **unlimited Internet usage**. You can also **access** company files at any time. Lucy will organize your **personal password**. And if you have any problem at all, call our service staff. Again, Lucy has the number. Just ask her to **put you through**.

direkten Zugriff auf das Internet – und **haben Sie keine Hemmungen**, damit zu arbeiten. Zu unserem Service-Paket gehört eine **unbeschränkte Internet-Nutzung**. Sie können außerdem jederzeit auf alle Firmendaten **zugreifen**. Lucy wird Ihnen Ihr **persönliches Passwort** geben. Wenn Sie irgendwelche Probleme haben sollten, rufen Sie einfach unser Service-Team an. Bitten Sie sie einfach, sich von ihr **durchstellen zu lassen**.

Background Information

»Programme« is in general the British spelling. But in computer applications the British use the American spelling, that is »program«.

3. Train Yourself

Wie lauten die Verben?

The office has the latest technology. It is ▒▒▒▒▒▒▒▒▒▒▒▒▒.
How do I ▒▒▒▒▒▒▒▒▒▒▒▒▒▒▒▒▒▒▒▒▒▒▒▒▒ the Internet?
What software has been ▒▒▒▒▒▒▒▒▒▒▒▒▒▒▒▒▒▒▒▒▒ ?

Background Information

A **CV – Curriculum Vitae –** is a written »Lebenslauf«. It should be brief and to the point. If you have to write one, remember it might be joining many others on a busy company director's desk. If you can't command his attention in one page then two or three aren't going to help. But avoid eye-catching tricks along the lines of »I'm just the person your company has been looking for«. Make sure there are no inexplicable gaps and also ensure that every claimed qualification can be supported by the **necessary certificates** or **diplomas**. Give two reliable references.

 **Talk Talk Talk**

M. (enters Peter's office) Lunch-time, Peter! Normally, we **go out** for sandwiches – there are some excellent sandwich bars in the area. But **let's get the week off to a good start**. Let me invite you to lunch at one of our wine bars. Forget the pubs at lunch-time. They're usually hopelessly overcrowded and you have to fight for a beer. Beer, anyway, **knocks me out** for the whole day ...

(In the wine bar)
M. Well, Peter, **what's it to be**? Can I **recommend** a very good claret. Or would you prefer a wine from your homeland?

P. No, I enjoy a Bordeaux. I'll join you in one.

M. And something with it? They do a rather fancy »Ploughman's«.

P. »Ploughman's«?

M. »Ploughman's lunch«. Basically bread and cheese – the kind of lunch the ploughman would take

M. (betritt Peters Büro) Zeit zum Mittagessen, Peter! Normalerweise lassen wir uns Sandwiches bringen – wir haben ein paar wirklich ausgezeichnete Sandwich-Bars in der Umgebung. Aber **gönnen wir uns zum Wochenauftakt** doch einmal etwas. Ich lade Sie zum Mittag in eine unserer Weinstuben ein. Die Pubs können Sie zur Mittagszeit vergessen. Sie sind normalerweise völlig überfüllt und Sie müssen um ein Bier kämpfen. Wen ich mittags ein Bier trinke **haut mich das** sowieso für den Rest des Tages **um** ...

(In der Weinstube)
M. Also, Peter, was **darf es denn sein**? Ich kann Ihnen einen sehr guten Rotwein **empfehlen**. Oder würden Sie einen Wein aus Ihrer Heimat vorziehen?

P. Nein, ich trinke gerne einen Bordeaux mit Ihnen.

M. Vielleicht noch irgendetwas dazu? Es gibt hier einen ziemlich guten »Ploughman's«.

P. »Ploughman's«?

M. Ein »Ploughman's Lunch«. Es besteht hauptsächlich aus Brot und Käse – eben die Art von

Telefonieren

with him into the fields in the old days. Now it's a staple of »**pub grub**«, but more and more wine bars are now offering it, although it's an **upmarket** »Ploughman's« – sometimes with French cheese. Sacrilege!

Mittags-Imbiss, die ein Ackersmann früher mit aufs Feld genommen hätte. Jetzt gehört er zum »pub grub« – zum »Kneipenfutter«, aber auch immer mehr Weinstuben bieten diesen Imbiss an. Allerdings ist es dann meist ein **aufgemotzter** »Ploughman's« – manchmal sogar mit französischem Käse. Was für ein Sakrileg!

 4. Train Yourself

1. Bei einer Einladung in einem Londoner Pub werden Sie von Ihrem Gastgeber gefragt, was Sie trinken möchten. Wie lautet die angemessene Antwort?

- Give me a beer.
- Would you please ask them to serve me a glass of beer.
- I'd like a beer, please.

2. Laden Sie nun Ihren Vorgesetzten ein!

- What's yours?
- Now, what would you like to drink?
- May I invite you to partake in something to drink?

 Talk Talk Talk

(Back at the office)
M. First things first, Peter. You'd better spend the afternoon making **contact** with various **estate agents**. Have you decided where you'd like to live?

(Zurück im Büro)
M. Immer eins nach dem anderen, Peter. Sie sollten heute Nachmittag erst einmal **Kontakt** zu verschiedenen **Maklern aufnehmen**. Haben Sie sich schon entschieden, wo Sie gerne wohnen würden?

P. It's a bit early for that, Mr Morgan. But I would like to make

P. Dafür ist es noch ein wenig zu früh, Mr Morgan. Aber ich würde

some initial inquiries. How should I go about it?

M. Lucy can help you there. She has a list of all the leading estate agents in London. Your **best bet** is to **give them all a call** and tell them roughly what you're looking for.

P. Thank you. I'll **tackle** Lucy about it right now ...

P. Lucy, could you please give me the numbers of some **leading** estate agents. I'd like to begin looking for some permanent accommodation.

L. My, you are in a hurry, Peter. But **don't put off until tomorrow what you can do today**. I'd start with Johnson and Partners if I were you. They **are represented** all over London. Here is their number. Can you manage or should I help you **deal with them over the phone**?

P. Oh, no, Lucy. I have to start somewhere. London estate agents can't be as frightening as Hamburg ones.

mich gerne schon mal etwas umschauen. Wie fange ich das wohl am besten an?

M. Dabei kann Lucy Ihnen helfen. Sie hat eine Liste mit den wichtigsten Wohnungsmaklern von London. Sie haben **die besten Chancen**, wenn sie einfach alle **anrufen** und ihnen grob sagen, was Sie suchen.

P. Vielen Dank. Ich werde Lucy gleich damit **überfallen** ...

P. Lucy, könnten Sie mir bitte die Telefonnummern von einigen der **führenden** Wohnungsmaklern geben? Ich würde gern damit anfangen, nach einer dauerhaften Bleibe zu suchen.

L. Meine Güte, Sie sind ja von der ganz schnellen Truppe, Peter. Aber es stimmt schon, **verschiebe nie auf morgen, was du heute kannst besorgen**. Ich würde an Ihrer Stelle mit Johnson and Partners anfangen. Sie **haben** überall in London ihre **Filialen**. Hier ist ihre Nummer. Kommen Sie zurecht, oder soll ich Ihnen helfen, wenn Sie **am Telefon mit ihnen verhandeln**?

P. Oh, nein, Lucy, Danke. Irgendwann muss ich schließlich damit anfangen, allein klar zu kommen. Und Londoner Makler können gar nicht so Furcht einflößend sein wie die in Hamburg.

Telefonieren

L. Then here's the number. **Can I** at least **connect you**?	L. Gut, hier haben Sie die Nummer. **Soll ich Sie** wenigstens **durchstellen**?
P. No, no. Let me try myself … **Hello, is that** Johnson and Partners? My name is Peter Brückner. I'm new in London and I am looking for permanent accommodation. I thought you might be able to help me. My company recommended you.	P. Nein, nein. Lassen Sie es mich selbst versuchen … **Hallo, spreche ich da mit** Johnson und Partners? Mein Name ist Peter Brückner. Ich bin gerade erst nach London gekommen und suche nun nach einer festen Bleibe. Ich dachte, Sie könnten mir vielleicht dabei helfen. Sie wurden mir von meiner Firma empfohlen.
(Johnson and Partners switchboard) I'm afraid you are **connected** at the moment to the **switchboard**. I'll have to **put you through** to one of our letting staff. What area are you interested in?	(Telefonzentrale von Johnson und Partners) Tut mir Leid, Sie sind momentan mit der **Vermittlungszentrale** unserer Firma **verbunden**. Ich werde Sie mit einem unserer Wohnungsvermittler **weiterverbinden**. An welches Wohngebiet hatten Sie denn gedacht?
P. Oh dear! I don't really know. Somewhere quite central but not too expensive.	P. Du meine Güte! Das weiß ich wirklich nicht. Relativ zentral, aber nicht zu teuer.
(Switchboard operator) Well, that makes things difficult. I'll ask Mr Johnson. **Please hold the line** a moment …	(Vermittler der Telefonzentrale) Tja, das macht es nicht gerade leichter. Ich werde Mr Johnson fragen. **Bitte bleiben Sie dran** …
P. Hello, hello! Damn, I think they have **cut me off**. Lucy, I need your help. **How can I get reconnected**?	P. Hallo, Hallo? Verdammt, ich glaube, die haben mich **aus der Leitung geworfen**. Lucy, ich brauche Ihre Hilfe. **Wie bekomme ich wieder eine Verbindung**?

L. **The line is still open**, Peter. You'll just have to wait. Didn't they tell you **to hold on**?

P. Yes, but **the line seems to have gone dead**. I think she's **put the phone down** on me! I'll **hang up** and try again ... Hello, Johnson and Partners? You seem to have cut me off ...

J. **Who's there**?

P. Peter Brückner, from Hamburg ...

J. Hamburg? You sound as if you are just around the corner. **Do you want to speak to me**?

P. I *am* just around the corner! **Who am I speaking to**?

J. Johnson! **What can I do for you?**

P. Mr Johnson himself? Oh, **I'm very sorry to trouble you**, but your **telephone operator** said she'd **connect** me to somebody who could help me with my **inquiry**.

J. What inquiry?

L. **Die Verbindung steht noch**, Peter. Sie müssen einfach warten. Haben sie Ihnen nicht gesagt, Sie sollen **in der Leitung bleiben**?

P. Ja, aber **die Verbindung scheint unterbrochen worden zu sein**. Ich glaube, Sie **hat einfach aufgelegt**! Ich **lege** jetzt auch **auf** und versuche es noch einmal ... Hallo, Johnson und Partners? Sie scheinen mich aus der Leitung geworfen zu haben ...

J. **Wer spricht da bitte**?

P. Peter Brückner, aus Hamburg ...

J. Hamburg? Sie klingen, als wären sie gleich um die Ecke. **Sie wollten mit mir sprechen**?

P. Ich *bin* gleich um die Ecke! **Mit wem spreche ich**?

J. Johnson! **Was kann ich für Sie tun**?

P. Mr Johnson persönlich? Oh, es **tut mir sehr Leid, Sie zu belästigen**, aber die **Dame in Ihrer Telefonzentrale** sagte, sie würde mich mit jemandem **verbinden**, der mir bei meiner **Anfrage** weiterhelfen könnte.

J. Was für eine Anfrage?

Telefonieren

P. I'm looking for somewhere to rent in London.	P. Ich suche eine Mietwohnung in London.
J. Where in London?	J. Wo in London?
P. Well, I haven't really decided yet. I thought I'd **look around** first.	P. Na ja, ich habe mich da noch nicht entschieden. Ich dachte, **ich sehe mich** erst einmal **etwas um** ...
J. My God, man! London's a big city, you know – a lot bigger even than your Hamburg. You have a good look around first and when you've found an area to your liking then **by all means** call us again. **Good day to you!**	J. Mein Gott, mein Bester! London ist eine große Stadt, wissen Sie – viel größer als Ihr Hamburg. Sehen Sie sich also bitte erst einmal gut um und wenn Sie ein Viertel gefunden haben, das Ihnen gefällt, dann rufen Sie uns **auf jeden Fall** wieder an. **Einen schönen guten Tag noch!**

 5. Train Yourself

1. Nachdem Sie einige Zeit vergeblich darauf gewartet haben, durchgestellt zu werden, beschließen Sie, es einfach noch einmal zu versuchen. Diesmal sind Sie erfolgreich. Was sagen Sie der Vermittlung?

Hello! I believe I was ▇▇▇▇▇ off when I ▇▇▇▇▇ the first time. I was told to ▇▇▇▇▇ the line, but then the phone ▇▇▇▇▇ dead. I decided to ▇▇▇▇▇ up and try to be ▇▇▇▇▇.

2. Sie haben jemanden am Telefon, der falsch verbunden wurde.
Er spricht Sie mit Mr Smith an und beschwert sich fürchterlich über eine falsche Lieferung. Wie führen Sie das Gespräch?

I'm sorry. You appear to have been wrongly ▇▇▇▇▇. If you'd like to ▇▇▇▇▇ I shall try to ▇▇▇▇▇ you ▇▇▇▇▇ to the person you are looking for. If you don't ▇▇▇▇▇ through then please ▇▇▇▇▇ again.

 **Talk Talk Talk**

(Steve to Peter)
S. Well, Peter. **How are you doing**? Found a place, or will you be making your bed at Buckingham Palace?

P. I've had terrible trouble, Steve. First of all I had difficulty **being put through** to the Estate Agency and then they seemed to be **put out** because I wasn't sure where I wanted to live.

S. Didn't you tell them Wimbledon? Don't listen to Melissa. She has no idea of the delights Wimbledon has to offer. Look, **give me a buzz** tonight after you get home and we'll fix something up. There are a few good pubs in my area. Not up to the standard of Morgan's wine bar, I'll admit. But at least the beer is good – even for a German's taste!

P. **That's very kind of you**, Steve. I'll certainly **give you a call** - that is, **if my phone is working** again. I've had such problems with the

(Steve zu Peter)
S. Also, Peter, **sind Sie weiter gekommen**? Haben Sie eine Wohnung gefunden oder werden Sie Ihr Lager im Buckingham Palace aufschlagen?

P. Ich hatte furchtbaren Ärger, Steve. Zuerst hatte ich Probleme, bei dieser Maklerfirma richtig **durchgestellt zu werden** und dann scheinen sie mich **aus der Leitung geworfen zu haben**, weil ich nicht wusste, wo ich wohnen wollte.

S. Warum haben Sie nicht einfach Wimbledon gesagt? Hören Sie bloß nicht auf Melissa. Sie hat keine Ahnung von den Vorteilen, die Wimbledon bietet. Passen Sie auf: **Rufen Sie** einfach **kurz durch**, wenn Sie heute Abend nach Hause kommen, und wir regeln das schon. Es gibt ein paar wirklich gute Pubs in meiner Gegend. Allerdings nicht gerade das Niveau von Morgans Wine Bar, das muss ich zugeben. Aber wenigstens ist das Bier gut – sogar für deutsche Geschmäcker!

P. **Das ist wirklich sehr nett von Ihnen**, Steve. **Ich rufe** ganz bestimmt **durch** – vorausgesetzt, mein **Telefon funktioniert wieder**.

Telefonieren

telephone system since I arrived that I'm beginning to believe it's jinxed.

Seit ich hier bin, habe ich solche Probleme mit dem Londoner **Telefonsystem** – ich glaube fast, es ist verhext.

S. **Not to worry**. Use pigeon post. There are enough of the blighters in Trafalgar Square.

S. **Nur keine Sorge**. Benutzen Sie einfach Brieftauben. Auf dem Trafalgar Square gibt es wahrlich genug von den Biestern.

P. Pigeon post?

P. Brieftauben?

S. Send the message by pigeon. Just my humour, Peter – I'm glad to have somebody new to try it out on. Sorry!

S. Ach, das ist nur meine Art von Humor, Peter – ich bin froh, das ich ein neues Opfer habe, an dem ich ihn ausprobieren kann. Tut mir Leid!

 6. Train Yourself

1. Ein Freund ruft an, um Sie zum Essen einzuladen. Wie lautet die angemessene Antwort?

Thank you ▨▨▨▨▨▨▨▨▨ *(very much or kindly?)*. It's very ▨▨▨▨▨▨▨▨▨ *(kind or accommodating?)* to think of me. I'd ▨▨▨▨▨▨▨▨▨ *(love or be enchanted?)* to come, but I'm not sure how long I shall be staying at the office. Can I ▨▨▨▨▨▨▨▨▨ *(call you or give you a telephone call?)* later?

2. Sie können die Einladung nicht annehmen, weil Sie zu beschäftigt sind. Wie würden Sie ablehnen, wenn die Einladung von Ihrem Chef käme?

- Sorry, I can't make it tonight.
- I'm busy - perhaps another time.
- I'd love to come, but I'm afraid I shall be working late.
- Can you call me later at the office and I'll let you know then.

 **Talk Talk Talk**

(The next day, in the office)
L. Good morning, Peter! You **look a bit down**. Anything wrong?

P. I was out with Steve last night and lost my briefcase. I think I left it on the tube.

L. Goodness me. Did it have anything valuable in it?

P. Just some **papers**. Thank goodness I always carry my passport and **wallet** on me. But I would like to try and get it back.

L. Then you must **call** the **Lost Property**. You might be lucky, although I wouldn't be too hopeful if I were you.

P. I'll **try them** right now. Can you **put me through**, Lucy?

L. Certainly. I have the number of London Transport right here. I'll **dial** it for you. Oh, dear the number is **engaged. I'll try again in a few minutes** ... Peter? I have London Transport on the line now.

(Am nächsten Tag im Büro)
L. Guten Morgen, Peter! Sie sehen **etwas deprimiert aus**. Stimmt etwas nicht?

P. Ich war gestern Abend mit Steve unterwegs und habe meine Aktentasche verloren. Ich glaube, ich habe sie in der U-Bahn liegen lassen.

L. Du liebe Güte. War etwas Wertvolles drin?

P. Nur ein paar **Unterlagen**. Gott sei Dank trage ich meinen Ausweis und meine **Brieftasche** immer bei mir. Aber ich würde gerne versuchen, sie zurückzubekommen.

L. Dann müssen Sie das **Fundbüro anrufen**. Vielleicht haben Sie ja Glück, obwohl ich mir an Ihrer Stelle keine zu großen Hoffnungen machen würde.

P. Ich **versuche es** sofort **bei ihnen**. Können Sie mich **durchstellen**, Lucy?

L. Natürlich. Ich habe die Nummer vom Londoner Nahverkehr gleich hier. Ich **wähle** für Sie. Oh, so ein Pech, die Leitung ist **besetzt. Ich versuche es in ein paar Minuten noch einmal** ... Peter? Ich habe

Telefonieren

25

P. (picks up phone in his office)

Hello, is that London Transport? Could you **put me through** please to your Lost Property Department? Thank you! Lost Property? **I wonder if you could help me.** I believe I lost my brief case late last night on the District Line between Wimbledon and Victoria. It's black hide with brass locks and it has the initials PB inscribed in gold lettering. Yes, I'll **hang on** ... You do? That's fantastic. I never really expected to have it returned. Thank you so much. I'll call today for it. What is **your address**? And until what time are you open. You close at eight? Fine, I shall **call by** around six.

jetzt die Verwaltungszentrale des Londoner Nahverkehrs am Telefon.

P. (nimmt in seinem Büro den Hörer ab)

Hallo, ist dort die Londoner Nahverkehrszentrale? Könnten Sie mich bitte zu Ihrer Fundstelle **durchstellen**? Vielen Dank! Hallo, ist dort die Fundstelle? **Ich frage mich, ob Sie mir helfen können.** Ich glaube, ich habe gestern Abend meine Aktentasche auf der Linie Wimbledon/Victoria verloren. Sie ist aus schwarzem Leder mit einem Messingverschluss und trägt goldene Initialen mit den Buchstaben PB. Ja, **ich warte** ... Sie haben sie? Das ist ja fantastisch! Ich hätte nie gedacht, dass ich sie wiederbekomme. Haben Sie vielen Dank. Ich hole sie heute noch ab. Wie ist denn **Ihre Adresse**? Und wie lange haben Sie geöffnet? Sie schließen um acht? Schön, ich werde so gegen sechs Uhr **vorbeikommen**.

7. Train Yourself

Eine ausländische Touristin hat ihren Regenschirm auf dem oberen Teil eines Londoner Busses liegen lassen und rief das Fundbüro des Londoner Nahverkehrs an. Sie wissen jetzt genug, um ihr Englisch korrigieren zu können – also an die Arbeit ...

Hello, am I talking to Lost Property? No? What number is on the line? Can you talk more slow! I need to say to Lost Property I have lost my umbrella! Please direct me to the right number! What means dial? Extension? Extend what? Please talk more clear! I repeat – I became this number from the book for telephones and now you say me I have not the right number!

False Friends

The English »**briefcase**« is the German »Aktentasche«. The English word for »Brieftasche« is »wallet«.

Another false friend is »**engaged**« which can't be translated into German as »engagiert«. »Engaged« means either »verlobt sein« or – as in our case – »(Leitung) besetzt sein«. The English word for »engagiert« is »dedicated« or »involved«.

 Talk Talk Talk

S. (enters office) Hello Lucy, hello Peter! Get home all right last night?

P. Yes, **no problem**, but I left my briefcase on the train. It's been **handed in** at the Lost Property, though.

S. Did you call them? They are usually so **busy** you have to wait an age to **get through**.

P. Lucy helped **connect** me. They were very helpful.

S. Lucky it was only the briefcase, my friend. We had **quite a bit** to drink, you know!

P. It's not the amount so much, it's the speed with which you English put it back.

S. (betritt das Büro) Hallo Lucy, hallo Peter! Sind Sie letzte Nacht gut nach Hause gekommen?

P. Ja, **kein Problem**, aber ich habe meine Aktentasche in der U-Bahn liegen gelassen. Zum Glück wurde sie beim Fundbüro **abgegeben**.

S. Haben Sie da angerufen? Normalerweise sind die so **beschäftigt**, dass man eine Ewigkeit warten muss um **durchzukommen**.

P. Lucy hat mir dabei geholfen, eine **Verbindung** zu bekommen. Sie waren wirklich sehr hilfsbereit.

S. Gut, dass es nur Ihre Aktentasche war, mein Freund. Wir haben **einiges** getrunken gestern Abend!

P. Ach, es war gar nicht mal die Menge, sondern das Tempo, mit dem ihr Engländer es 'runterkippt.

S. You have to be **quick on the downtake** to beat that damn bell they ring.

S. Tja, man muss einen **guten Zug am Leibe haben**, um diese verdammte Sperrstunden-Glocke zu schlagen.

P. I thought all that was now abolished with the new opening hours.

P. Oh, und ich dachte, mit den neuen Sperrstunden hätte sich das erübrigt?

S. **Fine thought!** They've relaxed the closing hours but they're still nothing like yours in good old Hamburg. And they still ring that bell for **last orders**. Gets on my nerves.

S. **Schön wär's!** Die Sperrstunden sind zwar etwas gelockert worden, aber das ist immer noch nichts verglichen mit den Kneipenöffnungszeiten in Ihrer alten Heimat Hamburg. Und es wird hier immer noch eine Glocke geläutet, um die **letzten Bestellungen** entgegenzunehmen. Das geht mir ganz schön auf die Nerven.

 Background Information

Drinking habits are very different in Britain to those in Germany, particularly in pubs. The British buy »rounds« when drinking in company, meaning each person in the group **pays in turn for all the others**. Under no circumstances try to pay only your own account – that is regarded as very bad behaviour! The practice of buying rounds can, of course, create problems, particularly if you're in a large group!

 **Talk Talk Talk**

M. Good morning all!

M. Guten Morgen zusammen!

S. My, you're **bright and breezy** this morning, Melissa.

S. Meine Güte, Sie sind ja heute **frisch wie der junge Morgen**, Melissa.

M. More than I can say for you. You look as if you haven't slept. Out **on the town** again?

S. Depends what you mean by town. I was showing a bit of it to our new colleague.

M. Showing him the pubs, **more like it**.

S. Nearly called you to ask you to join us.

M. You wouldn't have got far. I keep my **voice-mail** on to **keep** types like you **at bay**.

S. I'd have left you a sweet message, my dear – but I needed my **small change** for other things.

M. For the next beer, no doubt.

S. OK, next time I really will call and leave you a message.

M. You'll have to wait a long time for an answer, my lad.

M. Das ist mehr, als man von Ihnen sagen kann. Sie sehen aus, als hätten Sie kein Auge zugemacht. Sind Sie wieder mal **um die Häuser gezogen**?

S. So könnte man es auch sagen. Ich habe unserem neuen Kollegen ein bisschen von der Stadt gezeigt.

M. **Wahrscheinlich eher** die Kneipen.

S. Ich hätte Sie fast angerufen, um zu fragen, ob Sie mitkommen.

M. Na, da wären Sie nicht weit gekommen. Ich lasse extra meinen **Anrufbeantworter** immer laufen, um mir Typen wie Sie **vom Hals zu halten**.

S. Oh, ich hätte Ihnen schon eine süße Liebesbotschaft hinterlassen, meine Liebe – aber ich brauchte mein **Kleingeld** für etwas anderes.

M. Für das nächste Bier, keine Frage.

S. OK, nächstes Mal werde ich wirklich anrufen und Ihnen eine Nachricht hinterlassen.

M. Na, da werden Sie lange auf eine Antwort warten müssen, mein Guter.

Telefonieren

S. And if I call to invite you for a really exciting night out?

S. Und wenn ich Sie anrufe und zu einem wirklich aufregenden Abend einlade?

 Background Information

A telephone answering machine is also called »**voice-mail**« in England. If you leave a message on voice-mail, make sure you identify yourself clearly and also distinctly give the number where you can be reached, repeating it for emphasis. If you are leaving a mobile number on voice-mail it's especially helpful to enunciate each digit slowly and also repeat the full number.

 Vocabulary

to access	zugreifen auf
answering machine/answer-phone	Anrufbeantworter
to be represented all over a city	in der ganzen Stadt Filialen haben
to be speaking/calling/on the line	am Apparat sein
briefcase	Aktentasche
to call by	vorbeikommen
cell(ular) phone	Mobiltelefon, Handy
to connect sb.	jdn. durchstellen
to cut sb. off	jdn. aus der Leitung werfen
CV (curriculum vitae)	Lebenslauf
to deal with sb. over the phone	am Telefon mit jdm. verhandeln
to dial	wählen
estate agent	Wohnungsmakler
extension	Durchwahl
to get through	durchkommen
to give sb. a buzz	(ugs.) jdn. anrufen
to give sb. a call	jdn. anrufen
to hang up and try again	auflegen und es noch einmal versuchen
to hang/hold (on); hold the line	in der Leitung bleiben, warten
to have difficulty in reaching sb.	Probleme haben, jdn. zu erreichen
Hello, is that ...	Hallo, spreche ich mit ...

How can I get reconnected?	Wie bekomme ich wieder Verbindung?
inquiry	Anfrage
instant access	direkter Zugriff
leading	führend
to look in	hereinschauen
to lift	abnehmen (Hörer)
to make contact	Kontakt aufnehmen
May I help you?	Kann ich Ihnen behilflich sein?
meeting	Besprechung
to mend the lines	Leitungen reparieren
mobile (phone)	Mobiltelefon, Handy
not to get through	nicht durchkommen
operator	Vermittlung
personnel department	Personal-Abteilung
to phone to find out	anrufen, um nachzufragen
to put sb. through	jdn. durchstellen
to put the phone down	auflegen
to reach on the phone	telefonisch erreichen
to step into	hereinkommen
shortly	in Kürze, gleich
small change	Kleingeld
... speaking	... am Apparat
switchboard	Vermittlungszentrale
to tackle formalities	Formalitäten in Angriff nehmen
telephone number	Telefonnummer
telephone receiver	Telefonhörer
the line is still open	die Verbindung steht noch
the line went dead	die Verbindung wurde unterbrochen
the number is ringing	es wird gerade durchgeläutet
the number/line is engaged	es ist belegt
to trouble s.o.	jdn. belästigen
to try to get hold of sb.	versuchen, jdn. zu erreichen
tube (colloq.)	U-Bahn
unlimited usage	unbeschränkte Nutzung
voice mail	Anrufbeantworter
wrongly connected	falsch verbunden

Telefonieren

In the Sales Department
In der Verkaufsabteilung

 Here we go

Nach seinen ersten Telefonerfahrungen und den ersten kleinen Schwierigkeiten beim Zurechtfinden im britischen Alltags- und Geschäftsleben beginnt für Peter jetzt die zweite Woche im fernen London. Die nächste Zeit wird er im Büro von Steve Blackman assistieren, um einen Einblick in die Welt des Verkaufs zu bekommen.

 Talk Talk Talk

(Peter enters)
L. Good morning, Peter! Your second week already. What has Mr Morgan in mind for you?

P. **I'm joining** Steve in the Sales Department, but first I have to complete some **formalities** with the **Department of social security**. They have written to me with some forms. I have to get a **social security number**. I was so busy last week that I never got around to it.

L. Shall I help you? Just give me the **forms**.

(Peter kommt herein)
L. Guten Morgen, Peter! Das ist ja schon Ihre zweite Arbeitswoche. Was hat Mr Morgan für Sie geplant?

P. **Ich werde** Steve in der Verkaufsabteilung **unterstützen**, aber zuerst muss ich noch ein paar **Formalitäten** mit dem **Sozialversicherungsamt** abklären. Die haben mir ein paar Formulare geschickt. Ich brauche noch eine **Sozialversicherungsnummer**. Ich war letzte Woche so beschäftigt, dass ich mich noch gar nicht darum kümmern konnte.

L. Soll ich Ihnen dabei helfen? Geben Sie mir doch einfach die **Formulare**.

P. Thank you, Lucy, but I think I'll have to phone them first with some personal questions. It will be easier if I deal with them myself.

L. Then pour yourself a cup of tea and I'll put you through ...

P. ... Hello, is that the Department of Social Security? I have some questions **regarding** my **employment** in Britain. **Could you connect me with somebody who could help me**. No, I'm not applying for assisted housing – whatever that is. Hello! Who am I speaking to? The **Pensions Officer**? How was I put through to you? Can you reconnect me to the switchboard, please! Hello! Who? Maternity benefit?
Lucy, Lucy! Help, please!

P. Danke, Lucy, aber ich glaube, ich muss zuerst mal mit denen telefonieren, um ein paar persönliche Fragen zu klären. Es wird sicher einfacher sein, wenn ich das selbst regle.

L. Dann gießen Sie sich erst einmal eine Tasse Tee ein. Ich stelle Sie derweil durch ...

P. ... Hallo, spreche ich mit dem Amt für Sozialversicherungen? Ich habe ein paar Fragen **bezüglich** meiner **Arbeitsanstellung** in Großbritannien. **Könnten Sie mich bitte mit jemandem verbinden, der mir da weiterhelfen kann?** Nein, ich frage nicht wegen »Assisted Housing« an – was immer das sein mag. Hallo! Mit wem spreche ich bitte? Mit dem **Abteilungsleiter für Pensionsfragen**? Wieso hat man mich denn mit Ihnen verbunden? Könnten Sie mich bitte zur Telefonzentrale zurückverbinden? Hallo? Wer? Mutterschaftshilfe?
Lucy, Lucy! Helfen Sie mir bitte!

Telefonieren

 8. Train Yourself

Peter schafft es endlich bei der zuständigen Stelle durchzukommen. Wie entwickelt sich das Gespräch weiter?

Official: Good morning, can I be ▓▓▓▓▓?
P. Yes, please! I've been trying for ages to ▓▓▓▓▓ the right person. I hope I've now been ▓▓▓▓▓ correctly.
O. I can't understand how you had problems ▓▓▓▓▓ through to me. What is it you ▓▓▓▓▓?

P. I have just started work for a company in London. I'm German and I'm told I must obtain a social security number.

O. Is this your first ▩▩▩ to us?

P. Yes, I was too busy during my first week at work to spare the time to ▩▩▩ you.

O. Don't worry. Did we send you the necessary forms?

P. Yes, but I have so many questions I thought it better to ▩▩▩ you personally.

O. I can't really help you ▩▩▩ the phone. You'll have to ▩▩▩ by personally. Can you ▩▩▩ to make an appointment? I'll ▩▩▩ you ▩▩▩ to the secretary.

P. Hello, hello! Who am I ▩▩▩ to now? Maternity benefit! Oh, no!

 Talk Talk Talk

(Steve's Office)

P. Good morning, Steve. Mr Morgan tells me I'm working for you this week.

S. That's right, Peter. I hope you don't pick up any bad habits. I tried to call you at the weekend, but there was no reply. You don't have **voice-mail**?

P. Voice-mail? You mean an **answering machine**? I have ordered one from the **telephone people**, but it will take another week or so to install. I travelled down to Brighton at the weekend. German friends called me up on Saturday morning to invite me down there.

(Steves Büro)

P. Guten Morgen, Steve. Mr Morgan hat mir gesagt, dass ich diese Woche für Sie arbeite.

S. Stimmt, Peter. Hoffentlich gewöhnen Sie sich bei mir keine schlechten Eigenschaften an. Ich habe schon versucht, Sie am Wochenende anzurufen, aber da ging niemand ans Telefon. Haben Sie denn kein **Voice-Mail**?

P. Voice-Mail? Ach, Sie meinen einen **Anrufbeantworter**? Ich habe einen bei der **Telefongesellschaft** beantragt, aber es wird noch etwa eine Woche dauern, bis er angeschlossen ist. Ich bin über das Wochenende in Brighton gewesen. Freunde aus Deutschland hatten mich über das Wochenende dorthin eingeladen.

S. Well, I hope you had a relaxing time because we've got a busy week ahead of us. Our **top salesman** called in sick this morning, and I can't get hold of his **replacement**.

P. How can I help out?

S. Look, can you keep on trying his numbers. He's not even answering his **mobile**. Something must have happened to him over the weekend. He's usually very reliable and has his **report** on my desk first thing Monday mornings.

P. Report?

S. Each of our half dozen salespersons must submit a weekly **progress report**. Four are in. One man is sick – and one's gone missing! While I work through these reports can you try to **track** him **down**. Keep trying to get him on the phone. You can also **phone around** the other salespersons to see if they have any idea where he is.

P. No problem, Steve. Just give me the numbers.

S. Tja, ich hoffe, Sie haben sich gut erholt, denn wir haben eine anstrengende Woche vor uns. Unser **Top-Verkäufer** hat sich heute Morgen krank gemeldet und ich erreiche seine **Vertretung** nicht.

P. Wie kann ich da weiterhelfen?

S. Nun ja, Sie können versuchen, ihn weiter über seine Telefonnummer zu erreichen. Er geht nicht einmal an sein **Handy**. Irgendetwas muss ihm am Wochenende passiert sein. Er ist normalerweise sehr zuverlässig und ich habe seinen **Bericht** immer Montag früh auf dem Schreibtisch.

P. Berichte?

S. Jeder unserer sechs Vertreter und Vertreterinnen im Außendienst muss einen wöchentlichen **Erfolgsbericht** abliefern. Vier haben wir bereits. Einer unser Leute ist krank – und einer wird vermisst! Während ich mich durch diese Berichte arbeite, können Sie versuchen, ihn **aufzuspüren**. Versuchen Sie weiter, ihn ans Telefon zu bekommen. Sie können auch bei den anderen Vertretern **herumtelefonieren** – vielleicht haben die ja eine Ahnung, wo er stecken könnte.

P. Kein Problem, Steve. Geben Sie mir einfach die Nummern.

Telefonieren

S. Here's his mobile number. He has instructions to have it **switched on** at all times. And here is his home number. He has voice-mail and I've left **umpteen** messages on it already.

S. Hier ist seine Handy-Nummer. Er hat eigentlich Anweisungen, es Tag und Nacht **eingeschaltet** zu lassen. Und hier ist seine Nummer von zu Hause. Er hat einen Anrufbeantworter und ich habe bereits **zig** Nachrichten hinterlassen.

P. **I'll get down to it right away**. Is there anything I should know about him?

P. **Ich kümmere mich sofort darum.** Gibt es etwas, das ich über ihn wissen sollte?

S. His name is Joe Sampson. Single, lives alone in Newcastle and **covers** the entire north-east for us from there.

S. Sein Name ist Joe Sampson. Er ist Single und lebt allein in Newcastle. Das ganze Nord-Ost-Gebiet **fällt unter** seine **Zuständigkeit**.

 Background Information

Salesman or salesperson?
»-person« in combination instead of »-man« is used in Great Britain to avoid illegal or unnecessary discrimination on grounds of sex.

 9. Train Yourself

Peter schafft es endlich, Joe Sampson auf seinem Handy zu erreichen. Wie verläuft die weitere Konversation?

P. Hello, Mr Sampson? ▬▬▬ Peter Brückner, from ERGO in London. We have been trying to ▬▬▬ you for ages. Mr Blackman has ▬▬▬ several messages on your ▬▬▬ ▬▬▬. He hasn't received your weekly report either. Is anything wrong?

S. I've just come out of hospital. I slipped and injured my shoulder while putting up some cupboards on Saturday morning and the neighbours carted me off to hospital. I'm sorry I didn't have my ▬▬▬ phone with me. Have you been trying very long to ▬▬▬ me?

P. I've been trying for more than an hour to ▓▓▓▓▓ you, but I just couldn't ▓▓▓▓▓ through. I'll tell Mr Blackman you're OK, and I'm sure he'll be ▓▓▓▓▓ you shortly. He wants your weekly report!

 **Talk Talk Talk**

(Steve's office)
S. I'm glad to hear he's OK but he could have found some way of calling me. He should have that mobile on him and either have it switched on or check the voice-mail twice a day. That's part of his contract. You see the problems we have with the sales staff, Peter!

P. I asked him to call you right away, and he said he would. That'll be him now.

S. Hello, Joe? I was just telling Peter here we're glad to hear you are OK, but you had us worried. Now what about that report? No, I can't wait until you **punch it back into** the system and **email** it. That'll take hours. Fax it – as soon as possible, OK? Otherwise, did you have a good week? Give me a buzz later today and tell me all about it. And find an expert to put up those cupboards – you're paid to sell our systems!

(Steves Büro)
S. Ich freue mich zu hören, dass es ihm gut geht – aber er hätte eine Möglichkeit finden müssen, mich anzurufen. Er hätte sein Handy eingeschaltet haben müssen oder er hätte seinen Anrufbeantworter zweimal am Tag abhören sollen. Das gehört zu seinem Vertrag. Da sehen Sie mal, was wir für Probleme mit unseren Verkäufern haben, Peter!

P. Ich habe ihn darum gebeten, Sie umgehend anzurufen – und er sagte, er würde es sofort tun. Das müsste er sein.

S. Hallo Joe? Ich habe Peter gerade gesagt, dass wir froh sind, dass es Ihnen gut geht, aber wir haben uns Sorgen um Sie gemacht. Was ist jetzt mit dem Bericht? Nein, ich kann nicht warten, bis Sie ihn in den Computer **gehackt** haben und **per E-Mail herüberschicken**. Das wird ja Stunden dauern. Faxen Sie ihn – so schnell wie möglich, okay? Und hatten Sie ansonsten eine gute Woche? Rufen Sie mich doch später an und erzählen Sie mir darüber. Und suchen Sie sich gefälligst einen

Telefonieren

Fachmann, der Ihnen diese Regale aufstellt – Sie werden dafür bezahlt, unsere Systeme zu verkaufen!

 10. Train Yourself

1. Sie fühlen sich nicht wohl und beschließen, einen Arzt zu konsultieren. Rufen Sie Lucy an und sagen Sie ihr, dass Sie zu spät zur Arbeit kommen werden.

Hello, Lucy. It's Peter Brückner. I've just ▓▓▓▓▓▓▓▓ to say I shall be slightly late because I want to go to the doctor. Can you take any ▓▓▓▓▓▓▓▓ for me? If any of the salesmen ▓▓▓▓▓▓▓▓, please ▓▓▓▓▓▓▓▓ them to ▓▓▓▓▓▓▓▓ Dave, and he'll handle things. I have my ▓▓▓▓▓▓▓▓ with me, so please try to ▓▓▓▓▓▓▓▓ me on it if I'm needed urgently.

2. Formen Sie aus unten stehenden Sätzen einen einzigen Satz, indem Sie Konjunktionen verwenden *(and, but, so, because, that etc.).*

- I have a doctor's appointment.
- I shan't be at the office until later.
- I just called to say ...
- If there are any calls for me please take messages.

 Talk Talk Talk

(Steve's office)
S. Peter, let me now **induct** you into the very secret world of sales!

(Steves Büro)
S. So Peter, jetzt werde ich Sie in die Geheimnisse des erfolgreichen Verkaufens **einführen**.

P. Secret?

P. Geheimnisse?

S. Our business is so **innovative** and **competitive** that our sales people **play their cards very close to**

S. Unsere Branche ist so **innovativ** und es **herrscht** so **ein starker Wettbewerb**, dass unsere Ver-

the chest. I have difficulty myself **winkling out** the details of their reports. Sometimes I'm on the phone for hours **clarifying** and **elaborating points**. Reaching them is also a problem, although they are supposed to be on duty practically around the clock. I'll give you a **test run** first of all. Geoff Burnes says he's **on the brink** of **sealing a** big **contract** with Metropolitan Newspapers. We're trying to **break into** the provincial newspapers with a new copy-editing software system, called Quick-Ed. Give Geoff a call – at least, try to reach him – and ask if he has anything new to report **on that front**. There's absolutely nothing about it in his weekly report.

(Peter reports back after ten minutes)
P. I've tried his home number but he's not there. I left a message on his **answer-phone** and also on his mobile. I asked him to call back urgently.

S. OK, give me a few minutes while I just clarify one or two

käufer **ihre Geheimnisse für sich behalten**. Ich habe sogar selbst manchmal Probleme, die Details ihrer Berichte zu **enträtseln**. Manchmal verbringe ich am Telefon Stunden damit, bestimmte **Punkte** zu **klären** und **ausführlich auszuarbeiten**. Sie zu erreichen ist außerdem auch immer ein Problem, obwohl sie eigentlich rund um die Uhr im Dienst sein sollten. Ich werde sie erst einmal durch einen **Testlauf** schicken. Geoff Burnes sagt, dass er **kurz davor** steht, **einen Vertrag** mit Metropolitan Newspapers **abzuschließen**. Wir versuchen, mit unserem neuen redaktionellen Softwaresystem Quick-Ed **in den Markt** der provinziellen Zeitungen **vorzudringen**. Rufen Sie Geoff an – oder versuchen Sie wenigstens, ihn zu erreichen – und fragen Sie ihn, ob es **in dieser Sache** etwas Neues gibt. In seinem wöchentlichen Bericht steht absolut nichts darüber.

(Peter meldet sich nach zehn Minuten zurück)
P. Ich habe versucht, ihn zu Hause zu erreichen, aber er ist scheinbar nicht da. Ich habe sowohl auf seinem **Anrufbeantworter** als auch auf seinem Handy eine Nachricht hinterlassen. Ich habe ihn gebeten, dringend zurückzurufen.

S. Okay, geben Sie mir ein paar Minuten, in denen ich ein oder

Telefonieren

points in this other report ...	zwei Punkte in diesem anderen Bericht klären muss ...
(Peter's office phone rings) P. Hello, Peter Brückner here.	(Peters Telefon klingelt) P. Hallo, Peter Brückner am Apparat.
L. Oh, Peter! I have a very **agitated** Mr Burnes on the phone. He says he's been trying **for ages** to get through to Steve, but the line is constantly engaged.	L. Oh, Peter! Ich habe hier einen sehr **aufgeregten** Mr Burnes in der Leitung. Er meint, er würde jetzt schon **seit einer Ewigkeit** versuchen, zu Steve durchzukommen, aber die Leitung wäre ständig besetzt.
P. Steve has a lot of phoning to do this morning. Could you put Mr Burnes through to me please, Lucy. Hello, Mr Burnes?	P. Steve hat heute Morgen eine Menge zu tun. Könnten Sie Mr Burnes bitte zu mir durchstellen, Lucy? Hallo, Mr Burnes?
G. Yes, can I speak to Steve Blackman?	G. Ja, könnte ich bitte mit Steve Blackman sprechen?
P. **Not right now, his line is busy.** He's asked me to contact you and ask if you have anything new to report on the possible Metropolitan Newspapers contract.	P. **Er telefoniert gerade.** Er hat mich gebeten, Kontakt zu Ihnen aufzunehmen und Sie zu fragen, ob Sie etwas Neues über den möglichen Vertrag mit Metropolitan Newspapers zu berichten haben.
G. Good Lord! I've only just knocked on the door there. **Give me a break!** Tell Steve to call me back. But he'd better **make it snappy** – I'm back **on the road** as soon as I can get myself some lunch.	G. Meine Güte! Ich habe da doch erst vorsichtig an die Tür geklopft! **Machen Sie mal halblang!** Sagen Sie Steve bitte, er soll mich zurückrufen. Aber er **sollte sich besser beeilen** – ich bin gleich wieder **unterwegs** und versuche, mir etwas zum Mittagessen zu besorgen.

11. Train Yourself

1. Sie sollen einen Verkäufer Ihrer Firma anrufen und ihm mitteilen, dass der Verkaufsleiter mit seiner Leistung nicht zufrieden ist. Der Verkaufsbericht ist nicht vollständig. Wie drücken Sie sich hierbei taktvoll aber bestimmt aus?

Hello, Mr Burnes, Mr Blackman asked me to call and tell you he's not *(pleased, totally happy, quite content, at all satisfied)* with your report.
He wonders if you could *(kindly, please, immediately, right away, now, at your leisure)* take another look at it and *(improve, totally rewrite, elaborate on some of the points)*. Mr Blackman feels the report *(is not complete, has gaps, is sketchy)*. He'd like you to call him when it's ready – *(at your leisure, as soon as you can, immediately, right away, when you get the chance)*.

2. Sie kritisieren schriftlich einen Verkaufsbericht. Wie drücken Sie sich dabei taktvoll aber bestimmt aus?

After reading John Simmonds' report, I must say I am not at all *(happy, pleased, content, satisfied)* with it. He has not shown the necessary *(care, diligence, dedication)* in *(writing, constructing, penning)* it. I would like to suggest that he be *(asked, told, instructed, invited)* to rewrite it.

 **Talk Talk Talk**

(Steve's office)
S. Peter could you **man** my phone for a while, please? I have to step out on an errand. I'm expecting to hear from ABC Electronics about that new accounting system of ours they're installing. I'll ask Lucy to put all my calls through to you ...

(Two hours later)
P. Steve, **panic stations** at ABC! They can't install that software for **love nor money**! They sound very **irritated**. They can't read a thing on the discs and they're scared to **mess around** with it **for fear** their whole system will crash.

S. I'll handle it. Lucy, get me ABC right away please!
Hello, ABC? Could you put me through to the Accounting Department, please! The extension is engaged? I'll hang on, but please connect me as soon as you can. This call is urgent.

ABC. You're going through to Mr Baxter now, sir.

S. Hello, Mr Baxter? Steve Blackman here. **What seems to be the**

(Steves Büro)
S. Peter, könnten Sie bitte für eine Weile mein Telefon **übernehmen**? Ich muss etwas auswärts erledigen. Ich erwarte einen Anruf von ABC Electronics – es geht um unser neues Buchhaltungssystem, das bei ihnen installiert wird. Ich bitte Lucy, alle meine Anrufe zu Ihnen durchzustellen ...

(Zwei Stunden später)
P. Steve, es gibt eine **Krise** bei ABC! Sie können das Software System **auf Teufel komm raus** nicht installieren! Sie klingen ziemlich **verärgert**. Sie können nichts auf den Disketten lesen und haben eine **Heidenangst**, dass ihr ganzes System zusammenbrechen wird.

S. Ich kümmere mich schon darum. Lucy, verbinden Sie mich bitte sofort mit ABC!
Hallo, ABC? Könnten Sie mich bitte mit der Buchhaltung verbinden? Die Leitung ist besetzt? Ich warte, aber bitte verbinden Sie mich so schnell wie möglich. Es ist wirklich wichtig.

ABC. Ich verbinde Sie jetzt mit Mr Baxter, Sir.

S. Hallo, Mr Baxter? Hier spricht Steve Blackman. **Wo liegt denn das**

problem? Shut down your system, **reboot** and try again. Still no good? Look, what exactly have you got there? Accounting 2000 ER? Good lord, that's **our** system. You've got our entire **accounting** there! How on earth did that happen? It came in a bag with a packet of sandwiches? Wait a minute! I'll be damned! Your software is still sitting on my desk. Our courier grabbed the wrong package in his hurry to get to lunch. I'll send the right one round right away! I'll call you back to confirm it's on its way. Chip!!!

Problem? Fahren Sie ihr System herunter und **starten Sie es neu**. Es funktioniert immer noch nicht? Was für ein System haben Sie denn genau? Accounting 2000-ER? Du lieber Himmel, das ist unser System. Unsere gesamte **Buchhaltung** ist darauf gespeichert! Wie konnte das nur passieren? Es kam in einer Tüte mit ein paar Sandwiches? Moment mal! Das gibt's doch nicht! Ihre Software liegt immer noch auf meinem Tisch. Unser Kurier muss es so eilig gehabt haben, zum Mittagessen zu kommen, dass er das falsche Paket erwischt hat. Ich schicke Ihnen das richtige sofort vorbei! Ich rufe Sie zurück, sobald es unterwegs ist. Chip!!!

L. He's gone to lunch, Steve!

L. Er ist zum Mittag gegangen, Steve!

 12. Train Yourself

Stellen Sie aus den unten stehenden Sätzen ein Telefongespräch mit einer Kundenfirma zusammen!

(a) He's not there? Could you ask him to call me back as soon as possible, please.
(b) I just called to inquire how the new software is performing.
(c) No? Then I'll wait for Mr Baxter's call. Or perhaps I'll ring again later.
(d) Hello! ABC? Steve Blackman here. Could I speak to Mr Baxter, please?
(e) Oh, just one minute, please! Perhaps you have somebody else there who could help me with my inquiry?

False Friends

How irritating! No, »irritating« is not translated as »irritierend« in German. Irritating means »ärgerlich«. »They sound very irritated« is translated as »Sie scheinen sehr verärgert zu sein«. The German word »irritiert« is translated in English as »confused«.

 Talk Talk Talk

(Steve's office)
S. Well, Peter **let's get down to it!** This is my Monday routine. What a great way to start the week! We **call up** the individual salesmen's reports and **park** them in their individual files, which are subdivided into various folders. Let's start with Smales's. He's **responsible** for the Midlands, based in Birmingham. Last week he got as far as Stratford, **following up a lead** at a new electronics company there. He called in to report he was optimistic about the chances of **a deal**, so let's read what he has to say! But first we have to complete a **log** of his movements, day by day, then **match** these with his **expense-sheet**. That then goes to Accounting. At the end of the report, the salesman has to give an **assessment** of the week's work and a forward projection, but we usually put that on **file** in our own words.

(Steves Büro)
S. Na schön, Peter. **Stürzen wir uns in die Arbeit!** Das ist mein üblicher Montags-Trott. Was für eine Art, die Woche anzufangen! Wir **rufen** die einzelnen Berichte der Verkäufer **ab** und **legen** sie in ihren individuellen Ordnern **ab**, die wiederum in einzelne Abschnitte gegliedert sind. Fangen wir mit Smales an. Er sitzt in Birmingham und ist für die Midlands **zuständig**. Letzte Woche hat er sich bis nach Stratford vorgearbeitet, um dort einem **möglichen Kontakt** zu einer neuen Elektro-Firma zu **folgen**. In seinem Bericht klang er sehr optimistisch, was die Möglichkeiten über einen **Geschäftsabschluss** anbelangt, also lesen wir mal, was er zu sagen hat! Aber zuerst mal müssen wir einen **Ablaufplan** seiner Aktivitäten anfertigen, und zwar für jeden einzelnen Tag. Und dann müssen wir ihn mit dieser **Spesenabrechnung abgleichen**. Das Ganze wandert dann zur Buchhaltung. Am Ende seines Berichtes muss jeder Verkäufer

einen **Leistungsbericht** der vergangenen Woche abliefern und einen Kommentar über die zu erwartenden Entwicklungen abgeben. Aber das tragen wir gewöhnlich mit unseren eigenen Worten in die **Akten** ein.

Telefonieren

 13. Train Yourself

Der Bericht von John Smales richtet sich nach seinem Wochenplan. Können Sie aus den Einzelterminen einen vollständigen Bericht machen?

Monday: Birmingham. Call Texo. No reply. Try again tomorrow. PM: Cranford Foods, 2 PM. Contract changes good. Call again Friday.
Tuesday: AM Stratford. Taylor Electronics. Meeting set for Friday. Lunch: Stratford News Editor. Describe new copy-editing software. Interested! PM Back to Birmingham, call at phone company on way.
Weds. AM Dentist appointment! PM Met Birmingham Chamber of Commerce and Trade. Describe company objectives.
Thurs: AM Drive to Stratford for early start Fri.
Friday: Call Cranford Foods first thing – call again next Mon. 10 AM meeting with Taylor Electronics – full board! Prospects must be good!

 **Talk Talk Talk**

(Melissa enters office)
M. Morning Steve, good morning Peter!

S. My, you certainly seem to have had a fine weekend!

(Melissa betritt das Büro)
M. Guten Morgen, Steve, guten Morgen, Peter!

S. Meine Güte, Sie sehen aus, als hätten Sie ein großartiges Wochenende gehabt!

M. Not at all, nothing but work.

S. You're taking work home with you?

M. It's already there waiting for me. Look, I can't stand around here making polite conversation. I need to know if your people have made any progress with that new copy-editing software.

S. Peter can tell you more **on that score**. He's just spoken to the man responsible for the contract, Burnes. Burnes called me last week to say he was confident of getting the contract, but he didn't sound so optimistic when Peter contacted him this morning.

P. He was actually **very short** on the phone. He sounded really under pressure.

M. I'm not surprised! We're not the only company pushing new forms of this product. But if we can **get a lead** on the others we have a **head-start** in the market. **Keep me posted** on this one. If we

M. Ganz und gar nicht. Arbeit, nichts als Arbeit.

S. Sie nehmen Arbeit mit nach Hause?

M. Nein, sie wartet da schon auf mich. Okay, ich kann hier leider nicht nur herumstehen und ein Schwätzchen halten. Ich muss wissen, ob Sie Fortschritte mit der neuen Redaktions-Software gemacht haben.

S. Peter kann Ihnen mehr **über dieses Thema** erzählen. Er hat gerade mit dem Mann gesprochen, der für diesen Vertrag verantwortlich ist, mit Burnes. Burnes hat letzte Woche mit mir telefoniert, um mir zu sagen, dass er zuversichtlich sei, den Vertrag unter Dach und Fach zu bringen – aber er klang nicht mehr so optimistisch, als Peter heute Morgen mit ihm gesprochen hat.

P. Er war streng genommen sogar **ziemlich kurz angebunden**. Er klang, als würde er unter Druck stehen.

M. Das wundert mich nicht! Wir sind nicht die einzige Firma, die versucht, neue Versionen dieses Produkts auf den Markt zu bringen. Aber wenn wir es schaffen, den anderen ein wenig **voraus zu sein**,

score a hit I'd like to include the product in our new **promotion**.

können wir uns auf dem Markt einen **Vorsprung** verschaffen. **Halten Sie mich** über diese Sache **auf dem Laufenden**. Wenn wir **einen Erfolg verbuchen** können, würde ich dieses Produkt gern in unsere neue **Marktkampagne** aufnehmen.

S. Of course, I'll call you right away. But don't keep your hopes too high.

S. Natürlich, ich sage Ihnen sofort Bescheid. Aber machen Sie sich nicht zu viel Hoffnungen.

 14. Train Yourself

Vervollständigen Sie dieses Telefongespräch:

M. Hello, Mr Burnes. I'm ▒▒▒▒▒ after a meeting today with the Sales Department Chief. I'd like to clarify the state of the Metropolitan Newspapers negotiations. Mr Blackman said you ▒▒▒▒▒ him last week and that you were confident. But when Mr Brückner ▒▒▒▒▒ you today he said you didn't sound so confident.
B. When I ▒▒▒▒▒ to Blackman last week I ▒▒▒▒▒ just ▒▒▒▒▒ to the Chairman of Metropolitan Newspapers. The talks went very well, and I believe I shall be able to ▒▒▒▒▒ you next week with good news. I was under pressure when Mr Brückner ▒▒▒▒▒ this morning. Can you give him my apologies and tell him I shall ▒▒▒▒▒ back later today.

 Do's and Don'ts

Do insist on clarity in all telephone business dealings, and don't allow pressure to lead you into giving the wrong impression. Before making your call make a list on a notepad of all important points you have to discuss. Tackle them one by one, carefully noting the replies for reference. Following the conversation, write an immediate report on the exchange with the other party and if necessary, for complete clarity, formulate it as a business letter. If you record the conversation you should inform the other party before operating the tape recorder.

Talk Talk Talk

(Steve's office)
S. Now, Peter, if Melissa will allow us to get on with our work, I'll show you how we put the Department's own weekly report together.

P. That would really interest me. I don't know how you can **keep track of** what half a dozen salespeople out there in the field are up to.

S. There are plans to **update** the computer program we use to make it more **user-friendly**. Now, since we've actually spoken to Burnes this morning on the phone his report will be the most up to date. We go through it day by day, checking that every contact, every **lead** has been correctly **followed up**.

(Steves Büro)
S. So, Peter, wenn Melissa uns jetzt wieder an unsere Arbeit lässt, werde ich Ihnen zeigen, wie wir den Wochenreport unserer eigenen Abteilung zusammenstellen.

P. Das würde mich wirklich interessieren. Ich habe keine Ahnung, wie man den **Überblick darüber behält**, was ein halbes Dutzend Vertreter im Außendienst so treiben.

S. Es gibt Überlegungen, die Computerprogramme so **upzudaten**, dass sie etwas **benutzerfreundlicher** werden. Da wir ja heute Morgen mit Burnes telefoniert haben, wird sein Bericht sicher am aktuellsten sein. Wir werden ihn Tag für Tag durchsehen und aufpassen, dass jeder Vertrag korrekt ist und **jeder Ansatz** angemessen **weiterverfolgt wurde**.

 15. Train Yourself

Sie sollen Burnes anrufen um einige Punkte seines Berichts zu überprüfen. Wie führen Sie dieses Gespräch?

▒▒▒▒▒▒▒▒▒▒▒▒▒, Mr Burnes. ▒▒▒▒▒▒▒▒▒▒▒▒ Peter Brückner here. I ▒▒▒▒▒▒▒▒▒▒▒▒ you to elaborate on some of the points in your report. Take notes if you like and then ▒▒▒▒▒▒▒▒▒▒ me back later. I find it quicker to do this kind of thing ▒▒▒▒▒▒▒ the phone. ▒▒▒▒▒▒▒▒▒▒ you please tell me ▒▒▒▒▒▒▒▒ company you visited on Tuesday. Did you ▒▒▒▒▒▒▒▒▒▒ beforehand? Did they ask you to ▒▒▒▒▒▒▒▒▒▒ personally or were they happy to do business initially ▒▒▒▒▒▒▒▒ phone? Did you ▒▒▒▒▒▒▒▒▒▒▒▒ them back?

 **Background Information**

A German newspaper reported that the typical **English businessman-look** (dark suit, white shirt, laced-up black shoes) is on the way out. Again, the high-tech boom is responsible. The arrival of successful young »**dot.com**« **entrepreneurs** (see below) in central London has brought with it a tolerance of much more casual office-wear – jeans, T-shirts and trainers are acceptable even at board meetings. The »old guard« bemoan the passing of another British tradition – and with it a slice of English individuality. Even though the English businessman-look has a drab uniformity at first glance, closer inspection discloses flashes of individuality – ties and socks (both silk, please!) are chosen with as much care as their wives devote to selecting a new outfit.

»**Dot.com**« **or** »**.com**« is the latest addition to the English language, another product of the hi-tech boom. It's used as an adjective – as in »dot.com millionaire« or »dot.com business« – to describe anybody or anything having to do with high-tech.

 **Talk Talk Talk**

(Steve Blackman's phone rings)
S. Hello, Blackman here!

A. Mr Blackman. Accounting here! Arthur Smith speaking! There's an irregularity here in last week's **expenses return** by Jim Ives. Have you got a minute – or are you otherwise engaged?

S. Can you send Ives's file up? I'll look through it and then call you

(Steve Blackmans Telefon klingelt)
S. Ja, Blackman?

A. Mr Blackman. Arthur Smith von der Buchhaltung! Es gibt eine Abweichung in der **Spesenabrechnung** von Jim Ives aus der letzten Woche. Haben Sie eine Minute Zeit – oder sind Sie gerade zu beschäftigt?

S. Können Sie Ives Unterlagen einfach heraufschicken? Ich sehe sie

Telefonieren

back. Perhaps I overlooked something.

A. Fine, but can we clear this up today, before you send down last week's returns? We're pretty **inundated** down here – Miss Sykes is down with the flu. I don't have a soul to answer the phone, and it's been ringing all day.

(There's a knock at the door and Chip enters cautiously)

S. Well, hello Chip! Smith, you can borrow Chip if you like. He's got nothing to do apart from his sandwich round.

A. Oh, God, no! But wait a minute, has he really got nothing to do?

S. Well, he's just standing around. Wait a sec – I'll put this on **loudspeaker** …

A. Do you think he could run an **errand** for us?

S. Chip?
C. Sure.
A. Could he run down to the pizzeria on the corner and bring us back an order? I've been trying for the last

mir an und rufe Sie dann zurück. Vielleicht habe ich einfach etwas übersehen.

A. Gern, aber könnten wir das heute noch klären, bevor Sie die Abrechnungen der letzten Woche herunterschicken? Wir **ertrinken** hier unten **in Arbeit** – Miss Sykes liegt mit der Grippe im Bett. Ich habe hier keine Menschenseele, die ans Telefon gehen kann, und es klingelt den ganzen Tag.

(Es klopft an der Tür und Chip tritt vorsichtig ein)

S. Na so was, Hallo Chip! Smith, wenn Sie möchten, können Sie sich unseren Chip ausleihen. Er hat eh nichts zu tun – außer Sandwiches durch die Gegend zu fahren.

A. Oh Gott, bitte nicht! Aber warten Sie – hat er wirklich nichts zu tun?

S. Na ja, er steht nur herum. Sekunde bitte – ich schalte den **Lautsprecher** ein …

A. Meinen Sie, er könnte einen **Botengang** für uns erledigen?

S. Chip?
C. Klar.
A. Könnte er vielleicht schnell zur Pizzeria um die Ecke laufen und uns etwas zu Essen bringen? Ich versu-

half-an-hour to call them to place an order but they're just not answering ...	che jetzt schon eine halbe Stunde, dort etwas zu bestellen, aber es geht einfach niemand ans Telefon ...
S. Pizzas? Sandwiches are Chip's specialty – and that's just what I want to talk to you about now, Chip ...	S. Pizzas? Na, eigentlich sind ja Sandwiches Chips Spezialität – und genau darüber würde ich mit dir jetzt noch ein Wörtchen reden, Chip ...

 16. Train Yourself

1. Was können Sie mit diesem Chaos anfangen?

Hello, ▓▓▓▓▓▓▓ the Ergon Media Company?
No? ▓▓▓▓▓▓▓ to? ▓▓▓▓▓▓▓ to whom? Pronto Pizza?
But I ▓▓▓▓▓▓▓ the Ergon Media Company. What ▓▓▓▓▓▓▓ do you have? Well, that's the number I ▓▓▓▓▓▓▓. At least, that's the ▓▓▓▓▓▓▓ I always ▓▓▓▓▓▓▓ the Ergon Media Company on. I'll ▓▓▓▓▓▓▓ up and ▓▓▓▓▓▓▓ again. (After trying repeatedly) Damn, now I can't ▓▓▓▓▓▓▓ at all. The ▓▓▓▓▓▓▓ is always ▓▓▓▓▓▓▓, Lucy. Lucy? Where is the woman? (Chip calls out from the office) She's ▓▓▓▓▓▓▓ the phone, ordering pizza. Want one?

2. Multiple choice
Wählen Sie das richtige Wort.

a. Could you call the shop and give this order ▓▓▓▓▓▓▓ the phone *(on, with, over)*.
b. He's just come ▓▓▓▓▓▓▓ the phone, so he's ready to see you now *(off, from, away from)*.
c. If you can't contact me today ▓▓▓▓▓▓▓ phone you'll have to leave a message with my secretary *(per, via, with the, by, through the)*.
d. He's been ▓▓▓▓▓▓▓ the phone for hours, I can't think what he's ▓▓▓▓▓▓▓ about *(with, over, on, addressing) (speaking, thinking, talking)*.

 **Talk Talk Talk**

(Steve's office)
S. Well, there you have had an **object lesson**, Peter, in the frustrations of an average day in the Sales Department. (Phone rings) And here's another coming up ... Hello, Steve Blackman here. Can I help you? Mr Tomkins? Mr Tomkins of Arco? **What can I do for you?**

T. Your man in Sheffield promised to give me a call by the end of last week to **confirm the price and conditions** of the Accounting 2000 package. I haven't heard a thing from him.

S. Ferguson? He's normally very **reliable**. I'll try to reach him myself and get him to call you right away. Are you there all day?

T. I'll be **around**. If I'm not in the office tell him to **leave a message** with my secretary and I'll call him back. But I've so much going on at the moment that I expect to spend most of the morning on the phone, anyway. I just hope he catches me

(Steves Büro)
S. Tja, Peter – das war ein erster **praktischer Anschauungsunterricht** darüber, wie frustrierend ein typischer Tag in der Verkaufsabteilung sein kann. (Das Telefon klingelt) Und da kommt schon das nächste Problem ... Hallo, hier Steve Blackman. Kann ich Ihnen helfen? Mr Tomkins? Mr Tomkins von Arco? **Was kann ich für Sie tun?**

T. Ihr Mann in Sheffield hat mir versprochen, bis zum Ende letzter Woche zurückzurufen, um mir **den Preis und die Lieferbedingungen** für das Accounting 2000-Softwarepaket **zu bestätigen**. Ich habe noch kein Wort von ihm gehört.

S. Ferguson? Er ist normalerweise ziemlich **verlässlich**. Ich versuche, ihn selbst zu erreichen und sage ihm, dass er Sie sofort zurückrufen soll. Sind Sie den ganzen Tag im Büro erreichbar?

T. Ja, ich werde **da sein**. Sagen Sie ihm, falls ich nicht da sein sollte, soll er doch meiner Sekretärin **eine Nachricht hinterlassen** und ich rufe zurück. Aber hier ist gerade so viel zu tun, dass ich vermutlich ohnehin den größten Teil des Vormittags am

in a moment when I'm off the phone.

S. If I manage to get him on the phone right now I'll get him to call you immediately, so I hope you'll be hearing from him in a minute or two.

S. Lucy, can you get me Ferguson, please? Or, at least, try to reach him – either at home or on his mobile.

L. His home number is busy. **He's on the phone.** Shall I wait until **he's off**, or shall I try the mobile?

S. Get him on the mobile. I have to speak to him right away! Stan? I've had Arco on the phone **complaining** that you had promised them an Accounting 2000 package price last week. They're still waiting for your call.

F. What are they talking about? I called them last Thursday and told them the cost and explained conditions of sale and so on. They'll get it all in writing, but at least they got it over the phone.

Telefon verbringen werde. Ich hoffe nur, er erreicht mich, wenn ich gerade nicht spreche.

S. Wenn ich ihn sofort am Telefon erwische, sage ich ihm, dass er sie gleich zurückrufen soll. Ich hoffe also, dass Sie in den nächsten ein oder zwei Minuten von ihm hören.

S. Lucy, können Sie mich bitte mit Ferguson verbinden? Oder versuchen Sie wenigstens, ihn zu erreichen – entweder zu Hause oder über sein Handy.

L. Seine Privatnummer ist besetzt. Also **telefoniert er gerade**. Soll ich warten, bis **er aufgelegt hat** oder es auf dem Handy versuchen?

S. Holen Sie ihn ans Handy. Ich muss sofort mit ihm sprechen! Stan? Ich hatte gerade Arco am Telefon – sie haben sich **beschwert**, dass Sie ihnen schon letzte Woche ein Paketpreis für unser Accounting 2000 machen wollten. Sie warten immer noch auf Ihren Anruf.

F. Von was reden die eigentlich? Ich habe sie letzten Donnerstag angerufen, ihnen den Preis gegeben, die Lieferbedingungen erklärt und so weiter. Sie kriegen das natürlich alles noch einmal schriftlich, aber telefonisch habe ich ihnen bereits alles mitgeteilt.

Telefonieren

S. I'll get back to you on this one. Let me first call Arco. There seems to have been a **misunderstanding** here. But can you let them have what they want in writing as soon as possible?

S. Ich rufe Sie deshalb noch einmal zurück. Aber lassen Sie mich zuerst noch mal bei Arco anrufen. Da scheint es wohl ein **Missverständnis** gegeben zu haben. Aber könnten Sie denen trotzdem alle Daten so schnell wie möglich schriftlich geben?

F. Sure. No problem. They'll have it today by fax.

F. Natürlich, kein Problem. Sie bekommen es heute per Fax.

S. Lucy, be a dear and get me Mr Tomkins at Arco again. I've got something very important to clear up here. What, no reply? Then just keep trying please. God, what an **outfit**!

S. Lucy, seien Sie doch bitte so gut und holen Sie mir noch einmal Mr Tomkins von Arco an den Apparat. Ich muss hier etwas sehr Wichtiges klären. Was, es geht niemand dran? Dann versuchen Sie es bitte weiter. Gott, was für ein **Saftladen**!

 17. Train Yourself

Es gibt ein Missverständnis mit einem Kunden. Wie verläuft das Gespräch?

Hello, Arco? Could I ▇▇▇▇▇ to Mr Tomkins, please. Mr Tomkins, it's Jeffreys ▇▇▇▇▇. I ▇▇▇▇▇ if I ▇▇▇▇▇ trouble you with a small problem. Your office has just ▇▇▇▇▇ to ▇▇▇▇▇ that it is still waiting for word on the price of the system Arco are interested in. I ▇▇▇▇▇ several days ago, and although your phone was constantly ▇▇▇▇▇ I spoke to one of the clerks and ▇▇▇▇▇ him to ▇▇▇▇▇ you a message. Didn't you ▇▇▇▇▇ it? No, then I'll dig the information out again and ▇▇▇▇▇ you back. Oh, please don't ▇▇▇▇▇ up. Keep me on the ▇▇▇▇▇. I have to ▇▇▇▇▇ your accounting department.

Background Information

»**He's on the phone**« can mean either that the person referred to has a phone, possesses one, or that he is at that moment speaking on the phone. »**She's off the phone**« has only the meaning »she is no longer talking on the phone«.

Talk Talk Talk

(Steve's office)
S. OK, Peter, that's just the **regional sales operation**. Don't forget we're here in London.

P. So how do you handle things in London? I haven't seen a single representative here in the office. Do you just **phone around**?

S. **Cold-calling by phone?** Now that's one of your German jokes, I suppose! But you're right, we don't have any sales staff here at head office. There's no way we can cover London on a conventional basis. We **franchise** some of the most profitable business and put the rest in the hands of specific agencies.

P. How does that work?

(Steves Büro)
S. Okay, Peter, das waren nur die **Außenstellen unserer Verkaufsabteilung**. Vergessen Sie nicht, dass wir hier in London sind.

P. Und wie funktioniert das Ganze in London? Ich habe hier im Büro noch keinen einzigen Vertreter gesehen. **Telefonieren** Sie **einfach so herum**?

S. **Blindakquisition übers Telefon?** Das muss wohl deutscher Humor gewesen sein! Aber Sie haben Recht, wir haben hier im Büro kein Verkaufspersonal. Es gibt keine Möglichkeit, London mit konventionellen Methoden zu betreuen. Wir **vergeben Lizenzen** für die profitabelsten Geschäftsbereiche und übertragen den Rest an spezielle Agenturen.

P. Und wie funktioniert das?

S. In the case of our more successful lines – Accounting 2000, for example – we can **demand a franchise contract which guarantees us income**. Newer **lines** we have to push first of all through specialist agencies – but Melissa will be telling you more about that side of things. I'm meeting one of our **franchise-holders** for lunch. He called while you were busy with the files. I'll call him back and say there'll be two of us – three if Melissa wants to come.

S. Im Fall unserer erfolgreicheren Produkte – zum Beispiel Accounting 2000 – **fordern wir einen Lizenzvertrag, der uns einen bestimmten Gewinn garantiert**. Unsere neueren **Produktreihen** müssen wir zuerst über spezialisierte Agenturen auf den Markt bringen – aber Melissa wird Ihnen über diesen Aspekt des Geschäfts sicher noch mehr erzählen. Ich treffe mich mit einem unserer **Lizenznehmer** zum Mittagessen. Er hat angerufen, während Sie gerade mit den Akten beschäftigt waren. Ich rufe ihn einfach noch einmal an und sage ihm, dass wir zu zweit sein werden – drei, falls Melissa mitkommen möchte.

P. Now that would be nice – I **wonder** if she'll accept an invitation ...

P. Das wäre ja mal nett – **ich frage mich**, ob sie eine Einladung annehmen würde ...

 18. Train Yourself

Man bittet Sie in einem Restaurant anzurufen und einen Tisch für ein Geschäftsessen zu reservieren. Wie drücken Sie sich am besten aus?

Hello, is that Marco's Restaurant? I ▰▰▰▰▰ to reserve a table for four. We have business to discuss, so ▰▰▰▰▰ please give us a table in a quiet corner? I ▰▰▰▰▰ most grateful if you ▰▰▰▰▰ manage that for me. Shall I ▰▰▰▰▰ to confirm? At what time ▰▰▰▰▰ we arrive? ▰▰▰▰▰ the table ▰▰▰▰▰ free at that time? I'd better ▰▰▰▰▰ to make sure everything is all right – this is an important lunch for us!

Background Information

Cold-calling: Cold calling is a very expressive term used in sales and marketing to describe the practice of selecting numbers at random from the telephone directory and calling »cold«, without prior introduction. It's a particularly widespread practice in market research, where a cross-section of the public is contacted at random by telephone and asked to offer opinions or preferences. In sales strategy, specific sections of the market are selected and then contacted by telephone.

False Friends

»**I wonder**« can't be translated in German by »Ich wundere mich«. It has the meaning of »Ich frage mich, ob ...«. The German »sich wundern« translates as »surprised« or »amazed«. So »Ich wundere mich» becomes »I am surprised« or even »I am amazed«.

Talk Talk Talk

(Marco's Restaurant)
Marco, the restaurant manager:
Hello, Mr Blackman. I'm very pleased to see you again.

S. Hello, Marco. This is a new colleague, Mr Brückner, from Germany. You'll undoubtedly be seeing more of him.

M. How do you do, Mr Brückner? Welcome to Marco's. I hope you enjoy your visit! Mr Blackman, Miss Walker and your guest have already arrived and are at the bar. Let me take you to them.

(Marcos Restaurant)
Marco, der Restaurant-Manager:
Guten Tag, Mr Blackman. Ich freue mich, Sie wieder zu sehen.

S. Hallo Marco. Das ist ein neuer Kollege von mir, Mr Brückner, aus Deutschland. Sie werden ihn zweifellos noch öfters sehen.

M. Wie geht es Ihnen, Mr Brückner? Willkommen im »Marco's«. Ich hoffe, es wird Ihnen hier gefallen! Mr Blackman, Miss Walker und Ihr Gast sind bereits da und warten an der Bar. Ich werde Sie zu ihnen führen.

S. Don't bother, Marco. I know my way. We'll just have a quick aperitif and then place our order.	S. Machen Sie sich keine Umstände, Marco. Ich kenne den Weg. Wir werden uns nur einen kleinen Aperitif gönnen und dann unser Essen bestellen.
M. Hello, Steve. Hello, Peter. You're late, both of you! Mr Davis was even here before me.	M. Hallo, Steve. Hallo, Peter! Sie beide kommen aber reichlich spät! Mr Davis war sogar schon vor mir hier.
D. Don't worry! I think my secretary got the time wrong when you called. I did try to contact you but couldn't get through.	D. Keine Sorge! Ich glaube, meine Sekretärin hat sich nach Ihrem Anruf eine falsche Zeit notiert. Ich habe versucht, noch einmal anzurufen, aber ich kam nicht durch.
S. Davis, I'd like you to meet our new colleague, Peter Brückner. He's joined us from Germany.	S. Davis, ich würde Ihnen gerne unseren neuen Kollegen vorstellen, Peter Brückner. Er ist aus Deutschland zu uns gestoßen.
D. Germany! How do you do? How did Blackman here persuade you to swap Germany for grey London?	D. Aus Deutschland! Wie geht es Ihnen? Wie hat Blackman es geschafft, Sie aus Deutschland in unser graues London zu locken?
S. We persuaded him that the beer is better here. **By the way, mine's a** martini – stirred, not shaken!	S. Wir haben Ihn davon überzeugt, dass das Bier hier besser ist. **Übrigens, ich nehme** einen Martini – gerührt, nicht geschüttelt!

Background Information

Despite the casual nature of business dealings in Britain, you'll still hear just the **surname** being used in even mutual social dealings – and particularly between employees of rival firms. Don't take it as a sign of unfriendliness – it's said to be a throwback to English school tradition, where pupils are almost invariably addressed just by their surname. In fact, the surname can indicate a degree of intimacy which isn't necessarily expressed by the first name alone – and certainly not by the use of a »Mr« title. It's a further example of the subtle structure of English social behaviour. Avoid it until you're *really* part of the English scene!

Mine's a ... Like the use of just the surname, this way of ordering at the bar of a restaurant or a pub isn't as unfriendly or as rude as it sounds. In fact, it's often used among friends and colleagues. But avoid it until you really feel at home with the language!

 Vocabulary

accounting	Buchhaltung
assessment	Leistungsbericht
to be off the phone	aufgelegt haben, nicht sprechen
to be on the phone	gerade telefonieren
to break into	in den Markt vordringen
to call up sth.	etw. abrufen
cold-calling	Blindaquisition
competitive	wettbewerbsorientiert, konkurrenzfähig
to complain	sich beschweren
to confirm price and conditions	Preis und Lieferbedingungen bestätigen
to cover (a territory)	für (ein Gebiet) zuständig sein
deal	Geschäftsabschluss
Department of Social Security	Sozialversicherungsamt
to elaborate points	Punkte ausarbeiten

to email sth.	etw. per E-Mail schicken
errand	Botengang
expense sheet/expenses return	Spesenabrechnung
file (on s.o.)	Akte (über jdn.)
to follow up a lead	an einer Sache dranbleiben; eine Möglichkeit verfolgen
form	Formular
franchise contract	Lizenzvertrag
franchise holder	Lizenznehmer
to franchise	Lizenzen vergeben
to get down to sth. right away	sich sofort um etw. kümmern
to have a head-start	einen Vorsprung haben
to induct into sth.	einführen in etw.
innovative	innovativ
to keep sb. posted	jdn. auf dem Laufenden halten
to keep track of sth.	den Überblick behalten
to leave a message	eine Nachricht hinterlassen
log	Ablaufplan
loudspeaker	Lautsprecher/Mithörtaste
to man sb.'s phone	jds. Telefon übernehmen
panic stations	Krise
to phone around	herumtelefonieren
product line	Produktreihe
progress report	Erfolgsbericht
to punch sth. into	etw. einhacken
to put sth. on file	etw. in die Akten eintragen
to reboot	neu starten (PC)
regional operation	Außenstelle
to score a hit	einen Erfolg verbuchen
to seal a contract	einen Vertrag abschließen
to shut down	herunterfahren (PC)
social security number	Sozialversicherungsnummer
telephone company/people	Telefongesellschaft
test run	Testlauf
top salesman	Spitzenverkäufer
to track sb. down	jdn. aufspüren
user-friendly	benutzerfreundlich
umpteen	zig
to wake it snappy	sich beeilen

In Marketing
In der Marketing-Abteilung

 **Here we go**

Nachdem sich Peter in der Verkaufsabteilung einen Überblick verschafft hat, wird er nunmehr als Assistent in Melissa Walkers Marketing-Abteilung geschickt. Melissa trifft gerade die Vorbereitungen für die bevorstehende große Computermesse und Peters Beitrag zu diesem Projekt umfasst unter anderem natürlich auch jede Menge Telefongespräche ...

 **Talk Talk Talk**

(Marco's Restaurant)
M. Well, Peter, from Monday you're with me in Marketing.

S. Lucky chap!

M. He'll probably learn more from me than from you, my dear Steve. Peter, I hope you're now totally **at home** on the phone – we have a lot of phoning around to do next week.

P. I seem to have spent most of my time so far on the phone!

M. **We're preparing for the big computer fair** in the autumn. I'll

(Marcos Restaurant)
M. Tja, Peter, von Montag an arbeiten Sie mit mir in der Marketing-Abteilung zusammen.

S. Sie Glückspilz!

M. Er wird von mir wahrscheinlich mehr als von Ihnen lernen, mein lieber Steve. Peter, ich hoffe, Sie sind mittlerweile mit dem Telefon **vertraut** – wir werden nächste Woche eine Menge herumtelefonieren müssen.

P. Ich habe das Gefühl, bis jetzt sowieso die meiste Zeit nur am Telefon verbracht zu haben!

M. **Wir treffen alle Vorbereitungen für die große Computermesse** im

Telefonieren

want to speak to you about that, Mr Davis. Perhaps now's not the time – can I give you a call on Monday morning?

D. Certainly.

S. Davis is all mine today! I'd like to clear up those points in the **franchise** contract you're not happy with. You told me on the phone you are a bit doubtful about one or two clauses.
Davis, since I called I've read more carefully through them and I don't think there's much of a problem.

S. Good, well let's order – and then **down to orders!**

Herbst. Darüber wollte ich auch mit Ihnen sprechen, Mr Davis. Aber vielleicht ist jetzt nicht der richtige Zeitpunkt dafür – kann ich Sie am Montagmorgen anrufen?

D. Aber sicher.

S. Heute gehört Davis nur mir! Ich würde gerne die Details in dem **Franchise**-Vertrag klären, mit denen Sie noch nicht einverstanden sind. Sie haben mir am Telefon ja schon gesagt, dass Sie wegen ein oder zwei Paragraphen des Vertrages so Ihre Zweifel haben.
Davis, nachdem ich Sie angerufen hatte, habe ich sie noch einmal sorgfältig durchgelesen, und ich glaube nicht mehr, dass es da ein Problem geben wird.

S. Gut, lassen Sie uns bestellen – und dann **kommen wir zum Geschäftlichen!**

 19. Train Yourself

1. Steve Blackman unterhält eine Besprechung mit einem Kunden, dessen Englisch alles andere als korrekt ist. Können Sie es für ihn korrigieren?

Mr Blackman, I want speak this contract. It no good – makes me very unhappy. Paragraphs I not understand are one, three and six – what they mean? When I ring you yesterday, you say no problem – but when I do same today you speak not so happy. You say commission on whole order fifteen per hundred, but contract speak ten per hundred. Why this? I like call my office with answer – they waiting for my ring this afternoon. Can I get before then?

2. Geben Sie die korrekte Komparativform an und füllen Sie die Lücken!

It is (easy) ▒▒▒▒ to ▒▒ a number from home than from a telephone-box.

It is (complicated) ▒▒▒▒▒▒▒▒ to ▒▒▒▒▒▒▒▒ through on this phone.

Could you please speak (loud) ▒▒▒▒▒▒. The ▒▒▒▒▒▒ is very bad.

Please ▒▒▒▒▒▒▒▒▒▒▒▒▒▒▒▒▒▒▒▒▒▒ the line. Mr Jones won't be much (long) ▒▒▒▒▒▒▒▒▒▒▒▒▒▒▒▒▒▒▒.

You've ▒▒▒▒▒▒▒▒ me off. It's even (difficult) ▒▒▒▒▒▒▒▒ to ▒▒▒▒▒▒▒▒ out from this phone than from the other.

Could you please make sure your ▒▒▒▒▒▒▒▒▒▒▒▒▒▒▒▒ is (short) ▒▒▒▒▒▒▒▒▒▒▒▒▒▒▒▒ than yesterday's – it's (expensive) ▒▒▒▒▒▒▒▒ to ▒▒▒▒▒▒▒▒ America from Britain than from Germany.

Talk Talk Talk

(Melissa's office)
P. Good morning, Melissa. How are you today?

(Melissas Büro)
P. Guten Morgen, Melissa. Wie geht es Ihnen?

M. Fine, thanks, Peter. And you?

M. Sehr gut, danke, Peter. Und Ihnen?

P. I can't complain, although I was out with Steve again last night.

P. Ich kann nicht klagen, obwohl ich gestern Abend wieder mit Steve unterwegs war.

M. I sometimes think Steve has his main office in the pub. I'm afraid

M. Manchmal glaube ich wirklich, Steve hat sein wahres Büro in

this week will be much less exciting for you!

P. Oh, I don't know – marketing sounds very interesting.

M. Can be – but there's a lot of **slog**. As I told you, we're preparing for the big autumn fair, and the **work-load** is increasing daily.

P. What can I do to help?

M. I'm going to assign you Angela and ask you both to draw up a **press release** on ERGO **operations** – a **company profile**, that kind of thing. And I'd like you to organize a **press conference** at the Press Club and draw up a **hand-out** to be distributed there.

P. Oh dear, I've no experience of dealing with the press. And who's Angela?

M. She's been on holiday so you didn't get a chance to meet her until now. She joined us from Five Star magazine group, so when it comes to handling the press she's **tops** – she'll tell you what she wants done. She'll be spending

einem Pub. Ich fürchte, diese Woche wird längst nicht so aufregend für Sie werden!

P. Oh, ich weiß nicht – Marketing hört sich sehr interessant an.

M. Ja, das kann es sein – aber es gehört auch viel **Schufterei** dazu. Wie ich Ihnen schon sagte, bereiten wir uns auf die große Herbstmesse vor und das **Arbeitspensum** steigt von Tag zu Tag.

P. Wie kann ich helfen?

M. Ich werde Sie Angela zuteilen und Sie beide bitten, eine **Pressemitteilung** über die **Geschäftsaktivitäten** von ERGO zu entwerfen – ein **Geschäftsprofil**, etwas in dieser Art. Und ich hätte gerne, dass Sie im *Press Club* eine **Pressekonferenz** organisieren und ein **Informationsblatt** entwerfen, das wir dort verteilen können.

P. Oh weh, ich habe überhaupt keine Erfahrung im Umgang mit der Presse. Und wer ist Angela?

M. Sie war bis jetzt im Urlaub, also hatten Sie noch keine Gelegenheit, sie kennen zu lernen. Sie ist von der *Five Star Magazin*-Gruppe zu uns gestoßen – wenn es also darum geht, mit der Presse klar zu kommen, ist sie **unschlagbar**. Sie

most of her time on the phone, so you can help out there.	wird Ihnen schon sagen, was Sie für sie tun müssen. Angela wird wohl die meiste Zeit am Telefon verbringen, also können Sie ihr dabei aushelfen.
P. Well, I've now got a lot of telephone experience – just put me **by a phone**, **wind me up** and I go to work!	P. Tja, ich habe mittlerweile schon eine Menge Erfahrung mit dem Telefon – setzen Sie mich einfach **an ein Telefon**, **weisen Sie mich ein** und ich fange an zu arbeiten!
M. Fine, well, come and meet Angela ...	M. Sehr schön. Kommen Sie, ich stelle Ihnen Angela vor ...

Telefonieren

 20. Train Yourself

Sie wurden angewiesen, einen Vertreter der lokalen Zeitung zu einer Pressekonferenz einzuladen. Wie sieht dieses Gespräch aus?

Hello, is that the Southwark Advertiser? Could you ▓▓▓▓▓ me ▓▓▓▓▓ to the News Department, please. The number's ▓▓▓▓▓? I'll ▓▓▓▓▓ but please ▓▓▓▓▓ me as soon as possible. Thank you. News Department? Could I ▓▓▓▓▓ to the News Editor, please? His line is ▓▓▓▓▓? I'll ▓▓▓▓▓ if that's all right. Thank you. Hello, is that the News Editor? I would like to ▓▓▓▓▓ a representative of your newspaper to a press conference at the Press Club next Friday at 11 AM. You'll ▓▓▓▓▓ me ▓▓▓▓▓ to the Business Correspondent right now? That's very kind! Hello, ▓▓▓▓▓ the Business Correspondent? Ergo Limited here. We would like to ▓▓▓▓▓ you to a press conference next Friday. The first part, starting at 11 AM, will be a general background briefing ▓▓▓▓▓ record, where we will be distributing a press ▓▓▓▓▓. I can send you a general press ▓▓▓▓▓ right now, by fax. It contains all the relevant details. Can you ▓▓▓▓▓ me your fax ▓▓▓▓▓? You'll be ▓▓▓▓▓ from us right away.

Background Information

A **press release** is a written communication sent to newspapers and the media. A press hand-out is also a written communication, usually »handed out« at a press conference or press »briefing«. Businesses often use a release or a hand-out to communicate »background information« to the press. At international conferences, »off-the-record« briefings are often given to the press, meaning the sources of the information may not be quoted – the subject of the briefing is for »background information« only.

Talk Talk Talk

(Melissa's office)
M. Angela, I'd like you to meet Mr Peter Brückner, who has joined us from Germany.

A. How do you do? I had heard we were expecting a **colleague** from Germany. I'm very pleased to meet you. I do hope you enjoy your time with us and also your stay in England.

P. How do you do? **The pleasure's all mine.** I'm enjoying my time here so much that I fear I won't want to return to Germany!

M. You're obviously **settling in** very well!

P. (to Angela) I gather we shall be working together.

(Melissas Büro)
M. Angela, ich würde Ihnen gerne Mr Peter Brückner vorstellen, der aus Deutschland zu uns gekommen ist.

A. Wie geht es Ihnen? Ich habe schon gehört, dass wir einen neuen **Kollegen** aus Deutschland bekommen. Freut mich sehr, Sie kennen zu lernen. Ich hoffe, es gefällt Ihnen hier bei uns und in England.

P. Wie geht es Ihnen? **Das Vergnügen ist ganz auf meiner Seite.** Ich fühle mich hier so wohl, dass ich fürchte, gar nicht mehr nach Deutschland zurück zu wollen!

M. Sie haben sich offensichtlich schon sehr gut **eingewöhnt**!

P. (zu Angela) Soweit ich weiß, sollen wir zusammenarbeiten.

A. Yes, indeed – and we have a lot to do.

P. A lot of telephoning, I've been warned already. Although I'm **quite a hand** now on the phone.

A. Well, we'll see! Melissa will have told you that we are busy preparing for the autumn trade fair. As a **run-up** to that we want to publicize the company at a **press conference**. I thought you could take that over.

P. What's involved?

A. Basically, making sure every newspaper of the region is there.

P. **Invitations**?

A. Yes, but **to make doubly certain**, we **make a practice of following up** the invitations and press releases with either **personal calls or phone calls**. Obviously, it's difficult to visit all these newspapers personally – hence all the phone calls I referred to.

A. Ja, in der Tat – und es gibt eine Menge zu tun.

P. Eine Menge Telefoniererei, ich wurde bereits vorgewarnt. Allerdings habe ich jetzt mit dem Telefon **einige Erfahrung**.

A. Na, wir werden sehen! Melissa hat Ihnen wahrscheinlich schon erzählt, dass wir gerade voll damit beschäftigt sind, die Herbstmesse vorzubereiten. Als einen **ersten Schritt** dazu wollen wir die Firma auf einer **Pressekonferenz** vorstellen. Ich dachte, das könnten Sie vielleicht übernehmen.

P. Was gehört alles dazu?

A. Im Wesentlichen, dafür zu sorgen, dass jede Zeitung der Region teilnimmt.

P. **Einladungen**?

A. Ja, aber **um auf Nummer sicher zu gehen**, haben wir es uns **zur Regel gemacht**, nach den Einladungen und den Pressemitteilungen noch einmal mit **persönlichen Besuchen oder Anrufen nachzuhaken**. Natürlich ist es schwierig, bei diesen ganzen Zeitungen persönlich vorbeizuschauen – deshalb diese ganzen Telefonanrufe, die ich Ihnen zugeteilt habe.

Telefonieren

P. Who do we have to call?

A. We start in the **News Department** and **take it from there**. We try to get straight through to the **editor**, but we're lucky if we do. We usually have to try through his secretary or the News Editor. I warn you, you'll be hanging on that phone a great deal, being shunted from one number to another.

P. Wen müssen wir alles anrufen?

A. Wir fangen in der **Nachrichtenredaktion** an und **arbeiten uns von da aus weiter**. Wir versuchen zwar immer, direkt bis zum **Redakteur** durchzukommen, aber dazu gehört schon viel Glück. Wir müssen es gewöhnlich über seine Sekretärin oder seinen Nachrichtenredakteur versuchen. Ich warne Sie, Sie werden viel Zeit am Telefon verbringen und sich von einer Nummer zur nächsten abschieben lassen.

 21. Train Yourself

Sie sind im Norden Kents unterwegs und besuchen Zeitungsredaktionen im Zuge der Öffentlichkeitsarbeit. Am Nachmittag bemerken Sie, dass Ihnen für zwei Redaktionen die Zeit fehlt. Sie rufen im Büro an und bitten Ihre Kollegin, Ihren Zeitplan neu zu organisieren und die beiden Termine zu verlegen. Wie sieht dieses Telefongespräch aus?

Hello, Angela. I ▨▨▨▨ if you ▨▨▨▨ me a big favour. I'm never going to be able to get around to calling on the North Kent Times and the Dartford Herald this afternoon. Do you think you could give them each a ▨▨▨▨ and ▨▨▨▨ our meetings until tomorrow. I'd call them on my ▨▨▨▨ but I think it would look more businesslike if the ▨▨▨▨ came from the office. Just tell them I shall give them a ▨▨▨▨ first thing tomorrow morning before setting out. Whatever you do, don't allow them to cancel the meetings altogether. If there's any trouble you can ▨▨▨▨ me on my mobile. Perhaps you could ▨▨▨▨ my home number, anyway, and leave a message on the ▨▨▨▨.

Background Information

Make sure you know the precise difference between **postpone** and **cancel**. Mixing them up in business can lead to all kinds of problems! If you postpone an appointment you put it off until another time. If you cancel it you call it off altogether.

Talk Talk Talk

(Peter's Office – Angela enters)
A. Peter, if you're calling the papers there's one more thing you could do for me.

P. Certainly. What is that?

A. Could you also **contact the Advertising Departments** and inquire about the possibility of doing an **advertorial**?

P. An advertorial?

A. That's a combination of **advertisement and editorial copy**. It's a very effective and more reasonable way of advertising. Just ask them to send details of what they can offer.

P. Well, I'll try. Where do I start?

(Peters Büro – Angela tritt ein)
A. Peter, wo Sie gerade dabei sind, die Zeitungen anzurufen – es gibt da noch etwas, das Sie für mich tun könnten.

P. Sicher. Was denn?

A. Könnten Sie außerdem **Kontakt zu den Anzeigenabteilungen aufnehmen** und nachfragen, ob die Möglichkeit besteht, ein **Advertorial** zu schalten?

P. Ein Advertorial?

A. Das ist eine Kombination aus **Advertisement (Anzeige) und Editorial Copy (redaktionellem Beitrag)**. Eine sehr effektive und sinnvolle Art, Anzeigen zu schalten. Sagen Sie einfach, sie sollen uns ein Angebot mit den Möglichkeiten schicken.

P. Tja, ich kann's versuchen. Womit fange ich an?

A. Here's a list of newspapers we'd like coverage in. The numbers are there and in most cases a **contact name**. Just start at the top and work through the list. Sorry to **drop** this **on** you, but I have so much to do. And Melissa told me not to spare you.

A. Hier ist eine Liste mit Zeitungen, die nach Möglichkeit über uns schreiben sollten. Wir haben die Telefonnummern und in den meisten Fällen auch **den Namen eines Ansprechpartners**. Fangen Sie einfach oben an und arbeiten Sie sich dann nach unten durch. Tut mir Leid, dass ich das auf Sie **abwälzen** muss, aber ich habe einfach zu viel zu tun. Und Melissa hat mir gesagt, ich soll Sie nicht schonen.

P. Thank you, Melissa! Hand me the phone as you leave, Angela ...

P. Na, besten Dank auch, Melissa! Geben Sie mir doch bitte beim Herausgehen das Telefon, Angela ...

 22. Train Yourself

Peter hat Probleme beim Kontaktieren der ersten Zeitung, die er zu Anzeigen und redaktionellen Möglichkeiten befragen soll. Können Sie ihm helfen?

P. Hello, is ▨▨▨▨ the Barnett Chronicle? No? Who am I ▨▨▨▨ to? What ▨▨▨▨ do you have? That's the number I ▨▨▨▨. There must be some mistake. Oh, the Barnett Chronicle has moved? I didn't know. I'll ▨▨▨▨ directory inquiries and try and get the new ▨▨▨▨. Hello, directory inquiries? Could you ▨▨▨▨ me the new ▨▨▨▨ of the Barnett Chronicle, please. Double two nine eight three five? Could you ▨▨▨▨ that? Thank you.
(Peter dials the number) Hello, Barnett Chronicle? Could you ▨▨▨▨ me ▨▨▨▨ to the advertising department, please? Advertising department? No? What department am I ▨▨▨▨ to? Circulation department? I'm afraid I have been wrongly ▨▨▨▨. Are you able to ▨▨▨▨ me to the

advertising department? All right, I'll ▓▓▓▓▓▓▓▓▓▓▓▓▓▓. Hello, is that the advertising department? No? Where have I landed now? The news department? I keep on getting ▓▓▓▓▓▓▓▓▓▓▓▓ the wrong department. But wait! Don't ▓▓▓▓▓▓▓▓▓▓▓▓▓▓ off. I'd like to ▓▓▓▓▓▓▓▓▓▓▓▓ to your department, anyway.

Background Information

The English love to create **portmanteau words** – meaning words made up of at least two others with the same meaning (a portmanteau is a large travelling case, usually one with several compartments). **Advertorial** is a good example of a portmanteau word. An advertorial is – as Angela explained – a form of advertising incorporating both advertising and editorial copy. Although newspapers insist that it must be identified as an advertisement, usually in unobtrusive, small print, an advertorial can be a clever way of getting across a message without giving readers the impression they are reading an advertisement. Special editions on any subject from lines of business to entire economies are an ambitious form of advertorial. The most subtle form in the English press is to be found in most travel supplements. The next time you read an English newspaper try and spot the »advertorials«.

Talk Talk Talk

(Melissa enters)
M. Peter! Can the three of us have a meeting in my office in ten minutes to **review progress** on the trade fair, the press conference and the **general advertising and marketing programme**?

P. Certainly, I'll just **gather** my **papers** and join you ...

(Melissa tritt ein)
M. Peter! Können wir drei uns in zehn Minuten zu einer Besprechung in meinem Büro treffen, um über den **Fortschritt** der Messe, die Pressekonferenz und das **generelle Anzeigen- und Marketingprogramm zu sprechen**?

P. Sicher, ich **suche** nur meine **Unterlagen zusammen** und komme dazu ...

M. Angela, **let's hear from you first**. How far are you with the press conference and the press release?	M. Angela, **fangen Sie doch bitte an**. Wie weit sind Sie mit der Pressekonferenz und der Pressemitteilung?
A. I asked Peter to help me out with the press. The **release** is finished and ready for the print-shop.	A. Ich habe Peter darum gebeten, mir bei der Pressearbeit zu helfen. Die **Publikation** ist fertig und kann in Druck gehen.
M. I'll need to look at it first, please. Peter, how far are you with your inquiries?	M. Ich möchte zuerst noch einmal drübergehen. Peter, wie weit sind Sie mit Ihren Anfragen?
P. I've managed to get a few **quotes** on an advertorial campaign, but most of the people I spoke to were keen to **push** a special supplement to coincide with the fair.	P. Ich konnte ein paar **Preisangaben** für eine Werbekampagne in Erfahrung bringen, aber die meisten Zuständigen, mit denen ich gesprochen habe, würden eine Sonderbeilage lieber **verschieben** bis die Messe tatsächlich stattfindet.
M. The problem there is that we'll be sharing space with competitors, and we want to **go alone** on this one. We have a product we believe to be unique and we want to surprise the market with it. We can't do that if we share space in a newspaper **supplement** with half a dozen competitors. Call the papers again and put that to them. Anything else I should know about right now? No? Good! Let's get on with what we have to do then ...	M. Das Problem ist, dass wir dann Anzeigenplatz mit unseren Mitbewerbern teilen müssen und wir würden hierbei gern **allein in Erscheinung treten**. Wir haben ein Produkt, dass wir für einmalig halten und wir würden den Markt gern damit überraschen. Und das können wir nicht, wenn wir uns den **Anzeigenplatz** in den Zeitungen mit einem halben Dutzend Konkurrenten teilen müssen. Rufen Sie die Zeitungen noch einmal an und erklären Sie ihnen das. Gibt es sonst noch etwas, das ich wissen sollte? Nein? Gut! Dann machen wir uns wieder an die Arbeit ...

P. (alone with Angela). Wow, she certainly knows what she wants.	P. (allein mit Angela). Wow, sie weiß, was sie will.
A. Don't tell me! A real **hard cookie**! But you've seen nothing yet!	A. Wem sagen Sie das! Sie ist ein echt **harter Brocken**! Aber das war noch gar nichts!

 23. Train Yourself

1. Sie wurden gebeten, sich mit dem Redakteur der Lokalzeitung in Verbindung zu setzen und ihn zu einer Pressekonferenz inklusive Mittagessen einzuladen. Welche der folgenden Möglichkeiten würden Sie zu diesem Anlass wählen?

(a) Mr Norris, I want you to come to a press conference and lunch.
(b) Mr Norris, ERGO would be exceedingly grateful if you could spare the time to attend a press conference and lunch at our offices.
(c) Mr Norris, can you come to a press conference and lunch next week?
(d) Mr Norris, ERGO would like to invite you to attend a press conference at our offices next week. Lunch will also be served.

2. Mr Norris nimmt die Einladung an, aber Sie hätten dennoch gerne eine Bestätigung der Zusage durch seine Sekretätin. Wie formulieren Sie dies am diplomatischsten?

(a) Glad to hear you can come. Can your secretary confirm for us?
(b) Thank you for your acceptance, but we'd like your secretary to confirm.
(c) We are so glad to hear you can attend. Perhaps your secretary could confirm your attendance by telephone in the next few days.
(d) Great! Can your secretary confirm?

(James Morgan's office)	(James Morgans Büro)
J. Peter, **could you step into my office for a moment, please**?	J. Peter, **könnten Sie bitte kurz in mein Büro kommen?**

Telefonieren

P. Good morning, Mr Morgan.	P. Guten Morgen, Mr Morgan.
J. Good morning. I'm sorry to have neglected you these past few days, but you were **in good hands**. How are you **coming along**? No, no – I already know! I call both Steve and Melissa on a regular basis to check how you're doing. Both are highly satisfied.	J. Guten Morgen. Tut mir Leid, dass ich Sie in den letzten Tagen so vernachlässigt habe, aber Sie waren ja **in guten Händen. Wie kommen Sie klar**? Nein – das weiß ich ja längst! Ich rufe Steve und Melissa regelmäßig an, um mich zu erkundigen, wie Sie sich machen. Beide sind sehr zufrieden mit Ihnen.
P. Miss Walker, too?	P. Miss Walker auch?
J. She actually called me to say how happy she was with how well you are settling in. For Melissa, that's a very high compliment!	J. Sie hat mich sogar angerufen um mir zu sagen, wie froh sie ist, dass Sie sich so gut einfügen. Für Melissa ist das ein großes Kompliment!
P. I can believe it!	P. Das glaube ich!
J. Now, how about Steve? Do you approve of his operation?	J. Und was ist mit Steve? Billigen Sie seine Vorgehensweisen?
P. Approve? I'm here to learn, surely.	P. Billigen? Ich bin hier, um zu lernen.
J. You're right. Forget I asked! Steve is a very good Sales Manager, but he has his methods. Sometimes they can be rather unconventional.	J. Sie haben Recht. Vergessen Sie die Frage! Steve ist ein sehr guter Verkaufsleiter, aber er hat so seine eigenwilligen Methoden – manchmal können sie äußerst unkonventionell sein.
P. I can honestly say I didn't notice …	P. Ich kann mit gutem Gewissen sagen, dass mir das nicht aufgefallen ist …

J. Well, Miss Walker noticed you noticed! But don't let it bother you. **You're doing fine** and we're glad to **have you aboard** ...	J. Nun ja, Miss Walker ist es aufgefallen, dass es Ihnen aufgefallen ist! Aber machen Sie sich deshalb keine Gedanken. **Sie leisten gute Arbeit** und wir sind froh, Sie **an Bord zu haben** ...

 24. Train Yourself

James Morgan bittet Peter, zwei Vertreter anzurufen um diese zu fragen, warum ihre Berichte verspätet waren. Wie sehen diese Gespräche aus?

Hello, may I ▒▒▒▒▒ Donald Fyfe, please? Mr Fyfe, Mr Morgan asked me to ▒▒▒▒▒ you and ▒▒▒▒▒ about your weekly report. He's concerned that it is ▒▒▒▒▒ late. He says that you usually ▒▒▒▒▒ your report ▒▒▒▒▒ every week, but this week it hasn't ▒▒▒▒▒ yet. He would be ▒▒▒▒▒ if you ▒▒▒▒▒ it as soon as possible. He ▒▒▒▒▒ that you have a great deal to do at the moment, but the office does ▒▒▒▒▒ that report.

require, submit, speak to, grateful, very, appreciates, sent, arrived, promptly, inquire, call.

 Talk Talk Talk

(Melissa's office) M. Right, Peter. We're ready to make **final arrangements** for that press conference. I called the *Press Club* and confirmed the date. Can you **draw up a press release** for us, containing the invitation? Here are the details.	(Melissas Büro) M. Na schön, Peter. Wir sind jetzt so weit, die **letzten Vorbereitungen** für die Pressekonferenz zu treffen. Ich habe schon den *Press Club* angerufen und den Termin festgesetzt. Können Sie eine **Pressemitteilung** mit einer Einladung **entwerfen**? Hier haben Sie die Details.
P. Fine, but I'll need to clear up some details with the **Technical**	P. Gern, aber ich muss zuerst noch ein paar Einzelheiten mit der

Department first. I don't yet have all the facts about these two new systems. Who will be conducting the press conference?

M. Mr Morgan, but I'll also be there, and he'll certainly need your assistance.

P. He didn't tell me that when I called him yesterday.

M. Peter, you're officially his assistant. Are you nervous or something?

P. Do you think my English is up to it?

M. It'll do. You'll be identified as our German Assistant-Director, anyway.

P. Yes, that's just what worries me. I've read some strange comments about the Germans since getting here.

M. You're reading the wrong newspapers, Peter.

P. Well, you're the Marketing Director – give me some advice.

Technischen Abteilung klären. Ich habe noch nicht alle Fakten über diese beiden neuen Systeme. Wer wird die Pressekonferenz denn leiten?

M. Mr Morgan, aber ich werde auch dabei sein – und er wird sicherlich auch Ihre Hilfe brauchen.

P. Als ich ihn gestern angerufen habe, hat er mir das gar nicht gesagt.

M. Peter, Sie sind sein offizieller Assistent. Sind Sie vielleicht nervös?

P. Glauben Sie, mein Englisch ist gut genug?

M. Es wird reichen. Sie werden sowieso als unser Assistant Director aus Deutschland vorgestellt.

P. Ja, genau das macht mir ja Sorgen. Seit ich hier bin, habe ich schon einige sehr befremdliche Kommentare über die Deutschen gelesen.

M. Sie lesen die falschen Zeitungen, Peter.

P. Na ja, Sie sind der Marketing Direktor – geben Sie mir einen Rat.

M. My best advice, Peter, is to **keep your head down** at the press conference and let Mr Morgan do all the talking. Then you'll survive it ...

M. Mein bester Rat, Peter, ist es, sich auf der Pressekonferenz **zurückzuhalten** und das Reden Mr Morgan zu überlassen. Dann werden Sie das Ganze schon überleben ...

 25. Train Yourself

Können Sie Peter helfen, die Pressemitteilung und die Einladung zu entwerfen?

ERGO Limited. A press release.
You are ▓▓▓ to ▓▓▓ a press conference at the Press Club, Shoe Lane, on Friday, April 24, at 11 AM. ERGO will be ▓▓▓ its new software packages to the media. We feel sure the full range of our new products will be of ▓▓▓ to you, and our experts – led by Mr James Morgan, Managing Director, will be ▓▓▓ to answer your questions and ▓▓▓ any further information you ▓▓▓. The press conference will be ▓▓▓ by a luncheon, ▓▓▓ cordially invited to attend. ERGO would ▓▓▓ a reply by March 30.

Background Information

If you are involved in the **organization of a press conference**, make sure invitations are sent well in time, together with a request to reply by a set date. Be concise and clear about the purpose of the conference, which should be held in a neutral setting, such as a Press Club. Open the press conference with a brief introduction and summary of what you or your company has to make public, and then take questions. Ask questioners to identify themselves and their publications. Keep question-time to no longer than half an hour and signal the end of the press conference by announcing you can take »just two more questions« and making clear senior members of the company are prepared to be approached personally on specific topics – perhaps at an informal buffet or lunch.

 **Talk Talk Talk**

(Melissa's office)
M. Peter, could you help me out by giving the trade fair organizers a call and ask them if they've **got around** yet to **drawing up** a catalogue?

P. Certainly. Do you have the number?

M. Yes, and the **contact person**. Her name is Stella Barker. Her **extension** is three-o-five. You might have difficulty getting through – she's very busy right now. But please keep trying. I really need to know today how far she is with the catalogue.

P. I'll **get on to it** right away. I've nothing more **pressing** to do at the moment, anyway. A bit more phoning won't do any harm. It'll keep me in practice!

(Melissas Büro)
M. Peter, könnten Sie mir dabei helfen, die Organisatoren der Messe anzurufen und sie zu fragen, ob sie schon **dazu gekommen sind** einen Katalog **zusammenzustellen**?

P. Natürlich. Haben Sie die Nummer?

M. Ja – und die **Kontaktperson**. Ihr Name ist Stella Barker. Ihre **Durchwahl** ist Drei-Null-Fünf. Sie werden vielleicht Probleme haben, durchzukommen – sie ist gerade natürlich sehr beschäftigt. Aber bitte versuchen Sie es weiter. Ich muss wirklich heute noch wissen, wie weit sie mit dem Katalog ist.

P. Ich **kümmere mich** sofort **darum**. Ich habe im Augenblick sowieso nichts **Dringlicheres** zu tun. Ein bisschen mehr Telefonieren wird schon nichts schaden. So bleibe ich wenigstens in Übung!

 26. Train Yourself

1. Peter ruft die Messeorganisation an, um sich nach dem Katalog zu erkundigen. Er hat einige Schwierigkeiten zur richtigen Ansprechpartnerin, nämlich Stella Barker, durchzukommen. Können Sie ihm helfen?

Hello, is that the International Trade Fair Centre? Could you ▓▓▓▓▓▓ ▓▓▓▓▓▓ please to extension three-o-five? It's ▓▓▓▓▓▓▓▓▓▓?

I'll ▓▓▓▓▓▓. Hello, hello? Damn, I've been ▓▓▓▓▓▓. I'll have to try to ▓▓▓▓▓▓ her number direct. Still ▓▓▓▓▓▓. Right, here goes again! Hello, is that the International Trade Fair Centre? You ▓▓▓▓▓▓ me ▓▓▓▓▓▓ when I ▓▓▓▓▓▓ before. I am trying to ▓▓▓▓▓▓ Miss Stella Barker on three-o-five. I know the number is ▓▓▓▓▓▓. Can you ▓▓▓▓▓▓ her call? This is very important. You'll put me ▓▓▓▓▓▓ hold? But, please, I can't ▓▓▓▓▓▓ on for very long. As I said, this is important. Ah, ▓▓▓▓▓▓ at last. Is that the print department. Could I ▓▓▓▓▓▓ to Miss Stella Barker, please? She's just stepped out? Oh, no! Then I'll ▓▓▓▓▓▓ on. But please don't ▓▓▓▓▓▓ me off. I've been ▓▓▓▓▓▓ on this phone for what seems hours.

2. Als er Stella schließlich erreicht, ist er so frustriert, dass er zunächst atemlos probiert, seine Anfrage los zu werden!

Hello, Miss Barker. Peter Brückner here! Brückner of ERGO Limited. We are exhibiting at the electronics trade fair. I have an important question. Or, at least, my Marketing Director does. She's Miss Melissa Walker. Perhaps you know her. Anyway, it concerns the catalogue. She is worried about an apparent delay in its appearance. The appearance of the catalogue, that is. I mean, not the actual appearance of the catalogue but when it will be printed. Is the catalogue finished? When will it be appearing? Miss Walker says she wanted to see first of all the layout of the page where ERGO is advertising. She's worried there might be mistakes in it and wants to correct them, if there are any, that is. Although, we're sure there aren't any because we had a proof from you last week. But you can never be too sure, can you?

Doch dann holt er einmal tief Luft, entspannt sich und korrigiert seinen ersten Versuch. Helfen Sie ihm dabei!

 **Talk Talk Talk**

(Peter's office)
P. I had problems getting through to Stella Barker, but **she assured me**

(Peters Büro)
Ich hatte einige Probleme, zu Stella Barker durchzukommen, aber **sie**

the catalogues are ready and can be picked up from this afternoon. Or she'll **courier** them, if you like.

M. We'll send Chip round for them. Chip!

C. Miss Walker?

M. Drop what you're doing and get round to the International Trade Fair Centre right away. Miss Stella Barker will give you a batch of catalogues.

C. Righto! I'm on my way.

M. I would prefer to have seen a second **proof** of our **insertion** before the final printing. I just hope there are no further mistakes.

P. Miss Barker assured me the catalogue is now entirely free of mistakes.

M. Peter, in this business I have learnt **to trust no set of eyes but my own**.

P. Lovely eyes, too – oh, pardon me, that just slipped out!

hat mir versichert, dass die Kataloge fertig sind und heute Nachmittag abgeholt werden können. Wenn Sie wollen, kann sie die Kataloge auch **per Kurier schicken**.

M. Wir werden Chip danach schicken. Chip!

C. Miss Walker?

M. Lass' alles stehen und liegen und fahre sofort zum Internationalen Messezentrum. Miss Stella Barker wird dir dort einen Stapel mit Katalogen übergeben.

C. Geht klar! Bin schon unterwegs.

M. Ich würde gerne noch einen zweiten **Korrekturabzug** unseres **Inserates** sehen, bevor der Katalog endgültig in Druck geht. Ich hoffe, diesmal sind keine Fehler mehr darin.

P. Miss Barker hat mir versichert, dass der Katalog jetzt vollkommen fehlerfrei ist.

M. Peter, in diesem Geschäft habe ich gelernt, **nur das zu glauben, was ich mit eigenen Augen gesehen habe**.

P. Und mit wunderschönen Augen – oh, verzeihen Sie bitte, das ist mir so rausgerutscht!

M. Did Lucy put something stronger in your tea this morning? Compliments don't belong on your desk, Peter! Keep them for the evenings. Those long evenings at the pub with Steve.	M. Hat Lucy Ihnen heute Morgen etwas in den Tee getan? Komplimente haben am Schreibtisch nichts zu suchen, Peter! Sparen Sie sie für die Abende auf. Für diese langen Abende in den Pubs mit Steve.
P. You won't find me at the pub these days. I can't **get used to** the beer. And the way the English drink! Pubs get no complements from me.	P. In diesen Pubs werden Sie mich nicht mehr finden. Ich kann mich an dieses Bier nicht **gewöhnen**. Und die Art, wie Engländer trinken! Die Pubs können mir erst einmal gestohlen bleiben.

 27. Train Yourself

1. Sie wurden damit beauftragt, eine Anzeige von ERGO Limited für den Messekatalog zu entwerfen. In ihrem Notizbuch stehen die wichtigsten Anhaltspunkte, aber diese müssen erst in einen vollständigen Text umgewandelt werden. Wie sieht Ihr Textentwurf aus?

ERGO Limited, Carter's Lane, London NI. Tel. 171/385964, Fax. 171/385965. Website: http//www.ergo.uk. Email: Ergo@telkom.uk
British subsidiary of ERGO International, San Diego, USA, a leading manufacturer of communications technology.
Latest products on the market: Accounting 2000, updating earlier accounting program; Quick-Ed – entirely new editing program for magazines and newspapers. Very latest in easy editing and page makeup. Saves many man-hours in sub-editing phase of magazine and newspaper production. System can be viewed at Middlesex Echo – phone ERGO Limited for appointment to view.

2. Ein Zeitungsredakteur ruft an, um sich nach der Möglichkeit, das Quick-Ed Programm einmal in Betrieb zu sehen, zu erkundigen. Sie rufen beim »Middlesex Echo« zurück, um einen Termin zu vereinbaren. Füllen Sie die Lücken im Gesprächstext!

Hello, Middlesex Echo? Could you ▓▓▓▓▓▓ me ▓▓▓▓▓▓ to the Editorial Department, please? Hello, is that the Editorial Department? I'd like to ▓▓▓▓▓▓ the Editor, please. Yes, I'll ▓▓▓▓▓▓. Hello, is that the Editor, Mr Ponsonby? Good morning, Mr Ponsonby. My ▓▓▓▓▓▓ is Morgan, James Morgan, of ERGO Limited. You were kind enough to offer us the ▓▓▓▓▓▓ to demonstrate our Quick-Ed program **in situ** at the Middlesex Echo. Do you remember? I am ▓▓▓▓▓▓ now to inquire if I  bring along one of our potential clients to view the system at work. When? I'm not yet sure. I'm waiting for his ▓▓▓▓▓▓. He promised to ▓▓▓▓▓▓ me by today to suggest a ▓▓▓▓▓▓.
May I then ▓▓▓▓▓▓ you back and fix an ▓▓▓▓▓▓? Certainly, I'll ▓▓▓▓▓▓ your secretary. What ▓▓▓▓▓▓ does she have? Do I ▓▓▓▓▓▓ a zero before the local code? One question: how long can we spend in your editorial offices without being a nuisance. An hour or so? That's very kind of you! I'll be ▓▓▓▓▓▓ back later today to confirm the arrangements. When would it be convenient to ▓▓▓▓▓▓? I'll certainly ▓▓▓▓▓▓ by five o'clock.

Talk Talk Talk

(Melissa's office)
C. Here you are Miss. Here are the catalogues. They said there were six of them.

M. Thank you, Chip. I'd better call and confirm they have arrived, though.

(Melissas Büro)
C. Hier bitte, Miss – die Kataloge. Sie haben gesagt, es gäbe sechs Stück davon.

M. Danke, Chip. Aber ich rufe besser noch einmal an, und bestätige, dass sie angekommen sind.

C. Well, aren't *you* trusting? I came straight here with them.	C. Meine Güte, was für ein Vertrauen! Ich bin direkt mit den Dingern hierher gekommen.
M. **No reflection on** you, Chip. I made such a noise about these catalogues that I must confirm their arrival.	M. Das hat **nichts mit dir zu tun**, Chip. Ich habe so einen Aufstand wegen dieser Kataloge gemacht, dass ich den Erhalt jetzt auch noch einmal bestätigen muss.
C. Just as you like. **Will there be anything else**?	C. Ganz wie Sie wollen. **Gibt es sonst noch etwas?**
M. Chip, be a dear and run out for a sandwich for me. There's **no way** I'm going to get a lunch break today.	M. Chip, sei doch bitte ein Schatz und besorge mir ein Sandwich. Es besteht **keine Chance**, dass ich heute eine Mittagspause einlegen kann.
P. (appears in the door) I've just called out for a couple of ciabbatas – you're very welcome to share them, Melissa.	P. (erscheint in der Tür) Ich habe gerade ein paar Ciabbatas bestellt – Sie sind herzlich eingeladen, sie mit mir zu teilen, Melissa.
M. Peter, that's very kind of you. All right, Chip – you're **off the hook**! Now, let me finish off this catalogue business. Lucy, can you get me the International Trade Fair Centre? Do you have their number? Just dial the switchboard. Hello, is that the International Trade Fair Centre? Can you put me through please to Stella Barker ...	M. Sehr nett von Ihnen, Peter. Na schön, Chip – du bist **nochmal davongekommen!** Jetzt lasst mich diese Katalog-Geschichte zu Ende bringen. Lucy, können Sie mich mit dem Internationalen Messezentrum verbinden? Haben Sie deren Nummer? Rufen Sie einfach bei der Telefonzentrale an. Hallo, ist dort das Internationale Messezentrum? Können Sie mich bitte zu Stella Barker durchstellen ...

Telefonieren

28. Train Yourself

Stella Barker hat ungeduldig auf Peter Brückners Anruf gewartet, aber er hatte große Schwierigkeiten durchzukommen. Füllen Sie die Lücken im Text mit den passenden Wörtern!

P. Miss Barker, I'm terribly sorry to ▓▓▓▓▓▓ so late.

SB. I did wait in my office specifically for your ▓▓▓▓▓▓.

P. I had terrible difficulty ▓▓▓▓▓▓ through. Your number was constantly ▓▓▓▓▓▓ and when I ▓▓▓▓▓▓ the switchboard I found myself ▓▓▓▓▓▓ to a completely different number.

SB. I would have ▓▓▓▓▓▓ you, but I had a lot to do, anyway. It's not that important. But I can't ▓▓▓▓▓▓ right now. I'm in conference. Can I ▓▓▓▓▓▓ you back?

P. Certainly, but I shall be ▓▓▓▓▓▓ my phone for only another twenty minutes or so. If I don't ▓▓▓▓▓▓ from you in that time I'll try to ▓▓▓▓▓▓ you tomorrow.

SB. Tomorrow, I'm out and about. But you can ▓▓▓▓▓▓ my mobile. Do you have the number?

P. I think so. I'll check and call you back.

SB. No, please don't do that – I'm in conference, as I say. I never ▓▓▓▓▓▓ my mobile ▓▓▓▓▓▓ when I'm in conference. I find it so disturbing.
My number is – oh, dear, I've got it in the office next-door. Can you ▓▓▓▓▓▓?

P. I'm sorry, but I have to ▓▓▓▓▓▓ off. My director is signalling that he wants to speak to me and to ▓▓▓▓▓▓ the phone. If I don't ▓▓▓▓▓▓ from you I'll ▓▓▓▓▓▓ you tomorrow.

SB: That's fine. But don't forget to ▓▓▓▓▓▓ my mobile – if you find the ▓▓▓▓▓▓, that is!

Background Information

Mobile rules: there are no rules governing the use of a mobile telephone in Britain, apart from during the take-off and landing of an aircraft. But the sensitive businessperson follows certain rules:
1. He or she switches their mobile off in a restaurant – and of course in the cinema, theatre, opera house and concert hall.
2. In the office, it's considerate to switch the mobile off during important staff conferences. The secretary can be instructed to break in with calls requiring urgent attention.
3. Legislation making it illegal to use a mobile in the hand while driving is also being considered in Britain.

 **Talk Talk Talk**

(Melissa's office)
M. Well, Peter that's your week with me over! You survived it very well!

P. I enjoyed it very much, and I'm sure I learnt a lot – although I seem to have spent most of my time on the phone.

M. Don't worry, you'll soon get out and about. It's often necessary to lay the **groundwork** on the phone. At least, you have no difficulty there now.

(Melissas Büro)
M. Tja, Peter, Ihre Woche mit mir ist vorbei! Sie haben sich gut geschlagen!

P. Es hat mir viel Spaß gemacht und ich habe eine Menge gelernt – obwohl ich das Gefühl habe, die meiste Zeit am Telefon verbracht zu haben.

M. Keine Sorge, Sie werden bald etwas weiter herumkommen. Aber es ist oft unvermeidbar, die **grundlegende Arbeit** über das Telefon zu erledigen. Wenigstens haben Sie damit keine Probleme mehr.

P. There are still some points I'm not clear about. I'm still not used to being told »just one moment« when I dial a number and then having to hang on for what seems ages! And I wouldn't like to count the number of times I've been cut off or put through to the wrong extension. And then I can't stand it when the person on the other end of the line just answers »hello« without identifying himself or herself. It knocks me off balance for a moment and I have difficulty beginning the conversation.

P. Es gibt immer noch ein paar Punkte, mit denen ich nicht so recht klar komme. Ich habe mich immer noch nicht daran gewöhnt, gesagt zu bekommen, ich solle »einen Moment in der Leitung bleiben« – und dann eine Ewigkeit warten zu müssen! Und ich möchte gar nicht wissen, wie oft ich aus der Leitung geworfen oder falsch verbunden wurde. Und ich kann es nicht leiden, wenn die Person auf der anderen Seite der Leitung sich einfach nur mit »Hallo« meldet, ohne ihren Namen zu sagen. Das bringt mich immer für einen Moment aus der Fassung und ich habe dann Probleme, das Gespräch zu beginnen.

M. I know, and I quite agree. But at least you'll never make that mistake, will you?

M. Ich weiß, mir geht das ähnlich, aber wenigstens werden Sie diesen Fehler nicht machen, nicht wahr?

P. Well, I do have other problems when it comes to identifying myself. Spelling Brückner over the phone is not the easiest task here in Britain!

P. Tja, dafür habe ich Probleme, wenn ich meinen eigenen Namen am Telefon sage. Hier in England »Brückner« zu buchstabieren ist alles andere als einfach!

 Vocabulary

advertising department	Anzeigenabteilung; Werbeabteilung
advertorial	Mischung aus Anzeige und redaktionellem Beitrag
to be at home with sth.	mit einer Sache vertraut sein
businessperson	Geschäftsmann/-frau
to come along	sich entwickeln; Fortschritte machen

company profile	Firmenprofil
contact (name)	(Name eines) Ansprechpartner(s)
to conduct a press conference	eine Pressekonferenz leiten
to courier sth.	etw. per Kurier schicken
down to orders	zum Geschäftlichen kommen
to draw up	(einen Text) entwerfen
to drop on	(Arbeit) abwälzen
editor	Redakteur
fair	Messe
franchise	Franchise (Übertragung einer Lizenz)
to gather the papers	die Unterlagen zusammensuchen
to get around to	dazu kommen
to get on to	sich daran machen
to get used to	sich daran gewöhnen
to go alone	als Einziger vertreten sein
ground work	grundlegende Arbeit
hand-out	Handzettel; Informationsblatt
hard cookie	harter Brocken (anerkennend)
to have aboard	jmd. an Bord haben
he/she is tops	jmd. ist unschlagbar/ der, die Beste
in good hands	in guten Händen
insertion	Inserat
to keep your head down	sich zurückhalten
to make a practice of	es sich zur Regel gemacht haben
to make doubly certain	auf Nummer sicher gehen
news department	Nachrichtenredaktion
no reflection on	nichts zu tun haben mit (versichernd)
no way	unter keinen Umständen
off the hook	vom Haken/noch mal davon gekommen
operations	Geschäftsaktivitäten
personal call	Stippvisite
press conference	Pressekonferenz
press release	Pressemitteilung
pressing	etwas Eiliges/Wichtiges

print-shop	Druckerei
proof (in publishing)	Korrekturabzug
to push	hier: verschieben/aufschieben bis zum besten Zeitpunkt
quite a hand at	erfahren/geübt mit etwas
quote/quotation	hier: Aussage (sonst: Angebot)
release	Publikation
run-up	hier: für den Beginn/Anfang
to settle in	sich eingewöhnen
slog	harte Arbeit/Schufterei
special supplement	Sonderbeilage, Zeitungsbeilage
to take it from there	sich von da ab um etwas kümmern
technical department	Technische Abteilung
the pleasure is all mine	das Vergnügen ist ganz auf meiner Seite
work-load	Arbeitspensum

After-sales servicing
Kundenbetreuung

Telefonieren

 **Here we go**

Nach seinen Erfahrungen in der Marketing-Abteilung bei Melissa Walker tritt Peter nunmehr seine eigentliche Rolle als Assistent bei James Morgan, dem Managing Director bei ERGO Limited, an. Nun wird er zum ersten Mal persönlich mit Kundenproblemen und deren Lösung konfrontiert und erhält sogar seinen allerersten Außenauftrag ...

 **Talk Talk Talk**

(James Morgan's office)
J. Hello! Morgan here!

L. Oh, good morning, Mr Morgan. It's Lucy here. Mr Brückner called to say he would be a little late this morning because he has to call at the Social Security Office on the way in. I tried to put him through to you, but the line was busy, and he was in a hurry, **so I took the message**.

J. Fine, Lucy. Don't worry. I don't really have anything for him to do yet, even though this is his first day with me ...

(Peter enters after some time)
P. I really am sorry I'm so late, Mr Morgan. I hope Lucy told you the reason.

(James Morgans Büro)
J. Hallo! Morgan am Apparat!

L. Oh, guten Morgen, Mr Morgan. Hier ist Lucy. Mr Brückner hat mich angerufen, um zu sagen, dass er heute wohl etwas später kommen wird, weil er auf dem Weg zur Arbeit noch beim Sozialversicherungsamt vorbeischauen muss. Ich habe versucht, ihn zu Ihnen durchzustellen, aber die Leitung war immer besetzt und er hatte es sehr eilig – also **habe ich die Nachricht entgegengenommen**.

J. Schon gut, Lucy. Keine Sorge. Ich habe sowieso noch nichts Richtiges für ihn zu tun, obwohl heute sein erster Tag bei mir ist ...

(Nach einer Weile tritt Peter ein)
P. Tut mir wirklich Leid, dass ich so spät komme, Mr Morgan. Ich hoffe, Lucy hat Ihnen den Grund dafür gesagt.

J. No problem, Peter. Come in and make yourself at home. I'll call Lucy for some tea and then we'll **get down to business**.

P. **I'm looking forward to working more closely with you**, Mr Morgan. And I hope I can be of some help, too.

J. That you can be, Peter! Monday morning I just spend sifting through the **paperwork** that has to be attended to during the week. You can certainly take some of that work-load off me. You'll be very **au fait** by now with much of it after your time in Sales and Marketing.

J. Kein Problem, Peter. Kommen Sie rein und machen Sie es sich bequem. Ich bitte Lucy, uns einen Tee zu bringen und dann **machen wir uns an die Arbeit**.

P. **Ich freue mich schon darauf, enger mit Ihnen zusammenzuarbeiten**, Mr Morgan. Und ich hoffe, dass ich Ihnen eine Hilfe sein kann.

J. Oh, das werden Sie, Peter! Am Montagmorgen überfliege ich immer den **Papierkram**, der im Laufe der Woche erledigt werden muss. Sie können mir bestimmt etwas von dieser Arbeit abnehmen. Nach Ihrer Zeit im Verkauf und im Marketing werden Sie mit dem meisten davon schon **vertraut** sein.

 29. Train Yourself

1. Sie müssen im Büro anrufen, um mitzuteilen, dass Sie sich leider verspäten werden. Wie gehen Sie dies am elegantesten an?

Hello, Lucy? I've tried to ▆▆▆▆▆▆▆ Mr Morgan on his ▆▆▆▆▆▆▆, but the line is always ▆▆▆▆▆▆▆. I have to call at the Social Security Office on the way to work, so I'll be rather late. ▆▆▆▆▆▆▆ please leave a message for Mr Morgan? ▆▆▆▆▆▆▆ please tell him I tried to ▆▆▆▆▆▆▆ him but I couldn't ▆▆▆▆▆▆▆ through, and ▆▆▆▆▆▆▆ please tell him I shall be late in? If I'm delayed longer than half an hour or so I'll ▆▆▆▆▆▆▆ again. ▆▆▆▆▆▆▆ you ▆▆▆▆▆▆▆ able to do that for me? Thank you so much, Lucy!

2. Multiple choice
Finden Sie das richtige Wort für die Lücke!

Please ▓▓▓▓ I'm trying to connect you.	a) *wait* b) *hold on* c) *don't go away*
Can you ▓▓▓▓ another line?	a) *put through* b) *speak to* c) *try*
May I ▓▓▓▓ Mr Brown, please?	a) *speak to* b) *talk to* c) *contact*
The line is dead. I think I've been ▓▓▓▓.	a) *disconnected* b) *thrown out* c) *cut off*
Is he still ▓▓▓▓ the phone?	a) *on* b) *speaking on* c) *talking on*
Would you please ▓▓▓▓ the line. I'm busy.	a) *leave* b) *get off* c) *relinquish*
Please try to get them ▓▓▓▓ phone.	a) *by* b) *with the* c) *on the*

 **Talk Talk Talk**

(James Morgan's office)
J. Now, Peter. Let's look at some of this paperwork. Steve sends in at the start of every week a **round-up** of what his people have been up to the previous week, a progress report and a **projection**. He also copies me what he sends to **accounts**, a rough balance of outgoings, supported by receipts, and

(James Morgans Büro)
J. Also, Peter, nehmen wir uns mal etwas von dem Papierkram vor. Steve schickt mir zu jedem Wochenbeginn eine **Übersicht** darüber, was seine Leute in der Vorwoche alles getan haben, einen Fortschritts-Bericht und eine **Prognose**. Außerdem schickt er mir alles in Kopie, was er an die **Rech-**

an account of receipts, actual and expected. I try to get through it all on Monday morning, but it's usually Tuesday before I'm through. Anyway, Tuesday is our customary conference day.

P. How can I help you here?

J. Perhaps you'd like to take Steve's summary and match it with his accounts report. Accounting will pick up any irregularities, but it doesn't harm to be ahead of the **bean-counters**!

P. Bean-counters?

J. Oh dear, there's my time in the Far East showing me up again. That's what the accounting staff were called in Hong Kong, and the expression has travelled as far as the United States and Britain now!

(Phone rings) And there's the first distraction of the day. Hello, Morgan here! But Mr Thomson, we tried to get you all last week. You were never there. Look, can I call

nungsstelle weitergibt, eine grobe Aufstellung der Ausgaben, belegt durch Rechnungen, zusätzlich noch eine Zusammenstellung aller Rechnungen – der aktuellen und der noch erwarteten. Ich versuche, mich während des Montagmorgens da durchzuarbeiten, aber meistens brauche ich bis Dienstag, bevor ich damit fertig bin. Dienstag ist auf jeden Fall unser üblicher Konferenztag.

P. Wie kann ich dabei helfen?

J. Sie könnten vielleicht Steves Aufrechnungen übernehmen und sie mit der Summe seiner Rechnungsbeträge abgleichen. Die Rechnungsstelle wird zwar alle Unregelmäßigkeiten aufspüren, aber es kann nichts schaden, diesen **Erbsenzählern** einen Schritt voraus zu sein!

P. Erbsenzähler?

J. Oh je, da kommt meine Zeit im Fernen Osten wieder durch. So haben wir die Mitarbeiter der Rechnungsstelle in Hong Kong genannt und dieser Ausdruck hat sich inzwischen bis in die Vereinigten Staaten und nach England verbreitet! (Das Telefon klingelt) Und da haben wir ja schon die erste Ablenkung des Tages. Hallo, hier Morgan! Aber Mr Thomson, wir haben die ganze letzte Woche ver-

you right back? What's your extension? (Puts phone down). That, Peter, was a bean-counter!

sucht, Sie zu erreichen. Sie waren nie da. Hören Sie, kann ich Sie zurückrufen? Wie lautet denn Ihre Durchwahl? (Legt den Hörer auf) Das, Peter, war ein Erbsenzähler!

 30. Train Yourself

Sie wurden gebeten einen Verkäufer anzurufen, um ihn darauf hinzuweisen, dass sein Bericht nicht mit seiner Abrechnung übereinstimmt. Wie verläuft das Gespräch?

Hello, ▓▓▓▓▓ Mr Harper? I'm ▓▓▓▓▓ on the instructions of Mr Morgan to ▓▓▓▓▓ you for clarification of your report. Mr Morgan says it doesn't tally with your accounting. I think the best thing is for you to ▓▓▓▓▓ the company headquarters and ask to ▓▓▓▓▓ the head of accounting. When I ▓▓▓▓▓ to him this morning I must confess I didn't understand the problem. Would you mind ▓▓▓▓▓ him and ▓▓▓▓▓ him to sort the problem out, and then ▓▓▓▓▓ me to report on the situation. Mr Morgan also expects a ▓▓▓▓▓ from you later in the day. If he's not there ask to be ▓▓▓▓▓ to me. Oh, before you ▓▓▓▓▓ off please give me a ▓▓▓▓▓ where I can reach you this afternoon.

Background Information

Tally-ho! A tally in the business sense is an account or a reckoning. The verb »to tally« means »to make an account«, »to add up« – or, in the above context, »to make two separate things agree or correspond«. And tally-ho? That's a hunting term, describing a hunter's cry on sighting a fox!

 **Talk Talk Talk**

(Morgan's office)
J. Peter, may I hand Thomson on to you? He's an absolute nuisance! He's the accountant at Sparrow Technologies, and he's not happy with the software we sent him, nor with the **payment agreement**. I've told him we'll send one of our people round to **talk him through** the system and that our accounting will handle the payment problem. But he will insist on speaking to me. Give him a call, tell him you're my assistant and try and sort out his troubles. If you manage to get him off my back I'll buy you lunch tomorrow!

P. I'll do my best, Mr Morgan. But do you think I can do it all on the phone?

J. The alternative is a long journey – he's in Scotland!

(Morgans Büro)
J. Peter, kann ich diesen Thomson an Sie übergeben? Der Mann ist ein absoluter Nervtöter! Er ist Buchhalter bei Sparrow Technologies und er ist nicht zufrieden mit unserer Software – und auch nicht mit den **Zahlungsbedingungen**. Ich habe ihm gesagt, dass wir einen unserer Leute zu ihnen schicken werden, der ihnen das System **erklärt** und dass unsere Buchhaltung sich um die Zahlungsmodalitäten kümmern wird. Aber er besteht einfach darauf, mit mir zu reden. Rufen Sie ihn bitte an, sagen sie ihm, dass Sie mein Assistent sind und versuchen werden, seine Probleme zu lösen. Wenn Sie es schaffen, ihn mir vom Hals zu halten, lade ich Sie morgen zum Mittag ein!

P. Ich werde mein Bestes versuchen, Mr Morgan. Aber glauben Sie, ich kann das alles über das Telefon erreichen?

J. Die Alternative wäre eine lange Reise – er sitzt in Schottland!

 31. Train Yourself

Sie wollen sich nach den Kosten für eine Geschäftsreise nach Schottland erkundigen und rufen ein Reisebüro an, um nach der billigsten und schnellsten Reisemöglichkeit zu fragen. Wie verläuft das Gespräch?

Hello, ▓▓▓▓▓▓▓▓▓▓▓▓▓▓ the Oxford Street Travel Centre? I ▓▓▓▓▓▓▓▓▓▓▓▓ to travel to Scotland tomorrow, returning on Thursday. Do you have any special offers by air? The domestic desk? Can you ▓▓▓▓▓▓▓▓▓▓▓▓ me through? Yes, I'll ▓▓▓▓▓▓▓▓▓▓▓▓. Hello, is that the domestic desk? Do you have any special offers to Glasgow or Edinburgh? No, not by train! By air! I'm on the wrong ▓▓▓▓▓▓▓▓▓▓▓▓? Could you ▓▓▓▓▓▓▓▓▓▓▓▓ me through to the right extension then, please? Yes, I'll ▓▓▓▓▓▓▓▓▓▓▓▓. Hello, hello! Damn, I've been ▓▓▓▓▓▓▓▓. The phone is ▓▓▓▓▓▓▓▓▓▓▓▓. At this rate I'll never get to Scotland? I'll do it all ▓▓▓▓▓▓▓▓ phone.

 **Talk Talk Talk**

(Peter's office)
P. Hello, Mr Thomson? Mr Morgan asked me to call you and try and sort out your problems.

T. **Who am I speaking to**?

P. Oh, I am sorry – my name is Peter Brückner. I'm Mr Morgan's new assistant.

T. Well, I hope you can assist me with my troubles, young man!

P. I'll certainly try. What seems to be the problem?

T. Seems to be? Problem? I've got at least two for you to solve. Let's start with number one – the ac-

(Peters Büro)
P. Hallo, Mr Thomson? Mr Morgan hat mich gebeten, Sie anzurufen und zu versuchen, Ihre Probleme zu lösen.

T. **Mit wem spreche ich denn?**

P. Oh, tut mir Leid – mein Name ist Peter Brückner. Ich bin Mr Morgans neuer Assistent.

T. Tja, ich hoffe, Sie können mir auch bei meinen Problemen assistieren, junger Mann!

P. Ich werde es zumindest versuchen. Wo scheint es denn ein Problem zu geben?

T. Scheint? *Ein* Problem? Ich habe mindestens zwei, die Sie für mich lösen müssen. Fangen wir mit der

counting software you delivered. I can't install it.

Nummer Eins an – die Buchhaltungs-Software, die Sie mir geliefert haben. Ich kann sie nicht installieren.

P. We had a **call from a client with a similar problem**. He hadn't read our instructions carefully enough. A couple of phone calls put the matter right.

P. Wir hatten bereits einen **Anruf von einem anderen Kunden mit einem ähnlichen Problem**. Er hatte unsere Installationsanweisung nicht sorgfältig genug gelesen. Mit ein paar Telefongesprächen sollte das Problem zu lösen sein.

T. Phone calls? Phone calls? I want somebody round here **on the hop**, my man!

T. Telefongespräche? Ein paar Telefongespräche? Ich will jemanden hier an Ort und Stelle sehen, aber **in Nullkommanichts**, junger Mann!

P. Let's see. We have a man in Glasgow, who can call on you tomorrow.

P. Mal sehen. Wir haben einen Mitarbeiter in Glasgow, der morgen vorbeikommen könnte.

T. Tomorrow? Yesterday would have been better. But I'll **settle for** tomorrow.

T. Morgen? Gestern wäre besser. Aber ich werde mich mit morgen **zufrieden geben**.

P. I'll tell him to call you right away and tell you when he will be around.

P. Ich werde ihm sagen, dass er Sie sofort anrufen soll, um Ihnen zu sagen, wann er da sein kann.

T. I'll be waiting, young man, I'll be waiting ...

T. Ich warte, junger Mann, ich warte darauf ...

32. Train Yourself

The Pecking Order

1. Ordnen Sie die Berufe nach ihrem Rang im Unternehmen:

a. Secretary
b. Managing Director
c. Accountant
d. Department Head
e. Salesperson
f. Trainee salesperson
g. Assistant Managing Director
h. Chief Accountant
i. Chief Secretary

2. Ordnen Sie jeder dieser Personen Ihre korrekte Position zu!

Lucy ....
Peter Brückner ....
James Morgan ....
Jenkins ....
Joe Sampson ....
Melissa Walker ....
Chip ....
Mr Thomson ....
Steve Blackman ....
Geoff Burnes ....

 **Talk Talk Talk**

(Peter's Office)
P. Lucy, do you have the number of our man in Glasgow? McLeod is his name. Roy McLeod.

(Peters Büro)
P. Lucy, haben Sie die Nummer von unserem Mann in Glasgow? Sein Name ist McLeod. Roy McLeod.

L. I'll have it for you **in a jiffy**. Shall I call him for you and connect you?	L. Ich suche sie Ihnen im **Handumdrehen** heraus. Soll ich ihn für Sie anrufen und Sie gleich durchstellen?
P. That would be very kind of you, Lucy.	P. Das wäre sehr nett von Ihnen, Lucy.
L. Mr McLeod? ERGO Limited, London, here. Mr Brückner would like to speak to you. **Please hold the line. I'm putting you through right now** …	L. Mr McLeod? Hier ERGO Limited, London. Mr Brückner würde gern mit Ihnen sprechen. **Bitte bleiben Sie in der Leitung, ich stelle Sie durch** …
P. Hello, Roy McLeod? Peter Brückner here. I'm helping Mr Morgan out this week. Sparrow Technologies are giving us problems – at least, they say they have problems.	P. Hallo, Roy McLeod? Hier Peter Brückner. Ich assistiere Mr Morgan diese Woche. Wir haben Probleme mit Sparrow Technologies – zumindest sagen sie, dass sie Probleme hätten.
R. Are you dealing with Thomson?	R. Haben Sie es etwa mit Mr Thomson zu tun?
P. That's him, the company accountant. He has called several times, and frankly he's getting on Mr Morgan's nerves. Can you call round and try and sort things out.	P. Ganz genau, mit dem Buchhalter der Firma. Er hat schon mehrmals bei uns angerufen und, ehrlich gesagt, geht er Mr Morgan schon ziemlich auf die Nerven. Können Sie mal vorbeischauen und versuchen, das zu regeln?
R. I've been round there several times, didn't he tell you? The man is impossible, he can't operate a computer and he doesn't seem able to read. I helped him install Accounting 2000 and within a week	R. Ich war doch schon mehrfach da, hat er Ihnen das nicht gesagt? Der Mann ist einfach unmöglich; er kann nicht mit Computern umgehen und offensichtlich nicht einmal lesen. Ich habe ihm dabei gehol-

the whole system was down! But I'll give him a call – I hope I can do all this on the phone. He's got a fierce temper ...

fen, Accounting 2000 zu installieren und innerhalb einer Woche ist das gesamte System zusammengebrochen! Aber ich werde ihn anrufen – ich hoffe, ich kann das über das Telefon regeln. Der Mann hat ein ziemlich unbeherrschtes Temperament ...

33. Train Yourself

Sie sprechen am Telefon mit einem sehr verärgerten Mr Thomson von Sparrow Technologies. Wie würden Sie ihn beruhigen? Sie müssen Ihre Worte sehr sorgsam wählen!

Hello, Mr Thomson! Yes, I *(realize, understand, sympathize, know)* you have problems, and that is why I am calling. I do *(state, reassure, confirm, tell, assure)* you that we are doing everything we *(are able, know how, can, find possible)* to *(come to, reach, find, score)* a solution. I'm *(afraid, sorry to say, disappointed, concerned)* it won't be easy, but I can *(say, tell, assure, promise, guarantee)* you we won't *(give up, rest, stop work, be happy)* until you are entirely *(pleased, happy, satisfied)*.

Do's and Don'ts

»Sound« advice!

A telephone conversation puts a safe distance between the callers, but never allow that to affect your tone – particularly if you are talking in English. In business dealings, remain correct and polite at all times, even when provoked by difficult clients. Never, ever put the phone down in anger! However difficult or confrontational the conversation, direct it to a correct close. Remember the German saying: »Der Klügere gibt nach«. Interestingly, the nearest English equivalent has a martial ring: »Discretion is the better part of valour«. So discretion please, even in the most difficult telephone situation!

 **Talk Talk Talk**

(The bar of the Duke of Gloucester pub)
S. OK, what's yours, Peter?

P. No, it's my round, Steve.

S. Well, mine's a pint of best bitter. Now, tell me how you're getting along with Jimmy?

P. Jimmy?

S. Morgan. The old man!

P. Actually, he's very kind and helpful.

S. Well, I'm sure that's because you're being very kind yourself and helping him a lot!

P. I'm certainly helping him with the **work-load**. Phoning, sorting out problems over the phone – that kind of thing.

S. Such as?

P. Well, I had to call this very difficult type in Glasgow ...

(An der Bar vom Duke of Gloucester Pub)
S. Okay, was möchten Sie trinken, Peter?

P. Nein, diese Runde geht auf mich.

S. Na schön, dann nehme ich ein Pint Best Bitter. Na, erzählen Sie mal, wie kommen Sie mit Jimmy zurecht?

P. Jimmy?

S. Morgan. Der Alte!

P. Eigentlich ist er sehr nett und hilfsbereit.

S. Tja, das liegt sicher nur daran, dass Sie selber sehr freundlich sind und ihm viel Arbeit abnehmen!

P. Ich nehme ihm wirklich etwas von seinem **Arbeitspensum** ab. Telefonieren, versuchen, Probleme über das Telefon zu lösen – so was in der Art.

S. Zum Beispiel?

P. Na ja, ich musste diesen sehr schwierigen Typen in Glasgow anrufen ...

S. Don't tell me. Name of Thomson, perhaps?!

P. Yes. Fortunately, I was able to hand the problem on to McLeod.

S. McLeod can handle him. Thomson's our most difficult customer, and he doesn't like to sign a cheque!

P. That's the message I got from Mr Morgan.

S. Well, you're learning, my boy! Another?

P. Good lord, no! I'm due back in the office in five minutes.

S. Well, you're really a management type now. Has Jimmy given you a **pager** yet?

P. A pager?

S. Joking, Peter, joking! If Jimmy wants you you'll hear your mobile ringing frantically. He hasn't invested in pagers yet, thank goodness!

P. Well, he did mention something about »pagers«.

S. Oh, no! Spare me that! I some-

S. Nichts sagen! Heißt der zufällig Thomson?!

P. Ja. Zum Glück konnte ich das Problem an McLeod weitergeben.

S. McLeod kommt schon mit ihm klar. Thomson ist unser schwierigster Kunde und er schreibt nur sehr ungern Schecks aus!

P. Genau das hat Mr Morgan auch durchblicken lassen.

S. Tja, da lernen sie ja einiges, mein Junge! Noch eine Runde?

P. Gott bewahre, nein! Ich muss in fünf Minuten zurück im Büro sein.

S. Meine Güte, Sie sind ja schon ein richtiger Manager-Typ. Hat Jimmy Ihnen schon einen **Piepser** gegeben?

P. Einen Piepser?

S. Das sollte nur ein Scherz sein, Peter! Wenn Jimmy etwas von Ihnen will, werden Sie schon hören, wie Ihr Handy hektisch klingelt. Er hat bis jetzt noch kein Geld für Piepser ausgegeben, Gott sei Dank!

P. Na ja, er erwähnte mal irgendetwas über »Piepser«.

S. Oh, nein! Ersparen Sie mir das!

times long for the old days when you just left a number where you could be reached ...

Ich sehne mich manchmal nach den alten Tagen zurück, als man nur eine Nummer hinterließ, unter der man erreichbar war ...

 34. Train Yourself

Devious devices
Wie nennt man ...

- a device for taking messages which you can play back at your leisure? ....
- a device with which you can hold a conversation with somebody else who can be thousands of miles away or just around the corner? ....
- device on which you can be reached over short distances? ....
- an office installation for taking several different phone-calls simultaneously? ....
- a portable device for making and receiving calls? ....

Background Information

Pager? A pager – or a »beeper« – is a device which is carried by a person who must be reachable at all times – a doctor in a hospital, for instance, or the manager of a hotel. It emits a beep or other sound to alert the person carrying it that he or she is required. It is a »one-way« transmission device with a panel showing the number of the person calling. It normally has a limited range – within a building or, at most, a city block.

 **Talk Talk Talk**

(James Morgan's office)
P. I'm sorry I'm late back from lunch, Mr Morgan.

J. That's all right, Peter. Ask Lucy to get some tea ready and then let's get down to work ... I'd like you to take over the Accounting 2000 program for the next few days. We're having quite a lot of problems with it, chiefly because it does seem to be quite difficult to install.

P. Well, that certainly was Thomson's problem in Glasgow, but McLeod's working on it.

J. There are two Scots together. At least they're speaking the same language – or the same accent, that is!

P. I've looked at the installation instructions, and I must confess I had problems following them. Perhaps it's because they are written by the American **manufacturers**. They seem to assume a high degree of computer literacy.

(James Morgans Büro)
P. Tut mir Leid, wenn ich meine Mittagspause etwas überzogen habe, Mr Morgan.

J. Schon in Ordnung, Peter. Bitten Sie Lucy doch, uns etwas Tee zu kochen und dann machen wir uns an die Arbeit ... Ich hätte gern, dass Sie sich in den nächsten paar Tagen um das Accounting 2000-Programm kümmern. Wir haben einige Probleme damit, besonders, weil es schwer zu installieren zu sein scheint.

P. Tja, das war definitiv Thomsons Problem in Glasgow, aber McLeod arbeitet daran.

J. Na, zwei Schotten auf einem Haufen. Wenigstens sprechen sie dieselbe Sprache – oder wenigstens denselben Dialekt!

P. Ich habe selber einmal einen Blick in die Installationsanleitung geworfen und ich muss zugeben, dass ich Probleme hatte, ihr zu folgen. Vielleicht liegt es daran, dass sie von den amerikanischen **Herstellern** geschrieben wurde. Die scheinen es dort gewohnt zu sein, ganz selbstverständlich Fachbegriffe aus dem Computerbereich zu verwenden.

J. My, Peter! And you have assumed a high degree of English literacy since you have been with us! Congratulations!

P. I must thank you and my colleagues here if that is the case. I certainly feel very much at home in the English language now.

J. So tell me – **how do we go about tackling the** Accounting 2000 **problems**?

P. I think the best way would be to **assign** one of our computer staff to install each system personally. It will stretch the department and add to costs. But, in the end, I think it will benefit ERGO, in terms of **time, expense and customer-relations**.

J. I think you're right. Can I leave that in your hands? It will mean calling all our salesmen to alert them to what we intend to do.

P. McLeod should be installing Thomson's system right now and he'll call me back. I'll phone the

J. Meine Güte, Peter! Und Sie benutzen seit Sie hier sind ganz selbstverständlich Fachbegriffe aus der englischen Sprache. Kompliment!

P. Wenn das wirklich so ist, verdanke ich das Ihnen und meinen Kollegen hier. Ich fühle mich mittlerweile in der englischen Sprache wirklich zu Hause.

J. Also sagen Sie mir – **wie nehmen wir die Probleme** mit Accounting 2000 **am besten in Angriff**?

P. Ich glaube, der beste Weg würde es wohl sein, wenn wir einen Angestellten aus unserer Computer-Abteilung dazu **abstellen** würden, jedes System persönlich zu installieren. Das wäre natürlich eine zusätzliche Belastung für die Abteilung und würde das Budget strapazieren. Aber ich glaube, letztendlich würde ERGO davon profitieren – im Sinne von **Zeitersparnis, Kosten und Kundenbeziehungen**.

J. Ich glaube, Sie haben Recht. Kann ich das Ihnen übertragen? Es würde bedeuten, dass wir alle unsere Verkäufer sofort darüber informieren müssten, was wir vorhaben.

P. McLeod sollte in diesem Moment schon dabei sein, das System von Mr Thomson zu installieren und

others right away, and I'll follow up the calls with a **memo**.

danach wird er mich zurückrufen. Ich werde die anderen sofort anrufen und anschließend noch ein **Memo** verschicken.

 35. Train Yourself

Setzen Sie die richtige Form des Verbs »to call« ein:

I ▓▓▓▓▓▓▓▓▓▓▓▓▓▓▓▓▓ him yesterday but he wasn't there.
They told me he ▓▓▓▓▓▓▓▓▓▓▓▓▓▓ although I had instructed him not to.
He said he ▓▓▓▓▓▓▓▓▓▓▓▓▓▓ tomorrow.
I would ▓▓▓▓▓▓▓▓▓▓▓▓▓▓ if I had only known.
I wonder if she ▓▓▓▓▓▓▓▓▓▓▓▓▓▓ tomorrow.
He ▓▓▓▓▓▓▓▓▓▓▓ his mother every Sunday.
Do you think I shall disturb her if I ▓▓▓▓▓▓▓▓▓▓▓▓▓▓ tomorrow?
She ▓▓▓▓▓▓▓▓▓▓▓▓▓▓ constantly to find out if he is here.
If I inquire tomorrow I wonder if she ▓▓▓▓▓▓▓▓▓▓▓▓▓▓.
She ▓▓▓▓▓▓▓▓▓▓ always ▓▓▓▓▓▓▓▓▓▓▓▓▓▓ at this time in the past.
If I ▓▓▓▓▓▓▓▓▓▓▓▓▓▓ tomorrow do you think he will be at home?
I am ▓▓▓▓▓▓▓▓▓▓▓▓▓▓ to see how you are.
If I ▓▓▓▓▓▓▓▓▓▓▓▓▓▓ at the agreed time do you think he would have answered?
If I ▓▓▓▓▓▓▓▓▓▓▓▓▓▓ now do you think he will be at home?

 **Talk Talk Talk**

(Peter's office)
P. Hello, is Mr Burnes there, please? He's out? Oh, I'm speaking to Mrs Burnes? It's Peter Brückner of ERGO here. How are you? Could you ask your husband to phone me when he gets back, please? No, wait a minute, **don't bother** –

(Peters Büro)
P. Hallo, ist Mr Burnes zu sprechen? Er ist außer Haus? Oh, spreche ich mit Mrs Burnes? Hier spricht Peter Brückner von ERGO. Wie geht es Ihnen? Könnten Sie Ihren Mann bitten, dass er mich zurückruft, wenn er wieder nach

I'll call him on his mobile. **I'm sorry to have bothered you.** Goodbye ...

Hello, Geoff Burnes? Hi, it's Peter Brückner here. I thought I'd call you first just to **put you in the picture** regarding a **policy change** here. Since you're working on a contract right now, I thought you should know what's going on. If you get around to discussing a contract with Metropolitan Newspapers would you mention that ERGO will assign a computer specialist to install the software and stay on the job just as long as it takes **to break the system in**?

G. Sure, it's a good idea, obviously. But do we have the **manpower**?

P. Mr Morgan assures me that we'll make sure we have the staff to do the job.

G. I called him a couple of days ago to report on the Metropolitan Newspapers assignment. I'm getting nowhere fast.

Hause kommt? Nein, warten Sie, **machen Sie sich keine Mühe** – ich rufe ihn einfach auf seinem Handy an. **Bitte entschuldigen Sie die Störung**. Auf Wiederhören ...

Hallo, Geoff Burnes? Hi, hier spricht Peter Brückner. Ich dachte mir, ich rufe Sie erst einmal an, um Sie über eine kleine **Änderung unserer Geschäftspraktik ins Bild zu setzen**. Da Sie gerade an einem Vertragsabschluss arbeiten, dachte ich mir, Sie sollten wissen, was vor sich geht. Falls Sie über einen Vertragsabschluss mit Metropolitan Newspapers verhandeln sollten, würden Sie dann bitte auch erwähnen, dass ERGO einen Computerspezialisten abstellen wird, der die Software installiert und so lange dabei bleibt, wie es dauert, um **das System in Betrieb zu nehmen**?

G. Sicher. Das ist eine gute Idee. Aber haben wir dazu genug **Leute**?

P. Mr Morgan hat mir versichert, dass wir dafür sorgen werden, genug Personal zu haben, um diese Aufgabe zu bewältigen.

G. Ich habe ihn vor ein paar Tagen angerufen, um ihm einen Bericht über die Verhandlungen mit Metropolitan Newspapers abzugeben. So schnell werde ich da wohl nicht weiterkommen.

P. What seems to be the trouble?

G. There's a lot of scepticism that I can't **break down**. At first, they were **all ears**. But then there was a change at the top and I can't get near the new governor.

P. Governor?

G. The boss – the Managing Editor. He just doesn't seem to talk my language.

P. You have other assignments, don't you?

G. **You bet!** I'm busy with the accounting program and at least there I can report some progress.

P. Then **back off** the Metropolitan Newspapers assignment for now. I'll have a chat with Mr Morgan about it.

G. Gladly. Call me and tell me what he says.

P. I'll do that. Expect a call from me tomorrow morning at the latest. Will you be at home?

P. Wo liegt denn das Problem?

G. Sie haben eine Menge Zweifel, die ich nicht **zerstreuen** kann. Zuerst waren Sie **ganz Ohr**. Aber dann gab es einen Wechsel in der Führungsspitze und ich komme einfach nicht an den neuen Governor heran.

P. Governor?

G. Den Boss – den Herausgeber. Er und ich – wir scheinen einfach nicht dieselbe Sprache zu sprechen.

P. Sie haben doch noch andere Aufgaben, oder?

G. Na, **darauf können Sie wetten**! Ich bin sehr aktiv, was das Buchhaltungs-Programm angeht und wenigstens da kann ich einige Erfolge melden.

P. Dann **stellen Sie** die Verhandlungen mit Metropolitan Newspapers fürs Erste **zurück**. Ich werde mich mit Mr Morgan darüber unterhalten.

G. Aber gern. Rufen Sie mich an, und erzählen Sie mir, was er darüber sagt.

P. Das mache ich. Sie können spätestens morgen früh mit einem Anruf von mir rechnen. Werden Sie da zu Hause sein?

Telefonieren

G. If I'm not try me on my mobile, or leave a message with my wife.

G. Falls nicht, versuchen Sie es einfach auf dem Handy oder hinterlassen Sie meiner Frau eine Nachricht.

 36. Train Yourself

1. Sie müssen einen Verkäufer anrufen, um ihn über eine Änderung der Verkaufstaktik zu informieren. Bringen Sie die folgenden Sätze in die richtige Reihenfolge und füllen Sie die Lücken, um den Text zu einem verständlichen Gespräch zu machen.

He has decided on a new sales practice. Mr Morgan asked me to ▒▒▒▒▒ ▒▒▒▒▒▒▒▒▒▒▒▒▒ you. Mr Morgan wants you to ▒▒▒▒▒▒▒▒▒▒▒ Metropolitan Newspapers and ▒▒▒▒▒▒▒▒▒▒▒▒ them that they can expect a complete service package. Hello, is that Geoff Burnes? That means a computer specialist will spend just as long with them as they need. Can you ▒▒▒▒▒▒▒▒▒▒▒▒▒▒ me back to tell me how you get on? Until now, we offered only to install the system. He has already ▒▒▒▒▒▒▒▒▒▒▒▒ Metropolitan Newspapers to ▒▒▒▒▒▒▒▒▒▒▒▒▒▒▒ them that you will be ▒▒▒▒▒▒▒▒▒▒▒▒. Mr Morgan is worried about increasing complaints concerning the difficulty of operating the system.

2. Sie erstatten James Morgan einen Rückbericht über Ihr Telefonat mit Geoff Burnes. Wählen Sie Ihre Worte sorgfältig – in jeder Gruppe befindet sich mindestens ein »Außenseiter«. Finden Sie die Eindringlinge und streichen Sie sie!

(Hi. how do you do?, good morning, good day) Mr Morgan!
I (rang, called, contacted, got through to, found) Geoff Burnes, and (informed him of, told him about, described, talked about, reported on) the new sales initiative you have (decided on, drawn up, dreamt up).
He finds the idea (very interesting, of considerable use, exciting, very useful). But he would (like, welcome, wish for, appreciate) more information. Will you be (calling, ringing, contacting, buzzing) him?
Or shall we put it (in words, in writing, in written form, on paper) and (fax it, send it by fax, put in the fax machine, use the fax)?
He's (waiting, standing by, sitting, holding, impatient) for a reply. Shall I (contact, call, ring, telephone) him back?

 **Talk Talk Talk**

(Peter's office. Melissa enters)
M. Good morning, Peter. How are you getting along in **the hot seat**?

P. I'm tempted to say **it's not so hot**. I've run into my first difficulty.

M. Already?

P. I called Geoff Burnes, and I've had to **take him off one job**. Mr Morgan isn't around so I can't **clear it** with him, but I feel we have to act quickly here if we want to secure that Metropolitan Newspapers contract.

M. What's Geoff doing wrong?

P. Seems to be a personality problem. He can't **establish any rapport with** the man who'll decide for Metropolitan, the new **managing editor**.

M. Geoff's a good **sales rep**, but he can be abrasive. He's got enough **on his plate** anyway, hasn't he?

(Peters Büro. Melissa tritt ein)
M. Guten Morgen, Peter. Na, wie ist es, **im Rampenlicht zu arbeiten**?

P. Ich bin fast versucht zu sagen, **es ist gar nicht so schlimm**. Ich bin auf mein erstes Problem gestoßen.

M. Schon?

P. Ich habe gerade Geoff Burnes angerufen und ihn von einem **Auftrag abgezogen**. Mr Morgan ist nicht im Büro, also kann ich die Sache nicht mit ihm **abklären**, aber ich habe das Gefühl, dass wir schnell handeln müssen, wenn wir diesen Vertrag mit Metropolitan Newspapers noch unter Dach und Fach bringen wollen.

M. Was macht Geoff denn falsch?

P. Das scheint ein Problem mit der persönlichen Chemie zu sein. Er kann keinen **Draht zu** dem Mann **finden**, der jetzt für Metropolitan die Entscheidungen trifft, dem neuen **Herausgeber**.

M. Geoff ist ein guter **Außendienstmitarbeiter**, aber er hat seine Ecken und Kanten. Jedenfalls hat er **schon genug am Hals**, oder?

Telefonieren

P. Exactly. I told him to concentrate on the accounting system contracts. But I honestly don't know what to do about Metropolitan. Steve's on a **business trip** to the West Country. And Mr Morgan's off for the next three days. Shall I call him at home?

M. **At your peril**, Peter! He's playing golf and then he hates to be disturbed. You can't reach him anyway – mobile phones are banned from the golf course.

P. Then what shall I do?

M. You're his **stand-in**, Peter. It's your decision. But, if I were you, I'd take over the Metropolitan assignment myself. Give the Managing Editor a call. He can hardly refuse to take it. In Geoff's vocabulary, **get your foot in the door**! There's the telephone! Now **do your stuff**!

P. Ganz genau. Ich habe ihm gesagt, er soll sich besser auf die Verträge mit unserem Buchhaltungssystem konzentrieren. Aber ehrlich gesagt habe ich keine Ahnung, was wir mit Metropolitan anfangen sollen. Steve ist auf **Geschäftsreise** ins West Country. Und Mr Morgan hat die nächsten drei Tage frei. Ob ich ihn zu Hause anrufen sollte?

M. **Auf eigenes Risiko**, Peter! Er spielt Golf und hasst es, dabei gestört zu werden. Sie können ihn sowieso nicht erreichen – Handys sind auf dem Golfplatz nicht zugelassen.

P. Was soll ich dann tun?

M. Sie sind seine **Vertretung**, Peter. Es ist Ihre Entscheidung. Aber an Ihrer Stelle würde ich mich selbst um den Metropolitan-Vertrag kümmern. Rufen Sie den Herausgeber an. Er kann sich kaum weigern, Ihren Anruf entgegen zu nehmen. Wie Geoff es sagen würde: **Versuchen Sie, einen Fuß in die Tür zu bekommen!** Da steht das Telefon! Also **tun Sie, was Sie tun müssen**!

37. Train Yourself

1. Peter arbeitet allein an Lucys Schreibtisch, während sie Mittagspause macht. Das Telefon klingelt, Peter nimmt ab. Können Sie ihm helfen, den Anruf zu bewältigen, indem Sie die richtigen Wörter und Ausdrücke aussuchen?

Hello, ERGO Limited! Can I help you? You'd like to *(speak to, address, talk to)* Mr Blackman? I'll see if he's *(at his desk, in, at work)*.
I'm sorry, there's no *(response, reply, call back)*. He must be *(out, away, not at work)*. Or perhaps he's in another office. Shall I try another *(number, line, contact)* or would you like to *(wait, hang on, hold)*? You could leave a *(word, statement, message)* with me, if you *(prefer, like, desire)*. Right, I'll tell him to *(respond, get back, call back)*. Could you please give me your *(address, extension, number)*?

2. Finden Sie einfache Verben mit vergleichbarer Bedeutung!

to use the telephone ....
to be connected with somebody on the telephone ....
to wait while the operator tries to reach a number ....
to end a telephone conversation ....
to respond to the ringing of a telephone ....
to activate a telephone in order to reach a number ....

 Talk Talk Talk

(Peter's Office)
P. Hello! **Is that** Metropolitan Newspapers? Could you put me through please to the Managing Editor's Secretary. The line is busy. I'll wait, then ... **The line is still engaged? Then I'll call back later. What time would you suggest?** Good, perhaps you would be good enough to tell Mr Fothergill I called. It's Peter

(Peters Büro)
P. Hallo! **Bin ich verbunden** mit Metropolitan Newspapers? Könnten Sie mich bitte mit der Sekretärin des Herausgebers verbinden? Die Leitung ist besetzt. Schön, ich warte ... **Die Leitung ist immer noch besetzt? Dann rufe ich später noch einmal an. Welche Uhrzeit würden Sie denn vorschlagen?**

Brückner of ERGO Limited. I'm calling concerning the software program we introduced to Mr Fothergill. He'll know all about it. Just inform Mr Fothergill that I shall be calling back in an hour or two. Thank you!

Gut, vielleicht sind Sie so nett und richten Mr Fothergill aus, dass ich angerufen habe. Mein Name ist Peter Brückner von ERGO Limited. Ich rufe wegen der Software an, die wir Mr Fothergill schon einmal vorgestellt haben. Er weiß schon Bescheid. Bitte richten Sie Mr Fothergill nur aus, dass ich in ein oder zwei Stunden noch einmal zurückrufe. Vielen Dank!

 38. Train Yourself

1. Die Person, die Sie zu erreichen versuchen, ist gerade nicht verfügbar. Die Sekretärin geht ans Telefon. Was tun Sie?
- leave a message?
- say you'll call later?
- hang-up?
- leave a message and say you'll call later?

2. Was hat Peter bei folgendem Telefongespräch vergessen zu erwähnen?

Hello, is Mr Fothergill there? No? I'll call back later, then. When should I call? Fine, I'll do that. Thank you.

 Do's and Don'ts

If the person you wish to speak to is otherwise engaged or out of the office and you have to leave a message it's good form to give his or her secretary or representative an idea of the purpose of your call. When you finally succeed in reaching the person you wish to contact, he or she will be prepared for your call and will probably be better informed on the subject you wish to discuss. You'll save valuable time – and give a businesslike impression!

 **Talk Talk Talk**

(Peter's office)
P. Hello, Peter Brückner here. Mr Fothergill? **That's very kind of you indeed to call back personally.** I was about to call you. I hope your secretary told you the purpose of my call. Good. **I really am very concerned** that you are having doubts about our Quick-Ed copy-editing program. We have decided to assign a computer expert from our technical staff to accompany clients closely through installation and familiarization. The details are slightly complicated to explain on the telephone, and I'll gladly fax you our memorandum ...

(Peters Büro)
P. Hallo, Peter Brückner hier. Mr Fothergill? **Es ist sehr nett von Ihnen, persönlich zurückzurufen.** Ich wollte Sie gerade selber anrufen. Ich hoffe, Ihre Sekretärin hat Ihnen gesagt, warum ich angerufen habe. Gut. **Ich bin wirklich sehr bestürzt** darüber, dass Sie Zweifel an unserer Quick-Ed Redaktions-Software haben. Wir haben uns dazu entschlossen, jedem Kunden einen Computerexperten unserer Technischen Abteilung zur Seite zu stellen, bis die Installation abgeschlossen ist und die Käufer mit dem Umgang vertraut sind. Die Details sind am Telefon etwas schwer zu erklären, aber ich faxe Ihnen gerne unser Memorandum ...

 39. Train Yourself

Sie müssen anhand kurzer Aufzeichnungen, die Sie bei einer Besprechung gemacht haben, eine Aktennotiz erstellen. Wie sieht die endgültige Fassung der Notiz aus?

Quick-Ed program. Who interested? Installation. Who responsible? Advantages, drawbacks, complaints? Decisions: install at Metropolitan Newspapers, assign Ken Allington, chief computer analyst, to supervise installation/familiarization. Length of assignment? Depends on difficulties of acquainting Metropolitan staff with system. Costs/pricing? Subject of negotiations with Metropolitan. Next meeting: Tuesday, August 24.

Talk Talk Talk

(Peter's office)
P. Hello! Peter Brückner speaking. Mr Fothergill? Did you get my fax? Good. Do you have any questions? You want to see me personally? When? Oh dear, I'll have to clear this with Mr Morgan and Mr Burnes. You don't want anything to do with Mr Burnes? Well, this is all very delicate. But I'll certainly have to speak to Mr Morgan. He's back on Monday. I can let you have a firm reply on Tuesday. Can I call you then? Good, until Tuesday, then ...

(Melissa enters)
Melissa, that was Fothergill of Metropolitan. He wants to talk to me personally about that Quick-Ed offer.

M. That will mean a trip to Nottingham – your first **venture into the field**.

P. I know, and I'm not too happy about the prospect!

(Peters Büro)
P. Hallo, hier Peter Brückner. Mr Fothergill? Haben Sie mein Fax bekommen? Gut. Haben Sie Fragen dazu? Sie würden mich gern persönlich sprechen? Wann? Meine Güte, das muss ich erst mit Mr Morgan und Mr Burnes abklären. Sie wollen mit Mr Burnes nichts zu tun haben? Tja, das ist eine heikle Situation. Aber ich werde auf jeden Fall mit Mr Morgan sprechen müssen. Er ist Montag wieder im Büro. Ich kann Ihnen am Dienstag eine verbindliche Antwort geben. Kann ich Sie dann wieder anrufen? Gut, dann bis Dienstag ...

(Melissa tritt ein)
Melissa, das war Fothergill von Metropolitan. Er möchte mit mir persönlich über unser Quick-Ed-Angebot sprechen.

M. Das bedeutet eine Geschäftsreise nach Nottingham – Ihr erster **Außendiensteinsatz**.

P. Ich weiß, und ich bin nicht begeistert über diese Aussicht!

40. Train Yourself

1. Sie müssen selbst die Vorbereitungen für eine Geschäftsreise treffen. Als Erstes müssen Sie ein Hotelzimmer buchen. Wie gehen Sie es an?
Hello, is that the Hotel Astoria? I *(want, need, would like, request)* a room for the night of August 25. Yes, a single. You only have *(doubles, double-occupancy, two-person rooms)*? What is the extra charge for single *(use, occupancy, person-use)* of a double room? That's fine. I plan to *(come, arrive, get there, turn up)* on the afternoon of August 25.
Is dinner included in the room *(charge, fee, rate)*? Then I would like to *(have, occupy, reserve, take)* a table for myself and a business colleague. Does the hotel *(possess, claim, have)* a bar? And what other *(facilities, amenities, advantages, attractions)* does the hotel have?

2. Als Nächstes müssen Sie ein Auto mieten.

Hello, is that Star Hire? I would like to *(rent, have, hire, reserve)* a car for two days, August 24 and 25. Group two, please. What is your *(price, rate, fee, charge)* for that group? Does that *(mean, include, exclude, encompass)* tax and insurance? It's the *(complete, inclusive, all-in)(charge, fee, price, rate)*? Then please *(proceed, go ahead, carry on)* and *(book, reserve, keep, retain)* a group two car for me for those two days. I'd like to *(take delivery of, pick up, collect, drive off)* the car at 11 AM. Shall I *(send a fax to, fax, use a fax to)* you with *(a statement, confirmation, details)*? Then I'll *(ring, buzz, call, come through)* if I'm delayed. Otherwise, I shall be there *(on time, promptly, in time)*.

 Talk Talk Talk

(Peter's office)
P. Steve? Oh, thank goodness I've managed to reach you. Fothergill of Metropolitan Newspapers wants to meet me personally to discuss the Quick-Ed program. He doesn't want to deal with Burnes, apparently.

(Peters Büro)
P. Steve? Oh, Gott sei Dank, endlich erreiche ich Sie. Fothergill von Metropolitan Newspapers will mich persönlich treffen, um über unser Quick-Ed-Programm zu reden. Offensichtlich will er auf keinen Fall mit Burnes verhandeln.

S. Well, I can understand that Burnes may not **be his cup of tea**. I'd go myself, but I have a lot still to do down here. How soon does Fothergill want to meet you?	S. Tja, ich kann verstehen, dass er und Burnes **nicht auf einer Wellenlänge liegen**. Ich würde ja selber gehen, aber ich habe hier einfach zu viel zu tun. Wie bald will Fothergill Sie denn sehen?
P. Right away, he told me on the phone. Should I go up to Nottingham?	P. Am besten sofort, hat er mir am Telefon gesagt. Soll ich nach Nottingham hochfahren?
S. I don't think we've got any alternative. Get Lucy to **make the arrangements**. Good luck! You'll be OK.	S. Ich glaube nicht, dass uns eine Wahl bleibt. Lassen Sie von Lucy alle **Vorbereitungen treffen**. Viel Glück! Sie schaffen das schon.
P. Well, I'll do my best, but don't expect miracles! Lucy, I have to make a business trip to Nottingham. Could you help me with the arrangements? Could you call and reserve a hotel for me, and also a hire-car?	P. Ich tue mein Bestes, aber erwarten Sie keine Wunder! Lucy, ich muss auf eine Geschäftsreise nach Nottingham. Könnten Sie mir bei den Vorbereitungen helfen? Könnten Sie herumtelefonieren und mir ein Hotelzimmer und einen Wagen mieten?
L. Certainly, Peter. You look a bit nervous – let me make you a nice cup of tea and then you leave all the arrangements to me.	L. Aber sicher, Peter. Sie sehen ein wenig nervös aus – lassen Sie mich Ihnen ein schönes Tässchen Tee kochen und überlassen Sie mir alle Vorbereitungen.
P. That's very kind of you, Lucy. I have to make a few calls myself and it would help if you could get me a hotel room and a car.	P. Das ist sehr nett von Ihnen, Lucy. Ich muss selber ein paar Anrufe erledigen und es würde mir sehr helfen, wenn Sie sich um ein Hotel und einen Wagen kümmern würden.

 **Vocabulary**

accounts	Rechnungsstelle
all ears	ganz Ohr
to assign sb.	jdn. zu etw. abstellen
at your peril	auf eigene Gefahr
au fait	vertraut
to back off	zurückstellen
to be (my, your, his, her) cup of tea	auf einer Wellenlänge liegen; gut miteinander auskommen
bean-counters	Erbsenzähler (abfällig)
to break a system in	ein System in Betrieb nehmen
to break down	hier: zerstreuen, aus der Welt schaffen
to break in	einarbeiten
to clear sth.	etw. abklären
customer-relations	Kundenbeziehungen
Do your stuff!	hier: tun Sie, was Sie tun müssen/ für was Sie bezahlt werden!
expense	Kosten
to get down to business	zum Geschäft kommen
(the) hot seat	etwa: brenzlige Position (im Geschäftsbereich)
in a jiffy	im Handumdrehen
into the field	in der Praxis (hier besonders: im tatsächlichen Außendienst)
to make arrangements	Vorbereitungen treffen
managing editor	Herausgeber
manpower	Arbeitskraft/-kräfte; Mitarbeiter
manufacturers	Hersteller
memo	Memo
not so hot	nicht so toll (umgangssprachlich)
on his plate	auf sein Konto (gehen)
on the hop	in Nullkommanichts
pager/beeper	Piepser
paperwork	Papierkram
payment agreement	Zahlungsbedingungen

pecking order	Rangordnung
projection	Prognose
to put in the picture	ins Bild setzen, auf den neuesten Stand bringen
round-up	Zusammenstellung (eigentlich: Zusammentreiben von Vieh)
sales representative	Außendienstmitarbeiter
to settle for	sich zufrieden geben mit
stand-in	Vertretung
to take a message	eine Nachricht entgegennehmen
to take sb. off a job	jdn. von etw. abziehen
to talk through	einweisen; erklären
to tally	zusammen-, abrechnen; übereinstimmen
You bet!	Darauf können Sie/ kannst du wetten!

On a business trip
Auf Geschäftsreise

 **Here we go**

Peter macht sich auf seine erste Geschäftsreise. Er wird auf eigene Faust ein Verkaufsprojekt in Nottingham übernehmen. Trotz mangelnder Erfahrung gelingt es Peter mit großem persönlichen Einsatz zu einem erfolgreichen Abschluss zu kommen. Mr Morgan, Steve und vor allem Melissa sind stolz auf ihn und gratulieren. Und zu guter Letzt gibt Melissa noch ihr bestgehütetes Geheimnis preis ...

 Talk Talk Talk

(Peter's Office. Melissa enters)

M. Well, Peter, you're off on your Nottingham trip today. How do you feel?

P. Nervous! Everything is **arranged**, though. I've called to **confirm** my meeting with Fothergill, and I've called to confirm my hotel room. The car is waiting to be picked up.

M. When do you expect to be back?

P. The day after tomorrow. But I'll call to tell you when to expect me.

M. Well, I wish you all the luck in the world!

(Peters Büro. Melissa tritt ein)

M. Nun, Peter, heute steht Ihre Reise nach Nottingham an. Wie fühlen Sie sich?

P. Nervös! Obwohl alles **durchgeplant** ist. Ich habe noch einmal angerufen, um meinen Termin mit Fothergill **bestätigen** zu lassen. Dasselbe gilt für meine Zimmerreservierung. Das Auto steht abholbereit.

M. Was glauben Sie, wann Sie wieder zurück sind?

P. Übermorgen. Aber ich rufe an und sage Bescheid, wann Sie wieder mit mir rechnen können.

M. Tja, dann wünsche ich Ihnen alles erdenklich Gute!

P. Thanks, Melissa. That's kind of you. I'll probably need it.	P. Danke, Melissa. Sehr nett von Ihnen. Ich werde es wahrscheinlich brauchen.
M. Nonsense, you'll be all right. You know ERGO inside-out now. You'll be able to **manage** Fothergill.	M. Blödsinn, Sie schaffen das schon. Sie kennen ERGO jetzt in- und auswendig. Sie werden mit Fothergill schon **zurechtkommen**.
P. It's not really Fothergill I'm so worried about. It's the Quick-Ed system – I haven't had a lot of time to **acquaint myself** with it.	P. Es ist nicht einmal Fothergill, um den ich mir Sorgen mache – eher das Quick-Ed-System – ich hatte leider nicht viel Zeit, um mich damit **vertraut zu machen**.
M. But you'll have Duncan Wood from technical support to help you, I hear.	M. Aber Sie haben doch Duncan Wood von der Technischen Unterstützung dabei, damit er Ihnen helfen kann, habe ich gehört.
P. Yes, he's coming along tomorrow, after my first meeting with Fothergill. I've been trying to reach him on the phone, just to confirm the arrangements. You could really do me a favour if you tried to get him for me and ask him to call me at the hotel.	P. Ja, er kommt morgen dazu, nach meinem ersten Treffen mit Fothergill. Ich habe schon versucht, ihn telefonisch zu erreichen, um unsere Abmachungen zu bestätigen. Sie könnten mir wirklich einen großen Gefallen tun, wenn Sie versuchen würden, ihn zu erreichen und ihn zu bitten, mich im Hotel anzurufen.
M. Certainly, Peter. Anything else I can do?	M. Sicher, Peter. Kann ich sonst noch etwas tun?
P. Just **cross your fingers** for me!	P. **Drücken Sie mir die Daumen!**

41. Train Yourself

Peter ruft im Hotel an, um zu sagen, dass er spät ankommen wird. Wie verläuft das Gespräch?

Hello, is that the Hotel Astoria? Could you ▮▮▮▮ me please with the reception desk. Reception desk? I'm ▮▮▮▮ to say I shall be late arriving this evening. I asked my office to ▮▮▮▮ a message with you, but they said they had difficulty ▮▮▮▮ to you. Your telephone has been ▮▮▮▮ order all day? No wonder my office couldn't ▮▮▮▮ you. They thought the line was constantly ▮▮▮▮. Is the ▮▮▮▮ all right now? Does my room have an ▮▮▮▮? I shall need to use the ▮▮▮▮ a lot while I am staying at the hotel. Does my room have a direct ▮▮▮▮? Can a caller from outside ▮▮▮▮ straight through, without going ▮▮▮▮ the switchboard? I need to reserve a table in your restaurant, so could you please ▮▮▮▮ to the restaurant manager? Hello, is that the restaurant? I'm ▮▮▮▮ to the beer cellar? But I asked to be ▮▮▮▮ to the restaurant. Can you ▮▮▮▮ me, please? The line is ▮▮▮▮? Then I'll ▮▮▮▮. But please ▮▮▮▮ to the restaurant as soon as you can. I'm already running very late.

Background Information

Hotel practice. Hotels in Britain – and particularly in the United States – often demand a credit card number when a room is booked. Always state the approximate time you expect to arrive and call to inform the reception desk if you are delayed. Rooms not claimed after 6 PM can legally be relet by the hotel unless prior arrangements have been made. Rooms booked but not claimed can be charged at the full rate – deducted from the credit-card account of the »no-show«.

 **Talk Talk Talk**

(Car-hire company office)
P. Good morning! My office **has booked** a group two car for me for two days.

Clerk: May I have your name, sir?

P. Brückner. Peter Brückner, of ERGO Limited. My secretary called to make the booking.

Clerk: Here we are! May I see your **driving licence**, sir, and some form of other identification?

P. Here is my driving licence and my passport.

Clerk: Ah, you're German, sir! But your documents are European – they're fine. No problem. Just let me enter the details in the computer. There we are. The car is outside waiting for you, sir. Have a good journey ...

P. Oh, would you do me a favour and call my office to tell them I have picked the car up. I'm in such a hurry I really don't have the time.

(Im Büro der Autovermietung)
P. Guten Morgen! Mein Büro hat einen Wagen der Kategorie Zwei für zwei Tage für mich **gebucht**.

Schalterangestellter: Sagen Sie mir bitte noch Ihren Namen, Sir?

P. Brückner. Peter Brückner von ERGO Limited. Meine Sekretärin hat den Wagen gebucht.

Schalterangestellter: Da haben wir es ja! Dürfte ich bitte noch Ihren **Führerschein** und ein anderes Dokument sehen, das Ihre Identität bestätigt, Sir?

P. Hier sind mein Führerschein und mein Ausweis.

Schalterangestellter: Ah, Sie kommen aus Deutschland, Sir! Aber Ihre Dokumente sind in Europa ausgestellt – damit gibt es keine Probleme. Lassen Sie mich nur rasch die Details in den Computer tippen. Das war es schon. Der Wagen wartet draußen schon auf Sie, Sir. Gute Reise ...

P. Oh, könnten Sie mir wohl einen Gefallen tun und in meinem Büro anrufen und Bescheid geben, dass ich den Wagen abgeholt habe? Ich

Here's the number. Ask for Miss Lucy Scott. She is the secretary who called you to make the reservation.

bin so in Eile, dass ich wirklich keine Zeit mehr habe. Hier ist die Nummer. Fragen Sie einfach nach Miss Lucy Scott. Sie ist die Sekretärin, die bei Ihnen angerufen und die Buchung gemacht hat.

Clerk: Certainly, sir. Glad to. All part of the service!

Schalterangestellter: Natürlich, Sir. Sehr gern. Das gehört alles zum Service!

 42. Train Yourself

Multiple choice – Welches Wort passt in die Lücken?

Could I please ▮▮▮▮▮▮ a message for Mr Morgan?
1. *make*
2. *give*
3. *leave*
4. *send*

Can I tell him who's ▮▮▮▮▮▮?
1. *speaking*
2. *calling*
3. *talking*
4. *there*

Would you ▮▮▮▮▮▮ Miss Walker that I'll call back.
1. *mention*
2. *message*
3. *tell*
4. *instruct*

I'll ▮▮▮▮▮▮ the message to her.
1. *pass*
2. *give*
3. *send*
4. *hand*

You can reach me ▓▓▓▓▓▓▓▓▓▓▓▓▓▓▓ the number I gave you.
1. *with*
2. *during*
3. *at*
4. *using*

 Talk Talk Talk

(In the ERGO office. James Morgan enters)
L. Good heavens, Mr Morgan. We weren't expecting you back until next week!

J. The weather turned very nasty, Lucy, so I packed up and came home. I hate playing golf in the rain. Is everything all right? Are Melissa and Peter in?

L. Miss Walker is, but Mr Brückner is on his way to Nottingham.

J. Nottingham?

M. (enters) My, Mr Morgan! We didn't expect you until next week!

J. Good morning, Melissa. I would have called, but I didn't have my mobile with me. I never carry it on golfing trips, as you know. What's this about Peter on his way to Nottingham?

(Im Büro von ERGO. James Morgan tritt ein)
L. Meine Güte, Mr Morgan. Wir hatten Sie vor nächster Woche gar nicht zurück erwartet!

J. Das Wetter wurde so schlecht, dass ich einfach meine Sachen gepackt habe und nach Hause gefahren bin, Lucy. Ich hasse es, Golf im Regen zu spielen. Ist hier alles in Ordnung? Sind Melissa und Peter da?

L. Miss Walker schon, aber Mr Brückner ist auf dem Weg nach Nottingham.

J. Nottingham?

M. (tritt ein) Na so was, Mr Morgan! Wir hatten Sie vor nächster Woche gar nicht zurück erwartet!

J. Guten Morgen, Melissa. Ich hätte ja angerufen, aber ich hatte mein Handy nicht dabei. Ich nehme es nie auf meine Golf-Trips mit, wie Sie ja wissen. Was hat es damit auf sich, dass Peter auf dem Weg nach Nottingham ist?

M. He had to take a very **important decision** in a hurry, and he didn't want to break into your golf holiday. He wouldn't have been able **to get hold of** you, anyway.

M. Er musste in großer Eile eine **wichtige Entscheidung** treffen und er wollte Sie nicht während Ihres Golfurlaubs stören. Er hätte Sie ja sowieso **nicht erreicht**.

J. Well, that's true enough. Now come into my office and tell me what all this is about ...

J. Tja, das stimmt allerdings. Kommen Sie doch mit in mein Büro und erklären Sie mir, was überhaupt los ist ...

 43. Train Yourself

1. Ersetzen Sie die fehlenden Wörter anhand der Liste, die Sie unter der Übung finden.

I tried to ▓▓▓▓▓ you yesterday, but your phone seemed to be ▓▓▓▓▓. I'm calling today to ▓▓▓▓▓ that we shall be able to come to dinner, after all. James managed to ▓▓▓▓▓ his parents and ▓▓▓▓▓ them that we have to ▓▓▓▓▓ our visit until next week. We had terrible trouble ▓▓▓▓▓. When my mother is ▓▓▓▓▓ the phone she ▓▓▓▓▓ for hours. The line was constantly ▓▓▓▓▓. No sooner had we ▓▓▓▓▓ her and had a short ▓▓▓▓▓ with her than she was ▓▓▓▓▓ the phone again to a neighbour. I keep telling her she should ▓▓▓▓▓ less time on the phone, but she then says that's her main ▓▓▓▓▓ with the outside world.

getting through, reach, connection, spend, chat, engaged, out of order, on, got through to, talks, tell, postpone, say.

2. Setzen Sie das folgende Gespräch in die indirekte Rede!

I'm calling to confirm that we shall be coming tomorrow. I have to find out the most convenient rail con-

She said

nection. I think it will be easier and quicker to come by train than try the bus service. I called the bus station yesterday and discovered that we would have to change twice to get to you. I had always thought the bus service was much more efficient than that, but I was obviously wrong. What time do you expect us? Shall we bring anything? My aunt has given us some really good home-made wine, and we could bring a bottle or two. Ask Tom and then give me a call back. I really look forward to the evening. Who else will be there? I hope you have not invited the Smiths. I can't stand Nancy Smith. If they are coming then please put me at the other end of the table! And please seat me away from my dreadful husband – all he can talk about these days is the Stock Exchange …

 Talk Talk Talk

(James Morgan's office)
J. Lucy! Do you have the number of Peter's hotel?

L. Yes, shall I call it for you?

J. Yes please!

L. I **have** the Hotel Astoria **on the line**.

J. Is that the reception? Good. Could you put me through please

(James Morgans Büro)
J. Lucy! Haben Sie die Nummer von Peters Hotel?

L. Ja, soll ich für Sie dort anrufen?

J. Ja, bitte!

L. Ich **habe** das Hotel Astoria **in der Leitung**.

J. Ist dort die Rezeption? Gut. Bitte verbinden Sie mich mit dem

to Mr Brückner's room? He hasn't arrived yet? Then could I leave a message for him, please? He should phone me at the office or at home. James Morgan is the name. **Please make sure he gets the message.** It is very important. Thank you!

(Melissa enters)
M. I **couldn't help** overhearing your call. I hope Peter did the right thing.

J. Of course! He showed great initiative. I just want to call him to help him prepare for tomorrow's meeting with Fothergill.

M. He did seem very nervous.

J. And that's just what he should not be at a meeting like this. If I can do it on the phone, I'd like to try and **boost his confidence**.

M. Well, you're certainly the person to do that, James.

J. Frankly, I think you're better equipped. He seems to have **taken a real shine to** you, Melissa!

M. Oh, God – there's my phone. **Saved by the bell!**

Zimmer von Peter Brückner. Er ist noch nicht angekommen? Könnte ich dann bitte eine Nachricht für ihn hinterlassen? Er soll mich im Büro oder zu Hause anrufen. Mein Name ist James Morgan. **Bitte sorgen Sie dafür, dass er diese Nachricht bekommt.** Es ist wirklich sehr wichtig. Vielen Dank!

(Melissa tritt ein)
M. **Ich kam nicht darum herum**, Ihr Gespräch mitzuhören. Ich hoffe, Peter hat das Richtige getan.

J. Natürlich! Er hat eine großartige Initiative an den Tag gelegt. Ich wollte nur mit ihm telefonieren, um ihm dabei zu helfen, sich auf das morgige Treffen mit Fothergill vorzubereiten.

M. Er schien ziemlich nervös zu sein.

J. Und genau das sollte er bei so einem Meeting nicht sein. Wenn es über das Telefon überhaupt möglich ist, würde ich **sein Selbstvertrauen** gern etwas **aufbauen**.

M. Tja, wenn das jemand kann, dann sicherlich Sie, James.

J. Ehrlich gesagt glaube ich, dass Sie dafür besser geeignet sind. Er scheint **einen Narren an Ihnen gefressen zu haben**, Melissa!

M. Oh, Gott – mein Telefon klingelt. **Rettung in letzter Sekunde!**

Telefonieren

44. Train Yourself

Setzen Sie in den folgenden Sätzen die richtige Präposition ein!

She has been _____ the phone for a very long time. When she's finally _____ the phone, could you please put me _____.
Would you like to hang _____? As soon as she has hung _____ I'll try and get her _____ the line.
He's finally _____ the phone in his new house. Now he's rarely _____ the phone, his line is constantly engaged.
Would you like to hold _____? Mr Morgan is still _____ the phone. When he hangs _____ I'll tell him you are waiting _____ the other line.
_____ the start of our phone conversation I didn't realize who you were. Can you really feed all that information _____ the line. Wouldn't it be easier to put it _____ a fax? _____ the end of our chat on the phone I felt I knew him much better.

in, on, off, up, at, through, down.

 **Talk Talk Talk**

(Peter's hotel)
P. Hello, Mr Morgan? You asked me to call. I would have called you anyway, but I've just arrived at the hotel.

J. That's all right, Peter. I just wanted to talk to you about tomorrow's meeting with Fothergill.

(Peters Hotel)
P. Hallo, Mr Morgan? Sie haben mich gebeten, Sie zurückzurufen. Ich hätte auf jeden Fall noch angerufen, aber ich bin gerade erst im Hotel angekommen.

J. Schon in Ordnung, Peter. Ich wollte nur mit Ihnen über das morgige Treffen mit Fothergill reden.

P. I hope you didn't mind my going ahead and travelling up here. It did appear to be an urgent matter.

P. Ich hoffe, Sie haben nichts dagegen, dass ich auf eigene Faust hier hochgefahren bin. Es schien mir eine sehr dringende Angelegenheit gewesen zu sein.

J. You're right. You did the right thing. I just want to make sure you are **adequately briefed**.

J. Sie haben völlig Recht. Sie haben genau das Richtige getan. Ich wollte nur sicher gehen, dass Sie **angemessen vorbereitet** sind.

P. I have all the information with me, and I shall spend this evening **swatting up** on it.

P. Ich habe alle nötigen Informationen mitgenommen und ich werde den Abend damit verbringen, sie zu **büffeln**.

J. If you have any questions at all, call me at any time – either on my home number or on my mobile.

J. Wenn Sie noch irgendwelche Fragen haben, rufen Sie mich jederzeit an – entweder zu Hause oder über mein Handy.

Telefonieren

 45. Train Yourself

Welche Wörter passen in die Lücken?

I'm calling to ▒▒▒▒▒▒▒▒▒▒ a room for the night of August 24. Do you have a ▒▒▒▒▒▒▒▒▒▒?
Yes, we have one single and one double still ▒▒▒▒▒▒▒▒▒▒.
Could I ▒▒▒▒▒▒▒▒▒▒ the single room?
Certainly, in whose name should I ▒▒▒▒▒▒▒▒▒▒ the room?
Brückner. Peter Brückner.
When do you expect to ▒▒▒▒▒▒▒▒▒▒?
I'm leaving London within the next hour and expect to ▒▒▒▒▒▒▒▒▒▒ at the hotel by six o'clock.
We shall reserve the room for you until seven, just to be ▒▒▒▒▒▒▒▒▒▒.

129

If you are ▓▓▓▓▓▓▓▓▓▓▓▓ please ▓▓▓▓▓▓▓▓▓▓▓▓ and inform us.

Certainly. Could I also ▓▓▓▓▓▓▓▓▓▓▓▓▓▓▓▓▓▓ a table in the restaurant for two people?

What time would you like the table ▓▓▓▓▓▓▓▓▓▓▓▓▓▓▓▓?

Eight o'clock. My business partner might ▓▓▓▓▓▓▓▓▓▓▓▓ a little later than that. If he calls could you ▓▓▓▓▓▓▓▓▓▓ him a message?

Certainly. What shall we ▓▓▓▓▓▓▓▓▓▓▓▓▓▓▓▓ him?

That I have ▓▓▓▓▓▓▓▓▓▓▓▓▓▓ a table in the restaurant for eight o'clock.

reserve, sure, give, book, reserved, vacancy, arrive, call, give, tell, delayed, available.

 Talk Talk Talk

(Peter's hotel)
P. Hello, Mr Morgan? I'm sorry to disturb you, but I have one or two questions concerning tomorrow's meeting.

J. Go ahead?

P. I've established that the Metropolitan Newspapers's main newsroom has more than twenty terminals. Will the system support so many?

J. No problem.

P. I presume the quoted price is for one system, but Metropolitan is a fairly large group, as you know. Do we offer **discounted prices for larger orders**?

(Peters Hotel)
P. Hallo, Mr Morgan? Es tut mir Leid, Sie zu stören, aber ich habe ein oder zwei Fragen bezüglich des Meetings morgen.

J. Schießen Sie los!

P. Ich habe in Erfahrung gebracht, dass in der Hauptredaktion von Metropolitan Newspapers mehr als zwanzig Terminals im Einsatz sind. Unterstützt unser System so viele Computer?

J. Kein Problem.

P. Ich vermute, dass sich der angegebene Preis auf ein System bezieht, aber Metropolitan ist eine ziemlich große Gruppe, wie Sie ja wissen. Gewähren wir **für größere Abnahmen Mengenrabatt**?

J. Peter, I shall be **overjoyed** if we just get one system installed first of all. Concentrate on that initial order. Fothergill will just be **sounding you out** at first. If he likes the system the hard business negotiations will follow. **Stick now to** the quoted price.

J. Peter, ich werde **heilfroh** sein, wenn Sie es schaffen, zunächst einmal ein System installieren zu lassen. Konzentrieren Sie sich auf diese erste Bestellung. Fothergill will Sie zunächst **aushorchen**. Wenn ihm das System gefällt, werden noch harte Preisverhandlungen folgen. Halten **Sie zunächst mal** am alten Preis **fest**.

P. He asked me to call tonight to confirm the time of tomorrow's meeting. If he has any questions I can't answer may I call you back?

P. Er hat mich darum gebeten, heute Abend noch einmal durchzurufen, um den Termin des morgigen Meetings zu bestätigen. Kann ich Sie zurückrufen, falls er noch irgendwelche Fragen hat, die ich nicht beantworten kann?

J. I'm right by the phone – call at any time. But relax – and enjoy your evening.

J. Ich werde in der Nähe des Telefons bleiben – rufen Sie jederzeit an. Aber entspannen Sie sich – und genießen Sie Ihren Abend.

P. Thank you Mr Morgan. After supper, I'll be watching television there's a Mafia film on that I wanted to see.

P. Vielen Dank, Mr Morgan. Nach dem Abendessen werde ich noch etwas fernsehen – da läuft ein Mafia-Film, den ich gerne sehen würde.

J. Well, I hope that's the right choice under the circumstances!

J. Tja, ich hoffe, unter den gegeben Umständen ist das eine gute Wahl!

 46. Train Yourself

Füllen Sie die Lücken und setzen Sie die Verben ins Präsens:

I ▦▦▦▦▦▦▦▦▦▦ yesterday and asked if the hotel had a double room free for the night of April 4. I ▦▦▦▦▦▦▦▦▦▦ if the room had a telephone and a television set. I then said I would like to ▓▓▓▓▓▓▓▓▓▓ the room. I said I would be ▓▓▓▓▓▓▓▓▓▓ between 5 PM and 6 PM, and that if I were ▓▓▓▓▓▓▓▓▓▓ I would ▓▓▓▓▓▓▓▓▓▓ to advise the hotel of my late arrival. I asked if the room ▓▓▓▓▓▓▓▓▓▓ included breakfast and whether full English breakfast or continental was ▓▓▓▓▓▓▓▓▓▓. I told the reception clerk I liked to start the day on a full English breakfast because I often missed out on lunch.

rate, called, arriving, served, delayed, asked, reserve, call.

 **Talk Talk Talk**

(Astoria Hotel. Peter's room)
P. Hello! Yes, Peter Brückner speaking. Mr Meadows has arrived? Good, would you please tell him I'll be right down. Ask him to wait for me in the bar.

(Astoria Hotel. Peters Zimmer)
P. Hallo! Ja, hier spricht Peter Brückner. Ist Mr Meadows schon angekommen? Gut, würden Sie ihm bitte ausrichten, dass ich sofort herunterkomme? Bitten Sie ihn, an der Bar auf mich zu warten.

(Astoria Hotel bar)
P. Hello, Mr Meadows? I'm Peter Brückner, of ERGO. I'm very pleased to meet you.

(Hotelbar des Astoria)
P. Mr Meadows? Ich bin Peter Brückner von ERGO. Ich freue mich, Sie kennen zu lernen.

M. How do you do, Mr Brückner?

M. Wie geht es Ihnen, Mr Brückner?

P. What are you drinking? Will you join me in a sherry before we go in to eat?

P. Was möchten Sie gerne trinken? Trinken Sie mit mir einen Sherry, bevor wir etwas essen?

M. Gladly.

M. Aber gern.

P. I hope you didn't mind my calling you **out of the blue**, like that.

P. Ich hoffe, Sie hatten nichts dagegen, dass ich Sie einfach so **ohne**

I had very little notice of my trip to Nottingham.	**Vorwarnung** angerufen habe. Ich bin sehr kurzfristig zu meiner Reise nach Nottingham aufgebrochen.
M. Not at all. I'm very glad to help where I can.	M. Ganz und gar nicht. Ich freue mich, helfen zu können, wo ich nur kann.
P. Before joining Metropolitan Newspapers you were at the Middlesex Echo, am I right?	P. Bevor Sie zu Metropolitan Newspapers gegangen sind, waren Sie beim Middlesex Echo, stimmt's?
M. Yes. I was Executive News Editor there. Now, as you know, I'm Group Editor at Metropolitan.	M. Ja, ich war dort Nachrichtenredakteur. Jetzt bin ich, wie Sie sicher wissen, Leitender Redakteur bei Metropolitan.
P. During your time at the Middlesex Echo you **became acquainted** with our Quick-Ed editing system.	P. Während Ihrer Zeit beim Middlesex Echo konnten Sie sich doch schon mit unserem Quick-Ed-Redaktionssystem **vertraut machen**.
M. Indeed. **I was very impressed by** it.	M. In der Tat. Und **ich war sehr beeindruckt** davon.
P. I shall be meeting Mr Fothergill tomorrow. Does he know about your enthusiasm for Quick-Ed?	P. Ich werde morgen Mr Fothergill treffen. Weiß er, wie begeistert Sie von Quick-Ed sind?
M. I haven't really had the chance to talk to him about it yet.	M. Ich hatte bis jetzt noch nicht die Möglichkeit, mit ihm darüber zu reden.
P. Will you be at tomorrow's meeting?	P. Werden Sie beim Meeting morgen dabei sein?
M. No, I have to visit one of our publications in Newcastle.	M. Nein, ich muss eine unserer Publikationen in Newcastle besuchen.

Telefonieren

P. That's bad news. But you could really do me a big favour if you **get to** speak to Mr Fothergill on your return.	P. Das sind ja schlechte Neuigkeiten. Aber Sie könnten mir wirklich einen großen Gefallen tun, wenn sie **dazu kämen**, nach Ihrer Rückkehr mit Mr Fothergill zu reden.
M. And that is?	M. Und worüber?
P. Just tell him what you told me – that you are impressed by Quick-Ed.	P. Sagen Sie ihm einfach, was Sie mir gesagt haben – dass Sie von Quick-Ed sehr beeindruckt sind.
M. Certainly, there's no problem there.	M. Natürlich, da sehe ich kein Problem.
P. Then come, let's go and eat.	P. Dann kommen Sie, lassen Sie uns etwas essen.

47. Train Yourself

»Get« ist ein überbeanspruchtes Verb der englischen Sprache. Finden Sie dafür elegantere Ersatzformen in den folgenden Sätzen!

1. I think I can *get* him to sign.
2. I *got on* well in the examinations.
3. I *got* the flu while visiting London.
4. If you *get* more than sixty pounds for that antique I shall be surprised.
5. I don't think he'll ever *get over* her death.
6. He didn't *get* the joke. He has no sense of humour!
7. I don't know how he can *get by* in his work without the internet.
8. I've got to *get* that train.
9. He doesn't *get* much in that new job.
10. I tried several times to *get* you on the phone.

performed, obtain, becomes, catch, earn, reach, persuade, understand, cope, recover from, caught.

 **Talk Talk Talk**

(Metropolitan Newspapers head office)
P. Good morning! **I have an appointment to see** Mr Fothergill.

Receptionist: **What name shall I give**?

P. Brückner. Peter Brückner, of ERGO Limited.

R. Just one moment, please. I'll try to reach Mr Fothergill. Hello, Miss Sykes. I have a Mr Brückner here to see Mr Fothergill. You'll **be right down**. I'll tell him, then. Mr Fothergill's secretary is on her way down. She'll take you to Mr Fothergill's office.

P. Thank you very much.

S. Good morning! I'm Mr Fothergill's secretary. If you come with me I'll take you now to his office.

P. Thank you very much. I'm sorry I'm slightly late. I had difficulty calling a taxi from my hotel.

S. That's quite all right. Mr Fothergill was late, anyway, getting to the

(Hauptbüro von Metropolitan Newspapers)
P. Guten Morgen! **Ich habe einen Termin mit** Mr Fothergill.

Empfangsdame: **Wen darf ich melden?**

P. Brückner. Peter Brückner von ERGO Limited.

R. Einen Moment, bitte. Ich versuche, Mr Fothergill zu erreichen. Hallo, Miss Sykes. Ich habe hier einen Mr Brückner für Mr Fothergill. Sie **kommen gleich herunter**. Ich werde es ihm sagen. Mr Fothergills Sekretärin ist auf dem Weg nach unten. Sie wird Sie in Mr Fothergills Büro bringen.

P. Haben Sie vielen Dank.

S. Guten Morgen! Ich bin Mr Fothergills Sekretärin. Wenn Sie mich bitte begleiten würden, ich führe Sie in sein Büro.

P. Vielen Dank. Tut mir Leid, wenn ich ein wenig zu spät bin. Ich hatte Probleme, von meinem Hotel aus ein Taxi zu bekommen.

S. Das ist schon in Ordnung. Mr Fothergill ist heute ohnehin etwas

Telefonieren

office this morning. Apparently, he had a lot to do on the way.

später ins Büro gekommen. Offensichtlich hatte er auf dem Weg hierher sehr viel zu tun.

 48. Train Yourself

Ein anderes häufig gebrauchtes Verb des Englischen ist »to do«. Finden Sie auch hierfür elegantere Ersatzformen in den folgenden Sätzen.

1. *That will do*, Johnny! Now behave yourself!
2. I don't know if I can *do* it in the required time.
3. If you *do* the task correctly you'll get top marks!
4. That was quite a climb – I'm completely *done in*!
5. I think *I did* well in the exam.
6. The train *did* the distance in record time.
7. This is a very difficult puzzle. I just can't *do* it.
8. If you *undo* this catch, the door springs open.
9. *Do up* the buttons of your coat, it's very cold outside.
10. *Do it again*, please!

solve, covered, repeat, performed, release, that's enough, exhausted, fasten, complete (2x).

 **Talk Talk Talk**

(Mr Fothergill's office)
F. Come in, come in! How do you do, Mr Brückner. I'm very pleased to meet you!

(Mr Fothergills Büro)
F. Hereinspaziert! Wie geht es Ihnen, Mr Brückner. Ich freue mich, Sie kennen zu lernen!

Telefonieren

P. How do you do, Mr Fothergill? Thank you for this opportunity to meet you.	P. Wie geht es Ihnen, Mr Fothergill? Danke, dass Sie mir die Möglichkeit geben, mich mit Ihnen zu treffen.
F. A **face-to-face** meeting is much more satisfactory than a phone-call – that's my philosophy. Your people were always calling me up and trying to explain what you have to offer in a few minutes on the phone. You're the first to offer to travel up here to describe the system to me in person.	F. Ein **persönliches** Gespräch ist doch viel angenehmer als diese Telefoniererei – das ist meine Philosophie. Ihre Leute rufen mich andauernd an und versuchen, mir in ein paar Minuten am Telefon zu erklären, was sie mir anzubieten haben. Sie sind der Erste, der mir angeboten hat, hier hoch zu fahren und mir das System persönlich vorzustellen.
P. It's a pleasure, Mr Fothergill. We believe the system is so good that no effort can be spared in making its benefits known.	P. Ist mir ein Vergnügen, Mr Fothergill. Wir sind davon überzeugt, dass unser System so gut ist, dass keine Mühe ausgelassen werden sollte, um seine Vorzüge bekannt zu machen.
F. Well, young man, you've got two hours to do that. Miss Sykes! Can you bring in some coffee, please! And now **down to business** ...	F. Tja, junger Mann, dafür haben Sie jetzt zwei Stunden Zeit. Miss Sykes! Können Sie uns bitte einen Kaffee bringen! Und jetzt **kommen wir zur Sache** ...

 49. Train Yourself

Peter beginnt mit seiner Präsentation. Helfen Sie ihm bei der Wahl der richtigen Worte!

Let me begin by ▓▓▓▓▓ how the system ▓▓▓▓▓. There are just six discs to ▓▓▓▓▓. They ▓▓▓▓▓ the entire software. You can ▓▓▓▓▓ them in any drive. The discs ▓▓▓▓▓ individual files, ranging from rules to styles.

137

Let's ▓▓▓▓ with the first one. We'll ▓▓▓▓ it and then ▓▓▓▓ with it. You'll then ▓▓▓▓ how ▓▓▓▓ the system is.

explaining, understand, install, functions, start, contain, load, play, straightforward.

 **Talk Talk Talk**

(Hotel Astoria. Peter's room)
P. Good morning! Peter Brückner.

R. This is the reception. I have a call for you. **I'm putting the caller through now ...**

P. Hello! Brückner here!

J. Good morning, Peter. It's James Morgan here. I just called to find out how you got on yesterday.

P. Well, **the presentation went very well**, I think. In fact, Fothergill had allowed just two hours for the presentation and demonstration, but it actually went on all day and I had to extend my stay here by another night. I called Lucy and asked her to inform you. I hope she did.

J. Yes, indeed. That's fine. So what's your **general impression**?

(Hotel Astoria. Peters Zimmer)
P. Guten Morgen! Peter Brückner.

R. Hier ist die Rezeption. Wir haben ein Gespräch für Sie. **Ich stelle den Anrufer gleich durch ...**

P. Hallo! Brückner!

J. Guten Morgen, Peter! Hier spricht James Morgan. Ich rufe nur an, um zu fragen, wie es gestern gelaufen ist.

P. Nun ja, **die Präsentation lief sehr gut**. Tatsache ist, Fothergill wollte mir zunächst nur zwei Stunden für die Präsentation und die Vorführung geben, aber dann dauerte es den ganzen Tag. Ich musste meinen Aufenthalt hier um eine weitere Nacht verlängern. Ich habe Lucy angerufen und sie gebeten, Sie zu informieren. Ich hoffe, das hat sie getan.

J. Ja, das hat sie. Sehr schön. Und, wie ist Ihr **Gesamteindruck**?

P. I think they're interested, but I feel Fothergill will need some time to think it over.

P. Ich glaube, sie sind interessiert, aber Fothergill wird vermutlich noch etwas Zeit brauchen, um darüber nachzudenken.

J. Yes, he gives me the impression of being a very careful type who doesn't like to give up too easily in a **business negotiation**. Now, you have had a very tiring time – stay over another night and have a look around Nottingham. It's an interesting city, and don't miss out on a trip to Sherwood Forest. I'll expect you in the office the day after tomorrow ...

J. Ja, er macht wirklich den Eindruck, als wäre er ein sehr vorsichtiger Mensch, der in einer **geschäftlichen Verhandlung** nur ungern zu früh nachgibt. Aber hören Sie – das war eine sehr anstrengende Zeit für Sie – bleiben Sie doch noch eine weitere Nacht und schauen Sie sich Nottingham an. Eine sehr interessante Stadt – und lassen Sie sich einen Ausflug in den Sherwood Forest nicht entgehen. Ich erwarte Sie dann übermorgen zurück im Büro ...

 50. Train Yourself

Auch »to give« wird im Englischen häufig verwendet. Geben Sie in den folgenden Sätzen Alternativen an!

1. I *gave* him a wide berth when I saw him in the street. I can't stand the man.
2. *Give me a call* when you get home.
3. I *gave up* all claim to the property.
4. You know you're beaten! *Give in!*
5. I *gave up* my job at the Exchange after Lewis and Company *gave me the hint* that I could expect to earn much more there.

6. Please don't *give away* what I've just told you!
7. Hello! ERGO? Could you *give* me Mr Brückner, please?
8. The company *gave* nearly a million pounds to charity last year.
9. I'd *give up* smoking, if I were you.
10. *Give me word* when you're ready.

quit, disclose, avoided, relinquished, put me through to, surrender, inform, hinted, donated, call, stop.

 Talk Talk Talk

(The front office of ERGO Limited)
L. Oh, good morning, Peter! Did you have a good trip?

P. Well, I don't really know. I think it **went well** enough.

(James Morgan, Melissa and Steve Blackman all enter together)
J. Where's the champagne, Lucy?

L. I'll get it right now, Mr Morgan. How many glasses?

J. Five – no six, Chip deserves some bubbly, too. Chip!

C. Yes, Mr Morgan, right here. Champagne? Whose birthday?

(Empfangsbüro von ERGO Limited)
L. Oh, guten Morgen, Peter! Hatten Sie eine angenehme Reise?

P. Na ja, ich weiß nicht genau. Ich glaube, es lief **gut genug**.

(James Morgan, Melissa und Steve Blackman treten gemeinsam ein)
J. Wo ist der Champagner, Lucy?

L. Ich hole ihn sofort, Mr Morgan. Wie viele Gläser?

J. Fünf – nein, sechs. Chip hat sich auch etwas Schampus verdient. Chip!

C. Ja, Mr Morgan, bin schon da. Champagner? Wer hat denn Geburtstag?

J. No birthday, Chip, but still a very **good reason to celebrate**.	J. Kein Geburtstag, Chip, aber wir haben trotzdem einen sehr **guten Grund zum Feiern.**
P. Celebrate?	P. Feiern?
J. We've just **landed** the most promising order of the year.	J. Wir haben gerade die vielversprechenste Order des Jahres **unter Dach und Fach gebracht**.
M. Oh, come on, Mr Morgan. **Put him out of his misery!**	M. Oh, nun kommen Sie schon, Mr Morgan. **Lassen Sie ihn doch nicht länger zappeln!**
J. Fothergill called me last night and said he'd decided to install Quick-Ed in two of his newspapers, with an option to buy, at a small discount, for the rest of his group.	J. Fothergill hat mich gestern Abend angerufen und mir gesagt, dass er sich dazu entschlossen hat, Quick-Ed bei zwei seiner Zeitungen zu installieren – mit der Option, sie für einen kleinen Rabatt auch für den Rest seiner Verlagsgruppe zu kaufen.
P. Good heavens! He didn't seem that convinced when I left him.	P. Meine Güte! Er schien nicht so überzeugt zu sein, als ich ihn verlassen habe.
J. Fothergill is a cautious man, as I told you on the phone, Peter. But he liked your style. And he liked the product you demonstrated so ably. Well done.	J. Fothergill ist ein vorsichtiger Mann, wie ich Ihnen schon am Telefon sagte, Peter. Aber er mochte Ihren Stil. Und er mochte das Produkt, das Sie ihm so gekonnt vorgeführt haben. Gut gemacht.
S. You've become our star salesman, Peter. Must have been my training!	S. Sie sind jetzt unser Star-Verkäufer, Peter. Das muss an meinem Training liegen!

Telefonieren

J. Well, we'll drink to that, Steve.

M. *Ja, lasst uns anstoßen. Ein toller Erfolg, lieber Peter!*

P. *Bitte?* You speak German?

S. Melissa is as secretive as old Fothergill. I've just discovered why she could never join us in an after-work drink. She was studying German at night-school – every night!

M. And last night was the end of the course. So tonight I'm inviting you two to dinner.

S. But no German please, Melissa!

J. Schön, darauf sollten wir trinken, Steve.

M. *Ja, lasst uns anstoßen! Ein toller Erfolg, lieber Peter!*

P. *Bitte?* Sie sprechen Deutsch?

S. Melissa ist genau so geheimnistuerisch wie der alte Fothergill. Ich habe gerade herausgefunden, warum Sie nie mitgekommen ist, wenn wir einen Feierabend-Drink zu uns genommen haben. Sie hat an einer Abendschule Deutsch gelernt – jeden Abend!

M. Und letzten Abend war die letzte Unterrichtsstunde. Also lade ich Sie beide heute Abend zum Essen ein.

S. Aber bitte kein Deutsch, Melissa!

 **Vocabulary**

to acquaint oneself with	sich vertraut machen mit
adequately briefed	angemessen vorbereitet/ eingewiesen
to be right down	gleich herunterkommen
to become acquainted with sth.	vertraut werden mit
to book	buchen
to boost sb's confidence	Selbstvertrauen aufbauen (umgangssprachlich)
business negotiation	geschäftliche Verhandlung
can't help	nicht umhin kommen
to cross fingers	Daumen drücken

discounted prices for larger orders	Mengenrabatt
down to business	zur Sache/zum Geschäftlichen (kommen)
driving license	Führerschein
face to face	persönlich/ »von Angesicht zu Angesicht«
general impression	Gesamteindruck
to get hold of	erreichen
to get to	dazu kommen
to go well	gut laufen
to have an appointment to see sb.	einen Termin mit jdm. haben
head office	Hauptbüro
to have sb. on the line	jdn. in der Leitung haben
to land (an order)	»unter Dach und Fach bringen«/ »an Land ziehen«
to manage	schaffen/ in der Lage sein/ etw. in den Griff bekommen
out of the blue	ohne Vorwarnung/ »aus heiterem Himmel«
overjoyed	überglücklich
to put a caller through	einen Anrufer durchstellen
to put out of one's misery	jdn. nicht mehr länger zappeln lassen
saved by the bell	Rettung in letzter Sekunde
to sound out	aushorchen, ausfragen
to stick to	bei etwas bleiben
to swat up	büffeln, sich intensiv mit etwas beschäftigen
to take a shine to	einen Narren gefressen haben an etw./jdm.
What name shall I give?	Wen darf ich melden?

Telefonieren

Anfragen
Requests

 Here we go

Die schriftliche Korrespondenz stellt einen wichtigen Teil des Geschäftsalltags dar. Nachdem Peter bisher hauptsächlich damit beschäftigt war, Probleme auf telefonischer Ebene zu lösen, betraut ihn sein Vorgesetzter, James Morgan, nun mit der Aufgabe, sich um seinen persönlichen Postein- und Postausgang zu kümmern. Ein verantwortungsvoller Posten ...

 Talk Talk Talk

(The office of James Morgan, Managing Director of ERGO Limited)

(Das Büro von James Morgan, Managing Director von ERGO Limited)

J. Good morning, Peter. Have a good weekend?

J. Guten Morgen, Peter. Wie war Ihr Wochenende?

P. Good morning, Mr Morgan. Fine thanks. I took advantage of the rainy weather and **caught up on some letter-writing**. A lot of my friends in Germany haven't heard from me for some time now.

P. Guten Morgen, Mr Morgan. Danke, gut. Ich habe das Beste aus dem regnerischen Wetter gemacht und **ein paar überfällige Briefe geschrieben**. Viele meiner Freunde in Deutschland haben schon lange nichts mehr von mir gehört.

J. I hope you haven't got **writer's cramp**. And I hope you haven't grown tired of writing letters because that's just what I want you to take over from me this week. During my absence last week the **in-tray** has become full of letters waiting to be answered.

J. Ich hoffe, Sie haben keinen **Schreibkrampf** bekommen. Und ich hoffe, Sie sind das Schreibens dabei noch nicht leid geworden, denn genau das sollen Sie diese Woche für mich übernehmen. Während meiner Abwesenheit letzte Woche hat sich der **Eingangs-**

You know enough now about the business to reply to them for me. Just **dictate** them to Lucy and she'll **type** them **up** for you. When you've completed a **batch** put them in my **out-tray**. There are also some **emails to attend to**. You'll find them in the general ERGO **file**.

korb mit Briefen gefüllt, die darauf warten, beantwortet zu werden. Sie kennen das Geschäft jetzt gut genug, um sie für mich zu beantworten. **Diktieren** Sie sie einfach Lucy und sie wird sie für Sie **abtippen**. Wenn Sie einen **Stoß** fertig haben, legen Sie ihn einfach in meinen **Ausgangskorb**. Es gibt auch noch ein paar **E-Mails, die zu bearbeiten sind**. Sie finden sie im allgemeinen ERGO-**Ordner**.

P. I'll do my best, Mr Morgan. But there are just a few questions of **style** I'd like to sort out first. I'm still a bit uncertain how **to end a letter** in English – there seem to be so many different forms of closing a letter ... .

P. Ich werde mein Bestes tun, Mr Morgan. Ich habe aber noch ein paar Fragen bezüglich des **Schreibstils**, die ich vorher noch klären möchte. Ich bin mir immer noch ein bisschen unsicher, wie man **einen Brief** im Englischen **beendet** – es scheint so viele verschiedene Arten zu geben, einen Brief abzuschließen ... .

Korrespondenz

 Do's and Don'ts – A matter of form ...

When writing a **formal business letter**, the correct form of address is: **Dear Sir** or **Dear Madam**. The customary plural form is: **Dear Sirs/Mesdames.**
If you are writing a business letter **to a person you know by name** then you may now begin your letter in the following way:
Dear Mr (Smith, Brown). Difficulty is encountered by the British (and Americans) when a woman is addressed. If you are replying to a letter written by a woman who gave her name as Mrs then you can safely address her as: **Dear Mrs (Smith, Brown)**. A big problem arises when you have to reply to a letter signed **simply with surname and first name** – Joan Brown, for instance. Under no circumstances can you address her as Miss Brown. In the United States, the problem was

solved by inventing a new form – **Ms** – and this has also won wide acceptance now in Britain. So, replying to a letter signed by Joan Brown, you can safely address her as **Ms Brown**. Another alternative in use is to address her as: **Dear Joan Brown**.
Titles must always be used: Dear Lord Salisbury, Dear Sir John (here the surname is dropped!), **Dear Dr. Linklater, Dear Professor Maugham**.
Senior military ranks are also usually used in formal letter-writing: **Dear Major Rigby**.

And now – **how do you end a letter**?
Yours sincerely or **Yours faithfully**? The British use a simple rule in deciding whether to end a business letter with »**sincerely**« or »**faithfully**«. If the letter begins with a »**Dear Sir**« they avoid employing a further »S« by ending the letter »**Yours faithfully**«. The same rule applies if the letter begins »**Dear Madam**« or »**Dear Sirs/Mesdames**«.
»**Yours sincerely**« is reserved for letters addressed to persons by name: »Dear Mr Smith, Dear Mrs Brown etc.«. The form »**Yours truly**« is now found almost exclusively on letters sent by fax or electronic mail. The British have an almost limitless list of ways of ending letters addressed to persons by their first name: **Dear John ... with best wishes, with kind regards, with regards, all the best ...**

51. Train Yourself

Wie würden Sie die folgenden Briefe beenden?

1. Dear Major Trowbridge, I hope you got home safely after the wedding ...
2. Dear Sirs/Mesdames, We are writing to request ...
3. Dear James, Thank you for your invitation to dinner ...
4. Dear Sir Charles, My society would like to invite you to address ...
5. Dear Mr Spencer, We would like to place an order with your company for ...
6. Dear Mary, How pleased we were to hear your marvellous news ...
7. Dear Sir, We are writing to remind you that payment of the following account is due ...
8. Dear Lord Portbury, It would be a great honour for us if you were able to attend our open day ...

 **Talk Talk Talk**

(Peter's Office. Melissa, the Marketing-Manager, enters)	(Peters Büro. Melissa, die Marketing-Managerin, tritt ein)
M. Good morning Peter, you look busy.	M. Guten Morgen Peter, Sie sehen beschäftigt aus.
P. I have this **pile of letters to attend to**. They'll take a lot of **getting through**.	P. Ich muss diesen **Haufen Briefe bearbeiten**. Es wird eine Weile dauern, bis ich sie durch habe.
M. If you need any help or advice, give me a call – particularly if they concern marketing, of course.	M. Rufen Sie mich an, falls Sie Hilfe oder einen Rat brauchen – besonders, wenn es um Marketing-Fragen geht, versteht sich.
P. That's very kind of you, Melissa. But I must try first of all to master these things myself.	P. Das ist sehr nett von Ihnen, Melissa, aber ich sollte vor allem versuchen, solche Aufgaben selbst zu bewältigen.

 Peter's first letter is a **formal request** from a large retail company for information about ERGO's range of products:

Dear Sirs/Mesdames,

We would be most grateful if you sent us **at your convenience** full information about the range of the software products you are able to offer. We are particularly interested in any product you have which could lead to a streamlining of our sales and receipts accounting and recording systems.
Looking forward to your reply,
Yours faithfully,

John Mitchell,
Managing Director,
The Rosings Group

 **Talk Talk Talk**

(Peter's office)

P. Steve? Hello, how are you today? I have a request here for information on **our full range of products**, but with special interest in anything in the **retail trade** area. We do have a **sales and receipts accounting program**, don't we?

S. Yes, but we're not having a great deal of success with it. It's already a year old and, in computer terms, has long passed its **'sell-by' date**.
But I'm expecting an updated system from America at any time. **Can you put them off?**

P. Well, they seem to be in some hurry. Can I at least send off the other information?

S. Sure, but if they're retail trade they won't be interested in most of our other programs. But I'll let you have the lot. I'll tell you what – I'll do more. I have a new secretary.
She'll help you **draft that letter** in such a way they'll wait till next

(Peters Büro)

P. Steve? Hallo, wie geht es Ihnen heute? Ich habe hier eine Anfrage nach Informationen über unsere gesamte **Produktpalette**, besonders über alles, was den Bereich **Einzelhandel** betrifft. Wir haben doch ein **Verkaufs- und Quittungs-Buchführungsprogramm**, oder?

S. Ja, aber wir haben keinen besonderen Erfolg damit. Es ist bereits ein Jahr alt und hat für Computer-Verhältnisse sein **Verfallsdatum** schon lange überschritten. Allerdings erwarte ich täglich ein aktualisiertes System aus Amerika. **Können Sie die Leute noch ein bisschen hinhalten?**

P. Tja, sie scheinen es recht eilig zu haben. Kann ich ihnen wenigstens die anderen Informationen schicken?

S. Klar, aber wenn sie im Einzelhandel tätig sind, werden sie sich für die meisten unserer anderen Programme nicht sonderlich interessieren. Ich werde Ihnen trotzdem den ganzen Schwung geben. Ich sage Ihnen was – ich tue noch mehr. Ich habe eine neue Sekre-

Christmas for the retail sales program. Her name's Beryl ...

tärin. Sie wird Ihnen h**el**fen, **diesen Brief so zu entwerfen,** dass die glatt bis Weihnachten auf das Einzelhandels-Programm warten. Ihr Name ist Beryl ...

 Peter und Beryl machen sich an die Arbeit:

Dear Mr Mitchell,

Thank you for **your inquiry** of May 4. **We have great pleasure in enclosing** complete information on the full range of our products. You will, however, notice that one important product is missing: the ERGO retail sales and receipts logging and accounting program. This is because the program is being replaced by a revolutionary new software which will be reaching us from the United States shortly.

We would not want to interest you in a program which is so soon to be overtaken by the very latest technology, and we assure you that immediately we receive the new software we shall get again in touch with you and arrange to demonstrate the new development to you personally.

Assuring you of our best attention at all times,

Yours sincerely,

Peter Brückner,
Assistant Managing Director,
ERGO Limited

Background Information

The British use the american spelling for »programme« in context of computers »We want to install your **accounting program.**«

52. Train Yourself

Bestimmen Sie die Nomina der folgenden Verben nach diesem Beispiel:
I *instructed* him to send me the documents as soon as possible.
Lösung: *instruction*.

1. May I *request* a speedy reply?
2. I would like to *ask* you the following question ...
3. We are now forced to *demand* immediate payment of the outstanding account.
4. We have no alternative but to *refuse* payment until all the conditions have been met.
5. Our marketing department has had to *reject* your proposal.
6. There's no point in *denying* your responsibility in the following matter.
7. We have no choice but to *withhold* payment until the equipment is seen to perform correctly.
8. We are able to *offer* you the following terms: ...

 Talk Talk Talk

P. Well, that should do the trick. Thank you very much, Beryl.

B. That's quite all right, Mr Brückner. Any time. I'll put the letter in the **out-tray for posting**, shall I?

P. I think I'd better show it to Mr Morgan first.

B. Just as you wish. The letter is **stored** anyway. I created a **new file** for the Rosings Group. You'll find it there.

P. Okay, so dürfte es klappen. Vielen Dank, Beryl.

B. Gern geschehen, Mr Brückner. Jederzeit. Ich werde den Brief jetzt in den **Postausgangs-Korb** legen, in Ordnung?

P. Ich glaube, ich zeige ihn besser zuerst Mr Morgan.

B. Wie Sie wollen. Der Brief ist auf alle Fälle **abgespeichert**. Ich habe eine **neue Datei** für die Rosings Group angelegt. Da finden Sie ihn.

P. Well, I hope there'll be more to go in that file later on. Now for the next letter – oh dear, this one's a **complaint**.

P. Gut, ich hoffe, dieser Ordner wird später noch um einiges dicker werden. Jetzt aber zum nächsten Brief – oh weia, eine **Beschwerde**.

 Dear Sirs/Mesdames,

I regret to have to inform you that my company is **not** at all **pleased with** the way in which the servicing contract for the ERGO office-management system is being honoured. According to the contract, an ERGO representative should visit our offices in person once a month during the 12-month period after installation. Our system was installed seven months ago and your Newcastle representative, Mr Batty, has called on us personally just twice. He has phoned on occasion to check if the system is functioning satisfactorily. Fortunately, the system has given us no problems, but there are technical questions which we need to discuss on a one-to-one basis and not over the telephone.
I would be pleased if you rectified the situation and honoured the terms of the contract.
Hoping to hear from you forthwith,

Yours faithfully,
George Robertson,
Managing Director,
The Newcastle Fine Produce Company

P. Lucy, I have a letter here to dictate, but first of all could you get me Mr Batty in Newcastle on the phone?

P. Lucy, ich habe hier einen Brief zum Diktieren, aber könnten Sie mich bitte zuerst mit Mr Batty in Newcastle verbinden?

L. Certainly, Peter.

L. Natürlich, Peter.

P. Hello, is that Desmond Batty? Peter Brückner of ERGO here. We've had a complaint from Newcastle Fine Foods that you

P. Hallo, spreche ich mit Desmond Batty? Hier spricht Peter Brückner von ERGO. Wir hatten hier eine Beschwerde der Newcastle Fine

Korrespondenz

haven't been following up that office-management systems installation as required in the contract.

D. I established that the system is working well and there was really no need to call by on a regular basis. George Robertson appeared to be in agreement.

P. Well, he's written us a pretty stiff letter of complaint. Can I tell him you'll be calling by as arranged monthly?

D. Well, if that's really what he wants, then fine by me. But there's actually nothing to do.

P. I think he just wants the reassurance that somebody from ERGO is **on the spot** and taking a personal interest in his **office management**.

D. Fine, then tell him I'll come round tomorrow – and then once a month.

Foods darüber, dass Sie ihr Büromanagement-System nicht betreut haben, wie es im Vertrag vereinbart ist.

D. Ich habe mich davon überzeugt, dass die Anlage einwandfrei funktioniert und dass es wirklich keinen Grund gibt, regelmäßig vorbeizukommen. George Robertson schien damit einverstanden zu sein.

P. Tja, er hat uns einen ziemlich bestimmten Beschwerdebrief geschickt. Können Sie ihm mitteilen, dass sie in Zukunft wie vereinbart monatlich vorbeischauen?

D. Gut, wenn er das unbedingt will, dann ist mir das recht. Aber es gibt dort wirklich nichts zu tun.

P. Ich glaube er braucht lediglich die Gewissheit, dass jemand von ERGO **vor Ort** ist und persönliches Interesse an seinem **Büromanagement** zeigt.

D. Gut, dann sagen Sie ihm, dass ich morgen bei ihm vorbeikomme – und danach einmal im Monat.

 Dear Mr Robertson,

I am truly sorry you have had cause to complain about the way ERGO is honouring its contract with your company. There appears to have been a misunderstanding here. Mr Batty has not been calling personally as arranged because the system has been performing satisfactorily.

He most certainly would have visited your offices immediately if his help had been required.
I talked to Mr Batty by phone today and he promised to call personally next Monday and then once a month, as contractually arranged.
Assuring you of our best attention at all times,

Yours sincerely,
Peter Brückner

 53. Train Yourself

Welche Wörter passen in die Lücken?

Dear Sir,
We would be very ▒▒▒▒▒ if you ▒▒▒▒▒ us information about your company's full ▒▒▒▒▒ of ▒▒▒▒▒.
We are interested in various ▒▒▒▒▒ which have been ▒▒▒▒▒ by your company, and we are sure we could ▒▒▒▒▒ them in various ▒▒▒▒▒ of our ▒▒▒▒▒.
We have a board meeting ▒▒▒▒▒ for next Wednesday, so it would be particularly ▒▒▒▒▒ if you could ▒▒▒▒▒ to send the information material to us by then.
Looking forward to your ▒▒▒▒▒
Yours ▒▒▒▒▒

scheduled, faithfully, range, sent, reply, developed, areas, useful, operations, arrange, products, employ, grateful.

 **Talk Talk Talk**

(Steve enters Peter's office)

S. Still **submerged in letters**? It's nearly lunch-time – I feel like a beer and a steak-pie at the *Duke of Rutland*. Want to join me?

(Steve betritt Peters Büro)

S. Immer noch **unter einem Briefberg begraben**? Wir haben fast Mittag – ich hätte Lust auf ein Bier und eine Fleischpastete im *Duke of Rutland*. Möchten Sie mitkommen?

P. Oh, why not – I'll work late with the other letters if I have to.

B. Wait for me then, I've **worked up a thirst** myself.

S. **Make it snappy** then, Beryl ...

(The *Duke of Rutland* pub)
S. What's it to be, Peter, the usual?

P. Yes please, Steve.

S. And Beryl?

B. An alcohol-free, please, Steve. Writing letters in English must be quite different from how you compose letters in German, Peter?

P. There are small points of difference, but the general style is very similar. I had expected much less **formality** in English, but the rules are really just as rigid as in German.

S. You're right there about formality and rules. But they're really only a cover, you know – I'll give you an example. Look at this letter I got this morning from my local council ...

P. Oh, warum nicht – ich werde wegen der restlichen Briefe eben länger arbeiten, wenn es nötig ist.

B. Warten Sie auf mich, ich bin **vom Arbeiten ganz durstig** geworden.

S. Dann **machen Sie schnell**, Beryl ...

(Im *Duke of Rutland*-Pub)
S. Was darf's denn sein Peter, das Übliche?

P. Ja bitte, Steve.

S. Und Beryl?

B. Bitte ein Alkoholfreies, Steve. Briefe auf Englisch zu schreiben ist sicher etwas ganz anderes, als das in Deutsch zu tun, oder, Peter?

P. Es gibt ein paar kleine Unterschiede, aber der generelle Stil ist ganz ähnlich. Ich hatte im Englischen viel weniger **Förmlichkeit** erwartet, aber die Regeln sind tatsächlich ebenso streng wie im Deutschen.

S. Sie haben Recht, was die Formalitäten und Regeln angeht. Aber sie sind lediglich eine oberflächliche Hülle – ich werde es Ihnen demonstrieren. Schauen Sie sich diesen Brief an, den ich heute Morgen von meiner Stadtverwaltung bekommen habe ...

 Dear Sir,

It has been brought to our attention that you are parking your car illegally on council land at the end of Lansdowne Drive, Wimbledon. Although the land has not yet been fenced off there are two notices making it very clear that parking is prohibited. You have been observed on several occasions parking your car on this ground at night and driving your vehicle away the next morning before our parking wardens take up their duty. For security reasons, even night-time parking is prohibited. Hence, **we must ask you kindly to refrain from** parking your car on this terrain in the future. Failure to comply with our request will result in legal action having to be taken against you.

Yours faithfully,

Edmond Tracey,
Town Clerk

 54. Train Yourself

Finden Sie einfachere Wörter oder Ausdrücke:

1. prohibited
2. observed
3. on several occasions
4. take up their duty
5. refrain from
6. terrain

 Talk Talk Talk

B. So why are you getting so **het-up**, Steve? It looks like an **open-and-shut** case to me.

B. Warum **regen** Sie sich so **auf**, Steve? Für mich sieht das wie ein **ganz klarer** Fall aus.

Korrespondenz

S. No. That's not it. Look at the style of that letter. They're basically telling me: »Hey, you **berk**, stop parking your **lousy** car on our ground«. But this guy Tracey has wrapped the brick up in fancy paper.

S. Nein, darum geht es nicht. Sehen Sie sich den Stil an, in dem dieser Brief geschrieben wurde. Was sie mir eigentlich sagen, ist: »He du **Dussel**, hör endlich auf, dein **lausiges** Auto auf unserem Grundstück zu parken.« Aber dieser Tracey hat den Pflasterstein in Geschenkpapier verpackt.

B. Oh, come on, Steve. He's just being polite.

B. Ach, kommen Sie, Steve. Er ist doch nur höflich.

S. Yes, in that typically English way where it means **zilch**.

S. Ja, aber eben auf diese typisch englische Art und Weise, die ungefähr **gar nichts** bedeutet.

P. Well, I don't want to take sides here, but official letters like that are also **couched** in polite terms in Germany.

P. Na ja, ich möchte hier zwar keine Partei ergreifen, aber offizielle Briefe wie dieser sind in Deutschland auch in höfliche Formulierungen **eingebettet**.

 55. Train Yourself

1. Beryl kann Steve zu einem freundlichen Antwortbrief überreden. Können Sie die Lücken darin füllen?

Dear Mr Tracey,

Thank you for your letter of June 4. I am sorry you have had ▮▮▮▮ to ▮▮▮▮ me that I have been illegally parking on council land. In my ▮▮▮▮, I must say that I was ▮▮▮▮ that the land ▮▮▮▮ belonged to the council. I certainly saw no notices ▮▮▮▮ parking. I had ▮▮▮▮ that at night at least the land could be ▮▮▮▮ to park cars on. If this is not the case, I shall of course ▮▮▮▮ from parking my

car there in future. But may I take this ▬▬▬ to ▬▬▬ for more car-parking possibilities in Lansdowne Drive and the ▬▬▬.
Yours sincerely,

Steve Blackman

vicinity, opportunity, in question, cause, appeal, refrain, inform, used, unaware, prohibiting, assumed, defence.

2. In Großbritannien gibt es verschiedene Möglichkeiten zum Versenden eines Briefes. Wie kann man diese am besten umschreiben?

Registered post
(a) The recipient signs for the letter.
(b) The sender receives a receipt confirming the letter has seen sent.
(c) A description of the letter's contents is officially registered.

Recorded delivery
(a) The sender must sign a declaration assuming responsibility for the letter's delivery.
(b) The Post Office takes responsibility for the safe delivery of the letter.
(c) The recipient signs an official receipt confirming acceptance of the letter.

 Background Information

And don't forget to stamp your letters – but with which stamps? Letters are sent by two alternative routes:
a. First Class – guaranteeing next-day delivery.
b. Second Class – where delivery can take two or three days.

 Talk Talk Talk

(James Morgan enters Peter's office)
J. Peter, I have a letter here I'd like you to reply to today, if you can. It's a **job inquiry** which has

(James Morgan tritt in Peters Büro ein)
J. Peter, ich habe hier einen Brief, den Sie bitte noch heute beantworten sollten, wenn es Ihnen

been hidden among my **papers** for the past few days.

möglich ist. Es ist eine **Bewerbung**, die ein paar Tage lang unter meinen **Unterlagen** versteckt lag.

P. Certainly, Mr Morgan. But how should I reply to it?

P. Natürlich, Mr Morgan. Aber wie soll ich darauf antworten?

J. Just say we have no immediate vacancies but that we'll **put the application on file**. The young man certainly has qualifications which we might be able to use some time in the future. Just dictate the letter to Lucy.

J. Sagen Sie einfach, dass wir derzeit keine freien Stellen haben, **das Stellengesuch** jedoch **in die Datei aufnehmen**. Der junge Mann hat offensichtlich Qualifikationen, die uns in Zukunft vielleicht einmal nützlich sein könnten. Diktieren Sie den Brief einfach Lucy.

P. May I see the application?

P. Darf ich die Bewerbung mal sehen?

 Dear Sir/Madam,

I am writing to inquire if your company has **an opening for a trainee in business management**. I have just completed my Master's degree in Business Administration at the University of Aston and am looking for an opportunity to add practical experience now to the theoretical knowledge I built up in five years of study. Your company was recommended to me by the University's professional counselling service. I am attaching a brief **CV** which summarizes my educational background.

Yours faithfully,

Martin Russell

P. Lucy, could you **take a letter** please?

P. Lucy, können Sie bitte einen **Brief aufnehmen**?

L. Certainly, Peter …

L. Natürlich, Peter …

 Dear Mr Russell,

Thank you for your letter of May 22. **We regret to inform you** that at the moment we have no vacancy which would suit your qualifications. But we would be most interested in meeting you if such a vacancy occurred in the future and we shall be glad to put your inquiry in our files. **In the meantime**, please accept an up-to-date information brochure on ERGO Limited.

Yours sincerely,

Peter Brückner,
Assistant Managing Director

 56. Train Yourself

Der folgende Beschwerdebrief landet auf Peters Schreibtisch:

Dear Sir,

Your sales representative in Birmingham promised one month ago to call by our offices and explain the advantages of the ERGO Accounting 2000 package. We suspended inquiries we had begun with other companies pending the outcome of the meeting with your representative. To this date, no ERGO representative has reported to us. I **regret** to have to inform you that our Board has decided that unless we hear from your representative within one week of the date of this letter we shall be compelled to **strike** ERGO **from** our short-list of possible suppliers and look elsewhere for the product we urgently need.

Yours faithfully,

Eric Simpson,
Director,
Titan Products

Helfen Sie Peter dabei, James Morgan vom Inhalt des Briefes zu unterrichten, indem Sie die richtige Form der Verben in den Klammern benutzen!

Mr Simpson of Titan Products *(write)* to us *(complain)* that although our sales representative in Birmingham *(promise)* to call by his offices *(explain)* our Accounting 2000 system he *(not turn up)*. Mr Simpson *(tell)* us that Titan *(suspend)* inquiries with other possible suppliers until the company *(look at)* our product. He *(say)* the Titan Board *(decide ... give)* us one more week for our representative *(call)*. If he *(not do so)* within that time Titan *(strike)* us from its short-list of possible suppliers and *(look)* elsewhere for a supplier.

 **Talk Talk Talk**

(Melissa enters Peter's office)	(Melissa betritt Peters Büro)
M. How are you getting along, Peter, in your search for a place to live?	M. Wie kommen Sie bei Ihrer Suche nach einer festen Bleibe voran, Peter?
P. Two agents are now looking for me, but frankly I just get more confused with each letter I receive from them.	P. Ich habe jetzt zwei Makler, die für mich auf der Suche sind, aber ehrlich gesagt verwirrt mich jeder Brief mehr, den ich von ihnen bekomme.
M. What's wrong with them?	M. Was stimmt denn damit nicht?
P. Well, maybe I'm a bit too demanding but whenever they send me descriptions of property I might be interested in and I arrange for a viewing I never find what I expect. Here's the latest example ...	P. Tja, vielleicht verlange ich einfach zuviel, aber jedes Mal, wenn sie mir Beschreibungen von Wohnungen schicken, die mich eventuell interessieren könnten und ich einen Besichtigungstermin vereinbare, finde ich nicht das vor, was ich erwarte. Hier das jüngste Beispiel ...

Dear Mr Brückner,

We are very pleased to be able to offer you a **highly desirable** property in one of the areas which you indicated to us might be of most interest to you as a **permanent location** to live. The property is on the first floor of a magnificently converted Victorian-era mansion. It **boasts** a representative entrance hall, two **generously-proportioned** bedrooms, a stately living room with separate dining area, Adam fireplace and corniced, built-in book-shelves, a spacious kitchen with every possible modern appliance, a luxurious bathroom with jacuzzi, substantial brass fittings and pastel-toned suite. Panoramic views to Hyde Park.
We **urge** a very early viewing of this unique property and **would be pleased to arrange an appointment at your kind convenience**.

Yours sincerely,
…

 57. Train Yourself

Schreiben Sie den obigen Brief neu, indem Sie folgende Wörter und Ausdrücke durch diejenigen aus der unteren Auswahlliste ersetzen:

1. highly desirable
2. permanent location
3. boasts
4. generously-proportioned
5. urge

wanted, ask, recommend, luxurious, large, site, has, possesses, extensive, needed, attractive.

 **Talk Talk Talk**

M. Well? Looks quite a place!

M. Und? Hört sich doch gut an!

P. Doesn't it just? There were even a couple of photographs with the letter. Here …

P. Nicht wahr? Dem Brief waren sogar einige Fotos beigefügt. Hier …

M. Wow! Now that's something ...

P. The photographer who took them must have been quite something, too. They're not at all like what I saw with my own eyes!

M. You viewed the place?

P. Of course. Would you like *my* description of it?

M. I**'m dying to hear it!**

P. Right! Let's start with the entrance hall. »Representative« was the description. What it represented was a small space behind the front door, not large enough to put a hall-stand. Neither of the »generously-proportioned« bedrooms was larger than 12 square metres. »Stately« living room? It was **in a bit of a state**, that I'll admit. The »separate dining area« just didn't exist. The »Adam« fireplace was a plaster **mock-up**, and the bookshelves were a do-it-yourself job. Modern kitchen appliances? They might have been complete if there had been a dishwasher and a microwave. The »luxurious« bathroom was a converted cupboard with no window.

M. Donnerwetter! Das macht schon was her ...

P. Der Fotograf, der sie gemacht hat, muss auch ganz schön was her gemacht haben. Sie sehen nicht im geringsten so aus wie das, was ich mit meinen eigenen Augen gesehen habe!

M. Sie haben sich die Wohnung angesehen?

P. Natürlich. Würden Sie gern *meine* Beschreibung davon hören?

M. Ich **sterbe vor Neugier!**

P. In Ordnung! Beginnen wir mit der Eingangshalle. »Repräsentativ« lautete die Beschreibung. Was sie repräsentierte war ein kleiner Raum hinter der Eingangstüre, nicht einmal groß genug, um eine Garderobe hineinzustellen. Keines der »großzügig geschnittenen« Schlafzimmer war größer als zwölf Quadratmeter. Wohnzimmer in »prächtigem Zustand«? Es war **ein Zustand**, das muss ich zugeben. Der »separate Essbereich« existierte einfach gar nicht. Der steinerne Kamin war eine **Nachbildung** aus Gips und die Bücherborde waren selbst gemacht. Moderne Kücheneinrichtung? Sie wären vielleicht komplett gewesen, wenn es eine Geschirrspülmaschine und eine

And so on. Want to hear more?	Mikrowelle gegeben hätte. Das »luxuriöse« Badezimmer war ein umgewandelter Schrank ohne Fenster. Und so weiter, und so fort. Wollen Sie noch mehr hören?
M. (laughs). No, that's enough, Peter. You've learnt another important lesson in Britain – never trust an estate agent's **hype**. Or learn how to read between the lines.	M. (lacht). Nein, das reicht, Peter. Sie haben eine weitere wichtige, englische Lektion gelernt – traue nie den **Übertreibungen** eines Wohnungsmaklers. Oder lerne, zwischen den Zeilen zu lesen.
P. Between the lines?	P. Zwischen den Zeilen?
M. Estate agents have their own language. If the bedrooms had been really large they would have been described as »huge« not »generously proportioned«, that kind of thing.	M. Wohnungsmakler haben ihre eigene Sprache. Wären die Schlafzimmer tatsächlich groß gewesen, wären sie als »riesig« und nicht als »großzügig geschnitten« beschrieben worden oder etwas in der Art.
P. Oh dear! I don't think I'll ever find a place to live.	P. Ach du meine Güte! Ich glaube, ich werde nie eine richtige Bleibe finden.
M. Patience, Peter, patience – a very English virtue!	M. Geduld, Peter, Geduld – eine englische Tugend!

Background Information

As Peter has now discovered, there are **various forms of English, employed in distinct situations and most visible in written letters**. A letter containing a very real threat of **dire** action will be written in as polite a form as the most harmless **missive**. But of all the various forms of English employed in official communications the most curious and most difficult to construe is the language used by estate agents in describing the properties they hope to sell. If you are renting or buying property in Britain through the services of an estate agent you would be well advised to engage the additional advice of somebody fluent in English.

 ## 58. Train Yourself

Setzen Sie die korrekte Form des Verbs »to write« ein!

1. I would _____ if I had only known your address.
2. I'll _____ just as soon as I arrive.
3. He _____ regularly, won't he?
4. She has never _____ to me in that tone before.
5. I have better things to do than _____ to you all the time.
6. They _____ that they would be returning tomorrow.
7. I _____ to you right now, while waiting for the train.

 ## Talk Talk Talk

P. Melissa, now here's a letter I really don't understand at all. It seems to belong in your department, but I'm not sure.

M. Let me take a look ...

P. Melissa, ich habe hier einen Brief, den ich wirklich überhaupt nicht verstehe. Es scheint so, als würde er in Ihre Abteilung gehören, aber ich bin mir nicht sicher.

M. Zeigen Sie mal ...

 Dear Sirs/Mesdames,

Thank you for your letter of the 15th inst., **to which we now have pleasure in replying positively**. Your interest in participating in the joint InterConnect initiative has been noted and we have pleasure in enclos-

ing formal application forms. In view of the brief amount of time now remaining, may we urge you to forward us your application as soon as possible, together with the registration fee. The absolute deadline for applications is the 31st of July, and any applications received after that date can unfortunately not be accepted.
Looking forward to your reply,

Yours faithfully,
Robert Clarke

M. Oh dear, I don't know how that letter ended up on James's desk. I quite forgot that we had asked for information about participation in the InterConnect **marketing push**. I'll really have to get busy on this one – it's no wonder it had you puzzled, Peter.

P. Well, there's one expression – or abbreviation there – that really **foxed** me, is that what you say? That *inst*. What does that mean?

M. Oh, that! It's just a formal way of referring to the month – in this case our letter was dated the 15th of July, or the 15th *inst*. The form is becoming obsolete, but you'll still meet it and it's good for you to know what it means.

P. So today is the 21st *inst*.?

M. Oh je, ich weiß nicht, wie dieser Brief auf James Tisch gelandet ist. Ich hatte fast vergessen, dass wir um Informationen über die Teilnahme an der InterConnect-**Marketinginitiative** gebeten hatten. Darum muss ich mich wirklich kümmern – kein Wunder, dass Sie verwirrt waren, Peter.

P. Tja, es gibt da einen Ausdruck – oder Abkürzung – die mich wirklich **verblüfft** hat, ist das das richtige Wort? Dieses *inst*. Was bedeutet das?

M. Ach das! Das ist lediglich eine formelle Art und Weise, sich auf den jeweiligen Monat zu beziehen – in diesem Fall ist der Brief datiert auf den 15. Juli oder den 15. *inst*. Dieser Ausdruck ist langsam veraltet, aber er kommt manchmal noch vor und es ist gut, dass Sie jetzt wissen, was er bedeutet.

P. Also ist heute der 21. *inst*.?

M. Yes, but only in letter form – talking of which, do you have any more **to reply to**?

M. Ja, aber nur in schriftlicher Briefform – und da wir gerade davon sprechen, haben Sie noch welche **zu beantworten**?

P. Stacks – I'd better get down to them.

P. Haufenweise – ich kümmere mich besser darum.

M. Peter, a tip. Divide them up into categories. You'll save a lot of time that way. And then concentrate on those that have to be replied to urgently.

M. Peter, ein Tipp. Teilen Sie sie in Kategorien ein. So sparen Sie sich eine Menge Zeit. Und dann konzentrieren Sie sich auf diejenigen, die dringend beantwortet werden müssen.

P. Well, I suppose these **letters inquiring about** our products are the most pressing – I'll get down to those first ...

P. Tja, ich vermute, die **Briefe, in denen man sich nach** unseren Produkten **erkundigt**, sind die dringendsten – die werde ich zuerst bearbeiten ...

 59. Train Yourself

Wählen Sie die richtigen Wörter um die Lücken zu füllen!

1. We have pleasure in acknowledging ▬▬▬▬▬ of your letter.
2. Looking forward to a ▬▬▬▬▬ reply.
3. We would ▬▬▬▬▬ an ▬▬▬▬▬ reply.
4. Please be ▬▬▬▬▬ of our ▬▬▬▬▬ attention at all times.
5. Would you please ▬▬▬▬▬ to the above address.
6. We would be ▬▬▬▬▬ if you ▬▬▬▬▬ us information about your product-line.

reply, early, best, grateful, receipt, assured, appreciate, prompt, sent.

(Peter **tackles some letters of inquiry** ...)

(Peter **geht ein paar Anfragen durch** ...)

 Dear Sir,

My attention was caught by your company's advertisement in Techno-News. **I am particularly interested in** the Reddy program, which your company claims can contribute to large savings of time in sorting bulk orders. Our growth in wholesale trade has now reached the point where a highly-developed technological system is needed to keep pace with increasing orders. I would, therefore, be most obliged if you arranged to send me further, detailed information on the Reddy program.

Yours faithfully,

Frank R. Gilpin,
Managing Director,
Top Trading

P. (reaches for his telephone) Steve, do you have the **information brochures** and **catalogues** on the Reddy program?

P. (greift nach dem Telefonhörer) Steve, haben Sie die **Informationsbroschüren und die Kataloge** über das Reddy-Programm?

S. Hang on a moment, I'll have a look. Yes, I've got a pile of stuff here.

S. Bleiben Sie einen Augenblick dran. Ich sehe nach. Ja, ich habe einen Stapel von dem Zeug hier.

P. I have an **inquiry** here for as much information as we can send. Brochures and catalogues. I'll give you a copy of my reply – you'll want to alert your man in Birmingham, there could be a sale here.

P. Ich habe hier eine **Anfrage** nach so viel Informationen, wie wir schicken können. Broschüren und Kataloge. Ich werde Ihnen eine Kopie meiner Antwort geben – Sie werden Ihren Mann in Birmingham sicher darauf aufmerksam machen wollen, dass hier ein Geschäft zu Stande kommen könnte.

S. Yes, **please keep me in touch**. It's good of you to take over this **correspondence**, dear chap. I have so much to do at the moment.	S. Ja, **halten Sie mich auf dem Laufenden**. Es ist nett von Ihnen, diesen **Schriftwechsel** zu übernehmen, alter Freund. Ich habe im Augenblick so viel zu tun.
P. No problem, Steve. It's a pleasure.	P. Kein Problem, Steve. Ist mir ein Vergnügen.
P. Lucy, can you **take a letter**?	P. Lucy, können Sie **einen Brief aufnehmen**?
L. Peter, you have a **dictaphone** in your desk, you know. Why don't you use that? It'll save us both time.	L. Peter, Sie haben ein **Diktiergerät** in Ihrer Schreibtischschublade. Warum benutzen Sie es nicht? Damit würden wir beide Zeit sparen.
P. Well, bless my soul, I should have known a high-tech company would have a device like that.	P. Meine Güte, ich hätte wissen sollen, dass ein Hightech-Unternehmen so einen Apparat haben würde.
P. Well, here goes …	P. Also, los geht's …

 Reply to letter from Mr Frank Gilpin, Managing Director, Top Trading, Aston Road 20-14, Birmingham, dated the 14th of July.

Dear Mr Gilpin,

Thank you for your letter of July 14 (Lucy, make that 14th of July or 14.07., if you like, whatever our style is). **I have great pleasure in sending you full information** on the Reddy program which you requested. This is the **very latest development** in electronic order-sorting, and **we are sure it would match your requirements.**

If you have any further questions please do not hesitate to contact me. My telephone and telefax numbers are as above.

Yours sincerely,

Peter Brückner,
Assistant Managing Director,
ERGO Limited

P. Steve, how would you like a **copy** of this letter? A **hard copy** or shall I put it **on disc**?

P. Steve, in welcher Form hätten Sie die **Kopie** dieses Briefes gerne? **Auf Papier** oder soll ich sie **auf Diskette** speichern?

S. Can you create a file for Top Trading and save it in that? You'll find a general file for business inquiries under »ERGO-Inquiries«. I have access to that and it keeps me up to date on possible **sales follow-ups**. I'm sure we'll be hearing more from Top Trading – at least, I hope we do.

S. Könnten Sie eine Datei für Top Trading erstellen und ihn darin abspeichern? Unter »ERGO-Anfragen« finden Sie eine allgemeine Datei für Geschäftsanfragen. Ich habe Zugriff dazu und sie hält mich auf dem Laufenden über mögliche **Nachfolge-Verkäufe**. Ich bin mir sicher, wir werden noch mehr von Top Trading hören – wenigstens hoffe ich das.

 60. Train Yourself

Peter findet es einfacher, seine Briefe mit Hilfe des Diktiergeräts an Lucy weiterzureichen. Geben Sie in den folgenden Sätzen die korrekten Komparativformen an.

1. This letter was much *(clear)* than the first one.
2. His last letter was *(brief)* than usual, but still *(long)* than hers.
3. Although it was written by hand, the letter was *(legible)* than I thought it would be.
4. The tone of that letter was *(insulting)* than I expected.
5. Why was the letter *(lengthy)* than the others.
6. The letter arrived *(soon)* than I had expected.

(Peter takes the next letter from the pile ...)	(Peter nimmt den nächsten Brief vom Stapel ...)

 Dear Mr Morgan,

I am taking the liberty of writing to you following our meeting at the Chamber of Trade lunch. I was very interested in your description of the range of activities of your company, and I would like to learn more. I would be most honoured if you accepted an invitation to lunch with me at my club next week. May I suggest Friday?
Looking forward to hearing from you,

Yours sincerely,

Henry Rowbotham

 **Talk Talk Talk**

(Peter knocks at James Morgan's office and enters)	(Peter klopft an James Morgans Büro und tritt ein)
P. Mr Morgan, I believe this is a **personal letter** for you to answer. It was among the correspondence you gave me to attend to.	P. Mr Morgan, ich glaube dies ist ein **persönlicher Brief**, den Sie beantworten sollten. Er lag unter der Korrespondenz, die Sie mir zur Bearbeitung gegeben hatten.
J. Oh Peter, I wanted to talk to you about that. I can't face a meeting with that man Rowbotham. He has really absolutely no interest in ERGO – I think he's just looking for a drinking partner. Could you reply for me, telling him I am **indisposed** for the next couple of weeks.	J. Oh Peter, darüber wollte ich mit Ihnen sprechen. Ich möchte mich auf keinen Fall mit diesem Rowbotham treffen. Er hat absolut kein Interesse an ERGO – ich glaube, er sucht nur jemanden, der mit ihm einen Trinken geht. Könnten Sie für mich antworten und ihm mitteilen, dass ich die nächsten paar Wochen **unabkömmlich** bin?

P. I'll try, but I'd like to show you the letter before I send it ...	P. Ich werde es versuchen, aber ich würde Ihnen den Brief gerne zeigen, bevor ich ihn wegschicke ...

 Dear Mr Rowbotham,

Mr Morgan has asked me to reply to your letter and to your kind invitation to lunch. He is unable to do so himself because he is **unfortunately indisposed**. He much appreciates the interest you showed in the work of ERGO Limited, and he has asked me to forward to you all our available information on the activities of the company. **If you have further questions** on the company, **I shall be happy to answer** them for you.
Mr Morgan joins me in sending greetings,

Yours sincerely,

Peter Brückner,
Assistant Managing Director,
ERGO Limited

 **Talk Talk Talk**

J. **That'll do very well**, Peter. Thank you. But you might have opened yourself to an invitation to lunch with Rowbotham ...	J. **Sehr gut gemacht**, Peter. Allerdings könnten Sie sich jetzt selbst der Gefahr einer Einladung zum Mittagessen von Mr Rowbotham ausgesetzt haben ...
P. I think **I can handle that**, Mr Morgan. Don't worry. That was a comparatively easy one – let's see what's next in the pile ...	P. Ich denke, **damit komme ich klar**, Mr Morgan. Keine Sorge. Das war ein vergleichsweise einfacher Brief – mal sehen, was das Nächste auf dem Stapel ist ...

61. Train Yourself

Sie sind zum Essen mit dem Managing Direktor einer großen Firma, Mr Gerald Green, eingeladen. Nachdem Sie zuerst angenommen haben, stellen Sie fest, dass Sie an dem Tag auf Geschäftsreise außerhalb der Stadt müssen.

Wie würden Sie dementsprechend eine angemessene Absage formulieren?

....
....
....

 **Vocabulary**

berk	Dussel/Idiot (umgangssprachlich)
boast	prahlen (hier: etwas vorweisen können)
catch up on letter-writing	überfälligen Brief schreiben
to couch sth. in polite terms	etwas in höfliche Formulierungen einbetten
dire	grässlich/ hier: weitreichend, unangenehm
to draft	entwerfen
dying to	»sterben« etwas zu sehen/ hören etc.
to end a letter	einen Brief beenden
fine by me	ist mir recht
foxed	verblüfft
generously-proportioned	großzügig geschnitten
to get through	durchkriegen
het-up	aufgeregt/erhitzt über etwas
highly desirable	höchst attraktiv
hype	zielgerichtete Übertreibung/»Hype«

in a state	hier: in einem schlechten Zustand
indisposed	unpässlich, auch unabkömmlich
inquiry	Anfrage
to inquire about	sich erkundigen nach
in the meantime	in der Zwischenzeit
in-tray	(Post-)Eingangskorb
lousy	lausig, verflixt
Make it snappy!	Machen Sie schnell/fix!
marketing push	Marketing-Initiative
missive	Mitteilung
on occasion	bei Gelegenheit
on the spot	vor Ort
open-and-shut	klar und deutlich/ eindeutig
out-tray	(Post-)Ausgangskorb
permanent location	ständiger Wohnsitz
push	Initiative/ Vorstoß (besonders im Marketing)
refrain from	sich zurückhalten
to reply to	beantworten
»sell-by« date	Haltbarkeitsdatum
stacks	Stapel (hier: »stapelweise«)
strike from	ausstreichen/herausnehmen
streamlining	Leistungssteigerung
to tackle some letters	ein paar Briefe durchgehen
to type up	abtippen
urge	inständig bitten, drängen
work up a thirst	»sich durstig arbeiten«
writer's cramp	Schreibkrampf
zilch	Nichts (umgangssprachlich)

Recommendations and complaints
Empfehlungen und Reklamationen

 **Here we go**

Nachdem Peter jede Menge Briefverkehr für seinen Vorgesetzten zu erledigen hatte, konnte er sich schnell auf diesem Gebiet einarbeiten. Aber er muss nun leider der Tatsache ins Auge sehen, dass bei der Korrespondenz die Beschwerdebriefe eine wichtige Rolle spielen und dass der Anlass zu diesen Beschwerden schnellstmöglich aus der Welt geschafft werden muss ...

 Talk Talk Talk

(Peter's office)   (Peters Büro)

P. Well, it's good to find complimentary letters as well as complaints ...

P. Tja, es ist ja schön, neben Beschwerdebriefen auch einmal lobende Post zu bekommen ...

 Dear Sirs/Mesdames,

We are writing to compliment your company on the performance of your software package Accounting 2000 and the efficiency of the post-sales servicing. We first became aware of the program through the recommendation of Philips and Company, who also are highly pleased with the product. At a time when we were considering **subcontracting** a section of our accounting work, the program cut our work-load by a full thirty per cent and our two accountants are now able easily to **keep abreast** with the demands placed on them by our growing business. They are particularly happy with the **user-friendly** nature of the software and had no difficulty adjusting traditional accounting practices to the new technology.

Like you, we have great faith in the future of this new technology and would like to contribute to its progress. As a satisfied ERGO customer,

we can do much to **propagate** Accounting 2000 and would be happy to do so. An appropriate commission on orders completed as a result of our recommendation would be a material encouragement, and may we suggest a meeting to discuss a suitable arrangement of mutual benefit? Our Managing Director, Mr John Prestwick, can make himself available at any time during the next three weeks for such a meeting, which we believe could result in **considerable** advantages for both companies.

Yours faithfully,

Toby Samuels,
Company Secretary **(signing on behalf of Mr Prestwick)**

P. Hmm. This appears to be a problem letter as well as a complimentary one ...

(James Morgan's office)

P. Good morning, Mr Morgan. I have a letter here which I'm not sure how to respond to.

J. Let me see. Hmm, looks like a not-too-**subtle** attempt to make money out of us, doesn't it?

P. It does rather. But it puts us in a difficult position, don't you think?

J. How do you mean?

P. Well, if we refuse, Samuels or Prestwick could theoretically cause **problems** for us. I mean, it would

P. Hmm. Das scheint ein ebenso problematischer wie schmeichelhafter Brief zu sein ...

(James Morgans Büro)

P. Guten Morgen, Mr Morgan. Ich habe hier einen Brief, bei dem ich mir nicht sicher bin, wie ich darauf antworten soll.

J. Lassen Sie mal sehen. Hmm, sieht aus wie ein nicht besonders **subtiler** Versuch, Geld aus uns rauszukitzeln, stimmt's?

P. Ja, so ziemlich. Aber er bringt uns auch in eine **schwierige Lage**, meinen Sie nicht auch?

J. Wie meinen Sie das?

P. Nun ja, wenn wir uns weigern, könnten Samuels oder Prestwick uns theoretisch Ärger machen. Ich

be as easy to **rubbish** Accounting 2000 as to recommend it further, wouldn't it?

J. Rubbish? Your English vocabulary is widening by the day.

P. I have to thank Steve for that!

J. Perhaps Steve has a useful contribution to make here – I do agree with you that a suitable reply to the letter does pose problems.

P. I'll show the letter to Steve, then, and report back ...

meine, es wäre genauso einfach, Accounting 2000 **mies** zu **machen**, wie es weiter zu empfehlen.

J. Mies zu machen? Ihr Wortschatz wird von Tag zu Tag größer.

P. Das verdanke ich Steve!

J. Vielleicht kann Steve hier etwas Nützliches beisteuern – ich stimme mit Ihnen überein, dass eine passende Antwort auf den Brief Probleme aufwirft.

P. Dann zeige ich Steve den Brief und melde mich wieder ...

 Background Information

A matter of words ...
Slang has long crept into business English usage and even into formal business letters. The noun »rubbish« (Müll, Abfall) has given rise to a slang verb, to rubbish, meaning to talk badly about. It's another example of the flexibility of the English language, which accommodates quite easily the movement of words from one category to another (here from noun to verb).

 62. Train Yourself

Die folgenden Sätze sind einem Geschäftsbrief entnommen. Suchen Sie die Wörter aus, die am besten passen.

1. I would like to ▒▒▒▒▒ your company on the ▒▒▒▒▒ of its post-sales servicing.

a. recommend
b. praise
c. commend

a. promise
b. efficiency
c. efficacy

2. Please be ▒▒▒▒ enough as to send us information material as ▒▒▒▒ as possible.

a. gracious
b. generous
c. good

a. promptly
b. timely
c. rapidly

3. We have the ▒▒▒▒ duty to ▒▒▒▒ you that the delivery was not only late but incomplete.

a. unfortunate
b. unhappy
c. unpleasant

a. tell
b. inform
c. remind

4. Unless we ▒▒▒▒ satisfaction in this matter we shall be ▒▒▒▒ to instruct our lawyers to take action.

a. get
b. find
c. obtain

a. compelled
b. forced
c. obliged

 **Talk Talk Talk**

P. Hi Steve, did you read that letter? Do you have any ideas on how to reply to it?	P. Hallo Steve, haben Sie den Brief gelesen? Haben Sie irgend eine Idee, wie man darauf antworten soll?
S. Sure.	S. Sicher.
P. And?	P. Ja und?
S. Well, my first idea is **to junk** it.	S. Na ja, meine erste Idee war, ihn **wegzuschmeißen**.
P. Junk?	P. Wegzuschmeißen?

S. **Bin** it, crumple it up and **chuck** it in the waste-basket.

S. **Wirf** ihn **weg**, knüll ihn zusammen und **schmeiß** ihn in den Mülleimer.

P. No, come on – joking aside, I have to reply to it on Morgan's behalf.

P. Ach nein, kommen Sie schon – Spaß beiseite, ich muss ihn in Morgans Auftrag beantworten.

S. OK, I've drafted something that might **do the trick** ...

S. In Ordnung, ich habe da was ausgetüftelt, das **funktionieren könnte** ...

 Dear Mr Samuels,

Thank you very much for your letter of May 14. We at ERGO Limited **were delighted to hear of your satisfaction** with the accounting program 2000, and we appreciate very much that you took the trouble to write us such a letter of commendation.

Your proposal of commissions on contracts arising from your recommendation is basically acceptable to us, but **we must ask you to elaborate in more detail on what you have in mind**. Our commission policy and structure – in line with most other companies – is fairly complicated. For instance, we distinguish between recommendations and **referrals** which result in signed contracts. Furthermore, the commission structure is affected by the role of our salespeople in following up so-called leads. We would be happy to hear your ideas on this subject and would then be very pleased to take part in a meeting to discuss a further course of action.

Yours faithfully,

Peter Brückner,
Assistant Managing Director

P. So how does that letter solve the problem, Steve?

P. Und wie soll dieser Brief jetzt unser Problem lösen, Steve?

S. In two ways. First, we **blind them with science** – I'm sure they have never before had to distinguish between recommendations and referrals. And then we play the ball straight back into their court. I'd be surprised if we heard anything more.

P. But couldn't their proposal actually have won us more business?

S. Perhaps, but it would also have brought problems. The Accounting 2000 system is so successful **it sells itself. Personal recommendations** help, and they'll come anyway. But when you get into the **grey zone** of **direct referrals** which result in contracts you find yourself in tricky territory – ask any of our sales personnel.

S. In doppelter Hinsicht. Als erstes **verwirren** wir sie mit **Fachbegriffen** – ich bin mir sicher, sie mussten noch niemals zuvor zwischen Empfehlungen und Vermittlungen unterscheiden. Und dann spielen wir den Ball noch direkt zurück in ihr Spielfeld. Es würde mich wundern, wenn wir von denen noch mal irgend etwas hören würden.

P. Aber hätte uns ihre Anfrage nicht ein weiteres Geschäft eingebracht?

S. Vielleicht, aber es hätte uns auch Probleme eingehandelt. Das Accounting 2000-System ist so erfolgreich, dass **es sich** quasi **von selbst verkauft. Persönliche Empfehlungen** sind hilfreich und kommen so oder so. Aber wenn man in die **Grauzone direkter Vermittlungen** gerät, die auf Verträge hinauslaufen, gerät man auf unsicheren Boden – da können Sie jeden der Mitarbeiter aus dem Verkauf fragen.

Korrespondenz

 False Friends

Don't confuse **personal** and **personnel**!
»Personal« is an adjective, which has the general meaning of private, individual, peculiar or proper to a person. »Personnel« is a noun, meaning a group of employees in an enterprise. There is also a difference in pronounciation (pérsonal/personnél).

179

Recommendation and referral ...
If something is recommended its qualities are praised. The praise is a recommendation: »This is the best brand of tea I've found yet – I really do recommend it.«
If something is referred, attention is drawn to it – the act of referring becomes a referral, a common sales expression. »I gave their sales staff several names of companies who had expressed interest in the products on offer – I couldn't have given them a better list of referrals.«

 63. Train Yourself

»Personal« oder »personnel«? »Recommendation« oder »referral«? Wie lautet der richtige Begriff?

1. I told him I wanted to speak to him on a ▩ matter, affecting only him and me.
2. After assessing the ▩ performances of various staff members I told the General Manager I had to speak to him on a ▩ matter.
3. The company is interested only in how employees perform at their job ▩ problems never find their way into our ▩ files.
4. On the strength of the ▩ from this most important client, we asked the Head of Sales to establish contact with the company.
5. Our sales representative in Newcastle has passed on several ▩, which we shall be following up.
6. We thought it was a promising ▩ but when we called there appeared to be no interest.

 Talk Talk Talk

(Peter's Office)

M. Good morning, Peter. How's the letter-writing?

P. Hello, Melissa. It's like **painting the Forth Bridge**. I thought yester-

(Peters Büro)

M. Guten Morgen, Peter. Wie klappt es mit dem Briefe schreiben?

P. Hallo Melissa. Ungefähr so, als müsste ich **die Forth Bridge**

day I'd got the upper hand of the job, and now I've got this pile of **freshly-arrived correspondence** to tackle.

M. Eventually, we'll need an assistant to the Assistant General Manager. Can't James help?

P. **He's off this week** at a managerial symposium. I know he feels uncomfortable about leaving me with this work-load. Not to worry, I'll get through it.

M. Look, if you really do need any help let me know and I'll **assign** you Beryl again.

P. Thanks, Melissa, but I think I'll manage. You gave me some good advice when you said I should divide the correspondence into categories. The only problem is the biggest category seems to be letters of complaint. I had one warm letter of recommendation yesterday, but today the post brought a couple of real **stinkers**. Look at this one ...

anmalen (etwas schier Unmögliches schaffen). Gestern dachte ich noch, ich hätte die Oberhand über den Job gewonnen und jetzt habe ich diesen Stapel **frisch hereingekommener Briefe** zu bewältigen.

M. Am Ende werden wir noch einen Assistenten des Assistenten des leitenden Direktors brauchen. Kann Ihnen James nicht helfen?

P. **Er ist diese Woche außer Haus** auf einem Manager-Symposium. Ich weiß, ihm ist nicht wohl dabei, mich mit so einer Ladung Arbeit allein zu lassen. Aber keine Bange, ich werde schon damit fertig.

M. Passen Sie auf, falls Sie doch noch Hilfe brauchen, sagen Sie Bescheid und ich **teile** Ihnen Beryl noch einmal **zu**.

P. Danke Melissa, aber ich glaube ich kriege das hin. Sie haben mir wirklich einen guten Rat gegeben, als Sie sagten, ich solle die Korrespondenz in Kategorien aufteilen. Das einzige Problem dabei ist, dass die umfangreichste Kategorie die der Beschwerdebriefe zu sein scheint. Gestern hatte ich noch einen netten Brief mit Empfehlungen dabei, aber heute hat mir die Post ein paar richtig **harte Brocken** gebracht. Schauen Sie sich mal den hier an ...

Korrespondenz

Sirs!

More than one month has now passed since we requested you to send us complete information about your AGIT software program. To date, nothing at all has arrived, and unless we hear forthwith from you with complete documentation – i.e. information brochures and catalogues – we shall be compelled to turn elsewhere. We would regret having to do this, particularly in view of the recommendation we have received from two sources who are highly satisfied with the program. Hoping to hear from you without further delay,

We remain, Sirs,

Yours sincerely,

Severn and Sons,
Worcester

M. Looks like one for Steve.	M. Sieht nach einem Fall für Steve aus.
P. I think you're right. Something seems to have gone really wrong in the Sales Department.	P. Ich glaube, Sie haben Recht. Da scheint im Verkauf etwas richtig schief gegangen zu sein.
M. Why don't you call him in – you're theoretically the boss now James is **off base**. Come on, show us what you are made of?	M. Warum rufen Sie ihn nicht an – theoretisch sind Sie der Chef, jetzt wo James **nicht da** ist. Kommen Sie schon – zeigen Sie uns jetzt, woraus Sie geschnitzt sind?
P. Well, not with you around, Melissa.	P. Na ja, nicht so lange Sie hier sind, Melissa.
M. OK, but I'd like to know the outcome of this one.	M. In Ordnung, aber ich möchte wissen, was dabei rauskommt.

P. I'll keep you informed – as they seem to say all the time in this business …
(reaches for the phone) Hi, Steve, can I have a word with you?

P. Ich halte Sie auf dem Laufenden – wie man in diesem Geschäft hier immer zu sagen scheint …
(greift nach dem Hörer) Hallo Steve, kann ich kurz mit Ihnen sprechen?

Background Information

Painting the Forth Bridge …

The Forth Bridge, spanning the estuary of the Forth River in Scotland, was a masterpiece of engineering when built in 1889. The iron bridge is a mile long and its cantilever structure is so large it has to be constantly repainted. No sooner have painters completed the job than they have to start again. Thus if any job of work is compared with painting the Forth Bridge it means the task is virtually endless.

64. Train Yourself

Setzen Sie das folgende Gespräch ins Passiv!
Beispiel: They told us yesterday – we were told by them yesterday.

My company put the order in more than a month ago and they kept us waiting until today for delivery. The courier service delivered the package during our lunch break, so we were not able to check its contents immediately. When our sorting department opened the package they discovered that ATCO had sent the wrong product. We instructed the sorting department to contact you without delay, but your despatch department insisted they had sent the correct item.

Background Information

Commission or rebate?

»Commission« is a contractually-agreed percentage of the value of goods sold, paid to the seller – usually a sales representative – or his or her agent.

> »Rebate« is a reduction in the sales price of any goods, usually made on bulk orders.
>
> In American English, a »**commission house**« is a stockbroker's office that buys and sells stock for customers on a commission basis. A »**commission merchant**« is a person who buys or sells goods on behalf of others, receiving commission for his services.

65. Train Yourself

Commission oder **rebate**? Finden Sie das passende Wort!

1. The company employed him on a ▬▬▬ basis, and he had great success when he offered substantial ▬▬▬ to his customers.
2. On orders in excess of 100,000 dollars we are able to offer a ▬▬▬ of 15%. In view of the fact that our sales representatives are on 10% ▬▬▬, we regard this as a very generous offer.
3. Although he is our top salesman we really can't offer him more than 15% ▬▬▬, particularly as he has been offering customers such a generous ▬▬▬.

Talk Talk Talk

P. Hi, Steve. I've had a letter of complaint that seems to belong in your **department**.

P. Hallo Steve, ich habe hier einen Beschwerdebrief, der zu Ihrer **Abteilung** zu gehören scheint.

S. Let's have a **look-see**! Hmm, something seems to have gone wrong somewhere, doesn't it?

S. Lassen Sie uns **einen Blick darauf werfen**. Hm, sieht aus, als wäre irgendwo irgendetwas schief gegangen, nicht wahr?

P. You're telling me! If we overlook inquiries like this we really could **lose a lot of business**.

P. Was Sie nicht sagen! Wenn wir Anfragen wie diese hier übersehen, könnten wir **eine Menge Aufträge verlieren**.

S. Frankly, I can't recall ever hearing from a company called Severn & Sons. Letters inquiring **about our products** are usually answered **on the turn. I'll check this out.**	S. Ehrlich gesagt kann ich mich nicht daran erinnern, schon mal was von einer Firma namens Severn & Sons gehört zu haben. Briefe, in denen man sich **nach unseren Produkten** erkundigt, werden normalerweise **sofort** beantwortet. **Ich werde dem nachgehen.**
P. Thanks, Steve. Before replying to the letter I would appreciate hearing if we ever got the original inquiry.	P. Danke, Steve. Bevor ich antworte, hätte ich gerne gewusst, ob wir diese Anfrage wirklich jemals bekommen haben.
S. I might have a bit of a problem checking the correspondence received over the past month. But I'm sure Beryl will have no objection helping me out. But we can't rule out the possibility of the letter landing on the old man's desk and staying there. Perhaps he never got around to dealing with it himself.	S. Es dürfte schwierig werden, die Korrespondenz des letzten Monats zu überprüfen. Aber sicher wird Beryl nichts dagegen haben, mir zu helfen. Wir können die Möglichkeit nicht ausschließen, dass der Brief auf dem Schreibtisch des Alten gelandet und dort liegen geblieben ist. Vielleicht ist er nie dazu gekommen, sich selbst damit zu beschäftigen.
P. That's a possibility, of course. But let's start by checking your past correspondence.	P. Das ist natürlich eine Möglichkeit. Aber lassen Sie uns damit anfangen, die alte Korrespondenz durchzusehen.
S. No problem, Peter. I'll be starting on it just as soon as I've had my coffee.	S. Kein Problem, Peter. Ich werde gleich damit anfangen, wenn ich meinen Kaffee ausgetrunken habe.

Korrespondenz

66. Train Yourself

Was ist richtig? Das Gerund, der Infinitiv oder eine Kombination von Präposition und Gerund?

1. I really object *(have)* to do all this work alone.

2. It's no use *(object)* to the amount of work expected.

3. *(object)*, you should have first of all made sure what was expected.

4. I *(write ... inform)* you that the goods you ordered are now ready for dispatch.

5. *(inform)* us that the contract was ready *(sign)* they kept us waiting a further week.

6. We have great pleasure *(inform)* you that your order is ready for you *(collect)*.

7. *(order)* this item from your catalogue we forgot *(give)* the reference number.

8. We would like *(order)* 500 boxes of your company's Christmas crackers *(deliver)* by December 10.

9. *(order)* we would like first of all to know your conditions of sale.

10. We experienced problems *(contact)* you.

11. *(contact)* the company, we made sure we had their correct telephone number and address.

12. In order *(contact)* the company we had to call telephone inquiries to find out the right number.

 **Talk Talk Talk**

(Peter's office)	(Peters Büro)
P. Hello, Beryl! What can I do for you?	P. Hallo Beryl! Was kann ich für Sie tun?
B. Oh, Mr Brückner. **I'm very sorry to have to confess** that I've made a big **blunder**. Mr Morgan dictated to me a reply to that inquiry from Severn & Sons before he left for the seminar. He was in a hurry and I took a **notebook** I don't normally use. Afterwards, my attention was **diverted** by another task, and I quite forgot the letter. It was only when Mr Blackman asked me about it just now that I remembered. I just don't know how I made such a stupid mistake.	B. Oh Mr Brückner. **Es tut mir so Leid, es Ihnen sagen zu müssen**, aber ich habe mir einen großen **Patzer** geleistet. Mr Morgan hat mir eine Antwort auf die Anfrage von Severn & Sons diktiert, bevor er auf das Seminar gegangen ist. Er hatte es eilig und ich habe ein **Notizheft** genommen, das ich normalerweise nicht benutze. Danach ist meine Aufmerksamkeit auf etwas anderes **gelenkt** worden und ich habe den Brief fast vergessen. Erst als Mr Blackman mich eben danach fragte, fiel es mir wieder ein. Ich weiß gar nicht, wie mir so ein dummer Fehler passieren konnte.
P. Well, we all make mistakes, Beryl – I've made enough in my time. The biggest mistake of all is to try to cover one's mistakes up – and that mistake, at least, you did not make. I appreciate you coming so promptly to me, Beryl – we can **make up** a bit of **lost time** now. Where's that letter from Severn & Sons?	P. Tja, wir alle machen Fehler, Beryl – ich habe früher genug gemacht. Der größte Fehler ist es, zu versuchen den Fehler zu vertuschen – und diesen Fehler haben Sie wenigstens nicht gemacht. Ich finde es gut, dass sie sofort zu mir gekommen sind, Beryl – wir können jetzt einen Teil der **verlorenen Zeit wett machen**. Wo ist der Brief von Severn & Sons?

B. Mr Blackman's got it. He's ever so angry.

B. Den hat Mr Blackman. Er ist so was von wütend.

P. Anger isn't going to help us, Beryl. Get the letter – and get your notebook. But the right one, please!

P. Wut hilft uns nicht weiter, Beryl. Holen Sie den Brief – und ihr Notizheft. Aber bitte das richtige!

(Peter dictates a letter to Beryl …)

(Peter diktiert Beryl einen Brief …)

 To Severn & Sons, Worcester
Dear Sirs,

Thank you for your letter of May 18, to which **we are replying as a matter of utmost priority**. **We are extremely concerned** that you have been waiting so long for a reply to your original request. **I must confess** that your original letter was unaccountably overlooked, an oversight for which we must sincerely apologise. I am personally arranging for the immediate dispatch by express post of a complete information package on AGIT. We are very pleased to hear the product has been recommended to you, and we can assure you it is the very best of its kind. **If you have any further queries please do not hesitate to contact me** on my office extension. **I am directing my personal attention to this matter.**

Yours faithfully,

Peter Brückner,
Assistant Managing Director

 67. Train Yourself

Verbinden Sie die Wörter und Ausdrücke mit ähnlicher Bedeutung!

go wrong, query, hesitate, dispatch, overlook, rule out, blunder, check, normally, angry, make up, cover up, promptly, task

mistake, at once, question, malfunction, usually, furious, send, eliminate, job, put together, disguise, delay, fail to observe, examine

 **Talk Talk Talk**

(Peter's office. Melissa enters)	(Peters Büro. Melissa kommt herein)
M. Have your ears been burning?	M. Haben Ihnen die Ohren gebrannt?
P. What do you mean?	P. Was meinen Sie damit?
M. Oh, it's an expression we have when somebody is talking about us.	M. Oh, den Ausdruck benutzen wir, wenn jemand über uns spricht.
P. I'm burning, all right – but burning to get home. I'm **dog-tired**.	P. Ich brenne, das stimmt – aber ich brenne darauf, nach Hause zu kommen. Ich bin **hundemüde**.
M. Peter, your English is now quite amazing. You could pass for an Englishman – well, almost.	M. Peter, Ihr Englisch ist schon ziemlich beeindruckend. Sie könnten als Engländer durchgehen – na ja, fast.
P. I'll keep the almost – I'm German and I don't want to forget it! But why should my ears be on fire?	P. Ich bleibe bei dem fast – ich bin Deutscher und das will ich nicht vergessen. Aber warum sollten meine Ohren in Flammen stehen?
M. Burning, Peter, Burning. You've won a big admirer.	M. Brennen, Peter, brennen. Sie haben eine große Bewunderin dazugewonnen.
P. Well, that's nice to hear. But tell me more. Who?	M. Na, das höre ich gerne. Erzählen Sie mir mehr davon. Wer?
M. Beryl.	M. Beryl.
P. Beryl! But I've just **given** her a **telling off**!	P. Beryl! Aber ich habe ihr gerade eine **Standpauke gehalten**.

Korrespondenz

M. No, that's the point. You didn't. At least, she tells me you didn't. She says you treated her mistake with great understanding.	M. Nein, darum geht es. Das haben Sie nicht getan. Zumindest sagt sie, Sie hätten das nicht getan. Sie sagt, dass Sie mit ihrem Fehler sehr verständnisvoll umgegangen sind.
P. Well, there's no **crying over spilt milk** – now that's something else I've learnt here in England.	P. Na ja, was passiert ist, ist passiert – das ist noch etwas, das ich in England gelernt habe.
M. But you could have made things very difficult for her.	M. Aber Sie hätten ihr große Schwierigkeiten machen können.
P. But why should I? What would that achieve? She won't make the mistake again. And the mistake was quite easy to correct.	P. Warum sollte ich? Was würde das bringen? Sie wird den Fehler nicht noch mal machen. Und dieser Fehler war leicht wieder gutzumachen.
M. Peter, you're on the way to becoming a very good manager!	M. Peter, Sie sind dabei, ein sehr guter Manager zu werden!

 68. Train Yourself

1. Füllen Sie die Lücken in diesem Geschäftsbrief mit den richtigen Wörtern!

Dear Sirs,

I am writing to ▇▇▇ your letter of September 21 and to ▇▇▇ for the ▇▇▇ delay in ▇▇▇ the order ▇▇▇ for the start of the Christmas season. The problem ▇▇▇ in the late ▇▇▇ of important ▇▇▇ from our ▇▇▇ . We have ▇▇▇ a complaint with them and ▇▇▇ for a ▇▇▇ in their quoted price. This, of course, we shall ▇▇▇ directly on to you.
▇▇▇ again for any ▇▇▇ and ▇▇▇ you of our best attention,
Yours ▇▇▇ ,

forward, parts, assuring, pass, hope, suppliers, assuring, lay, arrival, acknowledge, regrettable, apologising, faithfully, discount, apologise, inconvenience, in time, lodged, dispatching.

2. Finden Sie das Gegenteil (Antonym) zum jeweiligen Wort:

1. late	insincere
2. delighted	easy
3. send	early
4. ask	right
5. sincere	depart
6. trust	forget
7. wrong	receive
8. difficult	reply
9. achieve	mistrust
10. remember	disappointed
11. arrive	fail

 Talk Talk Talk

(Peter's office. James Morgan enters)

J. Good morning, Peter! Everything under control?

P. Good morning, Mr Morgan. I think so. We had a couple of problems, problem letters – that kind of thing. But we sorted them out between us.

J. Well done. Don't give me the details – I'm still recovering from that seminar. Three days of inten-

(Peters Büro. Mr Morgan kommt herein)

J. Guten Morgen, Peter! Alles unter Kontrolle?

P. Guten Morgen, Mr Morgan. Ich denke schon. Wir hatten ein paar Probleme, problematische Briefe – und solche Sachen. Aber wir haben das unter uns ausgemacht.

J. Gut gemacht. Erzählen Sie mir keine Einzelheiten – ich erhole mich gerade noch von dem

sive lectures. My head's spinning. Lucy, where's that coffee?

L. Right here, Mr Morgan. My, you look really exhausted – can I get you a **pick-you-up**?

J. Not the kind I really need, Lucy. It's too early for alcohol! The coffee will help. Now, Peter, **I made some useful contacts** at the seminar, and I'd like you to follow up **some of the leads** for me.

P. Certainly, Mr Morgan. How can I help?

J. Two of the directors there represented very big companies and both expressed interest in the Accounting 2000 program. Can you write to them on my behalf giving them **background information**? I told them all I could, but we should get something to them in writing.

P. Certainly, Mr Morgan …
Lucy, I'll have two letters for you on the **dictaphone** later today. Will you have time to type them up for me?

Seminar. Drei Tage voller intensiver Vorträge. Mein Kopf dreht sich. Lucy, wo bleibt der Kaffee?

L. Hier, Mr Morgan. Sie sehen wirklich erschöpft aus, kann ich einen **Muntermacher** besorgen?

J. Nicht die Art, die ich eigentlich bräuchte. Es ist zu früh für Alkohol! Der Kaffee wird helfen. Also, Peter, ich **habe** auf dem Seminar **ein paar nützliche Kontakte geknüpft** und möchte, dass Sie **ein paar der wichtigsten** für mich weiterverfolgen.

P. Natürlich, Mr Morgan. Wie kann ich Ihnen helfen?

J. Zwei der Direktoren dort vertraten sehr große Firmen und beide zeigten Interesse am Accounting 2000-Programm. Könnten Sie ihnen in meinem Auftrag schreiben, um ihnen ein paar **Hintergrundinformationen** zu geben? Ich habe ihnen erzählt, was ich nur konnte, aber wir sollten ihnen etwas Schriftliches zukommen lassen.

P. Natürlich, Mr Morgan …
Lucy, später habe ich auf dem **Diktiergerät** noch zwei Briefe für Sie. Werden Sie dann Zeit haben, sie für mich zu tippen?

L. No problem, Peter. I'll keep the afternoon free for you.

L. Kein Problem, Peter. Ich halte mir den Nachmittag für Sie frei.

P. Well, here goes …

P. Also, los geht's …

 The first letter is to:

Mr Timothy Rogers,
Managing Director,
Newland Brokers Limited,
Basingstoke (I'll let you have the exact address later, Lucy!)

Dear Mr Rogers,

Our Managing Director, Mr James Morgan, has asked me to write to you to say how pleased he was to make your acquaintance at the managerial seminar last week in Brighton. He noted your interest in our software program Accounting 2000, which is my direct area of responsibility. Hence, **it is my pleasure to write to you** with a description of the program and some excerpts from the many testimonials and recommendations we have had from satisfied clients.
These include a letter from the North of England Land Recovery Service which is employing the Accounting 2000 system in every one of its 22 offices. The law company Spinks, Grobat and Renny has just installed the system in 12 of its subsidiary offices nationwide. You will find their testimonials among others in **Appendix** 2. The description of the program itself is attached as Appendix 1. Apart from these, we are taking the liberty of sending you ERGO's documentation on the Accounting 2000 system and our range of brochures.
If you have any further questions on the system please do not hesitate to call me on my direct line, or to write to me at the above address. Mr Morgan asks me to add his sincere greetings.

Yours sincerely,

Peter Brückner,
Assistant Managing Director,
ERGO Limited

P. The second letter, Lucy, is to Mr Thomas Rampton, of Rampton Industrial Machines. You'll find the address on his **letter-head** ...

P. Lucy, der zweite Brief geht an Mr Thomas Rampton von Rampton Industrial Machines. Die Adresse finden Sie auf dem **Briefkopf** ...

Dear Mr Rampton,

Our Managing Director, Mr James Morgan, has asked me to write to you **to express his appreciation for the extremely complimentary remarks you made to him**, at the managerial seminar, on the Accounting 2000 software program which we market.

He was sorry he did not have the opportunity or time to give you a full description of the program, and consequently he has asked me to send you the relevant information. Apart from documentation and brochures, I am sending you as **appendices** to this letter a brief outline of the program and its uses, and excerpts from letters of recommendation and testimonials. I have also taken the liberty of asking our Sales Department to instruct our representative in Derby to call you and, if you wish, make an appointment to make you personally more closely acquainted with the program. **Should you have any further questions or require additional information do not hesitate to contact me on my personal extension.**

Mr Morgan joins me in sending sincere greetings,

Yours sincerely,

Peter Brückner,
Assistant Managing Director

Background Information

Appendix - isn't that a useless body part?

»Appendix« has several meanings – and not only in the medical field. Apart from describing the small appendage of the large intestine, »appendix« means anything added – in business correspondence it describes any addition to the main letter, such as an additional sheet of paper containing extra information. The plural is appendices.

> **Recommendation or testimonial?**
> A recommendation in favour of a product can be either written or verbal - a testimonial is always in written form.

 69. Train Yourself

Setzen Sie in den folgenden Sätzen die richtige Form ein:

1. The company sent a ▩▩▩▩ placing on record its satisfaction with the product.
2. Acting on your ▩▩▩▩ I wrote to the company asking for further information.
3. Thank you for the ▩▩▩▩, which we have framed and put in a place of prominence at headquarters.

 Talk Talk Talk

(Peter's office. A knock on the door)

P. Come in – oh, it's you Chip. What can I do for you?

C. I had to pick up this letter from Torrence and Partners in Cheapside. They said it was important – I'd give it to Mr Morgan, but he isn't here. Lucy said you should handle it.

P. She's right. I'm handling most of Mr Morgan's correspondence, anyway. Let's see what this one is about.

C. Anything else, Mr Brückner?

(Peter Büro. Es klopft an der Tür)

P. Herein – ach, Sie sind es, Chip. Was kann ich für Sie tun?

C. Ich sollte diesen Brief von Torrence and Partners in Cheapside abholen. Sie sagten mir, es wäre wichtig – ich wollte ihn Mr Morgan geben, aber er ist nicht da. Lucy sagte, Sie sollten sich darum kümmern.

P. Sie hat Recht. Ich kümmere mich sowieso um den Großteil von Mr Morgans Korrespondenz. Lassen Sie uns mal sehen, worum es hier geht.

C. Ist sonst noch was, Mr Brückner?

P. Yes, Chip – be a good chap and run out for a couple of sandwiches for me. I'll have to lunch at my desk today. And this may be one of the reasons, if it's that urgent ...

P. Ja, Chip, seien Sie ein netter Kerl und holen Sie mir ein paar Sandwiches. Ich werde heute am Schreibtisch zu Mittag essen müssen. Und das hier könnte einer der Gründe dafür sein, wenn es schon so dringend ist ...

 Dear Sirs/Mesdames,

We are taking the liberty of returning to you by your company courier the Trigger software package which you delivered one week ago. There appears to be a fundamental fault which our computer specialist has been unable to rectify. We had no problem installing it but then had difficulty with the various configurations, which appear to be incompatible with our hardware. **We would be very pleased** if you checked the problem and informed us of the results of your investigation.
You will understand that we are withholding payment until the problem is solved.

Yours faithfully,

Charles Jospin,
p.p. Torrence and Partners

 Background Information

> **p.p.** at the foot of a letter is an abbreviation from the Latin »per procurationem«, meaning »officially acting for ...«
> **pp** without the full-stops is an abbreviation for the word »pages«.
> In informal correspondence, a **PS** (= postscript; an abbreviation of the Latinism Post Script) precedes an addition to the letter following the signature ...
> With very best wishes,
> John
> **PS** I forgot to tell you that Henry and Maud are getting married in the summer.

And now for some other »P« abbreviations you will meet in official correspondence:
p.a. – per annum, or annually, yearly
PA – Personal Assistant
p.c. or **pct** – per cent
pd – paid
p/e – price-earnings ratio
PO – Post Office
PPS – Additional postscript (Post Post Script), used when an additional topic is addressed following the signature at the end of a letter
PR – Public Relations
PRO – Public Relations Officer
pro tem (abbreviation of the Latinism pro tempore) – for the time being (»He was appointed director pro tem«)
proximo – Latinism used in naming dates, meaning »of the next month« – (»The goods will be delivered on the 6th proximo, precisely on the 6th of March«). The opposite is »ultimo« – »The goods were delivered on the 20th ultimo« (meaning the preceding month).

 70. Train Yourself

Der Schreiber des folgenden Briefes scheint die Abkürzungen, die er benutzt hat, durcheinander gebracht zu haben. Können Sie die richtigen Formen finden?

Dear Jack,

I have some good news for you. I've just been appointed *PO* of a big *PPS* company here in the city. I don't yet know what I'll be paid *PA*, but *pro forma* - or for the time being as they say - I'm happy. I am assured of a *p.c.* rise of 10 *p/e*, though. Give me a call some time and I'll tell you more.

Your good friend,
Jim

pps Can you make lunch next Tuesday?

 **Vocabulary**

appendix - appendices (pl.)	Anhang
to assign	unterzeichnen
to be off-base	nicht da sein; außer Haus sein
to bin	weg werfen
to blind with science	jdn. mit großen Worten beeindrucken
blunder	(schwerer) Fehler
brief	kurz
to chuck	zerknüllen
considerable	beachtlich
to divert	ablenken
dog-tired	hundemüde
do the trick	funktionieren
to give a telling off	eine Standpauke halten
grey zone	Grauzone
incompatible	unverträglich/ unvereinbar
to junk	wegwerfen
to keep abreast of	Schritt halten mit
letter-head	Briefkopf
look-see	kurzer Blick
to make up lost time	verlorene Zeit aufholen
not to cry over spilt milk	»was passiert ist, ist passiert«
on the turn	sofort, umgehend
pick-you-up	Muntermacher
to propagate	verbreiten
to rectify	richtig stellen
referral	Vermittlung
to rubbish	mies/schlecht machen
sign on behalf of	im Auftrag von ... unterschreiben
some of the leads	ein paar der Wichtigsten
stinker	harter Brocken
to subcontract	Unteraufträge vergeben
= to farm out	
subtle	subtil/feinsinnig
testimonial	Anerkennung/(positive) Referenz
user-friendly	benutzerfreundlich

Offers
Angebote

 Here we go

Neben den alltäglichen Dingen, die bei der Firmenkorrespondenz anfallen, wie Anfragen und Beschwerden, werden auf dem Postweg natürlich auch wichtige geschäftliche Verbindungen angebahnt. Peter bekommt von James Morgan die Aufgabe übertragen, sich um einen bedeutenden Franchise-Vertrag von ERGO Limited mit einem amerikanischen Softwareanbieter zu kümmern. Wird Peter es schaffen, diesen verantwortungsvollen Auftrag zur Zufriedenheit aller zu bewältigen?

 **Talk Talk Talk**

(James Morgan's office)

J. (speaks into telephone) Peter, could you step into my office, please!

P. (enters) Good morning, Mr Morgan. What can I do for you?

J. I've been asked by **head office** in America to inquire into the possibility of obtaining a franchise for the United States for a new software product which Newcom in Manchester **has just brought out**. It was favourably written about in the American magazine *Computer World*. We might be too late, nevertheless head office wants us to go ahead and approach Newcom. I'm

(James Morgans Büro)

J. (ins Telefon) Peter, könnten Sie bitte in mein Büro kommen?

P. (tritt ein) Guten Morgen, Mr Morgan. Was kann ich für Sie tun?

J. Ich wurde vom **Hauptbüro** in Amerika darum gebeten, herauszufinden, ob es möglich ist, die amerikanischen Franchise-Lizenzen einer neuen Software zu erwerben, die Newcom in Manchester **gerade herausgebracht hat**. In dem amerikanischen Magazin *Computer World* wurde sehr positiv darüber berichtet. Wir kommen damit vielleicht schon zu spät, aber das

really under pressure this week, therefore I'd like you to take this one over for me.	Hauptbüro möchte trotzdem, dass wir es versuchen und Newcom ansprechen. Ich bin diese Woche wirklich ziemlich im Stress, deswegen hätte ich gern, dass Sie die Sache für mich übernehmen.
P. Certainly, Mr Morgan.	P. Natürlich, Mr Morgan.
J. Head office faxed us the *Computer World* article. You'll find everything you need there – even the address of Newcom and the name of their **Project Manager**. I'd be glad if you could get on to it right away ...	J. Das Hauptbüro hat uns den Artikel aus der *Computer World* gefaxt. Sie finden darin alles, was Sie brauchen – selbst die Adresse von Newcom und den Namen ihres **Projektmanagers**. Es wäre schön, wenn Sie sich gleich darum kümmern könnten ...

 71. Train Yourself

»Therefore« oder »nevertheless«?
Setzen Sie das richtige Wort in die folgenden Sätze ein!

1. We experienced delays in deliveries from our suppliers, ▓▓▓▓ we were unable to complete your order in time.
2. Our production line let us down badly, ▓▓▓▓ we shall do everything possible to get the goods to you by the end of next week.
3. We regret that we have not yet received payment for the last shipment, ▓▓▓▓ we are not yet processing your second order.
4. Although we are far from happy with the performance of the C-100 model, we shall ▓▓▓▓ continue to work with it during its trial period.

Background Information

»**Nevertheless**« is often – and particularly in written English – replaced by »nonetheless« or (but more rarely) »notwithstanding«.
»**Notwithstanding**« has the same meaning as despite – but has the

distinction of normally »standing« at the start of the sentence ...
Notwithstanding (or despite) his objections, the company went ahead with its rationalization program. The company went ahead with its rationalization program despite his objections.
»Notwithstanding« is very rarely used in spoken English but is nevertheless often found in formal business correspondence.

 Talk Talk Talk

(Peter dictates a letter to Newcom) (Peter diktiert einen Brief an Newcom)

P. This letter is to Mr Trevor Payne, Project Manager of Newcom Technology – Lucy, you have the address on the fax.

P. Dieser Brief geht an Mr Trevor Payne, Projektmanager von Newcom Technology – Lucy, die Adresse finden Sie auf dem Fax.

 Dear Mr Payne,

Our attention was caught by the article on your company's software program »Instantweb«, which was carried by the American magazine Computer World. ERGO Limited markets in the United States and Britain a wide range of software products, including a successful newspaper copy-editing program which might well be complemented by »Instantweb«. In combination, the two programs could contribute to an easier and more rapid access to the Internet by newspaper editorial offices.
Our head office in the United States was particularly interested in this possibility and we **have been asked to approach you** with a view to obtaining the franchise for »Instantweb« in the United States. If the franchise is still available, we would be pleased to discuss with you all relevant details with a view to reaching a business contract of benefit to both enterprises.
I look forward to hearing from you,
Yours sincerely,

Peter Brückner,
Assistant Managing Director

Background Information

»Franchise« or **»licence«**?

A »franchise« is an official, contractual authorization to sell a company's products or services in a specified region or country.
A »licence« is the document of authorization.

72. Train Yourself

1. Im vorhergehenden Brief hat Peter einige Schlüsselsätze in der Passivform geschrieben. Das Aktiv ist jedoch dem Passiv immer vorzuziehen – also helfen Sie ihm und korrigieren Sie seinen Brief!

....

....

....

2. Die Konjunktionen *and, but, because, since.*

Verbinden Sie jeden der folgenden Satzteile damit!

1. We intend placing an order for items 1, 3 and 6 ▬▬▬▬ first of all we would like to see your full price list.
2. We would like to order 100 units ▬▬▬▬ look forward to a prompt delivery.
3. We regret having to return the delivered goods ▬▬▬▬ they arrived in a spoilt condition.
4. We regretfully have to cancel the contract ▬▬▬▬ you failed to honour an important clause.
5. We would normally have cancelled the contract ▬▬▬▬ we recognize you acted in good faith.
6. Thank you for your prompt reply ▬▬▬▬ we look forward to a fruitful co-operation.

Talk Talk Talk

(James Morgan's office. Peter enters)

P. Good morning, Mr Morgan. I'm afraid the reply from Newcom doesn't look very promising.

J. Let me see the letter ...

(James Morgans Büro. Peter tritt ein)

P. Guten Morgen, Mr Morgan. Ich fürchte, die Antwort von Newcom hört sich nicht sehr viel versprechend an.

J. Zeigen Sie mir mal den Brief ...

 Dear Mr Brückner,

Thank you for your letter of May 21. **We were naturally pleased to hear that** our new software program »Instantweb« had caught not only the attention of »Computer World« but of your company, too.

Because of the »Computer World« publicity, we have received approaches from various companies and are at this time **involved in negotiations** with some of them. Nonetheless, we are not ruling out your company, and would certainly welcome your more detailed proposals on a possible franchise for the United States.

Yours sincerely,

Trevor Payne

J. Hmm, how do we **take it from here**?

P. Well, as I see it, we have to convince them that we are the right company for the franchise. But how?

J. Hmm, wie sollen wir jetzt **weiter vorgehen**?

P. Nun ja, so wie ich das sehe, müssen wir sie überzeugen, dass wir die richtige Firma für ein Franchise sind. Aber wie?

J. Peter, let me think this one over, and I'll come back to you on it ...

J. Peter, lassen Sie mich über diese Sache nachdenken, ich komme dann wieder auf Sie zu ...

 73. Train Yourself

1. »Cost« or »price«? Füllen Sie die Lücken mit den richtigen Wörtern!

1. Would you please send us your current ▓▓▓▓ list.
2. We can't afford to pay such a high ▓▓▓▓.
3. Production ▓▓▓▓ were too high for the project to be a success.
4. We were able to keep ▓▓▓▓ stable by cutting production ▓▓▓▓.
5. The ▓▓▓▓ is as stated. It would push our ▓▓▓▓ to an intolerable level if we cut ▓▓▓▓ any further.
6. If the ▓▓▓▓ is right, my recommendation is to buy. The ▓▓▓▓ to you is low compared to what you can make on the deal.

2. Peter muss drei dringliche Geschäftsbriefe beantworten. Beachten Sie dabei besonders den Gebrauch der Wörter »consequent« und »consequence«.

1.
Dear Sirs/Mesdames,

Our accountants inform me that a mistake in our costing department has resulted in a credit in your favour amounting to $2,560. **Consequently**, we have pleasure in sending you forthwith a cheque in this amount ...

2.
Dear John,

Our conversation over dinner last night has given me food (no pun intended!) for thought. As a **consequence**, I'd like to put to you the following business proposition ...

3.
Sirs,

I have the unpleasant task of informing you that your company's failure to live up to the terms of the contract will have legal **consequences** ...

Finden Sie nun die richtige Form im folgenden Lückentext:

1. May we remind you of the legal ▓▓▓▓ that may arise as a result of your actions?
2. We have waited two weeks for a reply to our letter, ▓▓▓▓ we have no alternative but to look elsewhere.
3. ▓▓▓▓ to our last letter, and as a result of your latest offer, we are now able to place an order for 2,000 items.
4. We were most impressed by the results of the pilot project, ▓▓▓▓ we have pleasure in placing an immediate order.

 False Friends

The English word »**consequent**« has nothing at all in common with German »konsequent«. »Consequent« and »**consequence**« both describe anything that logically follows something else, the result of a previous happening or action.
So, in the above example, numbered 1, Peter writes that as a consequence – as a result – of an error in the costing department, his company is able to repay a sum of $2,500. In example 2, he informs John that as a consequence – as a result – of their dinner conversation he is able to make a business proposition. In example 3, he informs a company that failure to live up to contractual obligations will have legal consequences – will result in legal action.

 Talk Talk Talk

(John Morgan's office)

J. Peter, I think the only way to tackle the Newcom issue is to make a **personal visit**. I don't

(John Morgans Büro)

J. Peter, ich glaube, der einzige Weg, diese Newcom-Geschichte richtig anzugehen, ist ein **persön-**

| think any amount of letter-writing is going to solve this one. | **licher Besuch**. Ich denke, ein noch so großer Haufen Briefe wird uns in dieser Angelegenheit nicht weiterbringen. |

P. I **tend to** agree, but who should attempt it – Steve?

P. Ich **neige dazu**, Ihnen zuzustimmen, aber wer soll das versuchen – Steve?

J. Steve's a good **sales director**. But this isn't a sale – it's a much more complicated matter.

J. Steve ist ein guter **Verkaufsleiter**. Aber hier geht es nicht um einen Verkauf – das ist eine viel kompliziertere Angelegenheit.

P. So who have we got?

P. Wen haben wir denn sonst noch?

J. You, Peter. You!

J. Sie, Peter. Sie!

P. Me. A **franchise contract**? I hardly know what a franchise is!

P. Mich? Für einen **Franchise-Vertrag**? Ich weiß ja kaum, was ein Franchise ist!

J. I know we haven't spent a lot of time together, but I have observed one thing – you are very quick to learn, Peter. I'll give you three days to **swot** this subject up – and then Newcom is all yours!

J. Ich weiß, dass wir uns noch nicht lange kennen, aber eins ist mir aufgefallen – Sie lernen schnell, Peter. Ich gebe Ihnen drei Tage, um sich in dieser Sache **schlau zu machen** – und dann gehört Newcom Ihnen!

P. Oh, no! And if I don't succeed?

P. Oh, nein! Und wenn ich keinen Erfolg habe?

J. Steve tells me he has an opening in sales!

J. Steve hat mir gesagt, er hätte noch eine offene Stelle im Verkauf!

74. Train Yourself

»Swot« ist ein Slang-Ausdruck und bedeutet »intensiv lernen«. Finden Sie für die nun folgenden Slang-Ausdrücke und umgangssprachlichen Wörter formellere Begriffe:

1. There wasn't much to learn about the product. I got the **gist** of it in no time.
2. If you give me the **gen** I'll read up on the product at home tonight.
3. Give me the papers. I'd like to **take a look-see at** them.
4. I gave him the **low-down** on the terms of the contract.
5. Let's **gen** ourselves **up** on the background of the company before the meeting.
6. Just give me the **guts** of what the report has to say.

Alternativen:
examine, basic facts, information, inform, essence, inside information.

 Talk Talk Talk

(Peter's office)

P. I have an important letter for you, Lucy. Could you bring your notebook – and a cup of your excellent tea, if it's not too much trouble.

L. Certainly, Peter. I'll be right there …

P. The letter is to Mr Trevor Payne, Project Manager of Newcom Technology, Birmingham. You have the exact address **on file**, Lucy …

(Peters Büro)

P. Ich muss Ihnen einen wichtigen Brief diktieren, Lucy. Könnten Sie bitte Ihr Notizbuch mitbringen – und vielleicht eine Tasse Tee, wenn es nicht zu viel Mühe macht.

L. Natürlich, Peter. Ich komme sofort …

P. Der Brief geht an Mr Trevor Payne, Projektmanager von Newcom Technology, Birmingham. Die exakte Adresse haben Sie **in Ihren Unterlagen**, Lucy …

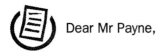 Dear Mr Payne,

Thank you for your letter of May 26. **We fully understand** that other companies have also expressed interest in the »Instantweb« program, **but we are confident that we are best placed to give it the fullest market exposure** in the United States. We have various ideas on how this could be achieved within the framework of a franchise agreement, and I would be very pleased to explain these to you in a personal meeting. **I would be only too happy** to travel to your offices in Manchester on any day of your choosing and shall keep my diary free for the next two or three weeks in anticipation of a favourable reply from you.
Looking forward to hearing from you,

Yours sincerely,

Peter Brückner

P. Lucy, could you give a copy of that to Mr Morgan, and if he has no alterations to make then could you send it today by express post to Newcom?	P. Lucy, könnten Sie Mr Morgan eine Kopie davon geben und den Brief, wenn er keine Änderungen mehr vornehmen will, noch heute per Express an Newcom schicken?
L. Certainly, Peter.	L. Aber sicher, Peter.
(James Morgan enters Peter's office)	(James Morgan betritt Peters Büro)
J. Peter, the letter is fine. I've asked Lucy to send it right away. Now, I want to give you this – it's **the current annual report** of Newcom. It will **put** you **in the picture** – it's always best to know as much as you can about the company you're dealing with. If there's anything that's new to you or that	J. Peter, der Brief ist sehr gut. Ich habe Lucy gebeten, ihn sofort abzuschicken. Jetzt möchte ich Ihnen dies hier geben – das ist der **aktuelle Jahresbericht** von Newcom. Er wird Sie **ins Bild setzen** – es ist immer gut, so viel wie möglich über die Firma zu wissen, mit der man es zu tun hat. Wenn es irgendetwas

you can't understand just let me know.

gibt, das neu für Sie ist oder das Sie nicht verstehen, lassen Sie es mich einfach wissen.

Background Information

An »**annual report**« is a full account of a company's activities over the previous year. It contains a balance sheet showing income, expenditure and the value of company assets. The final balance shows either a profit or loss and calculates a dividend payable to the company's shareholders. The annual report is presented at the annual meeting of shareholders, at which company officers also stand for re-election.

 75. Train Yourself

Peter ist sich immer noch nicht so ganz sicher, wie er mit den Begriffen aus dem Jahresbericht von Newcom umgehen soll. Können Sie ihm helfen, die Bedeutung der folgenden Wörter richtig zuzuordnen?

1. balance sheet
2. board of directors
3. chief executive
4. current assets
5. multinational
6. profit and loss account
7. subsidiaries
8. supervisory board

a. A statement showing a company's expenditure and income over a period of usually one year.
b. A company's total wealth, in terms not only of cash, cheques and payments due, but property, equipment, stocks of goods, raw materials, etc.
c. A body of elected officers who run the company and who stand for re-election at the annual meeting.
d. A company's additional, semi-autonomous offices, usually distributed in various different countries.

e. When a company has such a network of offices abroad it is referred to in this way.
f. A financial statement showing a company's income, expenditures, assets and debts.
g. A small group of officers whose job is to overlook the work of the Board of Directors.
h. The head of a company's Board of Directors.

 Background Information

»**Net**« or »**Gross**«?

In financial transactions and statements, »net« describes an amount entirely free of taxes, deductions, expenses etc. A company's net profit, for instance, is the amount of income remaining after deduction of all costs and expenses incurred in the production process.

»Gross« has the opposite meaning, describing the total of anything, the result before deductions. A company's **gross profit**, for instance, is the total amount earned before taxes and other deductions.

And **gross national product**? That's the annual total value of goods produced and services provided by an individual country. The gross national product of South Africa in the year following the fall of apartheid there was equivalent to 75 billion American dollars.

This figure (usually abbreviated to GNP) is often expressed in »**per capita**« (»per head«) terms. South Africa has a population of 31 million – therefore the GNP »per capita« in the relevant period was equivalent to 2,400 American dollars.

 **Talk Talk Talk**

(The offices of ERGO Limited)

L. Good morning, Peter. What a lovely day! Perhaps summer really is on the way. I have **a stack of** post for you!

(In den Büros von ERGO Limited)

L. Guten Morgen, Peter. Was für ein wunderbarer Tag! Vielleicht wird es wirklich langsam Sommer. Ich habe **einen ganzen Haufen** Post für Sie!

P. Thanks, Lucy. A pot of tea would also be welcome. And do you have any more of those biscuits your sister makes?	P. Danke, Lucy. Eine Tasse Tee wäre mir auch sehr recht. Und haben Sie vielleicht noch ein paar von diesen Keksen, die Ihre Schwester macht?
L. I kept some specially for you. Now you just take this **bundle** off to your office and I'll bring you tea **in a jiffy.**	L Ich habe extra für Sie ein paar aufgehoben. Nehmen Sie diesen **Packen** hier einfach mit in Ihr Büro und ich bringe Ihnen **in Windeseile** Ihren Tee.
P. Lucy, you're a treasure.	P. Lucy, Sie sind ein Schatz.
(Melissa enters) M. *»Schatz«* is the word! Don't you listen to his sweet words, Lucy. He's a German charmer!	(Melissa tritt ein) M. Ein »Schatz«, ja? Hören Sie nicht auf Ihn, Lucy. Er ist ein deutscher Charmeur!
P. I **met my match** when I tried to charm you, though, Melissa!	P. Ich habe **mir die Zähne ausgebissen**, als ich versucht habe, meinen Charme bei Ihnen wirken zu lassen, Melissa!
M. Well, perhaps I can't make tea like Lucy. I certainly can't make biscuits like her sister!	M. Tja, vielleicht kann ich nicht so gut Tee kochen wie Lucy. Und ganz sicher backe ich nicht so gute Kekse wie ihre Schwester!
P. But you can serve up a marvellous English roast. Steve and I really enjoyed our meal with you.	P. Aber dafür servieren Sie einen wunderbaren englischen Braten. Steve und ich haben das Essen mit Ihnen wirklich genossen.
M. Well, if you're a good boy we might just repeat the experience. Now, off to work with you!	M. Nun ja, wenn Sie immer schön brav sind, können wir dieses Erlebnis ja noch einmal wiederholen. Und jetzt an die Arbeit!

Korrespondenz

P. I'm just sorting my post now – here's a reply from Newcom ...

P. Ich sortiere gerade meine Post – hier ist eine Antwort von Newcom ...

 Dear Mr Brückner,

Thank you for your letter of June 2. I would be very happy to meet you at our offices here in Manchester on any day convenient to you next week to discuss franchise possibilities. **I would suggest a morning meeting** to allow us to continue the discussions over lunch and possibly into the afternoon. You would naturally be our guest for the entire day.
May I suggest that you call my secretary on the above extension to fix a day. If you require hotel accommodation in Manchester she will also be glad to accommodate your requirements.
Looking forward to meeting you and to fruitful discussions,

Yours sincerely,

Trevor Payne

 76. Train Yourself

Multiple Choice. Finden Sie die Lösung, die am besten passt:

1. My secretary will be glad to ▬▬▬▬▬ an appointment for you.
a. find
b. arrange
c. date

2. If you ▬▬▬▬▬ hotel accommodation please don't hesitate to let us know.
a. require
b. seek
c. demand

3. We would be very glad to ▓▓▓▓▓ your flight from London to Birmingham.
a. organize
b. find
c. book

 Talk Talk Talk

(Peter's office)

P. Lucy, could you put me through to Newcom, please? You have the number.

L. Certainly, Peter. Just one moment.

P. Hello, Newcom? **Could you put me through** please to extension 210. Hello, is that Mr Payne's office? It's Peter Brückner of ERGO Limited here. Mr Payne wrote to me to suggest that I make an appointment for a meeting next week. Next Thursday? Fine. At 11 AM? Yes, that suits me very well. No, I don't need hotel accommodation. I shall return to London the same day. Should I fax you **confirmation of my travel arrangements**? No? I'll do it all the same – I like to have these things on file. But thank you very much for all your help. I look forward to my visit to Newcom …

(Peters Büro)

P. Lucy, könnten Sie mich bitte zu Newcom durchstellen? Die Nummer haben Sie.

L. Natürlich, Peter. Einen Moment bitte.

P. Hallo, Newcom? **Könnten Sie mich bitte** mit der Durchwahl -210 **verbinden**? Hallo, bin ich verbunden mit Mr Paynes Büro? Hier spricht Peter Brückner von ERGO Limited. Mr Payne hat mir geschrieben, um einen Termin für die nächste Woche vorzuschlagen. Nächsten Donnerstag? Sehr schön. Um 11 Uhr? Ja, das passt mir sehr gut. Nein, ich brauche keine Hotelreservierung. Ich reise noch am selben Tag nach London zurück. Soll ich Ihnen eine **Bestätigung für die Details meiner Reise zufaxen**? Nein? Ich tue es trotzdem – ich habe so etwas immer gern schriftlich. Aber vielen Dank für Ihre Hilfe. Ich freue mich schon auf meinen Besuch bei Newcom …

Korrespondenz

Fax to:

Mr Trevor Payne,
Projects Manager,
Newcom,

Manchester

From:
Peter Brückner,
Assistant Managing Director
ERGO Limited,
London
Fax Nr. 003
Date: 04.06.2000

Dear Mr Payne,

This fax serves as confirmation that I will be travelling to Manchester next Thursday morning for a meeting with you at Newcom headquarters at 11 AM. Thank you very much for finding the time for a meeting, to which I look forward very much.

Yours truly,

Peter Brückner

 77. Train Yourself

Einladungen – Was gehört in die Lücken?

1. If it is ▬▬▬ for you, may I ▬▬▬ you for tea at the Dorchester next Tuesday afternoon at 4?
2. To ▬▬▬ the 25th anniversary of the company, we are ▬▬▬ all employees to a champagne ▬▬▬ in the conference room next Wednesday at 12 noon.

3. I would be very _____ if you and Mrs Smith accepted our _____ to dinner on the 25th. Cocktails at 7 PM.
4. Thank you for your _____ invitation to _____ the concert and supper-reception. My wife and I are very _____ to accept.
5. May we have the _____ of your _____ at dinner at the Ritz next Saturday?
6. Thank you so much for the invitation, but I'm _____ I am otherwise _____ on that evening.

honour, inviting, invitation, pleased, engaged, convenient, glad, kind, company, mark, reception, attend, afraid, invite.

 **Talk Talk Talk**

(Peter's office, John Morgan enters)

(Peters Büro, John Morgan tritt ein)

J. Well, Peter, all **geared up** for the Manchester meeting?

J. Nun, Peter, **alles bereit** für das Meeting in Manchester?

P. I'm as ready as I ever shall be, Mr Morgan.

P. Ich bin so bereit, wie ich nur sein kann, Mr Morgan.

J. Any questions before you set off? You've got an early start tomorrow and we won't be seeing each other before then. I have to leave the office in ten minutes.

J. Noch irgendwelche Fragen, bevor Sie losfahren? Sie müssen morgen früh los und wir werden uns davor nicht mehr sehen. Ich muss in zehn Minuten das Büro verlassen.

P. No, I think I shall be all right, Mr Morgan.

P. Nein, ich glaube, ich komme schon klar, Mr Morgan.

J. Then good luck, Peter. See you the day after tomorrow ...

J. Dann viel Glück, Peter. Wir sehen uns dann übermorgen ...

(Melissa enters after a while)

(Etwas später tritt Melissa ein)

M. You're off to Manchester tomorrow, then, Peter?	M. Sie brechen also morgen nach Manchester auf, Peter?
P. That's right. Wish me luck!	P. Stimmt. Wünschen Sie mir Glück!
M. I'll do better than that. Come on, I'll buy you one at the *Nag's Head* – one for the road.	M. Ich werde noch etwas viel Besseres tun. Kommen Sie, ich lade Sie auf einen Drink im *Nag's Head* ein – einen für unterwegs.
P. Actually, I might just have two – but that's very kind of you, Melissa. I accept **unconditionally**. But what about Steve?	P. Vielleicht nehme ich sogar zwei – aber das ist wirklich sehr nett von Ihnen, Melissa. Ich nehme **ohne zu zögern** an. Aber was ist mit Steve?
M. No, I want you all to myself for half an hour Peter – I want to make sure you're prepared for what awaits you in Manchester. I've had some dealings in the past with Newcom. They're tough customers.	M. Nein, ich möchte Sie für ein halbes Stündchen ganz für mich allein haben, Peter – ich möchte sicher sein, dass Sie auf das, was Sie in Manchester erwartet, auch gut vorbereitet sind. Ich hatte in der Vergangenheit schon öfter mit Newcom zu tun. Das sind schwierige Kunden.

 78. Train Yourself

1. James Morgan befragt Peter. Setzen Sie in die Fragen jeweils »some« oder »any« ein:

1. Did you make ▨▨▨▨ progress at the meeting?
2. Could you give me ▨▨▨▨ advice on how to tackle the problem?
3. I could only find ▨▨▨▨ entries in an old calendar.
4. I'd like to open the meeting to a general discussion of the issue and ask if there are ▨▨▨▨ questions.
5. Did the theatre production give you ▨▨▨▨ pleasure at all?

6. I was able to get ▬▬▬ meaning out of it.
7. Is there ▬▬▬ sense at all in that book? Well, I did find ▬▬▬ things of interest.
8. ▬▬▬ of the points in his lecture I found quite provocative.

2. Wählen Sie nun zwischen »something« oder »anything«:

1. Have you ▬▬▬ on your mind?
2. Do you have ▬▬▬ at all in that forgetful head of yours?
3. Would you like to see ▬▬▬ of the castle and grounds?
4. I can't see ▬▬▬ at all from where I'm standing.
5. May I ask you ▬▬▬ very important?
6. Ask me ▬▬▬ at all, I really don't mind.
7. Was there ▬▬▬ left over from the buffet after the guests had gone?
8. Did you have ▬▬▬ to eat on the plane?

 Talk Talk Talk

(Peter's Office)

P. Lucy, I have one important letter I must send before leaving for Manchester.

L. I'll be with you after I've made this one call, Peter.

P. I'll dictate it into the dictaphone, Lucy. Take your time.

(Peters Büro)

P. Lucy, ich habe hier noch einen sehr wichtigen Brief, den ich abschicken muss, bevor ich nach Manchester fahre.

L. Ich komme sofort zu Ihnen, nachdem ich diesen Anruf erledigt habe, Peter.

P. Ich spreche ihn einfach auf das Diktiergerät, Lucy. Lassen Sie sich Zeit.

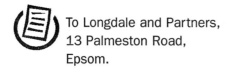 To Longdale and Partners,
13 Palmeston Road,
Epsom.

(Lucy, fill in the exact postal code for me from the letter-head, please!)

Dear Sirs,
Thank you for your inquiry about our Accounting 2000 Program. **I am arranging for you to receive all our available information on the system and for our regional sales representative**, Mr Simon Tucker, to call you and arrange for a meeting at which he will be happy to explain its qualities and functions and answer your questions.
Before contacting Mr Tucker, however, it would be useful for me to know the size of your accounting department and the nature of the accounting system you are now using. I shall be away for the next few days, but during my absence please feel free to contact our Sales Director, Mr Steve Blackman, who will be happy to answer any queries you may have.
Assuring you of my company's best attentions,

Yours faithfully,

Peter Brückner,
Assistant Managing Director

 79. Train Yourself

Before, after, during, while, meanwhile

Geben Sie die richtige Präposition und die richtige Verbform an:

1. ▓▓▓▓▓▓▓ *(reply)* in full to your letter, I would like to remind you of one or two relevant facts.
2. It was only ▓▓▓▓▓▓▓ *(read)* your letter that I became aware of the true state of the company's affairs.
3. ▓▓▓▓▓▓▓ the time it took you *(reply)* I was able to find answers to all my questions.

4. I must confess that I read your letter only ▨▨▨▨ (receive) the subsequent reminder.
5. ▨▨▨▨ (agree) in principle to your proposals, I must raise one or two objections.
6. ▨▨▨▨ (examine) your proposals, I shall respond in full; ▨▨▨▨ please allow me a little time to study the situation.
7. ▨▨▨▨ my time with the company, he ▨▨▨▨ (learn) a surprising amount.
8. ▨▨▨▨ (leave), I would just like to thank you for your splendid hospitality.
9. Here is the proposal. Please study it ▨▨▨▨ we (wait) in the Garibaldi Restaurant.
10. ▨▨▨▨ (study) the proposal, I believe my company is in the position of being able to accept it.

 **Talk Talk Talk**

(Peter prepares to leave the office. Lucy calls him back)

L. Oh, Peter! In this morning's post there was another letter from Longdale and Partners, which might **affect** your reply. I opened it because it was simply addressed to ERGO – but I think you should read it.

P. Lucy, I'm off to lunch now but give me the letter and I'll read it in my break.

L. Here it is. Are you having lunch with Miss Walker? She's already left, but she said she thought you were joining her.

(Peter will gerade das Büro verlassen, als Lucy ihn zurückruft)

L. Oh, Peter! In der Post von heute Morgen war ein Brief von Longdale and Partners, der **Auswirkungen** auf Ihre Rückantwort **haben** könnte. Ich habe ihn geöffnet, weil er nur an ERGO adressiert war – aber ich glaube, Sie sollten ihn besser lesen.

P. Lucy, ich bin gerade auf dem Weg zum Mittagessen, aber geben Sie mir einfach den Brief und ich lese ihn in meiner Pause.

L. Hier ist er. Gehen Sie mit Miss Walker zum Lunch? Sie ist schon gegangen, aber sagte, dass sie dachte, Sie würden mitkommen.

P. Yes, Lucy, that's why I'm in such a hurry. See you later ...	P. Ja, Lucy, deshalb habe ich es ja auch so eilig. Bis später ...
(At the *Nag's Head*)	(Im *Nag's Head*)
P. Hello, Melissa. Sorry I'm late but Lucy had an important letter to give to me.	P. Hallo, Melissa. Tut mir Leid, dass ich so spät komme, aber Lucy hat mir noch einen wichtigen Brief gegeben.
M. Important? Who from?	M. Wichtig? Von wem?
P. Longdale and Partners. They are interested in our Accounting 2000 program. It would be **a very important sale** for us.	P. Longdale and Partners. Sie sind an unserem Accounting 2000-Programm interessiert. Das wäre **ein sehr wichtiger Verkaufserfolg** für uns.
M. So what does the letter say?	M. Also, was steht in dem Brief?

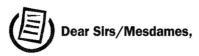 **Dear Sirs/Mesdames,**

Subsequent to our letter of June 6, requesting full information on your Accounting 2000 system, we have been approached by Redstar Technologies with a very attractive offer which will undoubtedly have an **effect** on our final decision. **In all fairness to your company, we do not want to take this decision before comparing the various systems on offer.** Our problem is that the Redstar Technologies offer combines a highly **competitive price with a firm deadline** for our decision. We normally resist pressure of this kind, but the attractive nature of the offer compels us to take rapid action. Would your company be in the position of demonstrating to us your Accounting 2000 system within one week of receipt of this letter? In the meantime, you could perhaps fax us relevant information on the system. **Additionally**, we would appreciate a call establishing direct communication between our accounting department and whoever is responsible in your company for the Accounting

2000 system. Our Chief Accountant, Mr Francis Staff, can be reached on extension 4435 (Fax. 2965-4436).
Thanking you in advance for your prompt attention to this matter,

Yours faithfully,

Matthew Gilpin,
Chief Executive

 False Friends

Be careful not to confuse »**affect**« and »**effect**«. The words are so similar that even the British have problems with them. »Affect« is most commonly used as a verb and »effect« is frequently the corresponding noun (although, to add to the confusion, it can also be used as a verb, meaning to bring about or accomplish something). To affect means to produce a result, a change or an »effect«. Mr Gilpin of Longdale and Partners says the offer from Redstar Technologies will inevitably **affect** his company's decision – will inevitably **have an effect** on it.

 80. Train Yourself

»Affect« oder »effect«?

1. Alcohol has a very strange ▬▬▬▬▬▬ on some people.
2. How will the downturn in profits ▬▬▬▬▬▬ the company's future?
3. What ▬▬▬▬▬▬ is Jim's promotion likely to have on his family?
4. Will the move to company headquarters in New York ▬▬▬▬▬▬ his future plans?
5. How can we ▬▬▬▬▬▬ this staff reshuffle without causing problems?
6. If you can ▬▬▬▬▬▬ this plan successfully you're assured of promotion.
7. The ▬▬▬▬▬▬ of the company move were quite unforeseen.
8. How is the Stock Market slump likely to ▬▬▬▬▬▬ exports?
9. How can we ▬▬▬▬▬▬ an export drive successfully?
10. The ▬▬▬▬▬▬ of the reorganization are still to be felt.

 **Talk Talk Talk**

(in the pub – continued ...)

P. Well, Melissa, what do you make of that?

M. Well, I wouldn't worry your head about it. You've got **bigger fish to fry**. This is Steve's problem.

P. But he's not around.

M. He's back tomorrow.

P. But I'm in Manchester.

M. Then I'll give him the correspondence.

P. You're a treasure. Another drink?

(im Pub – Fortsetzung ...)

P. Tja, Melissa, was halten Sie davon?

M. Na ja, ich würde mir deshalb nicht den Kopf zerbrechen. Sie haben **einen größeren Fisch am Haken**. Das ist Steves Problem.

P. Aber er ist nicht da.

M. Er kommt morgen zurück.

P. Aber ich bin in Manchester.

M. Dann werde ich ihm die Korrespondenz geben.

P. Sie sind ein Schatz. Noch einen Drink?

 Do's and Don'ts

Matthew Gilpin of Longdale and Partners begins his letter: »**Subsequent to ...**«. He could have just as well written: »**After sending you our letter of ...**«. English stylists actually prefer the latter version, arguing that it is simpler and easier to understand. In spoken English, »subsequent to« virtually never occurs, but it is a very entrenched form in official letter-writing – whatever the »stylists« say! Equally, »**Thank you for your letter of ...**« is often replaced by a very formal »**We acknowledge receipt of your letter of ...**« or »**We are in receipt of your letter of ...**«. The two forms are in common use, but you will be never wrong in writing a simple: »**Thank you for your letter of ...**«.

81. Train Yourself

Sie müssen einen Brief beantworten, in dem nach Informationen über ein neues Produkt gefragt wird, für das Ihre Firma wirbt. Wie beginnen Sie Ihren Brief? Machen Sie mindestens drei Entwürfe und benutzen Sie jeweils die folgenden Wörter: »pleased«, »pleasure« und »glad«.

 Vocabulary

to affect	beeinflussen
bundle	Bündel/Packen
confirmation	Bestätigung
effect	Auswirkung
(to be) geared up	bereit sein (etwa: seine Siebensachen zusammen haben)
gross profit	Bruttogewinn
gross national product (GNP)	Bruttosozialprodukt
to have bigger fish to fry	einen größeren Fisch am Haken haben (etwas Wichtigeres vorhaben)
in a jiffy	im Handumdrehen/in »Windeseile«
in the picture	im Bild sein/Bescheid wissen
market exposure	Markteinführung
to meet one's match	»seinen Meister treffen«
on file	in den Unterlagen
per capita	pro Kopf
sales director	Verkaufsleiter
(a) stack of	ein ganzer Haufen (von)
stock	Vorrat
to swot (colloquial)	»büffeln; pauken« (ugs.)
to take it from here	jetzt weiter vorgehen
to tend to	dazu tendieren/neigen
unconditionally	bedingungslos/ohne Vorbehalte

Letter of application
Bewerbungsschreiben

 Here we go

ERGO Limited ist auf der Suche nach einem neuen Mitarbeiter für die Marketingabteilung und hat aus diesem Grund eine Stellenanzeige in einer Zeitung geschaltet. Schnell treffen die ersten Bewerbungen bei der Firma ein und müssen nun sorgfältig geprüft und ausgewertet werden, und Mr Morgan ist davon überzeugt, dass Peter hierfür genau der richtige Mann ist ...

 Talk Talk Talk

(Peter enters the office)

L. Well, hello, Peter! **Did you have a successful journey** to Manchester?

P. I don't know yet if it was successful, Lucy. But the trip itself was fine.

L. Mr Morgan is waiting for you.

(Peter enters Morgan's office)

J. Good morning, Peter. How did the trip to Manchester go?

P. I think it's too early to say, Mr Morgan. But the **presentation went well enough** and certainly

(Peter betritt das Büro)

L. Na so was, hallo, Peter. **War Ihre Reise nach** Manchester **erfolgreich**?

P. Ich weiß noch nicht, ob sie erfolgreich war, Lucy. Aber die Fahrt selber lief sehr gut.

L. Mr Morgan wartet schon auf Sie.

(Peter betritt Morgans Büro)

J. Guten Morgen, Peter. Wie lief Ihr Ausflug nach Manchester?

P. Ich glaube, es ist noch zu früh, um etwas sagen zu können, Mr Morgan. Aber die **Präsentation ver-**

they showed great interest. As you know, we have some **stiff** competition here.

lief zufriedenstellend und **sie haben großes Interesse gezeigt**. Wie Sie ja wissen, haben wir dort **harte** Konkurrenz.

J. I agree, we can't expect **immediate results** with this assignment. I think we'll have to sit patiently by and just wait for a **decision** ...

J. Das sehe ich auch so, wir können bei diesem Auftrag keine **sofortigen Ergebnisse** erwarten. Ich denke, wir müssen einfach geduldig ausharren und auf eine **Entscheidung** warten ...

 82. Train Yourself

Im letzten Gespräch verwendet James Morgan die Begriffe »**immediate**« und »**immediately**«, »**patient**« und »**patiently**«. »Patient« und »immediate« sind Adjektive, die das Nomen näher bestimmen, »immediately« und »patiently« hingegen sind Adverbien, die das Verb näher bestimmen. Setzen Sie im folgenden Text entweder das richtige Adverb oder das richtige Adjektiv ein!

1. Thank you for waiting so *(patient)* for a reply to your letter.
2. I would be grateful for *(immediate)* action in this important matter.
3. We have been *(full)* employed in searching for the causes of the delay.
4. Would you please make sure we are informed *(prompt)*.
5. Our company expects *(complete)* compliance with the terms of the licence agreement.
6. The delay in deliveries cannot *(necessary)* be blamed on our department.
7. Their despatch department is *(usual)* very *(prompt)* in attending to our orders.
8. I am afraid I am not *(complete)* in agreement with your views on this matter.
9. We are happy to report that the performance of the A-300 is *(full)* satisfactory.
10. *(Happy)*, we can report outstanding interim financial results.
11. We would not have waited so *(patient)* if we had known.

12. The Birmingham office is *(unusual)* late in calling back.
13. They complain they were treated very *(bad)* by the new director.
14. *(Bad)* enough, but worse was to follow.

 **Talk Talk Talk**

(James Morgan's office)   (James Morgans Büro)

J. Peter, Melissa might have told you that **an opening** has arisen in the **Marketing Department, and we are advertising the post**. I'd like you to take over the **initial selection** process.

J. Peter, Melissa hat Ihnen ja vielleicht schon gesagt, dass sich **eine freie Stelle** in der **Marketing-Abteilung** ergeben hat und wir **für diese Stelle annoncieren**. Ich hätte gerne, dass Sie den **ersten Auswahlprozess** übernehmen.

P. Certainly, but what does that **entail**?

P. Sicher, was **gehört dazu**?

J. First of all, careful reading of the **applications**. With the employment situation as it is, we are expecting quite a number. There are already some on file, so please take those into consideration, too. When you have **sorted out a rough short list of candidates** let's then get together with Melissa and narrow down the selection process.

J. Zunächst einmal das sorgfältige Lesen der **Bewerbungen**. Bei der derzeitigen Situation auf dem Arbeitsmarkt erwarten wir eine ganze Menge davon. Wir haben bereits ein paar Bewerbungen in den Akten, also berücksichtigen Sie diese bitte auch. Wenn Sie **eine erste Auswahl der Bewerber zusammengestellt** haben, schließen Sie sich mit Melissa zusammen und grenzen die Auswahl weiter ein.

P. What should I be looking for?

P. Nach was soll ich denn Ausschau halten?

J. This is a trainee position. We are looking for a young person who

J. Es geht um eine *Trainee*-Position. Wir suchen nach einem

has just completed university or Technical College, preferably with a **degree in economics** or a **business-related discipline**. Melissa will be wanting somebody with marketing potential, with a **forceful personality** – and that sometimes is evident from the first page of a letter of application.	jungen Menschen, der gerade die Universität oder die Technische Hochschule abgeschlossen hat, am besten mit einem Abschluss in **Wirtschaftswissenschaft** oder einem anderen **wirtschaftlichen Ausbildungsfach**. Melissa wird jemanden mit Talent zum Marketing haben wollen, jemanden mit einer **ausgeprägten Persönlichkeit** – und so etwas wird manchmal schon auf der ersten Seite eines Bewerbungsanschreibens ersichtlich.
P. I'm not awfully sure just how forceful Melissa expects a trainee to be!	P. Ich bin mir nicht sicher, wie viel Persönlichkeit Melissa bei einem Trainee wirklich erwartet!

 83. Train Yourself

Suchen Sie in den folgenden Sätzen nach der richtigen Präposition:

1. If you're passing the library on the way to work could you look .... for me and collect anything they have on Adam Smith.
2. Just look .... yourself. You look .... if you've been dragged through a hedge backwards!
3. If you're in the neighbourhood tomorrow look .... and we'll have tea.
4. Could you look this .... in your dictionary for me?
5. They are real snobs. They look .... on anyone they feel is below their own social rank.
6. The problem with kids today is they have nobody to look .... to, that's what my dad says.
7. We'll certainly look .... this matter and see if we can find the cause of the problem.
8. Look ...., there's a car coming for us on the wrong side of the road!
9. Look very carefully .... these notes for me and look .... any mistakes.
10. Look .... you very carefully when you walk through this neighbourhood at night.

Background Information

And **look** here! There are some phrases to note, too!

Look here!	Now just look here, you can't tell me what to do.
Look sharp!	Look sharp, hurry up! Breakfast is in ten minutes!
Look alive!	Get a move on! We haven't got all day, you know!
Look daggers!	He looked daggers at me – he was obviously very annoyed.

 Talk Talk Talk

(James Morgan's office)

J. Here are the first applications, Peter. Go through them and make a first selection.

P. Righto (returns to his office). Lucy, be a dear and make me some tea, please. I shall be **tied down** in my office for some time. Now, let's look at these letters ...

(James Morgans Büro)

J. Hier sind die ersten Bewerbungen, Peter. Sehen Sie sie durch und treffen Sie eine Vorauswahl.

P. Klaro (geht in sein Büro zurück). Lucy, seien Sie bitte ein Schatz und kochen Sie mir einen Tee. Ich werde eine Weile in meinem Büro **eingebunden** sein. Gut, dann schauen wir uns mal diese Briefe an ...

Dear Sirs,

Having read your advertisement offering a position in your marketing department, I feel I might be just the person you are looking for. Although I **broke off** my university studies after one semester, I later gathered practical experience in marketing in the shoe department of Holly and Brights, **the big department chain**. After five years in this department, I feel the time has come **to move on to something more demanding**. Possibilities at Holly and Brights are limited, so I am looking for a position in a completely different area of business. I do have some experience of computer technology, having just invested in a PC.

My colleagues at Holly and Bright will testify as to my cheerful and helpful disposition. If you need any further information, please write to me *poste restante* at Herne Bay Post Office because I am in the process of moving address. From July 1, I can be contacted c/o Miss Judy O'Connell, at 35 Cedar Drive, Herne Bay.
Hoping to hear from you soon,

Yours very sincerely,

Bill Boulton

P. Well, I think we can forget that one, for a start. What else is in the post-bag?

P. Tja, ich denke, den können wir schon mal vergessen. Was haben wir denn sonst noch im Postsack?

 **Dear Sirs/Mesdames,**

Further to your advertisement in the Morning Echo, I would like to add my humble name to the list of those you will be interviewing for the vacancy in your marketing department. Perhaps I cannot claim the qualifications required and am a little too advanced in age (52) to hope for a post as trainee, but in my long career with J.P. Engineering I have always been ready to learn something new. You might have read reports that J.P. Engineering is preparing for **retrenchments**, and I feel that for my own security I must begin to look around for alternative employment.
I would therefore be very pleased if you could consider my application for the vacancy in your company. I can promise loyalty, hard work and a willingness to learn new technologies – even those related to the computer age, which I'm afraid has passed me by!

Your loyal and obedient servant,

Henry J. Jobson

Background Information

»**Poste restante**« (French for »Letters remaining«) describes the department in British Post Offices where letters can be sent and then collected personally by the **addressee**. Addressee? That's the person to whom the letter is sent.

»**c/o**« is short for »care of«. It is added to the address when the letter is to be delivered into the care of somebody other than the addressee:
Mr John Ripton,
c/o Mrs Jane Simpson,
The Oaks,
Bramley

Do's and Don'ts

»**Your loyal and obediant servant**«? You will still encounter this archaic way of signing off a formal letter. Variations include: Your loyal and dutiful servant! Charming and genteel as they sound, resist any temptation to use them!

84. Train Yourself

Let's take a break ...

»Break« als Verb oder Nomen ist oft in umgangssprachlichen Ausdrücken zu finden. Setzen Sie in den folgenden Sätzen die passende Form ein:

1. I'm tired. Let's take a ▓▓▓▓▓▓▓▓▓▓.
2. Jim and Jane aren't going out together any more. They ▓▓▓▓▓▓▓▓ off.
3. Police are investigating a ▓▓▓▓▓▓▓▓▓▓ at the local bank.
4. Police were called in to ▓▓▓▓▓▓▓▓▓▓ the demonstration.
5. I'll have to get a new car. Mine is constantly ▓▓▓▓▓▓▓▓▓▓.

6. The right wing of the party ▬▬▬▬ from the mainstream.
7. The ship was ▬▬▬▬ for scrap.
8. An epidemic of measles has ▬▬▬▬ in the north of the country.

 Talk Talk Talk

(Peter's office. James Morgan enters)

J. So how's it going, Peter? Have you found our ideal candidate yet?

P. I've only been through two letters so far, and they certainly don't qualify.

J. Mind if I look?

P. Not at all, help yourself!

(James Morgan reads the letters)

J. You know what dismays me, Peter? Some people seem incapable of reading an advertisement correctly. We were very clear indeed in stating our **requirements**. I just can't see how anybody could fail to understand. I'm just unable to explain it.

P. I think the letters were written from a position of despair. Boulton is obviously bored with his depart-

(Peters Büro. James Morgan tritt ein)

J. Wie läuft es, Peter? Haben Sie schon unseren Traumkandidaten gefunden?

P. Ich habe bis jetzt erst zwei Briefe durch und sie haben sich beide ganz sicher nicht qualifiziert.

J. Was dagegen, wenn ich mal einen Blick darauf werfe?

P. Überhaupt nicht, nur zu!

(James Morgan liest die Briefe)

J. Wissen Sie, was ich wirklich erschreckend finde, Peter? Einige Leute scheinen nicht in der Lage zu sein, eine Anzeige korrekt zu lesen. Wir haben unsere **Anforderungen** klar ausgedrückt. Es ist mir schleierhaft, wie jemand sie missverstehen kann. Ich kann so etwas einfach nicht erklären.

P. Ich denke, diese Briefe wurden aus der Verzweiflung heraus geschrieben. Boulton ist in seinem

ment store job, and Jobson fears he'll be out of a job before long.

Kaufhaus-Job offensichtlich gelangweilt und Jobson fürchtet, dass er bald ohne Job dastehen wird.

J. But that's no reason to regard us as an escape route ...

J. Aber das ist noch kein Grund, uns als letzten Ausweg zu missbrauchen ...

 85. Train Yourself

»**Incapable**« oder »**unable**«? Beide Wörter bedeuten im Englischen, dass man nicht in der Lage ist, etwas zu tun, obwohl »incapable« eine eher negative Bedeutung hat und mit »unfähig« übersetzt wird. »He is quite incapable of assuming the position of Managing Director« (Das soll heißen, dass er nicht die Fähigkeiten besitzt, Geschäftsführer zu werden). »Is she totally incapable of doing that job properly?«. »Incapable« verwendet man mit »of« und der Gerundform des Verbs; »unable« verlangt einen Infinitiv. Und nun sollten Sie dazu in der Lage sein, die folgenden Sätze zu vervollständigen!

1. I regret we are unable *(accept)* your kind invitation to dinner.
2. She is totally incapable *(tell)* him that she wants a divorce.
3. Are you incapable *(read)* the small print on the sales agreement?
4. I am afraid we are unable *(deliver)* by the date you mention.
5. He appears to be incapable *(be)* on time for any appointment.
6. I must confess I am unable *(see)* the purpose of your company's proposal.
7. That company appears incapable *(pay)* its debts on time.
8. I am very sorry I was unable *(make)* the appointment.

 **Talk Talk Talk**

P. Do we have a **regular form of letter to reply to unsuccessful applicants**?

P. Haben wir ein **standardisiertes Absageschreiben für abgelehnte Kandidaten**?

J. Yes, Lucy can help you there. But in the case of these two appli-

J. Ja, Lucy kann Ihnen da helfen. Aber ich denke, im Fall dieser

cants I think a personal letter might be kinder. See what you can do!

P. I'll do my best but I don't have much experience of this sort of thing ...

beiden Bewerber wäre ein persönlicher Brief freundlicher. Schauen Sie doch mal, was Sie machen können!

P. Ich versuche mein Bestes, aber ich habe nicht viel Erfahrung in solchen Dingen ...

 Dear Mr Boulton,

Thank you for your letter responding to our advertisement in the Morning Echo. **I regret to inform you that your impressive professional experience does not completely match the requirements of the position we are seeking to fill.**
Thank you, nonetheless, for your interest, and wishing you every success in your present career.

Yours sincerely,

Peter Brückner,
Assistant Managing Director

 Talk Talk Talk

(James Morgan's office. Peter enters)

P. Do you think this reply will do?

J. (reads it) I think that's very **well worded**. I don't see the point of being too **offhand**. A personal touch can't do any harm. You can

(James Morgans Büro. Peter tritt ein)

P. Glauben Sie, dass diese Antwort angemessen ist?

J. (liest den Brief) Ich finde, er ist sehr gut **formuliert**. Ich sehe keinen Grund dafür, zu **unpersönlich** zu sein. Ein persönlicher

use the same wording in the second letter.

Touch kann nichts schaden. Sie können dieselbe Formulierung beim zweiten Brief verwenden.

P. I'll give them to Lucy to type and then get **stuck into** the others ...

P. Ich werde sie Lucy zum Abtippen geben und mich dann in die anderen **vertiefen** ...

 86. Train Yourself

Ein Lebenslauf ist einer der wichtigsten Teile einer Bewerbung. Der englische Begriff dafür, »CV«, steht kurz für den lateinischen Ausdruck »Curriculum Vitae«. Suchen Sie im folgenden Lebenslauf die fehlenden Verben und setzen Sie sie in die korrekte Zeit!

Name: John Tatterell
I ▬▬▬▬ in Plymouth, Devon, on May 22, 1968. After ▬▬▬▬ Plymouth Grammar School for six years, I ▬▬▬▬ with A-Level passes in English, French and Social Studies. I ▬▬▬▬ one year off and ▬▬▬▬ extensively in North and South America. On ▬▬▬▬ to Britain in 1987, I ▬▬▬▬ for a course in business studies at Hendon Technical College. After ▬▬▬▬ the course in 1989, I ▬▬▬▬ Jackson and Tucker Limited as a management trainee. During my time there, I ▬▬▬▬ experience in all departments of the company and at present I ▬▬▬▬ as assistant to the Marketing Director. My French ▬▬▬▬ still fluent, and I ▬▬▬▬ German and Spanish during my spare time. My duties at Jackson and Tucker ▬▬▬▬ contacts with foreign clients and ▬▬▬▬ participation in trade fairs in mainland Europe. This work ▬▬▬▬ me to Milan, Munich, Stockholm and Copenhagen, and I ▬▬▬▬ very much at home in an international arena.

return, organise, gain, take, join, leave, employ, enrol, feel, be, attend, complete, include, study, be born, travel, maintain.

(Peter reads the next letter) (Peter liest den nächsten Brief)

 Dear Sirs/Mesdames,

I would be grateful if you considered my application for the position your company has advertised in the Morning Echo. As you will see from the **accompanying CV**, I have just left university with a Master's degree in Business Administration and am looking for a post which would allow me to **put into practice** what I have learnt over the past five years. With my background in computer studies, a company such as yours would offer the ideal opportunity for me. One year of my degree course was **devoted to** marketing and market research, and **I would be very happy to have the chance to work in the kind of area your advertisement describes**. I am available under the above address and telephone number to provide additional information, and of course I am available at any time to attend a personal interview.

Yours faithfully,

Roger Fenton

 **Talk Talk Talk**

(James Morgan's office) (James Morgans Büro)

P. Mr Morgan, this letter here sounds promising.

P. Mr Morgan, dieser Brief hier klingt viel versprechend.

J. Let's have a look! (He reads the letter). You're right. The young man seems to have the qualifications we are looking for. **Some practical experience** would have been desirable, but he would certainly get that here. Where's his CV?

J. Schauen wir mal! (Er liest den Brief) Sie haben Recht. Dieser junge Mann scheint genau die Qualifikationen zu haben, die wir suchen. Ein paar **praktische Erfahrungen** wären zwar wünschenswert gewesen, aber die wird er hier schon noch bekommen. Wo ist sein Lebenslauf?

CV - Roger Fenton.

Born: February 20, 1975, in Carlisle.
Education:
Primary: St. Christopher's Preparatory School, Carlisle.
Secondary: Carlisle Grammar School.
Certificates: 6 GSCEs (English Language, English Literature, History, Biology, Economics, French). 3 A-Levels: (English, Economics, Business Studies).
Universities: University of York. BA (Economics, American Studies); London School of Economics (MBA).
Additional studies and work experience: One year (1988-89) exchange student at Yale University, U.S.A. Six months (1985) practical experience in the Marketing Division of Santos Holdings, London.
References can be obtained from Professor Hamilton Harding of the University of York and Dr. Jonathan Digby-Smith, Managing Director, Santos Holdings.

 **Talk Talk Talk**

J. Quite impressive. Reads well, even though I do prefer a **written CV** instead of one in this **tabular form**. It makes it more difficult to assess the person behind the facts. But, of course, we'll be inviting him for an interview. Young Fenton certainly **falls into** the short-list category. You'll have **made up a file** already, Peter?

P. Well, this is the first application that qualifies, so I'll create a file right now and put the letter in it.

J. Recht eindrucksvoll. Liest sich sehr gut, obwohl ich einen **ausformulierten Lebenslauf** einem in dieser **tabellarischen Form** vorziehe. So ist es schwieriger, den Mensch hinter den Daten einzuschätzen. Aber natürlich werden wir ihn zu einem Gespräch einladen. Unser junger Mr Fenton **fällt** ganz sicher **in** die Vorauswahl. Haben Sie bereits **einen Ordner angelegt**, Peter?

P. Na ja, das ist die erste Bewerbung, die sich qualifiziert, also werde ich sofort einen Ordner

What about a reply to the application?	anlegen und den Brief einfügen. Wie sieht es mit einer Antwort auf die Bewerbung aus?
J. I think we can send out a standard reply to applicants we shall be inviting for an interview. I'll leave that to you ...	J. Ich denke, wir können an die Bewerber, die wir zu einem Gespräch einladen, einen Standardbrief schicken. Das überlasse ich Ihnen ...

 87. Train Yourself

Impression, impressive, impressively, to impress? Finden Sie die richtige Form (inklusive Präposition) für die folgenden Sätze:

1. I was very ▒▒▒▒▒▒▒▒ his performance.
2. I didn't find his performance as ▒▒▒▒▒▒▒▒ as the last time I saw him in the concert hall.
3. The new system has been functioning most ▒▒▒▒▒▒▒▒ since its installation.
4. What kind of ▒▒▒▒▒▒▒▒ did she leave ▒▒▒▒▒▒▒▒ you?
5. That's a very ▒▒▒▒▒▒▒▒ motorbike you've got there.
6. Were you really ▒▒▒▒▒▒▒▒ what she said?
7. I find it very difficult ▒▒▒▒▒▒▒▒ him with the facts.
8. Did you think our presentation left ▒▒▒▒▒▒▒▒ the audience?
9. I thought he spoke ▒▒▒▒▒▒▒▒ about a difficult subject.
10. They said they were very ▒▒▒▒▒▒▒▒ what he had to say.

(Peter dictates ...)	(Peter diktiert ...)

 Dear Mr Fenton,

We acknowledge receipt of your application for the position which has become available in our Marketing Department, and **we have pleasure in inviting you for an interview**, at a date yet to be set. Interviews will, however, be held during the last two weeks of July. If for any reason you are unable to come to London during this time, please let us know in

Korrespondenz

good time and we shall endeavour to organise our schedule to match yours.

Yours sincerely,

Peter Brückner,
Assistant Managing Director

(Peter opens another letter)   (Peter öffnet einen weiteren Brief)

 Dear Sirs,

My attention was caught by your company's insertion in the Morning Echo, advertising the vacancy in your Marketing Department. **I would be very grateful if you considered my application for the post.** For the past three years I have been employed by the Robinson public relations agency, mostly writing advertising copy (cf. accompanying CV). I would now like very much to make the change to the purely business sector and, in particular, the hi-tech field. For that reason, I would be very interested indeed in working for a company such as yours.
Hoping to hear from you soon,

Yours faithfully,

Nigel Branson

Nigel Branson's CV:

Nigel John Branson.

Born October 12, 1975, in Huddersfield, Yorkshire. Educated at St. Christopher's Preparators School and Huddersfield Grammar School, leaving in 1993 with 7 GSCEs and 3 A-Levels (English, History and Geography). Four years study (1993-97) at the University of Sussex, Brighton, graduating with BA (2/1 grade). In September, 1997, joined Robinson Public Relations, London, as copy-writer.

Background Information

The word »**acknowledge**« has several meanings in the business English vocabulary. In the above letter, it is used to register receipt of the job application – »We acknowledge receipt of your letter of ...«. In business letters it is a common substitute for: »Thank you for your letter of ...«

Other uses are seen in the following examples:
1. We acknowledge your company's complaints and will do all we can to rectify the situation (agree to the truth of).
2. The lawyers acknowledged the deed and added it to the file (gave it legal validity, accepted it as valid).
3. The accountant acknowledged his responsibility for the mistake in the annual report (admitted his guilt).
4. We acknowledge your efforts to correct the mistake (we express appreciation).
5. They acknowledged our presence at the concert (took notice of).
6. We acknowledge Mr Hoskins as the responsible officer in this case (recognise his authority).

The abbreviations **c.f.** and **cf.** have very different meanings in business English:
1. c.f. – »carried forward« – used in financial statements when a sum or figure is »carried forward« from one column or page to another.
2. cf – (as used in the above letter) »compare« (from the Latin imperative *confer* – compare). In Nigel Branson's letter, he uses the abbreviation to draw attention to the fact that his summarised career is dealt with in more detail in an accompanying CV.

88. Train Yourself

Das Wort »acknowledge« hat viele Synonyme, z. B.: *accept, admit, allow, avow, certify, concede, confess, confirm, grant, own, profess, recognise.*

Finden Sie in den folgenden Sätzen die korrekten Synonyme für dieses Wort!

1. Could your lawyer please acknowledge the validity of the will?
2. I acknowledge total responsibility for the errors in the report.
3. We acknowledge receipt of your letter of March 12.
4. The company acknowledged our authority to act in this matter.
5. He acknowledged our presence at the meeting but still ignored us.
6. The board acknowledged him as the best person to represent the company.
7. When finally charged with embezzlement, he acknowledged his guilt.
8. They acknowledged their admiration for the company's recovery.

 Talk Talk Talk

(Peter's Office. Melissa enters)

(Peters Büro. Melissa tritt ein)

M. Hope I'm not disturbing, but I was just passing the door and curiosity **got the better of** me. Have you found anyone promising?

M. Ich hoffe, ich störe nicht, aber ich kam gerade an Ihrer Tür vorbei und **konnte der Neugier nicht widerstehen**. Haben Sie schon jemand Vielversprechenden entdeckt?

P. Well, yes and no – at least we've got the start of a short-list of candidates. When are you joining the selection panel?

P. Tja, ja und nein – wenigstens konnten wir schon eine Vorauswahl-Liste anlegen. Wann werden Sie zur Bewerberauswahl dazukommen?

M. I'll be there at the interviews. I'm leaving the hard work to you. But there are rewards – come on, it's my round at the *Nag's Head* ...

M. Ich werde bei den Vorstellungsgesprächen dabei sein. Ich überlasse Ihnen die Knochenarbeit. Aber Sie sollen auch belohnt werden – kommen Sie, ich spendiere eine Runde im *Nag's Head* ...

(The *Nag's Head pub*)

(Im *Nag's Head Pub*)

Korrespondenz

M. Cheers, Peter! How many possibles have you got so far?	M. Prost, Peter! Wie viele mögliche Kandidaten haben Sie bis jetzt?
P. Just two, really, although a couple more are on file. They **wrote inquiring** about employment possibilities before we inserted the advertisement.	P. Erst zwei, obwohl wir noch ein paar in den Akten haben. Sie haben **Initiativbewerbungen** an uns geschickt, bevor wir die Stellenanzeige aufgegeben hatten.
M. And how many more applications have you got to read?	M. Und wie viele Bewerbungen müssen Sie noch lesen?
P. About half a dozen, I believe. James wants to **narrow** the shortlist **down** to no more than six, anyway.	P. Etwa ein halbes Dutzend, schätze ich. James möchte die Vorauswahl-Liste auf nicht mehr als sechs Bewerber **einschränken**.
M. Well, **keep me posted** – I'll be working with whomever is chosen for the job.	M. Na gut, **halten Sie mich auf dem Laufenden** – ich werde schließlich mit dem ausgewählten Bewerber zusammenarbeiten.
P. Don't worry – you can take over the selection process right now, if you want.	P. Keine Sorge – Sie können das Auswahlverfahren sofort übernehmen, wenn Sie wollen.
M. No thanks, Peter – that's your job!	M. Nein, vielen Dank, Peter – das ist Ihr Job!

 89. Train Yourself

Who, whom oder *whose*?
Füllen Sie die Lücken mit der korrekten Form!

1. With ▬▬▬▬ were you talking so long on the telephone?
2. To ▬▬▬▬ address did you send that letter?
3. ▬▬▬▬ did you talk to for so long on the phone last night?
4. Have you yet decided ▬▬▬▬ should head the company next year?

241

5. I never realised ▇▇▇▇ she really was.
6. ▇▇▇▇ would you like to accompany you to the dinner?
7. ▇▇▇▇ name is to appear at the top of the letter?
8. By ▇▇▇▇ did you say that book is written?
9. You never told me ▇▇▇▇ actually performed the part.
10. On ▇▇▇▇ shoulders will the blame ultimately rest?

 **Talk Talk Talk**

(Peter's office. Steve enters)

(Peters Büro. Steve tritt ein)

S. Hi, Peter! Are you still **head-hunting**?

S. Hi, Peter! Immer noch beim »**Head-hunting**«?

P. Hi, Steve! I haven't seen you for a while. Have you been **off-base**?

P. Hi, Steve! Lange nicht gesehen. Waren Sie **außerhalb** unterwegs?

S. I had to do the usual round of the sales posts. One of the guys had heard there was a place in marketing. He wants out of sales and would be interested in something else within the company. I told him to get an application in.

S. Ich habe die übliche Tour bei unseren Verkaufsstellen gemacht. Einer von den Kollegen hat gehört, dass es eine Stelle im Marketing gibt. Er möchte aus dem Verkauf heraus und ist an einer Anstellung in der Firma selbst interessiert. Ich habe ihm gesagt, er soll eine Bewerbung einreichen.

P. I'm working through them right now. But this position is for a young career-starter, you know.

P. Ich arbeite mich gerade durch. Aber diese Position ist für einen jungen Berufseinsteiger gedacht, wissen Sie.

S. Never too late to start, Peter old chap!

S. Es ist nie zu spät einzusteigen, Peter, alter Freund!

Background Information

Head-hunting
In this highly competitive professional world, more and more companies are engaging specialist firms to hunt specifically for the employees they need. The practice is called »head-hunting«.

 90. Train Yourself

Interest, interested, interesting ...
Vervollständigen Sie die folgenden Sätze mit den passenden Wörtern (und den Präpositionen, wenn möglich)!

1. The company found this proposal ▓▓▓ particular ▓▓▓.
2. The company found this proposal particularly ▓▓▓.
3. The company is particularly ▓▓▓ this proposal.
4. The company's ▓▓▓ has been caught ▓▓▓ the proposal.
5. She made an ▓▓▓ impression on us.
6. Would a brochure ▓▓▓ your company?
7. Would a brochure be of ▓▓▓ your company?
8. They sat through the whole lecture. They were very ▓▓▓.
9. They sat through the whole lecture. They found it very ▓▓▓.
10. Are you really ▓▓▓ what he has to say?
11. The suggestion aroused much ▓▓▓.
12. The audience found the suggestion very ▓▓▓.

 **Talk Talk Talk**

(Peter's office. Peter takes a fax from the machine)

P. Well, Steve's man lost no time ...

(Peters Büro. Peter nimmt ein Fax aus dem Gerät)

P. Na so was, Steves Spezi hat keine Zeit verloren ...

 Dear Mr Brückner,

Mr Blackman informs me that a position has become vacant in ERGO's Marketing Department, and I would be grateful if you were able to consider my application. Although I have been employed in sales for ERGO for the past five years I feel that in that time I have acquired skills which could benefit the company in a wider area. After five years in sales, I must confess that I would like to move on and gain further experience within the company.

My full details and work record are, of course, on file, so I shan't bother you with a CV, **but if you require any further information I am only too ready to supply it**.

Hoping for a favourable response,

Yours sincerely,

Dale Spinks

 Background Information

The expression »**only too**« is found frequently in business correspondence. It is a slightly archaic form, which can just as easily – only too easily – be substituted by »very«:
a) I shall be only too (very) pleased to comply with your wishes.
b) We shall be only too (very) ready for your comments.
c) We shall be only too (very) delighted to see you next Tuesday.
d) They were only too (very) glad to see the company fail.
e) He was only too (very) glad to call off the meeting.

 91. Train Yourself

Vervollständigen Sie folgende Sätze mit »only« oder »only too«:

1. I wanted to meet her before she left. Now it's too late.
2. They should be pleased they didn't take up that offer.

3. I'm grateful for the help you gave me.
4. It's not the anger it causes, but also the pain.
5. We've two miles to go before we get home.
6. I shall be glad to do that for you.

 Talk Talk Talk

(Peter's office. Chip, the courier-messenger, enters)

P. Hello, Chip! What can I do for you?

C. This package from Dickens and Jolly is for you – they asked me to deliver it personally. Oh, Mr Brückner, I hear there's a vacancy in the Marketing Department.

P. Oh, no, Chip, not you, too!

C. Good lord, you wouldn't catch me wanting to work in there **for all the tea in China**! I like my freedom, **buzzing about** the place on a motorbike is my idea of a job. I wouldn't last a morning in an office with Miss Walker. That miss and me would be a real mistake!

P. Chip, if you were as fast on your motorbike as you are with words

(Peters Büro. Chip, der Kurierbote, tritt ein)

P. Hallo, Chip! Was kann ich für dich tun?

C. Dieses Paket ist für Sie, von Dickens und Jolly – sie haben mich gebeten, es persönlich abzugeben. Oh, Mr Brückner, ich habe gehört, dass es eine freie Stelle in der Marketing-Abteilung gibt.

P. Oh, nein, Chip, nicht du auch noch!

C. Um Himmels Willen, **nicht für alles Geld der Welt** möchte ich hier arbeiten! Ich mag meine Freiheit und mit dem Motorrad **herumzufahren** ist meine Vorstellung von einem Traumjob. Ich würde es keinen Vormittag zusammen in einem Büro mit Miss Walker aushalten. Diese Dame und ich – das würde nicht gut gehen!

P. Chip, wenn du mit deinem Motorrad so schnell wärst wie mit

we'd have the most efficient courier service in London. But just watch what you have to say about Miss Walker, you mischievous miscreant!

deinem Mundwerk, wärst du der effektivste Kurierfahrer in London. Aber sei vorsichtig, was du über Miss Walker sagst, du schändliches Schandmaul!

C. Hey, you're not so bad with the words yourself! At least, for a German!

C. Hey, Sie können aber auch gut mit Worten umgehen! Wenigstens für einen Deutschen!

P. Out with you, before I find a missile to chuck at you ...

P. Raus mit dir, bevor ich etwas finde, dass ich nach dir werfen kann ...

 92. Train Yourself

Finden Sie die passenden Wörter zu den Umschreibungen.
Sie fangen alle mit der Vorsilbe »mis-« an, also keine »Missgriffe« bitte!

1. Do this and you pronounce a word incorrectly.
2. Bad luck strikes you if you experience this.
3. This person doesn't like people and avoids society.
4. If you shape or form something badly it will be ...
5. Give out money wastefully and you ...
6. A mixture or medley of anything.
7. Give somebody the wrong instructions or advice and you ...
8. A feeling of mistrust or apprehension.
9. Somebody who just doesn't belong in a particular place or environment.
10. A crime or evil act.
11. Bad behaviour.
12. Use the wrong name or word and you're guilty of a ...

misspend, misnomer, miscellany, misanthrope, mischance, misfit, misdeed, misconduct, misgiving, mispronounce, misshapen, misdirect.

Vocabulary

addressee	Adressat
to advertise a post	eine Stelle annoncieren
to break off	aufhören/abbrechen
(a) business-related discipline	wirtschaftliches Ausbildungsfach
to buzz about	umhersausen
a degree in economics	Abschluss in Wirtschaftswissenschaft
devoted to	gewidmet
discipline	hier: Fachgebiet
to entail	beinhalten/nach sich ziehen
to fall into	hineinfallen (im Sinne von »dazu gehören«)
for all the tea in China	(Redewendung) etwa: Für alles Geld der Welt
forceful	hier: ausgeprägt (Charakter)
to get the better of	etwas nachgeben, nicht widerstehen können
initial	anfänglich
to keep sb. posted	auf dem Laufenden halten/ informieren
to make up a file	einen Ordner anlegen
to narrow down	eingrenzen
off-base	außerhalb (einer Firma etc.)
offhand	unpersönlich
(an) opening	eine freie Stelle
requirements	Anforderungen
to put into practice	in die Praxis umsetzen
retrenchment	Einschränkung/Kürzung; Kostenreduzierung
to sort out	aussortieren
stiff	steif/hier: rauh, umkämpft
to stuck into sth.	sich in etwas vertiefen/ »hineinknien«
tabular	tabellarisch
(to be) tied down	in etwas eingebunden sein
well-worded	wohl formuliert

Letter of reply
Antwortschreiben

 Here we go

Viele Bewerbungen für die freie Stelle in der Marketingabteilung sind bei ERGO Limited eingegangen. Doch Dank Peters Hilfe konnten die vielversprechendsten Bewerber ausgemacht werden. Aber die Entscheidung fällt nicht leicht. Peter kann einen guten Vorschlag einbringen, der letztlich zum lang erwarteten Ergebnis führt, und dieses Ergebnis ist gleichzeitig noch für eine freudige Überraschung gut ...

 Talk Talk Talk

(The front office of ERGO Limited. Peter enters)

L. Good morning, Peter! Did you have a good weekend?

P. I visited my friends in Sussex. They took me hunting. What strange sports you English have!

L. You actually rode in the hunt?

P. I rode in a motor-car! I let the others risk their necks. And they were incapable of finding one single fox!

(Das Eingangsbüro von ERGO Limited. Peter tritt ein)

L. Guten Morgen, Peter! Hatten Sie ein schönes Wochenende?

P. Ich habe meine Freunde in Sussex besucht. Sie haben mich zur Jagd mitgenommen. Ihr Engländer habt schon seltsame Sportarten!

L. Sind Sie tatsächlich bei der Jagd mitgeritten?

P. Ich bin im Auto gefahren! Sollen die anderen ihren Hals riskieren. Die haben es nicht mal geschafft, einen einzigen Fuchs aufzuspüren!

J. Good morning, Peter – did I hear right? You went hunting? You insensitive chap! That's a very controversial way for a visitor to England to spend his weekends!

J. Guten Morgen, Peter – habe ich da richtig gehört? Sie waren auf einer Jagd? Sie unempfindsamer Kerl! Das ist schon eine sehr umstrittene Art und Weise für einen England-Besucher, seine Wochenenden zu verbringen!

L. Oh, don't you listen to Mr Morgan, Peter! He says golf is his sport, but I know for a fact that sometimes he goes shooting in Scotland!

L. Ach was, hören Sie nicht auf Mr Morgan, Peter! Er behauptet ja, Golf wäre seine Sportart, aber ich weiß ganz genau, dass er manchmal zum Schießen nach Schottland fährt!

J. Wrong again, Lucy. I only visit Scotland for the whisky. Talking of which, you can add a dash to my morning tea ...

J. Schon wieder falsch! Ich besuche Schottland nur wegen des Whiskys. Da wir gerade davon sprechen, Sie können mir einen Schuss davon in meinen Frühstückstee gießen ...

 93. Train Yourself

Wie lassen sich die Sätze durch die Vorsilben ab-, dis-, il-, im-, in-, un- verneinen?

1. She loves animals. She's ▭ capable of killing a fly.
2. He's so obstinate. He's quite ▭ pervious to any reasonable argument.
3. I'm away on business on that day, so I am ▭ able to accept the invitation.
4. The bill is much too high for the amount of work involved. It's ▭ proportionate.
5. I've never before seen them behave like that. It's quite ▭ normal.
6. The company gave him one month's notice – how ▭ sensitive.
7. He took the news without displaying any emotion, ▭ passively.

8. Despite the company's poor performance, the share price remained ▬▬▬ affected.
9. I wouldn't invest at this time, if I were you – the stock market seems very ▬▬▬ stable.
10. The contract is for three months only because the position is ▬▬▬ secure.
11. He was summarily sacked because of ▬▬▬ seemly behaviour.
12. The company could have kept him until the end of the month. I thought its treatment of him was quite ▬▬▬ gracious.
13. I can't read the letter - his handwriting is ▬▬▬ legible.
14. They allow smoking in the office. It's a very ▬▬▬ healthy environment.
15. I'll have to leave. The working atmosphere is quite ▬▬▬ tolerable.
16. He was very ▬▬ certain, unable to choose which course to follow.

 **Talk Talk Talk**

(Peter's office. James Morgan enters)

J. How far are you with the job applications, Peter?

P. Just two to go, unless any more arrive.

J. We'll have **to close the shortlist** this week. We've still got the interviews to organize.

P. At least one of the remaining letters looks quite promising, what do you think?

(Peters Büro. James Morgen tritt ein)

J. Wie weit sind Sie mit den Bewerbungen, Peter?

P. Es sind nur noch zwei zu erledigen, falls nicht noch mehr kommen.

J. Wir müssen die **Vorauswahl** noch diese Woche **abschließen**. Die Interviews müssen wir auch noch organisieren.

P. Zumindest einer der übrigen Briefe sieht viel versprechend aus, was meinen Sie?

Dear Sirs/Mesdames,

In response to your company's advertisement in the Morning Echo, I would like to apply for the vacant post. I have just graduated with a Master's Degree in Business Administration from the University of Essex and I am actively looking for a position in the Marketing Department of a company such as yours. I have practical experience of marketing, gathered during one year's job-training in the United States, where I worked in the Marketing Division of Johnson and Sears, one of the country's largest public relations companies. I attach a full CV, with references, and would be very happy to respond to any questions you may have.

Yours faithfully,

John Smith-Powell

P. But, **by way of contrast**, just look at this letter!	P. Schauen Sie sich **als Gegenbeispiel** mal diesen Brief an!

 Dear Sir/Madam,

Look no further. I am the man you want for the job you advertised in the Morning Echo. You won't find a better man for the position, or anyone more loyal. My marketing experience knows practically no boundaries – for the past three years I have been street-selling time-share deals, with great success. Just ask my employers – or my former employers, because their company has just been closed down, allegedly for illicit trading after a dissatisfied salesman blew the whistle. Hence, I'm available immediately. Please give me a call at the above number if you're interested – and interested you must be!

Yours in great expectation,

Thomas (Tom) Fosters

J. I don't believe it! We should frame that one, as an example of how *not* to get a job!	J. Das fasse ich ja nicht! Den sollten wir einrahmen als Beispiel dafür, wie man einen Job *nicht* bekommt.
P. But how do we reply to it?	P. Aber wie antworten wir darauf?
J. It doesn't really merit a reply. Or send the briefest of acknowledgements. Just one question, have you checked the email in-basket today?	J. Eigentlich verdient er gar keine Antwort. Oder schicken Sie ihm die kürzeste, die es nur gibt! Nur eine Frage, haben Sie heute schon in den E-Mail-Posteingang geschaut?
P. I've been so busy that I haven't got around to it. But I'll do it right away.	P. Ich war so beschäftigt, dass ich nicht dazu gekommen bin, aber das mache ich jetzt gleich.

 Do's and Don'ts

If you are writing a **job application** in English, don't be misled by your experience of English casualness and humour. In dealings as important as this, the British are as serious as the Germans. So abandon any idea of catching a prospective employer's attention with a »I am the person you're looking for« approach. Your application can be just as eye-catching if it is succinctly and correctly written.

 94. Train Yourself

Verbinden Sie in den folgenden Sätzen das Verb »to get« mit der jeweils passenden Präposition:

1. She'll get ▨▨▨▨▨ quite easily on that salary.
2. He is an impressive young man and will certainly get ▨▨▨▨▨ in life.
3. If you live beyond your means you'll soon get ▨▨▨▨▨ debt.
4. They want to get ▨▨▨▨▨ on the deal as quickly as possible.
5. So what are you getting ▨▨▨▨▨ to these days?

6. Get _____ it! You have to keep up with the times!
7. Are we all here? Right, let's get _____ to business.
8. The boss is fine. You'll have no problem getting _____ with him.
9. Can you get _____ the 1999 file for me please, Lucy!
10. I don't think he'll ever get _____ the death of his wife.
11. The songs from that new musical really get _____ your skin.
12. The new board chairman will find it difficult to get his views _____.

across, along, by, down, in, into, on, out, over, under, up, with.

Talk Talk Talk

(Peter's office.
James Morgan enters)

J. I don't want to rush you, Peter, but do you have any more applications to **shift through.**

P. No, I've gone through them all now and **whittled** them **down** to a **short-list** of seven. Here they are.

J. Fine, I didn't really expect you to get through them that quickly. This afternoon we'll have a meeting with Melissa and prepare the interviews. We can send out a **form-letter** inviting the short-listed candidates to an interview. I'll leave you to **draft** it ...

(Peter writes ...)

(Peters Büro.
James Morgan tritt ein)

J. Peter, ich will Sie nicht hetzen, aber haben Sie noch mehr Bewerbungen **durchzuschauen**?

P. Nein, ich bin sie alle durchgegangen und habe sie auf eine **Auswahlliste** von sieben **reduziert**. Hier sind sie.

J. Gut, ich hatte wirklich nicht erwartet, dass Sie so schnell damit fertig werden. Heute Nachmittag werden wir uns mit Melissa treffen und die Bewerbungsgespräche vorbereiten. Wir können den vorausgewählten Kandidaten einen **Formbrief** schicken, um sie zum Gespräch einzuladen. Sie können ihn **entwerfen** ...

(Peter schreibt ...)

 Dear ...

Following your application for the position of Assistant Marketing Officer at ERGO Limited headquarters here in London, **we have pleasure in inviting you** to an interview next week. Interviews are being held on Tuesday and Wednesday, August 14-15, between 9 AM and 3 PM. Would you please call our secretary, Ms Lucy Sparrow, to arrange a convenient day and time.
We look forward very much to meeting you and wish you every success with your application.

Yours sincerely,

Peter Brückner,
Assistant Managing Director

 95. Train Yourself

Haben Sie die erste Übung mit »to get« vervollständigt? Dann versuchen Sie sich jetzt an dieser Fortsetzung!

1. The company made good progress and rapidly got ▒▒▒▒▒ .
2. He got ▒▒▒▒▒ that tricky situation without much difficulty.
3. He is always getting ▒▒▒▒▒ trouble.
4. If I can find the time, I'll get ▒▒▒▒▒ to it.
5. Considering the seriousness of the crime, he got ▒▒▒▒▒ lightly.
6. The company soon went bankrupt. It got ▒▒▒▒▒ an enormous amount of money in no time at all.
7. Your company's sales people are on the road a lot. They certainly get ▒▒▒▒▒ .
8. Can you get ▒▒▒▒▒ those documents without attracting attention?
9. It's difficult to understand at first, but persist and you'll get ▒▒▒▒▒ .
10. She's in a very strange mood. What can have got ▒▒▒▒▒ her?
11. Grab a pen and get this ▒▒▒▒▒ in writing.
12. He got ▒▒▒▒▒ the boss by waiting until the last moment before handing in his notice.

13. Get all the letters ______ and let's make a short-list.
14. He got ______ that problem by just ignoring it.

around, at, back, down, into, off, through, on, out, round to, there, together.

Talk Talk Talk

(Peter enters office, Lucy greets him)	(Peter betritt das Büro, Lucy begrüßt ihn)
L. Good morning, Peter. Do you have a lot of work to do this morning?	L. Guten Morgen, Peter. Haben Sie heute Morgen viel zu tun?
P. Oh, the usual, Lucy. Why?	P. Ach, das Übliche, Lucy. Warum?
L. Oh, you'll soon see why!	L. Sie werden gleich sehen, warum!
(James Morgan enters)	(James Morgan kommt herein)
J. Well, Lucy, where is it?	J. Lucy, wo ist es?
L. Still on ice. I was waiting for Mr Brückner to arrive.	L. Noch auf Eis. Ich habe auf Mr Brückner gewartet.
J. Can't get started without him, can we. Right, Lucy, serve up!	J. Ohne ihn können wir nicht anfangen, nicht wahr. Gut, Lucy, servieren Sie.
P. Champagne again? Somebody's birthday?	P. Schon wieder Champagner? Hat jemand Geburtstag?
(Melissa and Beryl both enter)	(Melissa und Beryl kommen herein)
M. Not ours, anyway.	M. Wir jedenfalls nicht.

J. Peter, you're to blame. Keep this up and our champagne bill alone will **sink** the company?	J. Peter, Sie sind schuld. Machen Sie weiter so und unsere Champagnerrechnung wird die Firma **ruinieren**.
P. Me?	P. Ich?
J. You secured the Newcom Technology franchise, dear chap! Another coup for you – I'm beginning to worry about the security of my position here!	J. Sie haben uns den Newcom Technology-Franchise gesichert, mein Guter! Schon wieder ein Streich für Sie – ich fange an, mir Sorgen um die Sicherheit meiner Position hier zu machen!
P. The Newcom franchise. Good heavens! I'd forgotten all about it.	P. Die Newcom-Franchise. Gütiger Himmel! Das hatte ich schon ganz vergessen.
J. Well, Newcom hadn't. This letter came today – but first a glass of bubbly and then you and I are off for a celebration lunch ...	J. Nun, Newcom nicht. Dieser Brief kam heute an – aber erst ein Glas Champus und dann machen wir beide uns auf den Weg zu einem festlichen Mittagessen ...
(Peter reads the letter ...)	(Peter liest den Brief ...)

 Mr James Morgan,

Managing Director,
ERGO Limited

Dear Mr Morgan,

Following our very fruitful discussions with Mr Peter Brückner, your Assistant Managing Director, and consultations with our lawyers, we are pleased to inform you that we have decided to grant ERGO Limited the franchise for the distribution and marketing of our new product, »Instantweb«, in the United States. Mr Brückner presented a very

convincing argument in favour of ERGO, stressing the depth and breadth of the company's American experience and involvement.
We would like to propose a further meeting now between senior management representatives and lawyers representing both companies to complete the franchise formalities and draw up the relevant agreement and documentation. We would obviously be very happy to see Mr Brückner again as a member of your team.
In anticipation of a very successful co-operation,
I remain,
Yours sincerely,

Joshua Streatham,
Managing Director,
Newcom Technologies

Talk Talk Talk

J. Well, there you have it in **black and white**, Peter. Congratulations! You obviously made a big impression in Manchester.

J. Nun, hier haben Sie es **schwarz auf weiß**, Peter. Gratuliere! Sie haben offensichtlich in Manchester großen Eindruck gemacht.

M. Yes, here's to you Peter – you're becoming quite indispensable ...

M. Ja, auf Sie, Peter – Sie werden hier ziemlich unentbehrlich ...

Background Information

The word »**fruit**« has »**given fruit**« to various expressive words and expressions in English ...

Fruitful   meaning productive, beneficial. The board meeting was very fruitful.

Fruitless meaning the opposite. Their search for the cause of the problem remained fruitless.

Fruition meaning the enjoyment or attainment of something desired. He lived to see the fruition of all his plans.

In business English, the plural »**fruits**« has the meaning of results or revenues. »The fruits of the company's three-year existence were very impressive.«

96. Train Yourself

1. Setzen Sie die korrekten Formen von »fruit« ein!

1. The project failed after _____ attempts to get it started.
2. The company made a record profit after two very _____ years.
3. After ten years of hard work, we can now sit back and enjoy the _____ of those labours.
4. The plans finally came to _____ after much hard work.
5. I'm glad to hear your efforts were _____ .
6. I told them from the start that their efforts would be in vain and _____ .
7. Their hopes have been realised, they can finally see _____ .
8. I can promise you a _____ visit to our car assembly plant next week.

2. Versuchen Sie dasselbe mit »keep«!

1. I've always avoided dealing with that particularly company, and I'd advise you to keep _____ from them, too.
2. If the company keeps _____ this growth rate next year it will be able to report record profits.
3. If we can only succeed in keeping _____ production costs we shall be able to avoid making a loss.
4. If we keep _____ this course we can't go wrong.
5. Keep those particular salesmen _____ our premises.
6. It's hard work, I know, but try to keep _____ it.
7. Keep it _____ ! You haven't got much further to run.
8. If we want to avoid an accident, we'll have to keep _____ the crowds.

at, away, back, down, off, on, up.

 Background Information

Expressions with »**keep**«:
Keep your spirits up!   Cheer up!
Keep your end up!   Don't relax your efforts!

How are you keeping?	How is your health?
keep in good repair	maintain (a home, a car etc.)
keep up appearances	maintain a good appearance
keep in with somebody	remain on good terms with them
keep up your knowledge of something	Are you keeping up your Spanish?
keep up with the Joneses	meaning to work hard at remaining on terms of obvious social equality with the neighbours

 Talk Talk Talk

(Marco's restaurant)

J. Well, we certainly have something to celebrate today, Peter. By the way, I've asked Melissa to join us. She had some correspondence of her own to complete and said she'd be along then.

P. I'm glad to hear that. I do enjoy her company.

J. You'll be enjoying more of her company than ever in the weeks ahead. When this new trainee joins us I'd like you to help her acquaint him with the **ins and outs** of marketing – and sales, too, eventually. Steve will also be in on the induction of our new colleague.

(Marcos Restaurant)

J. Nun, heute haben wir wirklich etwas zu feiern, Peter. Übrigens, ich habe Melissa gebeten, uns Gesellschaft zu leisten. Sie hatte noch einige Korrespondenz zu erledigen und sagte, sie würde danach vorbei kommen.

P. Freut mich zu hören. Ich mag ihre Gesellschaft.

J. Sie werden ihre Gesellschaft in den nächsten Wochen öfter denn je genießen. Wenn der neue Trainee zu uns kommt, möchte ich, dass Sie ihr dabei helfen, ihn mit den **Details** des Marketings – und auch des Verkaufs – vertraut zu machen. Steve wird auch bei der Einführung unseres neuen Kollegen dabei sein.

P. Fine, I'll look forward to it.

P. Schön, ich freue mich schon darauf.

J. I'm sorry to have overloaded you with all that correspondence in the past couple of weeks. I don't know how I allowed it to **accumulate** like that. From now on, it will be a lot easier. I've asked Beryl to give you a hand.

J. Es tut mir Leid, dass ich Sie in den letzten Wochen mit dieser ganzen Korrespondenz so überladen habe. Ich weiß nicht, wie ich zulassen konnte, dass sich das so **ansammelt**. Von jetzt an wird es viel einfacher werden. Ich habe Beryl gebeten, Ihnen zur Hand zu gehen.

P. She's a very willing worker – I get on well with her.

P. Sie ist eine sehr bereitwillige Arbeitskraft, ich komme gut mit ihr aus.

J. Melissa tells me Beryl won't hear a word said against you – not that anyone is. Ah, here's Melissa now ...

J. Melissa sagt, Beryl duldet es nicht, dass auch nur ein schlechtes Wort über Sie gesprochen wird – nicht, dass das einer täte. Ah, da ist Melissa ja ...

 97. Train Yourself

1. Die »ins and outs«!
Die »ins and outs« bedeuten im umgangssprachlichen Englisch die Details von etwas, z. B. eines Dokuments. Setzen Sie die richtigen Begriffe mit »in« ein!

1. He couldn't stand his boss and ▓▓▓▓ him from the start.
2. She's a very capable worker and ▓▓▓▓ to do the job well.
3. Are they ▓▓▓▓ the secret?
4. He's really ▓▓▓▓ his boss and managed to get two pay rises in one year.
5. I just don't know what's going on - I'm completely ▓▓▓▓.
6. Now he has been promoted he is ▓▓▓▓.
7. They can't offer us serious competition - they're just not ▓▓▓▓.

8. The race will be close-run - there's not much _____.
9. She dresses well, in clothes that are really _____.
10. He's _____ big trouble if he tries to evade the tax authorities.

had it in for, has it in her, in clover, in fashion, in it, in on, in the dark, in with, in for, had it in.

2. Zeit zum Üben!
Vervollständigen Sie die folgenden Briefe!

Dear Sirs/Mesdames,

I _____ grateful if you _____ us information _____ your latest products.
   _____ we need the information as quickly as _____ , could you please _____ it by _____ post. A complete price list and an explanation of your _____ of payment would also be _____.

Yours _____,
...

Dear Mr Hancock,

With _____ to your letter of February 24, we have _____ in informing you that we have _____ to place an _____ with your company for 60,000 units. Would you please arrange to _____ our stock department to discuss delivery. We would obviously _____ delivery as soon as _____ , and are _____ to meet any extra _____ that this would involve. Invoices should be _____ to our finance department.

Yours _____,
...

appreciate, appreciated, contact, costs, decided, express, faithfully, forward, about, order, pleasure, prepared, reference, sent, since, sincerely, terms, would be, possible.

 **Talk Talk Talk**

(Marco's Restaurant)

M. Sorry I'm late. I find it more and more difficult to leave the office at lunch-time these days.

J. Anything urgent?

M. No, not at all, but it would be waiting for me if I **put** it **off** until after lunch. So what has Marco to offer today?

J. I always recommend his gnocchi – but while we're waiting just let's run through the interview procedure. I'm not very good at this. In all my time with the company, I've possibly only hired half a dozen people personally.

P. But who did the **hiring**?

J. We used to have a personnel officer – »human resources« officer, I suppose you'd call her these days. When she left we never filled the position.

P. So who hires?

(Marcos Restaurant)

M. Entschuldigung, dass ich zu spät komme. Ich finde es momentan zunehmend schwieriger, das Büro zur Mittagszeit zu verlassen.

J. Irgendetwas Dringendes?

M. Nein, überhaupt nicht, aber es würde auf mich warten, wenn ich es bis nach dem Essen **verschieben würde**. Also, was hat Marco heute anzubieten?

J. Ich empfehle immer seine Gnocchi – aber während wir warten, lassen Sie uns noch einmal den Gesprächsablauf durchgehen. Ich bin nicht sehr gut darin. Seit ich für die Firma arbeite, habe ich selbst vielleicht nur ein halbes Dutzend Leute eingestellt.

P. Aber wer hat die **Einstellungen** übernommen?

J. Wir hatten eine Personalbearbeiterin – heutzutage würde man sie wohl »Human Ressources«-Betreuerin nennen. Als sie ging, haben wir die Stelle nicht neu besetzt.

P. Wer führt also die Einstellungen durch?

J. You're looking at her right now.

P. Melissa?

J. Yes, but in this case she wants our advice, too – even though the vacancy is in her department. She's being as secretive as ever ...

J. Sie sehen sie gerade an.

P. Melissa?

J. Ja, aber in dem Fall möchte sie auch unseren Rat – obwohl die Stelle in ihrer Abteilung frei ist. Sie macht es wie immer geheimnisvoll ...

 98. Train Yourself

Im Gespräch erzählt Mr Morgan, dass er schon lange für die Firma arbeitet. Er verwendet dabei den Begriff »to work with«. »To work« hat noch andere Präpositionen, setzen Sie diese hier ein!

1. How long have you been working ▬▬▬ ERGO Limited?
2. I have been working ▬▬▬ the company for ten years now.
3. He works directly ▬▬▬ the foreman.
4. I've been working ▬▬▬ this project for five years.
5. He is a good draughtsman and works ▬▬▬ great accuracy.
6. She was working ▬▬▬ Jackson and Partners from 1993 until 1997.
7. Are they working ▬▬▬ this department?
8. He's working ▬▬▬ the Dagenham factory.
9. At the moment, I'm working ▬▬▬ a completely different project.
10. I've been working ▬▬▬ ERGO Limited one way or another for some time now.
11. He's ▬▬▬ work on that project at the moment.

at, by, for, in, on, under, with.

 **Background Information**

Further expressions with »**work**«:

a good day's work	a lot has been accomplished, achieved
have one's work cut out	have as much to do as one can manage
give somebody the works	give or tell him or her everything
work away on	continue to work on
work one's fingers to the bone	work very hard
work in	find a place for something
work out	calculate, solve
work off	get rid of

 **Talk Talk Talk**

(Back at the office)

S. Oh, Peter, this letter was among my batch today, but I think it's something for you to handle.

P. Steve, you've **made my day** – my week. I thought I'd got through all the correspondence. But give it here and I'll see what I can do.

S. By the way, a few pals and I are playing skittles tonight out in the country, at Farningham. Want to come along?

(Zurück im Büro)

S. Ach Peter, der Brief war heute in meinem Stapel, aber ich glaube, Sie sollten sich darum kümmern.

P. Steve, Sie haben **meinen Tag gerettet** – meine ganze Woche. Ich dachte, ich wäre mit der gesamten Korrespondenz fertig. Also geben Sie ihn schon her und ich sehe, was ich tun kann.

S. Übrigens, ein paar Kumpel und ich gehen heute zum Kegeln draußen auf dem Land, bei Faringham. Wollen Sie mitkommen?

Korrespondenz

P. Love to, Steve, but I'm otherwise engaged. Melissa has finally accepted an invitation to dinner.

P. Würde ich liebend gern, Steve, aber ich habe schon was anderes vor. Melissa hat endlich meine Einladung zum Abendessen angenommen.

S. Wow! Watch your step, though, Peter, my friend. She's a mankiller, that one.

S. Wow! Passen Sie auf sich auf, Peter. Die ist eine Männerfresserin.

P. I'll take my chance.

P. Das werde ich riskieren.

S. What can have led her to melt at last?

S. Was hat sie am Ende zum Schmelzen gebracht?

P. Oh, come on Steve, who's talking about melting?

P. Ach kommen Sie schon, Steve, wer redet denn von schmelzen?

(Melissa enters)

(Melissa kommt herein)

M. Who's melting? I am – it's even hotter today than yesterday. Who's going to run out for an ice?

M. Wer schmilzt? Ich schmelze jedenfalls – heute ist es noch heißer als gestern. Wer geht Eis holen?

S. Chip? Chip? Damn me, he's probably sitting on his motorbike right now licking a cornet. OK, you two, choc or vanilla?

S. Chip? Chip? Verdammt noch mal, er sitzt wahrscheinlich gerade auf seinem Motorrad und leckt ein Eis. Okay, ihr beiden, Schoko oder Vanille?

 99. Train Yourself

Peter verwendet den Ausdruck »to take one's chance«. Vervollständigen Sie die folgenden Sätze mit »take«!

1. I can't be hurried – this job is going to take ▓▓▓.
2. Are you tired already? Let's take ▓▓▓.

3. This is the third time this week she's turned up late – I shall have to take it _____ with her.
4. Take it _____ me, I predict trouble within one month.
5. His qualifications are excellent. He obviously has _____ it takes.
6. The forgery was a very good one. It took us all _____ .
7. The finances are in a mess, they need to be taken _____ hand.
8. Did you understand the lecture? Did you take it all _____ ?
9. He's got a new hobby – he's recently taken _____ collecting antique teapots.
10. I have something important to tell you, but can I really take you _____ my confidence?

The possibilities: a break, from, in, into, time, to, up, what.

 Background Information

Further expressions with »**take**«:

take for a ride	Deceive (»That swindler took us all for a ride«).
Take it or leave it.	Do as you please.
take it out on	Work off one's frustration by attacking or maltreating another (»He's so unhappy in his job that he takes it out on the dog when he gets home at night«).

 Talk Talk Talk

(Peter's office. He opens the letter given to him by Steve ...)   (Peters Büro. Er öffnet den Brief von Steve ...)

 Dear Sirs,

My company is endeavouring to organise a joint exhibit by office software producers and distributors at the upcoming Intertec electronics trade fair. A joint exhibit would reduce costs without necessarily

affecting competitiveness. In fact, we feel a combined stand at the fair would contribute to productive co-operation and a healthy exchange of ideas. A synergy could arise which could be of great benefit to all involved.
I would be very happy to hear your views on this proposal, and would be delighted to answer any questions you may have.

Yours faithfully,

Samuel Trotman,
Chief Executive,
Grant Technologies

(Steve's office. Peter enters) | (Steves Büro. Peter tritt ein)

P. Steve, why did you **pass me on** this letter? It looks like something for Melissa. | P. Steve, warum haben Sie diesen Brief **an mich weitergeleitet**? Sieht aus, als wäre er etwas für Melissa.

S. I'm sorry, Peter, but I'm not in Melissa's **good books** at the moment, and frankly I'm reluctant to drop any work on her desk. | S. Es tut mir Leid, Peter, aber ich stehe bei Melissa im Augenblick **nicht gut im Ansehen** und offen gesagt habe ich Hemmungen, ihr Arbeit auf den Schreibtisch zu legen.

P. OK, I'll be glad to tackle her on it. | P. Also, ich nehme das gerne in Angriff.

Background Information

Business word of the decade is »**synergy**«. It has long since grown out of its original medicine book context, where it meant the combined effect of medicines that exceeds the sum of their individual effects. In business terms, synergy means the combined positive effect of business co-operation. Two separate companies producing goods or services which can be profitably combined can co-operate and develop a successful synergy.

100. Train Yourself

Don't pass this by ...

Das Verb »pass« wird oft in geläufigen Ausdrücken verwendet. Vervollständigen Sie »pass« in den folgenden Sätzen durch die passenden Präpositionen: *through, up, on, by*.

1. He passed _____ the opportunity to take the company over.
2. The company passed _____ a very difficult phase.
3. He left without passing _____ any of the experience he had gained.
4. Success just passed him _____ .
5. Fancy passing _____ a chance like that!
6. They passed _____ without giving us so much as a nod of recognition.

 Talk Talk Talk

(Melissa's office. Peter enters)

P. Hello, Melissa. This letter seems to belong in your department, although I'd be happy to answer it.

M. Let me see (reads the letter). But this is crazy! What can this man Trotman be thinking about? The trade fair arrangements have long since been made. We've booked and paid for our stand – in fact, I've really got to get down to work on preparations for the fair. I really need that assistant – when are we interviewing the candidates?

(Melissas Büro. Peter tritt ein)

P. Hallo Melissa. Dieser Brief scheint in Ihre Abteilung zu gehören, ich kann ihn aber auch gerne beantworten.

M. Lassen Sie mich sehen (liest den Brief). Das ist ja verrückt. Was denkt sich dieser Trotman nur? Die Arrangements für die Messe sind schon lange erledigt. Wir haben unseren Stand gebucht und bezahlt, ich muss jetzt wirklich damit anfangen, an den Vorbereitungen für die Messe zu arbeiten. Ich brauche diesen Assistenten wirklich – wann führen wir die

	Bewerbungsgespräche mit den Kandidaten?
P. In a couple of weeks' time. It will be about six weeks before you get that help.	P. In ein paar Wochen. In etwa sechs Wochen bekommen Sie Hilfe.
M. Just as the trade fair opens.	M. Genau wenn die Messe öffnet.
P. Well, if there's anything I can do just say the word ...	P. Nun, wenn es irgend etwas gibt, das ich tun kann, sagen Sie es ...
M. Well, reply to that letter, **for starters!**	M. Na ja, beantworten Sie diesen Brief, **für den Anfang**!

 Dear Mr Trotman,

Thank you for your letter of August 3. We registered with interest your offer of co-operation in a combined presentation at the forthcoming electronics trade fair. However, we have to inform you that we have already booked our stand-space at the fair, and we shall therefore be exhibiting alone. Nevertheless, we do not rule out co-operation at a suitable level between our companies, and remain open to any proposal from your side.
Wishing Grant Technologies every success at the fair,

Yours faithfully,

Peter Brückner,
Assistant Managing Director

 Talk Talk Talk

(Melissa's office. Peter enters and presents her with the letter)   (Melissas Büro. Peter tritt ein und zeigt ihr den Brief)

M. (after reading the letter) Yes, that's fine Peter, thank you.	M. (nachdem sie den Brief gelesen hat) Ja, das ist gut so, Peter, ich danke Ihnen.
P. And that's my last letter for a week. I'm off on holiday tomorrow, Melissa.	P. Und das war mein letzter Brief für eine Woche. Ab morgen bin ich im Urlaub, Melissa.
M. Holiday already?	M. Urlaub, schon?
P. Just a week. I want to have a look at Scotland. I was never there.	P. Nur eine Woche. Ich möchte mir Schottland ansehen. Ich war noch nie dort.
M. You'll be back in time for the interviews?	M. Werden Sie rechtzeitig zu den Bewerbungsgesprächen zurück sein?
P. Yes, of course. I'll be **in** there **at the kill**, as I learnt on my hunting trip!	P. Ja, natürlich. Ich werde **beim Abschuss dabei sein**, wie ich bei meinem Jagdausflug gelernt habe.

 101. Train Yourself

Peter erzählt Melissa, dass er noch nie in Schottland war und verwendet dabei das Simple Past. Setzen Sie in den folgenden Sätzen das Verb in seiner korrekten Form ein!

1. I *(live)* in London for four years before moving to Glasgow.
2. I *(live)* in Hamburg now for five years.
3. *(Be)* you ever in Spain?
4. How long *(live)* you in London before moving to Germany?
5. I *(be)* in Paris during that very hot spell of weather.
6. *(spend)* you all your time in the mountains?
7. I *(live)* in Britain all my life.
8. Where *(spend)* you your holidays last year?
9. *(Be)* you ever to Africa?
10. I never *(live)* abroad.

Background Information

Holiday time:
On holiday – »I'm on holiday« - **but**
holidays – »Where will you spend your holidays this year?«
I'm **making** (or **taking**) a holiday from work.
Noun: a holidaymaker.

In American English, vacation is preferred to holiday. »In America, workers usually get two weeks' vacation a year«.
In American English, »vacation« is also a commonly-used verb – »They vacation every year at their beach cottage on Long Island«. »Holiday« is also used as a verb in British English, but not so commonly – »I holidayed in Mallorca last summer«.

Talk Talk Talk

(Two weeks later. James Morgan's office. Morgan, Melissa and Peter sit at a small conference table)

J. Right, how do we go about the selection process? Throw names in a hat? (laughs)

P. Well, in my view, there's only one person for the job.

J. And that is?

P. No, let's hear what Melissa has to say first.

M. I'm staying out of this first round.

(Zwei Wochen später. James Morgans Büro. Morgan, Melissa und Peter sitzen an einem kleinen Besprechungstisch)

J. Gut, wie treffen wir die Auswahl? Werfen wir die Namen in einen Hut? (lacht)

P. Also, meiner Meinung nach kommt für die Stelle nur eine Person in Frage.

J. Und das wäre?

P. Nein, lassen Sie uns erst hören, was Melissa zu sagen hat.

M. Ich setze in der ersten Runde aus.

J. But why? You've been strangely silent from the first.

J. Aber warum? Sie waren von Anfang an merkwürdig still.

M. Please, you two have your say and then I'll add my opinion.

M. Bitte sagen Sie beide erst etwas und dann sage ich meine Meinung dazu.

J. Well, Peter, that's it – who's your prize candidate?

J. Schön, Peter, los geht's – wer ist Ihr Wunschkandidat?

P. Can I make a suggestion? We all write the name of our preference on a slip of paper and then **disclose** our choices.

P. Kann ich einen Vorschlag machen? Wir schreiben alle den Namen der von uns bevorzugten Person auf ein Blatt Papier und **verdecken** unsere jeweilige Wahl.

J. Is this a German practice? Sounds like a betting syndicate to me. But I don't mind. All right with you, Melissa?

J. Ist das eine deutsche Vorgehensweise? Klingt für mich wie eine Wette. Aber mir soll es recht sein. Sind Sie einverstanden, Melissa?

M. On just one condition – that my selection is read last of all.

M. Unter einer Bedingung – dass meine Wahl als Letzte vorgelesen wird.

J. The suspense is killing me, but that's all right by me. Pencil and paper?

Die Spannung bringt mich um, aber ich bin einverstanden. Papier und Bleistift?

 102. Train Yourself

Peter Brückner schlägt vor, den richtigen Bewerber auszulosen und verwendet dabei den Begriff »disclose«. »Dis-« ist eine weit verbreitete Vorsilbe, die Substantiven, Adjektiven und Verben viele verschiedene Bedeutungen verleihen kann. Einerseits kann es sich hierbei um eine Unterscheidung von Etwas zu etwas Anderem handeln (»distinguish«), aber auch um ein Gegenteil oder die Umkehrung einer Handlung (»disable, dishonest«). Finden Sie nun in den folgenden Sätzen die richtige Form!

1. The trade union is not represented in that factory – the workers are totally ▨▨▨ .
2. The company ▨▨▨ all responsibility for the late deliveries.
3. We ▨▨▨ ourselves from his actions.
4. The management showed its ▨▨▨ by cancelling the usual holiday bonus.
5. The strike action ▨▨▨ production at the assembly plant.
6. He's a liar and a cheat, in fact an utterly ▨▨▨ person.
7. The projects manager ▨▨▨ all our ideas, he just ignored them.
8. We have a very generous expense allowance at our ▨▨▨ .
9. The entire board of directors was ▨▨▨ at the annual meeting.
10. The ▨▨▨ workers threatened strike action.
11. The office is in a completely ▨▨▨ state, with papers all over the place.
12. He's a very ▨▨▨ worker, with no system or routine.
13. The firm ▨▨▨ after trying for three years to recover its losses.
14. The factory was sold off and then ▨▨▨ piece by piece.
15. There's no ▨▨▨ in admitting you made a mistake.
16. The supporters were very ▨▨▨ by their side's defeat in the Cup.

disadvantaged, disclaimed, disgruntled, disheartened, dishonour, disintegrated, dismantled, dismissed, disorderly, disorganised, displeasure, disposal, disregarded, disreputable, disrupted, dissociated.

 Talk Talk Talk

(James Morgan's office)

J. Right, where are the slips of paper? Let's see what name is on yours, Peter! Good heavens! Martin Russell!

(James Morgans Büro)

J. Gut, wo sind die Zettel? Lassen Sie uns sehen, welcher Name auf Ihrem steht, Peter! Gütiger Himmel! Martin Russell!

P. Why the surprise?	P. Warum die Überraschung?
J. That's the young man I've chosen, too. Whose name is on your slip of paper, Melissa? Here with it! But you've written nothing down. No name at all. What does that mean?	J. Das ist der junge Mann, den ich auch gewählt habe. Wessen Name ist auf Ihrem Zettel, Melissa? Her damit! Aber Sie haben ja nichts hingeschrieben. Überhaupt keinen Namen. Was soll das bedeuten?
M. But since you two have **unanimously** chosen Martin Russell, my choice is **immaterial**.	M. Nachdem Sie beide **einstimmig** Martin Russell gewählt haben, ist meine Wahl **bedeutungslos**.
J. That's not true, you'll be working with him, Melissa.	J. Das ist nicht wahr, Melissa, Sie werden mit ihm zusammenarbeiten.
M. I'll have no problem at all working with young Martin Russell.	M. Ich werde keinerlei Schwierigkeiten haben, mit dem jungen Martin Russell zusammenzuarbeiten.
J. You know him?	J. Sie kennen ihn?
M. I have met him on a few occasions, yes. He's Beryl's nephew. That's why I had to withdraw from the final selection process. But since you two have both **plumped for** Martin it didn't make much difference, did it?	M. Ja, ich habe ihn bei ein paar Gelegenheiten getroffen. Er ist Beryls Neffe. Deswegen musste ich mich vom endgültigen Auswahlprozess zurückziehen. Aber nachdem Sie beide für Martin **gestimmt** haben, machte das keinen großen Unterschied, nicht wahr?
J. Well, I'll be damned. You're good for surprises, Melissa.	J. Ja, verflucht noch mal. Sie sind für Überraschungen gut, Melissa.
M. Can I go and tell Beryl? She'll be delighted. And you'll be delighted with Martin on the staff, too. He'll be a credit to ERGO!	M. Kann ich gehen und es Beryl erzählen? Sie wird begeistert sein. Und Sie werden begeistert sein, Martin als Angestellten zu haben. Er wird ein Gewinn für ERGO sein!

103. Train Yourself

Melissa erwähnt, dass ihre Wahl »immaterial« (nicht wichtig) ist, also »not material«. Setzen Sie die richtigen Negativpräfixe »un-«, »in-« oder »im-« in den folgenden Sätzen ein:

1. I find it extremely ▓▓ polite to smoke while others are eating.
2. The union's wage demands were ▓▓ moderate.
3. I find his remarks quite ▓▓ appropriate.
4. We could hardly understand a thing he said - he's very ▓▓ articulate.
5. Mozart's music made him ▓▓ mortal.
6. No, it can't be changed. It's ▓▓ alterable.
7. She won't forgive me - she's quite ▓▓ placable.
8. I won't accept such behaviour. It's quite ▓▓ tolerable.
9. The company president is totally ▓▓ pervious to such arguments.
10. The damage he did to the company is ▓▓ measurable.

 Vocabulary

to accumulate	ansammeln
to disclose	verdecken
to draft	entwerfen
for starters	für den Anfang
to hire	einstellen
in black and white	schwarz auf weiß
ins and outs	alle Details
in somebody's good books	bei jemandem gut im Ansehen stehen
immaterial	bedeutungslos
to make sb.'s day	einem den Tag retten
to plump for	stimmen für
to put off	verschieben
short-list	Auswahlliste
to shift through	durchschauen
to sink	ruinieren
to whittle down	reduzieren

Acquire customers
Kunden akquirieren

 Here we go

Nachdem Peter sich schon in viele Bereiche bei seiner Firma ERGO Limited eingearbeitet hat, ist sein Vorgesetzter James Morgan nun der Überzeugung, dass Peter sich näher mit der Verkaufsabteilung von Steve Blackman befassen sollte. Er muss sich jetzt Gedanken darüber machen, wie man eine Verkaufsstrategie am besten angeht und wie man Menschen dazu animiert, ein Produkt zu kaufen. Seine ersten Versuche startet er sogleich bei seinen eigenen Kollegen ...

 Talk Talk Talk

(James Morgan's office at ERGO Limited, Peter Brückner enters)

J. Good morning, Peter! Did you have a good weekend?

P. Very enjoyable, Mr Morgan. I spent it with my friends in Sussex again.

J. Not hunting, surely?

P. No, the season's over. We drove down to Brighton.

J. And what do you think of Brighton? It's been **run down** so much recently in the press.

(James Morgans Büro bei ERGO Limited. Peter Brückner tritt ein)

J. Guten Morgen, Peter! Hatten Sie ein schönes Wochenende?

P. Ich habe es sehr genossen, Mr Morgan. Ich habe es wieder mit meinen Freunden in Sussex verbracht.

J. Aber Sie haben doch nicht wieder gejagt?

P. Nein, die Saison ist vorüber. Wir sind runter nach Brighton gefahren.

J. Und was halten Sie von Brighton? In der Presse wurde in letzter Zeit viel **darüber hergezogen**.

P. Actually, I liked the place very much. It's got – what do you say, a **buzz**? Probably because of all the university students.

J. Brighton also knows how to sell itself – and that brings me to what I want to talk to you about, Peter. I'd like you to **immerse yourself** during the next few weeks in our **sales operation** and then report to me on your ideas on **how we could improve things in that area**.

P. Certainly, Mr Morgan, but what do you want me to do?

J. Steve Blackman's going down to the West Country next week for an **intensive seminar** in **salesmanship**. I'd like you to go with him. He's following that up with a tour of our **sales offices**. I'd like you write that down in your **schedule**, too.

P. Also eigentlich gefiel mir der Ort sehr gut. Er – wie sagt man – **er brummt**? Wahrscheinlich wegen all der Universitätsstudenten.

J. Brighton versteht es außerdem, sich selbst zu verkaufen – und genau darüber wollte ich mit Ihnen sprechen, Peter. Ich möchte, dass Sie sich während der nächsten paar Wochen **intensiv in unsere Verkaufsaktivitäten einarbeiten** und mir dann über Ihre Ideen berichten, **wie wir diesen Bereich noch verbessern könnten**.

P. Natürlich, Mr Morgan, aber was genau soll ich tun?

J. Steve Blackman fährt nächste Woche für ein **Intensiv-Seminar** über das **Verkaufsgeschäft** hinunter ins West Country. Ich möchte, dass Sie ihn begleiten. Er macht danach eine Tour zu unseren **Verkaufbüros**. Ich möchte, dass Sie auch das in Ihren **Terminkalender** eintragen.

Colloquial English

> Peter says that Brighton has got a **buzz**. This means it has a **lively atmosphere**.
> Also: The place was **buzzing**.
> »To **give someone a buzz**« means **to telephone**.

Verkaufsgespräche

Background Information

Many verbs in English include the prepositions »**up**« and »**down**«. Some such as »**drive up/down**« and »**go up/down**« have a literal sense of direction, i.e. Brighton is south of London, so Peter drove down to Brighton just as he would drive up to Edinburgh. Similarly, one would go up the mountain and then down again.

Others such as »**run down**« (generally used to mean »to discredit somebody or something«) have no obvious literal meaning. »To **write down**« means to make a note of something, or to copy something, »to **write up**«, on the other hand implies a longer process, e.g. »I'm writing up my reports at the moment«; direction has nothing to do with it.

Some other »up/down« phrasal verbs include:

to put up	to give accommodation to somebody
to put down	to belittle or make somebody feel inferior
to set up	to establish, install
to bring up	to introduce a new idea, to mention
to scale down	to reduce
to let down	to disappoint
to turn down	to reject or refuse

104. Train Yourself

Setzen Sie das korrekte »phrasal verb« in die folgenden Sätze ein.
Verwenden Sie folgende Begriffe: *run down, write down, write up, follow up, set up, scale down, let down, put up, put down, go up, go down, turn down.*

1. The management are ▒▒▒▒▒▒ operations in Eastern Europe and making many employees redundant.
2. Can you ▒▒▒▒▒▒ this ▒▒▒▒▒▒ please, Lucy, it's for a speech I'm preparing for the conference this weekend.
3. I think it's important to ▒▒▒▒▒▒ the subject of overtime in next week's meeting.

4. Where are you staying?
   Oh, they're ▮▮▮▮▮ me ▮▮▮▮▮ in the Hilton Hotel, would you believe!
5. We're ▮▮▮▮▮ a new franchise agreement to boost sales in the American market.
6. We don't want to ▮▮▮▮▮ Rothmans ▮▮▮▮▮!
   We told them our report would be there today!
   Send this express post immediately!
7. Peter ▮▮▮▮▮ his presentation with a quick tour of the department.
8. Simon was ▮▮▮▮▮ for the position of general manager. He was devastated.
9. Why are you so tired?
   I spent all night ▮▮▮▮▮ the new proposals for the merger.
10. He's not a popular member of the department because he's always ▮▮▮▮▮ colleagues behind their backs.
11. We can ▮▮▮▮▮ to Manchester tonight. It's only a two hour drive from London.
12. I'm ▮▮▮▮▮ to the shops! Does anybody want something?

 Talk Talk Talk

(Peter's office. Steve Blackman enters)

S. Come on Peter, **drop what you're doing** and follow me to my office – the *Nag's Head*. Buy me a beer and I'll tell you all you need to know about selling!

P. I **gather** we're off on a **sales trip** together. That should be fun.

(Peters Büro. Steve Blackman tritt ein)

S. Kommen Sie, Peter – **lassen Sie alles stehen und liegen** und folgen Sie mir in mein Büro – ins *Nag's Head*. Spendieren Sie mir ein Bier und ich verrate Ihnen alles übers Verkaufen, was Sie wissen müssen!

P. Ich **habe gehört**, dass wir zusammen auf eine **Verkaufsreise** gehen. Das wird bestimmt ein Spaß.

S. Don't count on it, Peter, my dear chap ...	S. Erhoffen Sie sich nicht zu viel, Peter, alter Freund ...
(In the pub) S. So what's it to be?	(Im Pub) S. Also, was darf's sein?
P. Oh, make mine a pint of best bitter – there's nothing waiting for me on my desk today.	P. Oh, ich nehme ein Pint *Best Bitter* – auf meinem Schreibtisch wartet heute keine Arbeit mehr auf mich.
S. Now, did the **old man** fill you in?	S. Also, hat **der Alte** Sie ins Bild gesetzt?
P. He said we'd be attending a sales seminar and then touring our **sales points** around the country.	P. Er hat mir gesagt, dass wir an einem Verkaufsseminar teilnehmen und dann unsere **Verkaufsstellen** in der Umgebung abklappern.
S. You're in for a grand tour. We start in Bournemouth – that's where the seminar is being held. Then we head for Plymouth, from where we cover the West Country. Then over to Cardiff, to see how Wales is being covered. Then up to Scotland, to Glasgow and Edinburgh. And all in two weeks. You'll need a holiday after that.	S. Machen Sie sich auf eine große Tour gefasst. Wir starten in Bournemouth – dort wird das Seminar abgehalten. Dann fahren wir weiter nach Plymouth, von wo aus wir das West Country abdecken. Dann rüber nach Cardiff, um zu sehen, wie Wales abgedeckt wird. Dann geht es hoch nach Schottland, nach Glasgow und Edinburgh. Und das alles in zwei Wochen. Danach werden Sie urlaubsreif sein.
P. Well, I was planning to get back to Hamburg for a short visit ...	P. Tja, ich hatte sowieso vor, für einen Kurzbesuch zurück nach Hamburg zu gehen ...

Background Information

The devolution of regional political powers in Britain in 1999 – giving Scotland its own Parliament and Wales a semi-autonomous National Assembly – led to a **boost** in business activity in Glasgow, Edinburgh and Cardiff. Many companies strengthened their presence in Wales and Scotland in anticipation of greater investment there.

105. Train Yourself

Steve sagt zu Peter, er solle alles stehen und liegen lassen. Er verwendet dabei den Ausdruck »drop what you're doing« im Sinne von »stop doing what you're doing right now«. Im Englischen gibt es viele solcher umgangssprachlicher Redewendungen. Finden Sie nun heraus, was nachstehende Wendungen bedeuten!

1. Drop in and see us.

2. Drop me a line.

3. Just another drop!

4. A drop-out.

5. Drop off to sleep.

6. Drop something off.

Talk Talk Talk

(Peter's office. Melissa Walker enters)

M. **Off on your travels again**, Peter, I hear!

(Peters Büro. Melissa Walker tritt ein)

M. Ich habe gehört, **Sie brechen schon wieder zu einer Reise auf**, Peter!

P. A bit further **afield** this time, Melissa. I shall actually get to see Wales and Scotland.	P. Diesmal geht es etwas weiter **hinaus**, Melissa. Ich werde tatsächlich Wales und Schottland sehen.
M. You'll love Scotland. Every German I ever met **fell** for the country. My German teacher was **wild about** Edinburgh. She told me nearly every Scottish city, town and village is twinned with a partner in Bavaria.	M. Schottland wird Ihnen gefallen. Jeder Deutsche, den ich bis jetzt kennen gelernt habe, **hat sich** in das Land dort **verliebt**. Meine Deutschlehrerin war ganz versessen auf Edinburgh. Sie hat mir erzählt, dass fast jede schottische Stadt und jedes Dorf eine Partnerstadt in Bayern hat.
P. I'm also looking forward to seeing Wales.	P. Ich freue mich auch darauf, Wales zu sehen.
M. Do you know, I've never been there. But the countryside around Snowdon and the other mountains is supposed to be beautiful.	M. Wissen Sie, ich war nie da. Aber die Landschaft um Snowdon und die anderen Berge müssen wirklich wunderschön sein.
P. Melissa, **when it comes to selling** a place I think I could learn a lot from you!	P. Melissa, **wenn es darum geht**, eine Gegend **anzupreisen**, könnte ich eine Menge von Ihnen lernen.
M. Don't laugh, Peter, but I once worked in marketing for the National Tourist Board! But I left before I could get to Wales ...	M. Lachen Sie nicht, Peter, aber ich habe einmal im Marketing für das Nationale Touristenbüro gearbeitet! Aber ich bin von dort weggegangen, bevor ich je nach Wales gekommen bin ...

Background Information

Twinning: Several regions in Great Britain have developed strong business ties to German states through twinning arrangements between cities and towns in both countries. A special relationship has arisen in this way between Scotland and Bavaria, where 20 cities and towns are twinned with Scottish communities. The most notable are the twinnings of Munich and Edinburgh, Nuremberg and Glasgow.

False Friends

Melissa asks »**Off on your travels?**« meaning »**Are you leaving to go travelling?**«. Saying to somebody »**Right, I'm off! See you later!** « is very common in English. (Be careful, however, you don't get confused with the meaning of »**off**« to describe rotten food! e.g. »Urgh! **This meat is off! It stinks!**«)

There are also several verbs which use the preposition »**off**«:

to call off	to cancel
to put off	to postpone
to take off	to increase rapidly
to pull off	to succeed in something
to set off	to start a journey
to switch off	to begin to relax

106. Train Yourself

Füllen Sie die Lücken mit oben stehenden »phrasal verbs«:

1. The deal was ▒▒▒▒ when the managing director suddenly resigned.
2. We ▒▒▒▒ in a hurry because Jonathon couldn't find his passport.
3. Everyone was delighted that we ▒▒▒▒ the deal so quickly. We expected the negotiations to take much longer.
4. During the last quarter sales have really ▒▒▒▒ and profits are up by 40 per cent.
5. The meeting was ▒▒▒▒ until next week when everybody could attend.
6. Due to the pressures of work it is vital to ▒▒▒▒ every now and again.

Background Information

Melissa also says, »**Every German I ever met fell for the country**«. This does not mean they fell down and hurt themselves but rather they had a strong initial liking for the country. The meaning is virtually the same as to **fall in love**.

Other phrases with »**for**« are:
to make up for	to compensate for
to make for	to result in
to bargain for	to take into account
to stand for	to represent (i.e. initials)
to put in for	to apply for

 107. Train Yourself

Wählen Sie die passenden »phrasal verbs« aus oben stehender Liste für die folgenden Sätze!

1. We hadn't ▒▒▒▒▒▒▒▒▒▒ stiff competition from our rivals and our sales reflected this.
2. The BBC ▒▒▒▒▒▒▒▒▒▒ British Broadcasting Corporation.
3. Did you hear? Tony's ▒▒▒▒▒▒▒▒▒▒ the new management position. I hope he gets it.
4. She visited the new location for the company's offices and ▒▒▒▒▒▒▒▒▒▒ it immediately. It was perfect.
5. The Internet ▒▒▒▒▒▒▒▒▒▒ much easier communication with potential customers all over the world.
6. The success of the new prototype ▒▒▒▒▒▒▒▒▒▒ all the disappointments of the past.

Talk Talk Talk

(Peter arrives at the office the next day. Lucy Scott, the secretary, greets him)

(Am nächsten Tag kommt Peter im Büro an. Lucy Scott, die Sekretärin, begrüßt ihn)

Verkaufsgespräche

L. Good morning, Peter. You're off for a grand tour of the country, I hear!

P. **News does travel fast**, Lucy!

L. Well, I should be the first to know – I'm making all the **travel arrangements** for you and Steve!

P. Lucy, for the next few days, until we leave, I'm going to use you as a **guinea-pig**, if you don't mind, to help me **prepare for the seminar**. I know nothing about salesmanship.

L. Nor do I, Peter!

P. But you buy things – so in that sense you're an expert in salesmanship. For instance, what **considerations make you decide** to buy one product rather than another?

M. (enters) That's my area, Peter. Marketing.

P. But **the two areas coincide**, don't they?

L. Look, this is getting too complicated for me. Tea, anyone?

L. Guten Morgen, Peter. Ich habe gehört, Sie brechen zu einer großen Tour durch das Land auf!

P. **Neuigkeiten verbreiten sich hier schnell**, Lucy!

L. Tja, ich sollte auch die Erste sein, die das erfährt – schließlich treffe ich die **Reisevorbereitungen** für Sie und Steve!

P. Lucy, wenn Sie nichts dagegen haben, werde ich Sie in den nächsten paar Tagen vor unserer Abreise als **Versuchskaninchen** missbrauchen, um mich **auf das Seminar vorzubereiten**. Ich weiß überhaupt nichts über das Verkaufsgeschäft.

L. Genau so wenig wie ich, Peter!

P. Aber Sie kaufen Dinge ein – in diesem Sinne sind sie eine Expertin im Verkaufsgeschäft. **Wie** zum Beispiel **treffen Sie eine Entscheidung** darüber, ein bestimmtes Produkt statt einem anderen zu kaufen?

M. (tritt ein) Das ist mein Fachgebiet, Peter. Marketing.

P. Aber **diese beiden Gebiete überschneiden sich**, oder?

L. Also das wird mir jetzt zu kompliziert. Möchte jemand Tee?

P. Now there's an example! Tea! What makes you buy that **brand** in preference to another, Lucy?	P. Ein gutes Beispiel! Tee! Warum kaufen Sie diese **Marke** statt einer anderen, Lucy?
M. But that's a supermarket product that sells itself through **clever packaging** and marketing. Salesmanship has nothing to do with it.	M. Aber das ist ein Produkt aus dem Supermarkt, das sich selbst durch eine **clevere Verpackung** und Marketing verkauft. Verkaufsgeschick hat damit überhaupt nichts zu tun.
P. Well, perhaps in this case not. But haven't you ever been approached in the supermarket or in a department store by a **sales representative** asking you to **try out a certain product**?	P. Gut, in diesem Fall vielleicht nicht. Aber ist in einem Supermarkt oder Kaufhaus denn nie ein **Verkäufer** an Sie herangetreten und hat Ihnen angeboten, **ein bestimmtes Produkt auszuprobieren**?
L. You're right. It happened to me this morning. There was a **stand** at the entrance to the food hall of our local department store and biscuits were being **handed out**.	L. Sie haben Recht. Das ist mir erst heute Morgen passiert. Am Eingang der Lebensmittelabteilung unseres Kaufhauses war ein **Stand** aufgebaut, an dem Kekse **verteilt** wurden.
P. Handed out, Lucy? Did everybody accept a biscuit?	P. Verteilt, Lucy? Hat denn jeder einen Keks angenommen?
L. Well, no. I didn't, for instance.	L. Tja, nein. Ich zum Beispiel nicht.
P. Why not?	P. Warum nicht?
L. I didn't like the look of the young girl handing them out. And she just sort of threw them at people!	L. Mir gefiel nicht, wie das junge Mädchen, das sie verteilte, aussah. Und sie hat sie den Leuten regelrecht aufgezwungen!
P. There you have it! A bad **sales-**	P. Da haben Sie es! Eine schlechte

person. Sloppy appearance and personal presentation and no motivation.	Verkäuferin. Schlampiges Erscheinungsbild, schlechte Präsentation und keine Motivation.
M. Wow, Peter! Do you really need to go to that seminar?	M. Wow, Peter! Müssen Sie wirklich noch an diesem Seminar teilnehmen?

Background Information

Peter asks Lucy in this section if she doesn't mind being used as a **guinea-pig** to help him prepare for a seminar. A »**guinea-pig**«, as well as being a small furry animal, can also refer to a person used in a scientific experiment, and this is obviously the meaning Peter has in mind.

There are many other words and expressions in English that refer to **testing/experimentation** and some are listed below:

to sound out	(colloquial) to discover somebody's intentions or opinions
to try out	to test something in order to see how useful or effective it is
to pilot	to judge how good something is before introducing it
to test the water	(colloquial) to find out people's opinions before introducing something
a prototype	The first example of something from which later forms are developed.
a sample	an example, usually given free, of an article or commodity being offered for sale so that possible buyers can examine or test it
a trial run	a practical test of something new, or unknown, to discover its effectiveness
a pitch	persuasive talk or arguments for financial gain

108. Train Yourself

Benutzen Sie die oben aufgeführten Wendungen (einschließlich »guinea-pig«) um die folgenden Lücken zu füllen. Verwenden Sie dabei jeden Begriff nur einmal!

1. Have you seen the ▨▨▨▨▨ of the new Amstrad computer? They're hoping to move into mass production with it next year.
2. I hear you're off to that sales conference in Paris next week. I don't know yet, I've got to ▨▨▨▨▨ it ▨▨▨▨▨ with the boss first.
3. The company is venturing the Eastern European market to ▨▨▨▨▨ the new product.
4. They made several ▨▨▨▨▨ in the domestic sector before launching the product abroad.
5. As I was saying, Peter, I need to ▨▨▨▨▨ with this one before we go ahead with production.
6. They're asking for students to be used as ▨▨▨▨▨ in their research into the common cold.
7. They're ▨▨▨▨▨ a new brand of biscuit in my local supermarket.
8. There are sales people handing out ▨▨▨▨▨ on every aisle.
9. The representative gave his sales ▨▨▨▨▨ about quality and quantity.

 **Talk Talk Talk**

(Beryl, Melissa's assistant, peeps into Peter's office)	(Beryl, Melissas Assistentin, wirft einen Blick in Peters Büro)
P. Good morning, Beryl. Care to join us in this illuminating conversation?	P. Guten Morgen, Beryl. Möchten Sie unserer erhellenden Diskussion nicht beitreten?
B. So what are you lot chatting about?	B. Über was quasselt ihr denn hier?

M. Selling, Beryl. Peter here is getting all **geared up** for that seminar he'll be attending with Steve.	M. Über das Verkaufsgeschäft, Beryl. Unser Peter **bereitet sich** auf das Seminar **vor**, an dem er zusammen mit Steve teilnehmen wird.
P. Beryl, when did you last buy anything because of a **convincing sales pitch**? And what did you buy?	P. Beryl, wann haben Sie das letzte Mal etwas wegen einer **überzeugenden Verkaufsstrategie** gekauft? Und was?
B. Let me see ... Well, funnily enough, I bought some lens-cleaning liquid from a **sales stand** in that shopping mall of Leicester Square only yesterday.	B. Mal sehen ... tja, komischerweise habe ich gestern eine Linsen-Reinigungsflüssigkeit an einem **Verkaufsstand** gekauft, der in dem Einkaufscenter am Leicester Square aufgebaut war.
P. Lens-cleaning liquid?	P. Linsen-Reinigungsflüssigkeit?
B. You know the stuff. You clean your spectacles with it. Or a camera lens.	B. Sie kennen doch dieses Zeug. Man kann damit seine Brille putzen. Oder ein Kamera-Objektiv.
M. Good lord! But why did you buy that, Beryl? You don't even wear spectacles!	M. Gütiger Himmel! Aber warum haben Sie das nur gekauft, Beryl? Sie tragen doch nicht einmal eine Brille!
B. I wear sunglasses, and they get very dirty here in London.	B. Ich trage Sonnenbrillen, und die werden hier in London sehr schnell schmutzig.
P. But why did you buy the liquid? That's what I'd like to know.	P. Aber warum haben Sie diese Flüssigkeit gekauft? Das würde ich gerne wissen.
B. The young man **made a very good sales pitch. He made out a**	B. Der junge Mann **hat sein Produkt sehr gut angepriesen. Er hat ein**

Verkaufsgespräche

very good **case for buying** the stuff.	sehr **gutes Argument dafür angebracht**, dieses Zeug **zu kaufen**.
P. How?	P. Und wie?
B. First of all, he **caught my attention** with a friendly smile and he approached me in a way where I didn't feel under pressure. He asked me if he could **demonstrate the effectiveness** of the liquid and I gave him my sunglasses. The cleaning fluid made a real difference. Then he **persuaded** me that it was worth using the liquid because the lenses of the sunglasses were expensive and should be treated well. He **made a very sensible and persuasive case for buying** his product.	B. Zunächst mal **hat** er **meine Aufmerksamkeit** mit einem freundlichen Lächeln **erregt** und er hat sich mir in einer Weise genähert, durch die ich mich nicht bedrängt fühlte. Er hat mich gefragt, ob er mir **die Wirksamkeit** der Flüssigkeit **vorführen** dürfte und ich habe ihm meine Brille gegeben. Die Reinigungsflüssigkeit hat wirklich gut gewirkt. Dann **überzeugte** er mich davon, dass es sich lohnen würde, die Flüssigkeit zu benutzen, da Sonnenbrillengläser teuer wären und gut gepflegt werden sollten. Er **hat sehr vernünftige und überzeugende Verkaufsargumente vorgebracht.**
P. And there you see a successful salesperson at work ...	P. Und da sieht man einen guten Verkäufer bei der Arbeit ...

Background Information

Beryl says that the salesman in Leicester Square **made a very good sales pitch and made out a very good case for buying** the lens-cleaning liquid.
We looked at the meaning of to make »a sales pitch« in the last section; »to make out a case for something« has a similiar meaning like »to make a sales pitch«, i.e. to argue in favour of something in order to persuade the other person. e.g. »He made a great case for including Jonathon on our new sales seminars.«

Other phrases with »**make**« include:

to make headway	to make progress
to make allowances for	to prepare for the possibility of someone/something in future plans
to make a bid for	to make an effort (usually financial) in order to achieve something
to make an impact	to make a strong impression
to make a point of	to do always something, or to take particular care in doing something
to make amends for	to correct a past mistake
to make a stand on	to unite in favour of something

 109. Train Yourself

Verwenden Sie die oben stehenden Wendungen in den folgenden Sätzen!

1. The managing director ▬▬▬▬▬▬▬▬▬ congratulating the sales staff for the new orders received from Japan.
2. The success of the new advertising campaign was responsible for ▬▬▬▬▬▬▬▬▬ into the virgin market.
3. The company ▬▬▬▬▬▬ takeover ▬▬▬▬▬▬ for Watsons Pharmaceuticals.
4. Susan ▬▬▬▬▬▬▬▬▬ for losing the last order by increasing her sales ratio by 20 per cent.
5. When dealing with overseas customers one must ▬▬▬▬▬▬ for different customs and tastes.
6. In order to ▬▬▬▬▬▬ successful ▬▬▬▬▬▬ one must have total belief in the product and in oneself.
7. The administrative personnel in the company ▬▬▬▬▬▬ on increased overtime and more flexible working hours.
8. At their meeting Rupert ▬▬▬▬▬▬▬▬▬ increased investment in the Eastern European market.
9. Michael's personal touch really ▬▬▬▬▬▬▬▬▬! The deal was agreed and signed within hours!

 **Talk Talk Talk**

(Chip, the courier, enters office)	(Chip, der Kurier, betritt das Büro)
M. Hello, Chip! You're just in time to take part in our own **sales seminar**.	M. Hallo, Chip! Du kommst gerade rechtzeitig, um an unserem privaten **Verkaufsseminar** teilzunehmen.
C. Seminar? What's that?	C. Ein Seminar? Was läuft da ab?
M. We'd like to ask you a couple of questions to support some theories we are developing.	M. Wir würden dir gerne ein paar Fragen stellen, um ein paar Theorien zu bestätigen, die wir gerade aufstellen.
C. Look, the only theory I want developed right now is the correct address for this packet Lucy gave me. I've biked halfway across London and there's no company at this address.	C. Also hören Sie, die einzige Theorie, die ich gerade bestätigt haben möchte ist die korrekte Adresse für dieses Paket, das Lucy mir gegeben hat. Ich bin mit dem Motorrad durch halb London gefahren, aber es gibt keine Firma an dieser Adresse.
L. Give it to me, Chip. I'll **sort** this **out** for you ...	L. Gib es mir, Chip. Ich **kläre** das für dich ...
M. And in the meantime you can answer some of our questions. For instance, when did you last buy anything from a salesperson, without actually choosing the item yourself?	M. Und in der Zwischenzeit kannst du ein paar unserer Fragen beantworten. Wann hast du zum Beispiel das letzte Mal etwas von einem Verkäufer gekauft, ohne dir das Produkt selbst ausgesucht zu haben?
C. I bought a few apples from a **barrow** in Shaftesbury Avenue this	C. Ich habe heute Morgen ein paar Äpfel von einem **Straßenstand** auf

morning, if that's what you're looking for. Anyone like one?	der Shaftesbury Avenue gekauft, wenn Sie das meinen. Möchte jemand einen?
M. Thanks, Chip. Now that's interesting. Why did you buy the apples? Did you suddenly have the urge to eat an apple? Did you go looking for apples?	M. Danke, Chip. Das ist ja interessant. Warum hast du diese Äpfel gekauft? Hattest du plötzlich Heißhunger auf einen Apfel? Bist du auf der Suche nach Äpfeln gewesen?
C. No, not exactly. This barrowboy was shouting out »apples, fresh from the farm«, and I suddenly thought I'd like to sink my teeth into one.	C. Nein, nicht ganz. Der Junge am Stand rief »Äpfel, frisch vom Bauernhof«, und plötzlich hatte ich den Wunsch, in einen davon hineinzubeißen.
P. And there you have it! Another example of **good salesmanship**. And you've sold me on those apples, Chip. Can I take you up on your offer of one?	P. Da haben wir es! Ein weiteres Beispiel für **gute Verkaufskunst**. Und du hast mir diese Äpfel gut verkauft, Chip. Gilt dein Angebot noch?
C. Help yourself, Mr Brückner. They really are good.	C. Bedienen Sie sich, Mr Brückner. Sie sind wirklich gut.

Verkaufsgespräche

 110. Train Yourself

»Let me, let him/her, let's, ...« – Schreiben Sie nachfolgende Sätze um, indem Sie »let« auf korrekte Weise in die Sätze einbauen.

1. Why don't we consider offering this new product for sale?

2. I'd just like to think the idea over.

   ....
   ....

3. Come in, sit down and look over this proposal with me.

   ....
   ....

4. It's a fine day – get out the car and join me for a drive into the mountains.

   ....
   ....

5. She should fax this cost analysis to the customer right away.

   ....
   ....

6. The company will just have to wait another week for delivery – they are always so impatient.

   ....
   ....

7. Allow me to explain what we have in mind.

   ....
   ....

8. Why don't we join in this new venture?

   ....
   ....

 Talk Talk Talk

(Steve Blackman arrives at office)

S. Hello, hello, hello! This is quite a **confab. What's on the agenda**?

M. We're treading on your territory, Steve – we're discussing what makes a good salesperson.

(Steve Blackman betritt das Büro)

S. Aber hallo! Hier findet ja eine richtige **Konferenz** statt. **Was steht denn auf der Tagesordnung?**

M. Wir dringen gerade in Ihr Gebiet ein, Steve – wir diskutieren darüber, was einen guten Verkaufsmitarbeiter auszeichnet.

S. You're looking at him right now, Melissa!

M. Modesty is not your strong point, is it Steve?

S. **Modesty is perhaps the last quality a good salesperson needs**. You have to think constantly **in terms of the best** – and that means thinking you're the best, too. Or at least, better than the opposition.

M. You'll get your chance to demonstrate that at that seminar you and Peter are attending.

S. My God, I'd quite forgotten that – it's next week, isn't it?

M. Don't worry. I know Lucy has made all the preparations for you, isn't that right, Lucy?

L. Yes – **hotel rooms are booked, train tickets are on my desk**, together with **details of your hire car** for the trip to Scotland. All you have to do is pack.

S. Sie haben gerade einen vor sich, Melissa!

M. Bescheidenheit ist nicht gerade Ihre Stärke, was, Steve?

S. **Bescheidenheit ist vielleicht die letzte Eigenschaft, die ein guter Verkäufer braucht.** Sie müssen ständig immer nur **in den Kategorien des Besten** denken – und das bedeutet auch, dass man sich selbst für den Besten halten muss. Oder zumindest, dass man besser ist als die Gegenseite.

M. Sie werden die Chance haben, das auf dem Seminar zu beweisen, an dem Peter und Sie teilnehmen.

S. Mein Gott, das hätte ich fast vergessen – es findet nächste Woche statt, oder?

M. Keine Sorge. Ich weiß, dass Lucy alle Vorbereitungen für Sie getroffen hat, stimmt's, Lucy?

L. Ja – **die Hotelzimmer sind gebucht und die Bahnfahrkarten liegen auf meinem Schreibtisch**, zusammen mit den **Details Ihres Mietwagens** für die Fahrt nach Schottland. Alles, was Sie noch tun müssen, ist Koffer packen.

Background Information

While discussing what makes a good salesperson, Steve and Melissa use the comparative form »**better**« and the superlative form »**the best**«. English language learners at this level will be more than familiar with the general rules regarding comparatives and superlatives, i.e. adding »**-er/the -est**« to short adjectives and »**more/the most**« to longer ones, e.g. **shorter – the shortest, more beautiful – the most beautiful**. »**Better**« and »**the best**« are irregular, as is »**bad – worse – the worst**« and »**far – further**« (or »**farther**«) – »**the furthest**« (»**the farthest**«), the remainder following the general rule.

111. Train Yourself

Untenstehend finden Sie nun durcheinander geratene Sätze, die solche Komparativ/Superlativ-Konstruktionen enthalten. Bringen Sie sie in die richtige Reihenfolge!

Beispiel: by this the memory living worst is disaster in far
This is by far the worst disaster in living memory.

1. practice on significantly more than was it the attractive paper was in the proposal

2. our is sales our office marketing nowhere big as near as office

3. most business the I seen is comprehensive far this journal by ever have

4. won the unquestionably Jones the account was ever most company had lucrative the

5. remain lower expected share little than a prices

....
....

6. diligent salesperson she the company was easily in most the

....
....

7. the trademark Marlboro the world unquestionably is recognized in the most

....
....

8. much than sales the better previous informed is incumbent director present the

....
....

9. really serious expected had it not as was as we

....
....

 Vocabulary

brand	Marke
to catch s.o.'s attention	jds. Aufmerksamkeit erregen
confab	Geplauder/eine »Expertenrunde« (umgangssprachlich)
to demonstrate the effectiveness	die Wirksamkeit vorführen
to drop	hier: fallen lassen (eine Tätigkeit stehen und liegen lassen/ auch: eine Bemerkung fallen lassen etc.)
to fall for	sich verlieben
to fill in	über etwas aufklären/ ins Bild setzen
to follow up	folgen lassen/auch: Verfolgung
further afield	weiter weg
to gather	hier: gehört haben

to gear oneself up for sth.	sich vorbereiten auf, sich einstellen auf
guinea-pig	Meerschweinchen, »Versuchskaninchen«
to hand out	ausgeben, verteilen
sth. has got a buzz	etwas brummt (vor Besuchern)/ hat Pep
to immerse oneself	sich in etwas versenken; sich intensiv vertraut machen
to make out a very good case	ein sehr gutes Argument dafür
packaging	Verpackung
run down	erschöpft, hier: schlecht gemacht
salesmanship	Verkaufsgeschäft; Verkaufen
salesperson	Verkäufer, Verkäuferin
sales operation	Tagesaktivitäten
sales pitch	Verkaufsargument; Verkaufsstrategie
sales points	Verkaufsstellen
sales representative	Verkäufer
sales stand	Verkaufsstand
sales trip	Verkaufsreise
schedule	Terminkalender
sloppy	schlampig, nachlässig
to sort out	klassifizieren, einteilen
to sort out sth. for sb.	für jdn. etw. erklären
What's on the agenda?	Was steht auf der Tagesordnung?
When it comes to selling ...	Wenn es darum geht ... anzupreisen
wild about	wild/verrückt nach

Demonstrate Products
Produkte präsentieren

Verkaufsgespräche

 Here we go

Peter hat seine ersten Schritte in der Verkaufsabteilung hinter sich gebracht und soll nunmehr sein Wissen und Verkaufsgeschick weiter vertiefen, indem er mit seinem Kollegen Steve Blackman auf ein Verkaufsseminar geschickt wird. Die Reisevorbereitungen sind bereits getroffen und Peter und Steve machen sich auf den Weg nach Bournemouth, wo das Seminar stattfinden soll. Peter ist gespannt, ob seine Fähigkeiten dieser Bewährungsprobe standhalten und hofft, sich weitere nützliche Kenntnisse aneignen zu können ...

 Talk Talk Talk

(Waterloo Station, London. Steve and Peter meet)

S. Hello there, Peter! You're **right on time**. We've got time for a coffee before the train goes.

P. Great! I didn't really **have time** for breakfast this morning.

S. Then come on. I'm buying ...

(In the train)

S. You certainly brought a lot of luggage, Peter.

(Waterloo Station, London. Steve und Peter treffen sich)

S. Hallo Peter! Sie kommen **gerade rechtzeitig**. Wir haben noch Zeit für einen Kaffee, bevor der Zug losfährt.

P. Toll! Ich **hatte** heute Morgen überhaupt keine **Zeit**, richtig zu frühstücken.

S. Dann kommen Sie. Ich zahle ...

(Im Zug)

S. Peter, Sie haben aber eine Menge Gepäck dabei.

299

P. If we are away for two weeks I'll need it all. And I've got all my books with me.

S. German books?

P. Some, but mostly ones I picked up in London. I want to understand what's going on, so I did a bit of preparation.

S. You'll have no difficulty. **I know the scene**, so stick with me.

P. Don't worry, Steve. I won't leave your side. You're the expert ...

P. Wenn wir zwei Wochen unterwegs sind, brauche ich das alles. Und ich habe alle meine Bücher dabei.

S. Deutsche Bücher?

P. Einige davon, aber die meisten habe ich aus London mitgenommen. Ich will genau wissen, was los ist, deshalb habe ich mich ein bisschen vorbereitet.

S. Sie werden keine Schwierigkeiten haben, **ich kenne mich aus**, also halten Sie sich an mich.

P. Keine Sorge, Steve. Ich werde nicht von Ihrer Seite weichen. Sie sind der Experte ...

 Background Information

Steve tells Peter that he's **right on time** and that they **have time** for a coffee before the train leaves. Peter is pleased because he didn't really have time for breakfast that morning.

»To **have time** for something« clearly means that the action can be carried out without being the participant being late, i.e. the coffee can be drunk and the train will still be there.

»To **be on time**« means to be somewhere at the precise time arranged. Contrast this with »**in time**«, meaning to be somewhere before or at the period of time arranged. e.g. The seminar starts at 8 o'clock. Peter is on time. He gets there at 8 o'clock exactly. Steve gets there at 7.50. He's in time for the seminar.

There are many other expressions with the word »**time**«. Some of them are listed below:

to kill time	to do something to pass the time
from time to time	sometimes, now and then
to pass the time of day	to meet someone you know and then talk about general or unimportant things, e.g. the weather
about time	when something is finally done which the speaker feels should have been done earlier
in the nick of time	at the last possible moment
for the time being	for the present; until the situation changes
to take one's time	not to hurry, to be slow and careful

112. Train Yourself

In fünf der folgenden Sätze verbergen sich Fehler. Finden Sie sie und schreiben Sie dann die fehlerhaften Sätze in korrekter Form!

1. We got there just for the time being. The train was just leaving.

2. The situation in the Japanese stock market seems healthy for the time being but who knows what will happen in the future?

3. About time the managing director pays us a visit to make sure everything is running smoothly.

4. We got there just to kill time! The meeting was just starting.

5. It's from time to time they fixed that photocopier! It's been playing havoc for ages!

6. It's important in sales to pass the time of day with a client before going for the hard sell.

7. The summer holiday period is always a slow time for the company. People have nothing to do and just sit around in the nick of time.

8. Every year I have to give a small speech at the company dinner. I always try to relax and take my time over my words but I still get nervous.

9. It's very important to be in the nick of time when meeting a client. It creates a very bad impression if one is late.

10. OK, do we have time for a final rundown of tomorrow's events?

Colloquial English

stick with me	stay with me
to get hold of the wrong end of the stick	to misunderstand something
a stick-in-the-mud	an unadventurous person who refuses to do anything unusual

 Talk Talk Talk

(Steve and Peter arrive at their hotel)

S. Good evening. We have **booked two rooms under the names** Blackman and Brückner. Our office called last week to make the **booking**.

(Hotel receptionist) Yes, here we are. Two single rooms. You're here for the seminar?

S. Yes, we're from ERGO Limited.

(Steve und Peter kommen in ihrem Hotel an)

S. Guten Abend. Wir haben **zwei Zimmer auf die Namen** Blackman und Brückner **gebucht**. Unser Büro hat die **Reservierung** letzte Woche telefonisch vorgenommen.

(Hotelangestellter an der Rezeption) Ja, da haben wir es. Zwei Einzelzimmer. Sind Sie wegen des Seminars hier?

S. Ja, wir sind von ERGO Limited.

(Receptionist) There's a **reception** in the lounge at six for participants.

(Hotelangestellter an der Rezeption) Es gibt für die Teilnehmer um sechs Uhr einen **Empfang** in der Lounge.

S. **That's just the ticket.** I need a drink after that journey. In fact, Peter, let's have a quickie in the bar before settling into our rooms.

S. **Das ist genau das Richtige.** Nach dieser Reise brauche ich einen Drink. Peter, lassen Sie uns einen kurzen Drink an der Bar nehmen, bevor wir auf unsere Zimmer gehen.

P. **My treat!** What will it be?

P. **Das geht auf meine Rechnung!** Was darf's sein?

S. A double Scotch for me. What about you?

S. Für mich einen doppelten Scotch. Und für Sie?

P. I'm so thirsty I'm going to have a beer. Are we having dinner here?

P. Ich habe solchen Durst, ich nehme ein Bier. Essen wir hier zu Abend?

S. The **seminar programme includes** all meals, but if the food is no good we can always eat out.

S. Im **Seminarprogramm sind** alle Speisen **inbegriffen**, aber sollte das Essen nicht gut sein, können wir immer noch auswärts essen.

False Friends

»**Receptionist**« and »**reception**« have the same root verb – to receive – but there similarity ends. A receptionist »**receives**« or welcomes guests at a hotel, patients at the doctor's or dentist's surgery, visitors to an office. A reception, in the normal sense, is an »**Empfang**«.

There are several words/expressions in English that come from the root word »to receive«, apart from »**reception**« and »**receptionist**«:

receptive	an adjective describing somebody who is quick or willing to receive new ideas

a recipient	a person who receives something.
a receiver	an official appointed by law to look after the property of a bankrupt
in receivership	to be under control of an Official Receiver
to receive (somebody)	to welcome guests (formal)
to be on the receiving end of something	to suffer something unpleasant
to reciprocate	to do something in return for something
in receipt of something	having received something (usually a letter – formal)

 113. Train Yourself

Füllen Sie die Lücken mit oben stehenden Begriffen!

1. We are ▬▬▬▬▬ your letter of March 13th concerning the proposed takeover ...
2. The company has gone ▬▬▬▬▬ after a disastrous slump in profits.
3. We were ▬▬▬▬▬ by the ambassador in his private office.
4. We would like ▬▬▬▬▬ the loyalty shown us by our clients by offering a new special offer.
5. There were nearly 50,000 ▬▬▬▬▬ last year of our advertising circular.
6. The ▬▬▬▬▬ was held in the hotel lounge.
7. I don't think the marketing director was very ▬▬▬▬▬ to our ideas.
8. Have you met our new ▬▬▬▬▬, Mrs Peters?
9. One of our clerical staff was ▬▬▬▬▬ a tongue – lashing from the sales director after mislaying an important document.
10. We had to call in the ▬▬▬▬▬ after the company was declared bankrupt.

 **Talk Talk Talk**

(At the reception, John Barlowe, who will **conduct the seminar**, welcomes Steve and Peter)

J. How do you do, I'm John Barlowe. I'll be conducting the seminar, so we'll be seeing quite a bit of each other in the next few days. Now, what are you having to drink?

S. That's very kind of you. I'm Steve Blackman, by the way, **Sales Director** of ERGO Limited, and this is our **Assistant Managing Director**, Peter Brückner, from Germany.

J. Germany? I've conducted a few seminars there. In English – for companies selling to Britain or the United States or looking for **market openings** there.
Very interesting they were, too.

P. I'm doing it the other way, by coming to England and getting **first-hand experience** with a company here.

J. Probably the **best way of going about it**, too. Do you have **sales experience**?

(Am Empfang begrüßt John Barlowe, der **das Seminar leiten** wird, Steve und Peter)

J. Wie geht es Ihnen? Ich bin John Barlowe. Ich werde das Seminar leiten, also werden wir uns in den nächsten Tagen wohl ziemlich oft sehen. Also, was möchten Sie trinken?

S. Das ist sehr nett von Ihnen! Ich bin übrigens Steve Blackman, **Verkaufsleiter** von ERGO Limited, und das ist Peter Brückner, unser **stellvertretender Geschäftsführer** aus Deutschland.

J. Deutschland? Ich habe dort ein paar Seminare abgehalten. Auf Englisch – da die Unternehmen Verkaufskontakte in England oder in den Vereinigten Staaten haben oder dort nach **Markteröffnungen** suchen. Sie waren auch sehr interessant.

P. Ich mache das genau andersherum, indem ich nach England gekommen bin und hier **eigene Erfahrungen** mit einem Unternehmen **sammle**.

J. Das ist wahrscheinlich auch **der beste Weg, die Sache anzugehen**. Haben Sie **Erfahrungen im Verkauf**?

Verkaufsgespräche

P. Only what I've learnt from Steve here, during a **secondment** to his department. The idea is for me to immerse myself totally in each **area of the business**. Sales is where I am now.	P. Nur das, was ich von Steve hier gelernt habe, während ich seiner Abteilung **unterstellt war**. Die Idee dahinter ist es, mich in jedes **Geschäftsgebiet** einzuarbeiten. Momentan bin ich im Verkauf.
J. I don't know if what I have to offer is really necessary for your work, but you'll find it interesting, I'm sure. I'll see you both at 9 AM sharp tomorrow, then. Enjoy the evening!	J. Ich weiß nicht, ob das was ich Ihnen anzubieten habe, für Ihre Arbeit wirklich notwendig ist, aber Sie werden es sicherlich interessant finden. Ich sehe Sie also beide morgen pünktlich um 9 Uhr vormittags. Genießen Sie den Abend!

Background Information

John Barlowe in this section of Talk Talk Talk, referring to Peter's methods of gaining business experience, says that **he's going about it in the right way.** »To go about doing something« means **the approach or the way in which something is done**. Other »go«-expressions include:

to go hand in hand	to be connected or closely related
touch and go	a very risky or uncertain situation
to let oneself go	to enjoy oneself in a free and natural manner
to go it alone	to do something without anyone's help
from the word go	from the beginning
to go all out	to attempt to do something with the greatest possible determination
to go over with a fine toothcomb	to check very carefully for mistakes
to go without saying	to be understood and agreed without needing to be mentioned or proved
to make a go of something	to make a success of something

114. Train Yourself

Verwenden Sie diese Wendungen in den folgenden Sätzen!

1. Right, George, I want you to ▓▓▓▓▓ this report ▓▓▓▓▓ and make sure there are no inaccuracies.
2. Everybody in the company ▓▓▓▓▓ to ensure the success of the new account.
3. It ▓▓▓▓▓ that a successful salesperson must believe in himself and in the product he is selling.
4. I really want to ▓▓▓▓▓ this. If it's a success we'll all reap the benefits.
5. After a brief training period the new salesperson was allowed to ▓▓▓▓▓.
6. It was ▓▓▓▓▓ whether the new proposals would be accepted.
7. Helen ▓▓▓▓▓ the job in a very unprofessional manner resulting in her contract being terminated.
8. The marketing campaign for Rise and Shine breakfast cereal was doomed to failure ▓▓▓▓▓. Consumer response was very disappointing.
9. At the office party everybody ▓▓▓▓▓ and there were some red faces next morning!
10. Belief in a product, the sufficient energy involved to sell it and good promotions work all ▓▓▓▓▓ in creating an effective salesperson.

 Talk Talk Talk

(John Barlowe welcomes participants at start of seminar)

J. I'd like to welcome you all to this **seminar on salesmanship**. I'm sure that at least I will enjoy it and also learn something from it. Salesmanship is an open-ended

(John Barlowe begrüßt am Anfang des Seminars die Teilnehmer)

J. Ich begrüße Sie alle bei unserem **Verkaufsseminar**. Ich bin mir sicher, dass wenigstens ich es genießen und etwas daraus lernen werde. Im Bereich des Verkaufs

area of study. There's no set **agenda**. There are no rules. Some successful sales people say you can't learn how to sell successfully. So I won't be lecturing you on the subject. I'll just **throw in ideas** and hope that you will contribute yours. Then we'll try to find **consensus**. But I have some **preliminary observations** I have formed during these seminars, which I have been holding now for more than ten years. Basically I sum them up with the acronym **PEP**. That stands for **Product, Energy, Promotion**. If you lack one you lack them all. Without a product, of course, you have nothing to sell – that's obvious. But it has to be a product you believe in, something you know you can sell. But how do you sell it? That's where energy comes in. You can have the best product in the world, but unless you go vigorously about selling it it's not going to move from the **warehouse floor**. And **that's where promotion comes in**. You can talk all day about your product but unless your energy is matched by promotional material it's all wasted effort. When all three are working together you have a recipe for success. Now, any questions?

lernt man nie aus. Es gibt keine feste **Tagesordnung**. Es gibt keine Regeln. Einige erfolgreiche Leute aus dem Verkauf meinen, man könnte nicht lernen, erfolgreich zu verkaufen. Deshalb werde ich Sie in dieser Sache auch nicht unterrichten. Ich werde nur **Ideen einbringen** und hoffe, dass Sie Ihrerseits weitere beisteuern. Dann werden wir versuchen, eine **Übereinstimmung** zu finden. Trotzdem habe ich in diesen Seminaren, die ich seit mittlerweile zehn Jahren abhalte, einige **grundlegende Feststellungen** definiert. Im Großen und Ganzen fasse ich sie mit dem Akronym **PEP** zusammen. Das steht für **Produkt, Energie, Promotion**. Wenn Ihnen eines davon fehlt, fehlen Ihnen alle. Natürlich haben Sie ohne ein Produkt nichts zu verkaufen – das ist offensichtlich. Aber es muss ein Produkt sein, an das Sie glauben – etwas, von dem Sie wissen, dass Sie es verkaufen können. Aber wie verkaufen Sie es? Hier kommt die Energie ins Spiel. Sie können das beste Produkt der Welt haben, aber wenn Sie sich nicht voller Energie daran machen, es zu verkaufen, wird es das **Lager** niemals verlassen. Und **an diesem Punkt kommt die Promotion ins Spiel**. Sie können den ganzen Tag über Ihr Produkt sprechen, aber so lange Ihre Energie nicht mit

	Promotion-Material einhergeht, ist alles vergebene Mühe.
	Wenn alle drei Elemente kombiniert werden, haben Sie ein Erfolgsrezept.
	Nun, irgend welche Fragen?
(A participant poses a question)	(Ein Teilnehmer stellt eine Frage)
P. In my time, I've actually been called upon to sell products I did not at all believe in, or at the very least didn't particularly interest me. But the **commission basis** was high, or the contract a particularly attractive one.	P. Zu meiner Zeit wurde ich dazu aufgefordert, Produkte zu verkaufen, an die ich überhaupt nicht glaubte oder die mich zumindest nicht besonders interessierten. Aber die **Provisionsrate** war hoch oder der Vertrag besonders verlockend.
J. And did you sell successfully?	J. Und waren Sie erfolgreich im Verkauf?
P. To be quite honest, no!	P. Ehrlich gesagt, nein!
J. And there you have it! Your **lack of interest in your product** was certainly clear in your **sales approach**.	J. Da haben Sie es! Ihr **mangelndes Interesse an Ihrem Produkt** hat sich in Ihrem **Auftreten** sicherlich niedergeschlagen.
P. But how can I **overcome** that problem?	P. Aber wie kann ich dieses Problem **lösen**?
J. Get to know your product thoroughly. Nothing is that uninteresting. Look for all its **attractive, positive features** and emphasize those. And that brings me to another point: get to know your **competition,** your **competitors'**	J. Lernen Sie Ihr Produkt richtig kennen. Nichts ist völlig uninteressant. Suchen Sie all seine **attraktiven, positiven Seiten** und betonen Sie sie. Und das bringt mich auf einen anderen Punkt: Machen Sie sich mit Ihrer **Konkurrenz** ver-

products. **Seek out** all the advantages of your own product. That will certainly **kindle interest** in it and help you sell ...

traut, mit Ihren **Konkurrenzprodukten**. **Finden Sie** alle Vorteile Ihres eigenen Produktes **heraus**. Das wird sicherlich Ihr **Interesse** daran **entfachen** und Ihnen beim Verkauf helfen ...

Background Information

Peter is told in this section of the dialogue **to seek out the advantages** of his product in order to help him sell. »**To seek out something**« is **to look for and to find**. Other prepositional verbs in a similar context include:

to search for	to look for thoroughly
to look into	to investigate
to look someone up	to visit when in the area
to run over	to check
to sort out	to find a solution
to check up on somebody	to ascertain whether a person is behaving in a suitable way or not
to hunt down	to find somebody/something after a lot of effort
to come across	to find accidentally

115. Train Yourself

Verwenden Sie diese Wendungen in den folgenden Sätzen:

1. I was looking through my old files the other day and I ▒▒▒▒▒ this letter from Bob Stevens detailing the Adams account. What luck!
2. Management are ▒▒▒▒▒ the problem but as yet don't seem to be any closer to finding a solution.
3. I don't think it's necessary for Tom to ▒▒▒▒▒ us. We're quite capable of doing the job on our own.
4. Don't forget to ▒▒▒▒▒ me ▒▒▒▒▒ the next time you're in New York!
5. Steve, I've got that presentation to do tomorrow, I don't suppose you'd mind ▒▒▒▒▒ it with me, would you?

6. I'm exhausted! I finally managed to ▒▒▒▒▒ that old client of ours! I've been trying all day! He must have moved houses five times!
7. There's something wrong with the printer, can you ▒▒▒▒▒ it ▒▒▒▒▒ ?
8. I've been ▒▒▒▒▒ that invoice all day and I still can't find it!
9. We need to ▒▒▒▒▒ new business opportunities to increase our share of the market.

 **Talk Talk Talk**

J. I hope you all enjoyed your lunch. Now we're going to play a little game I've made up. Divide yourselves up into groups of two please.

S. I'll stay with you Peter, if you don't mind.

J. I'm going to distribute these **envelopes**. In each one is the description of a product which your group – your company – has to sell. You'll have the afternoon to work out a **sales strategy** and tomorrow morning I want each group **to put its case**. Then we'll take a democratic vote to discover the most successful team, the company that is selling its product the best.

S. Here you are Peter. Open it up. What have we got to sell?

J. Ich hoffe, Sie haben Ihr Mittagessen genossen. Wir werden jetzt ein kleines Spiel spielen, das ich mir ausgedacht habe. Teilen Sie sich bitte in Zweiergruppen auf.

S. Peter, ich bleibe bei Ihnen, wenn Sie nichts dagegen haben.

J. Ich werde nun diese **Umschläge** verteilen. In jedem befindet sich die Beschreibung eines Produktes, das Ihre Gruppe – Ihr Unternehmen – verkaufen muss. Sie haben den Nachmittag über Zeit, eine **Verkaufsstrategie** auszuarbeiten und morgen früh möchte ich, dass jede Gruppe **Ihren Fall vorträgt**. Dann werden wir über das erfolgreichste Team abstimmen, über das Unternehmen, das sein Produkt am besten verkauft.

S. Hier bitte, Peter. Öffnen Sie es. Was müssen wir verkaufen?

P. It's a new kind of vacuum cleaner, as far as I can make out.

P. Es ist eine neue Art Staubsauger, soweit ich das beurteilen kann.

S. Oh, just the ticket! From **high-tech** to home-care. We've taken a big step back.

S. Na, genau das Richtige! Von der **Hochtechnologie** zur Hauspflege! Wir haben einen großen Schritt zurück gemacht.

P. I think the point of this vacuum-cleaner is that it is a high-tech product. But we'll need some time to study the **specifications** and all this literature on it.

P. Ich glaube, das Interessante an diesem Staubsauger ist, dass er ein hochmodernes Produkt ist. Aber wir werden ein bisschen Zeit brauchen, um die **näheren Angaben** und die entsprechende Literatur zu studieren.

S. I know just the place. I've discovered a very cosy bar just down the road. Let's take up a corner table there and **get down to work**!

S. Dafür kenne ich den idealen Ort. Ich habe die Straße herunter eine sehr nette Bar entdeckt. Setzen wir uns dort an einen Ecktisch und **fangen mit der Arbeit an**!

Background Information

Steve knows a nice cosy bar **to get down to work** for their sales strategy. This means **to begin seriously to deal with something**. Here are a few more phrasal verbs with the word »**down**«:

to back down	to yield in an argument
to put something down to	to explain the cause of
to come down on	to punish or blame someone for something
to bring down	to cause to become less
to stand down	to give up one's official position
to lay down	to state a rule (especially »lay down the law«)
to come down to	to be in the end a matter of

116. Train Yourself

Schreiben Sie die folgenden Sätze noch einmal und ersetzen Sie dabei die hervorgehobenen Wörter durch oben stehende Wendungen.

1. The Managing Director *is retiring* at the end of the year.

   ....

2. – I wonder why the sales figures this year are so low?
   – Personally, I *blame* the recession.

   ....

3. At the end of the day the success of a company all *depends on* the degree of efficiency in which it is run.

   ....

4. When a new manager takes over a company he must *enforce* the law to ensure that things run the way he wants them to.

   ....

5. If everybody refused to *compromise* during negotiations no deal would ever be reached.

   ....

6. (At the meeting) – Good morning everybody. Now I think we all know each other so let's *start* doing business.

   ....

7. – I think we should *reduce* the price in order to make it more cost-effective. Prices are too high for the consumer right now.

   ....

8. The Advertising Standards Council promised *to severely punish* any companies using underhand methods to sell their products.

   ....

 **Talk Talk Talk**

(Next morning at the seminar)   (Am nächsten Morgen beim Seminar)

J. Good morning, ladies and gentlemen! I hope you slept well and are prepared for a productive

J. Guten Morgen, meine Damen und Herren! Ich hoffe, Sie haben gut geschlafen und sind bereit für

morning. Let's get down to business. Mr Blackman and Mr Brückner - let's hear your **presentation** first.	einen produktiven Morgen. Kommen wir gleich zur Sache. Mr Blackman und Mr Brückner – lassen Sie uns als Erstes Ihre **Präsentation** hören.
S. We start from the assumption that because there are so many **brands and types** of vacuum cleaner on the market we have to persuade **potential agents and clients** that **it really is worth their while investing** in ours. Now how do we do that ? Over to you, Peter!	S. Wir beginnen mit der Annahme, dass wir, weil es so viele **Marken und Arten** von Staubsaugern auf dem Markt gibt, die **potenziellen Vertreter und Kunden** davon überzeugen müssen, **dass unserer wirklich sein Geld wert ist**. Nun, wie machen wir das? Ich übergebe an Peter!
P. With a product such as a vacuum cleaner we have to start at the level of the agent, **persuading** him or her **to carry our range**. The days of the door-to-door salesman are really over – at least, in Germany! We believe that our product, because of its **advanced technology**, using centrifugal force, offers a distinct break from conventional, increasingly old-fashioned models. It is cleaner, **more efficient and cost-effective**. For a start, there is no longer any need to use dust-bags, a huge advantage for the busy housewife – or, as we say in German, Hausmann!	P. Mit einem Produkt wie dem Staubsauger müssen wir auf der Ebene des Vertreters anfangen – ihn oder sie davon **überzeugen, unser Sortiment zu übernehmen**. Die Tage des von Tür zu Tür gehenden Vertreters sind vorbei – wenigstens in Deutschland! Wir glauben, dass unser Produkt, da es eine **fortschrittliche Technologie** besitzt und auf Zentrifugalkraft basiert, einen klaren Bruch mit den konventionellen, langsam altmodisch werdenden Modellen anbietet. Es ist sauberer, **effizienter und kosteneffektiver**. Erst einmal brauchen wir keinen Staubsaugerbeutel mehr, ein großer Vorteil für die beschäftigte Hausfrau – oder den Hausmann, wie wir in Deutschland sagen!

S. We concentrate our **sales pitch** in three directions: **savings** in time and effort, particularly important in the case of a domestic appliance, new technology that is going to replace old-fashioned systems, and a competitive, economical price. Shall I go on?	S. Wir konzentrieren uns mit unsere **Verkaufsstrategie** auf drei Richtungen: Einsparungen von Zeit und Energie, was bei Haushaltsgeräten besonders wichtig ist, neue Technologien, die altmodische Systeme ersetzen und ein konkurrenzfähiger, ökonomischer Preis. Soll ich fortfahren?
J. Please do! I'm on the point of buying one of your machines ...	J. Ja, bitte! Ich bin fast so weit, Ihnen eine Ihrer Maschinen abzukaufen ...

Background Information

Peter and Steve begin their presentation by asking the question: »How do we persuade potential clients that it really **is worth their while investing** in our vacuum cleaner when there are so many others on the market?«

If something **is worth your while doing** then you **should follow out the advice** because you will benefit in some way (often financially) from your efforts. The word »**worth**« itself refers to the **value of something**; either to the amount of money something can be sold for (a painting is worth a million pounds etc.), or the importance or usefulness of something (a person is worth employing). A very common expression in English combines the two: »**She's worth her weight in gold.**«

Other expressions with **worth** include:

for all (your) worth	a great deal of effort
for what it's worth	an expression used when the person is unsure how useful or important a piece of information may be
to be not worth the paper something is printed on	to have very little value (a document)

worthless	having no value in money, being of no use
to make something worth someone's while	(colloquial) to pay somebody to do something
to be worth (your) salt	to be good at your job
worthy	a) deserving respect, admiration or support b) suitable for (e.g. »The dinner was worthy of a king«)

 117. Train Yourself

Vervollständigen Sie nun die unten stehenden Sätze mit diesen Wendungen! Manchmal passen mehrere Begriffe:

1. The new salesperson is really ▓▓▓▓▓▓! He's not stopped all morning!
2. I don't think it's ▓▓▓▓▓ our ▓▓▓▓▓ going over these figures again until we've both had a good night's rest. We're both exhausted.
3. What do you think of the new merger, Peter? Well, ▓▓▓▓▓, I don't think it's been thought out properly ...
4. During my first year at the company I had to work ▓▓▓▓▓ my ▓▓▓▓▓ just to keep my head afloat.
5. The company invested a lot of time and effort in trying to find a ▓▓▓▓▓ successor to the outgoing sales director.
6. Julie, could you start earlier on the cleaning this week? We'll ▓▓▓▓▓.
7. This account is ▓▓▓▓▓. Sales figures for this quarter have been terrible.
8. There's a great danger of feeling ▓▓▓▓▓ after retirement from a company. One needs to remain active as much as possible.

 **Talk Talk Talk**

(Still at the seminar)

J. Right, let's hear the next team. Yes, fine, you two on my right ...

N. I'm Nigel Gibbs and this is my partner, Graham Cluver. Our job is to sell garden seeds. Unlike the company that preceded us, **our task is to market our product** using bright, promising **packaging and cataloguing**. Our products, basically seed packages, have to stand out and **attract attention** in the seed shops. We have to assume that our customers know what they are looking for and buy by sight. So our **sales approach** is to hire a good **marketing company** to design the packaging, the cover pictures and the catalogue.

G. I'd just like to add that planting instructions must be clearly written, and no **false promises** made. If we promise impossibly fast-growing and blooming sweet peas and they don't **match our claims** then

(Noch immer beim Seminar)

J. OK, lassen Sie uns das nächste Team hören. Ja gut, Sie beide zu meiner Rechten ...

N. Ich heiße Nigel Gibbs und das ist mein Partner Graham Cluver. Unsere Aufgabe besteht darin, Saatgut zu verkaufen. Im Gegensatz zu dem vorherigen Unternehmen **ist es unser Ziel, unser Produkt zu vermarkten**, indem wir glänzende, viel versprechende **Verpackung und Kataloge** verwenden. Unsere Produkte, in erster Linie Saatpackungen, müssen in Samenhandlungen ausgestellt werden und **Aufmerksamkeit erregen**. Wir müssen davon ausgehen, dass unsere Kunden wissen, was sie suchen und aufgrund ihrer Wahrnehmung kaufen. Deshalb besteht unsere **Verkaufsstrategie** darin, eine gute **Marketingfirma** damit zu beauftragen, die Verpackung, die Coverfotos und den Katalog zu entwerfen.

G. Ich möchte noch hinzufügen, dass die Pflanzanweisungen klar formuliert werden müssen und keine **falschen Versprechungen** gemacht werden dürfen. Wenn wir unglaublich schnell wachsende

we are working **counter-productively** and losing customers.

und ertragreiche Erbsen versprechen, die **unsere Ansprüche** dann nicht **erfüllen**, arbeiten wir **kontraproduktiv** und verlieren unsere Kunden.

 118. Train Yourself

Bringen Sie die nachfolgenden Sätze ins Passiv!

Beispiel: Somebody delivered the parcel at 4 o'clock.
The parcel was delivered at 4 o'clock.

1. Somebody last saw John getting into a taxi.

2. Somebody published the report last year.

3. Somebody will announce the departure time later on today.

4. They make Fiat cars in Milan.

5. My secretary is typing out the work as we speak.

6. We have sold 10,000 units so far this month.

 Talk Talk Talk

(Steve and Peter are talking in the hotel lounge after dinner)

(Steve und Peter unterhalten sich nach dem Abendessen in der Hotel-Lounge)

S. Last day then tomorrow, Peter. Have you enjoyed it? More important, have you learnt much from the seminar?

S. Morgen ist also der letzte Tag, Peter. Hat es Ihnen Spaß gemacht? Oder noch wichtiger, haben Sie auf dem Seminar viel gelernt?

P. Yes, I think so. I like the interactive nature of it. **It matches the**

P. Ich glaube ja. Ich mag seinen interaktiven Charakter. **Er passt**

subject of the seminar perfectly. After all, what is selling if not **interactive**?	perfekt zum Thema des Seminars. Außerdem, was ist Verkaufen – wenn nicht **interaktiv**?
S. You're right there! But I'm still looking forward to getting on the road again, to Cardiff. We'll see a real **salesman** at work there. He's as Welsh as they come and he has a **natural ability for selling**. A natural asset, too – **the gift of the gab!**	S. Da haben Sie Recht! Aber ich freue mich schon darauf, wieder weiter zu fahren, nach Cardiff. Da werden wir einen richtigen **Vertreter** bei der Arbeit sehen. Er ist ein Waliser, wie Sie ihn sich nicht besser vorstellen können und er hat eine **natürliche Begabung fürs Verkaufen**. Und auch einen natürlichen Vorzug – **die Gabe einer großen Klappe!**
(A seminar participant approaches)	(Ein Seminarteilnehmer kommt)
B. Hello, I'm Barry Smythe – I hope I'm not intruding, but I would like to meet you and have a word with you.	B. Hallo, ich heiße Barry Smythe – ich hoffe, ich störe Sie nicht, aber ich wollte Sie gerne kennen lernen und mich mit Ihnen unterhalten.
S. Certainly. Sit down and join us.	S. Aber sicher. Setzen Sie sich zu uns.
B. That's very kind. Oddly enough I've just **won the franchise** to sell a revolutionary new vacuum-cleaner, made in Germany. I was most impressed by your presentation. I'm putting together a sales team now. You wouldn't be interested in joining it, would you? Or perhaps working for us **on a consultancy basis**? With your German background, Mr Brückner, you'd be invaluable.	B. Sehr nett. Seltsamerweise habe ich gerade **die Konzession** für den Verkauf eines revolutionären, neuen Staubsaugers »Made in Germany« **bekommen**. Ich war von Ihrer Präsentation sehr beeindruckt. Ich stelle gerade ein Verkaufsteam zusammen. Sie wären wohl nicht daran interessiert einzusteigen, nicht wahr? Oder **auf beratender Basis** für uns zu arbeiten? Mit Ihrem deutschen Hintergrund, Mr Brückner, wären Sie unbezahlbar.

Verkaufsgespräche

S. (laughs) Vacuum-cleaners? **We're into computer software**, Mr Smythe. I found it difficult enough mastering that **business area**. Vacuum-cleaners are right **out of my league**. And Mr Brückner here is destined for much greater things. But thanks for the compliment, anyway. And good luck with that new vacuum-cleaner ...	S. (lacht) Staubsauger? **Wir arbeiten in der Software-Branche**, Mr Smythe. Ich fand es schwierig genug, dieses **Geschäftsfeld** zu meistern. Staubsauger sind einfach **nicht mein Spezialgebiet**. Und Mr Brückner hier ist für Größeres bestimmt. Aber auf alle Fälle bedanken wir uns für das Kompliment. Und viel Glück mit dem neuen Staubsauger ...

 Background Information

Peter says, »It matches the subject of the seminar **perfectly**«. »Perfectly«, as you know, is an adverb, the adjective is »perfect«. The opposite of »perfect« is »imperfect«.
Later, the adjectives »**real**« and »**natural**« are used. Their opposites are »unreal« and »unnatural«.

»**un-**« and »**in-**« are prefixes that are used to change the meaning of an adjective or adverb into an opposite one. For example: »important« – »unimportant«. Where a word begins with an »r« we generally use the prefix, »ir«, hence, regular – irregular and many words beginning in a vowel use »in« as in »inevitable« or »inarticulate«.

 119. Train Yourself

Multiple Choice – Welches ist das richtige Präfix?
Geben Sie in den nachfolgenden Sätzen das Gegenteil an, indem Sie das richtige Präfix wählen:

1. It is (*im-/un-/in-*) ▒▒▒▒▒▒▒▒▒▒▒▒▒▒ possible to get any work done with all this noise around me!

2. (*In-/im-/un-*) ▒▒▒▒▒▒▒▒▒▒▒▒▒▒ fortunately the company lost the contract last year.

3. (Ir-/un-/im-) _____ respective of the fact that the senior manager had a bad relationship with his staff, he also had difficulties with his superiors.

4. Julie would spend an (un-/im-/ir-) _____ ordinate amount of time talking on the phone rather than getting her work done.

5. We were (im-/un-/in-) _____ mobile for over half an hour the traffic was so bad.

6. I hadn't researched the subject of the meeting and so I felt very (un-/im-/ir-) _____ comfortable throughout its duration.

7. The manager thought it was very (un-/im-/ir-) _____ responsible of Peter to demand a pay-rise.

8. It was very (un-/in-/im-) _____ usual for Harold to be late but this time was the exception to the rule.

9. It is (in-/un-/im-) _____ acceptable for staff to wear (in-/im-/un-) _____ appropriate clothes for work.

 **Vocabulary**

advanced technology	fortschrittliche Technologie
agent	Vertreter
agenda	Tagesordnung
Assistant Managing Director	stellvertretender Geschäftsführer
to be out of s.o.'s league	nicht das Spezialgebiet von jdm. sein
to book	buchen
booking	Reservierung
brand	Marke
business area	Geschäftsgebiet, Geschäftsfeld
to carry s.o.'s range	jds. Sortiment übernehmen
client	Kunde
commission (basis)	Provisions(rate)
competition	Konkurrenz

competitors' products	Konkurrenzprodukte
consensus	Übereinstimmung, Konsens
cost-effective	kosteneffektiv
consultancy basis	beratende Funktion
counter-productive	kontraproduktiv
first-hand experience	eigene Erfahrungen
to get down to sth.	etw. angehen
to go about sth.	etw. angehen
to have time	Zeit haben
to kindle interest	Interesse entfachen
to know the scene	sich auskennen
to market	vermarkten
to match perfectly	perfekt passen
to match s.o.'s claim	jds. Ansprüche erfüllen
My treat!	Das geht auf meine Rechnung!
preliminary observations	grundlegende Feststellungen
promotional material	Promotionsmaterial
reception	Empfang
right on time	rechtzeitig
Sales Director	Verkaufsleiter
sales experience	Verkaufserfahrung
salesman	Vertreter
sales pitch/approach	Verkaufsstrategie
secondment	Abordnung, im Sinne von »jdm. unterstellt werden«
to seek out	finden, heraussuchen
seminar on salesmanship	Verkaufsseminar
specifications	nähere Angaben
task	Ziel
That's just the ticket.	Das ist genau das Richtige.
the gift of the gab	die Gabe einer großen Klappe
warehouse floor	Lager
to win the franchise	die Konzession bekommen

Make good deals
Geschäftsabschlüsse erzielen

Verkaufsgespräche

 Here we go

Nach seinem Verkaufsseminar ist Peter nun bestens gewappnet für einen Ausflug in die Praxis. Er fährt mit Steve nach Cardiff und startet von dort aus Besuche in die Verkaufsvertretungen von ERGO Limited. Dort wird er mit den alltäglichen Aufgaben und Problemen von Außendienstmitarbeitern konfrontiert und versucht, so viel wie möglich über die eigentliche Verkaufstätigkeit zu lernen und auch seine eigenen Erfahrungen einzubringen ...

 **Talk Talk Talk**

(Steve and Peter are on their way by train to Cardiff)

S. (sings softly) We're on the road again ...

P. You like being **out and about**, Steve.

S. Love it, Peter, dear chap! I love the independence, the feeling that I'm my own man, out there in a world full of challenges. I envy my **salespeople** – I'd like to do more selling myself. But somebody has to look after the shop.

(Steve und Peter fahren mit dem Zug Richtung Cardiff)

S. (singt leise) Und weiter geht die Reise ...

P. Sie sind wohl gern **unterwegs**, Steve.

S. Ich bin ganz versessen darauf, Peter, mein Bester! Ich liebe die Unabhängigkeit, das Gefühl, dass ich mein eigener Herr in einer Welt voller Herausforderungen bin. Ich beneide meine **Außendienstmitarbeiter** – ich würde gern viel öfter selbst auf Verkaufstour gehen. Aber irgendjemand muss ja dafür sorgen, dass der Laden läuft.

P. So tell me again what we can expect in Cardiff.

S. It's also a **one-man operation.** Trevor **does a good job** but he needs the occasional **check**, which we are doing. He has a **part-time sales force** and does reasonably good business. Wales is getting a lot of central government assistance, even though it has its own national assembly now. Some government departments moved to Wales in a decentralization process, and there's a lot of support for new small businesses. So there's **a lot of scope** for us there.

P. Dann erzählen Sie mir doch noch mal, was uns in Cardiff erwartet.

S. Ein **Ein-Mann-Betrieb.** Trevor **leistet gute Arbeit**, aber er braucht ab und zu einen **Kontrollbesuch**, und genau das tun wir. Er beschäftigt eine **Teilzeitkraft für den Verkauf** und das Geschäft läuft recht gut. Wales bekommt eine Menge Unterstützung von der Zentralregierung, auch wenn es jetzt seine eigene Nationalversammlung hat. Ein paar Dienststellen der Regierung sind im Rahmen eines Dezentralisierungsprogramms nach Wales gezogen und neue, kleine Betriebe werden kräftig unterstützt. Für uns gibt es dort also **ein breites Betätigungsfeld**.

Background Information

Steve tells Peter in this section of the dialogue that he loves being **out and about**, in other words **he likes to be outside**, travelling and meeting people, e.g. »I hate being stuck in this stuffy office, I'd rather be out and about«. There are several phrasal verbs with »**out**« and »**about**«:

to set about	to start working
to bring about	to cause to happen
to come about	to happen
to sort out	to find a solution
to bear out	to confirm the truth
to carry out	to complete a plan
to come out	to appear
to fall out with	to quarrel with somebody
to point out	to draw attention to the fact
to miss out on	to fail to get sth.

120. Train Yourself

Vervollständigen Sie nun die Sätze mit diesen Wendungen!

1. The problem was ▓▓▓▓▓ by Martin's resignation.
2. In the meeting it was ▓▓▓▓▓ that the deadline coincided with a national holiday.
3. The deal fell through and the managing director was anxious to know how this had ▓▓▓▓▓.
4. The quarterly prediction was ▓▓▓▓▓ by the eventual sales figures.
5. When the news ▓▓▓▓▓ everybody was in a state of disbelief.
6. Peter and Steve ▓▓▓▓▓ working as soon as they arrived at the hotel.
7. Now Susan, I don't want to ▓▓▓▓▓ with you but I'm not happy with your lack of punctuality.
8. We spent half the night trying to ▓▓▓▓▓ the discrepancy but still couldn't come to a solution.
9. Tom was very upset, it was the second time he had ▓▓▓▓▓ promotion.
10. The strategy was successfully ▓▓▓▓▓ and the new account was won.

 Talk Talk Talk

(Cardiff railway station)	(Im Bahnhof von Cardiff)
S. We'll grab a taxi to the hotel and then **give** our man Trevor Jones **a call**. He can come round to the hotel for a drink or we would even invite him for a meal. What do you think?	S. Wir schnappen uns ein Taxi zum Hotel und **rufen** unseren Trevor Jones dann **an**. Er kann dann auf einen Drink im Hotel vorbeikommen, wir könnten ihn sogar zum Essen einladen. Was halten Sie davon?

P. I'm easy. Perhaps it would be hospitable to invite him to join us for lunch, and at the same time we could get to know each other.

P. Mir ist das recht. Vielleicht wäre es ein Zeichen der Gastfreundschaft, ihn zum Mittagessen einzuladen und außerdem könnten wir uns dabei besser kennen lernen.

S. He's a nice fellow. I think you'll like him. An **easy-going** Welshman, but at the same time a good worker, a **good salesman** ... Here we are – the hotel. Let's get settled in first. I'll meet you in the bar in half an hour. And in the meantime I'll give Trevor a call ...

S. Er ist ein netter Kerl. Ich glaube, Sie werden ihn mögen. Er ist ein **unkomplizierter** Waliser, aber gleichzeitig ein guter Mitarbeiter und **Verkäufer** ... Da sind wir schon – das Hotel. Richten wir uns erst einmal ein. Wir treffen uns in einer halben Stunde in der Bar. Und in der Zwischenzeit rufe ich Trevor an ...

Background Information

On arrival at the hotel, Steve goes off to **give** Trevor **a call.** He could have said he was going to: **give** him **a ring, get on the phone** to him, or very colloquially, **give** him **a bell.**
Presuming Steve is ringing Trevor at his place of work, he may also need an extension number, to phone directly to his office or he might say, »Could you put me through to Trevor (surname)'s office please?«
»To put somebody through to« is **to connect** them with somebody.
If Trevor is **not available** the secretary or receptionist might reply:
»I'm sorry/afraid he's **otherwise engaged**,« or »He's **being held** up in a meeting at the moment« or »He's **unavailable** at the moment«.

If Trevor is speaking on the phone to somebody else the receptionist might say: »I'm afraid his **line's busy** right now/at the moment, can I take a message?« or »Can you **hold the line**?«
Let's imagine Steve is able **to get through to** Trevor (to establish contact with him). This could be the beginning of their conversation:

- Hello is that Trevor Jones?
- Speaking.

- Hello Trevor, Steve Blackman here. How are you?
- Fine Steve. And you?
- Oh, not so bad. I'm just ringing to set up some things for tonight.
- Fine, fire away Steve.
- Well ...

»**Speaking**« in this context is used to confirm that the caller has got through to the right person; it is only used in telephone conversations. »**Fire away**« means to continue talking and is quite colloquial, used here because Steve and Trevor already know each other.

 121. Train Yourself

Sie sehen nun drei Ausschnitte aus Telefonaten. Vervollständigen Sie sie mit den vorangegangenen Wendungen!

1.
- Hello, this is Graham Brown here, can you (a) ▬▬▬▬ to Geoffrey Barclay, please?
- Certainly, (b) ▬▬▬▬, please. (A few seconds later) I'm (c) ▬▬▬▬ but he's ▬▬▬▬ in a meeting. Can I (d) ▬▬▬▬?
- Yes, can you tell him Geoffrey Barclay from ERGO Ltd called? He's got my number. I'll (e) ▬▬▬▬ later.
- Of course, Mr Barclay.
- Thank you.

2.
- Hello, I'd like to speak with Peter Lownes, please.
- (f) ▬▬▬▬.
- Oh, Hello Mr. Lownes. This is Steve Blackman from ERGO Ltd. I spoke to you last week. There's just some details I'd like to go over with you.
- Hello Mr. Blackman. I remember our conversation very well. Now, (g) ▬▬▬▬.

3.
- Good afternoon, ERGO Ltd. Can I help you?
- Yes, this is Brenda Harte here from Heslop Communications, can I have

(h) ▒▒▒▒▒▒▒ 345, please?
- Certainly, one moment. (A few seconds later) Sorry, he's
(i) ▒▒▒▒▒▒▒ at the moment.
- Oh I see, well I'll try and (j) ▒▒▒▒▒▒▒ to him later. Thank you.

 Talk Talk Talk

(The hotel bar)

S. You've unpacked already, Peter? What are you drinking?

P. A pint of best bitter, please, Steve.

S. Ah, here comes Trevor now! Hello, Trevor. Good to see you again. How's business? Oh, meet my colleague and our assistant managing director, Peter Brückner. He's from Germany and I'm **showing him the ropes** in the **sales area**.

T. Pleased to meet you, Peter! How are you liking England?

P. Loving it. Even the weather!

T. You'll get to see some rough weather in the next couple of days. We have to **run up** to Swansea and a gale is forecast off the Atlantic.

(In der Hotelbar)

S. Schon ausgepackt, Peter? Was möchten Sie trinken?

P. Ein Pint vom besten Bitter bitte, Steve.

S. Ah, da kommt Trevor ja! Hallo, Trevor. Schön, Sie wieder zu sehen. Wie läuft das Geschäft? Oh, darf ich Ihnen meinen Kollegen, unseren stellvertretenden Geschäftsführer Peter Brückner vorstellen? Er kommt aus Deutschland und ich **mache ihn mit den Grundzügen** des **Verkaufsbereiches vertraut**.

T. Ich freue mich, Sie kennen zu lernen, Peter! Wie gefällt Ihnen England?

P. Ich liebe es. Selbst das Wetter!

T. In den nächsten Tagen werden Sie ein ziemlich stürmisches Wetter erleben. Wir werden hinauf nach Swansea müssen und es wurde ein Sturm über dem Atlantik vorhergesagt.

S. What will we be doing in Swansea?	S. Was werden wir denn in Swansea zu tun haben?
T. There's a new **financial services company** up there and it's expressed interest in that new **financial exchange software. It will take some selling**, but it will help to have you two along. Makes us look a serious team.	T. Es gibt da oben eine neue **Firma für Finanzdienstleistungen** und sie hat Interesse für dieses neue **Bilanzierungsprogramm** gezeigt. Es **wird einige harte Verkaufsgespräche geben**, aber es wird vielleicht nützlich sein, Sie beide dabei zu haben. Das wird uns den Eindruck eines ernsthaft bemühten Teams verleihen.

Background Information

Trevor says here that he has to **run up** to Swansea, in other words he has to drive there. »**Run up**« when used with the word »against« can also mean to encounter something, usually a problem, e.g. »The boss told me we had run up against a serious problem.«

Other phrases and expressions with »**run**« include:

to run over	to check something (also »run through« which has the the same meaning)
to run into	to meet somebody by chance
to run to	to have enough money for something
In the long run	after everything has been considered
to be in the running	to have a chance of winning something
to be run off one's feet	to be very busy
run-of-the-mill	ordinary or average
to run an eye over	to look quickly at something
to run its course	to continue to its natural end, to develop naturally

122. Train Yourself

Verwenden Sie diese Wendungen nun in der folgenden Übung!

1. The interviewees were so ▒▒▒▒▒▒▒▒▒▒▒▒▒ the director decided to re-advertise the position in order to seek out an exceptional candidate.
2. – I'm totally ▒▒▒▒▒▒▒▒▒▒▒▒▒ ! I haven't stopped all day!
3. – Hey, you'll never guess who I ▒▒▒▒▒▒▒▒▒▒▒▒▒ at that conference last weekend! Steve Jones!
4. The delegate ▒▒▒▒▒▒▒▒▒▒▒▒▒ final ▒▒▒▒▒▒▒▒▒▒▒▒▒ his notes and then began his speech.
5. The company decided against taking action and let the matter ▒▒▒▒▒▒▒▒▒▒▒▒▒.
6. Although the new software attracted a great deal of attention at its inception, sales were disappointing ▒▒▒▒▒▒▒▒▒▒▒▒▒.
7. Two new branches of the company were opened last year but due to high overheads, the shareholders felt they couldn't ▒▒▒▒▒▒▒▒▒▒▒▒▒ a third.
8. Two salespeople at ERGO Ltd are ▒▒▒▒▒▒▒▒▒▒▒▒▒ for the salesperson of the year award. They're both very excited.
9. (On the phone) – Oh hello John, Peter Davis here. Look, can we meet next week? We've ▒▒▒▒▒▒▒▒▒▒▒▒▒ some unforeseen difficulties with the Roberts account.
10. The itinerary for the day was ▒▒▒▒▒▒▒▒▒▒▒▒▒ several times before everybody was satisfied.

Talk Talk Talk

(The hotel lobby. Peter and Steve meet Trevor Jones)	(Die Lobby des Hotels. Peter und Steve treffen Trevor Jones)
S. Good morning, Trevor. You're bright and early.	S. Guten Morgen, Trevor. Sie sind ja ein echter Frühaufsteher.
T. The early bird catches the worm, **as they say in the trade**. But	T. Der frühe Vogel fängt den Wurm, **wie man in unserem Geschäft**

we're after more than worms, of course. The car is outside. We'll chat on the way to Swansea …

(During the journey)

T. Let me **fill you** both **in** on this job. This new software, Quickpay, is brand new and although it's revolutionary – perhaps precisely because it is so – it will take some selling at first. It attracted some attention in the **trade press** and I had a call from this Swansea company, LSD Financial Services. I sent them as much material on the system as I had – I want to talk to you about that Steve. It wasn't that good. Don't we have anything more? Something about the system's success in the States, perhaps?

S. I brought some new material with me. I haven't had a chance yet to give you it. It's an **up-to-date brochure**.

T. Great, that's just what I need. Now, let me explain our **strategy** in Swansea …

sagt. Aber wir sind natürlich hinter mehr her, als nur hinter ein paar Würmern. Das Auto steht draußen. Wir können auf dem Weg nach Swansea weiterreden …

(Während der Fahrt)

T. Ich werde Sie erst einmal über dieses Geschäft **ins Bild setzen**. Diese neue Software, Quickpay, ist brandneu und obwohl sie revolutionär ist – oder vielleicht gerade deswegen – wird das Ganze zunächst einige Überzeugungsarbeit erfordern. Ich habe in der **Fachpresse** damit für Aufmerksamkeit gesorgt und bekam dann einen Anruf von dieser Firma in Swansea, LSD Financial Services. Ich habe ihnen so viel Material über das System geschickt, wie ich hatte – darüber würde ich mit Ihnen gern reden, Steve. Es war nicht besonders gut. Haben wir denn nicht mehr? Vielleicht irgendetwas über den Erfolg des Systems in den Staaten?

S. Ich habe neues Material mitgebracht, aber hatte bisher noch keine Gelegenheit, es Ihnen zu geben. Es ist eine **hochaktuelle Broschüre**.

T. Großartig, das ist genau das, was ich brauche. Gut, dann lassen Sie mich Ihnen unsere **Strategie** für Swansea erklären …

Verkaufsgespräche

331

Background Information

During the car journey to Swansea Trevor **fills** Steve and Peter **in** on the new software system, Quickpay. **To fill somebody in** means **to inform them, to give them all the news**.
Other »**in**« phrases include:

to tie in with	to be in agreement with
to let somebody in on sth.	to allow somebody to be part of a secret
to go in for	to make a habit of doing something
to put in for	to apply for something (usually a job)
to stand in	to take the place of
to sleep in	to sleep later than usual
to come in for	to receive (usually criticism or blame)
to talk somebody into	to persuade
to take (it) out on	to make someone else suffer because of the way you feel

 123. Train Yourself

Verwenden Sie nun diese »phrasal verbs« in den folgenden Sätzen!

1. Tony Dale ▓▓▓▓▓▓▓▓ for the sales director while the latter was at a sales conference.
2. Peter ▓▓▓▓▓▓▓▓ accompanying him to the trade fair even though I was laden down with work.
3. I hear you've ▓▓▓▓▓▓▓▓ Jeremy's old job. Do you think you'll get it?
4. My God! I know the boss is particularly stressed at the minute but I wish he wouldn't ▓▓▓▓▓▓▓▓ me!
5. I don't usually ▓▓▓▓▓▓▓▓ lunchtime drinking but this was an important client and so I ordered an expensive bottle of claret.

6. If I ▓▓▓▓▓▓▓▓▓▓▓▓▓▓▓ a secret, do you promise to tell nobody?
7. A meeting was held in order to ▓▓▓▓▓▓▓▓▓▓ everybody ▓▓▓▓▓▓▓▓▓▓▓▓▓▓▓ on the new changes that were about to take place.
8. I missed the connecting train to the airport because I ▓▓▓▓▓▓▓▓ ▓▓▓▓▓▓▓▓▓▓▓▓▓▓▓▓▓.
9. OK, all of this ▓▓▓▓▓▓▓▓▓▓▓▓▓▓▓ perfectly with the plans we made yesterday. I think we should go ahead.
10. The new proposals ▓▓▓▓▓▓▓▓▓▓▓▓▓▓▓ some harsh criticism from the press.

Talk Talk Talk

T. We know LSD have been having problems with the security of their **credit accounts and debiting systems**. They deal with so many banks and financial institutions and their business **is expanding** so rapidly that their present **mainframe** is overworked. This piece of software offers a gateway, a portal for all kinds of internet financial transactions while guaranteeing total security. Its **greatest selling point** is its one hundred per cent security. All credit information is held by the participating banks and finance houses. No **coding information**, no **enciphered data** gets onto the internet. This is what appeals to firms like LSD - you'll see what I mean when we meet their **CEO**.

T. Wir wissen, dass LSD Probleme mit der Sicherheit ihrer **Kreditkonten und Abbuchungssysteme** hat. Sie haben mit so vielen Banken und Finanzinstituten zu tun und ihr Geschäft **expandiert** so schnell, dass ihr derzeitiges **Computersystem** überlastet ist. Unsere Software bietet eine Art Durchgang, ein Portal zu allen möglichen finanziellen Transaktionen über das Internet an, während es absolute Sicherheit garantiert. Das **wichtigste Verkaufsargument** ist seine hundertprozentige Sicherheit. Alle Kreditinformationen bleiben bei den teilnehmenden Banken und Finanzhäusern. Es gibt keinerlei **kodierte Information**, keine **verschlüsselten Daten** gehen in das Internet hinaus. Genau das ist für Firmen wie LSD so ansprechend –

	Sie werden verstehen, was ich meine, wenn wir ihren **CEO** treffen.
P. CEO?	P. CEO?
T. **Chief Executive Officer**. He's Welsh, like myself. David Powys is his name. You'll like him, he's OK. But he'll take some selling too ...	T. **Chief Executive Officer** (Generaldirektor). Er ist ein Waliser, genau wie ich. Sein Name ist David Powys. Sie werden ihn mögen, er ist in Ordnung. Aber auch er erfordert einige Überzeugungsarbeit ...

Background Information

Trevor says in this section of Talk Talk Talk that the **mainframe** at LSD is overworked. The **mainframe** is the central computer system. Other words and expressions with »**main**« include:

mainstay	the most important part of something providing support for everything else
domain	an area of interest over which a person has control
mainspring	the most important reason for something
mainstream	the way of life accepted by the most people
in the main	mostly
to maintain	to continue to keep/have in existence

124. Train Yourself

Fügen Sie nun diese Wendungen in die Sätze ein!

1. The company's ▓▓▓▓▓▓▓▓▓▓▓▓▓▓ was the microchip market, they were way ahead of their competitors.
2. ▓▓▓▓▓▓▓▓▓▓▓▓▓▓ I get home from work at about ten at night although sometimes even later.

3. Tony was the ▓▓▓▓▓▓▓▓▓▓ of the operation, without him we would never have clinched the deal.
4. The ▓▓▓▓▓▓▓▓▓▓ to the company's success was the hard work put in by everybody.
5. When the ▓▓▓▓▓▓▓▓▓▓ crashed there was panic as it contained just about every important piece of information.
6. At present, the company ▓▓▓▓▓▓▓▓▓▓ five members of staff in the sales department and three in logistics.
7. To be successful in selling one must be aware of current ideas and fashions in ▓▓▓▓▓▓▓▓▓▓ culture.

 Talk Talk Talk

(The offices of LSD, Trevor addresses the receptionist)

T. Good morning, we're here to see Mr Powys.

R. Is he expecting you?

T. Certainly. We have an **appointment** for 11 o'clock.

R. I'll call him ... Yes, Mr Powys is expecting you. If you'll follow me I'll take you to him now ...

(David Powys's office)

D. Good morning gentlemen! Did you have a good journey from Cardiff?

T. Fine, thank you Mr Powys. I'd like you to meet Steve Blackman, **Sales Director** of ERGO Limited,

(In den Büros von LSD, Trevor spricht eine Empfangsdame an)

T. Guten Morgen, wir möchten gern mit Mr Powys sprechen.

R. Erwartet er Sie?

T. Natürlich. Wir haben einen Termin für 11 Uhr.

R. Ich werde ihn anrufen ... Ja, Mr Powys erwartet Sie. Wenn Sie mir bitte folgen, ich werde Sie gleich zu ihm führen ...

(David Powys Büro)

D. Guten Morgen, meine Herren! Hatten Sie eine gute Fahrt von Cardiff hierher?

T. Ja, danke, Mr Powys. Ich würde Ihnen gerne Steve Blackman, den **Verkaufsleiter** von ERGO Limited

and Mr Peter Brückner, the company's assistant managing Director.	und Mr Peter Brückner, den stellvertretenden Geschäftsführer der Firma vorstellen.
D. My, Trevor – I may call you Trevor? – you're **rolling out the heavy guns**. Is this such a hard sell?	D. Meine Güte, Trevor – ich darf Sie doch Trevor nennen? – Sie **fahren ja schwere Geschütze auf**. Rechnen Sie mit so harten Verkaufsgesprächen?
T. Steve and Peter are touring Britain, looking at our sales operation, and I thought it would be a good idea **to bring them along with me** today. Don't worry – **they're as new to Quickpay as you are** ...	T. Steve und Peter reisen durch England, um unsere Verkaufsstellen zu inspizieren und ich dachte, es wäre eine gute Idee, **sie heute mitzubringen**. Keine Sorge – **sie verstehen von Quickpay so wenig wie Sie** ...

Do's and Don'ts

British businessmen (such as David Powys) are often quick to move from a formal form of address to the informal use of first names. As **a rule of thumb**, wait for them to **enter first into first-name terms**. You'll usually be invited to communicate on that level – »Call me John! Let's drop this mister stuff!«

Background Information

Trevor says to David Powys that Steven and Peter are as **new to** Quickpay as he (David) is. The phrase »**new to**« is an example of a very common language structure in English – an adjective (new) plus a preposition (to). Other commonly used prepositional phrases comprising of an adjective with a preposition include:
interested in
worried about
good/bad at

> wary of
> concerned with/about
> skilled in
> disappointed in
> impressed by
> surprised by
> pleased with
> successful in

 125. Train Yourself

Verwenden Sie die oben stehenden Ausdrücke in den folgenden Sätzen:

1. We are very _____ the new marketing manager. She has settled into her new job very well.
2. The company were _____ the low profits shown by the new product. They were expecting a lot more consumer interest.
3. We are certainly very _____ your proposal and will be discussing it properly at the next board meeting.
4. He is _____ employing graduates without any experience at all of a working environment even if they are well-qualified.
5. We were very _____ your presentation this morning. It showed very thorough research into possible new markets for the new product.
6. He is _____ the technical side of his job but _____ any aspect involving communication skills.
7. The company has always been _____ predicting market trends. They have always foreseen the appearance of new directions.
8. She is very _____ negotiating with customers who are often difficult. She is always calm and diplomatic.
9. We are very _____ one of our colleagues who appears to have reacted very badly to the break-up of his marriage.
10. He's _____ the job so he still has a lot to learn.
11. We were _____ the results of the survey – we hadn't expected so much consumer interest.

12. We are ▓▓▓▓▓▓▓▓▓▓▓▓ the effect on the surrounding countryside of the new development and the possible reaction of local residents.

 **Talk Talk Talk**

(Still at the office)   (Immer noch im Büro)

T. Now, David, you've read all the brochure material we sent you, **I take it** ...

T. Also, David, **ich vermute**, Sie haben das Prospektmaterial, das wir Ihnen geschickt haben, gelesen ...

D. If I hadn't, dear boy, you would not be sitting there now!

D. Wenn ich das nicht getan hätte, mein Lieber, würden Sie hier nicht sitzen!

T. Then do you have any questions?

T. Haben Sie irgendwelche Fragen?

D. Certainly. I understand well enough how this software will organize our payments system. That just seems to be **an advance on** your **accounting program**, which – as you know – we have been **happily using** for some time now. In that respect, the Quickpay software is an update, a new generation of software ...

D. Natürlich. Ich verstehe jetzt einigermaßen, wie diese Software unser Abbuchungssystem organisieren wird. Das scheint **eine Verbesserung** Ihres Abrechnungsprogramms zu sein, das wir – wie Sie ja wissen – jetzt schon seit einiger Zeit **voller Zufriedenheit benutzen**. In dieser Hinsicht ist die Quickpay-Software ein Update, eine neue Generation von Software ...

T. You are so right. You see, **you are getting double value** from this product ...

T. Sie haben absolut Recht. Sehen Sie, **Sie profitieren** von diesem Produkt gleich **doppelt** ...

D. Good heavens, Steve – it is Steve isn't it? – this man of yours knows how to sell!

D. Du lieber Himmel, Steve – Ihr Name ist doch Steve, oder? – Ihr Kollege versteht es wirklich, etwas an den Mann zu bringen.

338

S. He's one of our best – but of course he is selling a **top product** here. No problem for him.

S. Er ist einer unserer besten Leute – aber natürlich verkauft er hier auch ein **Spitzenprodukt**. Das ist kein Problem für ihn.

Background Information

In this section of Talk Talk Talk David says his company have been **happily** using their accounting programme for some time. (The British use the American spelling of »programme« in context of computers.) »**Happily**« is an adverb corresponding to the adjective »**happy**«. As you know an adjective describes a noun whereas an adverb describes a verb. Below are other pairs of adverbs and adjectives:

warm – warmly	private – privately	direct – directly
accurate – accurately	anxious – anxiously	polite – politely
obvious – obviously	rapid – rapidly	unfailing – unfailingly

126. Train Yourself

Suchen Sie in den folgenden Sätzen das passende Wort in Klammern aus, um den Satz zu vervollständigen.

1. In business it is always better to deal _____ (direct/directly) with the customer rather than going through a third party.
2. Although he publicly expressed interest in the merger, in _____ (private/privately) he wasn't too sure.
3. On arriving at the conference we received a _____ (warm/warmly) welcome from the organizers.
4. The company was _____ (unfailing/unfailingly) in its attempts to float its shares on the stock market.
5. We waited _____ (anxious/anxiously) for the results of the audit.
6. _____ (obvious/obviously) it is better to do one's homework before meeting a client.

7. John said he would ▓▓▓▓▓▓▓▓▓▓ (happy/happily) do the job as long as he was paid expenses.
8. He rose ▓▓▓▓▓▓▓▓▓▓ (rapid/rapidly) through the ranks until he became CEO at the age of 40.
9. The company's forecast was not very ▓▓▓▓▓▓▓▓▓▓ (accurate/accurately) and as a result staff reductions were predicted.
10. In response to the customer complaint a ▓▓▓▓▓▓▓▓▓▓ (polite/politely) letter was sent offering a full apology.

 **Talk Talk Talk**

D. What I'm not that clear about is the security mechanism. We are very worried by this increasing number of internet fraud cases. We actually lost some **client details** only a few weeks ago – an **e-mailing retailer got hold of** them. Very embarrassing for us. I must admit **we are in the market now for** a really effective secure payments system. Now, tell me how yours works.

T. First of all, we **move** all financial transaction handling **out of your control** and place it entirely in the hands of your bank. Your clients still believe they are dealing with you but in effect they and you are enjoying the complete security of the bank. One major High Street bank, by the way, is already using our system, but all banks now

D. **Was ich noch nicht ganz verstehe**, ist diese Sicherheitseinrichtung. Wir sind sehr besorgt über diese zunehmenden Fälle von Internet-Verbrechen. Tatsache ist, dass wir erst vor ein paar Wochen einige **Kundendaten** verloren haben – **ein Händler von E-Mail-Adressen** hat sie **in die Finger bekommen**. Äußerst peinlich für uns. Ich muss zugeben, dass **wir jetzt wirklich Bedarf nach** einem effektiven Sicherheitssystem für Finanztransaktionen **haben**. Also, erzählen Sie mir, wie Ihres funktioniert.

T. Zunächst einmal **nehmen** wir alle finanziellen Transaktionen **aus Ihrem Verantwortungsbereich heraus** und legen sie voll und ganz in die Hände Ihrer Bank. Ihre Kunden werden immer noch glauben, es mit Ihnen zu tun zu haben, obwohl sie in Wirklichkeit in den Genuss der vollen Sicherheit der Bank kommen. Eine der großen Banken

have pretty **foolproof security shields**.	in der High Street benutzt übrigens schon unser System, aber mittlerweile haben alle Banken ziemlich **narrensichere Sicherheitssperren**.
D. So tell me more about yours – why it's better than the rest.	D. Dann erzählen Sie mir mehr über Ihres – warum es besser als die anderen ist.
T. Well, let me tell you how it functions and you'll soon see why we are **leaders** in this field ...	T. Na schön, lassen Sie mich erklären, wie es funktioniert und Sie werden schon bald verstehen, warum wir die **Marktführer** in diesem Bereich sind ...

Background Information

David Powys in this section of the dialogue tells Steve and Peter about how an **e-mailing retailer got hold of** some client details causing him to be concerned about the company's security mechanism. In this context »**to get hold of**« means **to find something and use it**; it can also mean **to contact somebody**, e.g. »Did you get hold of Jeremy yesterday?« or **to take something in one's hands** »He got hold of the rope and pulled«. In this instance it is the first meaning we are concerned with.

Phrasal verbs and expressions with »**hold**« include:

to hold up	to delay
to hold with	to agree (usually with an idea)
to hold out	to offer (usually hope)
to hold forth	to speak for a long time (often pompously)
to hold one's own	to continue to defend oneself in a difficult situation
to hold one's breath	to wait anxiously for something
to get hold of the wrong end of the stick	to misunderstand something completely

Verkaufsgespräche

| to hold the fort | to look after a business or state of affairs while someone is away |

 127. Train Yourself

Ergänzen Sie folgende Sätze und verwenden Sie dazu obige Wendungen:

1. Have you heard about Michael leaving the company at the end of the year? Don't ▮▮▮▮▮. He's only thinking about it.
2. The managing director left his assistant to ▮▮▮▮▮ while he was away.
3. Sorry I'm late. I was ▮▮▮▮▮ in traffic.
4. I don't really ▮▮▮▮▮ the idea that staff should be asked to retire at 60.
5. At the conference the organizer ▮▮▮▮▮ for 45 minutes causing some delegates to nearly fall asleep!
6. Management don't ▮▮▮▮▮ much hope that the dispute will be settled by the end of the week.
7. You seem to have ▮▮▮▮▮ ! I never said I would be leaving the company! I said I was leaving to go on holiday!
8. My P.A. tried for half an hour to ▮▮▮▮▮ him but was constantly told to just hold the line.
9. The company seems to be ▮▮▮▮▮ despite the economic climate.
10. Somebody ▮▮▮▮▮ some sensitive information and is causing enormous headaches for the management.

 **Talk Talk Talk**

(The hotel bar)

S. I'm impressed, Trevor. You witnessed a good salesman at work today, Peter.

(In der Hotelbar)

S. Ich bin beeindruckt, Trevor. Sie haben heute einen guten Verkäufer bei der Arbeit gesehen, Peter.

Verkaufsgespräche

P. I know. I was also very impressed. It was very interesting, after all this theory, to see **sales techniques** put into practice.

T. Thanks, gents – but you gave me great support. I think Powys was also impressed – but by the heavyweight team we rolled out.

S. Like one of your famous rugby sides, eh, Trevor!

T. Actually, Steve, rugby and selling have some things in common. Believe me, I used to play for a crack Swansea side. Strategy is **of paramount importance**, for a start. You don't take the field without being fully prepared, with an action plan in your head. **Tactics are secondary.** Look at a **sales pitch** as another rugby ground. Know your strengths but also your weaknesses – there's nearly always a weak link. You have to find it and compensate for it. Then you have to know your opposition just about as well as you know yourself. Respect your opposition, too. Don't just **rubbish** the other side or its products. If you're selling, admit that there are similar, good products out there in the market place. Prove that your product is better.

P. Ich weiß. Ich war auch sehr beeindruckt. Nach der ganzen Theorie war es sehr interessant, die **Verkaufstechniken** einmal in die Praxis umgesetzt zu sehen.

T. Danke, Herrschaften – aber Sie haben mich auch großartig unterstützt. Ich glaube, auch Powys war beeindruckt – von dem hochkarätigen Team, mit dem wir angerollt sind.

S. Wie eines Ihrer berühmten Rugby-Teams, was, Trevor?!

T. Streng genommen, Steve, haben Rugby und der Verkauf einiges gemeinsam. Glauben Sie mir das, ich habe für ein erstklassiges Team aus Swansea gespielt. Zunächst einmal ist die Strategie **von entscheidender Bedeutung**. Man geht nicht aufs Spielfeld, ohne lückenlos vorbereitet zu sein, mit einem genauen Handlungsplan im Kopf. Die **Taktik ist dann zweitrangig**. Betrachten Sie ein **Verkaufsgespräch** als ein Rugby-Spielfeld. Kennen Sie Ihre Stärken, aber auch Ihre Schwächen – und es gibt fast immer eine Schwachstelle. Sie müssen sie erkennen und einen Ausgleich dafür suchen. Und dann müssen Sie auch Ihren Gegner so gut kennen wie sich selbst. Sie sollten Ihren Gegner auch respektieren. **Werten** Sie die Gegenseite oder ihre Produkte nicht einfach nur **ab**.

| | Wenn Sie etwas verkaufen, müssen Sie auch eingestehen, dass es ähnliche gute Produkte auf dem Markt gibt. Beweisen Sie, dass Ihr Produkt besser ist. |

P. I noticed you **adopted that approach** when you told David Powys banks are using systems that we did not supply.

P. Mir ist aufgefallen, dass Sie **diesen Ansatz benutzt** haben, als Sie David Powys sagten, dass Banken auch Systeme benutzen, die nicht von uns geliefert werden.

T. No sense in hiding that fact. He would discover it anyway, and then our **credibility** would be damaged or even destroyed. **Honesty pays in selling**, believe me!

T. Es hätte keinen Sinn gemacht, diese Tatsache zu verschweigen. Er hätte es so oder so herausgefunden und unsere **Glaubwürdigkeit** wäre damit angeschlagen oder sogar zerstört worden. **Ehrlichkeit im Verkauf zahlt sich aus**, glauben Sie mir!

S. We believe you, and I'm sure Powys did, too. Now what are we drinking?

S. Wir glauben Ihnen und ich bin sicher, dass Powys das auch getan hat. Also, was wollen wir trinken?

 Background Information

»**Honesty pays in selling**« according to Trevor, meaning that **it is advantageous to do so**. He could have said »**honesty pays dividends**«, another expression with the same meaning.
Let's look at some more »**pay**« expressions:

to pay lip-service	to say that one approves of or supports something while not doing anything about it
to pay the price for	to suffer because of a previous error or wrongdoing

to pay through the nose	to pay a very high price for something
to pay attention to	to take careful notice of
to pay off	when a risky course of action proves successful
to put paid to something	to stop or destroy something
there'll be hell to pay	informal expression meaning great trouble will result

 128. Train Yourself

Verwenden Sie obige Wendungen in folgenden Sätzen:

1. The company ▨▨▨▨▨ for a lack of investment when share prices plummeted (fell heavily).
2. ▨▨▨▨▨ if we lose this account!
3. Knowing one's strengths and weaknesses ▨▨▨▨▨ when one meets the client.
4. The company ▨▨▨▨▨ for their new security systems - the cost was far higher than expected.
5. The management ▨▨▨▨▨ to the idea without being convinced about its benefits.
6. The gamble ▨▨▨▨▨ when the deal was finally clinched and there was champagne all round to celebrate.
7. The economic crisis ▨▨▨▨▨ any plans the company had for expansion.
8. If a salesperson wants to learn the ropes he or she must ▨▨▨▨▨ to the advice of more experienced colleagues.

Talk Talk Talk

(The next day. The hotel's breakfast room)	(Am nächsten Tag. Im Frühstücksraum des Hotels)
S. Good morning, Peter. How are you feeling today?	S. Guten Morgen, Peter. Wie geht es Ihnen heute?

P. I shouldn't have had that third pint, Steve. I've got **a bit of a hangover**.	P. Ich hätte das dritte Pint nicht trinken sollen, Steve. Ich habe **einen kleinen Kater**.
S. You know my hangover cure? **Kippers**. They're over there on the buffet table.	S. Kennen Sie mein Heilmittel gegen Kater? **Kippers**. Da drüben am Buffet gibt es welche.
P. Kippers?	P. Kippers?
S. Smoked fish, dear boy! You must have eaten them in Hamburg.	S. Geräucherter Fisch (Bückling), mein Lieber. So etwas müssen Sie in Hamburg doch auch gegessen haben.
P. The only fish I ate in Hamburg were fresh, apart from pickled herring – Matjes. Have you ever tried those?	P. In Hamburg habe ich immer nur frischen Fisch gegessen, mal abgesehen von eingelegten Heringen – Matjes. Haben Sie die mal probiert?
S. Sounds dreadful. No, **I'll stick to kippers** – you should try them, too ...	S. Klingt furchtbar! Nein, **ich bleibe bei den Kippers** – Sie sollten sie auch einmal probieren ...
(A hotel employee approaches the table)	(Ein Hotelangestellter tritt an den Tisch)
E. Excuse me, sir. Are you Mr Blackman?	E. Entschuldigen Sie, Sir. Sind Sie Mr Blackman?
S. That's me.	S. Das bin ich.
E. I have a Mr Jones on the phone. He says it's urgent.	E. Ich habe einen Mr Jones am Apparat. Er sagt, es wäre dringend.
S. I'll be right there. Excuse me, Peter ...	S. Ich komme sofort. Entschuldigen Sie mich, Peter ...

Do's and Don'ts

A reminder for **business travellers** in Britain: when booking a hotel always make sure it serves a full English breakfast, a buffet if possible. And check whether it is included in the room rate. A full English breakfast will **keep** the busy businessman **going** all day - there's no need even to break for the proverbial business lunch! And if kippers are on the breakfast menu **give them a try**!

Background Information

Steve doesn't like the sound of Matjes, he says he'd rather **stick to** kippers. To »**stick to**« means to stay with something. Other phrases and expressions with »**stick**« include:

to stick one's neck out	to take a risk
to get hold of the wrong end of the stick	to misunderstand something
a stick-in-the-mud	a person who has fixed ideas and is unadventurous
to carry a big stick (over)	to use power or to enforce control strictly
to stick in one's oar	to try to concern oneself in the affairs of others
to stick to one's guns	to continue to support a particular course of action
to stick out like a sore thumb	to be totally out of place

 129. Train Yourself

Setzen Sie die Wendungen in die folgenden Sätze ein!

1. The management decided to _____ and go ahead with the takeover despite widespread protest.
2. I hadn't realized the dinner was going to be so formal and I _____.

3. It's impossible to come to any decisions at a meeting when everybody tries to ▒▒▒▒▒▒▒▒▒▒▒▒▒▒▒▒.
4. The company didn't want to be thought of as ▒▒▒▒▒▒▒▒▒▒▒▒▒▒▒▒▒▒▒▒▒▒▒▒▒▒▒▒ and so decided to take a risk.
5. I listened intently to the agenda for next week's meetings just so that I didn't ▒▒▒▒▒▒▒▒▒▒▒▒▒▒▒▒
6. I don't think we're off-course here, I think we should ▒▒▒▒▒▒▒▒▒▒▒▒▒▒▒▒▒▒▒▒▒▒▒▒▒▒ our present plan of action.
7. The new sales manager ▒▒▒▒▒▒▒▒▒▒▒▒▒▒▒▒▒▒▒▒▒▒▒▒ and issued a series of company policy statements to all members of staff.
8. I think we should ▒▒▒▒▒▒▒▒▒▒▒▒▒▒▒▒▒▒▒▒▒ on this one. If we don't take a risk, we'll regret it later.

 Talk Talk Talk

(Steve returns to the table)

S. You're not going to believe this, Peter!

P. What did Trevor Jones have to tell you?

S. Do you want the good news first or the bad news?

P. This early in the day **I'll go for** the bad news.

S. Trevor told me David Powys called him first thing this morning and said a **hacker** had **broken into** their system and stolen credit card information on more than 1,000 clients. There's mayhem today over at LSD. Poor old Trevor was practically weeping. He's **in a heck of a state**!

(Steve kehrt an den Tisch zurück)

S. Sie werden das nicht glauben, Peter!

P. Was wollte Trevor Jones denn?

S. Wollen Sie zuerst die gute oder die schlechte Nachricht hören?

P. So früh am Morgen **ziehe ich** die schlechte Nachricht **vor**.

S. Trevor hat mir erzählt, dass David Powys gleich heute Morgen angerufen hat und sagte, dass ein **Hacker** in ihr System **eingebrochen** wäre und Kreditkarteninformationen von mehr als 1000 Kunden gestohlen hat. Drüben bei LSD herrscht das absolute Chaos. Der arme alte Trevor war fast am

	Heulen. Er ist **in einem furchtbaren Zustand**!
P. Good Lord! That's terrible. The nightmare of every company. So what's the good news?	P. Mein Gott! Das ist ja entsetzlich. Der Alptraum jeder Firma. Und was sind die guten Nachrichten?
S. Powys wants our system installed right away. He didn't even ask for a **cost estimate**. Trevor is down there right now – it's the biggest **sale** he's made yet.	S. Powys will unser System sofort installiert haben. Er hat nicht einmal nach einem **Kostenvoranschlag** gefragt. Trevor ist schon rübergefahren – das ist sein bisher größter **Geschäftsabschluss**.
P. And what do we do?	P. Und was machen wir?
S. We're off to Scotland, boyo! With that contract **under our belts** we've got a great head start. How were the kippers?	S. Wir brechen auf nach Schottland, Kumpel! Mit diesem Vertrag **unter Dach und Fach** haben wir einen großartigen Start hingelegt. Wie waren die Bücklinge?

Background Information

A hacker has broken into the computer system of the company visited by Steve and Peter. If a hacker breaks into a computer system he or she penetrates its security system and gains access to files. »Break« is a verb with many additional meanings – many of them in the world of business and industry.

130. Train Yourself

Versuchen Sie nun »break« in den folgenden Sätzen korrekt zu verwenden. Benutzen Sie hierfür die folgenden Optionen: *broke the back, break the market, break the strike, break even, make or break, break.*

1. The company disregarded the terms of the contract and ▓▓▓▓▓ ▓▓▓▓▓▓▓▓▓▓ the agreement.

2. The costs were crippling for the company. They finally ▓▓▓ the management's ▓▓▓.
3. For a few years after its foundation, the company had an upward struggle. It was ▓▓▓.
4. The share price dropped so low that it threatened to ▓▓▓
5. The company managed to balance income and outgoings. It ▓▓▓ ▓▓▓.
6. The unions were not strong enough to continue the work stoppage. Management managed to ▓▓▓.

 Vocabulary:

accounting program	Abrechnungsprogramm
to adopt an approach	einen Ansatz benutzen
advance	Fortschritt
a lot of scope	ein breites Betätigungsfeld
appointment	Termin, Verabredung
to be in the market for	wirklich Bedarf haben nach
client details	Kundendaten
cost estimate	Kostenvoranschlag
credit accounts	Kreditkonten
easy-going	unkompliziert
enciphered data	verschlüsselte Daten
to expand	expandieren
to fill sb. in	jdn. ins Bild setzen
financial exchange software	Bilanzierungsprogramm
financial services company	Finanzdienstleister
to fire away	losschießen (ugs.)
to get double value from sth.	von etw. doppelt profitieren
to get hold of sth.	etw. in die Finger bekommen
to go for sth.	etw. vorziehen
Honesty pays in selling!	Ehrlichkeit zahlt sich im Verkauf aus!
in a heck of a state	in einem furchtbaren Zustand
It will take some selling.	Es wird einige harte Verkaufsgespräche geben.
kipper	Bückling

leader	hier: Marktführer
mainframe	Computersystem
of paramount importance	von entscheidender Bedeutung
one-man operation	Ein-Mann-Betrieb
out and about	unterwegs
to pay dividends	sich bezahlt machen
to roll out the heavy guns	schwere Geschütze auffahren
to rubbish	abwerten
sale	Geschäftsabschluss
sales area	Verkaufsbereich
salespeople	Außendienstmitarbeiter
secondary	zweitrangig
selling point	Verkaufsargument
(to) show sb. the ropes	jdm. etw. erklären (ugs.)
to stick to	hier: bleiben bei
trade press	Fachpresse
under our belts	unter Dach und Fach
up-to-date	hochaktuell

Verkaufsgespräche

Place proposals
Angebote unterbreiten

 **Here we go**

Peter und Steve befinden sich immer noch auf ihrer Rundreise durch die verschiedenen Verkaufsvertretungen von ERGO Limited. Sie sind gerade in Schottland angekommen, um sich mit Angus Fairbairn, ERGOs Mann, in Glasgow zu treffen. Zusammen mit ihm wird Peter Einblicke in das neue »Online-Geschäft« und in so genannte »Cyber Parks«, neue Online-Geschäftszentren, erhalten. Außerdem findet Peter Gefallen an Schottland, dem dortigen Lebensstil und den freundlichen Menschen. Es gibt noch viel Neues kennen zu lernen ...

 **Talk Talk Talk**

(The hotel lobby)

S. All **ready for off**, Peter?

P. Just **say the word**, Steve.

S. The car's waiting. I've paid the bill, called the office, told James the good news. Now let's conquer Scotland. Let's go ...

(In the car)

S. We'll **break the journey** in the Lake District. Glasgow is our first destination. We have two offices in

(Die Hotel-Lobby)

S. Sind Sie **fertig zum Aufbruch**, Peter?

P. **Wann immer Sie wollen**, Steve.

S. Der Wagen wartet. Ich habe die Rechnung bezahlt, im Büro angerufen und James die gute Nachricht überbracht. Lassen Sie uns Schottland erobern. Los geht's ...

(Im Wagen)

S. Im nordwestlichen Seengebiet **unterbrechen** wir **unsere Reise**. Unser erstes Ziel ist Glasgow.

Scotland, you know – one in Glasgow and the other in Edinburgh. Business has picked up since **devolution**. The Scots seem to be flourishing under Independence – well, semi-independence.	Wissen Sie, wir haben zwei Büros in Schottland – eines in Glasgow und das andere in Edinburgh. Die Geschäfte dort haben seit der **Dezentralisierung** angezogen. Die Schotten scheinen aufzublühen in ihrer Unabhängigkeit – na ja, Halbunabhängigkeit.

Background Information

1. Scotland and Wales were granted a form of independence in 1999. Scotland now has a Parliament with sweeping powers, while Wales has a National Assembly with a more limited form of independence. The process of granting the two regions semi-independence is described as **devolution**.

2. Steve wants **to break the journey** to Scotland by stopping in the Lake District. In this context **breaking the journey** means **to interrupt** it. There are various phrases and expressions with **break** in English, some of them are listed below:

to break off	to stop talking
to break down	to stop working
to break up	to come to an end
a breakthrough	an important discovery that helps to provide an answer to a problem
to break in (coll.)	to prepare or train
to break even	to have one's losses balanced by one's gains
to break new ground	to do something new or to make a discovery
to break the back of something	to complete the most difficult part of a job
to break the ice	to make a formal or nervous situation easier by a friendly act or conversation

Verkaufsgespräche

131. Train Yourself

Setzen Sie die »phrasal verbs« nun in die folgenden Sätze ein!

1. The company is ▓▓▓▓▓ by opening a new branch in the Czech Republic.
2. I've got a really heavy workload on at the moment. Why don't we meet tonight at my place and try to ▓▓▓▓▓ it?
3. Everybody felt nervous at the party until Tony ▓▓▓▓▓ by telling one of his famous bad jokes.
4. There was a minor crisis at work when the photocopier ▓▓▓▓▓.
5. The best management can hope for it that the company will ▓▓▓▓▓ at the end of the year.
6. The meeting finally ▓▓▓▓▓ at midnight.
7. I'm ▓▓▓▓▓ my new P.A. at the moment, just showing her the ropes, you know.
8. After days of negotiations the two sides in the dispute finally came to a ▓▓▓▓▓ and the problem was solved.
9. During the interview the Sales Director ▓▓▓▓▓ to attend to an important phone call.
10. I'm exhausted! Let's ▓▓▓▓▓ the journey and get some lunch!

 Talk Talk Talk

(Dining room of motel on road between Carlisle and Glasgow)

(Speiseraum im Motel an der Straße zwischen Carlisle und Glasgow)

S. Sorry about the Lake District, Peter. I didn't expect all hotels to be full. We should have called **beforehand** to book. It is a weekend, of course.

S. Peter, das mit dem Seengebiet tut mir Leid. Ich hatte nicht erwartet, dass alle Hotels voll belegt sein würden. Wir hätten **vorher** anrufen und buchen sollen. Es ist schließlich Wochenende.

P. Not to worry, Steve. We shall be comfortable enough here, and we'll have time enough for sightseeing when this trip is over. Tell me now what awaits us tomorrow.	P. Ärgern Sie sich nicht, Steve. Wir haben es hier bequem genug und noch genügend Zeit für die Sehenswürdigkeiten, wenn diese Reise vorbei ist. Erzählen Sie mir jetzt, was uns morgen erwartet.
S. Glasgow is **making a big bid** to become one of Europe's new »**cyber cities**«. A centre for high-tech business and industry. Its old industrial and shipbuilding base has all but vanished. Glasgow was one of the first centres of the **industrial revolution**. It doesn't want to be left behind by the **new revolution**.	S. Glasgow **bemüht sich sehr**, Europas neue »**Cyber-City**« zu werden. Ein Zentrum für Hightech-Geschäfte und Industrie. Die frühere Handelsbasis Industrie- und Schiffbau ist völlig verschwunden. Glasgow war eines der ersten Zentren der **industriellen Revolution**. Es möchte von der **neuen Revolution** nicht zurückgelassen werden.
P. So where do we come in?	P. Und wo kommen wir ins Spiel?
S. Our job is to help local business and industry achieve their ambition to be leaders in this new revolution. We have the products. We just have to persuade Glasgow companies that **it's worth their while** buying them.	S. Unsere Aufgabe ist es, dem örtlichen Handel und der Industrie dabei zu helfen, dass sie ihre Ziele erreichen und die Anführer dieser neuen Revolution werden. Wir haben die Produkte. Wir müssen lediglich die Glasgower Unternehmen davon überzeugen, dass **sie es wert sind**, gekauft zu werden.
P. And how do we do that?	P. Und wie machen wir das?
S. You'll see tomorrow when you meet Angus Fairbairn, our Glasgow **representative**.	S. Das werden Sie morgen schon sehen, wenn wir uns mit Angus Fairbairn, unserem Glasgower **Repräsentanten**, treffen.

Verkaufsgespräche

Background Information

Steve apologizes to Peter for not being able to find accommodation in the Lake District.
He says he should have called **beforehand** to reserve rooms.
»**Beforehand**« means **before something else has happened**, in this case before they arrived in the Lake District.
There are many other phrases and expressions with »**hand**«, let's look at some of them:

to have the upper hand	to have a position of power or control over someone
to put one's hand to	to begin or try to do a task or job
out of hand	out of control
to know something/somewhere like the back of one's hand	to know it very well
to show one's hand	to do or say something that reveals one's intentions
an old hand	a person with a long experience in a job or activity
to go hand in hand	to be connected or closely related
at first hand	directly with the person or operation involved
underhand	dishonest and usually done secretly

 132. Train Yourself

Verwenden Sie diese Wendungen nun in den folgenden Sätzen!

1. Steve and Peter are touring around the offices of ERGO Ltd to see things ▓▓▓▓▓▓▓▓▓▓▓▓▓▓▓▓▓▓▓▓.
2. Joseph is ▓▓▓▓▓▓▓▓▓▓▓▓▓▓▓▓▓ at the job. He's been here twenty years.
3. When negotiating deals it's vitally important not to ▓▓▓▓▓▓▓▓ ▓▓▓▓▓▓▓▓▓▓▓▓▓▓▓▓▓ too early.

4. The stationery budget is getting ▓▓▓▓▓▓▓▓▓▓▓▓▓▓▓▓▓▓▓▓▓▓▓▓▓▓▓▓!
   Could people please not waste paper.
5. Steve volunteered to show Peter and Trevor around the town as he ▓▓▓▓▓▓▓▓▓▓▓▓▓▓▓▓▓▓▓.
6. You should have rung me ▓▓▓▓▓▓▓▓▓▓▓▓▓▓▓▓▓▓▓▓▓. I can't really see you at the moment.
7. George is so flexible, he is always ready to ▓▓▓▓▓▓▓▓▓▓▓▓▓▓▓▓▓▓▓▓▓▓▓▓▓▓▓▓▓▓▓▓▓ anything that comes his way.
8. Good salesmanship ▓▓▓▓▓▓▓▓▓▓▓▓▓▓▓▓▓▓▓ with confidence and belief in the product.
9. The management were accused by the union of being ▓▓▓▓▓▓▓▓▓▓▓▓▓▓▓▓▓▓▓▓▓▓▓▓▓▓▓▓▓▓ in their dealings with workers.
10. To ▓▓▓▓▓▓▓▓▓▓▓▓▓▓▓▓▓▓▓▓▓ in the market we need to be cost-effective, otherwise we will lose clients.

 **Talk Talk Talk**

(In the car, entering Glasgow)

(Im Auto, beim Eintreffen in Glasgow)

S. We'll **make straight for** the office. Angus is waiting there for us ... Here we are. Our office is on the third floor. **Mind how you go.** They're renovating the lobby. Glasgow is one huge building site at the moment. It was recently Europe's »City of Architecture« – and the building seems to be still going on!
(Enters office) Angus, dear boy!

S. Wir machen uns **sofort auf zum** Büro. Angus wartet dort auf uns ... Hier ist es. Unser Büro ist im dritten Stock. **Passen Sie auf, wo Sie hintreten.** Die Lobby wird gerade renoviert. Glasgow ist momentan eine einzige große Baugrube. Vor kurzem war es Europas »Stadt der Architektur« und die Bautätigkeit scheint immer noch weiterzugehen!
(Betritt das Büro) Angus, mein Bester!

How are you? How good to see you again. **How's business**?

Guten Tag! Schön, Sie wieder zu sehen. **Wie gehen die Geschäfte**?

A. Mustn't grumble. But I'm making no promises, you know.

A. Kann nicht klagen. Aber versprechen kann ich nichts, wissen Sie.

S. **Canny** Scot, this Angus – be warned, Peter. Oh, Angus! This is Peter Brückner, our Assistant Managing Director, over from Germany.	S. Ein **vorsichtiger** Schotte, dieser Angus – seien Sie gewarnt, Peter. Oh, Angus! Das ist Peter Brückner, unser stellvertretender Geschäftsführer aus Deutschland.
A. Germany? Welcome to Scotland, Peter. Been here before?	A. Deutschland? Willkommen in Schottland, Peter. Schon mal hier gewesen?
P. No, my first visit. But I hope to be able to acquaint myself well with the country during this visit.	P. Nein, das ist mein erster Besuch. Aber ich hoffe, ich werde es schaffen, während meines Aufenthalts etwas von dem Land kennen zu lernen.
A. You'll see something of the Lowlands tomorrow, but the Highlands will have to wait. You'll have to come back.	A. Morgen werden Sie einen Teil des Tieflandes sehen, aber das Hochland wird noch warten müssen. Sie müssen unbedingt wieder kommen.
S. What's the Lowlands trip?	S. Worum geht es bei dem Trip ins Tiefland?
A. There are plans for a so-called **cyber-park** there. Big **subsidies** and **tax breaks** are being offered to new **IT companies setting up**. Our job is to make sure they are aware of the software and servicing support we can **provide**.	A. Es gibt Pläne bezüglich eines so genannten »**Cyber-Parks**«. Neuen **IT-Gesellschaften** werden hohe **Subventionen** und **Steuerunterbrechungen** angeboten, damit sie **sich** dort **niederlassen**. Unsere Aufgabe ist es, dafür zu sorgen, dass sie die Software- und Serviceleistungen kennen, die wir **bereitstellen** können.
S. That's a big undertaking.	S. Das ist eine gewaltige Aufgabe.

A. We go right to the heart of the operation. I have an appointment tomorrow with the planning and management board. You'll be there, too, of course.

A. Wir setzen direkt im Herzen des Vorhabens an. Morgen habe ich eine Verabredung mit dem Planungs- und Leitungsausschuss. Sie werden natürlich dabei sein.

S. As long as we're not in the way.

S. So lange wir dabei nicht im Weg stehen.

A. Not as long as Peter is there. A German as part of the team can't do any harm!

A. Nicht so lange Peter dabei ist. Ein Deutscher als Teil des Teams kann nicht schaden!

Background Information

In »**cyberspeak**«, **IT** stands for **Information Technology**. Here are some others from the **IT-vocabulary**:

ISP	Internet Service Provider
MSE	Medium and Small-sized Enterprises. Most of the new IT companies fall into this category
R&D	Research and Development. An R&D budget is an amount of money set aside by a company for the purpose of research and development of a product.
e-Commerce	electronic commerce, or the »business« of doing business electronically

E-Commerce is based on the **electronic processing and transmission of data**, including text, sound and video. It encompasses many diverse elements, including the electronic trading of goods and services, the online delivery of digital material, transfer of funds, share trading, auctions, direct consumer marketing and after-sales servicing – literally everything covered by the general term »business«!

Background Information

Steve says to Peter, »**Mind how you go**« when they arrive at the office building.

»To **mind** something« is to pay attention to it. Other phrases with »mind« include:

to bear in mind	to remember or continue to consider
to be in two minds	to be undoubtful or uncertain about sth.
to make up one's mind	to decide
to have something in mind	to intend to do sth.
to know one's mind	to know what one wants, to have clear and firm opinions
to speak one's mind	to speak honestly and openly
to slip one's mind	to forget something
to cross one's mind	to happen to come into one's thoughts
to set one's mind to something	to put all one's efforts into doing something

 133. Train Yourself

Fünf der folgenden Sätze haben Fehler. Finden und berichten Sie sie!

1. Before we get too optimistic about competing in the Japanese market one must bear in mind that this is virgin territory for us.

2. After months of deliberations management have finally crossed their minds to go ahead with the project.

3. – Peter, I'd like you to do an important job for us.
   – Yes, Mr Morgan, what exactly did you make up your mind?

4. Jenny is known for slipping her mind. If she's not careful she'll land herself in trouble one of these days.

5. – The thought crossed my mind that we need to diversify a little more.

6. He made up his mind to improve his computer skills and decided to enroll on a course immediately.

7. – Oh Peter, it nearly spoke my mind. I need those reports by Friday.

8. The company was knowing their minds about going ahead with the proposal or not.

Colloquial English

A **canny** person is somebody who thinks quickly and cleverly, especially in business or financial matters.

 Talk Talk Talk

(At the »Cyber-park« central offices)

A. OK, lads, **let me do the talking**. If there's anything you want to contribute wait until we have a break and then let's discuss it.

S. What did I tell you, Peter? A canny Scot!

A. Now come on, Steve. I've learnt a lot from you. Right, let's go in.

(In den »Cyber-Park«-Hauptbüros)

A. Okay, **lassen Sie mich das Reden übernehmen**. Falls Sie irgendwas beitragen wollen, warten Sie, bis wir eine Pause machen und lassen Sie es uns diskutieren.

S. Was habe ich Ihnen gesagt, Peter? Ein vorsichtiger Schotte!

A. Jetzt kommen Sie schon, Steve. Ich habe viel von Ihnen gelernt! In

(The three enter the offices. Receptionist greets them)	Ordnung, lassen Sie uns reingehen. (Die drei betreten die Büros. Der Mann am Empfang begrüßt sie)
R. Good morning, gentlemen! Can I be of assistance?	R. Guten Morgen, meine Herren! Kann ich Ihnen behilflich sein?
A. We have an **appointment** with the Managing Director, Mr Travis.	A. Wir haben einen **Termin** mit dem leitenden Direktor, Mr Travis.
R. Of course, you must be Mr Fairbairn, from ERGO ...	R. Natürlich, Sie müssen Mr Fairbairn von ERGO sein ...
A. And these are my colleagues, Mr Blackman, our **Sales Chief**, and Mr Brückner, our Assistant Managing director.	A. Und das sind meine Kollegen, Mr Blackman, unser **Verkaufsleiter** und Mr Brückner, unser stellvertretender Geschäftsführer.
R. Please follow me. Mr Travis is waiting in his office.	R. Bitte folgen Sie mir. Mr Travis wartet in seinem Büro.
(The three enter Travis's office)	(Die drei betreten Mr Travis Büro)
T. Good morning, gentlemen. You found us without difficulty?	T. Guten Morgen, meine Herren. Haben Sie gut zu uns gefunden?
A. Yes, thank you. May I introduce Mr Blackman and Mr Brückner, both from London.	A. Ja, danke. Darf ich Ihnen Mr Blackman und Mr Brückner aus London vorstellen.
T. Pleased to meet you. Now **down to business**. How does ERGO propose to help us **get** this operation **off the ground**?	T. Freut mich, Sie kennen zu lernen. **Kommen wir zum Geschäftlichen**. Welche Art von Hilfestellung kann uns ERGO bieten, um das Geschäft **in Gang zu bringen**?

Background Information

Mr Travis asks Angus how he can help his company **get** the operation **off the ground**, i.e. **to get something started** or **to put something into operation**. Let's look at some other expressions with »**ground**«.

to have grounds for (doing something)	to have a reason, justification
to cut the ground from under someone's feet	to spoil someone's argument or plan by anticipating it
to break new ground	to introduce or discover a new method or system
common ground	opinions or experiences shared by two or more people
to cover a lot of ground	to deal with many different subjects very thoroughly
to fall on stony ground	not to be listened to or taken notice of
to gain ground	to advance or make progress
to have one's feet firmly on the ground	to be realistic or practical
a happy hunting ground	a place where a person finds what he desires or is very successful

134. Train Yourself

Benutzen Sie die oben stehenden Wendungen in den folgenden Sätzen!

1. The north-east is a very ▒▒▒▒▒▒▒▒▒ for us. We always sell well up there.
2. It took three months to finally get the project ▒▒▒▒▒▒▒▒▒ ▒▒▒▒▒▒▒▒▒ due to frequent delays.
3. Our competitor ▒▒▒▒▒▒▒▒▒ when they introduced an almost identical system to ours.

4. The new computer security system will ▓▓▓▓ when it is launched. In the UK it is the first of its kind.
5. Tony's proposition for more parking spaces to be made available to junior staff ▓▓▓▓. The chairman swiftly moved on to the next matter on the agenda.
6. You can rely on Debbie to get things done with the minimum of fuss. She ▓▓▓▓.
7. If we want to ▓▓▓▓ on our competitors we're all going to have to make a supreme effort this year.
8. Establishing ▓▓▓▓ with a client is a good foundation for a successful sale.
9. The boss ▓▓▓▓ no ▓▓▓▓ for taking it out on us! We did the best we possibly could!
10. The meeting was very constructive and we ▓▓▓▓ ▓▓▓▓.

 Talk Talk Talk

(Still at »Cyber Park«)

A. Now, as I understand it, you'll have **broadband communications** here. Fibre optics?

T. Yes, the **preparatory work** has begun.

A. What ERGO is proposing is that we **come in on the ground-floor**, assisting you at every stage. We have **a broad palette** of programs, each suited to **tackling** every stage of your operation and **meeting the demands of** every company involved in what, we must all agree, is a major initiative.

(Immer noch im »Cyber Park«)

A. Nun, so weit ich Sie verstehe, werden Sie hier über **Breitband-Kommunikation** verfügen. Fieberglas?

T. Ja, die **Vorbereitungen** haben bereits begonnen.

A. Was ERGO Ihnen anbietet, ist eine **Zusammenarbeit von Anfang an**, wobei wir Sie auf jeder Stufe unterstützen. Wir haben **eine breite Palette** von Programmen, von denen jedes in der Lage ist, mit jeder Entwicklungsstufe Ihrer Operation **fertig zu werden** und **die Anforderungen** jedes Unternehmens **zu erfüllen** - was, wie wir

T. So how do you propose doing that?

A. I read your promotional material with interest. It is very comprehensive and informative. What I am proposing is that you expand your **dossier** now with our **brochure material**.

T. But I'm giving you exclusivity in that case.

A. Not necessarily. ERGO is **well aware** there are other software companies out there. We don't want to lock them out of this particular market. ERGO just believes that no other company has organized its large variety of products to **suit the** kind of **purpose** associated with a **venture** like yours.

T. Wait, wait. You're leaving me behind ...

uns wohl alle einig sind, ein Hauptanliegen sein muss.

T. Und wie wollen Sie das bewerkstelligen?

A. Ich habe Ihr Promotionmaterial mit Interesse gelesen. Es ist sehr umfassend und informativ. Was ich Ihnen anbiete ist, dass Sie Ihr **Dossier** jetzt um unsere **Broschüren** erweitern.

T. Aber damit würde ich Ihnen exklusive Privilegien einräumen.

A. Nicht unbedingt. ERGO ist sich **wohl bewusst**, dass es da draußen auch andere Softwarefirmen gibt. Wir wollen sie von diesem speziellen Markt nicht ausschließen. ERGO ist nur der Meinung, dass kein anderes Unternehmen sein umfassendes Angebot an Produkten so organisiert hat, dass sie **den Anforderungen entsprechen**, die eine **Unternehmung** wie die Ihre mit sich bringt.

T. Warten Sie, warten Sie. Da komme ich nicht mit ...

Background Information

Angus proposes ERGO Ltd **coming in on the ground floor** meaning **being involved at the initial stages**, another expression with »ground« to add to those learnt in the previous section of the dialogue.

Angus seemed to be very **well-versed** in Cyber-Parks's operations meaning **he knows a lot about it**. One could also say he is well-informed, which has a similar meaning.

»**Well-versed**« and »**well-informed**« are both **compound adjectives** formed from the adverb »well« (from »good«), and the past participle. They are usually hyphenated (-).
Here are some more examples:

well-established	existing for a long time
well-advised	careful, prudent
well-appointed	having all the necessary equipment, furniture, etc.
well-connected	friendly with or related to rich or influential people
well-timed	done or said at the right time
well-disposed (towards somebody)	sympathetic or friendly
well-thought-of	respected or liked

135. Train Yourself

Suchen Sie nun für die folgenden Sätze das richtige zusammengesetzte Adjektiv!

1. Being ▓▓▓▓▓▓▓▓▓▓▓▓▓▓ and having the right contacts is a great advantage to getting ahead in life.
2. The Marketing Manager was very ▓▓▓▓▓▓▓▓▓▓▓▓▓▓ in the company and everybody wished him well on his retirement.
3. The offer to take over the company was ▓▓▓▓▓▓▓▓▓▓▓▓▓▓ as just a week earlier it had been on the verge of bankruptcy.

4. The company was very ▅▅▅▅ and had been in existence for more than 200 years.
5. One would be ▅▅▅▅ to be thoroughly familiar with a client's background before attempting a sale.
6. The new office was ▅▅▅▅ and in a very desirable location.
7. Gordon was ▅▅▅▅ in every area of the company's operations and subsequently was offered the job.
8. I'm not particularly ▅▅▅▅ towards anybody who can't do their job properly.

 **Talk Talk Talk**

(Some two hours later)

T. I think we can break there for lunch. It will give me the opportunity to put the questions that have raised themselves in my mind …

(At lunch)

T. I liked your proposal, Mr Fairbairn – may I call you Angus? Please call me Alistair. But what worries me a little is the **servicing guarantees** you have to offer. There's no doubt that the **package** you have put together is a good one. In fact, I don't think it could be **bettered**. But we have a responsibility to our clients, the companies who will be setting up operations here. If we recommend your package and then if ERGO **falls down on its promises we are**

(Ungefähr zwei Stunden später)

T. Ich glaube, wir können jetzt Mittagspause einlegen. Dabei habe ich Gelegenheit, die Fragen zu stellen, die mir in den Kopf geschossen sind …

(Beim Mittagessen)

T. Ihr Angebot hat mir gefallen, Mr Fairbairn – darf ich Sie Angus nennen? Bitte nennen Sie mich Alistair. Was mir ein bisschen Sorgen macht, sind die **Service-Garantien**, die Sie zu bieten haben. Ich habe keinen Zweifel daran, dass das **Service-Paket**, das Sie zusammengestellt haben, gut ist. Ich glaube sogar, dass es gar nicht **besser sein** könnte. Aber wir haben eine Verantwortung gegenüber unseren Kunden, den Unternehmen die hier Geschäfte

first in the firing line. How are we to be protected?

S. May I answer this one, Angus? ERGO's **payment plan** includes insurance from one of Britain's leading companies. Our package also has the support of two major banks, which means **payment can be spread out** over a period of up to five years, a kind of leasing, if you like. You are of course aware that big tax breaks are available for the involvement of companies such as ours – not to speak of subsidies. But, of course, that's your territory.

T. Quite right! We have gone fully into all **funding questions** and **are satisfied on that score**. But, please, don't let your meal go cold. That roast beef is best Aberdeen, Angus!

machen werden. Wenn wir Ihr Paket empfehlen und ERGO dann **seinen Versprechungen nicht nachkommt, werden wir als Erste in der Schusslinie stehen.** Wie können wir uns davor schützen?

S. Darf ich die Frage beantworten, Angus? ERGO's **Finanzplan** beinhaltet die Versicherung durch eines unserer führenden britischen Unternehmen. Unser Paket wird auch von zwei großen Banken unterstützt, was einen **Zahlungszeitraum** von bis zu fünf Jahren zulässt – eine Art Leasing, wenn Sie so wollen. Sie wissen sicher, dass es bedeutende Steuererleichterungen für Unternehmen wie unseres gibt – ganz zu schweigen von Subventionen. Aber das ist natürlich Ihr Fachgebiet.

T. Sie haben Recht! Wir sind alle **Basisfragen** durchgegangen und **sind bis jetzt zufrieden**. Aber bitte, lassen Sie Ihr Essen nicht kalt werden. Das Roastbeef ist bestes Aberdeen-Rind, Angus!

 **Background Information**

In the last section we looked at compound adjectives formed from adverbs. In this section there is an example of a very common **adverb being used as a verb**, i.e. **better**. Mr Travis says that ERGO **couldn't be bettered**, in other words it **couldn't be improved**.

The second language point concerns the use of »**score**«. This word is more often associated with **sports**, e.g. scoring a goal in football or a try in rugby. Alistair Travis, however, says that he is **satisfied on that score** (i.e. with the question of funding). »**On that score**« means »**in that regard**« or »**as far as that is concerned.**« A »**score**« also means **twenty** e.g. »There were three score and ten at the party«, i.e. 70, although this usage is now very old-fashioned. More commonly we say »**scores**« to mean **many**, e.g. »There were scores of people at the match! I couldn't believe it.«
Below are some more common expressions with »**score**« and »**better**«.

to know the score	to know everything about the situation
to get the better of	to win a victory over somebody
to go one better	to improve on a previous success
to have seen better days	to be in a worse condition than it used to be
for better or worse	whether one likes it or not
to think better of	to decide not to do something

 136. Train Yourself

Verwenden Sie die Wendungen in der folgenden Übung!

1. We were going to invest in a computer training scheme before we discovered how much it would cost and then ▓▓▓▓▓▓▓▓▓▓▓▓▓▓▓▓▓▓▓▓▓▓▓▓▓▓ it.
2. My car ▓▓▓▓▓▓▓▓▓▓▓▓▓▓▓▓▓▓. Shall we take yours to Scotland?
3. Although sales in the last quarter were impressive the CEO wants us to ▓▓▓▓▓▓▓▓▓▓▓▓▓▓▓▓▓▓▓▓ and achieve the highest sales figures in the company's history.
4. You can trust James with the account, he ▓▓▓▓▓▓▓▓▓▓▓▓▓▓▓▓▓.
5. ▓▓▓▓▓▓▓▓▓▓▓▓▓▓▓▓▓ if the staff ask for salary increases we are going to have to listen to them.
6. I've never seen so many delegates as there were at last week's conference. There were ▓▓▓▓▓▓▓▓▓▓▓▓▓▓▓▓▓▓▓ of them!

7. Peter is the top salesman in the company nobody can ▒▒▒▒▒▒▒▒▒▒▒▒▒▒▒▒▒▒▒▒▒▒▒▒▒▒ him.
8. The company finally ▒▒▒▒▒▒▒▒▒▒▒▒▒▒▒▒▒▒▒▒ their main rival and succeeded in winning the contract.

 **Talk Talk Talk**

(Travis's office, the next day. Steve, Peter and Angus enter)

T. Good morning, gentlemen! Sleep well, I trust?

S. Very well, thank you Alistair. That Scottish beer knocked me out for the night. And the way they serve it – in jugs. Not like in England. I have difficulty there getting a proper pint.

T. (laughs) It's another example of our Scottish way with money. You get more beer and pay less!

S. I noticed that – and so does my head this morning. Not to worry! Let's get down to business.

T. I have invited the **Chief Executive** of one of our interested enterprises to join in the talks. You'll get an idea then of the kind of concerns **facing** these small com-

(Am nächsten Tag in Travis Büro. Steve, Peter und Angus treten ein)

T. Guten Morgen, meine Herren! Nehme an, Sie haben gut geschlafen?

S. Sehr gut, ich danke Ihnen, Alistair. Das schottische Bier hat mich für einen Abend ins Aus befördert. Und wie es serviert wird – in Krügen. Nicht wie in England. Dort habe ich Schwierigkeiten, ein ordentliches Pint zu bekommen.

T. (lacht) Noch ein Beispiel für unsere schottische Art, mit Geld umzugehen. Man bekommt mehr Bier und zahlt weniger!

S. Das habe ich gemerkt – und mein Kopf auch heute morgen. Aber keine Sorge! Lassen Sie uns zum Geschäft kommen.

T. Ich habe den **Hauptgeschäftsführer** von einem der interessierten Unternehmen mit zum Gespräch eingeladen. Dann bekommen Sie einen Eindruck von

panies in the new, electronic market place.	der Art der Bedenken, die diese kleinen Unternehmen auf dem neuen, elektronischen Weltmarkt **haben**.
S. We'll be most interested to meet him.	S. Wir sind sehr gespannt darauf, ihn kennen zu lernen.
T. Actually, it's a »she«! A very clever young woman who has **put** her fashion business **on-line** – even offers **on-line fashion parades**. You'll see.	T. Es ist übrigens eine »Sie«. Eine sehr kluge junge Frau, die mit ihrem Modegeschäft **online ist** – sogar **Online-Modeschauen** anbietet. Sie werden sehen.
S. Fascinating.	S. Faszinierend.
(The Telephone rings)	(Das Telefon klingelt)
T. That'll be her now ...	T. Das wird sie sein...

Background Information

Mr Travis in this section of the dialogue talks about the problems **facing** small companies in the electronic market place meaning the problems »**requiring attention**«.

»**To face up to something**« has the similar meaning of **accepting or dealing with something unpleasant**. A common expression is »**to face the facts**«, implying that the person involved **must deal with reality rather than trying to avoid it**.

Let's look at some more »**face**« expressions:

face the music	to deal with the difficulties or consequences of one's actions
face value	as sth. appears to be initially
a long face	a serious or unhappy expression on somebody's face
staring s.o. in the face	be obvious or clearly in view

to lose face	to lose the respect or good opinion of others
to show one's face	to appear or present oneself
to talk till someone is blue in the face	to talk endlessly without achieving the desired result
to have egg on one's face	to look stupid or foolish

 137. Train Yourself

Füllen Sie die Lücken mit diesen Wendungen!

1. How was your meeting with Jarvis yesterday?
   A waste of time. I ▨▨▨▨▨ and got absolutely nowhere.
2. You shouldn't take things ▨▨▨▨▨ without having thought about them first.
3. Disaster was ▨▨▨▨▨ us ▨▨▨▨▨ until Tony came up with a masterplan to save the company.
4. When the Chief Executive came into the meeting with ▨▨▨▨▨ we all knew something was wrong.
5. Graham lost one of the company's most valued clients and is now on his way to head office to ▨▨▨▨▨.
6. I really had ▨▨▨▨▨ when I turned up to a sales meeting in Cardiff and found out it was actually being held in Swansea.
7. Are you going to the staff Christmas party?
   Oh, I'll ▨▨▨▨▨ for an hour or so but I need to have an early night tonight.
8. We've got to ▨▨▨▨▨, unless we become more consumer friendly profits will continue to go down.
9. When dealing with Asian clients one must be aware that on no account can they be seen to ▨▨▨▨▨. This is very important in Asian societies.

 **Talk Talk Talk**

(Still at the office)

T. Good morning, Miss Sinclair. How nice to meet you again! (He introduces Steve, Peter and Angus to Bettina Sinclair)

B. I'm very interested in meeting you. It's actually the first time I've met practically the whole **executive and sales staff of a company** we want to do business with.

S. I just hope we have the necessary experience to **handle** a company such as yours. Fashion is not our **strong point**.

A. What Steve is trying to say is that we usually deal with companies of a lower market profile than yours. Fashion is an extremely **consumer-oriented area of business**.

B. Not necessarily. We are a **retail outlet** primarily, that's true. But we have struck very **productive** and **lucrative deals** with larger fashion firms. We aim exclusively at the upper end of the market.

(Immer noch im Büro)

T. Guten Morgen, Miss Sinclair. Wie schön, Sie wiederzusehen! (Er stellt Steve, Peter und Angus Bettina Sinclair vor)

B. Ich freue mich sehr, Sie kennen zu lernen. Es ist tatsächlich das erste Mal, dass ich quasi **die gesamte Geschäftsführung und den Verkaufsstab eines Unternehmens** treffe, mit denen wir Geschäfte machen möchten.

S. Ich hoffe nur, wir haben die nötige Erfahrung, um mit einem Unternehmen wie Ihrem **umzugehen**. Mode ist nicht unsere **stärkste Seite**.

A. Was Steve sagen will ist, dass wir für gewöhnlich mit Firmen zusammenarbeiten, die ein niedrigeres Marktprofil haben als Ihres. Mode ist ein extrem **konsumentenorientiertes Geschäftsgebiet**.

B. Nicht unbedingt. Es stimmt, wir sind in erster Linie eine **Einzelhandels-Niederlassung**. Aber wir haben uns sehr **produktive** und **lukrative Geschäfte** mit größeren Modefirmen erkämpft. Wir wollen

P. But how can you do that online? Surely your customers need the personal touch – the experience of actually attending one of your fashion shows.

P. Aber wie können Sie das online realisieren? Sicher brauchen Ihre Kunden den persönlichen Kontakt – die Erfahrung, wirklich bei einer Ihrer Modenschauen anwesend zu sein.

unbedingt an das obere Ende des Marktsegmentes vorstoßen.

B. That's true to a certain extent. And the one aspect of the business doesn't exclude the other. Let me explain ...

B. Das stimmt bis zu einem gewissen Grad. Und der eine Aspekt des Geschäftes schließt den anderen nicht aus. Lassen Sie mich das erklären ...

Background Information

Steve tells Bettina that fashion is not ERGO's **strong point**, meaning that it's not the **strongest feature or aspect** of the company. »**The point**« can mean the essential thing, the principal idea. So when a listener feels that a speaker is not dealing with the matter at hand, he can say »**That's not the point**« or »**What point are you trying to make?**«

Let's look at some common expressions with »**point**«:

to point out	to draw attention to a fact
to make a point of	to make sure that one does something or emphasizes something
to take someone's point	to understand or accept what somebody is saying
in point of fact	in reality, actually
beside the point	not directly concerned with the main point of a discussion
on the point of	about to (do something)
not to put too fine a point on it	to speak plainly and honestly
to point a finger	to blame/accuse somebody

138. Train Yourself

Verwenden Sie die Begriffe in der nun folgenden Übung!

1. The Sales Director was ▓▓▓▓▓ hiring the new salesperson when he changed his mind on receiving an unsatisfactory reference from his previous employer.
2. No-one's ▓▓▓▓▓ here but we must face the facts; our performance has not been good enough.
3. I ▓▓▓▓▓ writing all my appointments down in my diary just in case one of them slips my mind.
4. Excuse me. I ▓▓▓▓▓ about the need to be more cost-effective but surely, staff reductions are not the answer ...
5. We had planned to stay overnight in the Britannia Hotel but Peter ▓▓▓▓▓ that it would be quicker to take the overnight train instead.
6. ▓▓▓▓▓ Neil, your work here has not been up to standard and this is why I am asking for your resignation.
7. Microsoft is not just an enormously profitable company; ▓▓▓▓▓ it is the most lucrative in the world.
8. When it comes to making an impression on a potential customer the regional dialect of the salesperson is ▓▓▓▓▓. It is the personality that matters.

Talk Talk Talk

(Two hours later)

S. Miss Sinclair, that was a **fascinating account** of an **area of business** which is entirely new to us. Now tell us how ERGO can help you.

B. I understand you have a program which I think could have

(Zwei Stunden später)

S. Miss Sinclair, das war eine **faszinierende Einführung** in ein **Geschäftsgebiet**, das völlig neu für uns ist. Sagen Sie uns, wie ERGO Ihnen helfen kann.

B. Soweit ich weiß, haben Sie ein Programm, dass wie ich glaube **für**

been **tailored to our needs** - this **electronic accounting system**. I'm a **small operation**, basically a **one-person show**. I can't afford a proper **accounting staff**, although business is **increasing at an encouraging rate**. Doing **business on-line** can be extremely labour intensive. I must tell you that I have made inquiries with other companies such as yours, but one of the things I have learnt from business is compare, compare, compare – until you've run out of **comparison possibilities**.

S. Very Scottish, if I may say, Miss Sinclair. But now it's over to you, Angus.

A. Let me first of all give you all the literature we have on the program. I sent you an **introductory pamphlet**, which I hoped would arise your interest. It has I see. Now my second proposal is that you inform yourself fully about our **accounting program** and that we meet over lunch tomorrow to discuss the system further. My third proposal is that we visit your office to show you the program at work – I'm sure you'll be impressed.

unsere Bedürfnisse wie geschaffen ist – dieses **elektronische Buchungssystem**. Ich bin eine **kleine Geschäftseinheit**, eigentlich ein **Ein-Personen-Unternehmen**. Ich kann mir kein richtiges **Buchführungs-Personal** leisten, auch wenn das Geschäft **eine zunehmende Erfolgsrate aufweist**. **Online-Geschäfte** können sehr arbeitsintensiv sein. Ich muss sagen, ich habe Erkundigungen bei anderen Firmen wie Ihre eingezogen, denn eines der Dinge, die ich im Geschäft gelernt habe ist: vergleichen, vergleichen, vergleichen – bis einem die **Vergleichsmöglichkeiten** ausgehen.

S. Sehr schottisch, wenn ich so sagen darf, Miss Sinclair. Aber jetzt zu Ihnen, Angus.

A. Lassen Sie mich Ihnen zu allererst die Literatur geben, die wir über dieses Programm haben. Ich hatte Ihnen eine **kurze Einführung** geschickt, von der ich hoffte, sie würde Ihr Interesse wecken. Wie ich sehe, hat sie das getan. Mein zweites Angebot besteht darin, dass Sie sich selbst vollständig über unser **Abrechnungssystem** informieren und dass wir uns morgen zum Mittagessen treffen und das System weiter diskutieren. Mein drittes Angebot ist, dass wir zu

B. That's fine by me. But you'll have a bit of a journey – I work from home in the Highlands. In this business, as you know, **you can work from anywhere**. My office has a wonderful view of the mountains – something I can't enjoy in Glasgow.

B. Von mir aus gerne. Aber Sie haben eine etwas weitere Reise vor sich – ich arbeite von meinem Zuhause im Hochland aus. In diesem Geschäft **können SIe**, wie Sie wissen, **von überall aus arbelten**. Mein Büro verfügt über einen wunderbaren Blick auf die Berge – etwas, das ich in Glasgow nicht genießen kann.

S. You're very lucky. Can't ERGO follow that example, Peter?

S. Sie haben Glück. Kann ERGO das nicht auch machen, Peter?

P. If it did, I might find myself back in Hamburg – just when I'm getting to know and like London.

P. Wenn ERGO das täte, würde ich mich in Hamburg wiederfinden – und das gerade jetzt, wo ich London kennen und lieben gelernt habe.

A. **Give me** the Highlands.

A. **Auf in** die Highlands.

 139. Train Yourself

1. Steve macht Miss Sinclair zwei Vorschläge: »Now my second proposal is that you inform yourself fully about our accounting program and that we meet over lunch tomorrow to discuss the system further. My third proposal is that we visit your office to show you the program at work.« Es handelt sich hier um eine indirekte Form der Aufforderung.

Seien Sie direkter und formen Sie die Sätze entsprechend um!

2. Finden Sie die richtigen Begriffe!

a. a small booklet of information ....

b. a body of persons employed in an establishment, usually on management, administration, clerical, etc. work as distinct from manual ....

c. a descriptive report ....

d. an agency ....

e. the sale directly to the consumer or in small quantities ....

operation, retail, pamphlet, staff, account.

 Vocabulary

a broad palette	eine breite Palette
accounting system	Buchhaltungssystem
an important catch	ein wichtiger Fang
beforehand	im Voraus
to better	verbessern
to break	unterbrechen
broadband communications	Breitband-Kommunikation
chief executive	Hauptgeschäftsführer
to come in on the ground floor	von Anfang an zusammenarbeiten
consumer-orientated	konsumentenorientiert

Verkaufsgespräche

deal	Geschäft; Angebot
devolution	Dezentralisierung
Down to business.	Kommen wir zum Geschäftlichen.
to fall down on s.o.'s promises	jds. Versprechungen nicht nachkommen
to get sth. off the ground	etw. in Gang bringen
to handle	umgehen mit
How's business?	Wie gehen die Geschäfte?
to increase at an encouraging rate	hohe Zuwachsraten verzeichnen
introductory pamphlet	kurze Einführung
lucrative	lukrativ
to make a big bid	sich sehr bemühen
to make straight for	sich sofort aufmachen zu
to meet the demands of	die Anforderungen erfüllen
new revolution	neue Revolution
payment plan	Finanzplan
to provide	bereitstellen
to put on file	abspeichern
retail outlet	Einzelhandels-Niederlassung
sales chief	Verkaufsleiter
to set up	sich niederlassen
strong point	starke Seite
subsidies	Subventionen
to suit the purpose	den Anforderungen entsprechen
to tackle sth.	fertig werden mit etw.
tailored	maßgeschneidert
tax breaks	Steuererleichterungen
venture	Unternehmung
well aware	im Klaren darüber

Settle conditions of a contract
Vertragsbedingungen aushandeln

 Here we go

Immer noch in Glasgow, ist Peter fasziniert von den Möglichkeiten, die die neuen Internet-Verkaufsseiten eröffnen. Aber auch Kunden aus traditionellen Branchen, wie zum Beispiel Theaterdarsteller und ihre Agenten, haben mittlerweile Bedarf an Softwareprogrammen, um Ihre Daten modern verwalten zu können. Hamilton McDonald, der Partner von Angus in Edinburgh, ist gerade dabei, ein Geschäft in diesem Bereich abzuschließen und lässt Peter und Steve daran teilhaben, was die beiden hochinteressant finden; aber was Peter noch viel mehr interessiert, ist Melissa's unerwartete Anwesenheit in Edinburgh und der Grund für ihren Aufenthalt ...

 **Talk Talk Talk**

(Glasgow hotel. Breakfast room)

(Das Hotel in Glasgow. Im Frühstücksraum)

S. Well, that was one heck of an interesting excursion to the Highlands. It's remarkable how that young woman can operate so successfully from home.

S. Tja, das war ein ziemlich interessanter Ausflug in die Highlands. Schon erstaunlich, wie erfolgreich eine junge Frau von zu Hause aus arbeiten kann.

A. Modern technology. **Electronic commerce.** You can do business now from just anywhere – a pal of mine has a holiday home on the Isle of Mull and operates mostly from there.

A. Moderne Technologie. **Elektronischer Handel.** Man kann sein Geschäft von überall aus betreiben – ein Freund von mir hat ein Ferienhaus auf der *Isle of Mull* und arbeitet hauptsächlich von dort aus.

P. I've read several reports on these so-called »**cyber ports**« which are **springing up all over the place**. It's a really interesting development. At the time of the industrial revolution one hundred years or so ago **centres of business activity** grew around main **thoroughfares**, rivers and harbours. Glasgow is an example. In the **high-tech age** these **business centres** are being created at geographical locations where telecommunications are good and **a highly-qualified pool of labour** exists.

S. It's a very interesting development, I agree, Peter. But I'll have to have another pair of kippers before I can really **tune in to** this level of conversation …

P. Ich habe schon mehrere Berichte über diese so genannten »**Cyber Ports**« gelesen, die jetzt **überall aus dem Boden schießen**. Eine wirklich interessante Entwicklung. Vor etwa hundert Jahren, zurzeit der industriellen Revolution erwuchsen die **Handelszentren** an **Hauptverkehrsstraßen** an Flüssen und Häfen. Glasgow ist ein Beispiel dafür. Im **Zeitalter der Hochtechnologie** werden solche **Handelszentren** an geographischen Punkten errichtet, an denen die Telekommunikationsstruktur gut errichtet ist und wo **genügend hochqualifizierte Mitarbeiter** zu finden sind.

S. Eine sehr interessante Entwicklung, Peter, da stimme ich Ihnen zu. Aber ich brauche noch so ein paar *Kippers* – Bücklinge – bevor ich dieser Ebene der Konversation **folgen** kann …

Background Information

1. So-called »**cyber-ports**« are now being created throughout the world. They are an officially planned and organised version of the »Silicon Valley« IT (Information Technology) developments which have arisen almost spontaneously in California, southern France and, of course, in Germany (around Munich and in Baden-Wuerttemberg). Asia is a leader in this field, and »**cyber-ports**« are taking shape in Hong Kong, Singapore, Malaysia, Thailand and even in India (Bangalore).

2. Steve says to Peter that he'll have to have another pair of kippers before **tuning in to** Peter's conversation. »**To tune in**« means **to concentrate**. »**To have to do something**« means that **the person is obliged to do it** and in this example Steve is using the future form with »**will**«. Let's look at how this verb changes depending on the verbal tense:

Present Simple	have to (»must« is also possible here)
Past Simple	had to
Will-Future	will have to (*or* 'll have to)
Going to-Future	am/is/are going to have + infinitive
Past Perfect	had had to (*or* 'd had to)
Present Perfect	have had to ('ve had to)
Would/Could/May/Should/Might	+ have to

Note: although »**must**« and »**have to**« possess almost identical meanings, in the negative their meanings differ. »I don't have to speak French«, implies an absence of obligation, i.e. »I can if I want to but it's not obligatory«. »I mustn't speak French«, however, implies prohibition and is the same as »I can't speak French even though I want to« or »I'm not allowed to.«

 140. Train Yourself

Verwenden Sie in den folgenden Sätzen die jeweils richtige Form von »to have to«:

1. I don't know what's happening tomorrow, we ▓▓▓▓▓▓▓▓▓▓▓▓▓▓▓▓▓▓▓ get there early but I'll ring you tonight to confirm the time.
2. If you go to this business fair on the 24th you ▓▓▓▓▓▓▓▓▓▓▓▓▓▓▓▓▓▓▓ report back to us on any areas of interest, OK?
3. We ▓▓▓▓▓▓▓▓▓▓▓▓▓ keep ahead of any important developments in the marketplace.

4. Since the company relocated to a new site Helen ▒▒▒▒▒ live in a hotel.
5. Hello John, listen, I ▒▒▒▒▒ speak with you about a matter of the utmost urgency.
6. By the time the new computer arrived she ▒▒▒▒▒ to use the one in the office for two months.
7. All the candidates ▒▒▒▒▒ take an entrance exam first. If we did this the overall standard would be much higher.
8. The company ▒▒▒▒▒ have a complete overhaul of the computer systems when they crashed the day before.
9. We're ▒▒▒▒▒ work all weekend to get this work done by Monday.
10. If your performance doesn't improve I ▒▒▒▒▒ speak to the Managing Director.

 **Talk Talk Talk**

P. What **intrigues me**, Angus, is how a **sales team** operates in this new environment. Don't you have to adopt a whole new **strategy**? You can hardly go knocking on doors in a **virtual marketplace**, can you?

P. Was **mich besonders interessiert**, Angus, ist, wie ein **Verkaufsteam** in dieser neuen Umgebung überhaupt arbeitet. Muss man dazu nicht eine völlig neue **Strategie** entwickeln? Man kann an einem **virtuellen Markt** ja wohl kaum einfach an die Tür klopfen, oder?

A. Well, we saw yesterday that even the **virtual marketplace** doesn't make the tried and tested **personal approach** superfluous. A face behind the product will always be a central factor of successful selling. But, you're right, the **IT revolution** – if I can call it that – has added a new dimension to selling. Every company, large and small, now has a **website**. It's a necessity. Without it you can't

A. Tja, wir haben ja gestern selbst gesehen, dass selbst ein **virtueller Markt** den altbewährten **persönlichen Ansatz** nicht überflüssig macht. Das Gesicht hinter dem Produkt wird immer ein zentraler Faktor des erfolgreichen Verkaufens sein. Aber Sie haben Recht, die **IT-Revolution** – wenn ich es mal so nennen darf – hat dem Verkaufsgeschäft eine völlig neue Dimension gegeben. Jede Firma,

operate in this new marketplace. Just as we used to have to attend very closely to the content and **visual presentation** of our **marketing material – brochures** and the like – we now have to design, or have designed, a website that is also attractive, informative and **easily accessible**. ERGO is a good example. Whoever drew up our website knew what he or she was doing.

S. Melissa oversaw it.

A. Clever girl that. But I hear she might be moving ...

P. What? Where?

A. The **grapevine** extends even to Scotland. **Word** reached me from Edinburgh ...

S. Edinburgh! Look at the time. We've got to **get on the road** – we have to be there by 12.

egal ob groß oder klein, hat heute ihre **Website**. Das ist unumgänglich. Ohne diese kann man auf diesem neuen Absatzmarkt gar nicht aktiv werden. Genau so wie wir uns sehr sorgsam um die **visuelle Präsentation** unseres **Marketing-Materials** kümmern müssen – etwa in Form von **Broschüren** – müssen wir nun auch eine Website designen oder designen lassen, die genau so attraktiv, informativ und **leicht zugänglich** ist. ERGO ist ein gutes Beispiel dafür. Wer immer unsere Website entworfen hat, wusste, was er oder sie tat.

S. Melissa hatte die Gesamtleitung darüber.

A. Ein cleveres Mädchen. Aber ich habe gehört, dass sie vielleicht wechselt ...

P. Was? Wohin?

A. Die **Gerüchteküche** reicht selbst bis Schottland. Ich habe ein **Gerücht** aus Edinburgh gehört ...

S. Edinburgh! Es ist schon spät! Wir müssen uns **auf den Weg machen** – wir müssen um 12 dort sein.

Background Information

»**We've got to get on the road**« announces Steve when he realises they're running behind time. **Get**, in this context, means **to arrive**, e.g. »We have to get to Edinburgh by 12«.
This very common word can also be used to mean: **to become**, e.g. »I'm getting tired of this«; **to bring**, e.g. »Can you get me this file, please?«; **to buy**, e.g. »I got some great things in the shops yesterday«; **to receive**, e.g. »I got an e-mail from the Accounts Department«; **to obtain/achieve**, e.g. »I got my diploma last year in IT«; and **to catch**, e.g., »We got the train just on time«, amongst others!
»**Get**« is also used as a part of several »phrasal verbs«. Some are listed below:

to get over	to recover
to get by	to manage or to survive
to get through to	to establish contact
to get something over with	to come to the end of something
to get round to	to find time to do something
to get on	to make progress
to get together	to have a meeting or party
to get away with	to do something wrong without being caught or punished

141. Train Yourself

Verwenden Sie die oben stehenden »phrasal verbs« in der folgenden Übung!

1. Hello Frank! Len here. Listen, let's ▨▨▨▨▨▨▨▨ some time this week and go over the Johnson account. Then we can have a drink afterwards. What do you say?
2. How are you ▨▨▨▨▨▨▨▨ with your new life in Britain, Peter?

3. I'm busy right now but hopefully I'll ▓▓▓▓▓▓▓▓▓ to doing it next week. Is that OK?
4. I've been calling Steve all day and I still can't ▓▓▓▓▓▓▓▓▓ him.
5. Some companies use offshore accounts to ▓▓▓▓▓▓▓▓▓ paying less tax.
6. During the recession the company ▓▓▓▓▓▓▓▓▓ through a reduction of overheads and a reduced workforce.
7. It took Tony a long time to ▓▓▓▓▓▓▓▓▓ the shock of being made redundant.
8. I wasn't looking forward to doing the company accounts but I decided to start straight away and ▓▓▓▓▓▓▓▓▓ it ▓▓▓▓▓▓▓▓▓.

 Talk Talk Talk

(In the car, on the drive to Edinburgh)

(Im Wagen, auf der Fahrt nach Edinburgh)

S. In Edinburgh, we'll be meeting Angus's **sidekick**, Hamilton McDonald. If you think Angus is your true Scot, you wait till you meet Hamilton. He's such a nationalist that he thinks working for a **London-based** company is treason. But he likes the money! Isn't that so, Angus?

S. In Edinburgh treffen wir Angus' **Partner**, Hamilton McDonald. Wenn Sie glauben, dass Angus schon ein echter Schotte ist, dann warten Sie, bis Sie Hamilton kennen lernen. Er ist so ein Nationalist, dass er es schon für Verrat hält, für eine Firma zu arbeiten, die ihren **Hauptsitz in London** hat. Aber ihn lockt das Geld! Ist es nicht so, Angus?

A. You said it, Steve!

A. Sie sagen es, Steve!

P. He's obviously successful?

P. Er ist also offensichtlich erfolgreich?

S. Hamilton's so successful he could even sell you – what do you

S. Hamilton ist so erfolgreich, er könnte Ihnen sogar – was isst man

Verkaufsgespräche

eat out there in place of kippers? Matjes?	bei euch an Stelle von *Kippers*? »Matjes«? – ja, »Matjes« verkaufen.
P. Matjes, Steve. Matjes.	P. Matjes, Steve. Matjes.
S. Don't know how you can get your tongue around that language of yours, Peter, my friend. But Hamilton would and he'd **end up** exporting Matjes to Hamburg. Hamilton's his name – but I call him **ham** for short. In fact, he really is something of an actor – the marketplace is his personal stage.	S. Ich weiß nicht, wie Sie Ihre Zunge dazu bringen, Ihre Sprache zu sprechen, Peter, mein Freund. Aber Hamilton **könnte** es und **am Ende** würde er Matjes nach Hamburg exportieren. Er heißt zwar Hamilton – aber ich nenne ihn »ham« **– einen Schmierenkomödianten**. Er ist in der Tat etwas wie ein Schauspieler – der Markt ist seine private Bühne.
P. I can't wait to meet him.	P. Ich kann es gar nicht abwarten, ihn kennen zu lernen.
S. You'll need some preparation. Let's **pull in** here for a coffee. And drink it the local way – with a **dram of** whisky …	S. Sie müssen darauf vorbereitet werden. Lassen Sie uns für einen Kaffee **anhalten**. Wir trinken ihn auf die für die Gegend übliche Weise – mit einem **Schuss** Whisky …

Background Information

Steve suggests that they **pull in** for a coffee, meaning **to park** or **stop the car**. One can also say »pull up«, e.g. »Let's pull up over there.«. There are several other phrasal verbs with »pull«, including »**to pull out**« which means **to start the car moving** and is the opposite of **pull in/up**. Other ones are listed below:

to pull off	to manage, to succeed
to pull out all the stops	to use all one's energy and effort
to pull in one's belt	to spend less money
to pull one's socks up	to make a serious effort to improve one's behaviour or work
to pull someone's leg	to make fun of a person in a friendly way
to pull the carpet out from under someone's feet	to stop giving help or support without any warning
to pull one's weight	to take one's fair share of the work

 142. Train Yourself

Verwenden Sie die »phrasal verbs« mit »pull« in der unten stehenden Übung:

1. Unless Trevor ▓▓▓▓▓▓▓▓ he could find himself out of a job.
2. The slump in the company's fortunes seems to have been a result of people not ▓▓▓▓▓▓▓▓ their ▓▓▓▓▓▓▓▓.
3. Bob is known as the joker in the office, he's always ▓▓▓▓▓▓▓▓ people's ▓▓▓▓▓▓▓▓
4. We (a) ▓▓▓▓▓▓▓▓ of the motorway service-station at 2 o'clock and then had to (b) ▓▓▓▓▓▓▓▓ again when we realized we were short of petrol.
5. The sales team have ▓▓▓▓▓▓▓▓ it ▓▓▓▓▓▓▓▓! The new contract is worth millions to the company.
6. At the meeting the Chief Executive told the staff that they would have to ▓▓▓▓▓▓▓▓ their ▓▓▓▓▓▓▓▓ and wait until next year for a salary raise.
7. The bank ▓▓▓▓▓▓▓▓ our ▓▓▓▓▓▓▓▓ when they refused to give us any more credit.
8. We ▓▓▓▓▓▓▓▓ and worked through the night but the deal still fell through.

Talk Talk Talk

(Glasgow)

A. Here we are. Hamilton's office. You can park right outside ... Good morning, we're here to see Mr McDonald. **Is he in?**

Receptionist: A very good morning to you all. He certainly is in. Shall I call him for you?

A. Be a good woman and do that for us, if you please ...

Receptionist: He's expecting you. I'll take you up to his office ...

H. Good morning, Angus! How are you doing? I haven't seen you in months. You must be busy.

A. I've had a busy time lately, that's true. Right now I'm **showing my two colleagues from London around** – Steve Blackman and Peter Brückner.

H. How do you do! Welcome to Scotland. We've only had **contact on the phone**, Mr Blackman – Steve isn't it? But I don't know Mr Brückner.

(Glasgow)

A. Da wären wir. Hamiltons Büro. Sie können direkt davor parken ... Guten Morgen, wir möchten gern zu Mr McDonald. **Ist er da?**

Empfangsdame: Einen schönen guten Morgen zusammen. Natürlich ist er da. Soll ich ihm Bescheid sagen?

A. Seien Sie so gut und machen Sie das für uns ...

Empfangsdame: Er erwartet sie. Ich werde Sie zu seinem Büro führen ...

H. Guten Morgen, Angus! Wie geht es Ihnen? Wir haben uns seit Monaten nicht gesehen. Sie müssen ja ziemlich beschäftigt sein.

A. Ich hatte in letzter Zeit wirklich viel zu tun, das stimmt. Im Augenblick **führe** ich gerade zwei Kollegen aus London **herum** – Steve Blackman und Peter Brückner.

H. Wie geht es Ihnen? Willkommen in Schottland. Wir haben schon einmal **telefoniert**, Mr Blackman – Steve, nicht wahr? Aber Mr Brückner kenne ich noch nicht.

Verkaufsgespräche

S. Our new Assistant Managing Director.

S. Er ist unser stellvertretender Geschäftsführer.

H. Oh, I'd better **watch my way**, then, hadn't I?

H. Oh, dann sollte ich **besser aufpassen,** nicht wahr?

S. Don't worry, Hamilton. I've filled Peter in on the way from Glasgow – I told him you're one of our best but also one of our most theatrical sales people.

S. Keine Sorge, Hamilton. Ich habe Peter auf dem Weg von Glasgow hierher genau ins Bild gesetzt – und ihm erzählt, dass Sie einer unserer besten aber auch theatralischsten Verkäufer sind.

H. They go together, laddy. Actors are sales people – they're selling themselves, and that great illusion we call theatre. Funnily enough, I'm off to the theatre today to meet an agent – one of Britain's best. He wants to **computerize** his whole operation and I believe ERGO has just the product for him. **Care to come along?**

H. Das beides passt gut zusammen, Freundchen. Schauspieler sind auch Verkäufer – sie verkaufen sich selbst und die großartige Illusion, die wir Theater nennen. Komischerweise gehe ich heute tatsächlich zum Theater, um mich mit einem Künstleragenten zu treffen – einem der besten in England. Er will sein ganzes Geschäft **auf Computer umstellen** und glaubt, dass ERGO genau das richtige Produkt für ihn hat. **Möchten Sie nicht mitkommen?**

 Background Information

In this section of the dialogue Hamilton asks Steve, Angus and Peter if they would **care** to join him in his meeting with his agent. »**Care**« here means **to like**. One can say, »I don't care for this wine very much« or »Would you care to come to a concert tonight?« etc.
»**To take care**« means **to pay attention** or **to be careful** and one can also **take care of somebody**, meaning **to look after him/her**. The opposite of **careful** is **careless**.
»**To care (about)**« can also mean **to be interested in** or **sympathetic towards something**, e.g. »She really cares about the environment«.

To return to the original example, »**Care to come along?**« is a suggestion. Other ways to suggest something using the same verb phrase »come along«, include (in order of formality, the most formal first):

a) Would you like to come along?
b) Why don't you come along?
c) Let's go together.
d) How about you coming along?
e) Do you fancy coming along?

Notice how the first three examples use the verb in the infinitive, whereas (c) and (d) have the verb in the gerund (-ing).

 143. Train Yourself

Setzen Sie nun das Verb in Klammern entweder in den Infinitiv oder die Gerundform!

1. Hi Larry. Do you fancy _____ (join) me for lunch tomorrow?
2. Why don't you _____ (speak) to him first on the telephone and then we'll arrange a meeting?
3. Would you care to _____ (meet) me in the bar for a drink?
4. Let's _____ (make) an arrangement to go over the plans next week, shall we?
5. OK, Peter, how about you _____ (start) off the meeting today?
6. Would you like to _____ (attend) the conference with me as my P.A.?
7. Why don't we _____ (break) off for lunch now, I'm starving!
8. Do you fancy _____ (share) a bottle of the Beaujolais? It's an excellent year.

 **Talk Talk Talk**

(In the City Theatre)

H. Here we are – the City Theatre. You know, of course, Peter, about our Edinburgh Festival?

P. Yes, indeed. I always wanted to go but somehow never got the chance.

H. You'll have to wait till next year now – the Festival has just closed. Darryl Thomas, the famous theatrical agent, stayed behind to discuss this **possible contract**. We're meeting him in the General Manager's office …

H. Hello, Darryl – good to see you again! Did you enjoy the festival?

D. I did indeed, and it has **alerted me to** a lot of latent talent. I've got a lot to do.

H. Then let's not waste our time. Oh, let me introduce you to two colleagues from London …

D. ERGO are really here in force,

(Im *City Theatre*)

H. Da wären wir – das *City Theatre.* Ich vermute, Sie kennen unser Edinburgh Festival, Peter?

P. Ja, sicher. Ich wollte immer schon einmal hingehen, aber ich hatte noch nie die Gelegenheit.

H. Dann werden Sie jetzt bis zum nächsten Jahr warten müssen – das Festival ist gerade zu Ende gegangen. Darryl Thomas, der berühmte Theateragent, ist noch geblieben, um über den **möglichen Geschäftsabschluss** zu reden. Wir treffen uns mit ihm im Büro des General Managers …

H. Hallo, Darryl – schön, Sie wieder zu sehen! Hat Ihnen das Festival gefallen?

D. Allerdings, und **ich bin** dabei auf eine Menge schlummernde Talente **aufmerksam geworden**. Es wird viel für mich zu tun geben …

H. Dann sollten wir keine Zeit mehr verschwenden. Oh, darf ich Ihnen zwei Kollegen aus London vorstellen …

D. ERGO ist ja wirklich massiv

then. Am I such an **important catch** for you?

H. Darryl, you are so important that I've drawn up a **special deal**. This software has been practically **custom-made** for you and your company's **requirements**. Let me explain ...

vertreten. Bin ich denn wirklich so ein **wichtiger Fang** für Sie?

H. Darryl, Sie sind so wichtig, dass ich für Sie ein **Spezialangebot** entworfen habe. Diese Software wurde quasi für Sie und die **Ansprüche** Ihrer Firma **maßgeschneidert**. Lassen Sie mich das erklären ...

Verkaufsgespräche

 False Friends

Peter is very **interested** in going to the Edinburgh festival and he is probably **disappointed** that he will have to wait until next year. »**Interested**« and »**disappointed**« are past participles of the verbs »**to interest**« and »**to disappoint**« as in »They disappointed me when they cancelled the meeting«, or »The new book on business techniques really interested him«.
»**Disappointed**« and »**Interested**« describe how one feels about something, one's emotions.
Of course one can also use the same stems as adjectives, i.e. »**interesting**« and »**disappointing**« which describe nouns but not a person's feelings. Thus, it is possible to say »I am bored with this class« but not »I am boring with this class«. Similarly, »The book is fascinating« but not »The book is fascinated.«

 Background Information

Let's look at some pairs of past participles and adjectives commonly used in English:

interesting	interested
boring	bored
disappointing	disappointed
fascinating	fascinated
tiring	tired

worrying	worried
exciting	excited
confusing	confused
annoying	annoyed
frustrating	frustrated

 144. Train Yourself

Wählen Sie das richtige Wort aus der Klammer:

1. The seminar on sales techniques was _____ (fascinating/fascinated).
2. It was very _____ (disappointing/disappointed) to lose the sale after all the work we put in.
3. We found the new proposals for the planned takeover quite _____ (confusing/confused).
4. After the _____ (tiring/tired) journey I was ready for my bed.
5. All of the shareholders were terribly _____ (exciting/excited) at the news of the merger.
6. The effect on business of global communications via the internet is _____ (fascinating/fascinated).
7. My God! I've never been so _____ (bored/boring) in all my life! I thought his speech would never end!
8. There's no point _____ (worrying/worried) about what may or may not happen. To succeed one must take some risks.
9. I was incredibly _____ (annoying/annoyed) when I found out that my work had been accidentally erased from the computer.
10. There are some very _____ (interesting/interested) theories on effective business management in this book I am reading at the moment.

Talk Talk Talk

(Still in the theatre)

H. ... so you see, the system gives you a completely reliable **data base**. It gives a new dimension to the term »**multi-media**« because we are adding the element »theatre« to it. You can **put on file** not only the contents of your clients' **personal portfolios** but even video excerpts from roles they have played. You can download onto your **mini-digital PC** for use when you are on the road or attending festivals, or you can go directly online with it, delivering far more information to producers, directors and theatre managers than was ever possible by **conventional means**.

D. I like it, I do confess. But it's hideously expensive. I could **revamp** my whole office and take on an **extra pair of hands** for that price.

H. Darryl, I said you were an important client for us, and **I've drawn up a deal you can't refuse**. We **install the system**, you use it for six months, completely **free of charge**. If at the end of the six months you like it then you keep it

(Immer noch im Theater)

H. ... wie Sie sehen, garantiert Ihnen das System eine absolut verlässliche **Datenbank**. Es fügt dem Begriff »**Multi-Media**« eine völlig neue Dimension hinzu, da es über ein »theatralisches« Element erweitert ist. Sie können damit nicht nur **Daten** über Ihre Klienten **abspeichern**, sondern sogar Video-Ausschnitte der Rollen hinzufügen, die sie gespielt haben. Sie können das Ganze auf ihren **Mini-Digital-PC** herunterladen, wenn Sie unterwegs sind oder Festivals besuchen oder Sie können damit direkt online gehen und mehr Informationen an Produzenten, Regisseure oder Theatermanager weiterleiten, als es mit **konventionellen Mitteln** bisher möglich war.

D. Ich muss zugeben, es gefällt mir, aber es ist furchtbar teuer. Ich könnte für diesen Preis mein ganzes Büro **neu einrichten** und eine **zusätzliche Hilfskraft** einsetzen.

H. Darryl, ich habe ja gesagt, dass Sie ein wichtiger Klient für uns sind und **ich habe Ihnen ein Angebot zusammengestellt, dass Sie nicht ablehnen können**. Wir **installieren** Ihnen das **System** und Sie können es sechs Monate lang völlig **kosten-**

and, if you like, take advantage of our **extended payments plan**. If you don't like it, then **we'll just pick it up and shake hands**. But, in that case, I want a bundle of tickets for next year's Edinburgh Festival. Now is that a deal – or is that not a deal?

los benutzen. Wenn es Ihnen nach Ablauf der sechs Monate gefallen hat, können Sie es behalten und wenn Sie wollen auf unseren **Ratenzahlungsplan** zurückgreifen. Wenn es Ihnen nicht gefällt, **nehmen wir es einfach zurück und sind quitt**. Aber in diesem Fall will ich ein ganzes Bündel Tickets für das Edinburgh Festival im nächsten Jahr. Ist das ein Angebot oder nicht?

D. You old ham, Hamilton! I said I like it – now let me think about it. How long are you in Edinburgh?

D. Hamilton, Sie alter Schurke (eigentlich: Schmierenkomödiant!). Ich sagte doch, es gefällt mir – jetzt lassen Sie mich darüber nachdenken. Wie lange sind Sie in Edinburgh?

H. Just as long as it takes for you to make up your mind, Darryl laddy.

H. So lange, wie Sie brauchen, bis Sie sich entschieden haben, Darryl, alter Freund.

D. Look, there's a very fine Festival production which has extended its run at the Prince's Theatre. I'll get you tickets – it'll **give** Peter **an insight** into contemporary British theatre, unless London has already given him that.

D. Hören Sie, in der Verlängerung läuft noch eine exzellente Festival-Aufführung im *Prince's Theatre*. Ich werde Ihnen Tickets besorgen – es wird Peter **einen Einblick** in das zeitgenössische, britische Theater **geben**, wenn er den in London noch nicht bekommen hat.

P. I just haven't had the time, I do confess.

P. Ich muss zugeben, dass ich noch nicht die Zeit dazu hatte.

D. Then off you go tonight to the theatre. I'll give you a call at your hotel tomorrow morning. Agreed?

D. Dann heißt es für Sie heute Abend: auf ins Theater. Ich werde Sie morgen früh in Ihrem Hotel anrufen. Einverstanden?

Background Information

Darryl says to Peter that going to a play in Edinburgh will **give him an insight** into contemporary British theatre. **»An insight«** is **a clear understanding of a complex problem or situation**. Let's look at some other **»sight«** words and expressions:

foresight	the ability to judge what is going to happen in the future and plan one's actions based on this knowledge
hindsight	the ability to understand why or how something was done in the past and how it might have been done better
at first sight	when first seen
to lose sight of	to not pay attention to something or forget about
to be within sight	to be almost finished
to go sightseeing	to visit interesting places usually when on holiday
to set one's sights on	to try very hard to achieve something

 145. Train Yourself

Füllen Sie die Lücken der folgenden Sätze!

1. After spending two days working on the report the end was _____.
2. I had no time to _____ when I was in Copenhagen, all I saw was the office and my hotel room.
3. I think we've _____ of our initial goal to sell software of high quality at a price people can afford.
4. Paul had _____ being Company Director within ten years and was therefore devastated when he heard he'd been passed over for promotion.

5. In _____, we should have moved in to secure the contract earlier and then we wouldn't have lost out to Farrell and Sons.
6. Spending a month being shown around the various departments of the company will give you an _____ into how things work round here.
7. Charles had the _____ to sell his shares in the company long before the crash occurred.
8. _____ the plan seemed to be full of holes but after consideration, we decided to go ahead with it.

 Talk Talk Talk

(The hotel. At breakfast)   (Im Hotel, beim Frühstück)

A. Good morning, gentlemen. Slept well?

A. Guten Morgen, meine Herren. Gut geschlafen?

S. and P.: Very well, Angus. What's on the programme today?

S. und P.: Sehr gut, Angus. Was steht heute auf dem Programm?

A. The waiting game – waiting for Darryl's call. Actually, let's **take the morning off** and look around Edinburgh. You've never seen the city, Peter – it's a northern city but I'm sure quite unlike your Hamburg.

A. Das übliche Warten – auf Darryls Anruf. Lassen Sie uns einfach **den Morgen frei nehmen** und uns Edinburgh ansehen. Sie haben die Stadt ja noch nie gesehen, Peter – es ist eine Stadt des Nordens, aber ganz sicher anders als Ihr Hamburg.

P. I'd love to see around the city. I've read so much about it, of course.

P. Ich würde mir die Stadt liebend gern ansehen. Ich habe natürlich schon viel darüber gelesen.

S. Then off we go after breakfast.

S. Dann ziehen wir gleich nach

I'll call Hamilton – he can **double as a guide** for us. Angus, you'll be wanting to get back to Glasgow.

A. I've a lot waiting for me there, that's for sure. If you don't need me any more I'll **get on the road**.

(Later, on Edinburgh's Prince's Street)

P. Look, isn't that Melissa over there?

S. Good lord, yes. What's she doing here? I didn't know she intended coming to Scotland. Hey, Melissa.

M. Heavens above, what are you two boys doing in Edinburgh? You're supposed to be in Glasgow.

S. That was yesterday, Melissa. We're working. What are you up to?

M. **Secret assignment** – but I'll tell you later.

S. Over lunch?

M. Yes, why not.

dem Frühstück los. Ich rufe Hamilton an – er kann für uns auch den **Fremdenführer spielen**. Angus, Sie werden sicher zurück nach Glasgow fahren wollen.

A. Dort wartet wirklich genug Arbeit auf mich, so viel ist sicher. Wenn Sie mich nicht mehr brauchen, **mache** ich **mich** wieder **auf den Weg**.

(Später, auf der *Prince's Street* in Edinburgh)

P. Sehen Sie mal, ist das da drüben nicht Melissa?

S. Guter Gott, ja. Was macht sie denn hier? Ich wusste gar nicht, dass sie vorgehabt hatte, nach Schottland zu fahren. Hey, Melissa.

M. Du lieber Himmel, was macht ihr zwei Jungs denn in Edinburgh? Solltet Ihr nicht in Glasgow sein?

S. Das war gestern, Melissa. Wir arbeiten. Was machen Sie denn hier?

M. Ein **geheimer Auftrag** – aber ich werde es Ihnen später erzählen.

S. Beim Mittagessen?

M. Ja, warum nicht.

Verkaufsgespräche

S. At our hotel then. It's the Connaught …

(At the hotel)

Receptionist: You had a call from a Mr McGregor, sir.

S. That'll be to say Darryl has given his answer. I'll call right away … Hamilton? Any news. He did? He has? That's great … Peter, Ham **made the sale.** That's a **real feather in ERGO's cap.** Now to lunch - here's Melissa.

(At lunch)

S. Well, Melissa, what's this secret you're withholding from us?

M. I don't know how to tell you two boys this, but I'm leaving ERGO to come up here and work. It wasn't an easy decision, but the offer was too good to **turn down.**

P. I'm very sorry indeed to hear that Melissa.

S. So will James. When do you leave, Melissa?

S. Dann treffen wir uns in unserem Hotel. Es ist das Connaught …

(Im Hotel)

Empfangsdame: Ein Mr McGregor hat für Sie angerufen, Sir.

S. Wahrscheinlich wollte er uns mitteilen, dass Darryl ihm eine Antwort gegeben hat. Ich rufe gleich zurück … Hamilton? Gibt es etwas Neues? Hat er? Er hat? Das ist ja großartig … Peter, Ham **hat das Geschäft abgeschlossen.** Das ist ein **schöner Erfolg für ERGO.** Jetzt auf zum Mittagessen – da ist Melissa schon.

(Beim Mittagessen)

S. Also, Melissa, was für ein Geheimnis verbergen Sie vor uns?

M. Ich weiß gar nicht, wie ich euch beiden Jungs das beibringen soll, aber ich verlasse ERGO, um hier zu arbeiten. Es war keine leichte Entscheidung, aber das Angebot war zu gut, um »**Nein« sagen** zu können.

P. Es tut mir wirklich Leid, das zu hören, Melissa.

S. So wird es James auch ergehen. Wann verlassen Sie uns, Melissa?

M. In about six weeks.

M. In etwa sechs Wochen.

S. Just time enough to complete your marketing programme for the **trade fair**. At least, you'll be seeing a lot of her on that project, Peter. Don't look so crestfallen. In this game you win one and lose one ...

S. Gerade genug Zeit, um Ihr Marketing-Programm für die **Messe** fertig zu stellen. Wenigstens werden Sie sie bei diesem Projekt häufig sehen, Peter. Also schauen Sie nicht wie ein begossener Pudel. Mal gewinnt man in diesem Spiel, mal verliert man ...

Background Information

Melissa tells her colleagues in this section of the dialogue that she had an offer of work that was too good to **turn down**. »**To turn down**« is **to refuse or reject something or someone**. Let's look at some more expressions with »**turn**«.

to turn out	to happen in the end
to turn up (a)	to arrive
to turn up (b)	to discover by chance
to turn around	to cause a situation or organisation to improve
to turn in	to go to bed
turnover	the amount of business a company does in a period of time
to take turns	a number of people do the same thing one after the other

146. Train Yourself

Benutzen Sie diese Wendungen in den unten stehenden Sätzen!

1. The company's annual ▓▓▓▓▓▓▓▓▓▓▓▓▓▓▓ has been increasing every year.
2. On the way to the conference we ▓▓▓▓▓▓▓▓▓▓▓▓▓▓▓ with the driving so that nobody got too tired.

3. The new Chief Executive brought in new measures to try and ▓▓▓▓▓▓▓▓▓ the company's fortunes after a very disappointing year.
4. In the end everything ▓▓▓▓▓▓▓▓▓ fine and the deadline was met.
5. On business trips abroad I usually ▓▓▓▓▓▓▓▓▓ quite early so as to be fresh next day.
6. The candidate did himself no favours by ▓▓▓▓▓▓▓▓▓ late for the interview and wasting the interviewer's time.
7. The company ▓▓▓▓▓▓▓▓▓ the offer as it was felt it wouldn't be beneficial for the shareholders in the long-term future.
8. After searching all morning for my car keys they finally ▓▓▓▓▓▓▓▓▓ behind the sofa.

 Vocabulary

business centre	Handelszentrum
Care to come along?	Möchten Sie nicht mitkommen?
to computerize	auf Computer umstellen
conventional means	konventionelle Mittel
custom-made	maßgeschneidert
data base	Datenbank
to double as a guide	den Fremdenführer spielen
to draw up	entwerfen, zusammenstellen
easily accessible	leicht zugänglich
electronic commerce	elektronischer Handel
extended payments plan	Ratenzahlungsplan
free of charge	kostenlos
to get on the road	sich auf den Weg machen
to give an insight	einen Einblick geben
grapevine	Gerüchteküche *(fig.)*
hand	Hilfskraft
highly-qualified	hochqualifiziert
high-tech age	Zeitalter der Hochtechnologie
to intrigue	sehr interessieren
to make a sale	ein Geschäft abschließen
marketing material	Werbematerial

personal approach	persönlicher Ansatz
pool of labour	Arbeitskräfte
to pull in	anhalten
to revamp	neu einrichten
secret assignment	Geheimauftrag
sidekick (Am.)	Partner, Kumpel (ugs.)
special deal	Spezialangebot
springing up all over the place	überall aus dem Boden schießen
to take off	frei nehmen
to turn down	ablehnen
trade fair	Handelsmesse
virtual marketplace	virtuelle Verkaufsstellen
visual presentation	visuelle Präsentation
website	Website

Verkaufsgespräche

Informal meetings
Informelle Besprechungen

 Here we go

Bald soll die große Herbstmesse stattfinden und die Marketingabteilung ist vollauf mit den Vorbereitungen hierfür beschäftigt. Dies wird Melissas letzte Aufgabe für ERGO Limited sein und sie wird hierbei von allen kräftig unterstützt – insbesondere natürlich von Peter, der die Aufgabe hat, sich um sämtliche Pressemitteilungen und Informationen zu kümmern. Eine Aufgabe, bei der er sich für Melissa selbstverständlich sehr engagiert ...

 Talk Talk Talk

(ERGO's London office. Peter enters and is greeted by the secretary, Lucy)

(ERGOs Londoner Büro. Peter tritt ein und wird von Lucy, der Sekretärin begrüßt)

L. Why, Peter! You're back from your travels. Did you have a **good journey**?

L. Na so was, Peter! Sie sind wieder zurück. Hatten Sie eine **angenehme Reise**?

P. Very good, and it was fascinating, too.

P. Sie war sehr gut – und außerdem faszinierend.

L. Which part of the country did you like best?

L. Welcher Teil des Landes gefiel Ihnen denn am besten?

P. I fell in love with Edinburgh.

P. Ich habe mich in Edinburgh verliebt.

L. I've never been there, but now that Miss Walker is going to Scotland I might just visit her.

L. Ich war noch nie da, aber jetzt, wo Miss Walker nach Schottland geht, werde ich sie vielleicht mal besuchen.

P. So she is really **leaving us for** Scotland?	P. Sie **verlässt uns** also wirklich **Richtung** Schottland?
L. Yes, but Beryl will be **taking over**. My, you look quite **crestfallen**!	L. Ja, aber Beryl wird für sie **übernehmen**. Meine Güte, Sie sehen ja ganz **erschüttert** aus!
P. I shall certainly miss her.	P. Ich werde sie ganz bestimmt vermissen.
L. Well, you'll have the next few weeks in her company. Mr Morgan tells me you will be working with her in marketing.	L. Tja, aber Sie werden die nächsten paar Wochen in ihrer Gesellschaft verbringen. Mr Morgan hat mir gesagt, dass Sie mit ihr in der Marketing-Abteilung arbeiten werden.
P. Well, that will be something to look forward to ...	P. Tja, das ist etwas, auf das ich mich freuen kann ...

Background Information

Lucy tells Peter in this section of the dialogue that Beryl **will be taking over** Melissa's job after the latter has gone to Edinburgh. »**Take over**« here means **to do something instead of someone** else. It can also mean **to take control of something**, e.g. »The company has taken over new premises as part of its expansion programme.« Look at some other phrasal verbs using »**take**«.

to take on	to do something extra
to take to	to start to like something
to take off	when a plane leaves the ground or to increase suddenly in success or popularity to
take up	to fill space or time or to start doing something (often a hobby)

Präsentationen

to take in	to understand completely the meaning or significance of something
to take somebody up on	to accept an offer made by somebody
to take aback	to surprise somebody

 147. Train Yourself

Verwenden Sie oben stehende Wendungen in den folgenden Sätzen!

1. The director ▒▒▒ us all ▒▒▒ when he announced his decision to quit at the end of the year.
2. The mainframe ▒▒▒ too much space in the old office so it was reinstalled in the basement.
3. By accepting her new post Lucy will have to ▒▒▒ much more responsibility in day-to-day affairs.
4. As the plane ▒▒▒ I put my watch to an hour ahead to coincide with British time.
5. The company hopes to ▒▒▒ PMC Pharmaceuticals Ltd in order to try and corner the market.
6. The new product really ▒▒▒ after the new advertising campaign started on TV.
7. When Gary was promoted to Senior Director Julie was asked to ▒▒▒ his old job.
8. To combat the stresses of her executive lifestyle Barbara decided to ▒▒▒ yoga.
9. After listening to the guest speaker for over an hour or more it was hard to ▒▒▒ much more.

 **Talk Talk Talk**

(Peter's office. Melissa enters)

M. Hello again, Peter. **Back safe and sound**? Did you enjoy Scotland?

(Peters Büro. Melissa tritt ein)

M. Na, hallo Peter. Sind Sie **heil wieder zurück**? Haben Sie Schottland genossen?

Präsentationen

P. Loved it – particularly Edinburgh. A lovely city.

P. Ich war begeistert – besonders von Edinburgh. Eine wunderbare Stadt.

M. I think so, too. In fact, that's one of the reasons I'll be leaving London.

M. Das sehe ich auch so. Streng genommen ist das auch einer der Gründe, warum ich London verlasse.

P. We'll all **miss you**, you know.

P. Wir werden Sie alle **vermissen**, wissen Sie?

M. Oh, Edinburgh's **not too far away**. And I shall remain closely in touch with the company. In fact, I'm trying to persuade James to use the services of the company I shall **be joining**.

M. Oh, Edinburgh ist ja nicht **so weit weg**. Und ich werde in engem Kontakt mit der Firma bleiben. Tatsache ist, dass ich versuchen werde, James davon zu überzeugen, die Dienste der Firma in Anspruch zu nehmen, **bei der ich anfangen werde**.

P. That's a great idea! Do you think he will?

P. Eine großartige Idee! Glauben Sie, er wird es machen?

M. James would like to **build up** his own **marketing division**. In fact, he has big plans – and they involve you, you know. That's why we'll be working closely together for the next few weeks.

M. James würde gerne seine eigene **Marketing-Abteilung aufbauen**. Tatsache ist, dass er große Pläne hat – und die betreffen auch Sie, wissen Sie? Deshalb werden wir während der nächsten paar Wochen auch so eng zusammenarbeiten.

P. You don't know how glad I am to hear that, Melissa!

P. Sie können sich gar nicht vorstellen, wie froh ich bin, das zu hören, Melissa!

Background Information

Peter was a little »**crestfallen**« **(sad)** in the first section of the dialogue because of Melissa's imminent departure to Scotland. In this section he is rather happier to be **working closely** with her before she leaves. He tells her that everybody **is going to miss her**, meaning **they will be unhappy that she is no longer present**. One can also **miss a train** or **a bus** etc. when the person **arrives too late** and the transport **has already left** or **miss a meeting** with the meaning of **failing to do something that one has planned to do** or **one was expected to do**.
Let's look at some expressions now using »**miss**«:

to miss out on something	to fail to be included
to miss the boat	to fail to do something by being slow to act
to miss the mark	to fail to achieve what one intended to achieve
to miss a trick	to fail to notice an opportunity
hit or miss	a situation where there is an equal chance of success or failure
to give somebody or something a miss	to avoid
a near miss	a narrow escape
to miss the thread	to fail to follow the course or development of an argument, conversation etc.

 148. Train Yourself

Füllen Sie nun die Lücken mit diesen »phrasal verbs«!

1. Management spent so long running over the pros and cons of the proposed merger that they ▭▭▭▭▭▭▭▭▭▭ completely and TELEX Ltd went back on the deal.

2. Nobody could get the better of the CEO, he never ▓▓▓▓▓▓▓▓▓ ▓▓▓▓▓▓▓▓▓ .
3. Alice was quite upset when she ▓▓▓▓▓▓▓▓▓▓ promotion for the second year running.
4. On the way to the sales fair Mike and Tony had a ▓▓▓▓▓▓▓ ▓▓▓▓▓▓▓▓▓ when Mike failed to notice a truck pulling out onto the motorway in front of them.
5. I ▓▓▓▓▓▓▓▓▓▓ of their conversation and had to ask them to repeat the main points again.
6. The disappointing results of the consumer survey showed clearly that we had  by trying to launch the two products at the same time.
7. At the conference we ▓▓▓▓▓▓▓▓▓▓ the talk on sales targets ▓▓▓▓▓▓▓▓▓▓ and made our way to the bar.
8. The Managing Director pointed out the importance of thorough planning prior to the new sales campaign so as to avoid a ▓▓▓▓▓▓ ▓▓▓▓▓▓▓▓▓ situation.

🗨 Talk Talk Talk

(The ERGO office)	(Im Büro von ERGO)
M. Morning, Beryl! Have a good weekend?	M. Morgen, Beryl! Hatten Sie ein schönes Wochenende?
B. Lovely, thanks, Melissa.	B. Es war wunderbar, danke, Melissa.
M. Then we're all **in the mood** for a **productive week**, right? Let's look at the **strategy** for the **upcoming trade fair**. I've rather **neglected** that in the past couple of weeks. With Peter and Steve **dashing around the country** and James down with flu, poor Beryl and I were just about **running the office** solo. Peter will be joining us	M. Dann sind wir ja alle **in der Stimmung** für eine **produktive Woche**, nicht wahr? Werfen wir mal einen Blick auf unsere **Strategie** für die **bevorstehende Messe**. Ich habe das in den vergangenen paar Wochen eher **vernachlässigt**. Während Peter und Steve sich **quer im ganzen Land herumgetrieben haben** und James

for the next month, Beryl. That will **take us up to** when I have to leave the company. Then you're on your own.	mit der Grippe flach lag, mussten die arme Beryl und ich **das Büro** fast ganz allein **leiten**. Peter wird für den nächsten Monat zu uns stoßen, Beryl. Das **wird uns solange weiterhelfen**, bis ich die Firma verlasse. Dann sind Sie auf sich allein gestellt.
B. So don't you think of going back to Hamburg, Peter?	B. Sie denken also nicht daran, zurück nach Hamburg zu gehen, Peter?
P. No chance, Beryl. I like it too much here.	P. Keine Chance, Beryl. Es gefällt mir hier viel zu gut.
M. I'll take you up on that after the month is up, Peter. We have a lot of work ahead. First things first: we have **to plan the design and presentation of our stand at the trade fair**. We have to **prepare a press conference, a reception** – and we have **to draw up a presentation** which James will make to a **gathering** of top CEOs. Oh, and a **press release**, of course. Can you handle that **for starters**, Peter?	M. Ich werde Sie noch einmal darauf ansprechen, wenn dieser Monat vorbei ist, Peter. Vor uns liegt eine Menge Arbeit. Aber eins nach dem anderen: Wir müssen **das Design und die Präsentation unseres Messestandes planen**. Wir müssen **eine Pressekonferenz vorbereiten, einen Empfang** – und wir müssen **eine Präsentation entwerfen**, die James bei einem **Treffen** der leitenden Direktoren vortragen wird. Oh, und natürlich eine **Pressemitteilung**. Können Sie sich **für den Anfang** darum kümmern, Peter?
P. I'll give it a try. I just hope my English **is up to it** ...	P. Ich werde es versuchen. Ich hoffe nur, dass mein Englisch **dafür reicht** ...

Background Information

Look at some »up« expressions. In the last section of the dialogue Melissa said: »**That will take us up to when I have to leave the company**« - In other words **it will fill the time until she leaves the company**.
Below are some other »**up**« expressions.

to catch up on	to do something one hasn't had the chance to do before
to play up	to behave or work badly
to make up for	to compensate for something
to pick up	to improve
to give up	to stop doing something
to set up	to establish or create
to come up against	to encounter something (usually a problem)
to take up	to occupy time, to start a hobby
to turn up	to be discovered by chance
to add up	to make sense

 149. Train Yourself

Verwenden Sie diese Ausdrücke nun in der folgenden Übung!

1. The computer had been ▒▒▒▒▒▒▒ all morning and so very little work was done.
2. These figures don't ▒▒▒▒▒▒▒! 850 pounds on expenses for one weekend! This can't be right.
3. The new marketing strategy was ▒▒▒▒▒▒▒ so much of my time I had barely enough left to get myself some lunch.
4. The company ▒▒▒▒▒▒▒ a problem when it was discovered that nobody would be left to hold the fort while the sales team were away.
5. We ▒▒▒▒▒▒▒ some useful information while looking through old company records.

6. ERGO Ltd plans to ▉▉▉▉▉▉ a new branch in Glasgow next year.
7. Business finally seemed to be ▉▉▉▉▉▉ after a very slow year and profits were up by 20%.
8. I was forced to ▉▉▉▉▉▉ some work over the weekend having spent the previous two days showing our Japanese visitors around the city.
9. We never ▉▉▉▉▉▉ and were rewarded when the company finally reached its production targets.
10. To ▉▉▉▉▉▉ the unavoidable delay in the arrival of the necessary raw materials everybody had to work overtime.

 **Talk Talk Talk**

(Peter's office. Melissa's assistant, Beryl, enters)
B. May I come in, Peter? Melissa said I **should help you prepare the press release**.

P. That's very kind of you, Beryl. I'm sure **I could do with some help**. I've **no experience** here.

B. I've had some **dealings with the press**, so I'll certainly be able to help you with **a draft**.

P. Great! I must **confess**, I don't know where to start.

B. We'll begin by putting together **a company profile**. Then we'll look

(Peters Büro. Beryl, Melissas Assistentin, tritt ein)
B. Darf ich hereinkommen, Peter? Melissa hat gesagt, ich soll Ihnen **bei der Vorbereitung der Pressemitteilung helfen**.

P. Das ist sehr nett von Ihnen, Beryl. Ich bin sicher, **dass ich etwas Hilfe gebrauchen kann**. Ich habe überhaupt **keine Erfahrung** in so etwas.

B. Ich hatte schon gelegentlich **mit der Presse zu tun**, also werde ich Ihnen bei **dem Entwurf** sicher behilflich sein können.

P. Großartig! Ich muss **zugeben**, ich weiß gar nicht, wo ich anfangen soll.

B. Wir fangen damit an, **ein Profil der Firma** zusammenzustellen.

for **a hook on which to hang the release**.	Dann suchen wir nach **einem Aufhänger, an dem wir die Pressemitteilung festmachen können**.
P. A hook?	P. Einen Aufhänger?
B. That's what we call something that attracts attention to **a written piece of material** such as a newspaper report or article. Nobody is going to read our company profile unless we **direct attention to it** somehow.	B. So nennen wir etwas, das die Aufmerksamkeit auf **ein Schriftstück** lenkt, zum Beispiel auf eine Zeitungsmeldung oder einen Artikel. Kein Mensch wird unser Firmenprofil lesen, wenn wir nicht irgendwie die **Aufmerksamkeit darauf lenken**.

Background Information

Peter, in this section of the dialogue, tells Beryl that **he could do with some help**. This expression means **it would be acceptable or useful to him to receive some help**. There is often great confusion amongst language learners between when to use »**do**« and when to use the word »**make**«.

»**Do**« primarily means **to act, or carry out an activity;** »**make**« means **to create or invent something**. Contrast: »I **did** that report yesterday« and »I **made** some useful contacts at the trade fair«. However, there are many irregularities in the usage of these two verbs and they often seem to be used indiscriminately. Hence, the headaches for language learners! Some expressions with »**do**« and »**make**« which don't automatically follow the rules given above.

to make a phone-call	to do well / badly
to make a suggestion	to do business with
to make a complaint	to do (somebody) a favour
to make a decision	to do a test
to make a profit	to do one's best / worst
to make a mistake	to do the dishes
to make an effort	to do the laundry

150. Train Yourself

»Do« or »make«? Füllen Sie die Lücken mit dem richtigen Verb!

1. A dissatisfied customer phoned to the head office this morning to .... a complaint.
2. Last year Vacro Ltd .... a profit of over a million pounds.
3. Every hopeful candidate must .... an entrance test.
4. Lucy .... a phone call to set up the meeting.
5. It's been a pleasure to .... business with you.
6. Will you .... me a favour and take this up to Steve's office for me?
7. If I could just .... a suggestion here, what about the second option?
8. All the company asks of its employees is that they .... their best.
9. I want everybody to .... an extra effort this month!
10. Peter has .... well with the new account.
11. The Sales Director is constantly procrastinating. He can never .... a decision.
12. I .... a mistake by not following up the phone-call yesterday.

 Talk Talk Talk

(Peter's office. James Morgan enters)

P. Good morning, James. Are you feeling better?

J. Yes, thank you, Peter. It's good to see you again. **I gather** you had a very successful trip.

P. Yes, indeed. It was very informative.

(Peters Büro. James Morgan tritt ein)

P. Guten Morgen, James. Geht es Ihnen wieder besser?

J. Ja, danke, Peter. Schön, Sie wieder zu sehen. **Ich habe gehört**, Ihre Reise war erfolgreich?

P. Ja, allerdings. Sie war sehr informativ.

J. We're certainly **putting you through an intensive learning process**, and now you're in Melissa's hands.

P. Marketing is **the side of the business** that interests me most, actually, so I'm very interested in working with her again.

J. I think you'll make a good team. I'm just sorry we're losing Melissa. ERGO will certainly miss her.

P. I shall, too – I can tell you …

J. Wir **unterziehen Sie ja tatsächlich einem ziemlich intensiven Lernprozess** und jetzt sind Sie in Melissas Händen.

P. Streng genommen ist Marketing sogar **der Geschäftsbereich**, der mich am meisten interessiert, also bin ich auch sehr daran interessiert, wieder mit ihr zusammenzuarbeiten.

J. Ich glaube, Sie beide geben ein gutes Team ab. Ich bedaure nur, dass wir Melissa verlieren. ERGO wird sie ganz bestimmt vermissen.

P. Ich auch – das kann ich Ihnen versichern …

Background Information

In this section of the dialogue James Morgan says that **the company is putting Peter through an intensive learning process. To put somebody through something** is **to make somebody undergo an experience, or an operation**. In colloquial English we can say »**She put me through hell!**« in other words **she caused the person to have an unpleasant time**.

»**To put somebody through to somebody else**« means **to connect one person to another, usually by phone**. Operators and receptionists do this.

There are many phrases and expressions with »**put**«. Some of them are listed below.

to put up with	to tolerate
to put in for	to apply for a job
to put up	to give accommodation
to put by	to save money

Präsentationen

to put off	to postpone
to put off somebody	to discourage somebody
to put down to	to explain the cause of something
to put oneself out	to make an effort to help someone

 151. Train Yourself

Verwenden Sie nun diese »phrasal verbs« in den unten stehenden Sätzen!

1. I rang Fosters Ltd. and the receptionist ▓▓▓▓▓ me ▓▓▓▓▓ to the Sales Director.
2. The meeting was ▓▓▓▓▓ until next week.
3. On the trip to our branch in Newcastle Steven ▓▓▓▓▓ us ▓▓▓▓▓ in his flat.
4. Joan intended ▓▓▓▓▓ the new position at Ackroyd and Sons but was ▓▓▓▓▓ by the low salary and therefore decided to stay at ERGO Ltd.
5. The Director ▓▓▓▓▓ the slump in profits ▓▓▓▓▓ to the economic climate.
6. Everybody in the office ▓▓▓▓▓ themselves ▓▓▓▓▓ to help the new recruit and so he settled in very quickly.
7. In order to succeed in business one needs to ▓▓▓▓▓ oneself ▓▓▓▓▓ a great deal of hard work.
8. After ▓▓▓▓▓ part of his salary every month George was able to buy himself the new car he'd had his eye on.

 Talk Talk Talk

(Melissa's office. Peter enters) (Melissas Büro. Peter tritt ein)

M. Good morning, Peter. I've asked Beryl to **sit in on our meeting**, since you'll be **dealing**

M. Guten Morgen, Peter. Ich habe Beryl gebeten, **an unserem Meeting teilzunehmen**, da Sie

with her a lot. That's her now ...

B. Morning all!

M. Beryl, we have to discuss with Peter the form of the **initial** press release.

B. We've already begun work on it. **It's taking shape well**. Peter and I feel we **must base it on a new development** within the company. It seems to us that the new internet security software we've **taken on board fills the bill exactly**.

M. But it's not exactly a new development. We have a lot of **keen competition** in this field.

B. Yes, but don't forget our Swansea success. Our action plan is **to issue** a press release announcing our **penetration of the market** with this new software.

M. Steve tells me there has been another **important sale**. Shouldn't we be reporting on that?

jetzt **viel mit ihr zu tun haben werden**. Da kommt sie schon ...

B. Guten Morgen zusammen!

M. Beryl, wir müssen mit Peter die Gliederung der **ersten** Pressemitteilung besprechen.

B. Wir haben bereits mit der Arbeit daran begonnen. **Sie nimmt langsam Form an.** Peter und ich waren beide der Meinung, **dass sie auf einer neuen Entwicklung** innerhalb der Firma **basieren muss**. Wir sind zu dem Schluss gekommen, dass die neue Internet-Sicherheitssoftware, die wir **neu ins Programm genommen haben, genau das Richtige ist**.

M. Aber das ist nicht direkt eine Neuentwicklung. Wir haben eine Menge **scharfer Konkurrenz** in diesem Bereich.

B. Ja, aber vergessen Sie nicht unseren Erfolg in Swansea. Unser Vorgehensplan sieht vor, dass wir eine Pressemitteilung **herausgeben**, indem wir unser **Vordringen auf den Markt** mit dieser neuen Software bekannt geben.

M. Steve hat mir gesagt, dass es noch einen weiteren **wichtigen Verkaufsabschluss** gab. Sollten wir nicht auch darüber berichten?

Präsentationen

P. That's new to me. Where is Steve?

P. Das ist mir neu. Wo ist Steve?

B. He's in Southampton today. Back tomorrow.

B. Er ist heute in Southampton. Er kommt morgen zurück.

P. Then let's have a **definitive meeting** then ...

P. Dann lassen Sie uns morgen eine **endgültige Besprechung** abhalten ...

Background Information

Beryl says that the press release **is taking shape well**. When an idea or a plan **takes shape**, it means that **it starts to become reality**, or **to have an actual form**. Later in the conversation Beryl mentions the new internet security software that has been **taken on board**. »To take something on board« means **to accept or include something**.

Let's look at some more expressions with »**take**«:

to take a back seat	to have a position of less importance than others
to take for granted	to believe something to be true or certain without looking at the evidence
to take a shine to	to develop a liking for somebody or something
to take heart	to be encouraged
to take root	to become established or to begin to grow or develop
to take the plunge	to decide to do something risky or difficult
to take over	to gain control
to take stock	to consider carefully

152. Train Yourself

Verwenden Sie diese Varianten des Verbs »take« in der folgenden Übung!

1. After a series of disappointments the company ▧▧▧ at the government's new tax laws which would mean greater profits.
2. A large American conglomerate is trying to ▧▧▧ Walker's tobacco company.
3. After listening to all the proposals the shareholders decided to ▧▧▧ and vote the following day.
4. AKRON Ltd finally ▧▧▧ and floated the company on the stock market.
5. The original vision of the company is starting to ▧▧▧ but it is still in its early stages.
6. We can't ▧▧▧ our customers ▧▧▧! It's vital to maintain standards.
7. I was forced to ▧▧▧ in the discussions, being a junior in the firm.
8. Our new software is finally starting to ▧▧▧ in the Eastern European market after an intensive media campaign.
9. Last year ERGO Ltd ▧▧▧ five new members of staff.
10. The boss seems to have ▧▧▧ to the new P.A. He's always complimenting her on her work.

 Talk Talk Talk

(The next day. Peter's office. Steve enters)

P. Hi, Steve! We have to discuss this press release. I gather there has been another sale of the security software.

(Am nächsten Tag. Peters Büro. Steve tritt ein)

P. Hi, Steve! Wir müssen diese Pressemitteilung besprechen. Ich habe gehört, es gab einen weiteren Verkaufsabschluss für die Sicherheitssoftware.

S. Yes, I'm sorry I just haven't had time **to report in on it**. It's our most important sale **to date**. The Surrey Building Society **have taken it**. They have **branches** all over the country.

P. Let's get Melissa and Beryl in on this ...

P. Melissa, Beryl. Steve has given us the necessary hook for a press release. The Surrey Building Society have taken our security software. Steve tells me it's the first sale of its kind to any British financial institution. Isn't that worth a press release in which we can also **announce our participation** in the trade fair?

M. I think you're right, Peter. Can you **get to work on that**? Beryl can **help you out**.

P. I'll do my best. When would you like the text?

M. As soon as possible. Like yesterday?

S. Ja, tut mir Leid, dass ich noch keine Zeit hatte, **das zu melden**. Es ist unser **bis jetzt** wichtigster Vertragsabschluss. **Wir haben ihn mit** der Surrey Building Society **gemacht**. Sie haben überall im Land **Zweigstellen**.

P. Erzählen wir Melissa und Beryl davon ...

P. Melissa, Beryl. Steve hat uns den nötigen Aufhänger für eine Pressemitteilung gegeben. Die Surrey Building Society hat unsere Sicherheitssoftware gekauft. Steve hat mir gesagt, dass dies der erste Verkaufsabschluss dieser Art mit einer britischen Finanzinstitution ist. Ist das nicht eine Pressemitteilung wert, in der wir außerdem **unsere Teilnahme** an der Verkaufsmesse **ankündigen** können?

M. Ich glaube, Sie haben Recht, Peter. Können Sie **gleich damit anfangen**? Beryl kann Ihnen **dabei helfen**.

P. Ich tue mein Bestes. Bis wann hätten Sie den Text gern?

M. So schnell wie möglich. Wie wäre es mit gestern?

Background Information

Melissa asks Beryl to **get to work** on a press release for the trade fair, in other words **to start working** on it. Other expressions with »**work**« include:

to work out	to calculate
to work up to	to work towards a specific objective
to have one's work cut out	to be faced with something difficult to do
to be worked up	to be anxious, worried or excited
dirty work	the unpleasant or difficult part of a task
to work wonders	to work very effectively
out of work	to be unemployed

 153. Train Yourself

Füllen Sie die Lücken mit diesen Begriffen!

1. The company was forced to make staff reductions and put fifty people _____.
2. Everybody _____ their _____ when the new account came in.
3. Management _____ that the company had lost over 50,000 pounds last year.
4. Giving Christmas bonuses _____ for staff morale.
5. Stephanie was extremely upset when the receptionist took unpaid leave and she had to do her _____ for her.
6. Every April the CEO gets very _____ when the auditors pay us a visit.
7. I arrived at work at six in the morning and _____ the report immediately.
8. We're all _____ the Christmas season so nobody has any free time at all.

 **Talk Talk Talk**

(Melissa's office. Peter enters)	(Melissas Büro. Peter tritt ein)
P. Good morning, Melissa. Well, here is the **draft** of the press release.	P. Guten Morgen, Melissa. Tja, hier ist der **Entwurf** der Pressemitteilung.
M. My, Peter. That was quick. I didn't really expect it so soon.	M. Meine Güte, Peter. Das ging aber schnell. So früh hatte ich gar nicht damit gerechnet.
P. It will probably need **some work done on it**. You'll have to forgive my English.	P. Es wird wahrscheinlich **noch überarbeitet werden müssen**. Seien Sie nachsichtig mit meinem Englisch.
M. Don't be so modest, Peter. I haven't noticed any **failings** in your English. Let me see the draft …	M. Seien Sie nicht so bescheiden, Peter. Mir sind noch nie irgendwelche **Fehler** in Ihrem Englisch aufgefallen. Zeigen Sie mir mal den Entwurf …
British building society chooses American electronic security system …	**Britische Baugesellschaft entscheidet sich für Amerikanisches Sicherheitssystem …**
The Woking-based Surrey Building Society is **updating** its internet security with an American **electronic payment system**. The system, marketed in Britain by ERGO Limited, London, uses a fine mesh of technological checks **to safeguard** credit card and account details. The Surrey Building Society decided on the investment	Die Surrey Building Society aus Woking **verbessert** ihre Internet-Sicherheit mit einem amerikanischen **elektronischen Zahlungssystem**. Das System, das in England von ERGO Limited, London, vermarktet wird, benutzt ein ausgeklügeltes Netz aus technologischen Kontrollvorrichtungen, um Kreditkarten- und Abrechnungs-

following a series of reports of **internet thefts**. Hackers have managed **to tap into the account details** of several companies and individual clients. In one case, the credit card numbers of 5,000 clients of a Far Eastern bank were »stolen« by hackers. ERGO claims its **security system** protects **finance houses** from such abuses by a complicated architecture of **encoding and digital signatures**. The Surrey Building Society contract is the first of its kind in Britain, and ERGO describes it as an »**important breakthrough**«. The software will be demonstrated at the Electronics Fair at Earl's Court September 12-19, but in the meantime further details can be obtained from ERGO Limited, London.

daten **zu sichern**. Die Surrey Building Society entschied sich für diese Investition, nachdem eine Reihe von aufeinander folgenden **Internet-Diebstählen** bekannt wurden. Hacker hatten es dabei geschafft, **in die Konten** von diversen Firmen und deren privaten Kunden **einzudringen**. In einem Fall wurden die Kreditkartennummern von 5000 Kunden einer Bank im Fernen Osten von Hackern »gestohlen«. ERGO nimmt für sich in Anspruch, dass ihr **Sicherheitssystem Finanzgesellschaften** vor solchem Missbrauch durch ein kompliziertes System von **Codierungen und digitalen Unterschriften** schützt. Der Vertragsabschluss mit der Surrey Building Society ist der erste dieser Art in Großbritannien und ERGO bezeichnet ihn als »**wichtigen Durchbruch**«. Die Software wird vom 12. bis zum 19. September auf der »Electronics Fair« in Earls Court vorgestellt, aber in der Zwischenzeit sind weitere Informationen direkt von ERGO Limited, London, erhältlich.

Background Information

In the last section of the dialogue the press release mentions that ERGO Ltd have made an »**important breakthrough**«. A »**breakthrough**« is an important discovery that helps to solve a problem. Now look at some other expressions with »**break**«.

to break new ground	to do something new
to break even	to have one's losses balanced by one's gains
a break-down	a division of something into smaller parts
to break off	to stop talking
make or break	to cause either the complete success or ruin of a person or thing
a break-up	the coming to an end of a business or relationship
to break away	to separate from a group

 154. Train Yourself

Vervollständigen Sie die Sätze:

1. The financial collapse led to the ▓▓▓▓▓▓▓▓ of his business empire.
2. Five people ▓▓▓▓▓▓▓▓ from the company and set up their own business.
3. After the recent setbacks the most we can hope for this year is to ▓▓▓▓▓▓▓▓ .
4. The Marketing Manager ▓▓▓▓▓▓▓▓ the conversation to attend to a phone-call.
5. The company is ▓▓▓▓▓▓▓▓ by investing in the South American market.
6. This year is ▓▓▓▓▓▓▓▓ for MOSS Ltd. Either we see substantial improvements in the company's fortunes or everybody will be out of a job.
7. The new hardware equipment was hailed as a ▓▓▓▓▓▓▓▓ by the country's media.
8. Can I have a ▓▓▓▓▓▓▓▓ of the new sales figures?

 **Talk Talk Talk**

(Melissa's office)

M. I think that will do nicely, Peter. It reads very well. **Succinct and informative**.

P. Not **too succinct**?

M. Not at all. A press release should be as brief as possible, just long enough **to sum up** what you have to say and keep interest aroused. If more information is needed it's there for the asking.

P. So how do we **distribute** the release?

M. We have a **circulation list** of newspapers and **trade magazines**. Lucy faxes them with the release. Just give her the release. She knows what to do ...

L. Good morning, Peter. **You look busy, and you look as if you're about to give me some work.** So what can I do for you?

P. Lucy, this press release has to be sent out to the numbers on

(Melissas Büro)

M. Ich finde, das hört sich gut an, Peter. Es liest sich sehr gut. **Auf den Punkt gebracht und informativ**.

P. Nicht **zu knapp**?

M. Überhaupt nicht. Eine Pressemitteilung sollte so kurz wie möglich sein, gerade lang genug, um **aufzuführen**, was man zu sagen hat und das Interesse aufrechtzuerhalten. Wenn noch weitere Informationen gebraucht werden, kann ja noch nachgefragt werden.

P. Und wie **verteilen** wir jetzt die Pressemitteilung?

M. Wir haben eine **Verteilerliste** mit Zeitungen und **Fachmagazinen**. Lucy faxt sie mit der Pressemitteilung durch. Geben Sie ihr einfach den Pressetext. Sie weiß schon, was zu tun ist ...

L. Guten Morgen, Peter. **Sie sehen beschäftigt aus und so, als würden Sie Arbeit für mich haben.** Also, was kann ich für Sie tun?

P. Lucy, diese Pressemitteilung muss an die Faxnummern auf

your press circulation list. Could you manage it today?	Ihrem Presseverteiler geschickt werden. Schaffen Sie das heute noch?
L. Of course, Peter. Now, what about a nice cup of tea? I'm about to brew up. And I've brought some biscuits I made ...	L. Natürlich, Peter. Wie wäre es mit einer schönen Tasse Tee? Ich wollte gerade welchen kochen. Und ich habe ein paar selbstgemachte Kekse mitgebracht ...

Background Information

Lucy says that Peter **looks busy and looks as if he's about to give her some work to do**. »**Look**« here means the same as **to seem**, or **to appear**. E.g. »She looks tired«. Or »You look as though you're going to give me some work«.

»**To look like**« can also mean **to resemble**. E.g. »You look like your father«.

Let's examine some expressions with »**look**«.

to look forward to	to feel pleasure that something is going to happen (often used to end letters)
to take a look at	to examine
a look-in	a chance to do something or to succeed
to look the part	to have the appearance of being a particular kind of person
to look on the bright side	to be optimistic
look lively (colloquial)	to hurry
to look on	to consider
to look the other way	to pretend not to notice

155. Train Yourself

Vervollständigen Sie die Sätze mit oben stehenden Wendungen:

1. He bought a new suit in order to ▓▓▓▓▓▓▓▓▓▓▓ for his presentation to the Japanese visitors.
2. I asked my superiors to ▓▓▓▓▓▓▓▓▓▓▓ my new policy document.
3. Harry is popular with everybody in the department because he always ▓▓▓▓▓▓▓▓▓▓▓.
4. The Managing Director ▓▓▓▓▓▓▓▓▓▓▓ when certain malpractices came to light.
5. The company ▓▓▓▓▓▓▓▓▓▓▓ its Swansea operation as its most lucrative in the long-term.
6. ▓▓▓▓▓▓▓▓▓▓▓! We're going to miss the train!
7. I ▓▓▓▓▓▓▓▓▓▓▓ the meeting with Frank next Friday. It's going to be a success.
8. I will never get promoted. I just don't get ▓▓▓▓▓▓▓▓▓▓▓!

 Vocabulary

to announce s.o.'s participation	jds. Teilnahme ankündigen
branch	Zweigstelle
breakthrough	Durchbruch
to build up	aufbauen
circulation list	Presseverteiler
company profile	Entwurf
crestfallen	erschüttert
to dash around	sich kreuz und quer herumtreiben
to direct	anziehen, richten/lenken auf
draft	Entwurf
to draw up a presentation	eine Präsentation entwerfen
electronic payment system	elektronisches Zahlungssystem
failings	Fehler
for starters	für den Anfang
gathering	Treffen
hook	Aufhänger (auch fig.)

internet thefts	Internet-Diebstähle
to issue	herausgeben
keen competition	scharfe Konkurrenz
learning process	Lernprozess
marketing division	Marketingabteilung
penetration	Vordringen
press conference	Pressekonferenz
press release	Pressemitteilung
productive	produktiv
reception	Empfang
to report in on sth.	etw. melden
to run the office	das Büro leiten
safe and sound	heil
to safeguard	sichern
security system	Sicherheitssystem
to sit in a meeting	an einem Meeting teilnehmen
strategy	Strategie
succinct and informative	auf den Punkt gebracht und informativ
to sum up	zusammenfassen, hier: aufführen
to take over	übernehmen
to take sb. up	jdm. helfen, unter die Arme greifen
to take shape well	langsam Formen annehmen
to tap into	eindringen in
trade fair	(Handels-)Messe
upcoming	bevorstehend
to update	verbessern
to work together	zusammenarbeiten

Interview with the press
Interview mit der Presse

 Here we go

Peter steckt mitten in den Vorbereitungen für die Herbstmesse. Er hat schon eine Pressemitteilung veröffentlicht, die insbesondere bei Melissa auf große Zustimmung getroffen ist. Nun muss er auch persönliche Kontakte zur Presse aufnehmen und dem Reporter einer Computerzeitschrift Rede und Antwort stehen. Dieser interessiert sich sehr für die Arbeit von ERGO Limited, aber auch für Peters Lebenslauf, und er zeigt sich von Peters Leistungen sehr beeindruckt ...

 Talk Talk Talk

(Peter's office. Phone rings)

P. Brückner here. Yes, Lucy – please send him in ... Hello, Mr Tait. Please come in. Take a seat. Would you like tea or coffee?

T. No thank you, Mr Brückner – or should I call you Herr Brückner?

P. Good Lord no! I'm fully integrated now. I already feel very English.

T. May I make a note of that? You don't mind if I take notes?

(Peters Büro. Das Telefon klingelt)

P. Brückner am Apparat. Ja, Lucy – bitte schicken Sie ihn herein ... Hallo, Mr Tait. Kommen Sie doch herein. Nehmen Sie Platz. Möchten Sie gerne Tee oder Kaffee?

T. Nein, vielen Dank, Mr Brückner – oder soll ich Sie Herr Brückner nennen?

P. Guter Gott, nein! Ich habe mich bereits vollständig eingelebt. Ich fühle mich bereits wie ein Engländer.

T. Darf ich das notieren? Es macht Ihnen doch nichts aus, wenn ich Notizen mache?

P. Not at all. What would you like to know. **Fire away!**	P. Aber ganz und gar nicht. Was würden Sie denn gern wissen? **Schießen Sie los!**
T. How would you **assess the importance** for the new economy of this security system you are **marketing?**	T. Wie würden Sie **die Bedeutung** dieses von Ihnen **vermarkteten** Sicherheitssystems für die »New Economy« **einschätzen**?
P. **Internet fraud** is costing companies billions of dollars annually. If we can contribute to the international effort to combat this new kind of crime then I think **we are doing a great service**. Look at us, if you like, as a form of accident insurance. Our system **doesn't come cheap**, but it can **save the very existence** of a company.	P. **Internet-Betrügereien** kosten die Firmen jedes Jahr Milliarden von Dollars. Wenn wir es schaffen, etwas zum internationalen Kampf gegen diese neue Form des Verbrechens beizusteuern, dann glaube ich, **dass wir einen wichtigen Beitrag leisten**. Betrachten Sie uns, wenn Sie so wollen, als eine Art Unfallversicherung. Unser System **ist nicht gerade billig**, aber es kann für eine Firma **Existenz rettend** sein.
T. Can you explain that in a bit more detail?	T. Können Sie das etwas genauer erklären?
P. A Japanese bank discovered earlier this year that a **hacker** had managed to get into its **data system** and steal the **credit details** of thousands of its customers. **Credit card numbers** were among the stolen details. You can imagine the damage that caused to the bank, materially and also **in terms of** credibility. The bank nearly went bankrupt. With our system in place, that would not have happened.	P. Eine japanische Bank hat früher in diesem Jahr entdeckt, dass ein **Hacker** es geschafft hat, in ihre **Datenanlage** einzudringen und **Kreditinformationen** über Tausende ihrer Kunden zu stehlen. Zu den gestohlenen Daten gehörten auch **Kreditkartennummern**. Sie können sich vorstellen, was für einen Schaden die Bank dadurch erlitten hat – finanziell, aber auch **im Sinne der** Vertrauenswürdigkeit. Die Bank wäre beinahe bankrott

gegangen. Wäre unser System installiert gewesen, wäre so etwas niemals passiert.

Background Information

Peter tells Guy Tait **to fire away**, meaning to start asking questions. **To fire questions** at somebody is **to ask questions one after the other** (as in interviews for example). »**To fire**« also means **to dismiss somebody**. Let's look at some expressions with »**fire**«.

to be fired-up	to be excited
to set the world on fire	to have a great success
to get on like a house on fire	to enjoy someone's company very much
to play with fire	to take risks
a baptism of fire	a difficult introduction to something
in the firing line	a position where one is likely to receive punishment or come under attack
to have a few irons in the fire	to have many jobs, interests, or activities at the same time

156. Train Yourself

Verwenden Sie die oben stehenden Begriffe mit »fire« in der folgenden Übung:

1. Peter had a ▬▬▬▬▬▬▬▬▬▬▬▬▬▬ when he first came to England but he soon learnt the ropes.
2. At the press conference the business magnate told the journalists to ▬▬▬▬▬▬▬▬▬▬▬▬▬▬.
3. Some of the board thought that floating the company on the stock exchange was ▬▬▬▬▬▬▬▬▬▬▬▬▬▬.
4. In today's ever-changing job market it's good to have ▬▬▬▬▬▬▬▬▬▬▬▬▬▬.
5. Peter was incredibly ▬▬▬▬▬▬▬▬▬▬▬▬▬▬ when he heard about the recovery of his shares.

6. I met the new Logistics Director yesterday. We ▓▓▓▓▓▓ ▓▓▓▓▓▓▓▓▓▓▓▓▓▓▓▓▓▓▓▓▓▓ and I didn't leave until eight.
7. The company is in the ▓▓▓▓▓▓▓▓▓▓▓▓▓▓▓▓ over the enforced redundancies last week.
8. Tony's speech at the conference hardly ▓▓▓▓▓▓▓▓▓▓▓▓▓▓▓▓ ▓▓▓▓▓▓▓▓▓▓▓▓▓▓▓▓ but was well-received nevertheless.

Talk Talk Talk

(Peter's office)

T. The system itself is well explained and described in the material you sent me. I've asked our graphic designer **to do some illustrations** to accompany my article, and I'm sure you'll like them. We're doing **a double-page spread** on your system. I'm strictly on the **editorial side** of the magazine, so I am not supposed to mention the possibility of **advertising** with us. But I'm sure you'll be hearing from our **marketing people**. I've brought along a copy of the magazine.

P. I already know it. It's a good publication. What kind of **circulation**?

T. We sell about 120,000 and we have a very **broad reader-base**, from individual **PC-users** to

(Peters Büro)

T. Das System wird in dem Material, das Sie mir geschickt haben, gut erklärt und beschrieben. Ich habe unseren Grafik-Designer darum gebeten, **ein paar Illustrationen anzufertigen**, um meinen Artikel zu unterstützen und ich bin sicher, sie werden Ihnen gefallen. Wir werden einen **doppelseitigen Artikel** über Ihr System veröffentlichen. Ich gehöre ausschließlich der **redaktionellen Belegschaft** des Magazins an, also sollte ich nicht die Möglichkeit erwähnen, bei uns **Werbung** zu **schalten**. Aber ich bin sicher, dass Sie von unseren **Marketing-Leuten** hören werden. Ich habe Ihnen ein Exemplar des Magazins mitgebracht.

P. Ich kenne es bereits. Eine gute Zeitschrift. Wie hoch ist die **Auflage**?

T. Wir verkaufen etwa 120 000 Exemplare und wir haben eine sehr **breit gestreute Leserschicht**, von

Präsentationen

IT company chief executives.

P. I'll **hand** the magazine **over** to the head of our marketing division, Miss Walker. She'll probably want **to get in touch with you**. I think I can say we shall be looking at effective **publicity** for our product, and that will include **advertising**, of course.

T. From what I know, our **rates** are very **competitive**, and because you've been so co-operative and helpful I'm sure our marketing people will be able to make you an attractive offer. But, as I say, **that is out of my area**. But I would like to pass Miss Walker's name and contact details to our marketing people.

P. No problem. Here is her card ...

individuellen **PC-Benutzern** bis hin zu **Geschäftsführern der IT-Branche**.

P. Ich werde das Magazin an die Leiterin unserer Marketingabteilung, Miss Walker, **weiterleiten**. Sie wird wahrscheinlich **Kontakt zu Ihnen aufnehmen** wollen. Ich glaube sagen zu können, dass wir alle eine gute **Öffentlichkeitsarbeit** für unser Produkt anstreben und dass dazu natürlich auch **Anzeigen** gehören werden.

T. Soweit ich das weiß, sind unsere **Preise** sehr **konkurrenzfähig** und da Sie so kooperativ und hilfreich waren, bin ich sicher, dass unsere Marketing-Leute Ihnen ein sehr attraktives Angebot machen können. Aber, wie ich schon sagte, **das gehört nicht zu meinem Zuständigkeitsbereich**. Aber ich würde Miss Walkers Namen und ihre Kontaktinformationen gern an unsere Marketing-Leute weitergeben.

P. Kein Problem. Hier ist ihre Karte ...

Background Information

In this section of the dialogue Peter says that he intends to **hand** the magazine **over** to Miss Walker, meaning **to give her the responsibility or control of advertising in the magazine** but also **to**

433

give her the magazine itself. There are many expressions with »**hand**«, let's look at some of them.

to change hands	to change owners
to come in handy (colloquial)	to be useful
to have one's hands tied	to be unable to do something because of other responsibilities or duties
to have one's hands full	to be very busy
a show of hands	a vote in which each person shows his opinion by raising his hand
out of hand	out of control
a golden handshake	a large payment given to a person leaving a company
at first hand	directly through one's experience
to give somebody a hand	to help somebody
a free hand	freedom or permission to do what one wants
to have a hand in	to be concerned in something

 157. Train Yourself

Vervollständigen Sie die Sätze mit diesen Wendungen!

1. The meeting nearly got ▨▨▨▨▨ when Robert Kilbride suggested closing down the plant altogether.
2. The firm had ▨▨▨▨▨ several times before being taken over by Reynolds.
3. Francesca's knowledge of French ▨▨▨▨▨ when she was sent on a business trip to Paris.
4. The director believes in giving the creative team a ▨▨▨▨▨ in their department.
5. After thirty years with the firm Mark was given a ▨▨▨▨▨ of several thousand pounds.

6. After a ▓▓▓▓▓▓ the proposal was carried through by a vote of eight to two.
7. Peter! Can you ▓▓▓▓▓▓ me ▓▓▓▓▓▓ with this? I can't do it on my own.
   Sorry Steve, I've ▓▓▓▓▓▓ my ▓▓▓▓▓▓ at the moment.
8. It was believed that the CEO ▓▓▓▓▓▓ the decision to buy back the shares.
9. Management visited the factory to see ▓▓▓▓▓▓ what the problem was.
10. Melissa ▓▓▓▓▓▓ the project to Beryl when she was transferred to Scotland.
11. Because of the new Government guidelines the CEO's ▓▓▓▓▓▓ and he was unable to find a resolution to the matter.

Talk Talk Talk

(Peter's office)

T. Now, Mr Brückner, I would like to **incorporate** in my piece some biographical **information** about yourself. **Do you have** a CV **handy**?

P. Yes, of course. I'll ask our secretary **to dig it out** for you.

T. That will be useful. But allow me to ask you some personal questions. Your age?

P. 30, but sometimes I feel 50!

(Peters Büro)

T. Und jetzt, Mr Brückner, würde ich in meinen Artikel gern noch ein paar biografische **Informationen** über Sie selbst **einstreuen**. **Haben Sie** zufällig einen Lebenslauf **zur Hand**?

P. Ja, natürlich. Ich werde unsere Sekretärin bitten, einen für Sie **auszugraben**.

T. Das wäre sehr hilfreich. Aber erlauben Sie mir, Ihnen ein paar persönliche Fragen zu stellen. Wie alt sind Sie?

P. 30, aber manchmal fühle ich mich wie 50!

T. Living in London should make you feel ten years younger, not older!	T. Aber wenn Sie in London leben, sollten Sie sich doch zehn Jahre jünger fühlen und nicht älter!
P. Well, yes and no. It's a great city, of course, but very tiring to live and work in. You must know that.	P. Tja, ja und nein. Es ist natürlich eine großartige Stadt, aber es ist sehr anstrengend, hier zu leben und zu arbeiten. Das sollten Sie doch selber wissen.
T. I live outside, in the Sussex countryside. I have to **commute** to London, of course, but only four times a week. And when I'm out there in my home village I can really relax. Wouldn't you like to live in the country?	T. Ich lebe außerhalb, in der ländlichen Gegend um Sussex. Ich muss natürlich auch als **Pendler** nach London, aber nur viermal in der Woche. Und wenn ich dort draußen, in meinem Heimatstädtchen bin, kann ich mich hervorragend entspannen. Würden Sie nicht auch gern auf dem Land leben?
P. I'm from Hamburg, remember. I suppose I'm a city type. But London is not my favourite British city.	P. Ich komme aus Hamburg, vergessen Sie das nicht. Ich schätze, ich bin ein Stadtmensch. Aber London ist nicht meine bevorzugte britische Stadt.
T. Oh, what is?	T. Oh, welche denn?
P. I'd say that of all the cities I've seen so far – and I've been to a few – I like Edinburgh the best.	P. Ich würde sagen, dass mir von allen Städten, die ich bis jetzt gesehen habe – und ich habe schon einige gesehen – Edinburgh am besten gefallen hat.
T. That's interesting. Why Edinburgh?	T. Das ist ja interessant. Warum gerade Edinburgh?

P. There are many things about Edinburgh that remind me of Hamburg. It's a very northern city, with a northern feel about it. And there are other reasons, which I can't really talk about ...	P. Es gibt in Edinburgh eine Menge Dinge, die mich an Hamburg erinnern. Es ist eine sehr nordische Stadt, mit einem nördlichen Flair. Und es gibt noch andere Gründe, über die ich jetzt wirklich nicht reden kann ...

Background Information

Peter says he's going to ask his secretary to **dig out** his CV for Guy Tait, meaning **to look for and then find something**. We can also say to **dig up** information on something or somebody, which has a similar meaning of **retrieving or finding**. Let's look at some more expressions with »**dig**«. (Remember, the past tense of dig is **dug**.)

to dig one's own grave	to create a bad situation for oneself
to dig up the dirt on somebody	to find embarrassing facts about a person's life
to have a dig at somebody	to make a remark which is intended to embarrass or make fun of somebody
to dig one's heels in	to show great determination over something
to dig in	to start eating
to dig down deep	to give money
to give somebody a dig in the ribs	to push the side of the body with the elbow in order to get that person's attention

158. Train Yourself

Benutzen Sie diese »phrasal verbs« nun in der folgenden Übung!

1. At the staff Christmas dinner I had to ▒▒▒▒▒▒ Paul ▒▒▒▒▒▒ when he started talking about a sensitive issue.

2. The Press ▓▓▓▓▓▓▓▓▓▓▓▓ the CEO, forcing him to resign.
3. When Sarah announced she was leaving the firm everybody ▓▓▓▓▓▓▓▓▓▓▓▓ in order to buy her a going-away present.
4. What are these, Steve?
They're kippers! ▓▓▓▓▓▓▓▓▓▓▓▓!
5. When it came to asking for a rise, the Management ▓▓▓▓▓▓▓▓▓▓▓▓ and refused point-blank.
6. It took me ages to ▓▓▓▓▓▓▓▓▓▓▓▓ the information the Sales Director needed.
7. Why did Rupert lose his job?
Oh, he ▓▓▓▓▓▓▓▓▓▓▓▓ his ▓▓▓▓▓▓▓▓▓▓▓▓ by not reaching his quotas.
8. All the staff ▓▓▓▓▓▓▓▓▓▓▓▓ at Maureen when she came into work with a hangover.

 **Talk Talk Talk**

(Peter's office)

T. Now, tell me something about yourself. Hamburg-born?

P. I was born just outside, in a small town in Schleswig-Holstein, but I went to school and then to university in Hamburg.

T. And what did you study?

P. **Economics** and politics.

T. Economics I can understand. But politics?

P. Hamburg is a very political city. You can't grow up in or around

(Peters Büro)

T. Also, jetzt erzählen Sie mir etwas über sich selbst. Sind Sie in Hamburg geboren?

P. Ich bin ganz in der Nähe geboren, in einer kleinen Stadt in Schleswig-Holstein, aber ich bin in Hamburg zur Schule und später auf die Universität gegangen.

T. Und was haben Sie studiert?

P. **Wirtschaft** und Politik.

T. Wirtschaft kann ich noch verstehen. Aber Politik?

P. Hamburg ist eine sehr politische Stadt. Sie können gar nicht in oder

Hamburg without somehow getting involved in politics.	um Hamburg herum aufwachsen, ohne irgendwie mit Politik in Berührung zu kommen.
T. But you didn't choose a political career.	T. Aber Sie haben sich nicht dazu entschlossen, eine politische Karriere anzustreben.
P. Oh, no! I would not have made a good politician. Hamburg's also a great **trading centre**, as you must know. My father was in the **export-import business**, and I just followed him.	P. Oh, nein! Aus mir wäre kein guter Politiker geworden. Hamburg ist außerdem auch ein bedeutendes **Handelszentrum**, wie Sie wahrscheinlich wissen. Mein Vater war im **Export/Import-Geschäft** und ich bin einfach in seine Fußstapfen getreten.
T. And your excellent command of English?	T. Und ihr fabelhaftes Englisch?
P. It was my second language in school, and I continued to study it even at university. Then I spent a short break in America. And now here in London I've been able to perfect it – or at least perfect it as much as I shall ever be able to.	P. Es war meine erste Fremdsprache in der Schule und ich habe es sogar an der Universität weiter studiert. Dann verbrachte ich eine kurze Auszeit in Amerika. Und hier in London war ich jetzt in der Lage, es zu perfektionieren – oder es wenigstens so weit zu perfektionieren, wie es mir jemals möglich sein wird.
T. I must compliment you on your command of the language. You could write this piece yourself.	T. Ich muss Ihnen ein Kompliment für Ihr gutes Englisch machen. Sie könnten diesen Artikel auch selber schreiben.
P. Well, I did write the press release which you received.	P. Nun ja, ich habe die Pressemitteilung geschrieben, die Sie erhalten haben.

Präsentationen

T. Congratulations. It **caught my eye** ...

T. Meinen Glückwunsch. Sie **haben** damit **meine Aufmerksamkeit erregt** ...

Background Information

Guy Tait comments in this section of the dialogue that the press release had **caught his eye**, meaning it had **attracted his attention**. We have already looked at expressions with **hand** earlier in this chapter, now let's look at some with **eye**.

to see eye to eye	to be in agreement
to keep an eye on somebody or something	to watch carefully
to turn a blind eye	to take no notice of
to run an eye over	to look quickly at something
to look somebody straight in the eye	to look steadily at somebody without showing any emotion
to get one's eye in	to become skilful or experienced through practice
to set eyes on	to see (often for the first time)

159. Train Yourself

Vervollständigen Sie nun die Sätze mit diesen »phrasal verbs«.

1. The Assistant Director asked me to ▓▓▓▓▓▓▓▓ things while he was away on business.
2. The members of the board never ▓▓▓▓▓▓▓▓ on the long-term direction of the company which led to meetings often being prolonged for hours.
3. The first time I ▓▓▓▓▓▓▓▓ Melissa I knew she was perfect for the job.
4. It is often expedient to ▓▓▓▓▓▓▓▓ to certain work practices and therefore avoid confrontations.

5. Any new recruit to a company needs to ▓▓▓▓▓▓▓ his/her ▓▓▓▓▓▓▓ before any performance assessment can be given.
6. One feature of the new publicity campaign which really ▓▓▓▓▓▓▓ ▓▓▓▓▓▓▓ was the good use of computer-enhanced graphics.
7. The boss asked me to ▓▓▓▓▓▓▓ his presentation in order to check for any errors.
8. The junior staff member ▓▓▓▓▓▓▓ me ▓▓▓▓▓▓▓ and denied any involvement in the illegal downloading.

 Talk Talk Talk

T. Now, why did you decide to come to London? What are your plans here?

P. I wanted to **broaden** my **experience**, and London seemed the natural place to start. The company I worked for in Hamburg has contacts with ERGO Limited, and I was offered a position here as Assistant Managing Director.

T. And what are your duties?

P. Theoretically, I should be assisting and sometimes representing our Managing Director, but until now I have been busy **getting to know** the individual departments.

T. Will you be **specialising in any particular field**?

T. Und, warum haben Sie sich entschieden, nach London zu gehen? Was für Pläne haben Sie hier?

P. Ich wollte meinen **Erfahrungsschatz vergrößern** und London schien mir der geeignete Ort zu sein, um damit anzufangen. Die Firma, für die ich in Hamburg gearbeitet habe, hat Kontakte zu ERGO Limited und man hat mir hier den Posten als Assistant Managing Director angeboten.

T. Und was sind Ihre Aufgaben?

P. In der Theorie sollte ich unserem Managing Director assistieren und ihn gelegentlich repräsentieren, aber bis jetzt war ich damit beschäftigt, die einzelnen Abteilungen **kennen zu lernen**.

T. Werden Sie sich **auf einen bestimmten Bereich spezialisieren**?

P. It's too early to say. Marketing interests me a lot and that's the area I'm involved in right now, helping **to prepare for** our **participation in the trade fair.**

P. Es ist noch zu früh, um das zu sagen. Das Marketing interessiert mich sehr und es ist auch das Gebiet, mit dem ich im Augenblick beschäftigt bin, indem ich dabei helfe, unseren **Auftritt bei der Fachmesse vorzubereiten.**

T. We shall be **covering** the fair, of course, so we'll meet up again there.

T. Wir werden natürlich auch **über** die Messe **berichten**, also werden wir uns dort wiedersehen.

P. **You are very welcome to visit our stand.** And we shall be having a press conference and reception. You'll get an invitation, of course.

P. **Sie sind herzlich eingeladen, unseren Stand zu besuchen.** Und wir werden eine Pressekonferenz und einen Empfang abhalten. Sie bekommen natürlich eine Einladung.

T. I'll certainly look forward to that ...

T. Darauf freue ich mich schon ...

Background Information

»**Get**«, one of the most common words in English, has a whole range of meanings. In the dialogue Peter says that he is **getting to know** the various departments of ERGO Ltd, meaning he **is starting to know** them. One can also say that he is **getting to grips with** the departments. Let's look at some phrasal verbs with »**get**«, some of which you might have seen before, however revision is always useful for the language learner!

to get (a message) across — to communicate
to get round to — to find the time to do something
to get back to — to telephone later
to get down to (business) — to begin work

to get together	to meet each other
to get at	to mean (normally used in the continuous form i.e. getting)
to get by	to survive
to get on with someone	to co-exist, co-operate successfully
to get over	to recover from
to get through	to obtain a telephone connection

 160. Train Yourself

Füllen Sie die Lücken mit diesen Wendungen!

1. The new Sales Director is very easy ▬▬▬▬▬▬▬▬. He is always friendly to everybody.
2. Excuse me, but I don't understand. What exactly are you ▬▬▬▬▬▬▬▬?
3. Peter tried calling the office in Madrid several times but he couldn't ▬▬▬▬▬▬▬▬.
4. OK everybody, thanks for coming. Now, let's ▬▬▬▬▬▬▬▬ to business.
5. The board decided to ▬▬▬▬▬▬▬▬ next week to discuss the issue in more detail.
6. The CEO stressed the importance of ▬▬▬▬▬▬▬▬ the message ▬▬▬▬▬▬▬▬ clearly so as to avoid any misunderstandings.
7. During a recession it is often very difficult for small businesses to ▬▬▬▬▬▬▬▬.
8. It took me three days to ▬▬▬▬▬▬▬▬ to dealing with the matter.
9. It may take many months for the company to ▬▬▬▬▬▬▬▬ its current difficulties.
10. Sorry, he's in the middle of a meeting right now. He says he'll ▬▬▬▬▬▬▬▬ to you later.

 **Talk Talk Talk**

(Peter's office. Melissa enters)

M. Well, Peter. How did the interview go?

P. I think it went all right. I'm a bit **concerned** that the reporter might have concentrated too much on me and not paid enough attention to ERGO.

M. You're something of an exotic figure in this business, remember. A German **holding down a job** at the head of an **expanding company** in Britain. I suppose it's natural that he was **inquisitive**.

P. Well, I just hope I acquitted myself well.

M. I'm sure you did. There's a saying, you know: Any publicity is good publicity! I'm really pleased that your press release has already **attracted attention**.

P. *Our* press release, Melissa!

M. Let's not argue over that. I have another important **task** for you.

(Peters Büro. Melissa tritt ein)

M. Nun, Peter. Wie lief das Interview?

P. Ich glaube, es lief ganz gut. Ich mache mir nur etwas **Sorgen**, dass sich der Reporter vielleicht zu sehr auf mich konzentriert hat und ERGO dafür nicht genug Aufmerksamkeit gewidmet hat.

M. Vergessen Sie nicht, Sie sind in diesem Geschäft so etwas wie eine exotische Figur. Ein Deutscher, der **einen Job** in der Führungsspitze einer **expandierenden Firma** in England **hat**. Ich schätze, es ist nur normal, dass er **nachgebohrt** hat.

P. Tja, ich hoffe, ich habe mich gut aus der Affäre gezogen.

M. Da bin ich sicher. Sie wissen ja, wie man sagt: Jede Publicity ist gute Publicity! Ich bin wirklich froh, dass Ihre Pressemitteilung schon **Aufmerksamkeit erregt** hat.

P. *Unsere* Pressemitteilung, Melissa!

M. Streiten wir uns nicht deswegen. Ich habe noch eine wichtige **Aufgabe** für Sie.

P. Anything you say!	P. Was immer Sie sagen!
M. We have to prepare for the press conference and reception. James agrees it makes sense to hold it just before the fair opens.	M. Wir müssen die Pressekonferenz und den Empfang vorbereiten. James stimmt damit überein, dass es Sinn macht, beides noch vor der Messe abzuhalten.
P. How can I help?	P. Wie kann ich dabei helfen?
M. I'd like your **input**. We'll **call Beryl in for a meeting** and **thrash out** some ideas between us. Wait, I've got a better idea. It's nearly lunch-time. We'll have lunch together and have a brain-storming session over a plate of pasta …	M. Ich hätte gern Ihre **Anregungen** dazu. Wir werden Beryl **zu einem Meeting dazu rufen** und zwischen uns ein paar spontane Ideen **austauschen**. Warten Sie, ich habe eine bessere Idee. Es ist fast Mittagszeit. Wir gehen zusammen Essen und halten unser »Brainstorming« über einem Teller mit Pasta ab …

Background Information

Melissa says that she'll call Beryl and **thrash out** some ideas. »To thrash out« something is **to discuss it in detail until a solution is found**. Below are some expressions with »out«.

out of the blue	unexpectedly
out of date	old-fashioned
out of one's depth	in a situation which one can't understand or control because of a lack of knowledge or experience
to go all out	to attempt to do something with the greatest possible effort
out of the question	impossible, not to be considered
on the way out	to leave employment after having been dismissed
out in the cold	not included

Präsentationen

161. Train Yourself

Verwenden Sie diese Begriffe in den folgenden Sätzen!

1. Workers were left ▓▓▓▓▓▓▓▓ in the recent negotiations with management over wage freezes.
2. Did you hear that Davis is ▓▓▓▓▓▓▓▓ his ▓▓▓▓▓▓▓▓? He's leaving at the end of the week.
3. Management ▓▓▓▓▓▓▓▓ the details of the new policy statement for three hours before reaching agreement.
4. A staff retraining programme was thought necessary so that nobody would feel ▓▓▓▓▓▓▓▓ their ▓▓▓▓▓▓▓▓.
5. The recent deregulation of the markets within the European Union has inspired everybody to ▓▓▓▓▓▓▓▓ to increase exports.
6. The equipment in the office is totally ▓▓▓▓▓▓▓▓ and in need of replacement.
7. The idea of bringing down prices is ▓▓▓▓▓▓▓▓. The company wouldn't be able to break even.
8. ▓▓▓▓▓▓▓▓ the company announced an economy drive, resulting in protestations from workers.

Talk Talk Talk

(In the restaurant)

M. Right, now **down to business**. Any idea from you two on how to organise this press conference?

B. Where are we holding it?

M. I originally thought of the Press Club, but the **facilities** there aren't that good. I'd like to combine it with a bit of catering – some drinks and snacks.

(Im Restaurant)

M. Gut, **kommen wir zum Geschäftlichen**. Hat einer von euch beiden eine Idee, wie wir diese Pressekonferenz organisieren?

B. Wo halten wir sie denn ab?

M. Ich hatte zuerst an den Presse-Club gedacht, aber die **Räumlichkeiten** dort sind nicht so besonders. Ich würde das Ganze gern mit einem kleinen Imbiss verbin-

B. The best way into a reporter's **notebook** is through his stomach!

M. You're so right. That's my experience, too.

P. But that **smacks of bribery**!

M. Oh, Peter, you can't be serious. At least, you have **disqualified** yourself from organising the catering! Beryl, that's your area.

B. No problem. **What's my budget?**

M. I'll work that out later, at the office.

P. So what shall I do?

M. I'd like you to **direct the press conference** itself. A small **welcome address** and then **chair** the **question-and-answer session**. I'll see to the invitations.

P. But I've never chaired a press conference.

den – etwas zu trinken und ein paar Snacks.

B. Der beste Weg zum **Notizbuch** eines Reporters führt durch seinen Magen!

M. Da haben Sie völlig Recht. Genau das ist auch meine Erfahrung.

P. Aber das **klingt nach Bestechung**!

M. Oh, Peter, das kann nicht Ihr Ernst sein. Damit haben Sie sich zumindest von der Organisation des Imbisses **disqualifiziert**! Beryl, das ist Ihre Aufgabe.

B. Kein Problem. **Wie hoch ist mein Budget?**

M. Das klären wir später, im Büro.

P. Und was soll ich dann tun?

M. Ich hätte gern, dass Sie die **Pressekonferenz** selbst **leiten**. Eine kleine **Begrüßungsansprache**, dann werden Sie die **Fragestunde halten**. Ich kümmere mich um die Einladungen.

P. Aber ich habe noch nie eine Pressekonferenz geleitet.

Präsentationen

447

M. There's always a first time, Peter. Just give it some of your German **authority** – they'll be eating out of your hand!

M. Es gibt immer ein erstes Mal, Peter. Verleihen Sie dem Ganzen einfach etwas von Ihrer deutschen **Autorität** – und sie werden Ihnen aus der Hand fressen!

Background Information

Melissa begins the discussion about the forthcoming press conference by declaring, «Right, now, **down to business**« In other words, «**let's begin talking about the subject at hand**«. There are various other expressions with the word »**business**«. Let's look at some.

to be in business	to have something to do or work on after a period of activity
to be out of business	when a company closes
to go about one's business	to take care of one's affairs or work
to mean business	to be serious in one's intentions
to mind one's business	to carry on with one's affairs and not be concerned with those of other people
to have no business	to have no right to do or be doing something
like nobody's business	(colloquial) very fast or very much

162. Train Yourself

Füllen Sie die Lücken mit diesen «phrasal verbs».

1. He works ▮▮▮▮▮▮▮▮▮▮▮▮! He finished the report two days before the deadline.
2. When I rang the number listed in the phone book I found out the company had been ▮▮▮▮▮▮▮▮▮▮▮▮ for a long time and the premises now housed a nightclub!
3. When I asked why Peter had been promoted ahead of me I was told to ▮▮▮▮▮▮▮▮▮▮▮▮ my ▮▮▮▮▮▮▮▮▮▮▮▮ .

4. OK. Has everybody got a drink? Right, let's get ▮.
5. You ▮ looking in my personal file while I'm out the office!
6. Jonathan is a pleasure to work with. He always ▮ his ▮ with a smile on his face.
7. When the lease was renewed we knew we were back ▮ ▮.
8. The new Managing Director is totally dedicated to the job. You can tell he ▮.

 **Talk Talk Talk**

(Peter's office. Beryl enters)

P. You know, Beryl, I **haven't the foggiest idea** how to go about organizing this press conference thing.

B. Just leave it to Melissa.

P. I can't. She'll think I'm an idiot.

B. So what's troubling you?

P. I don't think I'm very good at **public speaking**. I've never really tried.

B. So how do you know you can't do it. And it's not as if you're making a speech. Leave that to James.

(Peters Büro. Beryl tritt ein)

P. Wissen Sie, Beryl, ich habe **nicht die geringste Ahnung,** wie ich es anfangen soll, diese Pressekonferenz zu organisieren.

B. Überlassen Sie es einfach Melissa.

P. Das kann ich nicht. Sie wird mich für einen Idioten halten.

B. Was bereitet Ihnen denn Kopfzerbrechen?

P. Ich glaube, ich kann nicht besonders gut **vor Publikum sprechen**. Ich habe es noch nie wirklich versucht.

B. Woher wollen Sie dann wissen, dass Sie es nicht können? Und es ist ja nicht so, als ob Sie eine Rede halten müssten. Überlassen Sie das James.

P. Can't you give me some tips?

B. First things first: **establish your authority**. Be polite, welcoming, but make clear you're **in charge**. I've seen press conferences fall apart in chaos because they weren't conducted **properly**. Some just ended up in shouting matches.

P. So how do I avoid that?

B. Give as many people as possible the opportunity to put their questions. **Identify the questioner** by pointing at her or him, and then have the questioner identify himself or herself. Restrict questions to one per person, unless there's room and time for more. And be firm when **closing the conference**. Make clear that only one or two more questions can be taken, and stick to that.

P. Beryl, how did you **come by** so much inside **information**?

B. Didn't Melissa tell you? I used to be a reporter on the South Downs Gazette …

P. Können Sie mir nicht ein paar Tipps geben?

B. Immer eins nach dem anderen: **Sichern Sie sich Ihre Autorität**. Seien Sie freundlich, einladend, aber machen Sie deutlich, dass Sie **die Verantwortung tragen**. Ich habe schon Pressekonferenzen gesehen, die im Chaos versunken sind, weil sie nicht **angemessen** geführt wurden. Einige endeten damit, dass man sich gegenseitig anbrüllte.

P. Und wie verhindere ich das?

B. Geben Sie so vielen Anwesenden wie möglich die Gelegenheit, ihre Fragen zu stellen. **Identifizieren Sie die Fragesteller**, indem Sie auf ihn oder sie zeigen und dann sorgen Sie dafür, dass der Fragensteller sich selbst identifiziert. Lassen Sie jeden nur eine Frage stellen, es sei denn, es gibt genügend Zeit für mehrere. Und seien Sie entschlossen, wenn es darum geht, **die Pressekonferenz zu beenden**. Machen Sie deutlich, dass nur noch ein oder zwei Fragen gestellt werden können und halten Sie sich auch daran.

P. Beryl, woher **wissen** Sie nur so viel **darüber**?

B. Hat Melissa es Ihnen nie gesagt? Ich war früher Reporterin bei der South Downs Gazette …

Background Information

Peter tells Beryl he hasn't got **the foggiest idea** how to organise the press conference, meaning he **doesn't know how to.** »**Not having the foggiest idea**« is colloquial; another similar expression is »**I don't have a clue**«.

Note: Beryl consoles Peter by telling him that at least he doesn't have to **make a speech.** We say »**make a speech**« rather than »**do a speech**«.

163. Train Yourself

Im ersten Teil des Buches wurden schon einmal Wendungen mit den Verben »do« oder »make« vorgestellt. Füllen Sie nun als kleine Wiederholung die Lücken mit dem richtigen der beiden Verben!

1. The business was so run down that nobody expected her to ▬▬▬▬▬▬▬▬ a success of it.
2. I went to the bank and ▬▬▬▬▬▬▬▬ out a cheque to Williams and Sons.
3. We ▬▬▬▬▬▬▬▬ a slight profit on the sale of the property.
4. How long have you been ▬▬▬▬▬▬▬▬ business with this firm?
5. Can you ▬▬▬▬▬▬▬▬ me a favour? Call Whitbreads and ask them if we can postpone the meeting until tomorrow.
6. We could ▬▬▬▬▬▬▬▬ with some more computers in this office.
7. Not much progress has been ▬▬▬▬▬▬▬▬ with the merger proposals.
8. I would like to ▬▬▬▬▬▬▬▬ a complaint about the merchandise that I bought in your shop last week.
9. We had to ▬▬▬▬▬▬▬▬ away with the old premises after cracks appeared in the ceiling.
10. Presentation can ▬▬▬▬▬▬▬▬ all the difference when launching a new product.

 **Talk Talk Talk**

(James Morgan's office. Peter enters)

J. Come in, Peter. Come in! Melissa tells me that you and Beryl are **shaping up well** in the preparations for the press presentation and the trade fair.

P. I must say Beryl has helped me **tremendously**.

J. She's a good girl, a great **asset** to the company. I'm very glad to have her on board. In fact, I reckon we make a good team, with your good self an essential part of it.

P. Thank you, James. I try my best – but sometimes I have my doubts. I hope I can manage this press conference. It's **new territory** for me.

J. Where are you **holding** it?

P. Melissa wants to hold it at the Landseer Hotel. The Landseer is a leader in hi-tech hotel installations. All rooms have **internet access**. The conference room is apparently the last word in **state-of-the-art**

(James Morgans Büro. Peter tritt ein)

J. Kommen Sie herein, Peter. Kommen Sie herein! Melissa hat mir gesagt, dass Sie mit den Vorbereitungen für die Pressepräsentation und die Messe **gut vorankommen**.

P. Ich muss sagen, dass Beryl eine **gewaltige** Hilfe war.

J. Sie ist ein gutes Mädchen, eine große **Bereicherung** für die Firma. Ich bin sehr froh, das sie bei uns ist. Ich glaube, dass wir ein gutes Team abgeben, wobei Sie ein wichtiger Teil davon sind.

P. Vielen Dank, James. Ich versuche mein Bestes – aber manchmal habe ich so meine Zweifel. Ich hoffe, dass ich mit dieser Pressekonferenz klar komme. Das ist **völliges Neuland** für mich.

J. Wo **halten** Sie sie denn **ab**?

P. Melissa möchte sie im Landseer Hotel abhalten. Das Landseer ist mit seinen Hightech-Installationen führend. Alle Zimmer haben **Internet-Anschluss**. Der Konferenzraum ist offensichtlich der letzte

technology. And they are renowned for their cuisine.	Schrei in Sachen **modernster** Technologie. Und sie sind bekannt für ihre Küche.
J. Don't you go spoiling those hacks – bread and cheese and a couple of beers is too much for them!	J. Verwöhnen Sie diese kleinkarierten Journalisten nicht – Brot, Käse und ein paar Bier sind schon zu viel für die!
P. Beryl has more than that in mind. But her catering plan is well within the budget.	P. Beryl hat da etwas mehr im Sinn. Aber ihr Verpflegungsplan ist noch innerhalb des Budgets.
J. Glad to hear it. We've **made some money on** these last few **deals**, but let's not forget the **housekeeping bills**.	J. Freut mich, das zu hören. Wir haben **mit den** letzten **Geschäftsabschlüssen** zwar **etwas Geld verdient**, aber vergessen wir nicht die **Haushaltsrechnungen**.
P. I think you'll find both Melissa and Beryl are very good **housekeepers**!	P. Ich glaube, Sie werden feststellen, dass Melissa und Beryl sehr gute **Haushälterinnen** sind!

Background Information

The ERGO press conference is **to be held** at the Landseer Hotel. If you **hold an event**, you organize it and carry it through.

164. Train Yourself

Finden Sie die korrekten Verben, um folgende Veranstaltungen »abzuhalten«:

1. an art exhibition   ....
2. an opera   ....
3. a football match   ....

4. a lecture ....
5. a wedding ....
6. a cocktail party ....
7. a film ....
8. a report ....

stage, mount, show, give, play, present, hold.

 Vocabulary

to advertise	Werbung schalten
advertising	Werbung, Anzeigen
to assess the importance	die Bedeutung einschätzen
asset	Bereicherung
to be in charge of sth.	die Verantwortung über etw. haben
to be inquisitive	nachbohren
bribery	Bestechung
to broaden	erweitern, vergrößern
to catch one's eye	jds. Aufmerksamkeit erregen
to chair	leiten, den Vorsitz führen
chief executive	Geschäftsführer
circulation	Auflage
come by information	etw. wissen über
to commute	pendeln
competitive	konkurrenzfähig
to cover sth.	hier: berichten über
credit details	Kreditinformationen
data system	Datenanlage
deal	Geschäftsabschluss
to direct sth.	etw. leiten
double-page spread	doppelseitiger Artikel
down to business	zum Geschäftlichen kommen
editorial	redaktionell
expanding company	expandierende Firma
to get in touch with sb.	Kontakt aufnehmen zu jdm.
to get to know	kennen lernen
hack	kleinkarierter Journalist

Präsentationen

hacker	(Computer-)Hacker
to hand over	weiterleiten
to have handy	zur Hand haben
to have not the foggiest idea	nicht die geringste Ahnung haben
to hold	abhalten, z. B. Konferenz
to hold down sth.	etw. innehaben, z. B. einen Job
housekeeping bill	Haushaltsrechnung
to incorporate information	Informationen einstreuen
input	Anregungen
in terms of	im Sinne von
internet access	Internet-Anschluss
internet fraud	Internet-Betrug
to make some money on	etw. Geld verdienen mit
marketing	vermarkten
marketing people	Marketing-Leute
public speaking	Sprechen vor Publikum
publicity	Öffentlichkeitsarbeit
question-and-answer session	Fragestunde
reader-base	Leserschicht
to shape up well	gut vorankommen
to specialise in a particular field	sich auf einen bestimmten Bereich spezialisieren
stand	(Messe-)Stand
state-of-the-art	hochmodern / Stand der Technik
That is out of my area.	Das gehört nicht zu meinem Zuständigkeitsbereich.
trading centre	Handelszentrum
to thrash out sth.	etw. gründlich diskutieren, hier: (Ideen) austauschen
welcome address	Begrüßungsansprache

Press conference
Pressekonferenz

 Here we go

Da Peter bisher, was Kontakte mit der Presse anbelangt, bestens zurechtkam, bekommt er nun von seinem Vorgesetzten, James Morgan, seine bisher schwierigste Aufgabe hinsichtlich der bevorstehenden Messe übertragen. Er soll eine Pressekonferenz leiten und vor einer ganzen Gruppe von Reportern ERGO Limited vertreten. Peter hat Bedenken, insbesondere weil er befürchtet, dass seine Sprachkenntnisse einer solchen Herausforderung nicht gewachsen sein könnten. Doch Mr Morgan und Melissa haben an Peters Fähigkeiten überhaupt keine Zweifel und so nimmt er auch dieses Problem in Angriff.

 Talk Talk Talk

(Hotel. Manager's office) (Büro des Hoteldirektors)

Hotel Manager Tim Ewing:
Please come in, and do tell me how we can help with the **function** you have in mind.

Hoteldirektor Tim Ewing:
Bitte kommen Sie doch herein und sagen Sie mir, wie ich Ihnen bei dem **Vorhaben** helfen kann, das Ihnen vorschwebt.

M. These are my colleagues, Peter Brückner and Beryl Platt.

M. Dies hier sind meine Kollegen, Peter Brückner und Beryl Platt.

E. Delighted to meet you!

E. Sehr erfreut, Sie kennen zu lernen!

M. We would like to hire your **function room** for a press conference, and also **arrange for a light buffet** with drinks.

M. Wir würden Ihren **Mehrzweckraum** gerne für eine Pressekonferenz buchen und außerdem einen **kleinen Imbiss** mit Getränken **bestellen**.

Präsentationen

E. What date do you have in mind?

M. We thought the 30th, if that suits you.

E. Let me look at my calendar. Yes, that day is free. You can have the conference room up until six in the evening, when we need it for a reception.

M. That's fine. We thought of having the press conference in the late morning. We can then **precede it** or **follow it** with drinks and snacks.

E. I'll **put** you **in touch** with our Food and Beverage Manager, who will advise you **on that score**.

M. That's your area, Beryl. Peter, I'll leave you to make final arrangements with Mr Ewing. I have to return to the office ...

E. Und welches Datum schwebt Ihnen da vor?

M. Wir dachten an den 30., wenn das für Sie machbar ist.

E. Lassen Sie mich kurz in meinen Kalender schauen. Ja, der Tag ist noch frei. Sie können den Konferenzraum bis sechs Uhr abends haben, danach brauchen wir ihn für einen Empfang.

M. Das passt sehr gut. Wir hatten geplant, die Pressekonferenz am späten Vormittag abzuhalten. Wir können den Imbiss und die Getränke dann entweder **vorher** oder **nachher** servieren lassen.

E. Ich werde Sie an unseren Bewirtungs-Manager **weiterleiten**, der Ihnen **diesbezüglich** behilflich sein kann.

M. Das ist Ihr Bereich, Beryl. Peter, ich lasse Sie hier, damit sie die restlichen Fragen mit Mr Ewing regeln können. Ich muss zurück ins Büro ...

Background Information

Tim Ewing promises **to put** Melissa **in touch** with the Food and Beverage Manager at the hotel. In other words he will **arrange communication** between them. Some more expressions with »**touch**« are listed below.

the common touch	the ability to act or talk on the level of ordinary people
in touch	having seen someone recently or having recent news or information (about a person, subject, etc.)
to lose touch	to be no longer regularly informed about somebody or something
touch and go	a very risky and uncertain situation
to lose one's touch	to lose one's usual skill
a soft touch	(colloquial) a person from whom it is easy to get what one wants
touch wood	(colloquial) an expression of hope that the good fortune one has just mentioned will continue. The speaker often touches an article made of wood for luck.

 165. Train Yourself

Verwenden Sie die Begriffe in der folgenden Übung.

1. I read the Financial Times every morning so that I don't _____ with the world of finance.
2. No decision has been made and so it's very _____ whether the project will get off the ground.
3. The company needed more office space and so Williams _____ them _____ with a building contractor he knew.
4. Well, _____ this time next year profits will have risen even more.
5. A successful salesperson needs to have the _____ when dealing with the general public.
6. Even though my ex-colleague is now working in Japan we still keep _____ regularly by e-mail.
7. Tony was a _____ when it came to lending people money.

8. Having not chaired a press conference for many years I was delighted when I made a success of it. I haven't ▓▓▓▓▓▓▓▓▓▓ my ▓▓▓▓▓▓▓▓▓▓.

 **Talk Talk Talk**

(Melissa's office. Peter enters)

M. **All settled**? Are we **ready for kick-off**?

P. I've arranged as much as I can. We have the conference room from 11 AM until 1 PM on the 30th. It holds up to fifty people so there should be plenty of room. There's a video-recorder and large TV screen, so we can show the company video.

M. Sounds fine. Now, what has Beryl achieved? I'll call her in …

B. Melissa?

M. **How are the** catering **arrangements coming along**?

B. I've arranged for soft drinks and water to be on the tables for the start of the press conference and then **at the close** we'll serve wine and canapes.

M. That sounds a good idea. I've been to conferences which have

(Melissas Büro. Peter tritt ein)

M. **Alles bereit**? Können wir jetzt **durchstarten**?

P. Ich habe geregelt, was ich konnte. Wir haben den Konferenzraum am 30., von 11 bis 13 Uhr. Er fasst bis zu 50 Leute, also sollten wir genügend Platz haben. Es gibt einen Videorekorder und einen großen Fernseher, also können wir das Firmenvideo vorführen.

M. Hört sich gut an. Und, was hat Beryl erreicht? Ich rufe sie herein …

B. Melissa?

M. **Was macht die Planung** der Bewirtung?

B. Ich habe dafür gesorgt, dass zum Beginn der Konferenz alkoholfreie Getränke und Wasser auf den Tischen stehen, **nach dem Ende** der Konferenz werden wir dann Wein und Kanapees servieren.

M. Das hört sich nach einer guten Idee an. Ich habe schon Presse-

developed into drunken parties because alcohol has been served **from the start**.	konferenzen erlebt, die zu Zechgelagen wurden, weil schon **vor Beginn** Alkohol serviert wurde.
P. I'll get about sending the invitations, then, should I?	P. Ich werde dann beginnen, die Einladungen abzuschicken, in Ordnung?
M. Yes, fine, you know Lucy has the **press distribution list**. She'll do it for you.	M. Ja, sehr gut, sie wissen ja, dass Lucy die **Verteilerliste für die Presse** hat. Sie wird das für Sie übernehmen.
P. Dear Lucy. I don't know what I'd do without her.	P. Die gute Lucy. Ich weiß gar nicht, was ich ohne sie tun würde.
M. Nor do I.	M. Genau so wenig wie ich.
P. Frankly, Melissa, I don't know what I shall do without you, either.	P. Ehrlich gesagt, Melissa, ich weiß auch nicht, was ich ohne *Sie* tun würde.
M. Now let's not get sentimental. **Down to work** ...	M. Nun lassen Sie uns nicht sentimental werden. Zurück **an die Arbeit** ...

Background Information

Melissa asks Beryl how the catering arrangements are **coming along**, in other words **how they are progressing**. We use this expression in the continuous form, (we can't say »It comes along fine, for example«). There are many expressions with »**come**«, some of them are listed below.

to come a cropper	to suffer failure or sudden misfortune
to come to nothing	to have no result

to come up in the world	to improve one's social rank, job or wealth
to come up roses	when something has a satisfactory ending
to come to a head	to reach the most important stage or part
to come to terms with	to accept that a state of affairs or difficulty is unavoidable and to deal with it rationally
come and go	to pass or disappear quickly
to come full circle	to return to the position where one started
to come to light	to be known by everyone

 166. Train Yourself

Verwenden Sie die »come«-Ausdrücke in der folgenden Übung!

1. The members of the board discussed the issue but couldn't decide on an appropriate course of action and so all their efforts _____.
2. The business world is slowly _____ with the impact of digital technology.
3. Despite Peter's misgivings about organizing the press conference, in the end everything _____.
4. Since arriving at the company in 1991 as a clerical officer, Trevor has really _____ and is now Human Resources Director.
5. Peter nearly _____ when he couldn't find his notes for his speech. Fortunately they were in the back seat of his car.
6. It has _____ that there are certain design faults in the new product.
7. Everything _____ when after weeks of rumours, Tom announced his departure for a rival company, causing commotion in the office.

8. Trends ▓▓▓▓▓▓▓▓▓▓▓▓▓▓▓▓▓▓ but there is no substitute for quality and reliability.
9. The company realised that after the recent slump everything had ▓▓▓▓▓▓▓▓▓▓▓▓▓▓▓▓▓ and profits were identical to the previous year.
10. The manager called me into her office to ask me how the report was ▓▓▓▓▓▓▓▓▓▓▓▓▓▓ .

 Talk Talk Talk

(Peter's office. James Morgan enters)

J. Good morning, Peter. How are the press conference arrangements coming along?

P. Fine, James. I think we're **up-to-date with everything** – thanks to Melissa and Beryl.

J. And the trade fair planning?

P. Melissa's **handling that**. She says you will be **addressing a seminar on** the »new economy« and the challenges it presents for companies like ERGO.

J. That's just what I want to talk to you about, Peter. It looks as if I won't be able to make it. My niece is marrying in Los Angeles on the very day of the seminar. It looks as if you will have to **spring in** in my place.

(Peters Büro. James Morgan tritt ein)

J. Guten Morgen, Peter. Was machen die Vorbereitungen für die Pressekonferenz?

P. Alles läuft hervorragend. Ich glaube, wir haben **alles so weit geregelt** – dank Melissa und Beryl.

J. Und die Planung der Verkaufsmesse?

P. **Darum kümmert** sich Melissa. Sie sagt, Sie würden **vor einem Seminar einen Vortrag über** »New Economy« **halten** – und welche Herausforderungen damit für Firmen wie ERGO verbunden sind.

J. Genau darüber wollte ich mit Ihnen sprechen, Peter. Es sieht aus, als würde ich das nicht schaffen können. Meine Nichte in Los Angeles heiratet genau am Tag des Seminars. Es sieht aus, als würden Sie an meiner Stelle **einspringen** müssen.

P. Me?	P. Ich?
J. I've no-one else, Peter. You are my assistant, you know.	J. Ich habe sonst niemanden, Peter. Sie sind schließlich mein Assistent.
P. But I've no experience at all of public speaking. And I know next to nothing on the **so-called** »new economy«.	P. Aber ich habe überhaupt keine Erfahrungen mit öffentlichen Reden. Und ich weiß über diese **so genannte** »New Economy« so gut wie gar nichts.
J. You can get all you need to know of the internet. And as for public speaking, Melissa tells me you can **present a case** very well.	J. Sie finden alles, was Sie darüber wissen müssen im Internet. Und was das Reden vor anderen angeht – Melissa hat mir erzählt, dass Sie sehr überzeugend **für eine Sache sprechen** können.
P. But not in front of a seminar audience. Impossible!	P. Aber doch nicht vor einem Seminar. Unmöglich!
J. You know what ERGO's company motto is? We make the impossible possible! It's **over to you**, Peter. Come on, don't look so down – let me invite you to lunch and we'll **talk it through** over some of Mario's pasta ...	J. Sie wissen doch, was das Motto von ERGO ist? Wir machen das Unmögliche möglich! Jetzt **liegt es an Ihnen**, Peter! Kommen Sie, schauen Sie nicht so zerknirscht – ich lade Sie zum Mittagessen ein und dann **reden** wir bei Marios Pasta **darüber** ...

Background Information

James Morgan invites Peter to a pasta restaurant **to talk through** his forthcoming seminar. »**To talk through something**« means **to discuss a subject in detail** often with an objective in mind, (in Peter's case his seminar). Below are some more expressions with »**talk**«.

to talk shop	to talk about your job with your colleagues while outside of work
to make small talk	to make polite conversation about unimportant matters
talk of the devil!	used when a person who has not been present suddenly arrives among a group of people who have just been talking about him/her.
the talk of the town	the subject of everybody's conversation
to talk down to	to speak to somebody in a superior manner
to talk round	to persuade somebody to do something
a talking-to	a severe talking-to with somebody who has done something wrong

 167. Train Yourself

Vervollständigen Sie die Sätze!

1. After working all day I often find it tedious when people insist on ▨▨▨.
2. We managed to ▨▨▨ Tom ▨▨▨ into staying with the firm after we agreed to some of his demands.
3. How was lunch with the members yesterday?
   Oh you know, the usual ▨▨▨. Nothing of any importance was discussed.
4. I gave that new temp a real ▨▨▨ yesterday. I can't bear staff coming in late.
5. Did you hear Peter got lost on his way to the conference? Oh! ▨▨▨ . Here he is now!
6. Our share of the domestic market is ▨▨▨ We've left our competitors way behind.
7. One thing that drives me mad is when management ▨▨▨ ▨▨▨ me. I hate to be patronised.

8. How are you feeling about your transfer to Brighton?
   Oh, much better, I ▓▓▓▓▓▓▓▓▓▓▓▓▓▓ the idea ▓▓▓▓▓▓▓▓▓▓▓▓▓▓ with my wife and she thinks it's for the best.

 **Talk Talk Talk**

(Mario's restaurant)

J. My, that was very good. Mario! Two espressos – and for me a glass of that excellent grappa of yours. One for you, too, Peter? Make that two. Now, **let's tackle** these fears of yours, Peter. What troubles you about speaking to an audience?

P. Well, I've never done it, **for a start**. And English is not my mother tongue. There are two reasons why I'm a bit apprehensive.

J. Your English is now fluent. Apart from which, the presence at the seminar of a London company's German **Executive Officer** is bound to impress. You speak well and coherently, your appearance is immaculate, your **manner of presentation** impeccable – so what's worrying you.

P. Well, that's your impression, and I'm flattered and very grateful. I've learnt a lot from you and my

(Marios Restaurant)

J. Das war wirklich sehr gut. Mario! Zwei Espressos – und für mich ein Glas von Ihrem exzellenten Grappa. Für Sie auch, Peter? Dann bitte zwei! Gut, dann **nehmen wir uns mal** Ihre Ängste **vor**, Peter. Was für Probleme haben Sie denn, vor Publikum zu sprechen?

P. Nun ja, **zuerst einmal** habe ich das noch nie gemacht. Und Englisch ist nicht meine Muttersprache. Das sind zwei Gründe, warum mir ein wenig mulmig dabei ist.

J. Sie sprechen jetzt fließend Englisch. Abgesehen davon wird es das Publikum sehr beeindrucken, wenn ein **leitender** deutscher **Angestellter** eine Londoner Firma beim Seminar repräsentiert. Sie sprechen sehr gut und flüssig, Ihr Erscheinungsbild ist makellos, Ihre **Präsentationsmethoden** perfekt – was also macht Ihnen Sorgen?

P. Nun ja, das ist Ihre Meinung und ich bin dankbar und fühle mich sehr geschmeichelt. Ich habe

work at ERGO. But I'm still not convinced I can do it.	durch meine Arbeit bei ERGO viel gelernt. Aber ich bin immer noch nicht sicher, ob ich das kann.
J. Of course you can. You'll have a kind of **dress rehearsal** at the press conference. You'll be **presiding** at that, won't you?	J. Natürlich können Sie das. Die Pressekonferenz wird doch so eine Art **Generalprobe** werden. Sie werden dabei **den Vorsitz führen**, nicht wahr?
P. I'll have Melissa as **back-up**.	P. Ich habe Melissa als **Rückendeckung** dabei.
J. You work well with Melissa, don't you.	J. Sie arbeiten gut mit Melissa zusammen, nicht wahr?
P. I think we **make a good team**, yes. We had our problems **at the outset**, but now we get along very well.	P. Ich glaube, wir **geben ein gutes Team ab**, ja. Wir hatten **am Anfang** unsere Schwierigkeiten, aber jetzt kommen wir sehr gut miteinander aus.
J. Yes, I had noticed ...	J. Ja, das war mir aufgefallen ...

Background Information

At the outset Peter had some problems with Melissa but now they get on very well together. »**At the outset**« means **in the beginning**. A similar word is »**onset**« which is **the moment something unpleasant begins**, e.g. »The negotiators were making good progress until the onset of a stalemate over the question of overtime«.
Let's look at some phrases and expressions with »**set**«.

to set up	to establish
to set out	to arrange or to start an action
to set about doing something	to start working
to set back	to delay

a setting	a location
to be (dead) set against	to oppose
to set off	to start a journey
to set one's sights on	to have something as a purpose

 **168. Train Yourself**

Benutzen Sie diese Wendungen nun in der Übung!

1. James was ▇▇▇▇▇▇ the idea of increasing clients' fees at first, thinking this would cause a drain on resources but he soon came round to the idea.
2. The ▇▇▇▇▇▇ for the press conference was outside in the Managing Director's own private grounds.
3. The CEO ▇▇▇▇▇▇ increasing productivity by 20% over the next two years.
4. It was a long drive to Newcastle so we ▇▇▇▇▇▇ early to avoid the traffic.
5. At a trade fair it is important to ▇▇▇▇▇▇ one's stall in the most appealing manner possible in order to attract potential clients.
6. The seminar has been ▇▇▇▇▇▇ until next week due to the speaker's unavailability.
7. At the moment we're trying to ▇▇▇▇▇▇ a new branch in Athens.
8. The ▇▇▇▇▇▇ of the economic slump was bad news for everybody involved with Hollins Ltd.
9. ▇▇▇▇▇▇ of the presentation the speaker welcomed those present and then ▇▇▇▇▇▇ outlining the company's latest project.

 **Talk Talk Talk**

(Peter's office. Melissa enters) | (Peters Büro. Melissa tritt ein)

M. Just one day **to blast-off**. Ten and counting. | M. Nur noch ein Tag **bis zum Start**. Der Countdown läuft.

Präsentationen

P. Don't make me more nervous than I already am, Melissa. How many can we expect at the press conference?	P. Machen Sie mich nicht nervöser als ich schon bin, Melissa. Wie viele Besucher erwarten wir bei der Pressekonferenz?
M. Sixty invitations **went out**. Around forty **acceptances**.	M. Es **sind** sechzig Einladungen **verschickt worden**. Und etwa vierzig **Zusagen** zurückgekommen.
P. Such a lot of interest in our operation?	P. So groß ist das Interesse an unseren Unternehmungen?
M. Not so much in ERGO as in the new **internet payment security software**. There was another spectacular internet theft last week, you remember. One hundred credit card numbers went missing. Companies are quaking. They're desperate for protection. We can hardly **keep up with** the **inquiries** – ask Steve, he's never worked so hard in his life.	M. Es geht gar nicht so sehr um ERGO als vielmehr um die neue **Sicherheitssoftware für den Geldtransfer im Internet**. Letzte Woche gab es wieder einen spektakulären Internet-Diebstahl, wie Sie sich erinnern werden. Einhundert Kreditkarten-Nummern sind dabei verschwunden. Die Firmen zittern vor Angst. Sie suchen verzweifelt nach Schutzprogrammen. Wir **kommen** bei den **Anfragen** kaum noch **hinterher** – fragen Sie Steve, er hat in seinem ganzen Leben noch nie so hart gearbeitet.
P. I wondered why I hadn't seen him for so long. I've been so **busy** preparing for the trade fair and the press conference that I must confess I haven't had time **to inquire about sales**.	P. Ich hatte mich schon gefragt, warum ich ihn so lange nicht mehr gesehen habe. Ich muss zugeben, dass ich mit der Vorbereitung der Messe und der Pressekonferenz so **beschäftigt** war, dass ich gar nicht mehr dazu gekommen bin, mich **nach den Verkaufszahlen zu erkundigen**.

M. Sales are **booming**. America is delighted and wants to give us more autonomy and a research and development budget. There's even talk about a **stock exchange listing**. And you know what that means, Peter?	M. Die Verkaufszahlen **schießen nach oben**. Amerika ist begeistert und will uns deshalb mehr Autonomie und ein Budget für Forschung und Entwicklung geben. Es wird sogar über einen **Börsengang** geredet. Und Sie wissen ja wohl, was das bedeutet, Peter?
P. Tell me.	P. Sagen Sie es mir.
M. **Share options** for us all.	M. **Optionen auf Belegschaftsaktien** für uns alle.
P. But you're leaving.	P. Aber Sie verlassen uns doch.
M. I'm **leaving my options open**, Peter my dear ...	M. Ich **lasse mir alle Möglichkeiten offen**, mein lieber Peter ...

Background Information

Melissa says that she's **leaving her options open**, meaning **she's waiting before making her choice**. A »**soft option**« is **an easy way of dealing with something**. E.g. when a difficulty arises, most people **choose the soft option**, however, this is not always possible. We also talk about **share options** meaning **the right to buy the shares in the future** or giving somebody **first option** on something, meaning giving them **first choice**.
But there are also a lot of possibilities on how to use the word »**open**«.
Let's take a look at some of them:

out into the open	revealed
with open arms	willingly and eagerly
open-minded	tolerant and accepting of new ideas

an open secret	something should be a secret but in fact everybody knows about it
an open market	a trading situation in a country which allows foreign companies to work freely there
to open up	to make something available
open-mouthed	astonished, surprised

 169. Train Yourself

Verwenden Sie diese Begriffe in den nachstehenden Sätzen!

1. The country is planning to ▓▓▓▓▓ its economy to foreign investment.
2. The plummeting sales figures left everybody ▓▓▓▓▓.
3. Peter was welcomed into the company ▓▓▓▓▓
4. One must be ▓▓▓▓▓ when making overseas business trips.
5. At last the secret was ▓▓▓▓▓ and everybody could get on with countering its effects.
6. It's always better to ▓▓▓▓▓ rather than investing everything in one outcome.
7. Multinationals in the West look forward eagerly to the day when China will become an ▓▓▓▓▓ without any trading blocks.
8. In ERGO Ltd it was an ▓▓▓▓▓ that Peter had fallen for Melissa although he wasn't aware of it.

 Talk Talk Talk

(Hotel conference room)   (Im Konferenzraum des Hotels)

P. Good morning, ladies and gentlemen. Thank you for accepting our invitation to **attend** this ERGO Limited press conference. I'd like **to start the proceedings** with a

P. Guten Morgen, meine Damen und Herren. Danke, dass Sie unserer Einladung gefolgt sind und an der Pressekonferenz von ERGO Limited **teilnehmen**. Ich würde die

short statement, introducing our company and explaining its work. Most of you already know us, either through personal contact or through our regular press releases. In the two years since we first established ourselves in London as a **subsidiary** of ERGO International we have **grown at an encouraging rate** and expect a 50 percent rise in **net profits** for **the current business year**. Although **we deal in a wide range** of state-of-the-art software products we are concentrating our efforts right now on an entirely new **internet security architecture**, with which we have **scored some remarkable successes**. **You are all** of course **aware** of the huge problem of internet theft and abuse. Probably every one of you here today has reported at one time or another on a case of internet theft. I have here in front of me your excellent Telegraph report, Mr Highsmith, on the most recent incident. I don't think I am exaggerating when I say that if the company **in question** had had our security architecture **in place** this theft would not have occurred – now, I see some hands already in the air, so I'll **take questions** …

Tagesordnung gern mit **ein paar kurzen Worten** über unsere Firma und ihre Arbeit **einleiten**. Die meisten von Ihnen kennen uns ja schon, entweder durch persönliche Kontakte oder unsere regelmäßigen Pressemitteilungen. Seit wir uns vor zwei Jahren als **Tochtergesellschaft** von ERGO International in London niedergelassen haben, konnten wir **sehr ermutigende Zuwachsraten verzeichnen** und erwarten im **laufenden Geschäftsjahr** eine Steigerung des **Reingewinns** von 50 Prozent. Obwohl wir **eine breite Produktpalette** von modernsten Softwareprodukten **anbieten**, konzentrieren wir unsere Anstrengungen derzeit auf eine völlig neue **Internet-Sicherheits-Architektur**, mit der wir schon **einige bemerkenswerte Erfolge erzielen konnten**. **Sie alle kennen** natürlich das gewaltige Problem von Internet-Diebstählen und -betrügereien. Wahrscheinlich jeder, der heute hier ist, hat bereits das eine oder andere Mal über einen Internet-Diebstahl berichtet. Ich habe hier Ihren exzellenten *Telegraph*-Bericht über den neuesten Vorfall dieser Art vorliegen, Mr Highsmith. Ich glaube, ich übertreibe nicht, wenn ich sage, dass es nie zu diesem Datendiebstahl gekommen wäre, wenn die **betreffende** Firma unsere Sicherheits-Architektur **verwendet** hätte –

ich sehe schon einige erhobene Hände, also **nehme** ich Ihre **Fragen** gern **entgegen** ...

Background Information

»**Architecture**« in e-commerce terms means **the structure of a software product**. It's an example of how Information Technology (IT) is expanding at such a rate that it is finding difficulty in developing a new vocabulary to describe its activities. Often, it has to call on »old«, well-known terms to achieve clarity. »**Architecture**« is one of these. A software product is so complicated in structure and operation that it can be described in layman's terms only by using an immediately-recognizable word like »**architecture**«.

170. Train Yourself

Geben Sie Synonyme für die folgenden Wörter und Ausdrücke aus dem vorhergehenden Text an.

1. *Start* the proceedings
2. *scored* some remarkable successes
3. *explaining* its work
4. *grown* at an encouraging rate
5. *deal in*
6. *concentrating* our efforts *on*
7. you *are* all *aware*
8. the *current* year
9. *expect* a 50 per cent rise
10. *in place*

established, open, describing, achieved, do business in, directing at, present, know, present, anticipate.

 **Talk Talk Talk**

(Hotel conference room)

P. Well, Melissa, **how** do you think the **press conference went**. Are you happy?

M. More than happy, Peter. You did remarkably well. James would be proud of you. I think we'll get some very favorable **press coverage** out of it.

B. Yes, **great stuff**, Peter! I thought you **handled some pretty difficult questions** in a masterly fashion. Couldn't have done better myself!

M. Modesty was never one of Beryl's **strong points**. Now be a good girl and get Peter a drink ... Peter, this is your day. Can I invite you to dinner tonight?

P. Good heavens, Melissa, what have I done to **deserve** this?

M. A working dinner, dear boy! The press conference was just the beginning – now we have to prepare for the trade fair. I have a few arrangements to discuss with you.

(Konferenzraum des Hotels)

P. Nun, Melissa, was denken Sie, **wie die Pressekonferenz gelaufen ist**? Sind Sie zufrieden?

M. Mehr als zufrieden, Peter. Sie haben sich bemerkenswert gut geschlagen. James wäre stolz auf Sie. Ich denke, wir werden mit ein paar sehr positiven **Berichten** daraus hervorgehen.

B. Ja, **großartige Leistung**, Peter! Ich finde, Sie haben **ein paar ziemlich schwierige Fragen** meisterhaft **beantwortet**. Ich hätte es selbst nicht besser gekonnt!

M. Bescheidenheit war noch nie Beryls **Stärke**. Jetzt seien Sie ein gutes Mädchen und holen Sie Peter einen Drink ...
Peter, heute ist Ihr großer Tag. Darf ich Sie heute Abend zum Essen einladen?

P. Du meine Güte, Melissa, womit habe ich mir denn das **verdient**?

M. Das wird ein Arbeitsessen, mein Junge! Die Pressekonferenz war erst der Anfang – jetzt müssen wir uns auf die Messe vorbereiten. Ich muss noch ein paar Vorberei-

Frankly, I'm too tired **to tackle** them at the office. I'm **taking** the afternoon **off**, and you can **pick** me **up** at my place at seven tonight ...

tungen mit Ihnen besprechen. Ehrlich gesagt bin ich zu müde, um sie im Büro in **Angriff zu nehmen**. Ich **nehme** mir **den Nachmittag frei** und Sie können mich heute Abend um sieben zu Hause **abholen** ...

P. But, Melissa ...

P. Aber, Melissa ...

M. No »buts« Peter. That's an order. From your Marketing Director. Beryl, hand him that wine - cheers, Peter. And well done!

M. Kein »Aber«, Peter. Das ist ein Befehl. Von Ihrer Marketing-Direktorin. Beryl, geben Sie ihm den Wein – Prost, Peter. Gut gemacht!

Background Information

Peter asks Melissa **how** she thought the press conference **went**. In other words **how was** the press conference. Let's look at some phrasal verbs with »**go**«.

to go in for	to make a habit of
to go on	to continue
to go round	to be enough
to go by	to pass
to go through	to experience
to go over	to check
to go back on	to break a promise
to make a go of	to be successful

 171. Train Yourself

Füllen Sie nun die Lücken!

1. Management ▧▧▧▧▧▧▧▧▧▧▧▧▧▧ their original promise to reinstate the two sacked workers which caused further protests outside the plant.

2. There weren't enough brochures to ▓▓▓▓▓▓▓ at the conference so some people had to share.
3. Two weeks ▓▓▓▓▓▓▓ before the electronic equipment finally arrived at its destination.
4. By using less expensive materials we finally ▓▓▓▓▓▓▓ bringing costs down.
5. The recession has ▓▓▓▓▓▓▓ for two years now and there's no sign of a recovery yet.
6. The company ▓▓▓▓▓▓▓ a huge improvement in efficiency.
7. Could you ▓▓▓▓▓▓▓ these sales figures once more for me?
8. I don't usually ▓▓▓▓▓▓▓ these American style positive thinking courses but I'll make an exception in this case.

 Talk Talk Talk

(Peter's office. James Morgan enters)

J. Hello, Peter. I **gather** the press conference was a success.

P. **Word gets back very quickly.** I thought it went quite well, yes.

J. Quite well? Melissa called to say the press was eating out of your hand. Still worried about that **trade fair symposium**?

P. **Funnily enough**, James, I think I've lost some of my **stage fright**

(Peters Büro. James Morgan tritt ein)

J. Hallo, Peter. Ich **habe gehört**, die Pressekonferenz war ein voller Erfolg.

P. **Die Nachrichten verbreiten sich hier ja schnell.** Ja, ich glaube, sie lief recht gut.

J. Recht gut? Melissa hat angerufen, um mir zu sagen, dass Ihnen die Pressevertreter aus der Hand gefressen haben. Machen Sie sich immer noch Sorgen wegen des **Seminars auf der Messe**?

P. **Seltsamerweise**, James, glaube ich, dass ich etwas von meinem

now. You're right, the press conference was a good preparation, a kind of dress rehearsal.

J. If you examine your **direction** of the press conference what do you think you have learnt from it?

P. I think the most important thing was to **establish authority**. I got the impression that the press **took me seriously**. They certainly listened **attentively** to what I had to say. The questions were intelligent and I found I was able to answer them without difficulty and in a way that was clearly understood. I surprised myself there, I must confess.

J. Well done! I really am glad we have you on board as my assistant. I'm confident you'll do well at the trade fair.

P. I'll certainly do my best. But I'm glad I'll have Melissa's **assistance**.

J. Ah, she's taking you out to dinner tonight, you lucky dog!

Lampenfieber verloren habe. Sie hatten Recht, die Pressekonferenz war eine gute Vorbereitung, eine Art Generalprobe.

J. Wenn Sie Ihre **Vorgehensweise** auf der Pressekonferenz im Nachhinein betrachten, was glauben Sie, daraus gelernt zu haben?

P. Ich glaube, das Wichtigste war, dass ich meine **Autorität etabliert** habe. Ich hatte den Eindruck, dass die Pressevertreter mich **ernst genommen** haben. Sie haben auf jeden Fall **aufmerksam** zugehört, was ich zu sagen hatte. Die Fragen waren intelligent und ich fand, dass ich sie ohne Schwierigkeiten und verständlich beantworten konnte. Ich muss zugeben, dass ich mich selbst überrascht habe.

J. Gut gemacht! Ich bin wirklich froh, das wir Sie als meinen Assistenten an Bord haben. Ich bin zuversichtlich, dass Sie sich bei der Messe gut schlagen werden.

P. Ich werde natürlich mein Bestes tun. Aber ich bin froh, dass ich Melissa als **Unterstützung** dabei habe.

J. Ah, sie geht heute Abend mit Ihnen Essen, Sie Glücklicher!

P. **News really does travel fast.** She told you that?

P. **Neuigkeiten verbreiten sich hier ja wirklich schnell.** Sie hat Ihnen das gesagt?

J. Actually, Beryl whispered something in my ear. Beryl was also so impressed with your **performance** that she's after you now, too. Aren't you the lucky man!

J. Streng genommen hat mir Beryl das zugeflüstert. Beryl war ebenfalls so beeindruckt von Ihrem **Auftritt**, dass sie jetzt auch hinter Ihnen her ist. Was sind Sie nur für ein Glückspilz!

 172. Train Yourself

Finden Sie die Antonyme (Gegensätze) zu folgenden Wörtern und Ausdrücken. »They seem easy – but be wary!«

1. impressed
2. well
3. worried
4. lost
5. you're right
6. learnt
7. established
8. attentively
9. understood
10. fast
11. lucky

 Vocabulary

acceptance	Zusage, z. B. bei einer Einladung
to address a seminar on sth.	vor einem Seminar einen Vortrag halten über
All settled?	Alles bereit?
to arrange for	bestellen
arrangements	Vorbereitungen, Planung
at the close	nach dem Ende

at the outset	am Anfang
to attend	folgen, z. B. einer Einladung
back-up	Rückendeckung
to be busy doing sth.	beschäftigt sein mit etw.
to boom	nach oben schießen, z. B. Verkaufszahlen
to come along	vorankommen, z. B. Vorbereitungen
current business year	laufendes Geschäftsjahr
to deal in a wide range of sth.	eine breite Produktpalette von etw. anbieten
to deserve sth.	etw. verdienen, z. B. Lob
direction	hier: Vorgehensweise
dress rehearsal	Generalprobe
executive officer	leitender Angestellter
for a start	zuerst einmal
from the start	vor Beginn
function	hier: Vorhaben
function room	Mehrzweckraum
to gather	gehört haben
to grow at an encouraging rate	sehr ermutigende Zuwachsraten zu verzeichnen haben
to handle sth.	sich um etw. kümmern
to inquire about	sich erkundigen nach
inquiries	Anfragen
internet payment	Geldtransfer im Internet
to leave one's options open	alle Möglichkeiten offen lassen
light buffet	kleiner Imbiss
to keep up with	Schritt halten mit
manner of presentation	Präsentationsmethode
net profits	Reingewinn
on that score	in diesem Punkt, hierbei
outset	Anfang
to present a case	für eine Sache sprechen
to preside	den Vorsitz führen
press coverage	Pressebericht
press distribution list	Verteilerliste für die Presse
proceedings	Tagesordnung
to put in touch with sb.	an jdn. weiterleiten

sales	Verkaufszahlen, Verkauf
to score success	Erfolg erzielen
security software	Sicherheitssoftware
share option	Option auf Belegschaftsaktien
short statement	ein paar kurze Worte
so-called	so genannt
stage fright	Lampenfieber
to spring in	einspringen
stock exchange listing	Börsengang
strong point	starke Seite (einer Person)
subsidiary	Tochtergesellschaft
to take off	frei nehmen
to take questions	Fragen entgegennehmen
to tackle sth.	sich etw. vornehmen, etw. in Angriff nehmen
to talk shop	fachsimpeln
to talk sth. through	etw. durchsprechen
up-to-date with everything	alles so weit geregelt
Word gets back very quickly/ News does travel fast	Neuigkeiten verbreiten sich schnell
You are all aware ...	Sie alle kennen ...

Präsentationen

Presentation at the trade fair
Präsentation auf der Messe

 Here we go

Nun hat die Herbstmesse endlich begonnen und Melissa, Beryl und Peter stecken bis zum Hals in Arbeit. Sie sind den ganzen Tag über am Messestand von ERGO Limited damit beschäftigt, potenzielle Kunden und Interessenten zu beraten und Informationsbroschüren zu verteilen. Außerdem gibt es viele Vorträge von Experten, die gehört werden wollen. Und genau dies beschäftigt Peter am meisten. Denn auch er soll vor den Messeteilnehmern eine Präsentation über ERGO abhalten und ist schon sehr aufgeregt, aber mit seiner Vorbereitung und Melissas Unterstützung sollte dies ein Leichtes für ihn sein ...

 Talk Talk Talk

(Olympia trade fair centre, London) (Olympia Handelsmesse-Zentrum, London)

P. Melissa, I've quite forgotten where our stand is. I can't even find it listed in **the trade fair catalogue**.

P. Melissa, ich habe ganz vergessen, wo unser Stand ist. Ich kann ihn nicht einmal in der Liste des **Messekatalogs** finden.

M. Oh, Peter! You're looking for it in completely the wrong section. Here, we're in Hall B, stand number 233.

M. Aber Peter! Sie suchen ihn ja in einem völlig falschen Bereich. Hier, wir sind in Halle B, Stand Nummer 233.

P. You need a map to find your way around here.

P. Man braucht ja einen Plan, um hier den Weg zu finden.

M. The catalogue has a map, at the end.

M. Im Katalog ist ein Plan, ganz hinten.

P. Some of the stands are already open. What about ours?

M. Don't worry. Beryl has been there since six this morning. Chip, too.

P. Chip?

M. We needed **all hands on deck**. Chip will just have to forget about **courier service** for the next few days. Here we are. The stand is there, on the right.

B. Hello, you two. I was beginning to get worried.

M. Worrying will **get you nowhere**, Beryl. What have we got to do?

B. Nothing, really. Everything is **set up**. Chip is **just fetching** another **batch of pamphlets** and other material. Then **we're ready for the off**. Coffee?

M. I don't mind if I do. Or is that for the **customers**?

B. We've got all kinds of **goodies** in the fridge. Plus coffee and biscuits. Help yourself.

P. Ein paar Stände haben schon geöffnet. Wie steht es mit unserem?

M. Keine Sorge. Beryl ist seit sechs Uhr morgens hier. Chip auch.

P. Chip?

M. Wir brauchten **alle verfügbaren Leute**. Chip wird den **Kurierdienst** für die nächsten paar Tage vergessen müssen. Wir sind da. Der Stand ist dort auf der rechten Seite.

B. Hallo Sie beide. Ich habe schon angefangen, mir Sorgen zu machen.

M. Sich sorgen **bringt nichts**, Beryl. Was gibt es für uns zu tun?

B. Eigentlich nichts. Alles ist **fertig**. Chip **holt gerade** noch einen **Stapel Broschüren** und anderes Material. Dann **können** wir **loslegen**. Kaffee?

M. Gerne, wenn ich darf. Oder ist der für die **Kunden**?

B. Wir haben viele **Leckereien** im Kühlschrank. Und Kaffee und Kekse. Bedienen Sie sich.

Präsentationen

Background Information

»**To have all hands on deck**« is a colloquialism meaning **to have everybody involved**. Another colloquialism used in the text is »**goodies**« meaning **nice things to eat**.
Beryl says we're **ready for the off**, meaning **ready to start**. Let's look at some more expressions with »**off**«.

off line	computers not connected to the main system
off the hook	out of a difficult situation
right off	immediately
on the off chance	with the possibility (that/of)
to break off	to stop talking
to carry off	to complete successfully
to put off	to discourage

173. Train Yourself

Verwenden Sie diese »phrasal verbs« nun in der folgenden Übung!

1. The team worked brilliantly and ▓▓▓▓▓▓▓▓ the deal in no time.
2. While I was talking to the Assistant Managing Director she ▓▓▓▓▓▓▓▓ to attend to a phone call.
3. I was rather ▓▓▓▓▓▓▓▓ by his abrupt manner and thought again about investing in his company.
4. We are planning to connect all our ▓▓▓▓▓▓▓▓ computers to the mainframe.
5. We got down to work ▓▓▓▓▓▓▓▓ in the hope of finishing everything by the next day.
6. Melissa got us ▓▓▓▓▓▓▓▓ by explaining to the Director that we weren't totally familiar with company procedures.
7. I brought my notes to the symposium ▓▓▓▓▓▓▓▓ that I might be called upon to say some words.
8. After the stall had finally been set up we were ▓▓▓▓▓▓▓▓

 **Talk Talk Talk**

Präsentationen

(At the ERGO stand)

M. When is your presentation, Peter? I've quite forgotten.

P. Tomorrow morning, at 11.

M. Want to **practise** it on me?

P. Good Lord, no, Melissa. I'm nervous enough.

M. Well, you can practise your **sales technique** right now. Here comes our first potential customer ...

Visitor: Good morning! I'm **collecting information on accounts programming**, and someone sent me to your stand. Do you have anything in that direction?

B. **I'll see to that.** If you have any questions, Mr Brückner here will be glad to help you.

P. Yes, of course. Don't hesitate to ask if you need more information.

V. Can you give me any **references**? This program is quite new to me.

(Am ERGO Stand)

M. Peter, wann ist Ihre Präsentation? Die hatte ich fast vergessen.

P. Morgen früh um 11.

M. Wollen Sie sie mir **probeweise vortragen**?

P. Guter Gott, nein, Melissa. Ich bin schon nervös genug.

M. Nun denn, Sie können Ihre **Verkaufstechnik** gleich jetzt üben. Da kommt unser erster potenzleller Kunde ...

Besucher: Guten Morgen! Ich **sammle Informationen über Buchhaltungs-Programme** und jemand hat mich zu Ihrem Stand geschickt. Haben Sie etwas in der Richtung?

B. **Ich kümmere mich darum.** Wenn Sie Fragen haben, wird Ihnen Mr Brückner hier gerne weiter helfen.

P. Aber natürlich. Zögern Sie nicht und fragen Sie, wenn Sie mehr Informationen brauchen.

V. Können Sie mir irgendwelche **Referenzen** nennen? Das Programm ist mir ganz neu.

P. Yes indeed. It has been **installed** in a number of companies. You'll find a list of them at the end of the first brochure. They are all ready **to vouch** for the **effectiveness** of the software.	P. Aber ja. Einige Firmen haben es bereits **installieren** lassen. In der ersten Broschüre finden Sie sie ganz hinten auf einer Liste. Sie können sich alle für die **Effektivität** der Software **verbürgen**.
(Six hours later)	(Sechs Stunden später)
P. We have an excellent **accounting program**. May I give you this **information brochure**? Please feel free to sit down and **glance through** it while we prepare you a cup of coffee. Or would you prefer tea?	P. Wir haben ein ausgezeichnetes **Buchführungs-Programm**. Dürfte ich Ihnen diese **Informations-Broschüre** mitgeben? Bitte setzen Sie sich und **sehen** Sie **sie durch**, während ich Ihnen eine Tasse Kaffee mache. Oder möchten Sie einen Tee?
V. A cup of tea would do nicely ...	V. Eine Tasse Tee wäre nett ...
P. Phew, Melissa, **I'm all in**. That was a long day.	P. Puh, Melissa. **Ich bin völlig fertig**. Das war ein langer Tag.
M. I know, my feet are killing me.	M. Ich weiß, meine Füße bringen mich um.
P. Come on, **my turn** to buy you dinner. What about you, Beryl?	P. Kommen Sie, **ich bin dran** mit Abendessen zahlen. Wie steht's mit Ihnen, Beryl?
B. I'll have to lock up here. You two **take off**. I think I'll go straight home ...	B. Ich mache hier dicht. **Gehen Sie** beide nur. Ich glaube, ich gehe gleich nach Hause ...

Background Information

Peter says that he's **all in**, meaning he's **very tired**. Beryl tells Peter and Melissa to **take off**, meaning to **leave**. »**Take off**« can also mean to **succeed**, e.g. »After a slow start to the year sales took off in a spectacular fashion.« Also when a plane **leaves the ground** we say »**it takes off**«.

Below are listed some expressions with »**take**«.

to take a leaf out of someone's book	to imitate another person's actions
to take advantage of	to make good use of something
to be taken aback	to be surprised
to take steps	to take action in order to achieve an objective
to take one's time	not to hurry
I take it	I suppose
to take a dim view of	to disapprove of
to take someone's word for it	to accept the statement of the person to be true
to take heart	to be encouraged

 174. Train Yourself

Füllen Sie nun die Lücken!

1. Hello, you're Mr Jones, ▨▨▨▨▨▨▨▨▨▨▨▨▨▨▨.
2. We all ▨▨▨▨▨▨▨▨▨▨ by the rise in profits at the end of the second quarter. It was very good news for the company.
3. The boss ▨▨▨▨▨▨▨▨▨▨ of anybody arriving late for work.
4. I trusted Fiona and decided to ▨▨▨▨▨▨▨▨ rather than look up the facts of the case myself.
5. We had worked hard all day and decided to ▨▨▨▨▨ early to avoid the rush-hour traffic.
6. We decided to ▨▨▨▨▨▨ our competitor's ▨▨▨▨▨▨ and invest more heavily in publicity campaigns.

7. ▒▒▒▒▒ your ▒▒▒▒▒! There's no rush! The meeting doesn't start for another twenty minutes.
8. We were quite ▒▒▒▒▒ when we saw the sales figures for the previous month. They were much higher than expected.
9. The company ▒▒▒▒▒ of the healthy economic climate by opening two new branches abroad.
10. Management are aware of the problem and are ▒▒▒▒▒ ▒▒▒▒▒ to rectify the situation.

 **Talk Talk Talk**

(Olympia trade fair centre. Conference room B)

P. Ahoi, Melissa! I'm **over here**!

M. Ah, Peter, I've been looking for you everywhere.

P. There are so many people here, and I hate crowds.

M. You can't avoid them at trade fairs. But I'm surprised to find so many have **turned up for** the symposium.

P. I'm surprised too – and a bit alarmed.

M. Oh, come on, Peter! We've been through all this. **You'll be fine.** When **are you on**?

P. On? When am I speaking, you mean. Here's the programme.

(Olympia Handelsmesse-Zentrum. Konferenzraum B)

P. Ahoi, Melissa. Ich bin **hier drüben**!

M. Peter, ich habe Sie überall gesucht.

P. Hier sind so viele Leute und ich hasse Menschenmengen.

M. Darum kommen Sie bei Handelsmessen nicht herum. Aber es wundert mich, dass so viele **sich** zum Symposium **sehen lassen**.

P. Ich bin auch überrascht – und ein bisschen panisch.

M. Ach kommen Sie schon, Peter. Das hatten wir doch alles schon mal. **Das wird schon klappen**. Wann **sind Sie dran**?

P. Dran? Sie meinen, wann ich spreche. Hier ist das Programm.

There are six of us **main speakers**, interspersed by **discussion sessions** and lunch. I'm first on this afternoon. **The topics range from** pretty technical subjects, such as **digitalisation, to** general themes **along the lines of** what I shall be **delivering**. I'm afraid I look pretty lightweight in this company. There's even a professor in cybernetics from Cambridge.	Es gibt sechs **Hauptredner**, unterbrochen durch **Diskussionsrunden** und Mittagessen. Ich bin heute Nachmittag der Erste. **Die Themen reichen von** sehr technischen Dingen wie **Digitalisierung bis hin zu** allgemeinen Themen, **also ungefähr das**, was ich **zu bieten** habe. Ich fürchte, ich werde in dieser Gesellschaft wie ein Leichtgewicht dastehen. Es ist sogar ein Kybernetik-Professor aus Cambridge hier.
M. Oh, come on! These intellectuals will be fascinated to hear from somebody in the business, somebody who has **to grapple with** the problems they know only from a **classroom setting.**	M. Ach, kommen Sie schon! Diese Intellektuellen werden fasziniert sein, jemandem der aus der Praxis kommt zuzuhören, jemandem der sich **mit** den Problemen **herumschlagen** muss, die sie nur aus dem **Unterricht** kennen.
P. Well, I don't know about that. I just wish I were on at the end of the day's programme – then perhaps most of them have packed up and gone home.	P. Na ja, ich weiß nicht. Ich wünschte nur, ich wäre am Ende des Tagesprogramms dran – dann hätten die meisten wahrscheinlich schon ihre Sachen gepackt und wären gegangen.
M. First speaker after lunch is also a good place to have – most of the participants will be **dozing off**!	M. Erster Redner nach dem Mittagessen ist auch gut – die meisten Teilnehmer werden **vor sich hin dösen**!
P. Now **you're kidding me**. But you'll have lunch with me?	P. Jetzt **machen Sie sich über mich lustig**. Aber Sie werden doch mit mir zu Mittag essen?

Präsentationen

M. If you like, with pleasure.

P. Then I really will be prepared for my appearance ...

M. Sehr gerne, wenn Sie wollen.

P. Danach werde ich bereit sein für meinen Auftritt ...

Background Information

Peter in this section of the dialogue explains how some of the subjects at the symposium are **along the lines of** what he is going to talk about, meaning **they are similar to his chosen subject**.
Let's look at some more expressions with the word »**line**«.

to be in line for	to have a good chance of something
to toe the line	to follow the rules, procedures
reading between the lines	deducing the meaning of something
to draw the line	to set limits to something
right down the line	completely, at every stage
in line	in accordance
to be in one's line	to be something one does well or enjoys doing

 175. Train Yourself

Vervollständigen Sie die Sätze!

1. The Manager makes us all ▒▒▒▒▒▒▒▒▒▒▒▒▒▒▒▒▒. He is completely inflexible with the staff.
2. Did you hear John's ▒▒▒▒▒▒▒▒▒▒▒ for the Assistant Director's job?
3. Helen made so much sense that I agreed with her ▒▒▒▒▒▒ ▒▒▒▒▒▒▒▒▒▒▒.
4. The boss doesn't mind occasional lateness but he ▒▒▒▒▒▒ ▒▒▒▒▒▒▒▒▒▒▒ at persistent unpunctuality.
5. ▒▒▒▒▒▒▒▒▒▒▒▒▒▒▒ I think the company could be in trouble, although nothing official has been said of course.

6. What's that new business book you're reading?
   Oh. It's ▨▨▨▨▨ of the one I read last month.
7. Our health and safety standards must be ▨▨▨▨▨ with Government regulations.
8. Public speaking is not really ▨▨▨▨▨. I get too nervous and forget what I was going to say.

 **Talk Talk Talk**

(Olympia trade fair centre. Symposium begins)

Chairman: **Ladies and gentlemen, learned colleagues, members of the press – I hope I've left no-one out**! Welcome! Welcome to this **exchange of views** on a subject not only **dear to our hearts** but **critical to our futures**. Indeed, critical to the future of mankind. The technological revolution. For what we are experiencing and witnessing today is **nothing short of** a revolution – comparable to the great industrial revolution of the 19th century. In fact, many experts say the industrial revolution **will appear as a very minor chapter** in the final history of the world when compared to what is **occurring** now. We shall be discussing this profound thought and also considering the **implications** for society, business and trade. This morning we shall be considering the social implications of this great development, beginning with a **treatise** by Professor Betram Smith-Fellowes

(Olympia Handelsmesse-Zentrum. Das Symposium beginnt)

Vorsitzender: **Meine Damen und Herren, geehrte Kollegen, Mitglieder der Presse – ich hoffe, ich habe niemanden ausgelassen**! Willkommen! Willkommen zu diesem **Meinungsaustausch** über ein Thema, das nicht nur **sehr wichtig für uns** ist, sondern auch **entscheidend ist für unsere Zukunft**. Sogar entscheidend für die Zukunft der Menschheit. Die technologische Revolution. Denn das, was wir heute an Erfahrungen und Beobachtungen machen, ist **nicht weniger** als eine Revolution – vergleichbar mit der großen industriellen Revolution des 19. Jahrhunderts. Tatsächlich meinen viele Experten, dass die industrielle Revolution, verglichen mit dem was jetzt **passiert**, in der gesamten Geschichte **eine viel geringere Rolle spielen wird**. Wir sollten diesen tief gehenden Gedanken diskutieren und auch in Betracht ziehen, **was das** für

Präsentationen

of the University of Exeter. This afternoon we shall be looking at the practical, pragmatic effects of the **information technology revolution** and the birth of what **is being called** a new economy. This session will begin with a presentation by Herr Peter Brückner, Assistant Managing Director of ERGO Limited, one of the **leading** companies **in this field**. Now, if I can invite Professor Smith-Fellowes **to take the rostrum** we can begin what I believe will be a highly interesting exchange ...

Gesellschaft, Geschäft und Handel **bedeutet**. Heute Morgen sollten wir die gesellschaftlichen Auswirkungen dieser großen Entwicklung betrachten, beginnend mit einer **Abhandlung** von Professor Betram Smith-Fellowes von der Universität Exeter. Heute Nachmittag werden wir die praktischen, pragmatischen Folgen der **Revolution der Informationstechnologie** und die Geburt dessen, **was wir** als »New Economy« **bezeichnen**, betrachten. Dieser Teil beginnt mit einer Präsentation von Herrn Peter Brückner, dem stellvertretenden Geschäftsführer von ERGO Limited, einer der **führenden** Firmen **auf diesem Gebiet**. Nun, wenn ich Herrn Professor Smith-Fellowes jetzt **zum Rednerpult bitten** darf, dann können wir mit etwas beginnen, von dem ich glaube, es wird ein höchst interessanter Austausch werden ...

 Background Information

The chairman says that the subject which will be talked about is **dear to their hearts**, meaning that **it is of importance to them**. One can also say **close to one's heart** or **near to one's heart**
Below are some more expressions with »**heart**«.

to set one's heart on	to wish for something strongly
to lose heart	to become discouraged
someone's heart is not in something	someone is not giving his/her complete interest or attention to something

at heart	in reality
someone's heart sinks	to be sad or disappointed
to one's heart's content	as long or as much as one wants
to take heart	to be encouraged

 176. Train Yourself

Füllen Sie die Lücken!

1. Although the new boss made us all toe the line ▓▓▓▓▓▓▓▓▓▓▓▓▓▓▓▓▓▓▓▓▓▓▓▓▓▓ he was a good-natured person.
2. Tom had his ▓▓▓▓▓▓▓▓▓▓▓▓▓▓▓▓▓▓▓▓▓▓▓▓ getting the promotion and his ▓▓▓▓▓▓▓▓▓▓▓▓▓▓▓▓▓▓▓▓▓▓▓▓ when he heard that Sandra had got the job.
3. We all ▓▓▓▓▓▓▓▓▓▓▓▓▓▓▓▓▓▓▓▓▓▓▓ at the excellent sales figures after expecting the worst.
4. Steve decided that his ▓▓▓▓▓▓▓▓▓▓▓▓▓▓▓▓▓▓▓▓▓▓▓▓▓▓▓ wasn't ▓▓▓▓▓▓▓▓▓▓▓▓▓▓▓▓▓▓▓▓▓▓ marketing and he decided to work in sales instead.
5. Lunch was an area ▓▓▓▓▓▓▓▓▓▓▓▓▓▓▓▓▓▓▓▓▓▓▓▓▓▓▓ our ▓▓▓▓▓▓▓▓▓▓▓▓▓▓▓▓▓▓▓▓▓ and everybody was pleased when 2 o'clock came around.
6. With ERGO's new security system installed a thief could try to break into the mainframe to ▓▓▓▓▓▓▓▓▓▓▓▓▓▓▓▓▓▓▓▓▓▓ but he wouldn't get very far.
7. It's important not to ▓▓▓▓▓▓▓▓▓▓▓▓▓▓▓▓▓▓▓▓▓▓ when things don't go your way.

Talk Talk Talk

(Olympia trade fair centre, dining room)	(Olympia Handelsmesse-Zentrum, Speisesaal)
M. So how do you think the morning went?	M. Na, wie ist der Morgen Ihrer Meinung nach gelaufen?

P. Well, I must say, I wasn't too **impressed with** that professor – Smith Fellowes, was that his name?	P. Na ja, ich muss sagen, ich war nicht übermäßig **beeindruckt von** diesem Professor – Smith Fellowes, war das sein Name?
M. You have difficulty remembering his name, too? I can't remember a thing of what he said. It was so dry and **delivered with a total lack of** enthusiasm for the subject. Sad, really, because he obviously is an **expert** in his field.	M. Sie können sich auch nicht mehr an seinen Namen erinnern? Ich erinnere mich an gar nichts mehr von dem, was er gesagt hat. Es war so trocken und **vermittelte so gar keine** Begeisterung für das Thema. Wirklich traurig, denn er ist offensichtlich ein **Experte** auf seinem Gebiet.
P. I think that at an occasion like this, presentation is the **top priority**. **After all**, we're here to **exchange ideas** and not just **pontificate** and **display** what knowledge we might have. I did like the second speaker, however – Tony Summerfield, from that research institute.	P. Ich glaube, bei einer Gelegenheit wie dieser ist die Präsentation **am wichtigsten**. **Schließlich** sind wir hier, um **Ideen auszutauschen** und nicht nur, um zu **dozieren** und zu **demonstrieren**, wie viel wir wissen. Aber den zweiten Redner – Tony Summerfield, von diesem Forschungsinstitut, mochte ich.
M. I liked his style, too. And his presentation was **cogent**, humorous and lively. **Made all the difference.**	M. Ich mochte seine Art auch. Und sein Vortrag war **schlüssig**, humorvoll und lebendig. **Das machte den Unterschied aus.**
P. He was no youngster, either. But what energy and commitment!	P. Er war ja auch kein junger Hüpfer mehr. Aber welche Energie und Hingebung!
M. Two other useful factors in a successful presentation. You have to believe in what you are saying and then **project** that belief with	M. Zwei weitere wichtige Faktoren für eine erfolgreiche Präsentation. Man muss an das glauben, was man sagt und diesen Glauben mit

the energy of a top actor. I've always felt that.	der Energie eines Spitzen-Schauspielers auf andere **übertragen**. Das war mir schon immer klar.
P. You should be speaking this afternoon instead of me.	P. Sie sollten heute Nachmittag an meiner Stelle sprechen.
M. Oh, no, Peter. I know how it should be done but don't ask me to do it – public speaking is not my force.	M. Aber nein, Peter. Ich weiß wie man es machen sollte, aber bitten Sie mich nicht, es zu tun – öffentlich zu sprechen ist nicht meine Stärke.
P. Well, we're about to discover if it's mine. Look at the clock. I've got ten minutes ...	P. Nun, wir werden herausfinden, ob es meine ist. Schauen Sie mal auf die Uhr. Ich habe noch zehn Minuten ...

Background Information

Peter says that «presentation is a top priority. **After all**, we're here to exchange ideas and not just pontificate ... «
»**After all**« here, means the **fact is**. It can also mean **despite problems or doubts**. For example, »We worked so hard on the project that we were able to finish in time **after all**.«
Let's look at some more expressions with »all«.

above all	most important of all
all in all	when everything is considered
all of a sudden	suddenly
all in good time	when the time is right
all over the place	everywhere
all the same	but in spite of that, anyway
the be-all and end-all	the most important aim or end

177. Train Yourself

Verwenden Sie diese Wendungen in der folgenden Übung!

1. Although we've had some ups and downs, ▒▒▒▒▒ it's been a very good year for the company.
2. I know you've not got much experience of public speaking, ▒▒▒▒▒ I'm sure you'll do a great job.
3. Excuse me you have said nothing about staff conditions. I'll come to that ▒▒▒▒▒, firstly I'd like to say ...
4. It's of great importance to come to a conference prepared. ▒▒▒▒▒ one never knows who one might meet.
5. We were having a coffee at the train station when ▒▒▒▒▒ we saw the train leave!
6. You need to be well-presented, have good social skills and a knowledge of the product but ▒▒▒▒▒ you must have motivation.
7. Can you tidy my desk, Beryl? I've got stuff ▒▒▒▒▒.
8. Having a good speaking voice is not ▒▒▒▒▒ of everything. One must know one's subject as well.

 Talk Talk Talk

(Olympia trade fair centre. Conference room)

Chairman: **I have great pleasure** now **in** introducing to you an expert from the private sector, the Assistant Managing Director of a company which **is riding the crest of this wave** we call the new economy. **What is more**, this young man is German, a **businessman** from Hamburg who has had the courage to leave his home country

(Olympia Handelsmesse-Zentrum. Konferenzraum)

Vorsitzender: **Es ist mir eine große Freude**, Ihnen jetzt einen Experten aus dem privaten Sektor vorzustellen, den stellvertretenden Geschäftsführer einer Firma, die **auf jener Welle mitschwimmt**, die wir die »New Economy« nennen. **Außerdem** ist dieser junge Mann ein Deutscher, ein **Geschäftsmann** aus Hamburg, der den Mut hatte

and **throw in his lot with** the British **subsidiary** of an American **concern**. I can't think of a better example of the **globalization** we're all talking about today. Ladies and gentlemen, I hand the rostrum with great pleasure over to Peter Brückner, Assistant Managing Director of Ergo Limited. Mr Brückner, **the floor is yours** …	sein Heimatland zu verlassen und **sein Schicksal** der britischen **Niederlassung** eines amerikanischen **Konzerns anzuvertrauen**. Ich kann mir kein besseres Beispiel für die **Globalisierung** vorstellen, als das, worüber wir heute sprechen. Meine Damen und Herren, ich überlasse das Rednerpodium Peter Brückner, dem stellvertretenden Geschäftsführer von ERGO Limited. Mr Brückner, **Sie haben das Wort** …
P. Mr Chairman, ladies and gentlemen. I am **both honoured and delighted** to be talking to you today. I was fascinated by this morning's proceedings and I think, in common with most of us, I learnt a great deal. We are living and working in an age which will surely rank as the most exciting and **profoundly innovative** in the history of the human race. It seems only yesterday that a **mouse** was just an annoying little rodent, a **keyboard** was an essential part of a piano and then of a **typewriter**, if you had **mail** the postman had called – and if you experienced a **crash** you, or your wife, had written off the car. You see, the information technology revolution has changed the very basis of our civilization – language.	P. Herr Vorsitzender, meine Damen und Herren, ich fühle mich **sowohl geehrt als auch erfreut**, heute mit Ihnen sprechen zu dürfen. Ich war fasziniert von den Vorgängen dieses Vormittags und glaube, wie die meisten von uns, dass ich viel gelernt habe. Wir leben und arbeiten in einem Zeitalter, das sicher als das aufregendste und **innovativste** in der Geschichte der Menschheit gilt. Es kommt mir vor wie gestern, dass die **Maus** nur ein nervtötendes kleines Nagetier war, eine **Tastatur** ein wichtiger Teil eines Pianos und dann einer **Schreibmaschine**, wenn Sie **Post** bekamen, dann kam auch der Postbote – und wenn Sie einen »**Crash**« miterlebt hatten, waren Sie, oder Ihre Frau, mit dem Auto angefahren. Wie Sie sehen, hat die Revolution der Informationstechnologie die eigentliche Basis unserer Zivilisation verändert – die Sprache.

Background Information

The chairman says that ERGO Ltd is riding the **crest of the wave**, meaning it is **enjoying success and good fortune**.
Let's look at some more expressions with »**wave**«.

to make waves	to make an impression
to be on someone's wavelength	to understand somebody
to wave one's magic wand	to do something that brings about a desired result as if by magic
to wave goodbye to something	the opportunity no longer exists for you
to waver	to hesitate

 178. Train Yourself

Füllen Sie die Lücken mit den oben stehenden Ausdrücken!

1. Our new publicity campaign really ▩▩▩▩▩▩▩▩▩▩ judging by the response it got.
2. When it came down to the crunch the CEO wasn't sure and he ▩▩▩▩▩▩▩▩▩▩ for a while before finally coming to a decision.
3. I really get on well with my new boss, we're on exactly the same ▩▩▩▩▩▩▩▩▩▩.
4. You can ▩▩▩▩▩▩▩▩▩▩ your chances of promotion if you don't make this deal.
5. It's not a case of ▩▩▩▩▩▩▩▩▩▩ my ▩▩▩▩▩▩▩▩▩▩. Everything must be checked with management first.
6. The company is ▩▩▩▩▩▩▩▩▩▩ at the moment. Profits are up and the shareholders are happy.

Talk Talk Talk

M. (whispers to Beryl) Beryl, he's good, he's more than good – he's really impressive. I didn't think **he had it in him**.

B. I did, from the start.

M. Beryl, are you more than a bit **taken with** our Mr Brückner?

B. Taken is the right word, Melissa. I wouldn't dare take him from you.

M. What are you talking about, you silly girl?

B. Shh. Just listen to that applause. We're not the only ones who are impressed by our Mr Brückner …

P. … and what I want to say to you today is follow the lead of the young **entrepreneurs** among us. If we don't we'll be **left behind**. This is their age, but **there's room** in it for the veterans among us, those from the old economy. **Flexibility** is the **key word**. Now can I suggest we **adjourn** and, after a coffee break, discuss this **concept**. I, **for one**, am very interested in what

M. (flüstert Beryl zu) Beryl, er ist gut, er ist mehr als gut – er ist wirklich beeindruckend. Ich hatte nicht geglaubt, **dass das in ihm steckt**.

B. Ich schon, von Anfang an.

M. Beryl, sind Sie mehr als nur ein bisschen **eingenommen für** unseren Mr Brückner?

B. Nehmen ist das richtige Wort, Melissa. Ich würde es nicht wagen, ihn Ihnen wegzunehmen.

M. Wovon sprechen Sie, Sie verrücktes Mädchen?

B. Pst. Hören Sie sich diesen Applaus an. Wir sind nicht die einzigen, die von unserem Mr Brückner beeindruckt sind …

P. … und was ich Ihnen heute sagen möchte ist: Folgen wir der Führung der jungen **Unternehmer** um uns herum. Wenn wir das nicht tun, **bleiben** wir **zurück**. Dies ist ihr Zeitalter, aber **es ist genug Platz** für die Veteranen unter uns, die aus der alten Wirtschaft. **Flexibilität** lautet das **Schlüsselwort**. Nun würde ich vorschlagen, **machen** wir eine **Pause** und diskutieren diesen

the rest of you have to say on the subject. Thank you for your attention (applause).

Ansatz nach einer Kaffeepause. Ich **für meine Person** interessiere mich sehr für das, was der Rest von Ihnen zu diesem Thema zu sagen hat. Danke für Ihre Aufmerksamkeit (Applaus).

M. Well, that was quite a presentation. It's a shame James couldn't be here.

M. Nun, das war aber eine Präsentation. Es ist eine Schande, dass James nicht dabei sein konnte.

B. He'll hear it, though. I arranged for it to be recorded.

B. Er wird es trotzdem hören. Ich habe sie aufnehmen lassen.

M. Did I call you a silly girl just now? Let's **amend** that to clever girl – now let's go and congratulate Peter ...

M. Habe ich Sie gerade ein verrücktes Mädchen genannt? **Ersetzen** wir das durch »schlaues Mädchen« – lassen Sie uns gehen und Peter gratulieren ...

 179. Train Yourself

Peter spricht von »flexibility« – dem Nomen, das von dem Adjektiv »flexible« abgeleitet ist. Finden Sie das richtige Adjektiv für die folgenden Nomina.

1. anger
2. pride
3. love
4. disappointment
5. industry
6. application
7. interest
8. gift
9. endowment
10. wealth
11. understatement

Vocabulary

a batch of sth.	ein Stapel von etw.
accounting program	Buchführungs-Programm
accounts programming	Buchhaltungs-Programm
to adjourn	Pause machen
all hands on deck	alle verfügbaren Leute
along the lines	ungefähr das
to amend	ersetzen
to appear as a very minor chapter	eine viel geringere Rolle spielen
to be all in	erschöpft, fertig sein
to be on	dran sein
to be taken with	eingenommen sein für
cogent	schlüssig
courier service	Kurierdienst
critical to s.o.'s futures	entscheidend für jds. Zukunft
customer	Kunde
dear to s.o.'s hearts	wichtig für jdn.
to deliver	hier: bieten, vermitteln
digitalisation	Digitalisierung
discussion session	Diskussionsrunde
to display sth.	etw. demonstrieren
entrepreneur	Unternehmer
exchange of views	Meinungsaustausch
for one	für meine Person
to glance through sth.	etw. überfliegen/durchsehen
globalization	Globalisierung
to grapple with sth.	sich mit etw. herumschlagen
I am both honoured and delighted to be (+ Gerund-Form)	Ich fühle mich sowohl geehrt als auch erfreut ...
I have great pleasure in (+ Gerund-Form)	Es ist mir eine große Freude ...
implications	Auswirkungen
to install	installieren, z. B. Computerprogramm
Ladies and gentlemen ...	Meine Damen und Herren ...
leading	führend
learned colleagues	gelehrte Kollegen

Präsentationen

main speaker	Hauptredner
my turn	ich bin dran
nothing short of	nicht weniger als
to pontificate	dozieren
to project	übertragen
to range from sth. to	reichen von etw. bis hin
references	Referenzen
to ride the crest of a wave	auf einer Welle mitschwimmen
rostrum	Rednerpult
sales technique	Verkaufstechnik
set up	fertig
to take off	sich entfernen, abheben
The floor is yours!	Der Platz gehört Ihnen!/ Sie haben das Wort!
topic	Thema
top priority	höchste Priorität, hier: am wichtigsten
trade fair catalogue	Messekatalog
treatise	Abhandlung
to vouch	sich verbürgen
whatismore	außerdem
with a total lack of	so gar kein

Present at the Chamber of Trade
Präsentation vor der Handelskammer

 Here we go

Allen seinen Befürchtungen zum Trotz schafft es Peter, seine Präsentation zu einem durchschlagenden Erfolg zu machen. Alle sind begeistert und loben Peter überschwänglich. Aber dessen Freude ist äußerst getrübt. Die Aussicht darauf, dass Melissa ihn und die Firma bald in Richtung Edinburgh verlassen wird, macht ihm das Leben schwer. Doch Peters Vorgesetzter, James Morgan, der von der Präsentation am tiefsten beeindruckt war, hat eine Überraschung für seinen Angestellten parat, die alle, und insbesondere Melissa und Peter, sprachlos werden lässt ...

 Talk Talk Talk

(ERGO Limited. The reception area. Peter Brückner enters)

(Der Empfangsbereich von ERGO Limited. Peter Brückner tritt ein)

Lucy: Oh, Peter! Everybody is talking about you today and the **speech** you **gave** at the trade fair.

Lucy: Oh, Peter! Alle hier reden heute über Sie und die **Rede**, die Sie auf der Messe **gehalten haben**.

P. It wasn't really a speech, Lucy. **It was** just **intended** to get people talking.

P. Es war nicht wirklich eine Rede, Lucy. **Sinn der Sache war** nur, die Leute zum diskutieren zu bringen.

L. Well, it certainly got our people talking. Melissa was full of it this morning. And Mr Morgan is **over the moon** – he wants to see you **right away**.

L. Tja, unsere Leute diskutieren ganz sicher darüber. Melissa redet heute Morgen über gar nichts anderes mehr. Und Mr Morgan ist **hin und weg** – er will Sie **sofort** sehen.

P. I'll have a cup of your tea first, please, Lucy.	P. Ich hätte zuerst gern eine Tasse Tee, wenn Sie so lieb wären, Lucy.
L. **Right away**, Peter. And a couple of my home-made biscuits?	L. **Schon unterwegs**, Peter. Und ein paar von meinen selbst gebackenen Biskuits?
J. Ah, Peter, hello! Step in, step in. Tell me all about the trade fair. I've heard Melissa's version and she was **highly complimentary** about you. She's given me a **recording** of your **address**, but I haven't had a chance to listen to it yet.	J. Ah, Peter, hallo! Kommen Sie herein, kommen Sie herein. Erzählen Sie mir alles über die Verkaufsmesse. Ich habe Melissas Version gehört und sie war **voll des Lobes** für Sie. Sie hat mir eine **Tonbandaufnahme** von Ihrer **Ansprache** gegeben, aber ich hatte noch nicht die Gelegenheit, sie mir anzuhören.
P. Oh, it wasn't that good. It was a very attentive and appreciative audience, that's all. I enjoyed the experience very much.	P. Oh, so gut war sie nun auch wieder nicht. Das Publikum war nur sehr aufmerksam und anerkennend, das ist alles. Ich habe diese Erfahrung sehr genossen.
J. You'll have other opportunities. I have to go to the States next week to discuss **expansion plans** and you'll be **standing in for** me again. I was invited to speak to the **Chamber of Trade** – can you take that over for me?	J. Sie werden dazu noch öfter Gelegenheit haben. Ich muss nächste Woche in die Staaten reisen, um über **Erweiterungspläne** zu diskutieren und Sie werden wieder **für** mich **einspringen** müssen. Ich wurde dazu eingeladen, vor der **Handelskammer** zu sprechen – können Sie das für mich übernehmen?
P. I'll do my best.	P. Ich werde mein Bestes tun.
J. Your best will be just right ...	J. Ihr Bestes wird genau das Richtige sein ...

Background Information

Peter is told here that he'll be **standing in** again in a week's time, meaning he'll be **taking the place of another person**. Other expressions with »**stand**« include:

to stand down	to withdraw or resign
to stand for	to represent (usually initials)
to stand out	to be distinctive or conspicuous
to stand by	to keep to an agreement
to stand a chance	to have a chance of winning or succeeding
to stand up and be counted	to make one's presence or opinions known
to make a stand	to be resolute about an opinion

180. Train Yourself

Füllen Sie die Lücken!

1. We allowed certain malpractices to go unchecked but ▓▓▓▓▓ ▓▓▓▓▓ against staff making private phone calls during office hours.
2. The company doesn't ▓▓▓▓▓ of competing in the electronics market unless the whole marketing strategy is changed.
3. After 20 years of working for EMC Chemicals Ltd, Paul decided to retire and ▓▓▓▓▓ at the end of the year.
4. Although Peter's speech was excellent overall one thing that really ▓▓▓▓▓ was his ability to explain his ideas clearly.
5. The initials CEO ▓▓▓▓▓ Chief Executive Officer.
6. Tony ▓▓▓▓▓ for Margaret while the latter was away on holiday.
7. The company ▓▓▓▓▓ their promise to give all the staff full-time contracts and saw the work-rate rise accordingly.
8. - If we want to break into the Japanese market we need to ▓▓▓▓▓ ▓▓▓▓▓ and that means a massive publicity campaign.

 **Talk Talk Talk**

(Peter's office. Steve enters)

S. Well, Peter my boy, I've been hearing glowing reports about your **performance** at the trade fair. Melissa was particularly impressed.

P. I know. I really do value her judgement, particularly when it comes to **presentation skills**. Her experience in marketing provides useful lessons for beginners like me.

S. You a beginner? No longer, Peter. You've **picked up** all the skills now **to run** this place **single-handed**. You'll be **taking over** sales next.

P. Don't worry, Steve. I know my limitations, and **salesmanship** is one of them. I fear I'm **pretty** bad at selling myself, **for starters**.

S. I wouldn't say that ...

P. I'm talking about my difficulties with Melissa.

S. Difficulties?

(Peters Büro. Steve tritt ein)

S. Na so was, Peter, mein Junge, ich habe schwärmerische Berichte über Ihren **Auftritt** auf der Messe gehört. Melissa war ganz besonders beeindruckt.

P. Ich weiß. Ich weiß ihre Beurteilung besonders zu schätzen, gerade wenn es um die **Fähigkeiten zur Präsentation** geht. Ihre Erfahrungen im Marketing sind sehr lehrreich für Anfänger wie mich.

S. Sie – ein Anfänger? Nicht mehr, Peter. Sie haben jetzt alle Fähigkeiten **erworben**, um diesen Laden auch **im Alleingang zu führen**. Als nächstes werden Sie noch den Verkauf **übernehmen**.

P. Keine Sorge, Steve. Ich kenne meine Grenzen und der **Verkauf** gehört ganz sicher dazu. Ich fürchte, **für den Anfang** bin ich schon **ziemlich** schlecht darin, mich selbst zu verkaufen.

S. Das würde ich nicht sagen ...

P. Ich spreche von meinen Schwierigkeiten mit Melissa.

S. Schwierigkeiten?

P. Look, Steve, I know I can **confide in** you. It must be pretty obvious now that I'm – do you say **bonkers**? – about Melissa. And now she's off to Scotland, damn it! And she still treats me as if I were just a colleague. I would have thought it's clear to her now how I feel.

P. Hören Sie, Steve, ich weiß, dass ich mich Ihnen **anvertrauen** kann. Es muss mittlerweile ziemlich offensichtlich sein, dass ich – wie sagt man – ziemlich **verknallt** in Melissa bin. Und jetzt geht sie nach Schottland, verdammt! Und sie behandelt mich immer noch, als wäre ich nur ein Kollege. Ich hätte gedacht, es müsste ihr mittlerweile klar sein, was ich empfinde.

S. Don't underestimate Melissa. She confided in me that she's very **fond of you.** I think she's going to Scotland with mixed feelings.

S. Unterschätzen Sie Melissa nicht. Sie hat mir gestanden, dass sie **sehr angetan von Ihnen** ist. Ich glaube, sie geht mit gemischten Gefühlen nach Schottland.

P. Then how do I get closer to her?

P. Aber wie komme ich ihr dann nur näher?

S. Leave it to your **good pal** Steve. I'll think of something ...

S. Überlassen Sie das Ihrem **guten Freund** Steve. Ich lasse mir etwas einfallen ...

Background Information

Peter says that he is **bonkers** about Melissa (meaning he's **crazy about** her) and asks if he can **confide in** Steve about her. To **confide in** somebody is to **tell somebody one's secrets or opinions**. We can also say »**to take somebody into one's confidence**« which has the same meaning. Be careful not to confuse **confide** with to **confine** which means to **keep within certain boundaries or limits**. The person one confides to is a **confidant** or **confidante** if that person is female and the adjective is **confidential**.
If a person is **confident** or has **confidence** then this person has **a**

Präsentationen

belief in his own abilities. The opposite of **confident** is **under-confident** or shy. Too much belief in one's abilities i.e. arrogance, is being **over-confident**.

To **confound** somebody is to **surprise** or **astonish** them. To **conform**, however, is to **comply in actions** or **behaviour**.

181. Train Yourself

Vervollständigen Sie die Sätze mit den richtigen Begriffen!

1. Due to Terry's inexperience in selling he was ▓▓▓▓▓ to observing other salespeople.
2. When making speeches it is important not to appear ▓▓▓▓▓ as this might be misconstrued for arrogance.
3. The CEO's sudden resignation ▓▓▓▓▓ everybody concerned with the company and was a total surprise.
4. The news was ▓▓▓▓▓ and for the eyes of management only.
5. Staff must ▓▓▓▓▓ to company dress codes on all occasions.
6. Simon ▓▓▓▓▓ in his superiors that he was having problems at home and was given a week's leave of absence.
7. Because of her trustworthy nature Theresa was the ▓▓▓▓▓ for half of the staff!
8. On first arriving at ERGO Ltd Peter was rather ▓▓▓▓▓ but the success of his speech made him believe in himself much more.

Talk Talk Talk

(James Morgan's office. Peter enters)

(James Morgans Büro. Peter tritt ein)

J. Now, Peter! About this Chamber of Trade speech. Any ideas?

J. Also, Peter, wegen dieser Rede vor der Handelskammer. Schon irgendwelche Ideen?

P. Since it's the Chamber of Trade, what about an address explaining the importance of the internet in **today's trading**?

J. Could you manage that?

P. I think so. I've been **reading up on** the subject, particularly on B2B.

J. B to B?

P. Business to business. It's the latest addition to the **e-commerce jargon**. It's actually written B2B, like this ...

J. Peter, you're leaving me behind. This is a new language to me.

P. It's a bit easier for me than learning English, though. And actually it's a fascinating study. I'd like to **refer to** it in the address to the Chamber of Trade. Is that all right?

J. **Fine by me**, Peter. I'm sure it will be a very interesting presentation. Reading up, reading into, reading in (a journalistic expression describing the act of catching up on **news files** before actually **getting down to work** in a newsroom).

P. Da es die Handelskammer ist, wie wäre es mit einer Ansprache über die Bedeutung des Internets im **modernen Handel**?

J. Trauen Sie sich das zu?

P. Ich glaube schon. Ich habe mich **in** das Thema **eingelesen**, besonders in »B2B«.

J. B to B?

P. »Business to Business«. Das ist die neueste Ergänzung zum **Jargon des e-Commerce**. Es wird tatsächlich so geschrieben: »B-2-B« ...

J. Peter, sie lassen mich langsam hinter sich. Das ist eine ganz neue Sprache für mich.

P. Für mich ist sie ein wenig einfacher, als Englisch lernen. Und es ist ein wirklich faszinierendes Gebiet. Ich würde in der Ansprache vor der Handelskammer gerne **darüber sprechen**. Ist das in Ordnung?

J. **Mir ist es recht**, Peter. Ich bin sicher, es wird eine sehr interessante Präsentation werden. »Reading up, reading into, reading in« (Eine journalistische Redensart, die beschreibt, wie man zuerst die **neuesten Meldungen** liest, bevor man **sich an die** eigentliche **Arbeit** in der Redaktion **macht**).

Präsentationen

Background Information

Peter says he's been **reading up on** B2B meaning he's been **acquiring information about the subject**. Let's look at some more expressions with »**read**«.

to read into	to infer a meaning not intended by the speaker
to read out	to read aloud
a read-out	information retrieved from a computer memory
to read through	to check a written text for mistakes
to take something as read	to regard something as being understood without necessarily being explained
readable	legible, able to be read
well-read	having knowledge gained from books

182. Train Yourself

Verwenden Sie diese Ausdrücke in der folgenden Übung!

1. Tony, would you mind ▬▬▬▬▬▬▬▬ my report before I give it to James?
2. This report is barely ▬▬▬▬▬▬▬▬! It looks like a spider crawled onto the page!
3. The computer ▬▬▬▬▬▬▬▬ confirmed our worst fears about profits being down again.
4. At the meeting the Sales Director ▬▬▬▬▬▬▬▬ the new policy document.
5. Martin is very ▬▬▬▬▬▬▬▬ and on our sales trip to Hereford was quoting Shakespeare all the way there.
6. Before delivering his speech Peter spent a week in the library ▬▬▬▬▬▬▬▬ the subject.

7. – James, I was hoping I could have next week off, I think I already explained to you about my home troubles.
   ▓▓▓▓▓▓▓▓▓▓▓▓▓▓▓▓ Gary. No problem. – Thanks, James.
8. It's important not to ▓▓▓▓▓▓▓▓▓▓▓▓▓▓ too much ▓▓▓▓▓▓▓▓▓▓▓▓▓▓ a situation until one knows all the facts.

 **Talk Talk Talk**

(Chamber of Trade auditorium)

Chairman: Ladies and gentlemen, colleagues, **distinguished** members of the press. It's my very **pleasant duty** today to introduce Mr Peter Brückner, Assistant Managing Director of ERGO Limited, a company which has **moved into the forefront**, into what we call the **cutting edge** of the high-tech business. Mr Brückner will be talking to us about the revolutionary possibilities **opened up** to us **business people** by the internet. I'm sure most of you will already be using the internet, in your **day-to-day business** or at home. I, for one, am constantly amazed by the possibilities offered by the internet and the mass of information I can obtain from it. Frankly, I don't know how I lived and worked before I and my **particular business went on-line**. But we are only at the start of this revolutionary era, which is moving ahead with enormous speed. **Who knows**

(Im Auditorium der Handelskammer)

Vorsitzender: Ladies and Gentlemen, verehrte Kollegen, **geschätzte** Vertreter der Presse. Es ist heute meine **angenehme Aufgabe**, Ihnen Peter Brückner vorzustellen, den stellvertretenden Geschäftsführer von ERGO Limited, einer Firma die sich **einen Platz an der Spitze** dessen **erobert** hat, was wir die **vorderste Front** des Hightech-Business nennen. Mr Brückner wird vor uns über die revolutionären Möglichkeiten sprechen, die sich uns **Geschäftsleuten** durch das Internet **eröffnet** haben. Ich bin sicher, dass die meisten von Ihnen bereits das Internet benutzen, in Ihrem **Tagesgeschäft** oder Zuhause. Ich für meinen Teil bin stets aufs Neue erstaunt über die Möglichkeiten, die das Internet bietet und die Masse an Informationen, zu denen ich dadurch Zugriff habe. Ehrlich gesagt weiß ich gar nicht mehr, wie ich leben und arbeiten konnte, bevor ich und mein **spezieller Geschäftszweig**

what tomorrow holds? And that question is at the heart of what Mr Brückner has to tell us today. Mr Brückner ...

»online« gegangen sind. Aber wir stehen erst am Anfang dieses revolutionären Zeitalters, das sich mit ungeheurer Geschwindigkeit weiter entwickelt. **Wer weiß, was morgen sein wird**? Und diese Frage ist **das Herzstück dessen**, was Mr Brückner uns heute zu sagen hat. Mr Brückner ...

P. Mr Chairman, ladies and gentlemen, colleagues, members of the press. **I am very honoured** to be speaking to you today. When I looked at the list of speakers who have addressed your distinguished body **over the years** I felt very inadequate indeed. But I did notice that I am the first to address you on what has **come to be known** as the new economy or e-commerce ...

P. Herr Vorsitzender, Ladies and Gentlemen, liebe Kollegen, geschätzte Vertreter der Presse. **Ich fühle mich sehr geehrt**, heute vor Ihnen sprechen zu dürfen. Als ich einen Blick auf die Liste der Sprecher geworfen habe, die vor Ihrem ehrenwerten Hause **im Laufe der Jahre** schon gesprochen haben, kam ich mir sehr unzulänglich vor. Aber mir ist auch aufgefallen, dass ich der Erste bin, der vor Ihnen über das spricht, was als »New Economy« oder E-commerce **bekannt geworden** ist ...

Background Information

In this section of Background Information we're going to look at some **adjectives** and their **opposites** including some examples from the last section of the dialogue.

fascinating	boring	enormous	tiny
adequate	inadequate	confusing	clear
confident	shy	generous	mean
superior	inferior	agitated	calm
hard-working	lazy	following	previous
modern	old-fashioned	fantastic	awful

 **183. Train Yourself**

Benutzen Sie diese Paare in der folgenden Übung!

1. I've never seen Tom so ▦▦▦▦▦ (agitated/calm)! What's the matter with him?
2. The rival company's offer was very ▦▦▦▦▦ (generous/mean) and so we decided to sell.
3. Our computers were becoming ▦▦▦▦▦ (old-fashioned/modern) and so we decided to have a new system installed.
4. I drank too much at the company's Christmas party and the ▦▦▦▦▦ (following/previous) day I had a terrible hangover.
5. The results were ▦▦▦▦▦ (fantastic/awful) and everybody celebrated as a result.
6. Brenda was very ▦▦▦▦▦ (hard-working/lazy) and was highly thought of by management.
7. Because Tony's sales record was ▦▦▦▦▦ (superior/inferior) to Greg's, he was given the promotion.
8. The development of the World Wide Web is ▦▦▦▦▦ (fascinating/boring) and has very important implications for business.
9. The company's debts were ▦▦▦▦▦ (enormous/tiny) and they had to declare themselves bankrupt.
10. Our performance during the last quarter was frankly ▦▦▦▦▦ (adequate/inadequate) and therefore I'm expecting a big improvement this quarter.
11. When I first arrived at the company I felt quite ▦▦▦▦▦ (confident/shy) but I soon grew in confidence.
12. The wording of the report was very ▦▦▦▦▦ (confusing/clear) and it took me a long time to understand the main points.

 **Talk Talk Talk**

(James Morgan's office. Peter enters)

J. Hello, Peter! Come in, come in! I've just been hearing **glowing** reports about your presentation at the Chamber of Trade function. I couldn't have done better myself. And that isn't **soft-soap**. You have really **advanced the company's cause** – and it's time for us to **reward you properly**.

P. James, it was a pleasure. My reward is being able to work with you and some marvellous colleagues here at ERGO.

J. No, no, no – now you are **handing out** compliments. You're a **sharp businessman**. I appreciate your loyalty. I appreciate it very much indeed. And that is another reason why I have reached an important decision about your future.

P. And that is? **I'm all ears**, as you say here in Britain!

J. Right, let me give it to you **straight from the shoulder**. ERGO's head office in America has decided to open an office in the new **techno-**

(James Morgans Büro. Peter tritt ein)

J. Hallo, Peter! Kommen Sie herein, kommen Sie herein! Ich habe gerade **überschwängliche** Berichte über Ihre Rede vor der Handelskammer gehört. Ich hätte es selbst nicht besser gekonnt. Und das ist keine **Weichspülerei**. Sie haben **dem Interesse der Firma** wirklich **gedient** – und es wird Zeit, **Sie dafür angemessen zu belohnen**.

P. James, es war mir ein Vergnügen. Meine Belohnung ist es, hier mit Ihnen und ein paar wunderbaren Kollegen bei ERGO arbeiten zu dürfen.

J. Nein, nein, nein – jetzt **verteilen** Sie Komplimente. Sie sind ein **geschickter Geschäftsmann**. Ich weiß Ihre Loyalität zu schätzen. Ich schätze sie sogar sehr. Und das ist ein weiterer Grund, warum ich eine wichtige Entscheidung über Ihre Zukunft hier getroffen habe.

P. Und das wäre? **Ich bin ganz Ohr**, wie man hier in England sagt.

J. Gut, ich werde es Ihnen **frei von der Leber weg** sagen. ERGOs Hauptbüro in Amerika hat sich entschieden, ein Büro in dem neuen

park in Glasgow, which you visited during your tour – you remember?	**Technologiepark** in Glasgow zu eröffnen, den Sie schon während Ihrer Tour besichtigt haben – erinnern Sie sich?
P. Indeed! I was very impressed with what is happening there.	P. Allerdings! Ich war sehr beeindruckt von dem, was dort passiert.
J. That's good to hear, because we'd like you to **take over** the ERGO office there.	J. Freut mich, das zu hören, denn wir möchten, dass Sie das ERGO-Büro dort **leiten**.
P. Me? Good Lord! But I still need **direction** here. How can I **run an office** – and in Scotland **of all places**.	P. Ich? Großer Gott! Aber ich brauche doch selbst hier noch **Anleitungen**. Wie soll ich da **ein Büro leiten** – und **dann auch noch** in Schottland.
J. We've **thought** that **over**. You'd be **working in close association** with Melissa.	J. Wir haben das Ganze **durchdacht**. Sie werden **eng** mit Melissa **zusammenarbeiten**.
P. Melissa? But she's taken a job in Edinburgh, and with another company.	P. Melissa? Aber sie hat doch einen Job in Edinburgh angenommen, bei einer anderen Firma.
J. We've given the ERGO **marketing account** to her company, and **in return** she'll **work closely with** us – with you, if you decide to take the Glasgow **post**.	J. Wir haben das **Marketing-Budget** von ERGO an ihre Firma vergeben und **im Gegenzug** wird sie **eng mit** uns **zusammenarbeiten** – mit Ihnen, wenn Sie sich entscheiden, den **Posten** in Glasgow anzunehmen.
P. How long have I got to decide?	P. Wie lange habe ich für die Entscheidung Zeit?
J. Two minutes!	J. Zwei Minuten!
P. Right, I **accept** …	P. Gut, ich **nehme an** …

Präsentationen

Background Information

In this section of Talk Talk Talk there are some colloquial expressions used. James says that he's going to give the news to Peter **straight from the shoulder**, meaning directly, without hesitation. He also compliments Peter and then assures him that this isn't **soft soap**, in other words, he is not being insincere and merely complimenting Peter to make him feel better. Finally, Peter announces that he's **all ears**, meaning that he's keen to hear what is being said. Let's look at some more expressions with »**ears**«.

wet behind the ears	inexperienced
up to the ears in something	completely concerned with something
to fall on deaf ears	to remain unnoticed or disregarded
to be music to one's ears	to receive good news
to prick up one's ears	to become suddenly very interested
walls have ears	a secret may become known to another person
to feel one's ears burning	to feel that one is being talked about

184. Train Yourself

Fügen Sie die oben stehenden »phrasal verbs« in die folgenden Sätze ein.

1. My superior couldn't talk to me because he was ▓▓▓▓▓▓▓▓▓▓▓▓▓▓▓▓▓▓▓▓▓▓▓▓▓▓▓▓▓ in sorting out the Macdonald report.
2. As soon as the conversation turned around to salary increases everybody present ▓▓▓▓▓▓▓▓▓▓▓▓▓▓▓▓▓▓▓▓▓▓▓.
3. I tried to get management on my side during the meeting but they weren't interested and my argument ▓▓▓▓▓▓▓▓▓▓▓▓▓▓▓▓▓▓▓▓▓▓▓.
4. The news of my promotion was ▓▓▓▓▓▓▓▓▓▓▓▓▓▓▓▓▓▓▓▓▓▓▓.

5. The Sales Director accused me of speaking too loudly and said »▒▒▒▒▒«.
6. After two months of working for the company Tony was still ▒▒▒▒▒ and needed further training.
7. I declared myself to be ▒▒▒▒▒ when Steve asked me if I would like to hear about the latest office gossip.
8. During the CEO's party I ▒▒▒▒▒ because I was sure I was being talked about.

 **Talk Talk Talk**

(Peter's office. Steve enters)

S. I've just heard we're losing you, too. **At this rate**, there won't be much of an office left here in London.

P. **I gather** James is looking for another German to replace me.

S. Another German? I thought one was enough – is this a German **takeover**?

P. Well, Steve, you know the **reputation** we have for hard work.

S. Oh, come on, Peter. It's been a **doddle** for you so far, admit it!

P. A doddle! That's a new one for me. But if you are trying to tell me it's been an **easy ride** you won't get another **round of beer** from me in your life.

(Peters Büro. Steve tritt ein)

S. Ich habe gerade gehört, dass wir Sie auch verlieren. **Wenn das so weitergeht**, wird hier in London kaum noch ein Büro übrig bleiben.

P. **Ich habe gehört**, dass James nach einem anderen Deutschen als Ersatz für mich sucht.

S. Noch ein Deutscher? Ich dachte, einer wäre genug – wird das eine deutsche **Übernahme**?

P. Tja, Steve, Sie kennen doch unseren **Ruf** für Fleiß.

S. Ach, kommen Sie, Peter. Bis jetzt war das doch alles ein **Klacks**, geben Sie es zu!

P. Ein Klacks! Dieser Ausdruck war mir neu. Aber wenn Sie mir damit sagen wollen, dass es bis jetzt eine **Kleinigkeit** war, werden Sie in ihrem ganzen Leben keine einzige

S. Oops! What a threat. **I was just about** to invite you down to the local to celebrate your **advancement** to the wilds of Scotland. But you'll be paying …	S. Uups! Was für eine Drohung. Und **ich wollte** Sie **gerade** in die Kneipe einladen, um Ihre **Beförderung** in die schottische Wildnis zu feiern. Aber Sie bezahlen …
P. Right, off we go – it might be the last round you'll ever **scrounge off** me.	P. Na schön, gehen wir – es könnte die letzte Runde sein, die Sie je von mir **schnorren** können.
S. Are you leaving that soon?	S. Gehen Sie denn so bald?
P. At the end of the month, James tells me.	P. Ende des Monats, wie James mir gesagt hat.
S. That's when Melissa is leaving, too. We can have a combined farewell party. We've got **to watch** the **business expenses**, you know…	S. Das ist genau dann, wenn auch Melissa geht. Dann können wir eine gemeinsame Abschiedsparty feiern. Wir **müssen** auf die **Spesenrechnung** achten, wissen Sie …

Background Information

A **doddle** is something that is very easy and which has exactly the same meaning as an **easy ride**. Another colloquial word used in this section is to scrounge, meaning to get something without payment.

Peter also says that the Germans have a **reputation** for hard work. One can also say the Germans **are reputed to** work hard or that they are **reputable** for working hard. »Reputation« (whether good or bad) is a noun, »reputed« is the past participle of the verb »repute«, and

> »reputable«, (or the opposite »disreputable«) is the adjective. One can also say that a person is of good or bad repute, a formal expression meaning that the person in question has a good or bad reputation.

 185. Train Yourself

Benutzen Sie die Redewendungen mit »repute« und die drei anderen umgangssprachlichen Ausdrücke in dieser Übung.

1. Tom never pays for his drinks! He prefers to ▓▓▓▓▓ one from his colleagues!
2. Mildred has a ▓▓▓▓▓ for working hard and always being on time.
3. The company were known to be ▓▓▓▓▓ and so we didn't do business with them.
4. I thought the presentation would be difficult but in the end it was a ▓▓▓▓▓ and I didn't have any problem with it at all.
5. Trevor is ▓▓▓▓▓ to be one of the best salespeople the company has ever had.
6. I wasn't expecting to be given an ▓▓▓▓▓ over my failure to close the deal but my superiors weren't too hard on me after all.

 Talk Talk Talk

(The ERGO office. A party is **in full swing**)

(Das Büro von ERGO. Eine Party ist **in vollem Gange**)

J. (**strikes** his wine glass) Just a minute, everybody. Can I have your attention, please? I'd just like to say a final farewell to Melissa and also to Peter. Final, of course, because they'll be leaving London **for pastures new**. But, of course, we'll be **keeping in relatively close touch**. Although Melissa will be

J. (**schlägt gegen** sein Weinglas) Einen Moment bitte, alle miteinander. Dürfte ich um Ihre Aufmerksamkeit bitten? Ich würde gern ein letztes Lebewohl zu Melissa sagen, ebenso wie zu Peter. Ein letztes Lebewohl natürlich deshalb, weil sie London verlassen und **zu neuen Ufern** aufbrechen. Aber

joining another company we haven't lost her entirely because she will be **in charge of** our **advertising account**. Peter will be **building** ERGO's **fortunes** in Scotland and he will continue to have the support of all of us here in London, not to mention the American **headquarters**. To both of you go our very warm wishes for a successful future in your different **endeavours** – in Edinburgh and in Glasgow. To you both – all the very, very best.

natürlich werden wir auch **relativ eng in Verbindung bleiben**. Obwohl Melissa einer anderen Firma **beitreten** wird, haben wir sie nicht ganz verloren, da sie **für** unser **Anzeigen-Budget verantwortlich** sein wird. Peter wird ERGOs **Interessen** in Schottland **vertreten** und weiterhin die volle Unterstützung von uns allen hier in London haben, ganz zu schweigen von der unseres amerikanischen **Hauptsitzes**. Wir wünschen Ihnen beiden das Beste für eine erfolgreiche Zukunft in Ihren neuen **Herausforderungen** – in Edinburgh und in Glasgow. Ihnen beiden – alles nur erdenklich Gute.

S. May I just add **a couple of words**? Peter, it's been a great pleasure to work with you – I was getting a bit worried that you were **shaping up** into such a good salesman that I was **in danger of** losing my job. Melissa, I'll miss your lovely face around the office – lucky Edinburgh to be getting you.

S. Darf ich auch noch **ein paar Worte** hinzufügen? Peter, es war ein großes Vergnügen, mit Ihnen zu arbeiten – ich hatte mir schon ein wenig Sorgen gemacht, Sie könnten **sich** zu einem so guten Verkäufer **entwickeln**, dass ich **Gefahr laufen** würde, meinen Job zu verlieren. Melissa, ich werde Ihr reizendes Gesicht im Büro vermissen – Edinburgh kann sich glücklich schätzen, Sie zu bekommen.

Beryl: You old **flatterer**! What about me then?

Beryl: Sie alter **Schmeichler**! Und was ist mit mir?

S. Beryl, sweetheart, I know I've no chance with you ...

S. Beryl, meine Liebe, ich weiß doch, dass ich keine Chance bei Ihnen habe ...

Lucy: And me? It's no more cups of tea for you, **my lad**.

Lucy: Und ich? Sie werden von mir keinen Tee mehr bekommen, **Freundchen**.

(Chip enters) Here are the train tickets for Miss Walker and Mr Brückner. I've just **picked** them **up** at the travel agency.

(Chip tritt ein) Hier sind die Bahnfahrkarten für Miss Walker und Mr Brückner. Ich habe sie gerade beim Reisebüro **abgeholt**.

S. Give them to me – I'm in charge of **company travel** arrangements at the moment ...

S. Gib sie mir – ich bin im Augenblick für die **Dienstreisen** in dieser Firma zuständig ...

Background Information

Steve in this section of Talk Talk Talk talks about Peter **shaping up** into being a good salesman. »To shape up« means the same as to become something.
We looked at some up expressions earlier. Here is a chance to revise these expressions and learn some new ones.

to pick up	to improve
to set up	to establish
to put somebody up	to provide accommodation
to shut up	to be quiet (colloquial)
to let up	to stop doing something
to bring up	to mention
to call up	to telephone
to turn up	to arrive
to come up	to occur (usually a problem)

186. Train Yourself

Benutzen Sie die oben stehenden »phrasal verbs« in den folgenden Sätzen.

1. Because we missed the train we ▓▓▓▓▓▓▓ late for the beginning of the presentation.
2. – Peter, I'm terribly sorry but something's ▓▓▓▓▓▓▓ and I can't meet you tomorrow.
3. I didn't have time to make a reservation in a hotel but luckily Tony ▓▓▓▓▓▓▓ me ▓▓▓▓▓▓▓ in his apartment for the night.
4. – Lucy, can you ▓▓▓▓▓▓▓ Rowntree Ltd and arrange a meeting for tomorrow?
5. Everything went well during the meeting until John ▓▓▓▓▓▓▓ the subject of voluntary redundancies.
6. The speech went on for hours and the speaker didn't ▓▓▓▓▓▓▓ the chairman requested him to!
7. A new branch of the company was ▓▓▓▓▓▓▓ in Paris last year.
8. The boss couldn't hear what he was saying and had to tell everybody to ▓▓▓▓▓▓▓!
9. After the recent recession business is now slowly ▓▓▓▓▓▓▓ and the forecast for next year is very promising.

Talk Talk Talk

(King's Cross station, London)

S. Hey, Peter! I'm over here.

P. Thank goodness, I was beginning to get worried. I quite forgot you had my ticket in all the excitement of the farewell party.

(King's Cross Station, London)

S. Hey, Peter! Ich bin hier drüben.

P. Gott sei Dank, ich fing schon an, mir Sorgen zu machen. Ich hatte im Trubel der Abschiedsparty ganz vergessen, dass Sie mein Ticket haben.

S. You can always **rely on** your good pal, Steve Blackman. Follow me to your train, sir!

P. But this is the train to Edinburgh.

S. Don't worry, you'll **end up** in Scotland, at least!

P. Good lord, look, there's Melissa. You told me she was taking an earlier train.

S. Probably missed it.

M. Hey, Steve, **what's going on**? You've still got my ticket you know.

S. **Here you are**, Melissa my dear. And here's yours, Peter. Here's your carriage.

M. You're travelling to Edinburgh, Peter?

S. He is now. Come on let's find your sleeper compartments. ERGO does nothing **in half measures**. It's first class for you two.

M. Hey, look, mine's right next to Peter. Steve, just what is going on?

S. **Auf** Ihren alten Freund Steve Blackman können Sie sich immer **verlassen**. Folgen Sie mir bitte zu Ihrem Zug, Sir!

P. Aber das ist der Zug nach Edinburgh.

S. Keine Angst, Sie werden schon noch in Schottland **ankommen**!

P. Mein Gott, sehen Sie doch, da drüben ist Melissa. Sie hatten mir doch gesagt, sie würde einen früheren Zug nehmen.

S. Wahrscheinlich hat sie ihn verpasst.

M. Hey, Steve, **was geht hier vor**? Sie haben immer noch mein Ticket.

S. **Hier bitte**, Melissa, meine Liebe. Und hier ist Ihres, Peter. Und hier ist Ihr Wagon.

M. Sie fahren nach Edinburgh, Peter?

S. Jetzt schon. Kommen Sie, lassen Sie uns Ihr Schlafabteil suchen. ERGO macht keine **halben Sachen**. Sie beide reisen erster Klasse.

M. Hey, sehen Sie mal, mein Abteil liegt direkt neben Peters. Steve, was soll das alles?

S. Don't worry, you're in separate compartments. But I have **booked** you dinner at the same table in the dining car. And there's a bottle of champagne waiting. And **unless** I get off this train right now I'll be travelling to Scotland with you. Goodbye – have a great journey. Oh, Peter, and there's a ticket from Edinburgh to Glasgow - **open dated**. Just in case you **fancy** spending the weekend in Edinburgh. But James says he wants you in the ERGO office in Glasgow on Monday **at nine sharp**.

S. Keine Sorge, Sie haben getrennte Abteile. Aber ich habe fürs Abendessen denselben Tisch im Speisewagen **reserviert**. Außerdem wartet schon eine Flasche Champagner auf Sie. Und **wenn** ich jetzt **nicht** sofort diesen Zug verlasse, werde ich mit Ihnen nach Schottland fahren. Auf Wiedersehen – ich wünsche Ihnen eine gute Reise. Oh, Peter, hier ist ein Ticket von Edinburgh nach Glasgow – **mit offenem Datum**. Nur für den Fall, dass Sie **Lust bekommen**, das Wochenende in Edinburgh zu verbringen. Aber James sagt, er will, dass Sie Montag Morgen **um Punkt Neun** im Glasgower Büro sind.

M. Steve, you're a **real rogue**!

M. Steve, Sie sind ein **echter Spitzbube**!

P. Steve, you're a **real pal** ...

P. Steve, Sie sind ein **echter Freund** ...

Background Information

Steve **booked dinner** for two at the restaurant, meaning he reserved a table for two people. There are many colloquial expressions using »**book**« as both verb and noun.

booked	charges recorded against s.o. (by the police)
by the book	according to the rules
everything in the book	everything possible
to throw the book at s.o.	(colloquial) to place every possible charge against s.o.; to punish severely

one for the books	something notably surprising, shocking, or unexpected
in his/her books	in his/her opinion
in s.o.'s good books	favourably regarded by s.o.
an open book	a person or subject that is well known or clearly understood
on the books	in an official record

 187. Train Yourself

Setzen Sie die Wendungen richtig ein!

1. John was ▨▨▨▨▨ for careless driving and failing to report an accident. The police ▨▨▨▨▨.
2. The teacher was very pedantic. He did everything ▨▨▨▨▨.
3. You can always tell what mood she's in. Her face is ▨▨▨▨▨.
4. In my opinion he's a crook, but ▨▨▨▨▨ he can do no wrong.
5. He likes the new secretary a lot. She's always ▨▨▨▨▨.
6. I don't want any misinterpretation of the result of the meeting. Let's get everything ▨▨▨▨▨.
7. He exceeded his annual sales target in just three months. That's ▨▨▨▨▨.
8. They really tried hard to sell that piece of equipment. They tried ▨▨▨▨▨.

 **Vocabulary**

a couple of words	ein paar Worte
address	Ansprache
to advance the company's cause	dem Interesse der Firma dienen
advancement	Beförderung
advertising account	Anzeigen-Budget

after all	schließlich
a sharp businessman	ein geschickter Geschäftsmann
to book	buchen, reservieren
to build s.o.'s fortunes	die Interessen von jdm. vertreten
business expenses	Spesenabrechnung
business people	Geschäftsleute
Chamber of Trade	Handelskammer
come to be known	bekannt geworden
company travel	Geschäftsreisen
to confide in s.o.	sich jdm. anvertrauen
day-to-day business	Tagesgeschäft
direction	hier: Anleitung
distinguished	geschätzt, verehrt
doddle	Klacks, Kleinigkeit
easy ride	Kleinigkeit, leichte Sache
endeavour	Herausforderung
expansion plans	Expansionspläne
fine by me	mir ist es recht
fond of	angetan von
forefront	vorderste Front
to hand out	verteilen (auch fig.)
to give a speech	eine Rede halten
glowing	überschwänglich
headquarter	Hauptsitz
highly complimentary	voll des Lobes
I am all ears	Ich bin ganz Ohr
I am very honoured	Ich fühle mich sehr geehrt
in charge of	verantwortlich
intended	Sinn der Sache
It's my pleasant duty	Es ist meine angenehme Aufgabe
jargon	Jargon
to join a company	einer Firma beitreten
marketing account	Marketing-Budget
to move into the forefront	sich einen Platz an der Spitze erobern
my lad	Freundchen
news file	neueste Meldungen
over the moon	hin und weg, begeistert

over the years	im Laufe der Jahre
pal	Freund, Kumpel
performance	Auftritt
to pick up	erwerben, z. B. Fähigkeiten; abholen
presentation skills	Fähigkeiten zur Präsentation
to read up on	sich einlesen
recording	Tonbandaufnahme
to refer to sth.	sich beziehen auf, hier: über etw. sprechen
reputation	Ruf, Ansehen
right away	sofort
rogue	Schurke
salesmanship	Verkauf
to scrounge off	schnorren
to shape up	sich entwickeln
single-handed	im Alleingang
soft-soap	Weichspülerei
to stand in for	einspringen für
straight from the shoulder	frei von der Leber weg
takeover	Übernahme
techno-park	Technologiepark
to think sth. over	etw. durchdenken
to work in close association/ closely with s.o.	eng zusammenarbeiten mit jdm.
pal	Freund, Kumpel
performance	Auftritt
recording	Tonbandaufnahme
reputation	Ruf, Ansehen
right away	sofort
rogue	Spitzbube
to scrounge off	schnorren
soft-soap	Weichspülerei
techno-park	Technologiepark

Auf einen Blick: Redewendungen rund ums Telefonieren

1. Anrufen

Good morning, can I speak to Mr Brückner, please?	Guten Morgen, kann ich bitte mit Mr Brückner sprechen?
Hello! Am I speaking to ARCO/Is this ARCO?	Hallo sprewche ich mit der Firma ARCO?
Peter Brückner here. Brückner of Ergo, may I speak to Mr Tomkins, please?	Hier Peter Brückner. Brückner von Ergo, kann ich bitte mit Mr Tomkins sprechen?
Is Ms Walker available?	Ist Ms Walker zu sprechen?
I'm calling on behalf of Mr Blackman.	Ich rufe im Auftrag von Mr Blackman an.

2. Anrufe entgegennehmen

Good morning, ERGO Limited. May I help you?	Guten Morgen, ERGO Limited. Kann ich Ihnen helfen?
How can I be of assistance?	Wie kann ich Ihnen helfen?
Who would you like to speak to?	Mit wem möchten Sie bitte sprechen?
May I ask who is calling?/Who is on the line? (US)	Mit wem spreche ich bitte?
Speaking.	Am Apparat.
I'm afraid Ms Walker is not in right now/in a meeting/ on holiday/at lunch/on business all week.	Es tut mir Leid, Ms Walker ist im Augenblick nicht im Büro/ in einer Besprechung/ im Urlaub/ zu

	Tisch/ die ganze Woche geschäftlich unterwegs.
I'll just find out if she is available/ back yet.	Ich werde gleich mal nachschauen, ob sie erreichbar ist/ schon zurück ist.

3. Verbinden

Could you put me through to Mr Tomkins, please?	Können Sie mich bitte zu Mr Tomkins durchstellen?
Can you connect me with the personnel department, please?	Können Sie mich bitte mit der Personalabteilung verbinden?
Please hold the line for a moment, I'll just put you through.	Einen Moment bitte, ich verbinde.
Who can I say is calling?	Wen darf ich melden?
May I put you through to her assistant/secretary?	Kann ich Sie mit ihrer Assistentin/ Sekretärin verbinden?
She has asked for no calls to be put through.	Sie hat mich gebeten, keine Anrufe durchzustellen.
One moment, please, I'll try her desk.	Einen Augenblick bitte, ich versuche, das Gespräch auf ihren Apparat zu legen.
I'm afraid the line is engaged.	Die Leitung ist leider belegt.

4. Rückrufe vereinbaren und Nachrichten hinterlassen

Could you please tell him to call me back this afternoon.	Könnten Sie ihm bitte sagen, dass er mich heute Nachmittag zurückrufen soll?

Ms Walker ist presently unavailable. Could you call back again this afternoon?	Ms Walker ist gerade nicht zu erreichen. Können Sie heute Nachmittag noch einmal anrufen?
Would you like to hold or should he call you back?	Möchten Sie warten, oder soll er Sie zurückrufen?
Can she call you back?	Kann sie Sie zurückrufen?
May I take your name and number and get someone to call you back?	Kann ich Ihren Namen und Ihre Telefonnummer notieren? Es wird Sie dann jemand zurückrufen.
In the office you can reach me on ..../My number at work is ...	Im Büro erreichen Sie mich unter ...
My home/private number is ...	Meine Privatnummer ist ...
My extension is .../The area code is ...	Meine Durchwahl ist .../Die Vorwahl ist ...
Could you give Mr Brückner a message, please?	Könnten Sie Mr Brückner bitte etwas ausrichten?
She's on the other line at the moment. May I take a message?	Sie spricht gerade auf der anderen Leitung. Kann ich ihr etwas ausrichten?

5. Termine vereinbaren

Can we arrange a meeting?	Können wir ein Treffen vereinbaren?
When would it suit you?	Wann würde es Ihnen passen?
Is next Tuesday OK with you?	Passt Ihnen nächsten Dienstag?
Let me check my appointment book.	Lassen Sie mich in meinem Terminkalender nachsehen.

I'll check with my secretary.	Ich frage bei meiner Sekretärin nach.
Could we make it a bit earlier/later?	Ginge es ein bisschen früher/später?
May I come and visit you?	Kann ich Sie besuchen kommen?
I think we should meet.	Ich glaube, wir sollten uns treffen.
I would like an appointment to see Mr Morgan, please.	Ich möchte bitte einen Termin bei Mr Morgan.
This is best discussed face to face.	Wir sollten es besser persönlich besprechen.
When could we meet?	Wann könnten wir uns treffen?
I'll just see if I have any appointments on that day.	Ich sehe nur nach, ob ich an dem Tag irgendwelche Termine habe.
Four o'clock next Thursday?	16 Uhr nächsten Donnerstag?
I'll see if he's free.	Ich sehe nach, ob er frei ist.
She won't be in until about 10 AM.	Sie wird vor 10 Uhr nicht hier sein.
She has a meeting in the city in the morning.	Sie hat vormittags eine Verabredung in der Stadt.
She has a meeting all day, how about Tuesday morning?	Sie hat den ganzen Tag eine Besprechung, wie wäre es mit Dienstag Vormittag?
She won't be back off holiday (US: back from vacation) until next Thursday.	Sie ist bis nächsten Donnerstag im Urlaub.

6. Anfragen

I'm ringing to enquire about .../ I'm calling regarding ...	Ich rufe an wegen ...
Can you tell me/ give me any idea when ...?	Können Sie mir sagen, wann ...?
Is there any chance of ...?	Gibt es irgendeine Möglichkeit ...?
We visited your stand last week at the Frankfurt fair.	Wir haben letzte Woche Ihren Stand auf der Frankfurter Messe besucht.
We saw your advertisement in the latest edition of	Wir haben Ihre Anzeige in der aktuellen Ausgabe von ... gesehen.
The British Chamber of Commerce was kind enough to pass on the name and address of your company.	Die britische Handelskammer hat uns freundlicherweise den Namen und die Adresse Ihrer Firma gegeben.
We have previously bought material from your competitors, but they are presently having difficulties with their production.	Wir haben früher Material von Ihren Konkurrenten gekauft, aber sie haben zur Zeit Produktionsschwierigkeiten.
We see a good opportunity to sell your products here in the German market.	Wir sehen gute Chancen, Ihre Produkte hier auf dem deutschen Markt zu vertreiben.
We would be interested in pocket notebooks, do you stock such items?	Wir sind an Taschennotizbüchern interessiert, führen Sie solche Artikel?
At the show in New York you let us have some samples; we would	Auf der Messe in New York haben Sie uns einige Muster mitgegeben;

now like to receive your offer for… Please send us a detailed offer based on …	wir würden jetzt gerne Ihr Angebot über … erhalten. Bitte schicken Sie Ihr detailliertes Angebot auf der Basis von …
We would need an offer for shipments ex works including price and present lead time.	Wir benötigen ein Angebot für Lieferungen ab Werk einschließlich Preisen und aktueller Lieferzeit.
Please quote on basis of a regular monthly quantity of 500 kg.	Bitte bieten Sie auf der Basis einer regelmäßigen monatlichen Menge von 500 kg an.
Do you offer a discount for large quantities?	Gewähren Sie Mengenrabatte?
We would appreciate you letting us have a company brochure and some samples showing your product range.	Wir wären Ihnen sehr dankbar, wenn Sie uns eine Firmenbroschüre und einige Muster Ihrer Produktpalette zukommen lassen würden.
Are you presently represented in the Japanese market?	Werden Sie zur Zeit im japanischen Markt vertreten?
Do you have the following material in stock: … ?	Haben Sie folgendes Material auf Lager: … ?
We have received an enquiry for two bottles of item 4379, is this presently available?	Wir haben eine Anfrage erhalten für zwei Flaschen vom Artikel 4379, ist er zur Zeit vorrätig?
Yes, this could be dispatched immediately.	Ja, wir könnten ihn sofort verschicken.
No, I'm sorry, we're completely out of this item at the moment.	Nein, tut mir Leid, wir haben diesen Artikel im Moment nicht mehr auf Lager.

Redewendungen

We will have this item ready for dispatch by the beginning of next week.	Dieser Artikel wird bis Anfang nächster Woche wieder lieferbar sein.
Would you be able to dispatch three units at the end of this week?	Könnten Sie Ende dieser Woche drei Einheiten zum Versand bringen?
Yes, of course, should I enter this for shipment?	Ja, natürlich, soll ich dies jetzt zur Lieferung eintragen?
We would need three boxes this week and two more boxes at the end of next week. Is this possible?	Wir bräuchten diese Woche drei Kartons und Ende nächster Woche weitere zwei Kartons. Wäre das möglich?
The three boxes will be OK, but the two additional boxes won't be here until the week after next.	Die drei Kartons gehen in Ordnung, aber die zwei weiteren Kartons sind vor übernächster Woche nicht hier.
Do you supply item 776 in 50-kg packets?	Liefern Sie Artikel 776 in 50-kg-Packungen?
Could you let us have the following samples?	Könnten Sie uns bitte die folgenden Muster zukommen lassen?
Yes, I'll make sure they are put in the post this afternoon.	Ja, ich werde dafür sorgen, dass sie heute Nachmittag mit der Post weggeschickt werden.
I only have the samples in brown, would this be acceptable?	Ich habe die Muster nur in braun, wäre das akzeptabel?
I'll have to check first whether we can accept this.	Ich muss zuerst überprüfen, ob wir dies annehmen können.

Do you have any special items that you would like to clear?	Haben Sie irgendwelche Sonderartikel, die Sie räumen möchten?	
We would be very interested in regularly receiving advertisements concerning special offers.	Wir wären sehr daran interessiert, regelmäßig Anzeigen über Sonderangebote zu erhalten.	
Please leave your e-mail address and I will put you on our mailing list.	Bitte hinterlassen Sie Ihre E-Mail-Adresse und ich werde Sie auf unsere Mailingliste setzen.	

7. Reklamationen

We are still waiting for .../We have not yet received ...	Wir warten immer noch auf .../ Wir haben ... immer noch nicht erhalten.
We were assured that it would be ready on time.	Man hat uns versichert, dass es rechtzeitig fertig werden würde.
I'm really sorry about that, but ...	Es tut mir wirklich Leid, aber ...
The quality of this material is not up to your usual standard.	Die Qualität dieses Materials entspricht nicht Ihrem üblichen Standard.
I cannot accept your claim.	Ich kann Ihre Reklamation nicht annehmen.
The material ordered was green and the material we have just received is brown.	Wir haben grünes Material bestellt und das Material, das wir bekommen haben, ist braun.
Please check what has happened.	Bitte überprüfen Sie, was genau passiert ist.
When could you dispatch the material in green?	Wann könnten Sie das Material in grün liefern?

Redewendungen

We could add this to your shipment tomorrow.	Wir können es Ihrer morgigen Sendung beifügen.
Both the order confirmation and the delivery note show three boxes, but we have only received two, what has happened?	Die Auftragsbestätigung und der Lieferschein zeigen beide drei Kartons, aber wir haben nur zwei bekommen, was ist passiert?
We ordered 5mm screws and you have sent us 6mm. We are prepared to keep these, but would need a delivery of 5mm screws by the end of this week.	Wir haben 5mm-Schrauben bestellt, und Sie haben uns 6mm-Schrauben geschickt. Wir wären bereit, diese zu behalten, bräuchten aber bis Ende dieser Woche eine Lieferung von 5mm-Schrauben.
Is there a chance that you could still use them?	Besteht die Möglichkeit, sie trotzdem zu verwenden?
Two of the chairs are badly damaged, the cushion material is ripped.	Zwei der Stühle sind schwer beschädigt, das Kissenmaterial ist aufgerissen.
Could you give them back to our driver when he comes on Friday? We will arrange for two replacement chairs to be dispatched tomorrow.	Könnten Sie sie am Freitag dem Fahrer wieder mitgeben? Wir werden dann morgen zwei Ersatzstühle wegschicken.
The paper we received is too thin. Could you send us a few leaves so that we can have our quality control people check this?	Das Papier, das wir bekommen haben, ist zu dünn. Könnten Sie uns ein paar Blätter zuschicken, damit unsere Leute in der Qualitätskontrolle diese überprüfen können?
The material is within our standard tolerance level.	Das Material liegt innerhalb unserer Standardtoleranzgrenze.

I will let you know.	Ich werde mich wieder melden/Ich werde Ihnen Bescheid geben.
I have passed this on to the person in charge and will get back to you when we have the results.	Ich habe es an die zuständige Person weitergeleitet und werde mich melden, wenn die Ergebnisse vorliegen.
You promised to get back to me. When will I hear from you?	Sie haben versprochen, sich noch einmal bei mir zu melden. Wann höre ich von Ihnen?
I have sent you an e-mail placing an order last week and I still haven't received any confirmation.	Ich habe Ihnen letzte Woche eine E-Mail über eine Bestellung geschickt und habe immer noch keine Bestätigung erhalten.
We had computer problems. We didn't get your e-mail.	Wir hatten Probleme mit dem Computer. Wir haben Ihre E-Mail nicht bekommen.

Auf einen Blick: Redewendungen rund um die Geschäftskorrespondenz

1. Geschäftsbriefe

Stil und Layout

Your Ref: ...
Our Ref: ...

Date: September 19, 2001

Miller Machines Inc.
Attn: Mr Anthony Brown
Purchasing Manager
5 Newton Street
Newport, Gwent

Dear Mr Brown,

Your enquiry dated April 4, 2001

Thank you for your letter of April 4, 2001 and the interest you showed in our products (...)

(...)

We enclose the requested company brochure and various catalogues. We hope that we have made you a favorable offer and look forward to hearing from you.

Sincerely,

Peter Brückner
Assistant Managing Director

Anrede

Dear Sir,	Sehr geehrter Herr ...,
Dear Madam,	Sehr geehrte Frau ...,
Dear Sir/Madam,	Sehr geehrte Damen und Herren,
Dear Mr (Mrs/Ms) Norman,	Sehr geehrte/r Herr/Frau Norman,
Dear Andrew,	Lieber Andrew,

Sirs, (distanziert)

Einleitende Phrasen

Thank you for your inquiry of May 4.

Thank you for your letter of May 14.
= We acknowledge receipt of your letter of ... /
We are in receipt of your letter of ... (very formal)
Thank you for your letter of ..., to which we now have pleasure in replying positively.

I regret to have to inform you that ...

I am writing to inquire if ...

We are writing to compliment your company on ...

Subsequent to our letter of June 6 ...
(after sending you our letter of)

Schlussformeln

We have great pleasure in enclosing complete information on ...

Should you have any further questions or require additional information do not hesitate to contact me on my personal extension.

Ms Walker asks me to add her sincere greetings.

Looking forward to hearing from you,
Yours sincerely,

Hoping to hear from you forthwith/soon,

Assuring you of our best attention at all times,
Yours sincerely,

Thanking you in advance for your prompt
attention to this matter,
Yours faithfully,

Mr Brückner joins me in sending greetings,

We remain, ... (distanziert)

Grußformeln

Yours sincerely,	Mit freundlichen Grüßen
Yours faithfully,	Mit freundlichen Grüßen
Yours truly,	Mit freundlichen Grüßen
Sincerely,	Mit freundlichen Grüßen
Best regards,	Mit freundlichen Grüßen
Kind regards,	Mit herzlichem Gruß
With kindest regards,	Herzliche Grüße/
	Mit herzlichen Grüßen

Abkürzungen

Encl.	Anlage
c.c.	Kopie an
Attn:	zu Händen von
dd (dated)	datiert
p.p.	i.A/i.V./ppa.

Bewerbungsschreiben

I noted with interest your advertisement for an Assistant Managing Director in today's Morning Post.
My attention was caught by your company's insertion in the Morning Echo, advertising the vacancy in your Marketing Department.

I am available under the above address and telephone number to provide additional information.

Antworten auf Bewerbungsschreiben

We acknowledge receipt of your application for the position which has become available in our Marketing Department, and we have pleasure in inviting you for an interview.

Following your application for the position of Assistant Marketing Officer, we have pleasure in inviting you to an interview next week.

We look forward very much to meeting you,
Yours sincerely,

Beispiel für einen Lebenslauf

Name:
Address:
Telephone number:
Email:

Born:

Education:
Primary:
Secondary:
Certificates:

Universities:
Additional studies and work experience:

References can be obtained from:

Vergessen Sie nicht das Datum und Ihre Unterschrift!

2. Faxmitteilungen

Mittlerweile ist auch in Großbritannien eine knappe Formulierung in Faxen weit verbreitet und akzeptiert. Die Formalia, die in Briefen zutreffen, sind daher nicht zwingend und können in einem Fax zu Gunsten einer kurzen, präzisen Formulierung aufgegeben werden.

FAX MESSAGE

Hans Müller GmbH
Seestraße 7
D-28717 Bremen

TO: Mr Mike Williams
Clark Industries

FROM: Mr Peter Brückner

DATE: September 19, 2001

Ref.: Conference

Dear Mr Williams,
We can attend the conference between the above dates. Please send details of accommodation and itinerary.
Thanks and regards,
Peter Brückner

Übertragungsfehler

Please refax.	Bitte noch einmal faxen.
Please repeat transmission.	Bitte Übertragung wiederholen.
The first transmission was difficult.	Die erste Übertragung war schwer leserlich.
Someone using this fax number tried to fax us this morning.	Jemand mit dieser Faxnummer hat heute Morgen versucht, uns zu faxen.
Our fax machine ran out of paper.	Unser Faxgerät hatte kein Papier mehr.
Please resend.	Bitte schicken Sie es noch einmal.

3. E-Mails

In Großbritannien und in den USA werden E-Mails in einem sehr viel informelleren Stil als in Deutschland geschrieben. Beispielsweise ist es üblich, den Adressaten mit Vornamen anzusprechen und sich informell zu verabschieden.

Re: Marketing concept
Date: 18 September 2001
From: viertill@gdf.bay.de
To: wyattjl@dds.bham.uk

Hi Jeremy,

Many thanks for your mail which I received yesterday.

I have taken into account the changes you suggested and have attached, in simple text format, what I would suggest should be the final draft of the marketing concept for your new range of products.

If you have any problems reading the attachment, please let us know and we can fax the relevant documents to you.

I look forward to hearing from you soon,
Till

Auf einen Blick: Redewendungen rund ums Verkaufen

1. Produkte präsentieren

Ladies and gentlemen, we are gathered here today to listen to Ms Walker's presentation on ...	Meine Damen und Herren, wir haben uns heute hier versammelt, um Ms Walkers Präsentation über ... zu hören.
It is my pleasure to introduce our guest, Ms Walker, to you.	Es ist mir eine Freude, Ihnen unseren Gast, Ms Walker, vorzustellen.
We are pleased to have Mr Brückner as our guest.	Wir freuen uns, Herrn Brückner als unseren Gast zu haben.
Could you please hold back all questions and comments until after I am done?	Könnten Sie bitte alle Fragen und Anmerkungen zurückhalten bis ich meinen Vortrag beendet habe.
Please feel free to interrupt me any time.	Falls irgendwelche Fragen aufkommen, scheuen Sie sich bitte nicht, mich zu unterbrechen.
There will be enough time for questions and comments after the presentation.	Im Anschluss an die Präsentation wird genug Zeit für Fragen sein.
After the first half of the presentation there will be a break of ten minutes.	Nach der ersten Hälfte der Präsentation wird es eine Pause von zehn Minuten geben.
I will begin my presentation by giving you an overview of ...	Ich werde meine Präsentation damit beginnen, Ihnen einen Überblick über ... zu geben.

We will use transparencies to present the facts.	Wir werden Folien verwenden, um die Sachverhalte darzustellen.
To show you ... I have brought some slides.	Um Ihnen ... zu zeigen, habe ich einige Dias mitgebracht.
This short film will introduce you to ...	Dieser kurze Film wird Sie mit ... vertraut machen.
I have brought a video to demonstrate ...	Ich habe ein Video mitgebracht, um zu zeigen ...

2. Kunden überzeugen

I think that/I believe that ...	Ich denke/glaube, dass ...
I am sure/certain that ...	Ich bin sicher, dass ...
I am absolutely sure that ...	Ich bin absolut sicher, dass ...
In my opinion ...	Meiner Ansicht nach ...
From my point of view ...	Nach meiner Auffassung ...
In my eyes ...	In meinen Augen ...
I presume/assume that ...	Ich nehme an/vermute, dass ...
As I see it ...	So wie ich das sehe ...
I am persuaded that ...	Ich bin überzeugt, dass ...
I am positive that ...	Ich bin mir ganz sicher, dass ...
The first reason for this I would like to mention is ...	Der erste Grund hierfür, den ich erwähnen möchte, ist ...
Second/Secondly there is ... to talk about.	Zweitens sollten wir über ... sprechen.
In addition, we shouldn't forget that ...	Zusätzlich sollten wir nicht vergessen, dass ...
Furthermore ...	Ferner/Des Weiteren ...
Moreover ...	Darüber hinaus ...
I would like to add ...	Ich würde gerne ... hinzufügen.
Not only ... but also ...	Nicht nur ... sondern auch ...
On the one hand ... on the other hand ...	Einerseits ... andererseits ...
In general ...	Im Allgemeinen ...
Generally speaking ...	Allgemein gesprochen ...

On the whole ...	Im Großen und Ganzen ...
All in all ...	Alles in allem ...
Nevertheless I should not forget to mention ...	Nichtsdestotrotz sollte ich nicht vergessen zu erwähnen ...
In spite of ...	Trotz ...
Despite the fact that ...	Trotz der Tatsache, dass ...
However ...	Aber/Trotzdem/Jedoch ...
Although ...	Obwohl ...
Instead of ...	Statt/Anstatt ...
Instead, ...	Stattdessen ...
Therefore ...	Deshalb/Deswegen ...
For that reason ...	Darum/Aus diesem Grund

3. Sie sind noch nicht ganz überzeugt!

I am not quite convinced.	Ich bin nicht ganz davon überzeugt.
I am not quite sure if I can agree.	Ich bin nicht ganz sicher, ob ich dem zustimmen kann.
What if you are wrong?	Was ist, wenn Sie sich irren?
I am afraid I cannot follow your argument.	Leider verstehe ich nicht, was Sie sagen wollen.
Could you please go more into detail?	Könnten Sie bitte mehr ins Detail gehen?
It might be better if ...	Es wäre vielleicht besser, wenn ...
Why dont't you tell us more about ...?	Warum erzählen Sie uns nicht mehr zu ...?
I wonder if you have taken into account that ...	Ich frage mich, ob Sie berücksichtigt haben, dass ...
Excuse me, Madam (Sir), may I interrupt you?	Entschuldigen Sie, darf ich Sie unterbrechen?

Sorry to break in, but ...	Tut mir Leid, dass ich Sie unterbreche, aber ...
Excuse me, may I ask you a question?	Entschuldigen Sie, darf ich Ihnen eine Frage stellen?
If I might just add something?	Wenn ich dazu etwas hinzufügen dürfte?
Before coming to a hasty decision we should leave it here.	Bevor wir zu einer übereilten Entscheidung kommen, sollten wir es hierbei belassen.
I am sorry, it is impossible to accept this offer.	Es tut mir Leid, das Angebot können wir nicht annehmen.
There seems to have been some slight misunderstanding. Could you please go back to your first point and clarify it?	Hier scheint ein kleines Missverständnis vorzuliegen. Würden Sie bitte Ihren ersten Punkt noch einmal erläutern?
We still have our doubts about ...	Wir haben immer noch Zweifel an ...
I am afraid that I cannot share your point of view.	Ihre Ansicht kann ich leider nicht teilen.

4. Neuheiten vorstellen

We are pleased to announce that this item is now available in three different new versions.	Wir freuen uns, Ihnen mitteilen zu können, dass dieser Artikel jetzt in drei neuen Ausführungen lieferbar ist.
We have developed a new series of machines for the cleaning industry.	Wir haben eine neue Reihe von Maschinen für die Reinigungsindustrie entwickelt.

We have updated our existing technology.	Wir haben unsere jetzige Technologie auf den neuesten Stand gebracht.
We are in the process of developing a new cleaning system.	Wir sind gerade dabei, ein neues Reinigungssystem zu entwickeln.
We have adjusted our machines to better suit the present market requirements.	Wir haben unsere Maschinen geändert, um den aktuellen Anforderungen am Markt besser zu entsprechen.
Would you be interested in seeing some brochures about this material?	Wären Sie daran interessiert, einige Broschüren über dieses Material zu sehen?
Should we send some with your next order?	Sollen wir Ihnen einige mit Ihrem nächsten Auftrag schicken?
We have now appointed a salesman to concentrate on your part of the country.	Wir haben jetzt einen Verkäufer für Ihren Teil des Landes eingestellt.
Could you send us some information on your new product, please?	Könnten Sie uns bitte Informationen zu Ihrem neuen Produkt zusenden?
This will enable you to benefit from on-the-spot service.	Sie werden jetzt die Vorteile des »Vor-Ort-Services« genießen können.
He can be contacted at the following telephone number:	Sie können ihn unter nachfolgender Telefonnummer erreichen:
We have just had our catalogues translated into English, we will let you have some with your next order.	Wir haben unsere Kataloge gerade ins Englische übersetzen lassen, wir schicken Ihnen einige mit Ihrem nächsten Auftrag zu.

Redewendungen

We are pleased to inform you that Mr Brückner is now responsible for all dealings with your company.	Wir freuen uns, Ihnen mitteilen zu können, dass Herr Brückner jetzt für Geschäfte mit Ihnen zuständig ist.
We are pleased to announce that you can now place your orders directly per internet. Just go to our homepage and click on »Orders«.	Wir freuen uns, Ihnen mitteilen zu können, dass Sie nun Ihre Bestellungen direkt über das Internet durchführen können. Gehen Sie einfach auf unsere Homepage und klicken Sie das Feld »Bestellungen« an.
We are pleased to announce that we have updated our existing technology and developed a new series of machines for the cleaning industry.	Wir freuen uns, Ihnen mitteilen zu können, dass wir unsere jetzige Technologie auf den neuesten Stand gebracht und eine neue Reihe von Maschinen für die Reinigungsindustrie entwickelt haben.

5. Angebote unterbreiten

Would you be prepared to accept this offer?	Wären Sie bereit, dieses Angebot anzunehmen?
Provided that ..., I will accept your conditions.	Vorausgesetzt, dass ..., werde ich Ihre Bedingungen akzeptieren.
To be honest, don't you think that his suggestion is more realistic?	Um ehrlich zu sein, denken Sie nicht, dass sein Vorschlag realistischer ist?
I still have to reject your offer.	Ich muss Ihr Angebot immer noch zurückweisen.
This is my last offer.	Das ist mein letztes Angebot.

I can see what you mean, but I still think ...	Ich verstehe was Sie meinen, aber trotzdem denke ich ...
I am afraid we cannot support your proposal.	Leider können wir Ihren Vorschlag nicht unterstützen.
Unfortunately we have to reject your offer.	Leider müssen wir Ihr Angebot ablehnen.
Would this be satisfactory for you?	Wäre das für Sie zufrieden stellend?
Last week you visited our stand at the Cologne fair and expressed interest in our products.	Letzte Woche haben Sie unseren Stand auf der Kölner Messe besucht und Interesse an unseren Produkten bekundet.
We noticed your advert (US: ad) in the latest edition of ...	Wir haben Ihre Anzeige in der letzten Ausgabe von ... zur Kenntnis genommen.
Mr Davis from Sundale mentioned that you had shown interest in our products.	Mr Davis von der Firma Sundale hat erwähnt, dass Sie sich für unsere Produkte interessieren.
You were advertising for partners in the European market.	Sie haben für Partner im europäischen Markt inseriert.
Thank you for your interest.	Vielen Dank für Ihr Interesse.
We would first of all like to tell you something about our company.	Wir würden Ihnen zuerst gerne ein bisschen über unsere Firma erzählen.
We were pleased to hear of your interest in our products, but would like more information as to your specific needs.	Wir haben uns über Ihr Interesse an unseren Produkten gefreut, möchten aber genauere Informationen über Ihre speziellen Anforderungen.

Redewendungen

We are a company specialising in the production of wooden furniture.	Wir sind eine Firma, die auf die Produktion von Holzmöbeln spezialisiert ist.
We are a leading manufacturer of locks for industrial purposes.	Wir sind ein führender Hersteller von Schlössern für industrielle Anwendungen.
We will then be in a position to make an offer based on the required application.	Wir werden dann in der Lage sein, Ihnen ein Angebot basierend auf der gewünschten Anwendung zu machen.
On what terms should we quote?	Zu welchen Bedingungen sollen wir anbieten?
Should we base our offer on full shipments or on smaller quantities?	Sollen wir auf der Basis von vollen Sendungen oder kleineren Mengen anbieten?
The present lead time is ex works three weeks after receipt of firm order.	Die aktuelle Lieferzeit ab Werk beträgt drei Wochen nach Erhalt des festen Auftrages.
At the moment there is a tremendous increase in raw material prices, but I'm sure that we can agree on a price.	Zur Zeit steigen die Rohstoffpreise erheblich an, aber ich bin sicher, dass wir uns preislich einigen können.
We offer a quantity discount if the annual quantity exceeds 50 units.	Wir bieten einen Mengenrabatt an, falls mehr als 50 Einheiten pro Jahr gekauft werden.
All our prices are quoted in German marks.	Alle Preise sind in DM-Währung errechnet.
You can also make payment in euro.	Sie können auch in Euro zahlen.

Our general payment term for overseas business is Letter of Credit, less 3% discount, or cash in advance.	Unsere allgemeinen Zahlungsbedingungen für Auslandsgeschäfte lauten gegen Akkreditiv, abzüglich 3% Skonto, oder Vorauskasse.
We would of course be delighted to send you our company brochure and some samples.	Wir würden Ihnen natürlich gerne eine Firmenbroschüre sowie einige Muster zusenden.
We will confirm this by fax.	Wir werden dies per Fax bestätigen.
We are pleased to offer as follows: All our prices are to be understood FOB German port including packing.	Wir bieten Ihnen freibleibend an: Unsere Preise verstehen sich FOB deutscher Hafen einschließlich Verpackung.
	(FOB steht für »Free on Board«. Transportkosten werden vom Auftraggeber übernommen bis die Ware am Bord des Schiffes ist. Die restlichen Frachtkosten werden vom Auftragnehmer übernommen.)
These prices are based on a minimum quantity of 50 units per order.	Diese Preise basieren auf einer Mindestabnahmemenge von 50 Stück pro Auftrag.
For CIF deliveries we would have to charge an extra 10% on list price.	Für CIF Lieferungen müssen wir einen Aufschlag von 10% auf den Listenpreis berechnen.
We hope that we have made you a favourable offer and look forward to hearing from you. Should we send you further details?	Wir hoffen, Ihnen ein günstiges Angebot gemacht zu haben, und würden uns freuen, von Ihnen zu hören. Sollen wir Ihnen weitere Informationen zusenden?

Redewendungen

Please visit our homepage. There you can find our latest price lists.	Bitte besuchen Sie auch unsere Homepage. Hier finden Sie unsere aktuellsten Preislisten.
This offer is subject to availability.	Dieses Angebot gilt, solange der Vorrat reicht.
Please advise whether this offer is of interest to you.	Würden Sie uns bitte mitteilen, ob dieses Angebot für Sie von Interesse ist.

6. Preise aushandeln

What is your current list price for item 472?	Wie ist der aktuelle Listenpreis für Artikel 472?
Our latest price list is from January of last year.	Unsere letzte Preisliste ist vom Januar letzten Jahres.
Would you be able to accept an order for 400 kg at the 500-kg price?	Können Sie einen Auftrag über 400 kg zum 500-kg-Preis annehmen?
Could you guarantee that you will take this quantity?	Können Sie garantieren, dass Sie diese Menge abnehmen?
We would then have to reduce the commission from 5% to 4%.	Wir müssten die Provision dann von 5% auf 4% reduzieren.
Our prices include 5% commission which will be paid monthly as agreed.	Unsere Preise verstehen sich einschließlich 5% Provision, die, wie vereinbart, monatlich bezahlt wird.
Commission will be paid on all orders.	Eine Provision wird auf alle Aufträge bezahlt.
The prices are subject to change.	Die Preise sind freibleibend.

At the moment the exchange rate is very weak, could you grant a currency rebate?	Zur Zeit ist der Währungskurs sehr schlecht, können Sie uns einen Währungsrabatt gewähren?
Unfortunately we have no other choice than to increase our prices.	Leider bleibt uns nichts anderes übrig, als unsere Preise zu erhöhen.
The increasing costs of raw materials make it impossible for us to hold our prices any longer.	Die zunehmenden Kosten für Rohstoffe lassen nicht zu, dass wir unsere Preise weiter halten können.
The costs of the required environmental measures force us to adjust our prices accordingly.	Die Kosten der erforderlichen Umweltmaßnahmen zwingen uns dazu, unsere Preise entsprechend zu korrigieren.
We are, however, prepared to guarantee these prices until the end of this year.	Wir sind jedoch in der Lage, diese Preise bis Jahresende zu garantieren.
After that time we would have to reconsider the cost situation.	Nach dieser Zeit müssen wir die Kostensituation neu überdenken.
We also accept payment in euro.	Wir akzeptieren auch Zahlungen in Euro.
Please keep exchange rates in mind when paying in euro.	Bitte bedenken Sie die Wechselkurse, wenn Sie in Euro bezahlen.

7. Abschlüsse erzielen

Wouldn't it be better if we tried to settle on a compromise?	Wäre es nicht besser, zu versuchen, uns auf einen Kompromiss zu einigen?
If you don't try to understand our point of view, we will not be willing to strike a compromise.	Wenn Sie nicht versuchen, unseren Standpunkt zu verstehen, werden wir nicht bereit sein, einen Kompromiss zu finden.
No, we will not support this compromise.	Nein, wir werden diesen Kompromiss nicht unterstützen.
What about leaving the differences aside and finding a solution.	Wie wäre es, wenn wir die Meinungsverschiedenheiten beiseite ließen und eine Lösung fänden?
This should be negotiable, don't you think?	Darüber sollten wir verhandeln können, denken Sie nicht?
I am afraid that we cannot come to an agreement.	Ich fürchte, wir können zu keiner Übereinstimmung kommen.
This sounds good to me and I think I can accept it.	Das klingt gut und ich denke, ich kann es akzeptieren.
Good then, I will accept your suggestion.	Also gut, ich werde Ihren Vorschlag annehmen.
I am glad that we found a common solution.	Ich bin froh, dass wir eine gemeinsame Lösung gefunden haben.
I see that we have come to an agreement.	Ich sehe, wir sind uns einig.

8. Zahlungsbedingungen verhandeln

cash in advance	Vorauskasse
cash on delivery (COD)	Per Nachnahme
cash against documents (CAD)	Kasse gegen Dokumente
Sixty days after date of invoice, net.	Sechzig Tage nach Rechnungsdatum, netto.
Today we have received a limit of DM 50,000. The order will be shipped with payment term 30 days after date of invoice, net.	Heute haben wir ein Limit in Höhe von DM 50.000 erhalten. Wir werden den Versand des Auftrages vornehmen mit Zahlungsbedingung 30 Tage nach Rechnungsdatum, netto.
No limit was granted.	Es wurde kein Limit gewährt.
We need a bank guarantee.	Wir benötigen eine Bankgarantie.
The pro forma invoice will be faxed.	Die Proformarechnung wird gefaxt.
When the invoice is paid, we will arrange for the goods to be sent.	Nachdem die Rechnung bezahlt ist, werden wir den Versand vornehmen.
Payable immediately after receipt of the goods.	Zahlbar sofort nach Erhalt der Ware.
Please open the L/C as follows: Part shipments allowed. Tolerance of 5% for quantity and amount. Latest date of shipment: 31.07.2001.	Bitte eröffnen Sie den L/C wie folgt: Teillieferungen erlaubt. Toleranzbereich von 5% für Menge und Betrag. Verschiffung spätestens am: 31.07.2001.

Would it be possible to issue the invoice in US dollars?	Wäre es möglich, die Rechnung in US Dollar auszustellen?
It is our company policy only to invoice in German marks.	Es entspricht unserer Firmenpolitik, nur in Deutschen Mark zu fakturieren.
What is your usual payment term?	Wie ist Ihre übliche Zahlungsbedingung?
We could offer you cash in advance less 3% discount.	Wir könnten Ihnen Vorauskasse abzüglich 3% Skonto anbieten.

Auf einen Blick: Redewendungen rund ums Präsentieren

1. Sitzungen planen

We will schedule our next quarterly meeting for ...	Wir werden unsere nächste Quartalbesprechung für ... ansetzen.
We should notify the participants of the next annual production meeting as soon as possible.	Wir sollten die Teilnehmer der nächsten Jahresproduktionsbesprechung so schnell wie möglich benachrichtigen.
Handouts containig the agenda should be sent out beforehand to everybody.	Handouts mit der Tagesordnung sollten vorab an alle verschickt werden.
Will all the staff be able to come?	Wird die ganze Belegschaft kommen können?
Shall we postpone the meeting?	Sollen wir die gesamte Besprechung auf später verschieben?
Should we settle on a later date?	Sollten wir uns auf einen späteren Termin einigen?
Would it be better to cancel the meeting altogether?	Wäre es besser die Besprechung ganz abzusagen?

2. Sitzungen moderieren

Begrüßen und Vorstellen

Ladies and gentlemen, welcome to today's meeting.	Meine Damen und Herren, ich begrüße Sie zu der heutigen Sitzung.

Ladies and gentlemen, I am happy to welcome you to our annual business meeting.	Meine Damen und Herren, ich freue mich Sie zu unserer jährlichen Geschäftsbesprechung willkommen zu heißen.
Welcome and thank you for coming today.	Herzlich willkommen und vielen Dank, dass Sie heute erschienen sind.
Ladies and gentlemen, we are gathered here today to listen to Mr Brückner's presentation on ...	Meine Damen und Herren, wir haben uns heute hier versammelt, um Herrn Brückners Präsentation über ... zu hören.
We have an extremely important session today.	Wir haben heute eine ausgesprochen wichtige Sitzung.
This month's meeting will have the following subject: ...	Die Besprechung dieses Monats hat folgendes Thema: ...
Mr Brückner's talk on ... will introduce us to today's topic.	Herr Brückners Vortrag über ... wird uns in das heutige Thema einführen.
It's my pleasure to introduce our guest, Ms Melissa Walker.	Es ist mir eine Freude, Ihnen unseren Gast, Frau Melissa Walker, vorzustellen.
We are pleased to have Ms Walker as our guest.	Wir freuen uns, Frau Walker als unseren Gast zu haben.
I'm sorry to announce that Ms Walker will be late.	Es tut uns Leid, Ihnen mitteilen zu müssen, dass Frau Walker sich verspäten wird.
We will begin the meeting in five minutes.	Wir werden in fünf Minuten mit der Besprechung beginnen.

Die Tagesordnung vorstellen

We will start even if not everybody has arrived.	Wir werden beginnen, auch wenn noch nicht alle da sind.
Handouts are provided for every member.	Jedes Mitglied bekommt ein Handout.
The agenda has been handed out in advance.	Die Tagesordnung ist schon vorab ausgeteilt worden.
Everybody should be in possession of a detailed description of today's topic.	Jeder sollte im Besitz einer detaillierten Beschreibung des heutigen Themas sein.
On the handout you can see this meeting's agenda.	Dem Handout können Sie die Tagesordnung dieser Besprechung entnehmen.
The meeting will follow the items on the agenda.	Die Sitzung wird den Punkten der Tagesordnung folgen.
Items can be added to today's agenda.	Der Tagesordnung können Punkte hinzugefügt werden.
Items can be deleted from the agenda.	Es können Punkte von der Tagesordnung gestrichen werden.

Protokollant bestimmen

We need somebody to keep the minutes.	Wir brauchen jemanden, der Protokoll führt.
Somebody has to be appointed to keep the minutes.	Irgendjemand muss dazu ernannt werden, Protokoll zu führen.
Mr Brückner would you be so kind to keep the minutes today?	Herr Brückner, wären Sie so freundlich, heute Protokoll zu führen.

If nobody volonteers I will have to appoint someone.	Falls sich niemand freiwillig meldet, muss ich jemanden bestimmen.

Diskussionen eröffnen

I hope that we will have an interesting discussion.	Ich hoffe, dass wir eine interessante Diskussion haben werden.
Due to the controversial topic of the presentation we will probably have a very lively discussion.	Aufgrund des umstrittenen Themas der Präsentation werden wir wahrscheinlich eine sehr lebhafte Diskussion haben.
There are still the following aspects of the problem to talk about.	Über folgende Aspekte des Problems müssen wir noch sprechen.
With this last statement we should open the discussion.	Mit dieser letzten Feststellung sollten wir die Diskussion eröffnen.
We can now discuss whatever you would like to be discussed.	Wir können jetzt alles diskutieren, was Sie zur Diskussion stellen möchten.
Now is the time to comment on Ms Walker's point of view, which she has elaborated on this past hour.	Jetzt ist der Zeitpunkt gekommen, Frau Walkers Ansicht zu kommentieren, die sie in der letzten Stunde ausführlich dargelegt hat.

Gesprächsergebnisse zusammenfassen

The following suggestions have been made:	Folgende Vorschläge sind gemacht worden:
To sum up ...	Um es zusammenzufassen ...

Die Sitzung schließen

Thank you, ladies and gentlemen, for being here today.	Meine Damen und Herren, vielen Dank, dass Sie heute gekommen sind.
Finally, all I have to say is that I think we should leave this aspect of the problem for the time being and call it a day.	Abschließend bleibt mir nur noch zu sagen, dass ich denke, wir sollten diesen Aspekt des Problems für heute beiseite lassen und Feierabend machen.
Goodbye, ladies and gentlemen, and thank you for being here. We will meet here again next week.	Auf Wiedersehen, meine Damen und Herren, vielen Dank, dass Sie hier waren. Nächste Woche treffen wir uns wieder hier.

3. Präsentationen führen

»warm up«

I am pleased to be here today/ I am glad to be here.	Ich freue mich heute hier zu sein/ Ich freue mich, hier zu sein.

Die Präsentation vorweg organisieren

Could you please hold back all questions and comments until after I am done.	Könnten Sie bitte alle Fragen und Anmerkungen zurückhalten bis ich fertig bin?
I would prefer answering any questions after having finished my talk.	Ich würde es vorziehen, Fragen erst zu beantworten, nachdem ich meinen Vortrag beendet habe.
If any questions arise please do not hesitate to interrupt me.	Falls irgendwelche Fragen aufkommen, scheuen Sie sich bitte nicht, mich zu unterbrechen.

Please feel free to interrupt me any time.	Bitte zögern Sie nicht, mich jederzeit zu unterbrechen.
There will be enough time for questions and comments after the presentation.	Im Anschluss an die Präsentation wird genug Zeit für Fragen sein.
After the first half of the presentation there will be a break of ten minutes.	Nach der ersten Hälfte der Präsentation wird es eine Pause von zehn Minuten geben.

Präsentieren

I will begin my presentation with giving you an overview of last year's development of the sales figures.	Ich werde meine Präsentation damit beginnen, Ihnen einen Überblick über die Entwicklung der Verkaufszahlen des letzten Jahres zu geben.
Before going into details I will give you the necessary background information.	Bevor ich ins Detail gehe, werde ich Ihnen die notwendigen Hintergrundinformationen geben.
In order to present the facts, I will use overhead foils.	Um die Fakten darzustellen, werde ich Overhead-Folien verwenden.
Pie charts are best suited for the presentation of percentages.	Kreisdiagramme sind am geeignetsten für prozentuale Darstellungen.
I will be using flip charts to illustrate …	Ich werde Flipcharts zur Verdeutlichung von … benutzen.
To show you … I have brought some slides.	Um Ihnen … zu zeigen, habe ich einige Dias mitgebracht.
This short film will introduce you to …	Dieser kurze Film wird Sie mit … vertraut machen.

I have brought a video to demonstrate ...	Ich habe ein Video mitgebracht, um zu zeigen, ...
From this table you can see ...	Aus dieser Tabelle können Sie ... entnehmen.
I almost forgot to tell you ...	Beinahe vergaß ich Ihnen zu sagen, dass ...

Präsentationen beenden

With the following quotation I will bring my presentation to an end.	Mit dem folgenden Zitat möchte ich meine Präsentation beenden.
Let me conclude with the following statement: ...	Lassen Sie mich mit der folgenden Feststellung abschließen: ...
You may now ask all questions that arose during my presentation.	Sie dürfen jetzt sämtliche Fragen stellen, die während meiner Präsentation aufgekommen sind.
I am now willing to answer any questions.	Ich bin jetzt bereit, Fragen zu beantworten.

4. Fragen einbringen

Excuse me, Madam (Sir), may I interrupt you?	Entschuldigen Sie, darf ich Sie unterbrechen?
Sorry to break in but ...	Tut mir Leid, dass ich Sie unterbreche, aber ...
Excuse me, may I ask you a question?	Entschuldigen Sie, darf ich eine Frage stellen?
I would like to say a few words.	Ich würde gerne einige Worte sagen.

There is something I would like to say.	Ich würde gerne etwas sagen.
If I might just add something.	Wenn ich dazu etwas hinzufügen dürfte?
I agree with most of what you presented here, yet don't you think that ...	Dem meisten von dem, was Sie hier vorgestellt haben, stimme ich zu, aber denken Sie nicht, dass ...
Everything you said is fine, but one should also take other aspects into account.	Was Sie gesagt haben ist schön und gut, aber man könnte auch andere Aspekte in Betracht ziehen.
I wonder if you have taken into account that ...	Ich frage mich, ob Sie berücksichtigt haben, dass ...
Could you please go more into detail?	Könnten Sie bitte mehr ins Detail gehen?
Why don't you tell us more about ...?	Warum erzählen Sie uns nicht mehr zu ...?

5. Standpunkte erläutern

For this two factors are responsible: First, ... Second, ...	Hierfür sind zwei Faktoren verantwortlich: Erstens, ... Zweitens, ...
I believe that there are several reasons: Firstly, ... Secondly, ...	Ich glaube, dass es verschiedene Gründe gibt: Erstens, ... Zweitens, ...
The main reason for this is ... Furthermore, ... Consequently, ... Therefore, ... In addition, ...	Der Hauptgrund hierfür ist ... Darüberhinaus/des Weiteren ... Folglich ... Deshalb/deswegen ... Zusätzlich ...

Business- und Internet-Trendwörter von A bis Z

A

Accelerator »Gaspedal« oder »Beschleuniger«; hinter dem Begriff Accelerator versteckt sich eine Person oder ein Unternehmen, das einem Start-up Infrastruktur in Form von Räumen und Computern zur Verfügung stellt, aber auch beim Aufbau des Geschäfts beratend zur Seite steht. Dadurch soll der Aufbau der Firma wesentlich beschleunigt werden, um z. B. den First Mover Advantage zu nutzen. Als Gegenleistung erfolgt meist eine Beteiligung am Unternehmen.

Ad Click »Werbeklick«; das Internet macht Werbeeinblendungen klickbar und damit den Erfolg messbar: Bei den »Ad Clicks« wird gezählt, wie viele Besucher einer Seite ein dort geschaltetes Banner anklicken und sich zu dem dahinter stehenden Angebot weiterleiten lassen. Die »Ad Click Rate« setzt dies in Relation zu denjenigen Usern, die eine Anzeige nur gesehen haben, meist über einen Monat hinweg gemessen. Wenn zwei von 100 Besuchern klicken, also nur 2 Prozent, dann gilt das bereits als eine gute Rate.

Added Value Der so genannte »Zusatzwert« ist eine Art Geschenk an den Kunden. Der eigentliche Zweck dieser Eigenschaft ist es, ein Produkt oder eine Dienstleistung gegenüber den Konkurrenzprodukten hervorzuheben. Der Added Value soll dem Kunden auch einen Gegenwert für seine Kommunikationskosten bieten.

Ad Impression Die Ad Impressions geben die Anzahl der Sichtkontakte von Internet-User mit einem Banner wieder. Anders als bei den Messeinheiten Visits und Page Impressions erfassen die Ad Impressions auch bei dynamischen, für jeden Nutzer individuell zusammengestellten Angeboten, die Zahl der Werbekontakte.

Ad Server Der Werbeserver ist ein zentraler Computer, der festlegt, welcher Internet-Surfer wann welche Werbung (Banner) zu sehen bekommt. Dafür benutzt der Ad Server zum Beispiel Cookies, um den Benutzer zu identifizieren und ihm auf seine Person abgestimmte Angebote zu unterbreiten. Außerdem kann der Ad Server den

Erfolg der Werbung messen, indem er feststellt, wie oft ein Banner angeklickt wird (Ad Click).

ADSL Asymmetric Digital Subscriber Line; neue Technik zur Datenübertragung, die die herkömmliche Telefonleitung besser ausnutzen soll. Im Gegensatz zum normalen Internetanschluss verläuft der Datenstrom asymmetrisch: mit einer hohen Übertragungsrate vom Internet zum Benutzer und mit einer niedrigen vom Benutzer zum Internet. Datenpakete wie z. B. Software oder Filme lassen sich so mit der zehnfachen ISDN-Geschwindigkeit herunterladen.

Analyst Fachmann, der Aktiengesellschaften und Aktienmärkte professionell beobachtet und versucht, Kursentwicklungen vorherzusagen. Aufgrund von Unternehmensdaten, aber auch anhand des grafischen Verlaufs der Kurse (so genannte »Charts«), gibt der Analyst Kaufs- oder Verkaufsempfehlungen. Oft lösen erst diese Bewertungen eine Kursveränderung aus.

ASP Application Service Provider; Anbieter von Applikationen (Anwendungen). Dahinter steckt der Gedanke, dass für bestimmte Aufgaben nicht immer ein dickes Software-Paket gebraucht wird, sondern nur spezielle Teile eines Programms. Diese schlanken Software-Pakete kann man bei einem ASP kaufen oder mieten und bekommt sie über das Internet zur Verfügung gestellt. Bei Privatanwendern hat sich dieser Gedanke bisher aber noch nicht so stark durchgesetzt wie bei Firmen.

Averaging Englisch für »den Durchschnitt bildend«. Die Optimierung des durchschnittlichen Einstandspreises von Wertpapieren oder Investmentzertifikaten durch regelmäßigen gleichbleibenden Zukauf.

B

B2B Business-to-Business; Geschäftsbeziehung und Handel zwischen zwei Firmen, meist über das Internet. Anders als bei den häufig mit viel Werbeaufwand lancierten B2C-Marktplätzen, findet das B2B-Geschäft fast im Verborgenen statt. Das sollte aber nicht darüber hinweg täuschen, dass manche Experten ihm ein wesentlich größeres Geschäft und mehr Gewinn zutrauen als z. B. den E-Tailern, die sich an Privatkonsumenten wenden. B2B-Marktplätze gibt es in unterschiedlichen Ausprägungen, so z. B. zwischen einem Hersteller und seinen Lieferanten, als Portal einer bestimmten Branche oder als Barter-Plattform.

B2C Business-to-Consumer; hier handeln Firmen direkt mit dem Kunden und versteigern beispielsweise im Internet Flugtickets, Stereoanlagen etc., oft aus Restbeständen oder mit kleinen Fehlern.

B2G Business-to-Government; Privatfirmen vermitteln übers Internet Dienstleistungen oder Waren an die öffentliche Hand; ein noch kaum erschlossenes Geschäftsfeld im E-Commerce, von dem sich Experten aber viel versprechen: Das Bundeswirtschaftsministerium schätzt den bundesweiten Bedarf allein im Beschaffungswesen auf rund 400 Milliarden Mark im Jahr.

Back End 1. Bezeichnet alles, was im Back-Office-Bereich passiert, also die Abwicklung von Bestellungen, Logistik, Lieferkontakte, Beschaffung usw. »Front End« heißen dagegen Aktivitäten, die auf Kundenkontakt ausgerichtet sind, also die Neukundengewinnung oder das Erschließen neuer Geschäfte. – 2. Bei Software bezeichnet man mit »Back End« Programme, zu denen der Benutzer keinen direkten Kontakt hat. Sie arbeiten meist im Hintergrund und stellen anderen Programmen Daten zur Verfügung – zum Beispiel »Front End«-Programmen, mit denen der Benutzer in Interaktion tritt.

Banner Werbeflächen auf Internetseiten, die von einem Ad Server möglichst zielgruppengerecht eingespielt werden und meist interaktiv sind. Viele Banner enthalten auch animierte Grafiken, um mehr Aufmerksamkeit auf sich zu lenken.

Barter Englisch für »Kompensationsgeschäft«. Das Internet lässt den Tauschhandel wieder aufleben. Das Prinzip: Ein Anbieter verkauft seine Waren oder Dienstleistungen nicht gegen Geld, sondern tauscht sie gegen andere Waren oder Dienstleistungen, die er braucht. Also: ein Friseur, der verreisen will, bezahlt sein Hotelzimmer, indem er der Hotelchefin die Haare schneidet. Eine einfache Form des Barters ist der »Bannerbarter«: Internetfirmen tauschen

Werbebanner aus und weisen auf ihrer Website gegenseitig auf ihre Angebote hin.

BCC Blind Carbon Copy; Kopie einer E-Mail, bei der der Empfänger nicht sehen kann, an wen sie noch verschickt wurde.

Beauty Contest Schönheitswettbewerb, bei dem es allerdings weniger um Schönheit als um Geld geht. Um das Geld der Banken, die ein Unternehmen bei einem Börsengang als Begleiter (so genannte Konsortialpartner) gewinnen will.

Below the Line Marketingmaßnahme, die nicht auf eine breite öffentliche Wahrnehmung zielt, sondern auf eng umrissene Kundengruppen. Diese versucht man direkt und ohne Streuverluste zu erreichen – z. B. mit »Direct Mail«. Wenn es gelingt, die Zielgruppe genau einzugrenzen (durch Techniken wie Data Mining), kann diese Marketingform deutlich wirksamer sein als herkömmliche Methoden »Above the Line«. Nicht zu verwechseln mit »unterschwelliger Werbung«, mit der in den 60er Jahren erfolglos experimentiert wurde. Dabei versuchte man, suggestive Einzelbilder unterhalb der Wahrnehmungsschwelle in Filmbotschaften einzuschleusen, die direkt auf das Unterbewusstsein wirken sollten.

Benchmarking Vom Englischen »benchmark« = »Maßstab«; Methode zur Wettbewerbsanalyse und Verbesserung des eigenen Unternehmens. Beim Benchmarking werden bestimmte Größen wie Produktionskosten, aber auch das Produkt selbst ständig mit dem besten (Konkurrenz-) Unternehmen (»best practice«) verglichen. Anschließend wird daran gearbeitet, den Abstand zu verringern.

Betaversion Bei einer Betaversion handelt es sich um eine neue Software, die erstmals an Konsumenten geliefert wird, obwohl sie noch unausgereift ist. Die Benutzer erhalten die Betaversion meist kostenlos und testen im Gegenzug das Produkt unter Praxisbedingungen. Mithilfe des Feedbacks wird dann ein »Release Candidate« und schließlich die »Final Version« entwickelt. Natürlich gibt es auch eine Alphaversion. Dieser Begriff bezeichnet den noch stark fehlerbehafteten Vorgänger der Betaversion.

Blamestorming Vom Englischen »to blame« = »beschuldigen«; die Technik kennt man vom »Brainstorming«: Eine Gruppe lässt den Gedanken freien Lauf, um auf neue, kreative Ideen zu kommen. Beim »Blamestorming« ist das Ziel ein anderes: den Schuldigen für das Scheitern eines Projektes zu benennen. Es ist also eine Art kollektiver Pranger, der aber reinigende Wirkung auf das Team haben soll.

Blue Chips Aktien von erstklassigen, besonders bekannten und großen Unternehmen, auch »Standardwerte« genannt. Der Ausdruck kommt aus den US-Spielcasinos: Dort haben die blauen Spieljetons den höchsten Wert.

Books on Demand »Bücher auf Nachfrage«; Bücher, die erst auf Bestellung produziert werden. Dadurch entfallen Massenproduktions- und Lagerkosten, weil ja keine Bücher mehr auf Vorrat hergestellt werden müssen. Die nötige Technik liefert das Internet: Autoren hinterlegen dort ihre Druckvorlagen, auf Bestellung wandern die Daten in die Druckerei, das fertige Buch wird an den Kunden geschickt. So werden auch Kleinstauflagen von Büchern wirtschaftlich, die sonst nie gedruckt worden wären.

Brain Drain Beschreibt den Verlust an klugen Köpfen, den Abfluss an Wissenskapital. Nicht nur aus Unternehmen werden die Besten von Headhuntern immer wieder abgeworben. Auch Staaten leiden unter dem »Brain Drain«: Ihre jungen Experten verlassen wegen besserer Verdienstmöglichkeiten das Land und gehen in die wirtschaftlich starken Regionen. Diese verzeichnen dann einen »Brain Gain«, einen Zuwachs an Wissen.

Brand Reputation Management Weil Marken so wertvoll sind (Branding), müssen sie gepflegt und weiterentwickelt werden. Beim Brand Reputation Management wird versucht, das ganze Unternehmen auf die Verbesserung des Markenimages auszurichten. Das schließt z. B. auch Auftritte des Vorstands oder den Kundenkontakt mit ein. Wenn die Marke sich als besonders dynamisch und modern darstellt, muss sie das auch durch ihre Mitarbeiter nach außen vertreten. Natürlich gehören dazu auch klassische Werbemaßnahmen, die allerdings nicht nur auf die kurzfristige Aufmerksamkeit zielen, sondern auch auf die langfristige Bedeutung für den Ruf eines Unternehmens.

Branding Vom Englischen »brand« = »Marke«; lässt sich am besten mit »Markenplatzierung/Markenführung« übersetzen. Dahinter steckt die Erkenntnis, dass der Markenname, sein Image und sein Bekanntheitsgrad häufig fast die Hälfte des Produktwertes ausmachen (Goodwill), weil Kunden die Produkte oft nur noch durch die Marke unterscheiden können. Bei einigen weltbekannten Firmen ist der Wert der Marke oft sogar noch deutlich höher. Firmen versuchen deshalb, z. B. durch Namensgebung und Logo, ein neues Produkt zu einer Marke aufzubauen oder an eine ihrer bestehenden Marken anzulehnen.

Break-Even-Point Der Punkt, an dem der Kaufmann sich zu freuen beginnt: Erstmals sind Kosten und Gewinne eines Unternehmens gleich groß. Wenn der Break-Even-Point erreicht ist, kommt also langsam Geld in die Kasse, das Geschäft beginnt sich zu rentieren.

Bricks and Mortar »Ziegel und Mörtel«; gemeint ist damit kein Maurerbetrieb, sondern schlichtweg all die handfesten Firmen der so genannten »Old Economy«, die in der realen Welt durch Fabrikgebäude, Lagerhallen und sichtbare Produkte präsent sind. Im Gegensatz zu den »New Economy«-Unternehmen, die weitgehend im Internet existieren und häufig mit unsichtbaren Datenströmen handeln.

Bridge Financing »Überbrückungsfinanzierung«; mit diesem Geld bereitet ein Unternehmen den Börsengang vor. Meist ist es kein Überbrückungskredit, die Geldgeber wollen stattdessen am Unternehmen beteiligt werden.

Browser Software, die es ermöglicht, die Inhalte des World Wide Web zu betrachten. Zu den bekanntesten Web-Browsern zählen Netscape Navigator und der Internet Explorer.

Burn Rate »Brennrate«; was hier »verbrennt«, ist Geld: Die Burn Rate zeigt, wie viel Verlust ein Unternehmen – meist pro Monat – macht.

Gerade bei Internet-Start-ups (Start-up) haben die Investoren am Anfang eine hohe Burn Rate hingenommen, ja sogar positiv bewertet: Sie galt als Zeichen dafür, dass die Firma in schnelles Wachstum investiert und, zum Beispiel durch teure Marketingkampagnen, ihren Bekanntheitsgrad steigert. Wer aber nur Geld verbrennt, hat am Ende natürlich keines mehr. Dann spricht man vom »Fume Day«, dem Tag, an dem sich das Kapital in Rauch aufgelöst hat. Das eigentliche Ziel ist aber, irgendwann mehr einzunehmen als auszugeben und dadurch den Break-Even-Point zu erreichen.

Burnout Wörtlich: »Ausbrennen«; Folge von zu viel Stress durch Arbeit und Informationsflut. Die Symptome sind ähnlich wie bei einer Depression: Antriebsschwäche, Schlafstörungen, Angstzustände.

Business Angel Kein völlig uneigennütziger Engel, sondern letztlich ein Geschäftsmann, der auch am Gewinn interessiert ist: Mit »Business Angel« bezeichnet man private Investoren eines Start-ups. Sie bringen meist Beträge bis zu einer halben Million Mark mit, aber zusätzlich noch Management-Erfahrung und Beratung (Smart Money). Im Gegenzug werden sie an der Firma beteiligt. Meistens ist ein Business Angel seinem Unternehmen stärker verbunden als die Investoren von Venture Capital. Er sucht deshalb nur selten nach der schnellen Mark, sondern denkt etwas langfristiger.

Business Plan In einem Business-Plan sind auf wenigen Seiten Geschäftsidee, Konzept und Ziele eines Start-ups zusammengefasst. Er dient dazu, Investoren von einem Unternehmen zu überzeugen und sie zur Zahlung von Risiko-Kapital (Venture Capital) zu bewegen.

Buy Back Bei einem Buy Back kauft eine Aktiengesellschaft bzw. die Altgesellschafter ihre eigenen Aktien zurück. Die Börsen werten dies häufig als Signal für einen steigenden Kurs, weil das Unternehmen offensichtlich an seine Aktien glaubt. Tatsächlich steigt oft durch den Kauf selbst der Kurs deutlich an. Vorsicht ist allerdings geboten, wenn das Unternehmen für den Buy Back seine Investitionen vernachlässigt. Dann handelt es sich wahrscheinlich um den Versuch, den eigenen Aktienkurs zu stützen, eine langfristige positive Entwicklung bleibt aber meistens aus.

BWQ Buzz-Word-Quotient; ironischer Seitenhieb auf den Anteil an Modewörtern in einem Text oder in einer Rede.

C

C2C Consumer-to-Consumer; Geschäft zwischen zwei einfachen Endverbrauchern: Herr A will sein Auto verkaufen, Frau B kauft es. Das lokale Anzeigenblatt, in dem solche Angebote bisher inseriert waren, soll in Zukunft von C2C-Plattformen im Internet abgelöst werden.

Calendar Server Der »Kalender-Server« ist ein Programm, das die Terminverwaltung über das Internet sowohl von Gruppen und Abteilungen, als auch von ganzen Unternehmen weltweit ermöglicht.

Call Optionsgeschäft an der Börse. Gibt dem Anleger das Recht, eine bestimmte Aktie zu einem vorher festgelegten Zeitpunkt und zu einem fest vereinbarten Preis zu kaufen. Wenn der Kurs über diese Preisschwelle steigt, vervielfältigt sich der Wert des Call. Es handelt sich aber wegen des Zeitlimits um ein hochriskantes Spekulationsgeschäft, denn wenn der tatsächliche Aktienkurs bei Ablauf des Call unter dem vereinbarten Preis liegt, ist die Option völlig wertlos.

Carried Interest Ein Bonus für Manager eines Investmentfonds (aber auch im Zusammenhang mit Venture Capital gebraucht). Der »Carried Interest« (auch »Carry« genannt) ist eine erfolgsabhängige Prämie, die Manager werden also direkt an den Gewinnen des Fonds beteiligt, wovon man sich einen besonderen Einsatz für den Erfolg verspricht.

Cash Cow Gut eingeführtes Produkt oder Geschäft, das ohne große Anstrengungen einen ständigen Fluss von Gewinnen erzeugt, also eine (Geld-)Kuh, die nur noch gemolken werden muss.

CC Carbon Copy; heißt wörtlich »Kohlepapierdurchschlag«; da im elektronischen Zeitalter kaum noch jemand weiß, was das überhaupt ist, benutzt man »CC« einfach als Bezeichnung für die Kopie einer E-Mail, die außer an einen Hauptadressaten auch noch an andere Empfänger geht.

Changeability Anpassungsfähigkeit an berufliche und technologische Veränderungen. Weil Wissen immer schneller veraltet und ständig neue Technologien entwickelt werden, ist Changeability eine Grundvoraussetzung für die Arbeitswelt von morgen.

Churn Rate Ein Maßstab für die Kundenbindung. Gemessen wird, wie viele neue Kunden im Schnitt ein Angebot benutzen und wie viele damit wieder aufhören oder zu Konkurrenten wechseln. Je höher die Churn Rate desto illoyaler das Kundenverhalten.

Clicks and Mortar Wortspiel mit Brick and Mortar, der Bezeichnung für die althergebrachte Wirtschaftswelt einerseits, und den Mausklick (»Clicks«), Symbol für die Online-Wirtschaft andererseits. Mit »Click and Mortar« oder auch »Bricks and Clicks« bezeichnet man Unternehmen, die sowohl in der einen als auch in der anderen Welt zu Hause sind. Also z. B. den Online-Broker, der in mehreren Großstädten Kundenzentren einrichtet.

Clickability »Klickbarkeit« heißt, dass der Name einer Internetmarke leicht einzutippen und eingängig sein soll.

CLM Career Limiting Move; ein Fehlverhalten, das die Karriere beendet.

Co-Branding Gemeinsamer Auftritt von mehreren Marken, die z. B. eine Website gemeinsam betreiben oder als Sponsoren einer Veranstaltung zusammenarbeiten. Co-Branding soll die positiven Attribute einer Marke auf die jeweils anderen übertragen.

Collaborative Filtering Eine Technik, die beim E-Commerce eingesetzt wird. Dabei analysieren die Unternehmen das Kaufverhalten ihrer Kunden. Sucht sich ein Käufer dann ein Produkt aus, werden ihm andere Produkte empfohlen, die – laut Analyse – seinem Kaufverhalten und Geschmack entsprechen, nach dem Motto: »Kunden, die dieses Buch bestellt haben, haben auch die Bücher X und Y gekauft.«.

Computer Literacy »Computer-Alphabetismus«; die Fähigkeit, mit einem Computer umzugehen.

Content Im Internet-Zeitalter bezeichnet das englische Wort für »Inhalt« das Text-, Bild- und Filmmaterial auf einer Website. Da es ohne Inhalte keine Website geben kann, erwarten die Experten einen Aufschwung für die Unternehmen, die Inhalte bereitstellen bzw. die Rechte an Inhalten haben. Häufige Schlagworte hierzu sind: »Content is the key« und »Content is king«, was etwa so viel bedeutet wie »Der Inhalt ist der Schlüssel zum Erfolg« und »Der Inhalt ist das Wichtigste«. Durch die Verbindung mit dem Medienunternehmen Time Warner gelang es zum Beispiel dem Online-Dienst AOL, sich den Zugang zu wertvollem Text- und Filmmaterial zu sichern.

Content Billing Abrechnungsverfahren für die Datenübertragung, bei dem der Nutzer nur für die übertragenen Inhalte bezahlt, aber nicht für die Verbindungszeit. Vor allem Anbieter von mobilen Datendiensten (beispielsweise per UMTS) setzen entsprechende Abrechnungssysteme ein oder kündigen sie an.

Content Syndication Bereitstellen von Inhalten für Websites. Diese Texte, Bilder oder Filme können idealerweise von verschiedenen Angeboten benutzt und dadurch mehrfach verwertet werden, z. B. Online-Horoskope oder Wetterberichte. Die Content Syndication funktioniert ähnlich wie eine Nachrichtenagentur bei Zeitungen: Sie stellt Inhalte zur Verfügung, die dann im Layout des Kunden erscheinen. Der Nutzer merkt idealerweise nicht, dass die selben Inhalte mehrfach verwendet werden.

Cookies Englisch für »Kekse«. Server sorgen dafür, dass diese Krümel auf der Festplatte eines Internetsurfers zurückbleiben. Beim nächsten Kontakt kann der Surfer identifiziert werden. Das kann einerseits eine Erleichterung sein, weil bestimmte Daten nicht immer wieder eingegeben werden müssen, andererseits fühlen sich manche Kunden von Cookies ausspioniert. Die meisten Browser erlauben es deshalb, die Datenkekse abzuweisen.

Co-Shopping So nennt man es, wenn Verbraucher nach dem Motto »gemeinsam sind wir stärker« handeln. Eine Co-Shopping-Plattform im Internet versammelt z. B. 50 Interessenten für den Kauf einer neuen Kaffeemaschine und versucht dann beim Hersteller Mengenrabatt herauszuhandeln.

Cracker »Computerfachleute«, die sich durch ihre Fähigkeiten illegal Zutritt zu fremden Computernetzen verschaffen und dort Daten und Informationen manipulieren und zerstören.

Cubicles »Zellen«, »Kabinen«; Aufteilung eines Großraumbüros in viele gleich große (oder eher kleine) Arbeitsplätze. Die Stellwände aus Pappe oder Sperrholz sollen dem Mitarbeiter das Gefühl von Privatsphäre geben, erzeugen aber meist ein Gefühl von Beklemmung.

Customer Relationship Management (CRM) Bündelt alle Maßnahmen, die zum Erhalt, zur Pflege und zum Ausbau des Kundenkontaktes dienen. Dazu gehören zum Beispiel die Erreichbarkeit für Kundenanfragen über Internet oder Call-Center, aber auch das Datamining. Ziel ist es, dem Kunden personalisierte, auf ihn zugeschnittene Angebote unterbreiten zu können.

Customizing Anpassen von Angeboten auf die Bedürfnisse und Vorlieben des einzelnen Kunden. Dazu wird entweder explizit nach den Wünschen gefragt oder das Verhalten des Konsumenten auch ohne sein Einverständnis durchleuchtet und analysiert.

D

Data Mining Bezeichnet das Graben nach Kundendaten – ob mit oder ohne dessen Wissen. Ziel ist, ein Benutzerprofil von den Besuchern einer Website anzulegen. So soll das Marketing besser auf den einzelnen Kunden zugeschnitten werden.

Daytrading Aktienspekulation, die versucht, die kurzfristigen Kursschwankungen innerhalb eines Tages zu nutzen. Seit über das Internet Kurse in Echtzeit verfügbar sind, werden auch immer mehr Privatanleger vom Daytrading-Fieber gepackt – mit zum Teil verheerenden Folgen, denn diese Geschäfte sind hochriskant. In den USA bewegen Daytrader zwar mittlerweile schon ein Viertel des Börsenvolumens, viele von ihnen müssen aber nach kurzer Zeit aufgrund hoher Verluste das Geschäft aufgeben.

Denial-of-Service-Attacke Form eines Hacker-Angriffs; dabei wird der Server eines Unternehmens von verschiedenen Computern aus mit Anfragen bombardiert, bis er unter der Last der zu verarbeitenden Daten zusammenbricht.

Digital Divide Die »digitale Spaltung« teilt die Gesellschaft in Menschen, die Ahnung von und Zugang zu Computern haben und Menschen, bei denen das nicht der Fall ist. Politiker und Wissenschaftler befürchten, dass diese Spaltung in Zukunft zu sozialen Spannungen führen wird. Allerdings erinnert die Theorie des Digital Divide ein wenig an die Wissenskluft (»Knowledge Gap«), die Wissenschaftler beim Aufkommen des Massenmediums Fernsehen vorhergesagt hatten.

Digitale Signature Die »digitale Unterschrift« soll bei Geschäften im Internet die Unterschrift ersetzen. Es handelt sich also um Daten, die eindeutig einem Benutzer zugeordnet sind: Das kann zum Beispiel ein Code sein, der auf einer Chipkarte gespeichert ist, oder der Fingerabdruck, der von einem Lesegerät auf der Maus eingescannt und übertragen wird.

Domaingrabbing Das Sichern von Domain-Namen ohne die Absicht, sie tatsächlich zu nutzen. Der Domaingrabber hofft vielmehr, seine Ware teuer verkaufen zu können. In Einzelfällen gab es dabei spektakuläre Erfolge, zum Beispiel bei der Veräußerung von »business.com« für mehrere Millionen Dollar. Vorsicht geboten ist allerdings bei geschützten Markennamen und ihren Abwandlungen. Hier sahen Gerichte schon den Tatbestand der Erpressung erfüllt und verhängten entsprechende Strafen. Analog zum Markenrecht gilt, dass sich zwar jeder prinzipiell jeden Markennamen schützen lassen darf. Allerdings muss erkennbar sein, dass er auch vorhat, diesen Namen zu benutzen.

Dot Bomb Klingt explosiv, ist aber meist eher harmlos und Mitleid erregend: ein Dotcom nach der Pleite.

Dotcom Kommt von der Endung ».com«, mit der Internetadressen von (US-amerikanischen) kommerziellen Anbietern enden. Gemeint sind neu gegründete Firmen (Start-up-Unternehmen), deren Geschäftsfelder vor allem im Internet liegen. Zu Beginn der Interneteuphorie galten die Gründer von Dotcoms als sichere Millionäre. Manche Firmen hängten sich sogar ein ».com« an den Namen und konnten so ihren Aktienkurs steigern.

Dot-conomy Verschmelzung von »dotcom« und »economy« (Wirtschaft). Dieser Kunstbegriff bezeichnet die Start-up-Szene, fasst also die große Anzahl der Firmen zusammen, die mit dem Internet oder im Internet Geschäfte machen (wollen).

Down Round Wenn ein Start-up-Unternehmen eine »niedrigere Runde« dreht, laufen die Geschäfte nicht besonders gut. Die Kapitalgeber sehen den Wert des Unternehmens dann nämlich als geringer an als bei der ersten Finanzierungsrunde.

Due Diligence »Gebührende Sorgfalt«; damit wird die genaue Prüfung und Bewertung eines Unternehmens bei Übernahmen, Fusionen oder vor Börsengängen bezeichnet. Die Untersuchung ist sehr detailliert und auf rechtliche, wirtschaftliche und organisatorische Merkmale ausgerichtet, aber auch auf die Unternehmenspsychologie oder -kultur. Für das Image einer Firma kann es verheerend sein, wenn sie nach der Due Diligence nicht aufgekauft oder der Börsengang abgesagt wird.

E
Early Adopter Zielgruppe, die einen neuen Trend mit als erste aufgreift und dadurch für seine Verbreitung sorgt.

Early Majority Nette Marketingbezeichnung für die »Mitläufer«, die einem Produkt zum breiten Durchbruch verhelfen, nachdem Trendsetter es bekannt gemacht haben.

Early Stage Investment Finanzierung eines Unternehmens in der frühen Entwicklungsphase. Sie beginnt mit der Unterstützung für die Konzeption der Geschäftsidee (Seed Capital) und geht bis zum Start der Produktion und der Vermarktung, dem Start-up-Investment.

E-Commerce Elektronischer Handel. Überbegriff für geschäftliche Transaktionen im Internet.

E-Day Abgeleitet vom D-Day, dem Tag der Landung alliierter Truppen in der Normandie im Zweiten Weltkrieg. Journalisten bezeichneten mit E-Day den 10. Januar 2000, an dem die Übernahme des Mediengiganten Time Warner durch den Online-Dienst AOL bekannt gegeben wurde. Es war das erste Mal, dass ein erst sechs Jahre altes Internet-Unternehmen einen Konzern der Old Economy kaufte.

E-Government Das Abwickeln von Verwaltungsaufgaben über das Internet; soll die Behörden modernisieren und das Ende der Papierbürokratie bedeuten – aber das papierlose Büro ist bis heute auch ein leeres Versprechen geblieben.

Empowerment »Ermächtigung«; bezeichnet die Idee, auch einfachen Beschäftigten eines Unternehmens eigene Entscheidungsfreiheit und einen gewissen Handlungsspielraum zu geben. Sie sollen dadurch eigenverantwortlicher und unternehmerischer handeln, motivierter und effizienter arbeiten.

Entrepreneur »Entrepreneur« heißt eigentlich nur »Unternehmer«, klingt aber viel trendiger.

Equity Story »Equity« bezeichnet die Interessen von Kapitalgebern eines Unternehmens, beispielsweise von Aktionären. Die »Equity Story« soll ihnen zum Beispiel vor einem Börsengang klar machen, warum sich eine Investition lohnt und was an dem Geschäftsmodell so besonders ist.

E-Tailer Verschmelzung von »retailer« (Einzelhändler) und »E-Commerce«. Gemeint sind Internet-Anbieter, die wie Einzelhändler Waren oder Dienstleistungen über das Netz verkaufen, z. B. Bücher, CDs oder Flugtickets.

Exit Im Flugzeug ein Notausgang, im Wirtschaftsleben ein häufig lukrativer Ausstieg aus einer Unternehmensbeteiligung. Dabei unterscheidet man grundsätzlich vier Exitstrategien. 1. Buy Back: Die Altgesellschafter kaufen ihre Anteile zurück. 2. Trade Sale: Die Anteile werden an einen industriellen Investor verkauft. 3. Secondary Purchase: Die Anteile werden an einen anderen Finanzinvestor verkauft. 4. Going Public: Die Anteile werden an die Börse gebracht und dort an andere Investoren verkauft.

Extranet 1. Das Extranet bringt Internet und Intranet zusammen und ist z. B. für Außendienstmitarbeiter wichtig. 2. Zusammenschluss von den Intranets zweier Firmen oder Anbindung von mobilen Mitarbeitern, Heimarbeitern und Franchise-Betrieben ans Intranet.

F

Family, Friends and Fools »Familie, Freunde und Verrückte« sind die erste Adresse bei der Suche nach Firmenkapital. Mit ihrer Hilfe und mit eigenem Geld können Start-up-Unternehmer ihre Idee so weit entwickeln, dass sie einen ausgearbeiteten Business-Plan vorlegen können. Dieser ist die Voraussetzung, um an Venture Capital zu kommen.

FAQs Frequently Asked Questions; Fragen, die so häufig gestellt werden, dass die Betreiber einer Website sie schon mal vorsorglich beantwortet haben und online verfügbar machen.

Feasibility Study Machbarkeitsstudie, in der analysiert wird, ob ein Projekt technisch umzusetzen ist und sich wirtschaftlich trägt.

First Mover Advantage Man könnte den First Mover Advantage auch als »Gnade des frühen Markteintritts« bezeichnen: Ein Unternehmen ist entweder durch ein neuartiges Produkt oder durch Expansion in fremde Märkte Pionier. Dadurch kann es vor den Me-too-Anbietern einen Standard setzen und zum Beispiel einen Netzwerkeffekt erzeugen. Wenn ein Unternehmen First Mover in einem Markt ist, wird häufig auch seine Aktie höher bewertet.

Flat Round Eine »flache Runde« macht kein Start-up-Unternehmen glücklich. Die Bewertung der Firma durch die Kapitalgeber liegt im Falle einer Flat Round bei der zweiten Finanzierungsrunde auf dem Niveau der ersten, anstatt, wie ursprünglich erhofft, darüber.

Flatrate Pauschaltarif zum Surfen im Internet ohne zeitliche Beschränkung. Der Online-Handel verspricht sich von einer Flatrate den Durchbruch, entsprechende Angebote sind in Deutschland aber noch sehr dünn gestreut.

Friends and Family Im Gegensatz zu Family, Friends and Fools sind dies die Mitarbeiter und engen Weggefährten von Firmengründern, die bei einem Börsengang besonders bedacht werden. Für viele Beschäftigte sind solche Stock Options der wichtigste Anreiz bei einem Start-up zu arbeiten.

FUD-Factor FUD steht für »fear, uncertainty, doubt«, also Angst, Unsicherheit und Zweifel. Diese Gefühle versuchen Marketingexperten beim Kunden auszulösen – in Hinblick auf ein Produkt, mit dem der Konkurrent zuvorgekommen ist. Durch gezieltes Streuen von Fragen wie »Ist es sicher? Funktioniert es auch unter harten Belastungen?« versuchen sie die Kaufentscheidung zu verzögern, bis die eigene Firma ihr Produkt marktreif hat.

G

Global Knowledge Economy In dem Begriff drückt sich die Erwartung aus, dass sich die Welt zu einer globalen Wissensgesellschaft entwickelt, in der Informationen staatenübergreifend per Internet ausgetauscht werden und die Wirtschaft weltweit vernetzt ist. Um eine Global Knowledge Economy zu verwirklichen, wären aber große Anstrengungen nötig: Denn bisher haben 60 Prozent der Weltbevölkerung noch nie telefoniert, 40 Prozent leben sogar ohne Strom.

Globalization Service Dieser Service passt Websites den verschiedenen Sprach- und Kulturräumen an, zum Beispiel bei großen Suchmaschinen. Ziel ist es, durch Berücksichtigung der regionalen Eigenheiten eine möglichst große Zahl von Nutzern anzusprechen.

Goodwill Immaterielle Werte einer Firma, die man nur schwer in Geld messen kann: Beziehungen zu Kunden, Geschäftspartnern, Behörden, Bekanntheitsgrad der Marke.

Guerilla-Marketing Diese Marketingstrategie setzt nicht auf teure Werbekampagnen, sondern auf ausgefallene, aber auffällige Aktionen – wenn möglich kostenlos.

H

Hotlist Dieser Begriff bedeutet so viel wie »Lesezeichenliste«. Eine Reihe vom User bevorzugter und deshalb zum leichten Wiederfinden gespeicherter Web-Sites.

Hurdle Rate Die »Hürdenrate« wird üblicherweise vom Vorstand vorgegeben. Sie bezeichnet eine Mindestrendite, die eine Investition, ein Unternehmensbereich oder ein Projekt erreichen muss. Sollte die Hürde nicht übersprungen werden, versuchen Controller und Berater die Leistung zu verbessern. Sollte das nicht gelingen, droht der Verkauf oder die Einstellung der Produktion. Prestige-Projekte dürfen manchmal auch einfach unter der Hürde durchschlüpfen: Wenn solche Investitionen besonders imageträchtig sind, akzeptieren manche Unternehmen auch ein Minusgeschäft.

Hypergrowth Extremes, explosionsartiges Wachstum einer Branche oder eines Unternehmens.

I

Incubator Eigentlich stammt der Begriff aus der Medizin und bezeichnet einen Brutkasten. In der New Economy sind Inkubatoren aber Büroräume, in denen Start-up-Unternehmen in Rekordzeit aufgebaut werden sollen. Sie erhalten dort nicht nur Infrastruktur wie Computer und Telefon, sondern auch geschäftliche Unterstützung in Form von Beratung und natürlich Kapital. Während Inkubatoren früher vor allem an US-Universitäten angegliedert waren, werden die erfolgreichsten mittlerweile von Venture-Capital-Gesellschaften betrieben. Sehr früh, bereits in den 60ern, wurde das Inkubator-Modell vom israelischen Staat zur Wirtschaftsförderung angewandt.

Infomediar Mischwort aus »Information« und »Intermediar« (Vermittler). Es kennzeichnet eine Art Online-Mittelsmann zwischen Verkäufer und Kunden, der auf der einen Seite Kundendaten sammelt (Data Mining) und auf der anderen Seite für diese Kunden versucht, günstige Konditionen bei Geschäften zu erhalten. Sowohl bei B2C- als auch bei B2B-Geschäften schalten sich Infomediare ein.

Information Architect Er kümmert sich um die Präsentation der Informationen auf einer Website. Die Schwierigkeit dabei ist, den Ausgleich zu finden zwischen den Interessen der Benutzer, der Sponsoren und der Grafiker, die die Seite gestalten.

Information Fatigue Syndrome (IFS) Stress-Syndrom, das durch Informationsüberflutung ausgelöst wird. Ergebnis von Rational Overchoice. (Siehe auch Burnout)

Infotisement Zusammensetzung aus »information« und »advertisement« (Anzeige, Annonce). Gemeint sind Texte, meist in E-Mail-Newslettern, die wie ein redaktionelles Angebot wirken, aber Werbung für eine Firma oder ihr Produkt machen.

Initial Public Offering (IPO) Die Neuemission von Aktien eines Unternehmens. Dabei setzen die Banken, die den Börsengang begleiten, den Herausgabekurs fest. Interessenten können die Aktien vor dem Börsengang bestellen und erhalten sie dann zugeteilt – bei zu großem Interesse manchmal deutlich weniger, als sie bestellt haben. Viele Start-ups arbeiten sehr schnell auf das IPO hin.

Innovators Bezeichnung für eine sehr kleine, aber sehr risikofreudige und meist reiche Gruppe von Konsumenten, die ein neues Produkt zuerst ausprobiert.

Intangible Assets Immaterielle Werte eines Unternehmens, zum Beispiel Patente und Markenrechte sowie die Kundenbeziehungen. Da bei den jungen Start-up-Unternehmen häufig noch keine materiellen Werte verfügbar sind, kommt es bei der Bewertung der Firmen sehr stark auf die »Intangibles« an.

Intelligent Agent Software-Entwickler arbeiten an Programmen, die zu den Suchmaschinen der Zukunft werden sollen und die die Informationsflut (Rational Overchoice) beherrschen. Einmal mit dem Interessenprofil des Anbieters gefüttert, durchstöbert der digitale Helfer selbstständig das Netz und filtert die besten Antworten heraus.

Internet Business Solutions (IBS)) Ein Unternehmen, das kleinen und mittelgroßen Betrieben Dienstleistungen über das Internet anbietet, z. B. Buchhaltung oder Reiseorganisation und -abrechnung. Dies versetzt auch Kleinunternehmen in die Lage, eigentlich teure Software für diesen Bereich einzusetzen, die noch dazu immer auf den neuesten Stand ist.

Internet-Speed Durch immer neue technische Möglichkeiten des Internet wird das Arbeitstempo immer weiter beschleunigt – bis an die Grenze: Datenpakete in Glasfasernetzen erreichen bereits die schnellstmögliche Geschwindigkeit, die Lichtgeschwindigkeit. Die Menschen können dabei nur noch durch Multitasking mithalten. Allerdings warnen Psychologen schon vor Techno-Stress und Burnout.

Intranet Firmeneigenes Internet.

IRC Abkürzung für »Internet Relay Chat«. Echtzeit-Chat (Realtime) im Internet. Um daran teilnehmen zu können, ist ein IRC-Client notwendig. Chats können aber auch über einen normalen Browser geführt werden.

J
Jobber Klingt nach einem einfachen Arbeiter, ist aber manchmal ein rücksichtsloser Spekulant: Jobber sind Wertpapiermakler oder Börsenmitglieder, die nur im eigenen Namen Geschäfte abschließen dürfen.

Jump Der direkte »Sprung« von einer Internetseite zu einer anderen mittels Link, ohne dass der User zwischenzeitlich offline geht.

K

Knowledge-Commerce »Handel mit Wissen«. In der Informationsgesellschaft gilt Wissen als die wichtigste Ware von allen. Internet- oder Intranet-Plattformen für Knowledge-Management sollen diejenigen, die das Know-how haben, mit denjenigen zusammenbringen, die nach der Lösung für ein Problem suchen.

Knowledge-Management Wissensmanagement; soll Karten für den Informationsdschungel anlegen. Dazu wird das Wissen in einem Unternehmen systematisch gesammelt, analysiert, aufbereitet und anderen Mitarbeitern zur Verfügung gestellt. Wissensmanagement soll verhindern, dass in einer Abteilung eines Unternehmens über eine Problemlösung nachgedacht wird, die in einer anderen Abteilung schon gefunden wurde. Schwierigkeiten bereitet aber noch die Frage, wie man das Wissen aus den Köpfen der Mitarbeiter am besten ins Intranet bekommt – denn nicht alles lässt sich in Worten oder Bildern ausdrücken und ausdrucken.

L

Laggards Konsumentengruppe, die wenig an Information über neue Produkte interessiert ist und die meist nur eine geringe Kaufkraft hat. Die »Zauderer« kaufen dann ein Produkt, wenn der Markt bereits gesättigt und der Trend vorbei ist.

Last Mover Advantage Scherzhaft gemeintes Gegenteil zu First Mover Advantage. Bezeichnet den Unternehmer, der als letzter ein neues Geschäftsfeld entdeckt und betritt. Sein Vorteil kann aber sein, dass er aus den Fehlern der First Mover gelernt hat.

Late Majority Gruppe von Konsumenten, die wartet, bis ein Produkt sich bewährt hat.

Launch Markteinführung eines neuen Produkts. Um Anlaufschwierigkeiten zu vermeiden, entscheiden sich Firmen häufig für einen Softlaunch, d. h. sie präsentieren erst einmal ein Basisprodukt oder ein eingeschränktes Angebot auf dem Markt, bei einem neuen Computerprogramm z. B. eine Betaversion.

Letter of Intent (LOI) »Absichtserklärung«. Üblicherweise wird damit eine vorläufige Bestellung bestätigt; Unternehmen in der Mergermania verschicken aber den LOI, wenn sie die Absicht erklären, sich an einem anderen Unternehmen zu beteiligen oder es zu übernehmen.

Leveraged Buyout Unternehmensübernahme, die durch Schulden finanziert wird. Nach dem erfolgreichen Leveraged Buyout verkauft der Neueigentümer häufig Teile des übernommenen Unternehmens, um die Schulden zu tilgen.

Load, fire, alm »Laden – schießen – und dann erst zielen.« Beschreibt eine Firmenstrategie, die vor allem auf schnelle Entscheidungen setzt, um den First Mover Advantage zu nutzen.

Lock-up Period »Verschluss-Zeit«; Frist nach einem Börsengang (Initial Public Offering), in der die Alteigentümer keine Aktien verkaufen dürfen. Am Neuen Markt in Deutschland sind zum Beispiel mindestens sechs Monate festgelegt. So soll verhindert werden, dass die anderen Aktionäre durch einen Börsengang übervorteilt werden. Aber auch danach ist Vorsicht angebracht: Denn wenn die Alteigentümer nach Ablauf der Frist viele Anteile auf den Markt werfen, kann der Kurs der Aktie unter Druck geraten.

M

M-Commerce Handel über mobile Geräte, momentan also vor allem das Handy. Mit der wachsenden Bandbreite in den Handy-Netzen durch neue Techniken wie UMTS werden völlig neue M-Commerce-Angebote möglich, zum Beispiel lokale Ausgehtipps samt Stadtplan und Kartenreservierung. UMTS soll selbst die Übertragung von Filmen aufs Handy erlauben.

Moral-Plus-Produkte Produkte, die zusätzlich zu ihrem Gebrauchswert einen moralischen Zweck erfüllen: Es handelt sich z. B. um Produkte, die besonders umweltschonend hergestellt werden oder bei denen ein Teil des Gewinns einem wohltätigen Zweck zugeführt wird. Der moralische Nutzen kann in der unübersichtlichen Warenwelt manchmal auch als Unique Selling Proposition dienen.

Multitasking Das Erledigen mehrerer Aufgaben zur gleichen Zeit. Eine Anforderung, die man früher vor allem bei der Entwicklung von Computer-Chips stellte (mehrere Programme und Funktionen sollten gleichzeitig ablaufen können), die aber wegen der Beschleunigung der Arbeitsprozesse immer mehr auf die arbeitenden Menschen übertragen wird.

N

Naming Englisch für »Benennung«. Das kreative Erfinden trendiger Namen für neue (oder alte) Produkte und Dienstleistungen. Große Unternehmen verfügen über eigene »Naming-Abteilungen«, denen wir Begriffe wie »City Call« statt »Ortsgespräche« oder »Service Point« statt »Informationsschalter« verdanken.

Nasdaq 1971 gegründete Computerbörse in den USA. Die Abkürzung steht für »National Association of Securities Dealers Automated Quotation System«. Im Nasdaq werden vor allem Aktien der Technologiebranche gehandelt. Es war Vorbild für andere Börsen der so genannten Wachstumswerte, wie z. B. den Neuen Markt und wurde durch den Aufschwung der Aktien von Internetfirmen zum Inbegriff des Börsenbooms.

Netizen Englisches Kunstwort aus »net« (Internet) und »citizen« (Bürger). Jeder, der zur weltweiten Gemeinde der Internetbenutzer gehört.

O

One-to-One-Marketing Werbemaßnahme, die direkt auf einen Kunden zugeschnitten ist. Möglich wird dies durch Methoden wie Data Mining und Techniken wie Collaborative Filtering. Die Gefahr dabei ist, dass sich der Verbraucher ausspioniert und (durch Spam) belästigt fühlt.

P

P2P Peer-to-Peer; mit einer einfachen Software lassen sich völlig neue Netze knüpfen: Peer-to-Peer-Programme erlauben es, aus den Computern zahlreicher Privatpersonen ein weltweites Netz aufzubauen.

Darin kann jeder auf bestimmte, freigegebene Bereiche fremder Festplatten zugreifen. Die Informationen müssen also nicht auf teuren Servern abgelegt werden.

Pac Man So nennt man die Verteidigung gegen eine feindliche Übernahme, wenn das Zielunternehmen seinerseits versucht den Angreifer zu schlucken. Der Begriff geht zurück auf eines der ersten populären Computerspiele, in dem sich eine großmäulige Spielfigur durch ein Labyrinth frisst.

Page Impression Früher als Page Views bezeichnet. Page Impressions liefern das Maß für die Nutzung einzelner Seiten eines Internet-Auftritts. Die Summe aller Page Impressions gibt Aufschluss über die Attraktivität des Angebotes. Wichtiger Wert für die Mediaplanung von Online-Werbekampagnen.

Parkinson's Law Dieses Gesetz besagt: »Jede Arbeit füllt die dafür vorgesehene Zeit vollständig aus.« In einer Abwandlung für die Informationstechnik: »Jede Datenmenge wächst, bis sie den vorhandenen Speicherplatz vollständig ausfüllt.«

PDA Personal Digital Assistant. Mini-Computer im Taschenformat, mit dem der Benutzer Termine und Adressen verwalten oder E-Mails schreiben kann. Die Eingabe erfolgt dabei häufig über einen berührungsempfindlichen Bildschirm und einen dazu passenden Stift. Auf dem Markt sind schon Modelle mit aufsteckbaren Digitalkameras, integrierten MP3-Spielern oder ein PDA, der ins Mobiltelefon eingebaut ist. Der bekannteste Vertreter ist der »Palm Pilot«.

Permission Marketing »Marketing nach Erlaubnis«; der Kunde wird dabei nicht mit unverlangter Werbung (Spam) überschüttet, sondern erst um sein Einverständnis gefragt, beispielsweise einen Newsletter zu beziehen. Davon erwartet man eine größere Aufgeschlossenheit des Kunden für die Werbebotschaft, weil sie nicht unerwartet oder ungelegen kommt.

PGP Pretty Good Privacy; populäres Programm zur Verschlüsselung von E-Mails.

Phantom Stock Plan Mitarbeiterbeteiligung ohne Beteiligung: Bei einem derartigen Plan (meistens für höhere Manager) erhalten die Begünstigten nicht wirklich Aktien, sondern nur Scheinaktien. Diese folgen zwar auch dem Börsenkurs, können aber nicht an der Börse gehandelt werden. Die Gewinne werden dann mit dem Gehalt ausbezahlt.

Point of Delivery (POD) Lieferpunkt; Ort, an dem eine bestellte Ware ausgeliefert wird. Zahlreiche E-Commerce-Betreiber setzen zum Beispiel große Hoffnungen auf das Tankstellennetz. Weil es dicht ist und die Tankstellen rund um die Uhr geöffnet sind, könnte ein Kunde seine bestellte Ware dort jederzeit abholen. Solche Abholmodelle sind auch billiger, als die letzte Meile zu überwinden und direkt an die Haustür des Kunden zu liefern.

Portal Internetangebot, das sich seinen Kunden als Einstiegsseite ins World Wide Web empfiehlt. Auf Portalen ist meist eine breite Palette an verschiedenen Themen dargeboten, die es möglichst allen Surfern recht machen sollen (horizontales Portal). Daneben gibt es aber auch vertikale Portale, die sich mit einem Themengebiet an eine klar umrissene Zielgruppe wenden. Wichtig vor allem im B2B-Bereich.

Post Merger Management Das »Management danach« ist bei einem Firmenzusammenschluss (= Merger) mindestens genauso wichtig wie die Verhandlungen davor. Häufig kommt es nämlich nach einer Fusion zu einem regelrechten Mitarbeiterschwund und zu Problemen durch unterschiedliche Firmenkulturen.

Post Money Valuation Bewertung einer Firma nach einer Finanzierungsrunde.

Pre Money Valuation Bewertung einer Firma vor einer Finanzierungsrunde.

Public Affairs Alles, was die Außenwahrnehmung eines Unternehmens beeinflussen kann. Weil diese auch für das Geschäft wichtig ist (Brand Reputation Management), beschäftigen viele Firmen PR-Agenturen oder eine eigene PR-Abteilung.

Put Optionsgeschäft an der Börse. Gibt dem Anleger das Recht, eine bestimmte Aktie zu einem vorher festgelegten Zeitpunkt und zu einem fest vereinbarten Preis zu verkaufen. Sinkt der Kurs unter diese Preisschwelle, steigt der Wert des Put. So lässt sich auch bei sinkenden Kursen Geld verdienen. Puts werden deswegen häufig zur Absicherung von Depots gegen fallende Kurse benutzt. Sie sind aber ein hochriskantes Spekulationsgeschäft.

R

Rational Overchoice Die rasante Zunahme verfügbarer Informationen. Selbst bei größter Anstrengung kann der Einzelne nicht mehr alle für die Lösung eines Problems relevanten Informationen verarbeiten. Deshalb wird versucht, mit technischen Filtern (Intelligent Agent) den Informationsfluss zu kanalisieren. Wenn das nicht gelingt, droht das Information Fatigue Syndrome.

Relaunch Neustart/Neupositionierung eines Produkts oder einer Marke. Kommt ursprünglich aus dem Zeitungsbereich und meint eine veränderte Aufmachung eines eingeführten Titels im Hinblick auf Layout aber auch die inhaltliche Ausrichtung.

Re-Start-up Firmengründung von Unternehmern, die mit einer ersten Start-up-Idee gescheitert sind. Vorteil eines solchen Neuanfangs kann sein, dass die Betroffenen bereits Erfahrungen gesammelt haben und außerdem gute Kontakte haben.

Return on Investment (ROI) Verhältnis vom Nettogewinn zum eingesetzten Kapital. Der ROI ist ein Maßstab für die Rentabilität einer Investition und macht unterschiedliche Anlagemöglichkeiten vergleichbar.

Rich Media Oberbegriff für Töne und bewegte Bilder auf einer Internetseite; im Gegensatz zu reinem Text und Grafiken, die man als »Poor Media« bezeichnen müsste.

Rocket Science »Raketenwissenschaft« (so die wörtliche Übersetzung) muss nicht unbedingt dahinter stecken. Von »Rocket Science« ist die Rede, wenn eine Firma eine echte technische Neuerung zu bieten hat und nicht nur eine Geschäftsidee. Das kann zum Beispiel eine bahnbrechende Software-Entwicklung sein.

S

Seed Capital Zum Zeitpunkt der »Anfangsfinanzierung« liegt lediglich die Geschäftsidee vor. Durch das Seed Capital soll diese start-up-fähig (Start-up) werden. Dafür greift der Gründer häufig auf sein eigenes Kapital zurück oder fragt Family, Friends and Fools nach Unterstützung. Möglicherweise findet sich auch ein Business Angel. Für Venture Capital-Geber (Venture Capital) sind die Summen, um die es dabei geht, meist zu klein, um den Prüfungsaufwand zu rechtfertigen.

Shill Bidding Das provozierte Hochbieten bei Versteigerungen, das vor allem im Internet leicht möglich ist. Der Auktionator treibt so den Preis und damit seinen Profit in die Höhe.

Short Position/Short Sale »Blankoverkauf«; Termingeschäft, bei dem auf fallende Kurse spekuliert wird. Dabei stellt ein Marktteilnehmer eine Aktie zum Verkauf, die er noch gar nicht besitzt (und geht damit eine Short Position ein). Der Short Seller verpflichtet sich, die Aktie zu einem festgelegten Zeitpunkt zu kaufen und dadurch die Position wieder zu schließen. Wegen der Unberechenbarkeit der Börse ein sehr riskantes Geschäft.

Silent Commerce Transaktion von Rechner zu Rechner, ohne Eingriff des Menschen. So könnte zum Beispiel der Computer des Herstellers beim Zulieferer automatisch den benötigten Nachschub bestellen, Auftragsabwicklung, Rechnungsstellung, selbst die Bezahlung ließen sich automatisieren. Ein anderes häufig genanntes Beispiel für Silent Commerce ist der Kühlschrank, der selbstständig nachbestellt, wenn ein Lebensmittel zur Neige geht. Entsprechende Systeme sind in der Testphase.

Silver Customer Wörtlich: »Silberner Kunde«; silbergrau sind seine Schläfen und versilbern soll er das Geschäft eines Werbetreibenden. Mit der wachsenden Überalterung der Gesellschaft gerät die Zielgruppe der über Fünfzigjährigen ins Visier der Wirtschaft. Und auf einmal stellt man fest, dass die Silver Customer über beträchtliches Vermögen verfügen und auch bereit sind, es auszugeben.

Smart Money »Kluges Geld« gibt es eigentlich nicht; wenn aber ein Kapitalgeber außer seinen Investitionen auch Ideen, Erfahrung und gute Ratschläge mitbringen kann, dann hat ein Unternehmen »Smart Money« gefunden.

Snailmail »Schneckenpost«; ironischer Ausdruck für das klassische Postwesen, bei dem die Briefe noch per Hand ausgeliefert werden. Snailmail ist das Gegenstück zum E-Mail, bei dem sich Texte in Sekundenschnelle weltweit verschicken lassen.

Spam Das sind unverlangt zugesandte Werbe-E-Mail (Ad Mail). Ähnlich wie eine Postwurfsendung. Weil aber elektronische Post soviel einfacher und billiger zu verschicken ist, wird bei manchen Kunden der E-Mail-Eingang geradezu überflutet. Für die Herkunft des Begriffs gibt es zwei Erklärungen: Zum einen könnte es aus »to spill over« (überlaufen) und »to cram« (verstopfen) zusammengesetzt sein.

Spinnwebsite Über einen solchen Internetauftritt legt sich der virtuelle Staub der Jahrzehnte: Seit Ewigkeiten haben die Verantwortlichen einer solchen Site die Inhalte nicht mehr aktualisiert, die Links verweisen ins Nichts und die Informationen sind veraltet.

Spin-off Geschäftliche Abtrennung einzelner Bereiche vom Mutterhaus. Zwei Anlässe gibt es dafür: 1) Ein Produkt oder eine Abteilung passt nicht mehr zum Unternehmen. 2) Das Produkt ist so stark, dass es zum Beispiel durch einen Börsengang mehr Profit bringt. Noch dazu, weil dann der Kapitalbedarf auf dem freien Markt gedeckt werden kann und gleichzeitig der Verkauf von Produkten und Dienstleistungen auch an direkte Konkurrenten der Muttergesellschaft möglich wird.

Start-out Eigentlich das Gleiche wie ein Start-up, nur wird ein Start-out von einem schon bestehenden Unternehmen gegründet. Die Firmen versprechen sich davon kreative Impulse durch den Gründergeist.

Start-up Auch wenn der Begriff fast schon mystifiziert wird: Er heißt eigentlich nichts anderes als »Unternehmensgründung«. Gemeint sind aber in der Regel Firmen, die in der IT- oder Internet-Branche tätig sind und die von oft jungen Unternehmern gegründet werden.

Stock Options Aktienoptionen; Modell der Mitarbeiterbeteiligung: Statt mehr Geld gibt es Aktien des eigenen Unternehmens. Einige US-Firmen haben bei Managern die Entlohnung fast gänzlich auf Aktien umgestellt. Bei guten Börsenkursen macht das die Beteiligten schnell zu Millionären. Bei fallenden Kursen kann es dazu führen, dass der CEO auf einmal weniger verdient als die unteren Angestellten.

Streaming Wörtlich: Strömen; Technik, die es erlaubt, Filme oder Töne in Echtzeit über das Internet zu verbreiten. Dazu wird ein Film komprimiert und in einzelne Datenpakete zerlegt. Während das erste Datenpaket schon im Programmfenster abgespielt wird, lädt der Computer die anderen im Hintergrund nach. Es entsteht ein kontinuierlicher Datenstrom, der Stream.

Synergy Vorteil, der durch das gemeinsame Nutzen vorhandener Ressourcen entsteht. Zwei Einheiten sollen dadurch zusammen wesentlich mehr schaffen, als zwei jeweils getrennte Einheiten (»1+1=3-Effekt«). Vor allem Firmenfusionen werden häufig mit Synergieeffekten begründet, wie beispielsweise gemeinsames Marketing, bessere Ausnutzung von Entwicklungskapazitäten oder leichtere Finanzierungsmöglichkeiten als größere Unternehmenseinheit. In der Praxis sind solche Effekte aber schwierig zu realisieren. Gegenteil von Wheel Reinventions.

T

Target »Ziel«; Unternehmen, das ins Fadenkreuz einer feindlichen Übernahme gerät.

Targeting Marketing, das speziell und trennscharf auf eine Zielgruppe zugeschnitten ist.

T-Commerce Handel über den Fernseher als Distributions- und Vermarktungsmedium. Weil Fachleute in Zukunft die Verschmelzung von Internet- und Fernsehdiensten sowie Breitband-Verbindungen mit hohen Übertragungsraten erwarten, wird interaktives Fernsehen möglich. Dadurch eröffnen sich neue Marketingmöglichkeiten: beispielsweise ein Werbespot, bei dem der Zuschauer mit einem Klick weitere Informationen zum Produkt erhält und auch direkt bestellen und bezahlen kann, ohne vom Fernsehsessel aufstehen zu müssen.

Think Tools Techniken, die komplexe Denkprozesse softwaregestützt sichtbar machen. Dadurch sind diese Prozesse nachvollziehbar und können eingesetzt werden, um neues Wissen zu erzeugen.

Third Place Der »dritte Platz« eines Arbeitnehmers neben Wohnung und Arbeitsplatz. Die Amerikaner, die diesen Begriff geprägt haben, verstehen darunter einen informellen Versammlungsort, eine soziale Drehscheibe jenseits von beruflichen Zwängen und häuslichen Verpflichtungen. In den USA wurde zum Beispiel die Coffeeshop-Kette »Starbucks« zu einem Synonym für den »Third Place«, in Deutschland könnte es die Stammkneipe sein.

Tribes »Stämme«; neue Zielgruppenkategorisierung, die auf den Medientheoretiker N. Bolz zurückgeht. Dahinter steckt die Erkenntnis, dass herkömmliche Einteilungen (beispielsweise nach Alter oder Einkommen) wegen der zunehmenden Individualisierung nicht mehr greifen. Mit dem weniger präzisen Begriff der unterschiedlichen Stämme kann die Wirklichkeit besser beschrieben werden. Dabei muss sich das Marketing laut Bolz nicht bemühen, die Stämme um jeden Preis zu verstehen – wichtiger ist, eine authentische Sprache zu sprechen.

U
UMTS Was die Fachleute als »Universal Mobile Telecommunications System« bezeichnen, steht für den Mobilfunk der dritten Generation. Dank der hohen Datenübertragungsraten werden völlig neue Anwendungen möglich. So können problemlos Fotos, Straßenkarten, ja sogar Filme in Fernsehqualität übertragen werden.

Unique Selling Proposition »Alleinstellungsmerkmal«; einzigartiges Verkaufsversprechen, das ein Produkt gegenüber anderen auszeichnet und nicht ohne Weiteres von der Konkurrenz kopiert werden kann. In Umlauf gebracht wurde der Begriff von Rosser Reeves mit dem Buch »Reality and Advertising« von 1960.

Uphill Communication »Bergauf-Kommunikation«; Gespräche und Besprechungen, oft mit Kunden, die sich als extrem mühsam und fruchtlos erweisen.

V

Vaporware »Dampfware« nennt man Software (oder Hardware), von der nichts bleibt als die heiße Luft der Vorankündigung. Manche Unternehmen setzen den Dampfstoß sogar gezielt ein: Sie halten sich damit die Konkurrenz vom Leib, weil die Kunden lieber auf das Update der bekannten Software warten, als zum neu entwickelten Produkt der Konkurrenten zu wechseln.

Venture Capital (VC) »Risikokapital«; gängige Art der Finanzierung von Start-ups, die nicht über genügend Eigenkapital verfügen. VC-Geber haben sich darauf spezialisiert, riskante Jungunternehmen zu finanzieren, die oft nicht mehr vorweisen können als eine Idee und einen Business Plan. Die Erfolgsquote der Venture Capital-Geber liegt bei etwa 1:9. Das heißt, dass das Geld in acht von neun Fällen unwiederbringlich verloren ist. Der eine Fall, der zu einem Erfolg wird, gleicht dies durch immens hohen Gewinn allerdings aus.

Venture Management Davon spricht man, wenn ein Risikokapitalgeber nicht nur Kapital mitbringt, sondern einem jungen Unternehmen auch mit Beratungsleistung zur Seite steht und seine Erfahrungen aus der Wirtschaftspraxis teilt.

Visit »Besuch«; Anzahl der Besucher auf einer Website. Ähnlich wie die Einschaltquote beim Fernsehen bestimmt sie maßgeblich die Preise für Werbebanner (Banner) auf einer Website – egal, ob der Besucher das Banner beachtet hat oder nicht.

Voice XML Weiterentwicklung von HTML, die Internetseiten mit Sprachausgabe möglich machen soll.

Vulture Capital »Geierkapital«; ironische Bezeichnung für Geldgeber, die bei einem Start-up nur auf die schnelle Mark aus sind. Die Strategie heißt also: so schnell wie möglich an die Börse, abkassieren und weiter.

W

WAP Wireless Application Protocol; was bis vor kurzem nur mit dem Computer möglich war, lässt sich mittlerweile auch mit dem Handy bewerkstelligen: das Surfen im Internet.

Webinar Ein Seminar, das im Internet abgehalten wird, zum Beispiel an einer Virtuellen Universität.

Webisodes Zusammensetzung aus »web« und »episodes«; damit ist eine Art Fernsehserie im Internet gemeint.

Weblift Ein Facelift für eine Website, also die Auffrischung derselben. Wie bei anderen Medien spricht man auch von einem Relaunch.

Web-Mall »Einkaufszentrum«; ähnlich wie im realen Leben bieten auch in der Web-Mall verschiedene Firmen ihre Produkte zum Kauf an. Inzwischen werden viele Malls durch Portale zusammengefasst, so dass sich der Kunde problemlos über ein breites Angebot informieren kann.

Webucation Verschmelzung aus »web« (für »Internet«) und »education« (»Erziehung«, »Ausbildung«); Weiterbildungsangebote im Netz. Laut Einschätzung von Managementberater Peter Drucker gibt es für Webucation »einen globalen Markt, der potenziell Hunderte von Milliarden Dollar wert ist.«

Wetware Ohne Wetware gäbe es keine Hard- und Software. Wetware bezeichnet den Menschen und sein Gehirn, ohne das die ganzen wunderbaren Computer und ihre Programme nichts taugen würden.

Wheel Reinventions Die »Neuerfindung des Rades« kann im 21. Jahrhundert kein großer Erfolg mehr sein. Deswegen bezeichnet man mit diesem Begriff auch (überflüssige) Doppelarbeit. Das Gegenteil eines Synergie-Effekts.

White Knight So romantisch können »feindliche Übernahmen« enden: In Gestalt des Weißen Ritters übernimmt ein Unternehmen eine bedrohte Firma – mit Einverständnis des Managements und natürlich an Stelle des unerwünschten Käufers.

Wildcard 1. Begriff aus der Szenario-Technik, bei der man mit »Worst Case« und »Best Case«-Überlegungen versucht, die Zukunft zu planen. Die Wildcard ist dabei ein sehr unwahrscheinliches Ereignis, das aber im Falle seines Eintretens einen sehr nachhaltigen Effekt auf die Zukunft hat. Zum Beispiel hielt man die Mikrowellentechnik lange Zeit für eine Wildcard, weil niemand glaubte, dass sie sich durchsetzen würde. Als sie es schließlich tat, hat sie die Ernährungsweise der westlichen Welt grundlegend verändert. 2. Platzhalter, der ein einzelnes Zeichen oder eine ganze Zeichenfolge z. B. bei einer Sucheingabe ersetzt, man versteht darunter v. a. die Zeichen »?« und »*«.

Win-win-Situation Situation zum beiderseitigen Vorteil. Die in der Wirtschaft ansonsten allgegenwärtige Logik des Nullsummenspiels – was der eine gewinnt, muss ein anderer irgendwo verlieren – ist hier außer Kraft gesetzt. Oft das Ergebnis eines Synergie-Effekts.

Worcation Zusammensetzung aus »work« (»Arbeit«) und »vacation« (»Urlaub«); angenehme Form der Heim- oder Telearbeit, die gern auch an Third Places geleistet wird.

Workflow »Arbeitsfluss«; bei Computerprogrammen bezeichnet er jene Arbeitsschritte, die notwendig sind, um das gesteckte Arbeitsziel zu erreichen.

Wysiwyg Steht für »What you see is what you get«. Meint den Sachverhalt, dass die Bildschirmdarstellung eines Dokumentes der Druckversion entspricht. Im erweiterten Sinn aber auch, dass ein bestelltes Produkt in Wirklichkeit genauso aussieht wie im Katalog.

Y

Yettie Abkürzung für »Young entrepreneurial, tech-based twenty-somethings« – junge, unternehmerische, technikorientierte Mittzwanziger. Der Begriff soll zum ersten Mal im März 2000 im amerikanischen Magazin »Talk« aufgetaucht sein. Der »Yettie« soll den typischen Internet-Gründer beschreiben und ist ungefähr das, was der »Yuppie«, der »Young urban professional«, in den 80ern war.

Z

Zip Dieses Kürzel hängt am Namen von Daten, die nach einem bestimmten Verfahren komprimiert wurden. Durch dieses Verfahren lassen sie sich leichter übers Internet verschicken.

 **Anhang**

1. Englische Kurzgrammatik

Das Adjektiv

Das Adjektiv (Eigenschaftswort) wird gebraucht, um ein Substantiv näher zu bestimmen; im Englischen verändert das Adjektiv seine Form nicht.

This car is expensive.	Dieses Auto ist teuer.
This is an expensive car.	Dies ist ein teures Auto.

Die Steigerung des Adjektivs

Grundform	1. Steigerungsstufe	2. Steigerungsstufe
tall	*taller*	*tallest*
cheap	*cheaper*	*cheapest*
happy	*happier*	*happiest*

Alle einsilbigen Adjektive und alle zweisilbigen Adjektive, die auf *-y* enden, werden durch das Anhängen von *-er* und *-est* gesteigert. Alle anderen Adjektive, d.h. alle zweisilbigen, die nicht auf *-y* enden und alle drei- und mehrsilbigen Adjektive werden mit *more* und *most* gesteigert:

stupid	*more stupid*	*most stupid*
dangerous	*more dangerous*	*most dangerous*

Bei der Steigerung mit *-er* und *-est* treten folgende Veränderungen der Schreibweise auf: Folgt am Wortende einem Konsonanten ein *y*, so wird dieses in der Steigerung zu *i*. Folgt einem kurzen Vokal ein Konsonant am Wortende, so wird dieser verdoppelt. Endet das Adjektiv auf ein *e*, das nicht gesprochen wird, so entfällt dieses:

easy	*easier*	*easiest*
big	*bigger*	*biggest*
pure	*purer*	*purest*

Folgende Adjektive werden unregelmäßig gesteigert:

good	*better*	*best*
bad	*worse*	*worst*
much	*more*	*most*
many	*more*	*most*
little	*less*	*least*

Das Adverb

Die abgeleiteten Adverbien

Die abgeleiteten Adverbien werden durch das Anhängen von *-ly* an das Adjektiv gebildet:

slow	*slowly*	langsam
nice	*nicely*	nett

Endet das Adjektiv auf *-y*, so wird *-y* zu *-i*:

easy	*easily*	leicht

Endet das Adjektiv auf *-le* und steht davor ein Konsonant, so entfällt das *-e*:

simple	*simply*	einfach

Endet das Adjektiv auf *-ic*, wird *-ally* angehängt:

basic	*basically*	grundsätzlich

Endet das Adjektiv auf *-ll*, wird nur ein *-y* angehängt:

full	*fully*	voll

Die ursprünglichen Adverbien

Neben den abgeleiteten Adverbien gibt es die sogenannten ursprünglichen Adverbien, die nicht von einem Adjektiv abgeleitet werden (z. B. *yesterday* – gestern, *here* – hier).

Von den ursprünglichen Adverbien können einige auch als Adjektiv verwendet werden. Eine einzige Form dient hier also als Adjektiv und als Adverb:

It is a daily newspaper.	Es ist eine Tageszeitung.
It appears daily.	Sie erscheint täglich.

Die wichtigsten davon sind:

fast	schnell	*straight*	gerade
long	lang	*daily*	täglich
low	niedrig	*weekly*	wöchentlich
monthly	monatlich		

Unregelmäßig gebildete Adverbien und Sonderformen

Eine wichtige Besonderheit stellen Adverbien dar, die die gleiche Form wie das entsprechende Adjektiv haben, zusätzlich jedoch noch eine mit *-ly* gebildete Form besitzen. Diese Gruppe ist besonders wichtig, weil die mit *-ly* abgeleiteten Adverbien eine andere Bedeutung haben. Zu dieser Gruppe zählen:

Adjektiv und Adverb		Adverb	
hard	schwer/hart	*hardly*	kaum
late	spät	*lately*	kürzlich
fair	fair	*fairly*	ziemlich

Die Steigerung der Adverbien

Alle einsilbigen Adverbien werden mit *-er* und *-est* gesteigert:

Grundform	Komparativ	Superlativ
early	*earlier*	*earliest*
früh	früher	am frühesten

Alle anderen Adverbien werden mit *more* und *most* gesteigert:

carefully	*more carefully*	*most carefully*
vorsichtig	vorsichtiger	am vorsichtigsten

Folgende Adverbien werden unregelmäßig gesteigert:

well	*better*	*best*
gut	besser	am besten
much	*more*	*most*
viel	mehr	am meisten
badly	*worse*	*worst*
schlecht	schlechter	am schlechtesten
a little	*less*	*least*
ein wenig	weniger	am wenigsten

Die amerikanische Rechtschreibung

Bei vielen Wörtern, deren *ae* oder *oe* mit dem Laut [i:] ausgesprochen wird, entfällt im amerikanischen Englisch das *a* bzw. das *o*:
    diarrhoea (UK)   *diarrhea (US)*

In nichtbetonten Silben mit einem ursprünglich doppelten *l* steht im amerikanischen Englisch nur ein *l*:
    travelled (UK)   *traveled (US)*

Bei betonten Silben, die auf *-l* enden, hat amerikanisches Englisch ein doppeltes *l*:
    fulfil (UK)   *fulfill (US)*

Wörter, die im britischen Englisch auf *-our* enden, werden im amerikanischen Englisch mit *-or* geschrieben, wenn dieser Laut [ə] ausgesprochen wird:
    colour (UK)   *color (US)*

Die Endung *-re* wird im amerikanischen Englisch zu *-er*, wenn vor dem *-re* ein Konsonant steht:
    centre (UK)   *center (US)*

Der Artikel

Der bestimmte Artikel

Für den bestimmten Artikel gibt es im Englischen nur eine einzige Form, die für Feminina und Maskulina, sowie im Singular und im Plural gleich ist.

Singular		Plural	
the tree	der Baum	*the trees*	die Bäume

Abstrakta (z. B. *life, love, peace*), Stoffnamen (z. B. *ice, milk*) und Gattungsnamen (z. B. *children, women*) stehen ohne den bestimmten Artikel, wenn sie im allgemeinen Sinn gebraucht werden, und mit bestimmtem Artikel, wenn sie näher bestimmt sind:

Life is hard.	Das Leben ist schwer.
The life of a politician	Das Leben eines Politikers
can be very dangerous.	kann sehr gefährlich sein.

Besonderheiten beim Gebrauch des bestimmten Artikels

Wie im Deutschen haben manche geografische Bezeichnungen keinen bestimmten Artikel.
Bei *all, both, half, twice, double* wird der bestimmte Artikel nachgestellt.

Der unbestimmte Artikel

Der unbestimmte Artikel lautet *a* und wird nur bei der Einzahl von zählbaren Begriffen gebraucht (z. B. *a house*).
Vor Vokalen lautet der unbestimmte Artikel *an*. Ausschlaggebend ist dabei nicht der Buchstabe, mit dem das folgende Wort beginnt, sondern dessen Aussprache (z. B. *an old house*).

Besonderheiten beim Gebrauch des unbestimmten Artikels

Abweichend vom Deutschen steht im Englischen der unbestimmte Artikel bei Berufsbezeichnungen und bei Konfessionen:

He is a teacher.   Er ist Lehrer.

Nach *half, quite, rather, such* steht der unbestimmte Artikel:

half a bottle of milk   eine halbe Flasche Milch

Bei Ausrufen steht nach what und bei zählbaren Substantiven der unbestimmte Artikel:

What a lovely day!   Was für ein schöner Tag!

Pluralbildung

Gewöhnlich wird der Plural eines Substantivs gebildet, indem man *-s* an die Singularform anhängt:

ship – ships   *table – tables*

Dennoch gibt es einige Ausnahmen. Endet das Substantiv auf einen Zischlaut (*-s, -x, -ch, -sh, -z*), hängt man *-es* an das Wort an:

bus – buses   *tax – taxes*

Wenn das Substantiv auf einen Konsonanten und *-y* endet, so wird *-y* im Plural zu *-ies*. Endet das Substantiv auf einen Vokal und *-y*, so wird im Plural *-s* angehängt:

hobby – hobbies   Aber: *boy – boys*
lady – ladies   *valley – valleys*

Die Pluralform der Substantive, die auf -f oder -fe enden, wird normalerweise gebildet, indem man das -f oder -fe durch -ves ersetzt:

  half – halves   Aber: *belief – beliefs*
  wife – wives   *chief – chiefs*

Substantive, die auf -o enden, bilden den Plural entweder mit -os oder mit -oes:

  radio – radios   Aber: *potato – potatoes*
  piano – pianos   *tomato – tomatoes*

Unregelmäßige Pluralformen

Neben den verschiedenen Formen der Pluralbildung mit -s gibt es im Englischen eine ganze Reihe von unregelmäßigen Pluralformen wie z. B.:

Singular	Plural	Singular	Plural
man	men	mouse	mice
woman	women	goose	geese
foot	feet	ox	oxen
tooth	teeth	child	children
louse	lice		

Substantive, die im Plural die gleiche Form besitzen

Es gibt im Englischen Substantive, die im Singular und im Plural die gleiche Form besitzen. Das ist beispielsweise bei einigen Tiernamen der Fall:

sheep   das Schaf/die Schafe
deer   der Hirsch/die Hirsche

Das Verb

Verbarten und Verbformen

Die Verben »to have«, »to be« und »to do«

Die Hilfsverben *do, be* und *have* haben eine besonders wichtige Funktion, weil mit ihnen die Fragen, die Verneinung, alle zusammengesetzten Zeiten und das Passiv gebildet werden können. Darüber hinaus sind diese drei Verben auch Vollverben.

to have

Infinitiv		Imperfekt	Partizip	Perfekt
have	haben	*had hatte*	*had*	gehabt
Gegenwart		Kurzform	Verneinung	Kurzform
I have	ich habe	*I've*	*I have not*	*I haven't*
you have	du hast			
he has	er hat	*he's*	*he hasn't*	
she has	sie hat			
it has	es hat			
we have	wir haben			
you have	ihr habt			
they have	sie haben			

Imperfekt		Kurzform	Verneinung	Kurzform
I had	ich hatte	*I'd*	*I had not*	*I hadn't*
you had	du hattest			
he had	er hatte			
she had	sie hatte			
it had	es hatte			
we had	wir hatten			
you had	ihr hattet			
they had	sie hatten			

Die Verwendung von »to have« als Hilfsverb

Die Formen der Gegenwart von have werden für die Bildung des Perfekts verwendet: *I have learnt.*

Mit der Imperfektform *had* wird das Plusquamperfekt gebildet: *I had learnt.*

to be

Infinitiv		Imperfekt	Partizip Perfekt	
to be		*was/were*	*been*	
sein		war/waren	gewesen	
Gegenwart		Kurzform	Verneinung	Kurzform
I am	ich bin	*I'm*	*I am not*	*I'm not*
you are	du bist	*you're*	*you are not*	*you aren't*
he is	er ist	*he's*	*he is not*	*he isn't*

she is	sie ist	*she's*	*she is not*	*she isn't*
it is	es ist	*it's*	*it is not*	*it isn't*
we are	wir sind	*we're*	*we are not*	*we aren't*
you are	ihr seid	*you're*	*you are not*	*you aren't*
they are	sie sind	*they're*	*they are not*	*they aren't*
Imperfekt			Verneinung	Kurzform
I was	ich war		*I was not*	*I wasn't*
you were	du warst		*you were not*	*you weren't*
he was	er war		*he was not*	*he wasn't*
she was	sie war		*she was not*	*she wasn't*
it was	es war		*it was not*	*it wasn't*
we were	wir waren		*we were not*	*we weren't*
you were	ihr wart		*you were not*	*you weren't*
they were	sie waren		*they were not*	*they weren't*

Die Verwendung von »to be« als Hilfsverb

Mit *to be* werden die Verlaufsform (*progressive form*) und das Passiv gebildet: *He is working. It is made of wood.*

to do

Infinitiv		Imperfekt	Partizip Perfekt
do	tun	*did* tat	*done* getan
Imperfekt		Verneinung	Kurzform
I did	ich tat	*I did not*	*I didn't*
you did	du tatst	*etc.*	*etc.*

Die Verwendung von »to do« als Hilfsverb

do und die Vergangenheitsform *did* werden für die Bildung der Fragen und der Verneinung bei Vollverben verwendet.

Die Vollverben

Jedes Vollverb besitzt drei Formen, mit denen sich alle Zeiten und Aussageweisen bilden lassen. Diese Formen sind Infinitiv, Imperfekt und Partizip Perfekt. Durch die unterschiedliche Bildung des Imperfekts und des Partizips Perfekt lassen sich die Vollverben in zwei Gruppen einteilen: Die regelmäßigen Vollverben bilden das Imperfekt und das Partizip Perfekt mit der Endung *-ed*:

Infinitiv	Imperfekt	Partizip Perfekt
wait	*waited*	*waited*

Die unregelmäßigen Vollverben bilden das Imperfekt und das Partizip Perfekt mit eigenen Formen. (siehe Tabelle S...)

Das Präsens

Bejahte Form	Verneinte Form	Frage
I take	*I don't take*	*Do I take?*
you take	*you don't take*	
he/she/it takes	*he/she/it doesn't take*	*Does he take?*
we take	*we don't take*	*Do we take?*
you take	*you don't take*	
they take	*they don't take*	

Das Imperfekt

Das Imperfekt wird bei den regelmäßigen Verben durch Anhängen von *-ed* an das Verb gebildet. Bei den unregelmäßigen Verben werden besondere Formen für das Imperfekt verwendet. Die Formen des Imperfekts bleiben in allen Personen unverändert.

Das Perfekt

Das Perfekt wird gebildet aus dem Präsens des Hilfsverbs *have* und dem Partizip Perfekt des Vollverbs.

Das Plusquamperfekt

Das Plusquamperfekt wird gebildet mit der Past Tense-Form *had* des Hilfsverbs *have* und dem Partizip Perfekt des Vollverbs.

Das Futur I (Will-Future)

Das *Will-Future* wird in allen Zeiten mit *will* und dem Infinitiv des Verbs gebildet.

Das Futur II (Future Perfect)

Das Futur II wird gebildet mit *will* und dem Infinitiv des Perfekts.

Der Konditional I
Der Konditional I wird gebildet mit *would* und dem Infinitiv des Verbs.

Der Konditional II
Der Konditional II wird gebildet mit *would, have* und dem Partizip Perfekt des Vollverbs.

Die Verlaufsform (Progressive Form)
Die Verlaufsform wird mit den jeweiligen Formen von *to be* und dem Partizip Präsens gebildet.

Präsens
I am writing.
Ich schreibe gerade.

Imperfekt
I was writing.
Ich schrieb gerade.

Perfekt
I have been writing.
Ich habe geschrieben.

Plusquamperfekt
I had been writing.
Ich hatte geschrieben.

Futur I
I will be writing.
Ich werde schreiben.

Futur II
I will have been writing.
Ich werde geschrieben haben.

Konditional I
I would be writing.
Ich würde schreiben.

Konditional II
I would have been writing.
Ich hätte geschrieben.

Die Zahlen

Die Grundzahlen

0	nought, zero	13	thirteen	50	fifty
1	one	14	fourteen	60	sixty
2	two	15	fifteen	70	seventy
3	three	16	sixteen	80	eighty
4	four	17	seventeen	90	ninety
5	five	18	eighteen	100	one hundred
6	six	19	nineteen	101	one hundred and one
7	seven	20	twenty	200	two hundred
8	eight	21	twenty-one	1,000	one thousand
9	nine	22	twenty-two	1,001	one thousand and one
10	ten	etc.		1,000,000	one million
11	eleven	30	thirty		
12	twelve	40	forty		

2. Unregelmäßige Verben im Englischen

	Präteritum	Partizip
arise	arose	arisen
awake	awoke	awoken
be	was/were	been
bear	bore	borne/born
beat	beat	beaten
become	became	become
beget	begot	begotten
begin	began	begun
bend	bent	bent
beseech	besought	besought
bet	bet/betted	bet/betted
bid	bade	bidden
bind	bound	bound
bite	bit	bitten
bleed	bled	bled
blow	blew	blown
break	broke	broken
breed	bred	bred
bring	brought	brought
build	built	built
burn	burnt/burned	burnt/burned
burst	burst	burst
buy	bought	bought
can	could	-
cast	cast	cast
catch	caught	caught
chide	chid	chidden/chid
choose	chose	chosen
cleave	clove/cleft	cloven/cleft
cleave (adhere)	cleaved/clave	cleaved
cling	clung	clung
come	came	come
cost	cost	cost
creep	crept	crept
cut	cut	cut

deal	dealt	dealt
dig	dug	dug
do	did	done
draw	drew	drawn
dream	dreamt/dreamed	dreamt/dreamed
drink	drank	drunk
drive	drove	driven
dwell	dwelt	dwelt
eat	ate	eaten
fall	fell	fallen
feed	fed	fed
feel	felt	felt
fight	fought	fought
find	found	found
flee	fled	fled
fling	flung	flung
fly	flew	flown
forbid	forbade	forbidden
forget	forgot	forgotten
forsake	forsook	forsaken
freeze	froze	frozen
get	got	got (US gotten)
give	gave	given
go	went	gone
grind	ground	ground
grow	grew	grown
hang	hung	hung
have	had	had
hear	heard	heard
heave	heaved/hove	heaved/hove
hide	hid	hid
hit	hit	hit
hold	held	held
hurt	hurt	hurt
keep	kept	kept
knit	knit/knitted	knit/knitted
know	knew	known
lay	laid	laid

lead	led	led
lean	leant/leaned	leant/leaned
leap	leapt	leapt
learn	learnt/learned	learnt/learned
leave	left	left
lend	lent	lent
let	let	let
lie	lay	lain
light	lit	lit
lose	lost	lost
make	made	made
may	might	-
mean	meant	meant
meet	met	met
mow	mowed	mowed/mown
pay	paid	paid
put	put	put
quit	quit	quit
read	read	read
rend	rent	rent
rid	rid	rid
ride	rode	ridden
ring	rang	rung
rise	rose	risen
run	ran	run
say	said	said
see	saw	seen
seek	sought	sought
sell	sold	sold
send	sent	sent
set	set	set
sew	sewed	sewn
shake	shook	shaken
shave	shaved	shaved/shaven
shed	shed	shed
shine	shone	shone
shoe	shod	shod
shoot	shot	shot

show	showed	shown
shrink	shrank	shrunk
shut	shut	shut
sing	sang	sung
sink	sank	sunk
sit	sat	sat
slay	slayed	slain
sleep	slept	slept
slide	slid	slid
sling	slung	slung
slink	slunk	slunk
slit	slit	slit
smell	smelt/smelled	smelt/smelled
smite	smote	smitten
speak	spoke	spoken
speed	sped	sped
spell	spelt/spelled	spelt/spelled
spend	spent	spent
spin	span	spun
spit	spat	spat
split	split	split
spoil	spoilt/spoiled	spoilt/spoiled
spread	spread	spread
spring	sprang	sprung
stand	stood	stood
steal	stole	stolen
stick	stuck	stuck
sting	stang	stung
stink	stank	stunk
strew	strewed	strewed/strewn
stride	strode	stridden
strike	struck	struck
string	strung	strung
strive	strove	striven
swear	swore	sworn
sweep	swept	swept
swell	swelled	swollen/swelled
swim	swam	swum

swing	swang	swung
take	took	taken
teach	taught	taught
tear	tore	torn
tell	told	told
think	thought	thought
throw	threw	thrown
thrust	thrust	thrust
tread	trod	trodden
understand	understood	understood
wake	woke	woken
wear	wore	worn
weave	wove	woven
weep	wept	wept
win	won	won
wind	wound	wound
wring	wrung	wrung
write	wrote	written

3. Wichtige Abkürzungen

abbrev.	*abbreviation*	Abkürzung
AC	*alternating current*	Wechselstrom
a/c	*account*	Konto
A.D.	*anno Domini*	A.D.
a.m./AM	*ante meridiem*	vormittags
amt.	*amount*	Menge
approx.	*approximately*	ca.
attn.	*to the attention of*	z.Hd.
Ave.	*Avenue*	Allee
b.	*born*	geboren
B.A.	*Bachelor of Arts*	akademischer Grad vor dem M.A.
BBC	*British Broadcasting Corporation*	BBC
B.C.	*before Christ*	v. Chr.
bn	*billion*	Milliarde
BR	*British Rail*	Britische Eisenbahngesellsch.
Bros.	*brothers*	Gebrüder
Capt.	*Captain*	Kapitän

c	*circa*	circa
cd	*cash discount*	Rabatt für Barzahlung
CD	*compact disc*	CD
CEO	*Chief Executive Officer*	Generaldirektor
CET	*Central European Time*	MEZ
cf.	*confer*	vgl.
CIA	*Central Intelligence Agency*	CIA (der amerikanische Geheimdienst)
c/o	*care of*	bei, c/o
Co.	*company*	Fa.
C.O.D.	*cash on delivery*	per Nachnahme
cp.	*compare*	vergleiche
CV	*Curriculum vitae*	Lebenslauf
D.A.	*district attorney*	Staatsanwalt
dir.	*director*	Direktor
dbl.	*double*	doppel
D.C.	*direct current*	Gleichstrom
Dept.	*department*	Abteilung
dupl	*duplicate*	Durchschrift
E.C.	*European Community*	Europäische Gemeinschaft
EDP	*Electronic Data Processing*	EDV
EEMU	*European Economics and Monetary Union*	EWWU, Europäische Wirtschafts- und Währungsunion
e.g.	*exempli gratia*	z. B.
encl.	*1. enclosed*	anbei
	2. enclosure	Anlage
esp.	*especially*	besonders
etc.	*et cetera*	usw.
EU	*European Union*	Europäische Union
extn.	*extension*	Durchwahl, Nebenstelle
FBI	*Federal Bureau of Investigation*	FBI (Bundespolizei in den USA)
FRG	*Federal Republic of Germany*	Bundesrepublik Deutschland
ft.	*foot*	Fuß
GNP	*gross national product*	Bruttosozialprodukt
HP	*Hire Purchase*	Ratenkauf

Anhang

H.R.H.	*His/Her Royal Highness*	Seine/Ihre Königliche Hoheit
ID	*identification*	Ausweis
i.e.	*id est*	das heißt
inc.	*incorporated*	eingetragen
incl.	*including*	einschließlich, inklusive
IOU	*I owe you*	Schuldschein
IQ	*intelligence quotient*	Intelligenzquotient
Jr.	*junior*	Junior
lb.	*pound*	Pfund
Ld	*Lord*	Herr (Teil eines Titels)
Ltd.	*limited*	GmbH
m	*million*	Million
MD	*Medicinae Doctor*	Dr. med.
m.p.h.	*miles per hour*	Meilen pro Stunde
Mr	*Mister*	Herr
Mrs	(nur als Abkürzung)	Frau
Ms	(nur als Abkürzung)	Frau (auch für Unverheiratete)
Mt	*mount*	Teil des Namens vor einem Berg
n/a	*not applicable*	nicht zutreffend
NATO	*North Atlantic Treaty Organization*	NATO
NB	*nota bene*	bitte beachten
nec	*necessary*	notwendig
no.	*number*	Nr.
oz.	*ounce*	Unze
p.	*1. page*	Seite
	2. pence	Penny
p.a.	*per annum*	jährlich
PC	*personal computer*	Personalcomputer
pd	*paid*	bezahlt
p.m./PM	*post meridiem*	nachmittags, abends
p.o.	*post office*	Post
pp.	*pages*	Seiten
PTO	*please turn over*	bitte wenden
Rd.	*road*	Straße
Ref.	*reference*	Bezug
regd.	*registered*	eingetragen
ret.	*retired*	in Ruhestand
ROM	*read-only memory*	ROM

rpm	revolutions per minute	Umdrehungen pro Minute
RSVP	répondez s'il vous plaît	u.A.w.g.
RV	recreational vehicle	Wohnmobil
sq.	square	Quadrat
Sr.	Senior	Senior (nach einem Namen)
St.	1. Saint	St.
	2. Street	Str.
tel./Tel.	telephone	Telefon
TV	television	Fernsehen
U.K.	United Kingdom	Vereinigtes Königreich
USA	United States of America	USA
VAT	value-added tax	Mwst.
VCR	video cassette recorder	Videorekorder
vol	volume	Band
VP	vice president	Vizepräsident
vs.	versus	gegen
yd.	yard	Yard
yr	year	Jahr
ZIP code	Zone Improvement Plan	Postleitzahl

4. Maße und Gewichte in Großbritannien und den USA

Gewichte

100g	= 3,527 oz	1 kg		= 2,205lb
1oz (ounce, Unze)				= 28,35g
1lb (pound, Pfund)				= 453,59g
1cwt (hundredweight, Zentner)		short		= 100lb = 45,359kg
		long		= 112lb = 50,802kg
1tn (ton, Tonne)		short		= 907,2kg
		long		= 1016,0kg

Längenmaße

1 in (inch, Zoll)	= 2,54 cm	1mm	= 0,039 in
1ft (foot, Fuß)	= 30,48 cm (12 in)	1cm	= 0,033 ft
1yd (yard, Elle)	= 91,44 cm (3ft, feet)	1m	= 1,09 yd
1 mi (mile, Meile)	= 1,610 km	1km	= 0,62 mi

Flächenmaße

1 in² (square inch)	=	6,45 cm²	1 cm²	=	0,155 in²
1 ft² (square foot)	=	9,288 dm²	1 dm²	=	0,108 ft²
1 yd² (square yard)	=	0,836 m²	1 m²	=	1,196 yd²
1 acre		= 0,405 ha	1 ha	=	2,471 acres
1 mi² (square mile)		2,589 km²	1 km²		0,386 mi²

Raummaße

1 in³ (cubic inch)	=	16,386 cm³	1 cm³	=	0,061 in³
1 ft³ (cubic foot)	=	28,320 dm³	1 dm³	=	0,035 ft³
1 yd³ (cubic yard)	=	0,765 m³	1 m³	=	1,308 yd³
1 bu (bushel)	=	35,24 l	1 m³	=	28,38 bu

Hohlmaße

1 gill = 0,118 l
1 pt (pint) = 0,473 l (4 gills)
1 qt (quart) = 0,946 l (2 pt)
1 gal (US gallon) = 3,787 l (4 qt)
1 l = 8,747 gills = 2,114 pt = 1,057 qt = 0,264 gal

5. Feiertage
Großbritannien

New Year's Day	(Neujahrstag)
Good Friday	(Karfreitag)
Easter Monday	(Ostermontag)
May Day	(Maifeiertag)
Spring Bank Holiday	(Pfingstmontag)
August Bank Holiday	(letzter Montag im August)
Christmas Day	(1. Weihnachtstag)
Boxing Day	(2. Weihnachtstag)

In England wird der Maifeiertag am ersten Montag im Mai gefeiert und nicht am 1. Mai. Pfingstmontag ist normalerweise der letzte Montag im Mai. »August Bank Holiday« ist immer der letzte Montag im August. »Boxing Day« wird so genannt, wegen des alten Brauchs, an diesem Tag an das Personal kleine Geschenke (Weihnachtsschachteln), also boxes zu verschenken.

Vereinigte Staaten

New Year's Day	(Neujahrstag)
Martin Luther King Day	(3. Montag im Januar)
President's Day	(3. Montag im Februar)
Memorial Day	(letzter Montag im Mai)
Independence Day	(4. Juli)
Labor Day	(1. Montag im September)
Columbus Day	(2. Montag im Oktober)
Veterans' Day	(11. November)
Thanksgiving	(4. Donnerstag im November)
Christmas Day	(1. Weihnachtstag)

Columbus und Veterans' Day sind nur behördliche Feiertage, d.h. dass zum Beispiel keine Post ausgetragen wird, viele Banken und Geschäfte aber trotzdem geöffnet haben.

6. Suchmaschinen

Am besten geeignet für die Suche im Internet sind die so genannten Suchmaschinen (search engines). Sie bieten Ihnen die Möglichkeit, gezielt Informationen zu suchen, oder mit Hilfe von Schlagwörtern Dinge zu finden, von denen Sie wissen, dass sie irgendwo im Internet vertreten sind. Suchen Sie zum Beispiel die Adresse einer Firma, können Sie entweder mit Hilfe der Suchmaschine ein Branchenverzeichnis aufrufen und dort den Namen der Firma eingeben. Oder Sie geben den Namen direkt in die Eingabezeile ein und lassen danach suchen. Bei der Suche mit Schlagwörtern erhalten Sie eine Liste, die Ihnen über die sogenannten »links« eine direkte Verbindung z. B. zu der Homepage der gesuchten Firma ermöglicht. Allerdings ist es sinnvoll, die Suche von vornherein so eng wie möglich einzugrenzen, denn wer möchte schon ein Suchergebnis von oft einigen tausend gefundenen Übereinstimmungen durchsehen?
Für die Suche stehen verschiedene Suchmaschinen zur Verfügung. Einige sind besonders für die internationale Suche geeignet, wie zum Beispiel »AltaVista« und »Lycos«, bei denen man die Suche aber auch auf Deutschland beschränken kann. Für Deutschland sind vor allem »Fireball«, »Nathan« und der »DINO-Lotse« empfehlenswert. Letzterer beinhaltet unter anderem den »Branchen-Dino«, der vor allem die

Suche nach Firmen erheblich erleichtert. Neben den umfassenden Suchmaschinen gibt es auch die thematischen Verzeichnisse, wie »Yahoo« und der »DINO-Katalog«. Im Unterschied zu den Suchmaschinen, können Sie sich hier einen Überblick über die Angebote im Internet verschaffen oder Informationen in einem größeren Zusammenhang suchen. Aber auch hier gilt: je eingeschränkter und konkreter die Suchbegriffe, desto besser die Chancen, ein zufriedenstellendes Suchergebnis zu erhalten.

Die wichtigsten Suchmaschinen:

AltaVista	http://www.altavista.com
DirectHit	http://www.directhit.com
Excite	http://www.excite.com
FindWhat	http://www.findwhat.com
Google	http://www.google.com
HotBot	http://www.hotbot.com
InfoSeek	http://www.infoseek.de
Internet Keywords	http://www.internetkeywords.com
ixquick	http://www.ixquick.com
Kanoodle	http://www.kanoodle.com
LookSmart	http://www.looksmart.com
Lycos	http://www.lycos.com
MetaCrawler	http://www.metacrawler.com
OpenDirectory	http://www.opendirectory.de
Savvy Search	http://www.savvysearch.com
GoTo	http://www.goto.com
WebCrawler	http://www.webcrawler.com
Yahoo	http://www.yahoo.com

 **Abschlusstest**

1. Finden Sie in den folgenden Übungen das richtige Wort oder die richtigen Wörter für die Leerstellen:

1. Could you please _____ on this number.
   (reach me/speak to me/call me/contact me)

2. I tried all day to _____ you, but I didn't _____.
   (find … succeed/speak to … connect/reach … get through/dial … find you)

3. The line was always _____.
   (out of order/engaged/not connected/unavailable)

4. Hello, this is ATP Limited, _____?
   (can I be of assistance/what can I do/what do you want/who do you want)

5. I called previously, but I was _____.
   (disconnected/cut off/thrown out/cut short)

6. After completing the call I _____.
   (cut off/cut short/hung up /left the line)

7. She has been _____ the phone for hours.
   (at/with/over/on)

8. This is the number. Could you please _____ it for me.
   (ring/dial/find/reach)

9. Could you please _____ Mr Jobson.
   (pass me to/find me/dial me/put me through to)

10. The line is _____. Would you like to _____?
    (out of order … stand by/busy … hold/not working … hang on/unavailable … wait)

11. The line is ▮▮▮▮. The Post Office is working on the problem.
    (not open/not working/out/out of order)

12. Does his office have ▮▮▮▮?
    (an extension/another number/a switch-board connection/a secondary phone)

13. Could I please ▮▮▮▮ a message?
    (give/leave/hand on/say)

14. Could you please ▮▮▮▮ this message to Mrs Smith?
    (say/transfer/hand over/give)

2. Sie haben eine Liste mit Leuten, denen Sie Briefe oder E-Mails schreiben müssen. Wie beginnen und beenden Sie Ihre Briefe?

1. To Mr Smith, General Manager of Acorn Foods? ▮▮▮▮ ... ▮▮▮▮.

2. To your good friend John Trebbit? ▮▮▮▮ ... ▮▮▮▮.

3. To the Management of Callout Electronics? ▮▮▮▮ ... ▮▮▮▮.

4. To Rosemary Charles, Chairlady of the Society of American Women for World Action? ▮▮▮▮ ... ▮▮▮▮.

5. An e-mail to Donald Higgins, a colleague? ▮▮▮▮ .. ▮▮▮▮.

6. To the General Manager, Sun Hotels? ▮▮▮▮ ... ▮▮▮▮.

3. Ihre Marketing-Abteilung erhält den folgenden Brief. Wie entwerfen Sie ein Antwortschreiben?

Manchester, 28 July, 2000
Dear Sirs,

We would be very grateful if you sent us the fullest information you have on your range of products, including price list, delivery terms and dates and guarantee details. Are you able to arrange with our Mr Jones a suitable time and place for a meeting to discuss the possibility of further co-operation between our two companies? We look forward to your reply.

Yours faithfully,
Thompson and Partners

....
....
....
....
....

4. Wird der folgende Brief dem Schreiber den gewünschten Job bescheren, was meinen Sie? Können Sie ihn verbessern?

Dear gentlemen,

I have read with a lot of interest the announcement you positioned in the newspaper of last week seeking an office assistant. I have much experience of office and I sure I might be the man you require. Up to now I work as stores manager of Hancock and Sons, just round corner from you – very convenient! I work in stores but often in office, so I know way around. My English not yet very good but I try to learn more. I make 300 pounds the week. You offer me more I your man.

With many greetings,

5. *Write* or *draft*? *Type up* or *take down*? Setzen Sie die richtigen Formen in die folgenden Sätze ein.

1. Miss Manners, would you please bring in your notebook and pencil and ▓▓▓▓▓▓ a letter for me?

2. I ▓▓▓▓▓▓ them a letter of complaint, but I did it in the heat of the moment and I should have ▓▓▓▓▓▓ it first and then looked at it again the next day.

3. Miss Manners, would you please ▓▓▓▓▓▓ that letter as soon as possible. I promised Hatcher and Company we would ▓▓▓▓▓▓ to them today.

4. Just ▓▓▓▓▓▓ the version you want to send and I'll get Miss Manners to ▓▓▓▓▓▓ the letter.

5. Before you ▓▓▓▓▓▓ that letter ▓▓▓▓▓▓ this version first, and then ▓▓▓▓▓▓ it ▓▓▓▓▓▓. If there are any additions I'll just ▓▓▓▓▓▓ them in.

6. Finden Sie die richtigen Lösungen zu den Sätzen und ergänzen Sie sie!

1. Our foreign visitors were ▓▓▓▓▓▓ *(put down/put by/put up)* in the Brighton Hotel.

2. Tony was looking forward ▓▓▓▓▓▓ *(by/to/in)* meeting the new Sales Director.

3. Before putting the product on the market it was tried ▓▓▓▓▓▓ *(out/by/over)* on over a thousand people.

4. The new publicity campaign really made ▓▓▓▓▓▓ *(amends/a difference/a bid)* for the previous disastrous campaign.

5. You get in touch with Mr Greaves and in the ▓▓▓▓▓▓ *(meantime/meanwhile/meaning)* I'll try and find his contract.

6. Have a guess who I ran ▓▓▓▓▓▓▓▓ *(down/by/into)* last week? George Partridge.

7. The Managing Director finished his speech by asking if ▓▓▓▓▓▓▓▓ *(anyone/someone/no-one)* had any questions.

8. Beryl was the ▓▓▓▓▓▓▓▓ *(mainframe/mainstay/mainstream)* of the company and made sure everything ran smoothly.

9. Peter was new ▓▓▓▓▓▓▓▓ *(on/over/to)* the job and therefore was worried ▓▓▓▓▓▓▓▓ *(about/in/to)* his performance.

10. It is important to be ▓▓▓▓▓▓▓▓ *(privately/unfailingly/warmly)* polite when dealing with a new client.

11. We were held ▓▓▓▓▓▓▓▓ *(up/down/by)* traffic and arrived at the conference two hours late.

12. Sales figures were ▓▓▓▓▓▓▓▓ *(completely/slightly/remarkably)* higher than last quarter but head office were still not happy.

13. ▓▓▓▓▓▓▓▓ *(In the meantime/From time to time/In the nick of time)* I do research on my chosen subject but not as much as I should do.

14. On arriving at the hotel the ▓▓▓▓▓▓▓▓ *(receptionist/receiver/receptive)* showed us where our rooms were.

15. I went ▓▓▓▓▓▓▓▓ *(by/over/to)* the report three times before I found the error.

16. Management are currently ▓▓▓▓▓▓▓▓ *(looking into/seeking out/searching for)* the possibility of opening a new branch in Glasgow.

17. We must persuade possible investors that it is worth _____ (doing/their weight in gold/their while) to put money into our company.

18. Operator: Can you _____ (hold/get/put) the line, please? He's in a meeting at the moment.

19. We had to pay through the _____ (mouth/nose/ear) to rent out the conference hall.

20. There was a _____ (breakdown/breakup/break-off) in communications between the two sides and the matter had to got to an industrial tribunal.

21. Right from the start there was something very _____ (upper hand/red-handed/underhand) about the entire process.

22. The company finally got the project _____ (on/out/off) the ground after months of debating.

23. Bankruptcy was _____ (staring us in the face/face to face with us/facing up to us) and therefore we had to call in the receiver.

24. If we want to compete effectively in the marketplace we _____ (will have to/will have had to/are having to) transform our entire corporate structure.

25. Tony was the star of the company after pulling _____ (off/out/around) a great victory in securing increased revenue for ERGO Ltd.

26. I found the trade fair _____ (fascinating/fascinated) but became extremely _____ (boring/bored) on the way home.

27. After the end of the recent economic crisis there was a noticeable _____ (turnover/turnaround/turndown) in the company's fortunes.

28. _____ (How's things/How's life/How do you do), Mr Jones? It's a great pleasure to meet the Senior Director of Jennings Ltd.

29. This computer has _____ (seen better days/gone one better/bettered). We must order a new one.

30. _____ (Would/Do/Can) you mind I'm trying to work here!

31. After thirty years in the company Giles has finally decided to _____ (stand down/stand by/stand out and retire).

32. Peter _____ (confounded/confided/conformed) in Steve that he was bonkers about Melissa.

33. I _____ (read up on/read out/read into) the history of the company thoroughly before attending the interview.

34. Everybody held _____ (the fort/the wrong end of the stick/their breath) when the results of the promotions were disclosed.

35. Sales _____ (took out/took off/took over) so suddenly that everybody was astonished.

36. Peter was very disappointed when he heard he had just missed _____ (out/over/by) on being selected for the Paris trip.

37. Tony was told to _____ (talk up/call up/bring up) the question of publicity during his meeting with the rival company.

38. The seminar was _____ (put off/put by/put out) until next week due to the unavailability of one of the speakers.

39. After various meetings the figures for the annual budget were starting to take _____ (down/through/shape).

Abschlusstest

40. The company was working ▓▓▓ (down/up/towards) to the busiest period of the year.

41. It looks ▓▓▓ (as if/when if/likely) this is the end of the road for Jacobs and Sons.

42. Management decided to ▓▓▓ (do/make/have) a stand against bad timekeeping at work.

43. Business is starting to pick ▓▓▓ (up/out/through) after a very slow start to the year.

44. – Roger, there's something I'd like to say to you if that's OK.
    – Sure, fire ▓▓▓ (off/out/away).

45. Steve handed responsibility for the running of his department ▓▓▓ (off/towards/over) to Peter while he was away.

46. The company ▓▓▓ (dug up/came up/set up) some very interesting information about one of its new employees.

47. The trade fair was a great success but what really seemed to catch ▓▓▓ (the attention/the worm/the eye) was the company's video presentation.

48. Nowadays it seems like multinational companies are ▓▓▓ (putting over/taking over/setting over) smaller operations every other week.

49. As soon as Tony arrived at the company he started to ▓▓▓ (invent/achieve/make) waves.

50. The subject was very dear to our ▓▓▓ (hearts/heads/minds) as it would have a great influence on our futures.

51. Right from the ▓▓▓ (onset/outset/offset) there were problems with the new contract.

52. The Marketing Director was very popular amongst the staff because every time anybody had a problem to discuss he was always _____ (up to his ears/with his ear to the ground/all ears).

53. It was _____ (in touch/touch and go/out of touch) whether the new project would get off the ground.

54. _____ (All in all/After all/All in), when one considers how much worse it could have been, I think we did a great job.

55. While Jonathon looked after the accounts department Peter _____ (watched/kept/gave) an eye on the sales department.

56. – How long have you been _____ (making/doing) business with Kelly Ltd?

57. These days everybody has got to _____ (mind/watch/toe) the line or they are out of a job.

58. All the work Tony had put in finally paid _____ (off/in/out) when he received the promotion.

59. I am really _____ (seeing/watching/looking) forward to the symposium at the end of the year.

60. The work was exhausting but Jerry made a _____ (go/start/try) of it and the results were spectacular.

61. – Beryl _____ (did/made) an appointment over the phone for the following day.

Glossar

acceptance	Zusage, z. B. bei einer Einladung
to access	zugreifen auf
account credit	Kreditkonten
accounting	Buchhaltung
accounting program	Buchführungs-Programm
to accumulate	ansammeln
accounts	Rechnungsstelle
a couple of words	ein paar Worte
to acquaint oneself with	sich vertraut machen mit
address	Ansprache
to address a seminar on sth.	vor einem Seminar einen Vortrag halten über
adequately briefed	angemessen vorbereitet/ eingewiesen
to adjourn	Pause machen
to adopt an approach	einen Ansatz benutzen
advance	Fortschritt
advanced technology	fortschrittliche Technologie
to advance the company's cause	dem Interesse der Firma dienen
advancement	Beförderung
to advertise	Werbung schalten
to advertise a post	eine Stelle annoncieren
advertising	Werbung, Anzeigen
advertising account	Anzeigen-Budget
advertising department	Anzeigenabteilung; Werbeabteilung
advertorial	Mischung aus Anzeige und redaktionellem Beitrag
to affect	beeinflussen
after all	schließlich
agenda	Tagesordnung
agent	Vertreter
all ears	ganz Ohr
all hands on deck	alle verfügbaren Leute
All settled?	Alles bereit?
a lot of scope	ein breites Betätigungsfeld

to amend	ersetzen
an important catch	ein wichtiger Fang
to announce s.o.'s participation	jds. Teilnahme ankündigen
answering machine/answerphone	Anrufbeantworter
to appear as a very minor chapter	eine viel geringere Rolle spielen
appearance	Aussehen; Erscheinung (zeitl.)
appendix, appendices (pl.)	Anhang
appointment	Termin, Verabredung
to arrange for	bestellen
arrangements	Vorbereitungen, Planung
a sharp businessman	ein geschickter Geschäftsmann
to assess the importance	die Bedeutung einschätzen
assessment	Leistungsbericht
asset	Bereicherung
to assign	unterzeichnen
to assign sb.	jdn. zu etw. abstellen
assistant managing director	stellvertretender Geschäftsführer
at the outset	am Anfang
to attend	folgen, z. B. einer Einladung
at your peril	auf eigene Gefahr
au fait	vertraut
to back off	zurückstellen
back-up	Rückendeckung
a batch of sth.	ein Stapel von etw.
to be all in	erschöpft, fertig sein
to be busy doing sth.	beschäftigt sein mit etw.
beforehand	im Voraus
to be in charge of sth.	die Verantwortung über etw. haben
to be inquisitive	nachbohren
to be off the phone	aufgelegt haben, nicht sprechen
to be on	dran sein
to be on the phone	gerade telefonieren
berk	Dussel/Idiot (umgangssprachlich)
to be taken with	eingenommen sein für
to be at home with sth.	mit einer Sache vertraut sein
to be represented all over the city	in der ganzen Stadt Filialen haben
to be right down	gleich herunterkommen
to be speaking/calling/on the line	am Apparat sein

Glossar

bean-counters	Erbsenzähler (abfällig)
to become acquainted with sth.	vertraut werden mit
to be in the market for	wirklich Bedarf haben nach
to be out of s.o.'s league	nicht das Spezialgebiet von jdm. sein
to better	verbessern
to bin	wegwerfen
to blind with science	jdn. mit großen Worten beeindrucken
blunder	(schwerer) Fehler
boast	prahlen
to book	buchen, reservieren
booking	Reservierung
to boom	nach oben schießen, z. B. Verkaufszahlen
to boost sb.s confidence	Selbstvertrauen aufbauen (umgangssprachlich)
to bother	stören
brand	Marke
branch	Zweigstelle
to break	unterbrechen
to break a system in	ein System in Betrieb nehmen
to break down	hier: zerstreuen, aus der Welt schaffen
to break in	einarbeiten
to break into	in den Markt vordringen
to break off	aufhören/abbrechen
breakthrough	Durchbruch
bribery	Bestechung
bright and breezy	frisch wie der junge Morgen
brief	kurz
briefcase	Aktentasche
to bring out	herausbringen
broadband communications	Breitband-Kommunikation
to broaden	erweitern, vergrößern
broad palette	eine breite Palette
to build s.o.'s fortunes	die Interessen von jdm. vertreten
to build up	aufbauen
bundle	Bündel/Packen

business area	Geschäftsgebiet, Geschäftsfeld
business centre	Handelszentrum
business expenses	Spesenabrechnung
business negotiation	geschäftliche Verhandlung
business people	Geschäftsleute
businessperson	Geschäftsmann, -frau
business-related discipline	wirtschaftliches Ausbildungsfach
to buy a round (of drinks)	eine Runde bezahlen
to buzz about	umhersausen
to call by	vorbeikommen
to call up sth.	etw. abrufen
to call out for	bringen lassen
can't help	nicht umhin kommen
Care to come along?	Möchten Sie nicht mitkommen?
to carry s.o.'s range	jds. Sortiment übernehmen
to catch one's eye	jds. Aufmerksamkeit erregen
to catch s.o.'s attention	jds. Aufmerksamkeit erregen
catch up on letter-writing	überfällige Briefe schreiben
cell(ular) phone	Mobiltelefon, Handy
to chair	leiten, den Vorsitz führen
Chamber of Trade	Handelskammer
to check out	nachgehen
chief executive	Geschäftsführer
to chuck	zerknüllen
circulation	Auflage
circulation list	Presseverteiler
to clear sth.	etw. abklären
client	Kunde
client details	Kundendaten
cogent	schlüssig
cold-calling	Blindakquisition
to come along	vorankommen, z. B. Vorbereitungen Fortschritte machen
come by information	etw. wissen über
come to be known	bekannt geworden
to come in on the ground floor	von Anfang an zusammenarbeiten
commission (basis)	Provisions(rate)
to commute	pendeln

company profile	Firmenprofil
company travel	Geschäftsreisen
competition	Konkurrenz
competitive	wettbewerbsorientiert, konkurrenzfähig
to complain	sich beschweren
complaint	Beschwerde
competitors' products	Konkurrenzprodukte
to computerize	auf Computer umstellen
to conduct a press conference	eine Pressekonferenz leiten
confab	Geplauder/eine »Expertenrunde« (umgangssprachlich)
to confide in s.o.	sich jdm. anvertrauen
confirmation	Bestätigung
to confirm price and conditions	Preis und Lieferbedingungen bestätigen
to connect sb.	jdn. durchstellen
consensus	Übereinstimmung, Konsens
considerable	beachtlich
consultancy basis	beratende Funktion
consumer-orientated	konsumentenorientiert
contact (name)	(Name eines) Ansprechpartners
conventional means	konventionelle Mittel
cost-effective	kosteneffektiv
cost estimate	Kostenvoranschlag
to couch	formulieren, »sprachlich einbetten«
counter-productive	kontraproduktiv
courier service	Kurierdienst
to courier sth.	etw. per Kurier schicken
to cover (a territory)	für (ein Gebiet) zuständig sein
to cross fingers	Daumen drücken
credit details	Kreditinformationen
crestfallen	erschüttert
critical to s.o.'s futures	entscheidend für jds. Zukunft
(my, your, his, her) cup of tea	auf einer Wellenlänge
current business year	laufendes Geschäftsjahr
customer	Kunde

customer-relations	Kundenbeziehungen
custom-made	maßgeschneidert
to cut sb. off	jdn. aus der Leitung werfen
CV (curriculum vitae)	Lebenslauf
data base	Datenbank
to dash around	sich kreuz und quer herumtreiben
data system	Datenanlage
day-to-day business	Tagesgeschäft
deal	Geschäftsabschluss
to deal in a wide range of sth.	eine breite Produktpalette von etw. anbieten
to deal with sb. over the phone	am Telefon mit jdm. verhandeln
degree in economics	Abschluss in Wirtschaftswissenschaft
to deliver	hier: bieten, vermitteln
to demonstrate the effectiveness	die Wirksamkeit vorführen
Department of Social Security	Sozialversicherungsamt
to deserve sth.	etw. verdienen, z. B. Lob
devolution	Dezentralisierung
devoted to	gewidmet
to dial	wählen
dictaphone	Diktiergerät
digitalisation	Digitalisierung
dire	grässlich/ hier: weitreichend, unangenehm
direction	hier: Vorgehensweise; Anleitung
to direct sth.	etw. leiten
discipline	hier: Fachgebiet
to disclose	verdecken
discount prices for larger orders	Mengenrabatt
discussion session	Diskussionsrunde
to display sth.	etw. demonstrieren
distinguished	geschätzt, verehrt
to divert	ablenken
doddle	Klacks, Kleinigkeit
dog-tired	hundemüde
do the trick	funktionieren
to double as a guide	den Fremdenführer spielen

double-page spread	doppelseitiger Artikel
Do your stuff!	hier: Tun Sie, was Sie tun müssen/für was Sie bezahlt werden.
Down to business.	Kommen wir zum Geschäftlichen.
down to orders	zum Geschäftlichen
draft	Entwurf
to draft	entwerfen
to draw up a presentation	eine Präsentation entwerfen
to draw up	(einen Text) entwerfen
dress rehearsal	Generalprobe
driving license	Führerschein
to drop	hier: fallen lassen (eine Tätigkeit stehen und liegen lassen/ auch: eine Bemerkung fallen lassen etc.)
to drop on	(Arbeit) abwälzen
dying to	»sterben« etwas zu sehen/ hören etc.
easily accessible	leicht zugänglich
easy-going	unkompliziert
editor	Redakteur
easy ride	Kleinigkeit, leichte Sache
editorial	redaktionell
effect	Auswirkung
to elaborate points	Punkte ausarbeiten
electronic commerce	elektronischer Handel
electronic payment system	elektronisches Zahlungssystem
to email sth.	etw. per E-Mail schicken
enciphered data	verschlüsselte Daten
to end a letter	einen Brief beenden
endeavour	Herausforderung
to entail	beinhalten/ nach sich ziehen
entrepreneur	Unternehmer
errand	Botengang
estate agent	Wohnungsmakler
exchange of views	Meinungsaustausch
executive officer	leitender Angestellter

to expand	expandieren
expanding company	expandierende Firma
expansion plans	Expansionspläne
expense sheet/expenses return	Spesenabrechnung
expense	Kosten
extended payments plan	Ratenzahlungsplan
extension	Durchwahl
face to face	persönlich / »von Angesicht zu Angesicht«
failings	Fehler
fair	Messe
to fall down on s.o.'s promises	jds. Versprechungen nicht nachkommen
to fall for	sich verlieben
to fall into	hinein fallen (im Sinne von dazu gehören)
far afield	weit weg
fine by me	mir ist es recht
file	Akte
to fill sb. in	jdn. ins Bild setzen/ aufklären über etw.
financial exchange software	Bilanzierungsprogramm
financial services company	Finanzdienstleister
to fire away	losschießen (umgangssprachlich)
first-hand experience	eigene Erfahrungen
to follow up a lead	an einer Sache dranbleiben; eine Möglichkeit verfolgen
fond of	angetan von
for all the tea in China	(Redewendung), etwa: Für alles Geld der Welt
for a start	zuerst einmal
forceful	hier: ausgeprägt (Charakter)
form	Formular
formal	formell
for one	für meine Person
for starters	für den Anfang
forefront	vorderste Front
foxed	verblüfft

franchise	Franchise (Übertragung einer Lizenz)
franchise contract	Lizenzvertrag
franchise holder	Lizenznehmer
to franchise	Lizenzen vergeben
free of charge	kostenlos
from the start	vor Beginn
function	Vorhaben
function room	Mehrzweckraum
to gather	hier: gehört haben
gathering	Treffen
to gather the papers	die Unterlagen zusammensuchen
(to be) geared up	bereit sein (etwa: seine Siebensachen zusammen haben)
general impression	Gesamteindruck
generously-proportioned	großzügig geschnitten
to get around to	dazu kommen
to get double value from sth.	von etw. doppelt profitieren
to get down to business	zum Geschäft kommen
to get down to sth.	etw. angehen
to get down to sth. right away	sich sofort um etw. kümmern
to get hold of sth.	etw. in die Finger bekommen
to get in touch with sb.	Kontakt aufnehmen zu jdm.
to get on to	sich daran machen
to get on the road	sich auf den Weg machen
to get the better of	etwas nachgeben, nichts widerstehen können
to get through	durchkriegen
to get to	dazu kommen
to get to know	kennen lernen
to get sth. off the ground	etwas in Gang bringen
to get used to	sich daran gewöhnen
to give an insight	einen Einblick geben
to give a speech	eine Rede halten
to give a telling off	eine Standpauke halten
to give sb. a buzz	(ugs.) jdn. anrufen
to give sb. a call	jdn. anrufen
to glance through sth.	etw. überfliegen/durchsehen
globalization	Globalisierung

glowing	überschwänglich
to go about sth.	etw. angehen
to go alone	als Einziger vertreten sein
to go for sth.	etw. vorziehen
to go well	gut laufen
grapevine	»Gerüchteküche«
to grapple with sth.	sich mit etw. herumschlagen
grey zone	Grauzone
groundwork	grundlegende Arbeit
to grow at an encouraging rate	sehr ermutige Zuwachsraten zu verzeichnen haben
guinea-pig	Meerschweinchen, oft im Sinne von »Versuchskaninchen«
hack	kleinkarierter Journalist
hacker	(Computer-)Hacker
hand	Hilfskraft
to handle	umgehen mit
hand-out	Handzettel; Informationsblatt
to hand out	ausgeben, verteilen
to hand over	weiterleiten
to handle sth.	sich um etw. kümmern
to hang up and try again	auflegen und es noch einmal versuchen
to have bigger fish to fry	einen größeren Fisch am Haken haben (etwas Wichtigeres vorhaben)
to have handy	zur Hand haben
to have not the foggiest idea	nicht die geringste Ahnung haben
to have sb. on the line	jdn. in der Leitung haben
to have time	Zeit haben
hold; hold the line	in der Leitung bleiben, warten
hard cookie	harter Brocken (anerkennend)
to have a head-start	einen Vorsprung haben
to have aboard	jmd. an Bord haben
to have an appointment to see sb.	einen Termin mit jdm. haben
to have difficulty in reaching sb.	Probleme haben, jdn. zu erreichen.
to have sth. pressing to do	etwas Eiliges/Wichtiges zu tun haben

head office	Hauptbüro
headquarter	Hauptsitz
he/she is tops	jmd. ist unschlagbar/der, die Beste
Hello, is that ...	Hallo, spreche ich mit ...
het-up	aufgeregt/erhitzt über etwas
(the) hot seat	brenzlige Position (im Geschäftsbereich)
highly complimentary	voll des Lobes
highly desirable	höchst attraktiv
highly-qualified	hochqualifiziert
high-tech age	Zeitalter der Hochtechnologie
to hire	einstellen
to hold	abhalten, z. B. Konferenz
to hold down sth.	etw. innehaben, z. B. einen Job
Honesty pays in selling!	Ehrlichkeit zahlt sich im Verkauf aus!
hook	Aufhänger (auch fig.)
housekeeping bill	Haushaltsrechnung
How's business?	Wie gehen die Geschäfte?
How can I get reconnected?	Wie bekomme ich wieder Verbindung?
hype	zielgerichtete Übertreibung/ »Hype«
I am all ears	Ich bin ganz Ohr
I am both honoured and delighted to be (+ Gerund-Form)	Ich fühle mich sowohl geehrt als auch erfreut ...
I have great pleasure in (+ Gerund-Form)	Es ist mir eine große Freude ...
immaterial	bedeutungslos
to immerse oneself	sich in etwas versenken; intensiv vertraut machen
implications	Auswirkungen
in a heck of a state	in einem furchtbaren Zustand
in a jiffy	im Handumdrehen/ in »Windeseile«
in a state	hier: in einem schlechten Zustand sein
in black and white	schwarz auf weiß
in charge of	verantwortlich

incompatible	unverträglich/ unvereinbar
to incorporate information	Informationen einstreuen
to increase at an encouraging rate	hohe Zuwachsraten verzeichnen
indisposed	unpässlich (hier: unabkömmlich)
initial	anfänglich
input	Anregungen
to inquire about	sich erkundigen nach
inquiry	Anfrage
ins and outs	alle Details
in sb.'s good books	bei jdm. gut angeschrieben sein
insertion	Inserat
to install	installieren, z. B. Computer Programm
instant access	direkter Zugriff
intended	Sinn der Sache
in terms of	im Sinne von
internet access	Internet-Anschluss
internet fraud	Internet-Betrug
internet payment	Geldtransfer im Internet
internet thefts	Internet-Diebstähle
in the meantime	in der Zwischenzeit
in the picture	im Bild sein/ Bescheid wissen
in-tray	(Post-)Eingangskorb
to intrigue	sehr interessieren
introductory pamphlet	kurze Einführung
into the field	in der Praxis
to issue	herausgeben
It's my pleasant duty...	Es ist meine angenehme Aufgabe...
It will take some selling.	Es wird einige harte Verkaufsgespräche geben.
jargon	Jargon
job inquiry	Bewerbung
to join a company	einer Firma beitreten
to junk	wegwerfen
keen competition	scharfe Konkurrenz
to keep abreast of	Schritt halten mit
to keep sb. posted	jdn. auf dem Laufenden halten

Glossar

to keep track of sth.	den Überblick behalten
to keep up with	Schritt halten mit
to keep your head down	sich zurückhalten
to kindle interest	Interesse entfachen
kippers	Bücklinge
to know the scene	sich auskennen
Ladies and gentlemen …	Meine Damen und Herren …
to land (an order)	»unter Dach und Fach bringen«/ »an Land ziehen«
leader	hier: Marktführer
leading	führend
learned colleagues	gelehrte Kollegen
learning process	Lernprozess
to leave a message	eine Nachricht hinterlassen
to leave one's options open	alle Möglichkeiten offen lassen
letter-head	Briefkopf
to lift	abnehmen (Hörer)
light buffet	kleiner Imbiss
log	Ablaufplan
look-see	kurzer Blick
loudspeaker	Lautsprecher/Mithörtaste
lousy	lausig, verflixt
lucrative	lukrativ
mainframe	Computersystem
main speaker	Hauptredner
to make a big bid	sich sehr bemühen
to make a practice of	es sich zur Regel gemacht haben
to make arrangements	Vorbereitungen treffen
to make a sale	ein Geschäft abschließen
to make contact	Kontakt aufnehmen
to make doubly certain	auf Nummer sicher gehen
to make it snappy	sich beeilen
Make it snappy!	Machen Sie schnell/fix!
to make out a very good case	ein sehr gutes Argument dafür
to make sb.'s day	einem den Tag retten
to make some money on	etw. Geld verdienen mit
to make straight for	sich sofort aufmachen zu
to make up a file	einen Ordner anlegen

to make up lost time	verlorene Zeit aufholen
to man sb.'s phone	jds. Telefon übernehmen
to manage	schaffen/in der Lage sein
managing editor	Herausgeber
manner of presentation	Präsentationsmethode
manpower	Arbeitskraft/-kräfte; Mitarbeiter
manufacturers	Hersteller
to market	vermarkten
market exposure	Markteinführung
marketing account	Marketing-Budget
marketing material	Werbematerial
marketing people	Marketing-Leute
marketing push	Marketing-Initiative
marketing division	Marketingabteilung
to match perfectly	perfekt passen
to match s.o.'s claim	jds. Ansprüche erfüllen
May I help you?	Kann ich Ihnen behilflich sein?
meeting	Besprechung
to meet one's match	seinen Meister treffen
to meet the demands	die Anforderungen erfüllen
memo	Memo
to mend the lines	Leitungen reparieren
missive	Mitteilung
mobile (phone)	Mobiltelefon, Handy
to move into the forefront	sich einen Platz an der Spitze erobern
my lad	Freundchen
My treat!	Das geht auf meine Rechnung!
my turn	ich bin dran
to narrow down	eingrenzen
net profits	Reingewinn
news department	Nachrichtenredaktion
news file	neueste Meldungen
new revolution	neue Revolution
no reflection on	nichts zu tun haben mit
nothing short of	nicht weniger als
no way	unter keinen Umständen
not so hot	nicht so toll (umgangssprachlich)

not to cry over spilt milk	»was passiert ist, ist passiert«
not to get through	nicht durchkommen
off-base	außerhalb (einer Firma etc.)
offhand	unpersönlich
off the hook	vom Haken sein/noch mal davon gekommen sein
of paramount importance	von entscheidender Bedeutung
one-man operation	Ein-Mann-Betrieb
on file	in den Unterlagen
on his plate	auf sein Konto (gehen)
on occasion	bei Gelegenheit
on that score	in diesem Punkt, hierbei, diesbezüglich
on the hop	in Nullkommanichts
on the spot	vor Ort
on the turn	sofort, umgehend
open-and-shut	klar und deutlich/ eindeutig
opening	freie Stelle
operations	Geschäftsaktivitäten
operator	Vermittlung
out and about	unterwegs
out of the blue	ohne Vorwarnung/ »aus heiterem Himmel«
outset	Anfang
out-tray	(Post-)Ausgangskorb
overjoyed	überglücklich
over the moon	hin und weg, begeistert
over the years	im Laufe der Jahre
pager/beeper	Piepser
packaging	Verpackung
pal	Freund, Kumpel
panic stations	Krise
papers	Unterlagen
paperwork	Papierkram
to pay dividends	sich bezahlt machen
payment agreement	Zahlungsbedingungen
payment plan	Finanzplan
pecking order	Rangordnung

penetration	Vordringen
per capita	pro Kopf
performance	Auftritt
permanent location	ständiger Wohnsitz
personal approach	persönlicher Ansatz
personal call	Stippvisite
personnel department	Personalabteilung
to phone around	herumtelefonieren
to phone to find out	anrufen, um nachzufragen
to pick up	erwerben, z. B. Fähigkeiten; abholen
pick-you-up	Muntermacher
to plump for	stimmen für
to pontificate	dozieren
pool of labour	Arbeitskräfte
preliminary observations	grundlegende Feststellungen
to present a case	für eine Sache sprechen
presentation skills	Fähigkeiten zur Präsentation
to preside	den Vorsitz führen
press conference	Pressekonferenz
press coverage	Pressebericht
press distribution list	Verteilerliste für die Presse
press release	Pressemitteilung
print-shop	Druckerei
proceedings	Tagesordnung
productive	produktiv
product line	Produktreihe
progress report	Erfolgsbericht
to project	übertragen
projection	Prognose
promotional material	Promotion-Material
proof (in publishing)	Korrekturabzug
to propagate	verbreiten
to provide	bereitstellen
public speaking	Sprechen vor Publikum
publicity	Werbung
to pull in	anhalten
to punch sth. into	etw. einhacken

push	Initiative/Vorstoß (bes. im Marketing)
to push	hier: verschieben/aufschieben bis zum besten Zeitpunkt
to put into practice	in die Praxis umsetzen
to put in touch with sb.	an jdn. weiterleiten
to put off	verschieben, hinhalten
to put on file	abspeichern
to put a caller through	einen Anrufer durchstellen
to put in the picture	ins Bild setzen, auf den neuesten Stand bringen
to put out of one's misery	jdn. nicht mehr länger zappeln lassen
to put the phone down	auflegen
question-and-answer session	Fragestunde
quite a hand at	erfahren/geübt mit etwas
quote/quotation	hier: Aussage (sonst: Angebot)
to range from sth. to	reichen von etw. bis hin
range of products	Produktpalette
to reach on the phone	telefonisch erreichen
to read up on	sich einlesen
reader-base	Leserschicht
to reboot	neu starten (PC)
reception	Empfang
recording	Tonbandaufnahme
to rectify	richtig stellen
to refer to sth.	sich beziehen auf, hier: über etw. sprechen
references	Referenzen
referral	Vermittlung
refrain from	sich zurückhalten
regional operation	Außenstelle
to regret	bedauern
release	Publikation
to reply to	beantworten
to report in on sth.	etw. melden
reputation	Ruf, Ansehen
request	Anfrage

requirements	Anforderungen
retail outlet	Einzelhandels-Niederlassung
retail (trade)	Einzelhandel
retrenchment	Einschränkung/Kürzung; Kostenreduzierung
to ride the crest of a wave	auf einer Welle mitschwimmen
right away	sofort
rogue	Spitzbube
rostrum	Rednerpult
round-up	Zusammenstellung (eigentlich: Zusammentreiben von Vieh)
to rubbish	mies/schlecht machen
to run the office	das Büro leiten
run-up	hier: für den Beginn/Anfang
to revamp	neu einrichten
right on time	rechtzeitig
roll out the heavy guns	»schwere Geschütze auffahren«
safe and sound	heil
to safeguard	sichern
sale	Geschäftsabschluss
sales	Verkaufszahlen, Verkauf
sales approach	Verkaufsstrategie
sales area	Verkaufsbereich
sales chief	Verkaufsleiter
sales director	Verkaufsleiter
sales experience	Verkaufserfahrung
sales manager	Verkaufsleiter
salesmanship	Verkauf
salesperson	Verkäufer
sales pitch	Verkaufsargument
sales points	Verkaufsstellen
sales stand	Verkaufsstand
sales strategy	Verkaufsstrategie
sales technique	Verkaufstechnik
sales trip	Verkaufsreise
saved by the bell	Rettung in letzter Sekunde
schedule	Terminkalender
to score success	Erfolg erzielen

Glossar

to scrounge off	schnorren
to seal a contract	einen Vertrag abschließen
to score a hit	einen Erfolg verbuchen
secondary	zweitrangig
secondment	Abordnung, im Sinne von »jdm. unterstellt werden«
secret assignment	Geheimauftrag
security software	Sicherheitssoftware
security system	Sicherheitssystem
to seek out	finden, heraussuchen
»sell-by« date	Haltbarkeitsdatum
selling point	Verkaufsargument
seminar on salesmanship	Verkaufsseminar
to set up	sich niederlassen
to settle for	sich zufrieden geben mit
to settle in	sich eingewöhnen
to shape up	sich entwickeln
share option	Option auf Belegschaftsaktien
to shift through	durchschauen
short-list	Auswahlliste
short statement	ein paar kurze Worte
to shut down	herunterfahren (PC)
shortly	in Kürze, gleich
to show sb. the ropes	jdm. etw. erklären (ugs.)
sidekick	Partner, Kumpel
single-handed	im Alleingang
to sink	ruinieren
to sit in a meeting	an einem Meeting teilnehmen
slog	harte Arbeit/Schufterei
sloppy	schlampig, nachlässig
small change	Kleingeld
so-called	so genannt
social security number	Sozialversicherungsnummer
soft-soap	»Weichspülerei«
some of the leads	ein paar der Wichtigsten
to sound out	aushorchen, ausfragen
to sort out	aussortieren
... speaking	... am Apparat

special deal	Spezialangebot
to specialise in a particular Field	sich auf einen bestimmten Bereich spezialisieren
special supplement	Sonderbeilage
specifications	nähere Angaben
to spring in	einspringen
springing up all over the place	»überall aus dem Boden schießen«
stage fright	Lampenfieber
(a) stack of	ein ganzer Haufen (von)
stacks	Stapel (hier: »stapelweise«)
stand	(Messe-)Stand
to stand in for	einspringen für
state-of-the-art	hochmodern
to step into	hereinkommen
stiff	steif (hier: rau, umkämpft)
to stick to	hier: bleiben bei
stinker	harter Brocken
stock	Vorrat
stock exchange listing	Börsengang
to store	abspeichern
straight from the shoulder	frei von der Leber weg
strategy	Strategie
streamlining	Leistungssteigerung
strike from	ausstreichen/herausnehmen
strong point	starke Seite (einer Person)
to stuck into sth.	sich in etwas vertiefen/ »hineinknien«
to subcontract	Unteraufträge vergeben
submerged in letters	unter einem Briefberg begraben
subsidiary	Tochtergesellschaft
subsidies	Subventionen
subtle	subtil/feinsinnig
succinct and informative	auf den Punkt gebracht und informativ
to suit the purpose	den Anforderungen entsprechen
supplement	Zeitungsbeilage
to sum up	zusammenfassen, hier: aufführen
to swat up	büffeln, sich intensiv mit

switchboard	Vermittlungszentrale
to swot	»büffeln«, »pauken« (umgangssprachlich)
tabular	tabellarisch
to tackle formalities	Formalitäten in Angriff nehmen
to tackle some letters	ein Paar Briefe durchgehen
tailored	maßgeschneidert
to take a letter	einen Brief aufnehmen
to take a message	eine Nachricht entgegennehmen
to take a shine to	einen Narren gefressen haben an etw./jdm.
to take if from here	jetzt weiter vorgehen
to take it	annehmen
to take it from there	sich von da ab um etwas kümmern
to take off	frei nehmen; sich entfernen, abheben
to take over	übernehmen
takeover	Übernahme
to take questions	Fragen entgegennehmen
to take sb. off a job	jdn. von etw. abziehen
to take sb. up	jdm. helfen, unter die Arme greifen
to take shape	Gestalt annehmen (fig.)
to talk shop	fachsimpeln
to talk sth. through	etw. durchsprechen
to talk through	einweisen; erklären
to tally	abrechnen; übereinstimmen
to tap into	eindringen in
task	Ziel
tax breaks	Steuererleichterungen
technical department	Technische Abteilung
techno-park	Technologiepark
telephone company/people	Telefongesellschaft
telephone number	Telefonnummer
telephone receiver	Telefonhörer
to tend to	dazu tendieren/neigen
test run	Testlauf
testimonial	Anerkennung/ (positive) Referenz

etwas beschäftigen

That is out of my area.	Das gehört nicht zu meinem Zuständigkeitsbereich.
That's just the ticket.	Das ist genau das Richtige.
The floor is yours!	Der Platz gehört Ihnen!/ Sie haben das Wort!
the gift of the gab	die Gabe einer »großen Klappe«
the line is still open	die Verbindung steht noch
the line went dead	die Verbindung wurde unterbrochen
the number is ringing	es wird gerade durchgeläutet
the number/line is engaged	es ist belegt
the pleasure is all mine	das Vergnügen ist ganz auf meiner Seite
to think sth. over	etw. überdenken
to thrash out sth.	etw. gründlich diskutieren, hier: (Ideen) austauschen
(to be) tied down	in etwas eingebunden sein
topic	Thema
top priority	höchste Priorität, hier: am wichtigsten
top salesman	Spitzenverkäufer
to track sb. down	jdn. aufspüren
trade fair	Handelsmesse
trade fair catalogue	Messekatalog
trade press	Fachpresse
trading centre	Handelszentrum
treatise	Abhandlung
to trouble s.o.	jdn. belästigen
to try to get hold of sb.	versuchen, jdn. zu erreichen
to turn down	ablehnen
tube (colloq.)	U-Bahn
to type up	abtippen
umpteen	zig
unconditionally	bedingungslos/ ohne Vorbehalte
under our belts	unter Dach und Fach
unlimited usage	unbeschränkte Nutzung
upcoming	bevorstehend
to update	verbessern
up-to-date	hochaktuell

up-to-date with everything	alles so weit geregelt
urge	inständig bitten, drängen
user-friendly	benutzerfreundlich
venture	Unternehmung
virtual marketplace	virtuelle Verkaufsstellen
visual presentation	visuelle Präsentation
voice mail	Anrufbeantworter
to vouch	sich verbürgen
warehouse floor	Lager
website	Website
welcome address	Begrüßungsansprache
well aware	im Klaren darüber
well-worded	wohl formuliert
whatismore	außerdem
What name shall I give?	Wen darf ich melden?
What's on the agenda?	Was steht auf der Tagesordnung?
When it comes to selling ...	Wenn es darum geht ... anzupreisen
to whitle down	reduzieren
wild about	wild/verrückt nach
to win the franchise	die Konzession bekommen
with a total lack of	so gar kein
Word gets back very quickly/ News does travel fast.	Neuigkeiten verbreiten sich schnell.
to work in close association / closely with s.o.	eng zusammenarbeiten mit jdm.
work-load	Arbeitspensum
work up a thirst	sich durstig arbeiten
writer's cramp	Schreibkrampf
wrongly connected	falsch verbunden
to work together	zusammenarbeiten
You are all aware ...	Sie alle kennen ...
You bet!	Darauf können Sie/ kannst du wetten!
zilch	Nichts (umgangssprachlich)

 **Lösungen**

Übung

1. 1. Good morning! May I help you? This is Peter Brückner speaking. I'm calling to find out when I should start. I tried to call Mr Morgan yesterday. I couldn't get through. The phone seemed to be out of order. Mr Morgan will be calling in shortly.
2. It's Peter Brückner speaking. I tried to call yesterday but I couldn't get through. Should I try to call Mr Morgan at home? Has the office tried to contact me?

2. Good morning. How do you do. Good morning. Hi. Hello.

3. Well-equipped. Access. Installed.

4. 1. I'd like a beer, please.
2. Now, what would you like to drink?

5. 1. Cut. Called. Hold. Went. Hang. Reconnected.
2. Connected. Hang on/hold. Put. Through. Get. Try.

6. 1. Very much. Kind. Love. Call you.
2. I'd love to come, but I'm afraid I shall be working late.

7. Hello! Is that Lost Property? No? What number is that? Could you please speak more slowly? I have to report to Lost Property that I have lost my umbrella. Could you please connect me to/with the correct/right number. What do you mean by dial? And what is an extension? Could you please speak more clearly. I obtained the number from the telephone directory, and now you are telling me I have the wrong number!

8. Of assistance. Contact. Connected. Getting. Want/require. Call. Call. Call. On. Call. Call. Put ... through. Speaking.

9. It's. Reach. Left. Voice-mail/answerphone. Mobile. Call. Call. Get. Calling.

10. 1. Called. Calls. Call. Tell. Contact. Mobile. Reach.
2. I just called to say that I shan't be at the office until later because I have a doctor's appointment and if there are any calls for me please take messages.

11. 1. Totally happy. Please. Elaborate on some of the points. Is not complete. When you get the chance. 2. Happy. Care. Writing. Asked.

12. d, a, b, e, c.

13. On Monday I was in Birmingham and called Texo, but there was no reply. I decided to call again on Tuesday afternoon. On Monday afternoon I was at Cranford Foods, where changes were made satisfactorily to the contract. I agreed to call again on Friday. On Tuesday morning I called in at Taylor Electronics in Stratford and we set a meeting for Friday. I had lunch with the Stratford News Editor and described to him the new copy-editing software. He expressed interest. In the afternoon I returned to Birmingham, calling in at the telephone company en route. On Wednesday morning I had a dental appointment. In the afternoon I described the company objectives to the Birmingham Chamber of Commerce and Trade. On Thursday I drove to Stratford in order to make an early start on Friday. Early on Friday morning I called Cranford Foods and agreed to call again on Monday. The full board of Taylor Electronics turned up for the 10 AM meeting, indicating that prospects are good.

14. Calling. Called. Contacted. Spoke. Had ... spoken. Call. Called. Call.

15. Hello. It's. Am calling. Call. On. Would. Which. Call. Call. By. Call.

16. 1. Is that. Who am I speaking. Speaking. Called. Number. Dialled. Number. Get. Hang. Try. Get through. Line/number. Busy/engaged. On. 2. a: Over; b: Off; c: By; d: On, talking.

17. Speak. Here. Wonder. Could. Called. Say. Called. Engaged. Asked/told. Leave. Get/receive. Call. Hang. Line. Contact.

18. Would like. Would you. Would be. Could. Phone. Should. Would ... be. Call.

19. 1. Mr Blackman, I want to discuss this contract. It's not satisfactory, and I'm not happy with it. I don't really understand what clauses one, three and six mean. When I rang you yesterday you assured me there was no problem. but when I called today you didn't sound so confident. You told me the commission on the whole order is 15 per cent, but the contract speaks of 10 per cent. Why this discrepancy? I'd like to give an explanation to my office, which is waiting for my call this afternoon. Could you give me an explanation before then?
2. Easier. Dial/call. More complicated. Get. Louder. Line. Hold. Longer. Cut. More difficult. Dial/call. Call. Shorter. More expensive. Call.

20. Put ... through. Engaged/busy. Hold. Connect. Speak. Busy/engaged. Hold. Invite. Put ... through. Is that. Invite. Off the. Hand-out. Release. Give. Number. Hearing.

21. Would be grateful. Did. Call. Postpone. Mobile. Call. Call. Reach. Call. Answerphone.

22. That. Talking. Number. Dialled. Call. Number. Give. Number. Repeat. Put ... through. Speaking. Connected. Connect. Hold. Put through to. Ring. Speak.

23. 1. d   2. c.

24. Speak to. Call. Inquire. Very. Submit. Promptly.
Arrived. Grateful. Sent. Appreciates. Require.

25. Invited. Attend. Introducing. Interest. Happy. Provide. Require. Followed. Which you are. Appreciate.

26. 1. Put me through. Engaged/busy. Hold. Cut off. Dial. Engaged. Cut ... off. Called. Contact. Busy. Interrupt. On. Hold. Through. Speak. Hold. Cut. Hanging.

2. Hello, Miss Barker. It's Peter Brückner, of ERGO Limited, here. ERGO is exhibiting at the electronics trade fair. My Marketing Director, Miss Melissa Walker, has an important question concerning the catalogue. She would like to know when the catalogue will be printed. She says she would like to see first of all the layout of the page on which ERGO is advertising. She found no mistakes in the proof you sent her last week, but she would like to be doubly certain.

27. 1. Quick-Ed: The software system for easy editing and page makeup, for newspapers and magazines. The Quick-Ed system saves many man-hours in sub-editing. Quick-Ed was developed by the company that marketed the accountancy program Accounting 2000 - ERGO International, San Diego, USA. The Quick-Ed system can be viewed in use at the Middlesex Echo. Sole U.K. suppliers of Quick-Ed: ERGO Ltd., Carter's Lane, London N1. Tel. 171/385964, fax 171/385965. Website: http://www.ergo.com. Email: Ergo@telkom.com. 2. Put ... through. Speak to. Hold. Name. Opportunity. Phoning. Could. Call. Call. Date. Call. Appointment. Call. Extension/number. Dial. Calling. Phone. Call.

28. Call. Call. Getting. Engaged/busy. Reached. Connected. Phoned. Talk. Call. By. Hear. Reach. Try. Switch ... on. Hold. Ring. Use. Hear. Call. Try. Number.

29. 1. Call. Mobile. Busy/engaged. Could I. Could you. Call. Get. Could you. Call. Would ... be 2. b; c; a; c; a; b: c.

30. Is that. Calling. Ask. Contact. Speak to. Spoke. Calling. Asking. Call. Report. Connected. Ring. Number.

31. Is that. Plan. Put. Hold/hang on. Extension. Put. Hold/hang on. Cut off. Dead. By.

32. 1. b; g; d; h; c; e; f; i; a.
2. Secretary; Assistant Managing Director; Managing Director; Accountant; Salesman; Marketing Department Director; Courier; Accountant; Sales Department Director; Salesman.

33. Understand. Assure. Can ... find. Afraid. Assure. Give up. Satisfied.

34. Answerphone. Telephone. Pager. Switchboard. Mobile or cell phone.

35. Called. Had called. Would call. Have called. Will call. Calls. Call. Calls. Will call. Has ... called. Call. Calling. Had called. Call.

36. 1. Hello, is that Geoff Burnes? Mr Morgan asked me to call you. He has decided on a new sales practice. Mr Morgan wants you to contact Metropolitan Newspapers and tell them that they can expect a complete service package. That means a computer specialist will spend just as long with them as they need. Until now, we offered only to install the system. Mr Morgan is worried about increasing complaints concerning the difficulty of operating the system. He has already contacted Metropolitan Newspapers to tell them that you will be calling. Can you call me back to tell me how you get on?
2. Hi. How do you do? Found. Talked about. Dreamt up.
Of considerable use. Wish for. Buzzing. In words. Put it in the fax machine, use the fax. Standing by, sitting, holding, impatient, contact, telephone.

37. 1. Speak to. In. Reply. Out. Line. Hold. Message. Like. Call back. Number.
2. Call, phone. Get through. Hold. Hang up. Answer. Dial.

38. 1. Leave a message and say you'll call later.
2. Peter has failed to identify himself!

39. The meeting discussed the Quick-Ed program, its advantages and drawbacks and reviewed complaints. Possible purchasers were listed. It was decided to assign Ken Allington, Chief Computer Analyst, to supervise the installation of a system at Metropolitan Newspapers and to familiarize staff with the system. The duration of his assignment will depend on the difficulty he has in acquainting the staff with the system. Costs and pricing will be the subject of negotiations with Metropolitan Newspapers. It was decided to meet again on Tuesday, August 24.

40. 1. Would like. Doubles. Occupancy. Arrive. Rate. Reserve. Have. Facilities. 2. Hire. Rate. Include. Inclusive. Rate. Go ahead. Reserve. Collect. Fax. Confirmation. Call. Promptly.

41. Connect. Calling. Leave. Getting through. Out of. Reach. Engaged/busy. Line. Extension. Phone. Line. Call/phone. Through/via. Put me through. Speaking. Connected. Connect. Engaged/busy. Hold. Put me through.

42. 3; 2; 3; 2; 3.

43. 1. Reach. Out of order. Say. Reach. Tell. Postpone. Getting through. On. Talks. Engaged. Got through to. Chat. On. Spend. Connection.
2. She said she was calling to confirm that they would be coming the next day. She had to find out the most convenient rail connection. She thought it would be easier and quicker to come by train than try the bus service. She had called the bus station the day before and had discovered that they would have to change twice to get to you. She had always thought the bus service was much more efficient than that, but she had obviously been wrong. She asked what time we expected them and should they bring anything. Her aunt had given them some really good home-made wine and she said they could bring a bottle or two. She told me to ask Tom and then give her a call back. She said she was really looking forward to the evening and asked who else would be there. She hoped we had not invited the Smiths. She said she couldn't stand Nancy Smith. If they were coming she asked to be put at the other end of the table and also to be seated away from her husband. She said all he could talk about these days was the Stock Exchange.

44. On. Off. Through. On. Up. On. On. Off. On. On. Up. On. At. Down. In. At

45. Book. Vacancy. Available. Reserve. Reserve/book. Arrive. Arrive. Sure. Delayed. Call. Reserve/book. Reserved. Arrive. Give. Tell. Reserved.

46. Called. Asked. Reserve. Arriving. Delayed. Call. Rate. Served.
I am calling to ask if you have a double room free for the night of April 4. Has the room a telephone and a television set? I would like to reserve the room. I shall be arriving between 5 PM and 6 PM. If I am delayed I shall call to advise you of my late arrival. Does the room rate include breakfast and do you serve full English breakfast or continental? I like to start the day on a full English breakfast because I often miss out on lunch.

47. 1. Persuade. 2. Performed. 3. Caught. 4. Obtain. 5. Recover from. 6. Understand. 7. Cope. 8. Catch. 9. Earn. 10. Reach.

48. 1. That's enough. 2. Complete. 3. Complete. 4. Exhausted. 5. Performed. 6. Covered. 7. Solve. 8. Release. 9. Fasten. 10. Repeat.

49. Explaining. Functions. Load. Start. Install. Contain. Start. Install. Play. Understand. Straightforward.

50. 1. Avoided. 2. Call. 3. Relinquished. 4. Surrender. 5a. Quit. 5b. Hinted. 6. Disclose. 7. Put me through to. 8. Donated. 9. Stop. 10. Inform.

51. 1. Yours sincerely; 2. Yours faithfully; 3. With best wishes; 4. Yours sincerely; 5. Yours sincerely; 6. With best wishes; 7. Yours faithfully; 8. Yours sincerely.

52. 1: request; 2: request; 3: demand; 4: refusal; 5: rejection; 6: denial; 7: withholding; 8: offer.

53. grateful; sent; range; products; products; developed; employ; areas; operations; scheduled; useful; arrange; reply; faithfully.

54. 1: banned; 2: seen; 3: several times; 4: start work; 5: stop; 6: land.

55. 1. cause; inform; defence; unaware; in question; prohibiting; assumed; used; refrain; opportunity; appeal; vicinity. 2. b; c.

56. has written; to complain; promised; to explain; has not turned up; tells; had suspended; looked at; says; decided to give; to call; had not done so; would strike; look.

57. 1: attractive; 2: site; 3: has; 4: large; 5: recommend.

58. 1: have written; 2: write; 3: will write; 4: written; 5: write; 6: wrote; 7: am writing.

59. receipt; prompt; appreciate; early; assured; best; reply; grateful; sent.

60. clearer; more brief; longer; more legible; more insulting; lengthier; sooner.

61. Dear Mr Green,
Thank you again for your invitation to lunch, which I originally very gratefully accepted. However, a very urgent business engagement has in the meantime cropped up and upset my plans. I regretfully have to cancel my plan to join you for lunch. Please excuse any inconvenience this might cause. I hope I may make amends and reciprocate by inviting you to lunch at the earliest opportunity.
With best regards,
...

62. 1: c, b; 2: c, c; 3: c, b; 4: c, a.

63. 1: personal; 2: personal, personal; 3: Personal, personnel; 4: recommendation; 5: referrals; 6: referral.

64. My company was told to put the order in more than a month ago and we were kept waiting until today for delivery. The package was delivered by the courier service during the lunch break, so its contents could not be checked immediately. When the package was opened by our sorting department it was discovered that the wrong product had been sent by ATCO. The sorting department was instructed to contact you without delay, but your dispatch department insisted that the correct item had been sent.

65. 1: commission, rebates; 2: rebate, commission; 3: commission, rebate.

66. 1: having; 2: objecting; 3: Before objecting; 4: am writing to inform; 5: After informing ... ready to sign (or ready for signing); 6: in informing ... to collect; 7: In ordering, to give; 8: to order, to be delivered; 9: Before ordering; 10; contacting; 11: Before contacting; 12: to contact.

67. malfunction, question, delay, send, fail to observe, eliminate mistake, examine, usually, furious, job, put together, disguise, at once.

68. 1. acknowledge, apologise, regrettable, dispatching, in time, lay, arrival, parts, suppliers, lodged, hope, discount, pass, apologizing, inconvenience, assuring, faithfully. 2. 1: early; 2: disappointed; 3: receive; 4: reply; 5: insincere; 6: mistrust; 7: right; 8: easy; 9: fail; 10; forget; 11: depart.

69. 1: testimonial; 2: recommendation; 3: testimonial.

70. PRO; PR; p.a.; pro tem; p/e; p.c.; PS

71. 1: therefore; 2: nevertheless; 3: therefore; 4: nevertheless; 5: therefore.

72. 1. An article on your company's software program, »Instantweb«, which the American magazine Computer World carried, has caught our attention ... This possibility particularly interested our Head Office in the United States, which has asked us to approach you with a view to obtaining the franchise for »Instantweb« in the United States. 2. 1: but; 2: and; 3: because; 4: since; 5: but; 6: and.

73. 1. 1: price; 2: price; 3: costs; 4: prices, costs; 5: price, costs, prices; 6: price, cost. 2. 1: consequences; 2: consequently; 3: Consequent; 4: consequently.

74. 1: basic facts; 2: information; 3: examine; 4: inside information; 5: inform; 6: essence.

75. 1: a; 2: c; 3: h; 4: b; 5: e; 6: f; 7: d; 8: g.

76. 1: b; 2: a; 3: c.

77. 1: convenient, expect; 2: mark, inviting, reception; 3: glad, invitation; 4: kind, attend, pleased; 5: honour, company; 6: afraid; 7: engaged.

78. 1. 1: any; 2: any; 3: some; 4: any; 5: any; 6: some; 7: any, some; 8: some. 2. 1: something; 2: anything; 3: something; 4: anything; 5: something; 6: anything; 7: anything; 8: something.

79. 1: Before replying: 2: after reading; 3: During ... to reply; 4: after receiving; 5: Before agreeing; 6: After examining, meanwhile; 7: During, has learnt; 8: Before leaving; 9: while ... are waiting; 10: After studying.

80. 1: effect; 2: affect; 3: effect; 4: affect; 5: effect; 6: effect; 7: effects; 8: affect; 9: effect; 10: effects.

81. Dear Sirs/Mesdames,
Thank you for your interest in our new product and your request for information. We are pleased to be able to send you our latest information on the product, and will be happy to answer any further inquiries you may have ...
Alternativen zum zweiten Satz: We have pleasure in sending you our latest information ...; We are glad to be able to send you our latest information ...

82. 1: patiently; 2: immediate; 3: fully; 4: promptly; 5: complete; 6: necessarily; 7: usually, prompt; 8: completely; 9: fully; 10: Happily; 11: patiently; 12: unusually; 13: badly; 14: Bad.

83. 1: in; 2: at, as; 3: by; 4: up; 5: down; 6: up; 7: into; 8: out; 9: at, for; 10: around.

84. 1: break; 2: have been broken; 3: break-in; 4: break up; 5: broken; 6: has broken away; 7: broken up; 8: broken out.

85. 1: to accept; 2: of telling; 3: of reading; 4: to deliver; 5: of being; 6: to see; 7: of paying; 8: to make.

86. was born; attending; left; took; travelled; returning; enrolled; completing; joined; gained; am employed; is; am studying; includes maintaining; organizing; has taken; feel.

87. 1: impressed by; 2: impressive; 3: impressively; 4: impression, on; 5: impressive; 6: impressed by; 7: to impress; 8: an impression on; 9: impressively; 10: impressed by.

88. 1: certify; 2: admit; 3: confirm; 4: accepted; 5: recognised; 6: accepted; 7: admitted; 8: avowed.

89. 1: whom; 2: whose; 3: Whom; 4: who; 5: who; 6: Who; 7: Whose; 8: whom; 9: who; 10: whose.

90. 1: of ... interest; 2: interesting; 3: interested in; 4: interest ... by; 5: interesting; 6: interest; 7: interest to; 8: interested; 9: interesting; 10: interested in; 11: interest; 12: interesting.

91. 1: I only wanted to meet her before she left. Now it's too late.
2: They should be only too pleased they didn't take up that offer.
3: I'm only too grateful for the help you gave me.
4: It's not only the anger it causes, but also the pain.
5: We've only two miles to go before we get home.
6: I shall be only too glad to do that for you.

92. 1: mispronounce; 2: mischance; 3: misanthrope; 4: misshapen; 5: misspend; 6: miscellany; 7: misdirect; 8: misgiving; 9: misfit; 10: misdeed; 11: misconduct; 12: misnomer.

93. 1: incapable; 2: impervious; 3: unable; 4: disproportionate; 5: abnormal; 6: insensitive; 7: impassively; 8: unaffected; 9: unstable; 10: insecure; 11: unseemly; 12: ungracious; 13: illegible; 14: unhealthy; 15: intolerable; 16: uncertain.

94. 1: by; 2: on; 3: into; 4: in; 5: up; 6: with; 7: down; 8: along; 9: out; 10: over; 11: under; 12: across.

95. 1: on; 2: through; 3: into; 4: down; 5: off; 6: through; 7: around; 8: out; 9: there; 10: into; 11: down; 12: back; 13: together; 4: round.

96. 1.1: fruitless; 2: fruitful; 3: fruits; 4: fruition; 5: fruitful; 6: fruitless; 7: fruit; 8: fruitful 2.1: away; 2: up; 3: down; 4: on; 5: away from; 6: at; 7: up; 8: back.

97. 1.1: had it in for; 2: had it in; 3: in on; 4: in with; 5: in the dark; 6: in clover; 7: in it; 8: in it; 9: in fashion; 10: in for.
2. would be; sent; about; since; possible; forward; express; terms; appreciated; faithfully.
reference; pleasure; decided; order; contact; appreciate; possible; prepared; costs; sent; sincerely.

98. 1: at; 2: with; 3: under; 4: in; 5: with; 6: at; 7: in; 8: at; 9: on; 10: with; 11: at.

99. 1: time; 2: a break; 3: up; 4: from; 5: what; 6: in; 7: in; 8: in; 9: to; 10: into.

100. 1: up; 2: through; 3: on; 4: by; 5: up; 6: by.

101. 1: lived; 2: have been living; 3: Were; 4: did you live; 5: was; 6: Do you spend; 7: have lived; 8: did you spend; 9: Have you ever been; 10: have never lived.

102. 1: disgruntled; 2: disclaimed; 3: dissociated; 4: displeasure; 5: disrupted; 6: disreputable; 7: disregarded; 8: disposal; 9: dismissed; 10: disadvantaged; 11: disorderly; 12: disorganised; 13: disintegrated; 14: dismantled; 15: dishonour; 16: disheartened.

103. 1: im; 2: im; 3: in; 4: in; 5: im; 6: un; 7: im; 8: in; 9: im; 10: im.

104. 1. scaling down; 2. write ... down; 3. bring up; 4. putting ... up; 5. setting up; 6. let ... down; 7. followed up; 8. turned down; 9. writing up; 10. running down; 11. go up; 12. going down

105. 1. To visit us; 2. To write to us; 3. One last drink; 4. A loser or a failure (He dropped out of college.); 5. To fall asleep; 6. Deliver something (»Oh Tony, can you drop these letters off at the post office for me?«)

106. 1. called off; 2. set off; 3. pulled off; 4. taken off; 5. put off; 6. switch off

107. 1. bargained for; 2. stands for; 3. put in for; 4. fell for; 5. makes for; 6. makes up for

108. 1. prototype; 2. sound … out; 3. try out; 4. trial runs; 5. test the water; 6. guinea-pigs; 7. piloting; 8. samples; 9. pitch

109. 1. made a point of; 2. making headway; 3. made a … bid; 4. made amends; 5. make allowances; 6. make a … pitch; 7. made a stand; 8. made a case for; 9. made an impact

110. 1. Let's consider offering this new product for sale.
2. Let me just think the idea over.
3. Come in, sit down and let's look over this proposal.
4. It's a fine day – let's get out the car and go for a drive into the mountains.
5. Let her fax this cost analysis to the customer right away.
6. Let the company wait another week for delivery – they are always so impatient.
7. Let me explain what we have in mind.
8. Let us join in this new venture.

111. 1. The proposal was significantly more attractive on paper than it was in practice.
2. Our marketing office is nowhere near as big as our sales office/ Our sales office is nowhere near as big as our marketing office.
3. This is by far the most comprehensive business journal I have ever seen.
4. The Jones account was unquestionably the most lucrative the company had ever won.
5. Share prices remain a little lower than expected.

6. She was easily the most diligent salesperson in the company.
7. The Marlboro trademark is unquestionably the most recognised in the world.
8. The present sales director is much better informed than the previous incumbent.
9. It was not really as serious as we had expected.

112. 1. We got there just in time; 2. correct; 3. from time to time; 4. in the nick of time; 5. about time; 6. correct; 7. killing time; 8. correct; 9. on time; 10. correct

113. 1. in receipt of; 2. in receivership; 3. received; 4. to reciprocate; 5. recipients; 6. reception; 7. receptive; 8. receptionist; 9. on the receiving end of; 10. receiver

114. 1. go over … with a fine toothcomb; 2. went all out; 3. goes without saying; 4. make a go of; 5. go it alone; 6. touch and go; 7. went about; 8. from the word go; 9. let themselves go; 10. go hand in hand

115. 1. came across; 2. sorting out; 3. check up on; 4. look … up; 5. running over; 6. hunt down; 7. sort … out; 8. searching for; 9. look into

116. 1. The Managing Director is standing down at the end of the year.
2. — Personally I put it down to the recession.
3. At the end of the day the success of a company all comes down to the degree of efficiency in which it is run.
4. When a new manager takes over a company he must lay down the law.
5. If everybody refused to back down during negotiations no deal would ever be reached.
6. Now I think we all know each other so let`s get down to business.
7. I think we should bring down the price in order to make it more cost-effective.
8. The Advertising Standards Council promised to come down hard on any companies using underhand methods to sell their products.

117. 1. worth his salt/his weight in gold; 2. worth … while; 3. for what it's worth; 4. for all … worth; 5. worthy; 6. make it worth your while; 7. not worth the paper it's printed on; 8. worthless

118. 1. John was last seen getting into a taxi.
2. The report was published last year
3. The departure time will be announced later on today.
4. Fiat cars are made in Milan.
5. The work is being typed out as we speak.
6. 10,000 units have been sold so far this month.

119. 1. im-; 2. un-; 3. ir-; 4. in-; 5. im-; 6. un-; 7. ir-; 8. un-; 9. in-

120. 1. brought about; 2. pointed out; 3. come about; 4. borne out; 5. came out; 6. set about; 7. fall out; 8. sort out; 9. missed out on; 10. carried out

121. 1. a. put me through; b. hold the line; c. sorry, being held up; d. take a message; e. give him a call, give him a ring, get on the phone to him
2. f. speaking; g. fire away; 3. h. extension; i. unavailable, otherwise engaged; j. get through

122. 1. run-of-the-mill; 2. run off my feet; 3. ran into; 4. ran an eye over; 5. run its course; 6. in the long run; 7. run to; 8. in the running; 9. run up against; 10. run over/run through

123. 1. stood in; 2. talked me into; 3. put in for; 4. take it out on; 5. go in for; 6. let you into; 7. fill … in; 8. slept in; 9. ties in; 10. came in for

124. 1. domain; 2. In the main; 3. mainstay; 4. mainspring; 5. mainframe; 6. maintain; 7. mainstream

125. 1. pleased with; 2. disappointed in; 3. interested in; 4. wary of; 5. impressed by; 6. good at, bad at; 7. successful in; 8. skilled in; 9. worried about; 10. new to; 11. surprised by; 12. concerned about

126. 1. directly; 2. private; 3. warm; 4. unfailing; 5. anxiously;
6. Obviously; 7. happily; 8. rapidly; 9. accurate; 10. polite

127. 1. hold your breath; 2. hold the fort; 3. held up; 4. hold with;
5. held forth; 6. hold out; 7. got hold of the wrong end of the stick; 8. get hold of; 9. holding its own; 10. got hold of

128. 1. paid the price; 2. There will be hell to pay; 3. pays dividends;
4. paid through the nose; 5. paid lip-service; 6. paid off;
7. put paid to; 8. pay attention

129. 1. stick to their guns; 2. stuck out like a sore thumb; 3. stick their oar in; 4. stick-in-the-muds; 5. get the wrong end of the stick;
6. stick to; 7. carries the big stick; 8. stick our necks out

130. 1. broke; 2. broke the back; 3. make or break; 4. break the market; 5. broke even; 6. break the strike

131. 1. breaking new ground; 2. break the back of; 3. broke the ice;
4. broke down; 5. break even; 6. broke up; 7. breaking in;
8. breakthrough; 9. broke off; 10. break

132. 1. at first hand; 2. an old hand; 3. show one's hand; 4. out of hand; 5. knows it like the back of his hand; 6. beforehand;
7. put his hand to; 8. goes hand in hand; 9. underhand;
10. have the upper hand

133. 1. correct; 2. made up their minds; 3. have in mind; 4. speaking her mind; 5. correct; 6. correct; 7. slipped my mind; 8. in two minds

134. 1. happy hunting ground; 2. get ... off the ground; 3. cut the ground from under our feet; 4. break new ground; 5. fell on stony ground; 6. has her feet firmly on the ground; 7. gain ground;
8. common ground; 9. has ... grounds; 10. covered a lot of ground

135. 1. well-connected; 2. well-thought-of ; 3. well-timed;
4. well-established; 5. well-advised; 6. well-appointed;
7. well-versed; 8. well-disposed

136. 1. thought the better of; 2. has seen better days; 3. go one better; 4. knows the score; 5. For better or worse; 6. scores; 7. better; 8. got the better of

137. 1. talked till I was blue in the face; 2. at face value; 3. staring … in the face; 4. a long face; 5. face the music; 6. egg on my face; 7. show my face; 8. face the facts; 9. lose face

138. 1. on the point of; 2. pointing a finger; 3. make a point of; 4. take your point; 5. pointed out; 6. Not to put too fine a point on it; 7. in point of fact; 8. beside the point

139. 1. Inform yourself fully about our accounting program, and let's meet over lunch tomorrow to discuss the system further. Let's then visit your office to show you the program at work.
2. a. pamphlet; b. staff; c. an account; d. operation; e. retail

140. 1. might have to; 2. will have to; 3. have to/must; 4. has had to; 5. have to/must; 6. had had to; 7. should have to; 8. had to; 9. going to have to; 10. will have to

141. 1. get together; 2. getting on; 3. get round; 4. get through to; 5. get away with; 6. got by; 7. get over; 8. get … over

142. 1. pulls his socks up; 2. pulling … weight; 3. pulling … legs; 4. a) pulled out b) pull in/up; 5. pulled … off; 6. pull in … belts; 7. pulled the carpet from under our feet; 8. pulled out all the stops

143. 1. joining; 2. speak; 3. meet; 4. make; 5. starting; 6. attend; 7. break; 8. sharing

144. 1. fascinating; 2. disappointing; 3. confusing; 4. tiring; 5. excited; 6. fascinating; 7. bored; 8. worrying; 9. annoyed; 10. interesting

145. 1. in sight; 2. go sightseeing; 3. lost sight; 4. set his sights on; 5. hindsight; 6. insight; 7. foresight; 8. At first sight

146. 1. turnover; 2. took turns; 3. turn around; 4. turned out; 5. turn in; 6. turning up; 7. turned down; 8. turned up

147. 1. took us all aback; 2. took up; 3. take on; 4. took off; 5. take over; 6. took off; 7. take over; 8. take up; 9. take in

148. 1. missed the boat; 2. misses a trick; 3. missed out on; 4. near miss; 5. missed the thread; 6. missed the mark; 7. gave ... a miss; 8. hit or miss

149. 1. playing up; 2. add up; 3. taking up; 4. came up against; 5. turned up; 6. set up; 7. picking up; 8. catch up on; 9. gave up; 10. make up for

150. 1. make; 2. made; 3. do; 4. made; 5. do; 6. do; 7. make; 8. do; 9. make; 10. done; 11. make; 12. made

151. 1. put ... through; 2. put off; 3. put ... up; 4. putting in for, put off; 5. put ... down; 6. put ... out; 7. put ... through; 8. putting by

152. 1. took heart; 2. take over; 3. take stock; 4. took the plunge; 5. take shape; 6. take ... for granted; 7. take a back seat; 8. take root; 9. took on board; 10. taken a shine to

153. 1. out of work; 2. had ... work cut out; 3. worked out; 4. works wonders; 5. dirty work; 6. worked up; 7. got to work on; 8. working up to

154. 1. break-up; 2. broke away; 3. break even; 4. broke off; 5. breaking new ground; 6. make or break; 7. breakthrough; 8. break-down

155. 1. look the part; 2. take a look at; 3. looks on the bright side; 4. looked the other way; 5. looked on; 6. Look lively; 7. look forward to; 8. a look-in

156. 1. baptism of fire; 2. fire away; 3. playing with fire; 4. a few irons in the fire; 5. fired-up; 6. got on like a house on fire; 7. firing line; 8. set the world on fire

157. 1. out of hand; 2. changed hands; 3. came in handy; 4. free hand; 5. golden handshake; 6. show of hands; 7. give ... a hand, got ...

hands full; 8. had a hand in; 9. at first hand; 10. handed over; 11. hands were tied

158. 1. give … a dig in the ribs; 2. dug up the dirt on; 3. dug down deep; 4. Dig in; 5. dug their heels in; 6. dig up; 7. dug … own grave; 8. had a dig at

159. 1. keep an eye on; 2. saw eye to eye; 3. set eyes on; 4. turn a blind eye; 5. get … eye in; 6. caught my eye; 7. run an eye over; 8. looked … in the eye

160. 1. to get on with; 2. getting at; 3. get through; 4. get down; 5. get together; 6. getting … across; 7. get by; 8. get round; 9. get over; 10. get back

161. 1. out in the cold; 2. on … way out; 3. thrashed out; 4. out of … depth; 5. go all out; 6. out of date; 7. out of the question; 8. out of the blue

162. 1. like nobody's business; 2. out of business; 3. mind … business; 4. down to business; 5. have no business; 6. goes about … business; 7. in business; 8. means business

163. 1. make; 2. made; 3. made; 4. doing; 5. do; 6. do; 7. made; 8. make; 9. do; 10. make

164. 1. mount; 2. stage; 3. play; 4. give; 5. hold; 6. hold; 7. show; 8. present

165. 1. lose touch; 2. touch and go; 3. put … in touch; 4. touch wood; 5. common touch; 6. in touch; 7. soft touch; 8. lost … touch

166. 1. came to nothing; 2. coming to terms; 3. came up roses; 4. come up in the world; 5. came a cropper; 6. come to light; 7. came to a head; 8. come and go; 9. come to full circle; 10. coming along

167. 1. talking shop; 2. talk … round; 3. small talk; 4. talking-to; 5. Talk of the devil; 6. the talk of the town; 7. talk down to; 8. talked … through

168. 1. dead set against; 2. setting; 3. set his sights on; 4. set off; 5. set out; 6. set back; 7. set up; 8. onset; 9. At the outset, set about

169. 1. open up; 2. open-mouthed; 3. with open arms; 4. open-minded; 5. out into the open; 6. leave one's options open; 7. open market; 8. open secret

170. 1. open; 2. achieved; 3. describing; 4. increased; 5. do business in; 6. directing ... at; 7. you all know; 8. present; 9. anticipate; 10. established

171. 1. went back on; 2. go round; 3. went by; 4. made a go of; 5. gone on; 6. went through; 7. go over; 8. go in for

172. 1. unimpressed; 2. badly; 3. unworried; 4. found; 5. you're wrong; 6. forgot; 7. unestablished; 8. unattentively; 9. misunderstood; 10. slow ; 11. unlucky

173. 1. carried off; 2. broke off; 3. put off; 4. off line; 5. right off; 6. off the hook; 7. on the off chance; 8. ready for the off

174. 1. I take it; 2. took heart; 3. takes a dim view; 4. take her at her word; 5. take off; 6. take a leaf out of ... book; 7. Take ... time; 8. taken aback; 9. took advantage of; 10. taking steps

175. 1. toe the line; 2. in line; 3. right down the line; 4. draws the line; 5. Reading between the lines; 6. along the lines; 7. in line; 8. in my line

176. 1. at heart; 2. heart set on, heart sank; 3. took heart; 4. heart ... in; 5. dear to ... hearts; 6. his heart's content; 7. lose heart

177. 1. all in all; 2. all the same; 3. all in good time; 4. All of a sudden; 5. after all; 6. above all; 7. all over the place; 8. the be-all and end-all

178. 1. made waves; 2. wavered; 3. wavelength; 4. wave goodbye to; 5. waving ... magic wand; 6. on the crest of a wave

179. 1. angry; 2. proud; 3. beloved; 4. disappointed; 5. industrious; 6. applied; 7. interesting; 8. gifted; 9. endowed; 10. wealthy; 11. understated

180. 1. made a stand; 2. stand a chance; 3. stand down; 4. stood out; 5. stand for; 6. stood in; 7. stood by; 8. stand up and be counted

181. 1. confined; 2. over-confident; 3. confounded; 4. confidential; 5. conform; 6. confided; 7. confidante; 8. under-confident

182. 1. reading through; 2. readable; 3. read-out; 4. read out; 5. well-read; 6. reading up on; 7. Take it as read; 8. read ... into

183. 1. agitated; 2. generous; 3. old-fashioned; 4. following; 5. fantastic; 6. hard-working; 7. superior; 8. fascinating; 9. enormous; 10. inadequate; 11. shy; 12. confusing

184. 1. up to the ears; 2. pricked up their ears; 3. fell on deaf ears; 4. music to my ears; 5. Walls have ears; 6. wet behind the ears; 7. all ears; 8. felt my ears burning

185. 1. scrounge; 2. reputation; 3. disreputable; 4. doddle; 5. reputed; 6. easy ride

186. 1. turned up; 2. come up; 3. put ... up; 4. call up; 5. brought up; 6. let up; 7. set up; 8. shut up; 9. picking up

187. 1. booked, threw the book at him; 2. by the book; 3. an open book; 4. in her books; 5. in his good books; 6. on the books; 7. one for the books; 8. everything in the book

Die Lösungen zum Abschlusstest

1. 1. call me; 2. reach ... get through; 3. engaged; 4. can I be of assistance; 5. cut off; 6. hung up; 7. on; 8. dial; 9. put me through; 10. busy ... hold; 11. out of order; 12. an extension; 13. leave; 14. hand over

2. 1. Dear Mr Smith. Yours sincerely.
2. Dear John. Best regards.

3. Dear Mesdames/Sirs. Yours faithfully.
4. Dear Ms Charles. Yours sincerely.
5. Dear Donald. Yours truly.
6. Dear Sir. Yours faithfully.

3. Musterentwurf:

Dear Sirs,

Thank you for your letter of 28 July. We have pleasure in enclosing the latest and fullest information on our range of products, together with the additional material you requested: price list, delivery terms and dates and guarantee details. We would be pleased to arrange a meeting with Mr Jones at his convenience to discuss the possibility of further co-operation between our two companies.

Yours faithfully,

4. Musterentwurf:

Dear Sirs,

I read with interest your insertion in last week's newspaper advertising the vacant post of office assistant, and I would be grateful if you considered my application for the job. I am currently employed by Hancock and Sons as store manager, but my employment here has given me the opportunity to acquaint myself with office routine. My salary with Hancock and Sons is 300 pounds a week. Although my English is not yet fluent I am learning the language and hope to gain proficiency soon.

Yours faithfully,

5. 1. take down; 2. wrote, drafted; 3. type up, write; 4. draft, type up; 5. write, take down, type ... up, write.

6. 1. put up; 2. to; 3. out; 4. amends; 5. meantime; 6. into; 7. anyone; 8. mainstay; 9. to, about; 10. unfailingly; 11. up; 12. slightly; 13. from time to time; 14. receptionist; 15. over; 16. looking into; 17. their while; 18. hold; 19. nose; 20. breakdown; 21. underhand; 22. off; 23. staring us in the face; 24. will have to; 25. off; 26. fascinating, bored; 27. turnaround; 28. How do you do; 29. seen better days; 30. do; 31. stand down; 32. confided; 33. read up on; 34. their breath; 35. took off; 36. out; 37. bring up; 38. put off; 39. shape; 40. up; 41. as if; 42. make; 43. up; 44. away; 45. over; 46. dug up; 47. the eye; 48. taking over; 49. make; 50. hearts; 51. outset; 52. all ears; 53. touch and go; 54. all in all; 55. kept; 56. doing; 57. toe; 58. off; 59. looking; 60. go; 61. made